AMERICAN HISTORY:

Recent Interpretations

BOOK II: SINCE 1865

BOOK II: SINCE 1865

Second Edition

Edited by ABRAHAM S. EISENSTADT   Brooklyn College

AMERICAN HISTORY:

Recent Interpretations

New York, Established 1834   THOMAS Y. CROWELL COMPANY

For Elizabeth, Laura, Jonathan

First Printing, October, 1969

Second Printing, March, 1970

Library of Congress Catalog Card Number: 69-13256

Designed by Herbert E. Caswell

Manufactured in the United States of America

*Preface
to the
Second
Edition*

In preparing a second edition of this anthology, I have tried to achieve the purposes that guided me in preparing the first edition: above all, to afford the novice the opportunity of meeting first hand many of today's principal writers of American history, and of becoming familiar with many of the newer viewpoints on the American past. The criteria I observed in drawing up my original list I have observed again in revising it; I refer the reader to the preface to the first edition for a statement of these criteria. The newer selections, which constitute more than half of the revised edition and which represent the historical literature of the 1960's, have been culled almost entirely from periodicals; in a few instances, however, selections have been taken from recent books of notable importance, because they better served the purposes of the anthology than what the periodicals offered.

It is a commonplace that every age is one of transition, and it is fair enough to expect that what historians are writing about our past is similarly undergoing change. While the change is far from being radical, it has however been characterized by an increasing concern with two new themes of major significance: 1) Out of the whole conflict over the Negro's place in today's America, a new view has emerged of his role in the American past. If some younger historians are urging the thesis that the Negro is central to American history, many more are exploring anew those elements in our society's development in which the Negro's centrality is universally recognized: the colonial economy, the ante-bellum plantation system, the Civil War and Reconstruction, the New South, and the shaping of Negro life in the Southern and

Northern communities during the first half of the twentieth century. 2) America's role vis-à-vis the new world of nations has served today's historians as a point of departure in reconsidering some basic aspects of the American past, viz.: the diplomacy of the American Revolution, the formation of parties in the new republic, the beginnings of the whole process of industrialization, the conduct of our foreign affairs, the premises and policies of American imperialism, and the impact of our revolutionary origins on the evolution of our institutions and values.

I should like to express my gratitude to the individuals whose help made it possible for me to prepare this new edition. I am, as ever, indebted to the authors whose writings are represented in the anthology and to the journals and publishing houses which permitted me to reprint these writings. I am indebted, too, to the staffs of the Brooklyn College Library, the New York Public Library, and the Baker Library of Dartmouth College, for serving me generously in my work, at their respective libraries, in the recent literature of American history. Three individuals at the Thomas Y. Crowell Company were particularly helpful to me: Mr. Stanley Duane, who patiently and perseveringly urged me on, Miss Penelope Post, whose editorial suggestions were most helpful in improving the manuscript, and Mrs. Phyllis Greenbaum, who lent me her invaluable assistance with unfailing good humor. I am grateful, too, to Mrs. Barbara Berg, for checking a variety of details, and to Mrs. Freda Limberg, for her usual job of superb typing. I wish, finally, to thank my younger colleagues at Brooklyn College, Thomas B. Furcron, James P. Johnson, and Samuel T. McSeveney, who were kind enough to read the introductory notes to the newer selections and to let me have the benefit of their criticism.

August, 1969   A.S.E.

Preface to the First Edition

This collection is designed to meet the need for supplementary readings in basic courses in American history. The need for such readings is clear enough. A textbook has, after all, the limitations of its author's knowledge and approach. A class in history requires the stimulus of different views and expert knowledge, both of which may be found in a book of collateral readings. Such a book affords, moreover, a satisfactory answer to the question of how to bring large groups of students in touch with a wide range of literature and opinion under conditions of limited library facilities.

The basic problem in editing a book of supplementary readings is to define what one seeks to achieve and how one seeks to do it. The editing of this book has been guided by the following purposes:

The collection as a whole undertakes to present the newer viewpoints in American history. All too frequently the textbook is based on approaches that have to be substantially modified if not altogether discarded. The selections in this book, on the other hand, date almost entirely from 1945—for the greater part, indeed, from 1950. They constitute in this way an anthology of American historical writing since World War II. They indicate the newer directions of American historical thought.

The selections have been drawn, wherever possible, from a broad field of periodicals which include the following:

Agricultural History   *Journal of Religion*
American Archivist   *Journal of Southern History*

American Heritage
American Historical Review
American Scholar
Atlantic Monthly
British Journal of Sociology
Business History Review
Centennial Review
Columbia University Forum
Commentary
Current History
Daedalus
History and Theory
Indiana Magazine of History
Journal of American History
Journal of Economic History
Journal of the Illinois State Historical
    Society
Journal of Negro Education

Labor History
Marine Corps Gazette
Mississippi Valley Historical Review
Pacific Affairs
Pacific Historical Review
Pacific Northwest Quarterly
Political Science Quarterly
Proceedings of the American
    Antiquarian Society
Proceedings of the American
    Philosophical Society
Proceedings of the South Carolina
    Historical Association
Progressive
U.S. Naval Institute Proceedings
William and Mary Quarterly
Wisconsin Magazine of History

It is in the rich essay literature of such periodicals that the new American history is being defined. It is in this essay literature, too, that the contributions of the foremost historians will often be found at their condensed and argumentative best. Though clearly of great importance, these writings are usually inaccessible to the class. Many college libraries do not have the wide collection of periodicals from which the readings in this volume have been taken; and even if they did, it would be very difficult, if not impossible, for large classes to use them at any given time. In the relatively few instances where selections were taken from recent books, the reason has generally been that these selections recommended themselves as clearly preferable to what was afforded by the periodicals.

The anthology consists entirely of complete essays. Each selection is a self-contained unit. The excerpts and fragments that usually make up a book of readings have been avoided. In composing an anthology of essays the purpose has been to do justice to their writers by letting them speak their minds fully on subjects on which they are authorities, without the arbitrary interruption of an editor. The desire has also been to do justice to the instructor and his students by letting them read and analyze in its entirety a noteworthy essay by a major historian on an important issue in the American past.

The choice of a particular essay has been made for one or more definite reasons. The essay is concerned with a major problem, development, or individual in American history. It summarizes the findings of an expert in the specific area of his research. It is often revisionist in approach. It is well written. It presents a provocative thesis, designed to stimulate the mind of the student and the discussion of the class. It has, as Carl Becker put it, something to say and says it in its own way.

The essays as a whole seek to present history as wider in scope than merely past politics. In order to underscore the historian's interest in all aspects of human activity, the editor has included a relatively larger number of selections dealing with economic, social, religious, and intellectual developments in the American past.

Introductory notes have been written for all of the essays. The notes discuss the contribution and approach of the historian who wrote each essay. They define the nature and importance of the subject with which the essay is concerned. They suggest lines of inquiry about the subject, both in its particular context in the American past and in the broader frame of American historical development. The effort has been to see the significance of a historical issue for our own times, not only for the purpose of using the student's interest in the present as a point of departure for his study of the past but also to encourage him to see the present in its deeper perspective as a phase of the past in evolution. The effort has also been made to throw open to the student the challenging questions posed by the study of history—such questions, for example, as whether the past is to be explained by determinism or by accident, what the nature and meaning of causation are, how much the great man influences the course of historical development, and whether or not an objective truth about the past can be attained. In terms of its introductory notes, therefore, the collection may be used as a "problems" approach to the study of the American past and may serve also as a primer for the study of the historical discipline.

The attempt has been made throughout to include articles of a high level of competence and interest and to represent as many approaches, to canvass as many problems, and to seek as catholic an orientation toward the whole American past as is possible. The footnotes that originally appeared with the essays have, as a rule, been omitted for reasons of length; in a few instances, however, where the theme of the essays is historiographical, the footnotes have by necessity been retained. Full information is given with each essay concerning the journal from which it has been taken, and the footnotes accompanying the essay may, of course, be readily consulted there. Obvious typographical errors have been corrected and abbreviations have been spelled out, but all stylistic preferences have been retained.

It is my hope that this volume will afford the student a broad and deep outlook on the American past as well as a real sense of the vitality of its study today. I also hope that he will thereby be encouraged to seek out its wider reaches and dimensions on his own.

November, 1961   A.S.E.

Contents

Changing Patterns of Life and Thought

The Era of Progressivism and War, 1900–1920

Normalcy and New Deal

World War II

The Course of Recent Politics

Contemporary Society

Part 1
THE GROWTH AND IMPACT OF INDUSTRY, 1865–1920

1

The Dark and Bloody Ground of Reconstruction Historiography
BERNARD A. WEISBERGER

2

The South's New Leaders
JOHN HOPE FRANKLIN

The years which followed Appomattox were no less dramatic or important than those which had preceded it. Appomattox meant an end of the trials of war and a beginning of the problems of peace. How would the victory of the North be translated into deeper economic and social terms? Would the triumph of arms also be a triumph in peace? Would the South lose the war but win the peace? What commercial and industrial policies would the new nation pursue? What would be the status of the freedman? What would the defeat of the Southern aristocracy mean for the social structure of the new America? How much had the compound of American society been altered by the chemism of war? Whatever the deeper problems resulting from the war, the most immediate one was that of Reconstruction. How

SOURCE: *The Journal of Southern History*, XXV (November, 1959), 427–447. Reprinted by permission.

were the defeated states to be governed? On what terms were they to be brought back into the Union?

Because Reconstruction dealt with problems that had been central to the war, its history has been as much a matter of controversy as the war itself. For many decades, historians tended to view Reconstruction as an age of political failure, a regrettable period in our history, in which the North inflicted a humiliating, almost barbarous rule upon the South. Seen in a bleak retrospect, the "reprehensible" deeds of the Radical Republicans in Congress and of "carpetbaggers," "scalawags," and Negroes in the Southern states appeared to be the outward and visible signs of the gracelessness of a generation. It is true enough that this unfavorable view has, in certain respects, been increasingly modified during the past decade, but until very recently historians have resisted a comprehensive reappraisal of the age. The reason is suggested by Professor Bernard A. Weisberger, of the University of Rochester, in the first of the following essays. An excellent writer on the history of American journalism, Professor Weisberger is also a specialist in the Civil War and Reconstruction era. With regard to what he calls "the dark and bloody ground of Reconstruction historiography," he pleads for historians to come to terms with some basic problems in the American past.

To understand the age of Reconstruction, submits Professor Weisberger, we must answer questions which go to the root of all American history. What, to begin with, is our view of the Negro, his nature, his potentialities, his personality? How far, moreover, does the corruption that seems to have been so widespread during Reconstruction tend to be part of the American democratic process? In what way were post-war relations between the federal government and the states merely a step along the road of a long-term evolution? To what extent are we still interpreting Reconstruction in the light of economic and social concepts whose validity is questionable and which we no longer apply to other areas of American history? What, in general, are the deeper personal values by which we construe the American past and what, in particular, are the values of those whose interpretations have dominated Reconstruction historiography? It is the sum of Professor Weisberger's suggestion that our views on one part of American history ought to be consistent with our views on the rest of it.

The answers to Professor Weisberger's questions rest, in the main, on what historians think about such fundamental issues as the nature of the Civil War, the justifiability of the Southern cause, and the whole issue of race relations. The new orientation that has been emerging in recent years is more positive in its assessment of the Radical Republican program and policies, and of the achievements of Reconstruction. The first major book to offer a comprehensive statement of this orientation was John Hope Franklin's Reconstruction: After the Civil War *(1961). Professor Franklin is one of our most distinguished scholars in the field of Southern and Negro history, and the author of several notable volumes, including* **From Slavery to Freedom** *(third edition, 1967),* **The Militant South** *(1956), and* **The Emancipation Proclamation** *(1963).* **His** Reconstruction, *as Daniel J. Boorstin has noted, sees the era in broad perspective, as a phase in national development, rather than "as a chapter in regional history—or, we might even say, in regional punishment or crucifixion. . . ."; it gives an account in refreshing detail of the forward steps taken, in the South, in important areas of social and economic life during the late 1860's and early 1870's. In the chapter reprinted below, Professor Franklin undertakes to correct the errors of fact and understanding that have for a long time affected our view of the South's new leaders after the Civil War: the Negroes, the "carpetbaggers," and the "scalawags."*

The South has been in a state of radical transition in recent years; it is being made over by powerful internal forces and by the impact on American policy of the opinion of a largely non-white world. Industrialization and desegregation are two significant aspects of the restyling of Southern life. In this sense we are witnessing a second and more profound Reconstruction. It is imperative for an honest consideration of what is occurring today that we review the first Reconstruction and that we understand what its men, its problems, and its achievements really were.

BERNARD A. WEISBERGER

Twenty years ago, as the exciting thirties drew to a close, the dry bones began to stir in that notable valley of historical skeletons, the Reconstruction period. In February 1939, the *Journal of Southern History* carried an article by Francis B. Simkins describing a number of "New Viewpoints of Southern Reconstruction."[1] Frankly facing the fact that "the main issue of the Reconstruction period, the great American race question," like Banquo's ghost, would not down, Simkins asked for a fairer analysis of Reconstruction's achievements and failures and an end to the notion that encouraging the Negro in voting and office-holding was somehow a crime of crimes. By adopting a more "critical, creative and tolerant attitude," he said, historians of the South could better discharge their "great civic obligation."

In the following year, Howard K. Beale took up this theme with a brisk, provocative essay, "On Rewriting Reconstruction History," in the *American Historical Review*.[2] Forthrightly, Beale asked if it were "not time that we studied the history of Reconstruction without first assuming, at least subconsciously, that carpetbaggers and Southern white Republicans were wicked, that Negroes were illiterate incom-

---

[1] *Journal of Southern History*, V (February 1939), 49–61.
[2] *American Historical Review*, XLV (July 1940), 807–27.

petents, and that the whole white South owes a debt of gratitude to the restorers of 'white supremacy'?" He then posted a list of questions previously ignored except in scattered numbers of the *Journal of Negro History* and in W. E. B. Du Bois' 1935 volume, *Black Reconstruction.* What was the *whole* story of popular government in the South from 1865 to 1900? What were the economic connections of the so-called Redeemers? How much of the famed Reconstruction debt went for gilt spittoons and legislative boodle, and how much for social, educational, and industrial rebuilding? Where did the poor white fit into the picture? What lessons could be learned by considering Reconstruction anew, this time as a short-lived revolution which placed power in inexperienced hands?

These questions struck to the heart of the prejudiced version of Reconstruction laid down around the turn of the century by Rhodes, Burgess, and Dunning, developed by Fleming and some of the individual state historians of the period, and widely popularized, in 1929, by Claude Bowers' zestful work of imagination, *The Tragic Era.*[3] That story is familiar. It told of how "Vindictives" and "Radicals" in Congress shouldered aside Johnson and the Supreme Court and imposed "Carpetbag" and "Scalawag" and "Negro" governments on the South by the bayonet. These new governments debauched and plundered a proud but helpless people until finally, desperately harried whites responded with their own campaigns of violence and persuasion. These respectable folk at last took advantage of mounting Northern disgust with "carpetbag crimes" to restore "home rule" unopposed.

The Beale and Simkins articles seemed to indicate that professional historians were ready to overhaul this operatic version of events—perhaps to use the perspective gained at the end of one decade of swift social change in the careful examination of an earlier period of upheaval. Yet now, twenty years after these premonitory signs, the indicated tide of revision has not fully set in. Certainly the work still needs to be done. The New Deal, the Second World War, and the Cold War have all set in motion what some have called a "New Reconstruction" of the South—with fresh patterns in industry, urban life, population movement, agrarian practice, social and political leadership, and

---

[3] Claude G. Bowers, *The Tragic Era; the Revolution after Lincoln* (Boston, 1929). To particularize individual monographs on Southern Reconstruction here would involve the compilation of a virtually complete critical bibliography of works on the subject up to 1939, whereas this article aims at a detailed examination only of studies appearing since that date. Accordingly, the reader's familiarity with the earlier works is assumed. They are conveniently listed in a number of places, notably in James G. Randall, *The Civil War and Reconstruction* (Boston, 1953), 881–935.

capitalization forming almost faster than the census takers can reveal them. The school desegregation crisis has, since 1954, moved the race question into disturbing but unescapable prominence. It is more important than ever that progress be made towards understanding the issues raised in the "old" Reconstruction of 1865 to 1877. Yet something seems to have blunted the purpose of the historical guild, and the discovery of what this something is deserves professional attention.

Certainly it is no lack of revisionary work on the monographic level. There is plenty of that, some of it brilliant. One is almost tempted to cite the leading journals *passim* for fear of overlooking meritorious pieces, but short of that, one may point to at least half a dozen books and twice that many articles of genuine significance. There are, for one thing, three path-breaking books by C. Vann Woodward dealing with economic leadership, political organization, and racial adjustment in the post-Appomattox South.[4] Among articles on more specialized topics, there is, to begin with, an outstanding survey of the attitudes dominating the historical approach to Reconstruction by T. Harry Williams, fit to stand in the good company of the Beale and Simkins articles.[5] David Donald gave impetus to a study of Southern Republicans, in 1944, with a piece on Mississippi "scalawags," and he has since given fresh scrutiny to the relationships between the Radicals, Lincoln, and Johnson.[6] Thomas B. Alexander surveyed the role of the Whigs in Tennessee Reconstruction and found a more complex story than had hitherto been suggested.[7] The oft-maligned agents of the Freedmen's Bureau had been made the subjects of a judicious plea in defense by John and LaWanda Cox.[8] Northern philanthropists and educators, alternately hailed as agents of progress and damned as Yankee marplots, have also undergone dispassionate examination by

---

[4] *Reunion and Reaction; the Compromise of 1877 and the End of Reconstruction* (Boston, 1951); *Origins of the New South, 1877–1913* (Baton Rouge, 1951); *The Strange Career of Jim Crow* (New York, 1955).

[5] "An Analysis of Some Reconstruction Attitudes," *Journal of Southern History*, XII (November 1946), 469–86.

[6] "The Scalawag in Mississippi Reconstruction," *Journal of Southern History*, X (November 1944), 447–60; "Why They Impeached Andrew Johnson," *American Heritage*, VIII (December 1956), 20–25; "The Radicals and Lincoln" in *Lincoln Reconsidered* (New York, 1956), 103–27.

[7] "Whiggery and Reconstruction in Tennessee," *Journal of Southern History*, XVI (August 1950), 291–305.

[8] "General O. O. Howard and the 'Misrepresented Bureau,'" *ibid.*, XIX (November 1953), 427–56. The Coxes believe that "even the most friendly studies of the Bureau have exaggerated its weaknesses and minimized its strength." LaWanda Cox has also contributed fresh material on the motivation of postwar reformers in "The Promise of Land for the Freedman," *Mississippi Valley Historical Review*, XLV (December 1958), 413–40.

such scholars as Henry L. Swint and Ralph Morrow.[9] Both Swint and Morrow have published full-dress books on the subjects of their articles, and, indeed, monographs continue almost regularly to break up the fallow ground.[10] George R. Bentley has brought up to date Paul Pierce's half-century-old work on the Freedmen's Bureau.[11] Otis Singletary has submitted the fullest report so far on Negro militiamen in the occupied states of the South.[12] Vernon Wharton has, it may be hoped, provided a pilot project for the studies of the Negro as voter and officeholder in his book on Negroes in Mississippi during and after the Radical heyday.[13] Fresh biographies, both of major and minor actors, have also appeared. Robert Durden has revealed the paradox of a Negro-hating Radical in his life of James S. Pike, and Jonathan Daniels has contributed a portrait of a "carpetbagger," Milton S. Littlefield, the delicious wickedness of which should not obscure its real importance.[14] At least two writers have grappled, since 1940, with the contradictions of Thaddeus Stevens: Richard Current in a sharply critical book, and Ralph Korngold in a rather saccharine tribute.[15] Two recent biographies of Benjamin F. Butler also bear witness to the dangers of attempting to "typecast" an important Radical.[16] Still more

---

[9] Henry L. Swint, "Northern Interest in the Shoeless Southerner," *Journal of Southern History,* XVI (November 1950), 457–71; Ralph Morrow, "Northern Methodism in the South during Reconstruction," *Mississippi Valley Historical Review,* XLI (September 1954), 197–218.

[10] Henry L. Swint, *The Northern Teacher in the South, 1862–1870* (Nashville, 1941); Ralph Morrow, *Northern Methodism and Reconstruction* (East Lansing, 1956). Before leaving the subject of periodical articles, it is well to note that this sampling takes no note of articles in the journals of various state historical societies or of professional associations for the study of economics, sociology, and political science. Nor is any attempt made here to list new works of which the author is aware on subjects related to Reconstruction indirectly—studies of pardon, amnesty, and loyalty oaths after the war, of railroad financing in the Southern states, or of aspects of the national battles over land, currency, and tariff reforms. Such a listing would unduly prolong this article, but would also add support to one of its contentions, that abundant material for a fresh synthesis of the period is available.

[11] George R. Bentley, *A Historian of the Freedmen's Bureau* (Philadelphia, 1955).

[12] *Negro Militia and Reconstruction* (Austin, 1957).

[13] *The Negro in Mississippi, 1865–1890* (Chapel Hill, 1947).

[14] Robert F. Durden, *James Shepherd Pike: Republicanism and the American Negro, 1850–1882* (Durham, 1957), a significant part of which appeared as "The Prostrate State Revisited: James S. Pike and South Carolina Reconstruction," *Journal of Negro History,* XXXIX (April 1954), 87–110; Jonathan Daniels, *Prince of Carpetbaggers* (Philadelphia, 1958).

[15] Richard N. Current, *Old Thad Stevens; A Story of Ambition* (Madison, 1942); Ralph Korngold, *Thaddeus Stevens; A Being Darkly Wise and Rudely Great* (New York, 1955).

[16] Robert Holzman, *Stormy Ben Butler* (New York, 1954); Hans L. Trefousse, *Ben Butler, the South Called Him Beast!* (New York, 1957).

light on Reconstruction may be expected when David Donald's forth-coming life of Sumner appears.

Varied as are all these works in quality, aim, and scope, their total impact clears the air. They show, first of all, that the so-called "scala-wags" were not all the ragged underlings of Southern society, but included—at least early in the period—many erstwhile Southern Whigs, high in status and thoroughly baptized in the church of the Lost Cause. The nucleus of a Southern Republican party, they were displaced by extremist pressure from overardent Radicals, both Negro and white, on the one hand, and die-hard "white line" supporters on the other. Often, however, the issues on which they were challenged had as much to do with patronage and with profit as with race.[17] Sec-ondly, the Republican state governments chosen under the operation of the Reconstruction Acts of 1867 were not composed exclusively of corruptionists, white or Negro, and achieved a number of praise-worthy social and educational reforms.[18] Thirdly, such corruption as did exist was shared in by many white and respectable Southerners, later to become "Bourbons," who did not scruple to profit by the lavish gifts of the sinful "carpetbag" governments to Southern development companies. Moreover, when restored to control, these "Conservatives" continued to keep the doors of the state treasuries hospitably open to

---

[17] Evidence for this statement is scattered widely through the works already referred to. Donald, "Scalawag in Mississippi Reconstruction," 60, declares that in that state, "the importance of the former Whigs has generally been neglected." Alexander, in "Whiggery and Reconstruction in Tennessee," 305, suggests "the possible value of reviewing Reconstruction in all southern states to appraise the role of persistent Whiggery." Insofar as the business com-munity of the South was identified with the Whigs, this view finds support in T. Harry Williams' study, "The Louisiana Reunification Movement of 1873," *Journal of Southern History,* XI (August 1945), 349–69, wherein he finds in Re-construction "still another group whose importance has not been recognized— the business men, not closely affiliated with politics, who saw the strife of parties and races destroying the stability they desired. . . ." (369). Woodward, in *Reunion and Reaction,* significantly entitles one chapter "The Rejuvenation of Whiggery," and begins his *Origins of the New South* with a quotation from a contemporary Southern source concerning a marriage whose "high contract-ing parties were Whiggism and Democracy," and whose presumable offspring was Conservatism.

[18] This point was so widely conceded as early as 1939 as to require little documentation here. It is cogently stated in Simkins, "New Viewpoints of Southern Reconstruction," Beale, "On Rewriting Reconstruction History," and Williams, "An Analysis of Some Reconstruction Attitudes," already cited. Vernon Wharton, after a close study of one "reconstructed" state, reaches a conclusion probably applicable to most of the former Confederate common-wealths: "Altogether, as governments go, that supplied by the Negro and white Republicans in Mississippi between 1870 and 1876 was not a bad government." *The Negro in Mississippi,* 179.

businessmen who had formerly supported the Radicals.[19]   Fourthly, the restored "Conservatives" were willing to live with Negro suffrage, provided they could control its outcome.   The "sin" of enfranchising the illiterate freedman was apparently washed whiter than snow, once he switched to the Democratic ticket.[20]   Fifthly, life somehow went on under "bayonet rule."   Crops, capital, and order *were* restored, after all, and there were cakes and ale as well as heartbreak and ugliness. Violence there was; but the legend of Negro militiamen's "atrocities," perpetuated in Thomas Dixon's *The Klansman,* is as baseless as the implication in Albion Tourgée's *A Fool's Errand* that every square Southern mile contained a secretly buried victim of the Klan.[21]   Lastly, neither in Congress nor in the South were the Radicals the purposeful and unified group of conspirators that they have been made out to be by friendly biographers of Andrew Johnson.[22]   Johnson himself, pilloried though he was by his enemies, added to his own woes by personal hardheadedness, political stumbling, and a blind belief that the

---

[19] This point forms almost the entire thesis of Woodward's *Reunion and Reaction,* and is explored in depth in *Origins of the New South,* 1–74, as well as in the opening chapters of the same author's *Tom Watson, Agrarian Rebel* (New York, 1938).   Daniels' *Prince of Carpetbaggers* is an excellent detailed account of the financial relationships between white Democrats and "carpetbaggers" in North Carolina and Florida.

[20] Negroes "continued to vote in large numbers in most parts of the South for more than two decades after Reconstruction."   Woodward, *Strange Career of Jim Crow,* 35.

[21] E. Merton Coulter, who most certainly believes Reconstruction to have been a severe time of trial for the South, nevertheless thoroughly documents the return to normal life in *The South during Reconstruction, 1865–1877* (Baton Rouge, 1947).   He declares (ix): "There were . . . with all the political and constitutional abnormalities of the times, the ordinary activities of the people, as they sowed and reaped, went to church, visited their neighbors, sang their songs, and sought in a thousand ways to amuse themselves."   As for the question of placing the role of the Negro militia in its true proportions, Singletary observes that the Radical governors rarely used the troops available to them under state law, and notes that the real affront, for white Southerners, was the simple presence of Negroes in uniform.   "For even had the militia refrained from committing a single act antagonistic to the whites, in all probability they would still have been destroyed."   *Negro Militia and Reconstruction,* 152.   The use of Federal troops is a matter deserving greater study, and as for riots and incidents not involving the use of uniformed soldiery, the responsibility is not easily pinned on one side or the other.

[22] David Donald notes, in *Lincoln Reconsidered,* 103–27, that the concept of the "malevolent Radical" comes in part from the need to find new antagonists, in every generation, for the noble figure of Lincoln in the Lincoln-myth.   Certainly close study of the lives of eminent Radicals reveals plenty of dissension among them; as for the Southern Radicals in the statehouses, their factional feuds in every state suggest, in the words of a recent article, "a much more complex social, economic and political evolution than is found in partisan accounts."   Jack B. Scroggs, "Southern Reconstruction: A Radical View,"

incantation of constitutional formulas could change the brute facts of power distribution.[23]

This is a good record of piecemeal accomplishment. Yet in two significant areas, the professional record remains poor. For one thing, there has been no synthesis of this material in a good general history of Reconstruction. The one full-scale treatment by an academic historian since 1940 is E. Merton Coulter's *The South during Reconstruction, 1865–1877.* Regrettably, Professor Coulter chose to begin with a veteran's indignant rejection of the entire notion of revision. There could be, he said, "no sensible departure from the well-known facts of the Reconstruction program as it was applied to the South. No amount of revision can explain away the grievous mistakes made in this abnormal period of American history."[24] This attitude seems excessively conservative. If modern historical scholarship teaches anything, it teaches that "well-established" facts are constantly changed in implication as new facts are unearthed, and that there are several sensible departures from any set of facts, depending upon whose definition of "sensible" is employed.[25] Rich though it may be in material, *The South during Reconstruction* is no contribution to understanding. In point of fact it is something of a setback. Appearing as it

---

Journal of Southern History, XXIV (November 1958), 428. Both Williams and Donald warn against facile generalization. "Southerners differed among themselves on the issues of Reconstruction in about the same degree as did groups in the North," says Williams in "An Analysis of Some Reconstruction Attitudes," 486, while Donald reports that the "difficulties of making an adequate study of a Reconstruction election in the South have seldom been realized." "The Scalawag in Mississippi Reconstruction," 458. James M. Dabbs, a temperate Southerner of today, also underscores the complexity of the story in *The Southern Heritage* (New York, 1958), 105.

[23] The most intelligent critical discussion of Johnson to appear recently is David Donald's "Why They Impeached Andrew Johnson," *American Heritage.* A good, new biography of the impeached President is needed. The two most frequently cited nowadays suffer from the vigor of their efforts to defend him unreservedly. They are, George F. Milton, *The Age of Hate; Andrew Johnson and the Radicals* (New York, 1930) and Lloyd P. Stryker, *Andrew Johnson; A Study in Courage* (New York, 1929). An interesting minor revision of the Johnson story has lately been contributed by Ralph J. Roske, "The Seven Martyrs?" *American Historical Review,* LXIV (January 1959), 323–30, who challenges the view that the seven Republicans who voted for his acquittal were "relentlessly persecuted . . . until they were forced altogether from the American political scene" (323). He denies that their later careers were marked by "unrelieved martyrdom."

[24] Coulter, *South during Reconstruction,* xi.

[25] A searching critique both of Coulter's "facts" and his deductions therefrom is John Hope Franklin's "Whither Reconstruction Historiography," *Journal of Negro Education,* XVII (February 1948), 446–61. For a briefer statement of Coulter's conventional view of Reconstruction, see A. B. Moore, "One Hundred Years of Reconstruction of the South," *Journal of Southern History,* IX (May 1943), 153–80.

does in the *History of the South* series published by the Louisiana State University Press—a set of works which must long remain the standard repository of Southern history—it would have been more enduring had it maintained a more judicious attitude. Since 1947 the only other general book on Reconstruction is Hodding Carter's *The Angry Scar; the Story of Reconstruction.*[26] Carter, a literate and "moderate" Mississippi editor, provides a book which is a distinct improvement in fairness on the earlier "nonprofessional" study of Bowers. Yet it is still marked by a defensive spirit, and more to the point, its incorporation of fresh research is at best uneven.

The other failure of historians to deal adequately with Reconstruction is evident in textbooks, many of which play old tunes on worn keys. This is especially lamentable since the text is so often the college graduate's only exposure to the literature of history. Some volumes designed for classroom use attempt balanced discussions—notably (though not exclusively) the works of Freidel, Current, and Williams, of Hofstadter, Aaron, and Miller, of Billington, Loewenberg, and Brockunier, and of Leland D. Baldwin.[27] Others lean heavily on stereotyped reactions. For one thing, the terms "Carpetbagger" and "Scalawag" are sometimes used as if they were genuine proper nouns and not cartoonists' labels. It is true that they are now so familiar as perhaps not to need quotation marks, and yet by the same token we should expect to find Jacobin, Doughface, and Gold Bug in current and unqualified usage to describe certain groups in our history. Negro suffrage is generally deplored and credited only to opportunistic, if not openly base, motives. Thus, John D. Hicks traces "an infinite amount of abuse" to "premature" voting by the freedmen, while Morison and Commager explain that it was instituted by the Radicals "to secure

---

[26] New York, 1959.

[27] Frank Freidel, Richard N. Current, and T. Harry Williams, *A History of the United States* (2 vols., New York, 1959), II, 23–27; Richard Hofstadter, Daniel Aaron, and William Miller, *The United States: The History of a Republic* (Englewood Cliffs, N.J., 1957), 404–405; Ray A. Billington, Bert J. Loewenberg, and Samuel Brockunier, *The United States; American Democracy in World Perspective* (New York, 1947), 261–85; Leland D. Baldwin, *The Stream of American History* (2 vols., New York, 1953), I, 911–15. The first two of these books stress economic turmoil as the basis for a good deal of political misbehavior usually imputed to "carpetbag" villainy or Negro ignorance. Baldwin declares that one "can find what he seeks when he examines the role of the Negroes in the reconstruction period. . . . If it was Negro votes that made some astonishing steals possible, it should be remembered that it was white men who got the bulk of the swag." Billington, Loewenberg and Brockunier point out that the "reconstruction record, written under the tutelage of scholars of Bourbon lineage seeking a gentlemanly road to reunion, has long demanded reappraisal." Another sympathetic and careful presentation of the Reconstruction period is to be found in Carl N. Degler, *Out of Our Past* (New York, 1959).

the colored vote at the earliest opportunity," which is partly true but does not explain why the Fourteenth Amendment offered the South the opportunity to reject Negro enfranchisement if Southerners were willing to pay the price of reduced representation in Congress.[28] Riegel and Long deplore the handiwork of the "ill-trained Negro freedman, intoxicated by his first breaths of liberty," while Carman and Syrett, generally fair, nevertheless ring the changes on the gross extravagance of the "black and tan" legislatures.[29] Thomas A. Bailey's *The American Pageant,* a highly popular one-volume text, belongs to the Burgess era. "The Radicals," it declares, "would 'Republicanize' the South by making the freedman an unwitting tool of their own schemes, and ride into power on his lash-scarred back." The "gun-supported reconstruction of the South, begun so brutally in 1867 . . . under the stern eye of bayonet-bearing Union soldiers," resulted in Southern legislatures which sometimes "resembled the comic opera."[30] No doubt this is as stirring, for students, as a showing of *The Birth of a Nation,* but it is not much more accurate.

In sum, although the foregoing survey does not pretend to cover the textbook situation completely, teachers of American history have not taken into account the newest modifications of the "Carpetbag–bayonet rule–Negro domination" legend either in general works for the broad public or in texts designed for college students. The question of "why" is a challenging one. Part of the answer appears to lie in a professional conservatism which we historians of America too often permit to close our minds to new approaches in the entire range of our work. "He that is unjust in the least," Scripture says, "is unjust also in much." If we have been unjust to some actors in the Reconstruction story, it is because we have not come to terms with some larger problems of United States history.

In the first place, white historians have shied away from grasping the nettle of race conflict, mainly because of the difficulty of recognizing their own emotional involvement in the problem. Yet this unwillingness to dwell on the almost universal nineteenth-century conviction of the Negro's innate inferiority often leads to a slipshod evaluation of materials. It is proper to take account of the frankly political motives

---

[28] John D. Hicks, *The American Nation; a History of the United States from 1865 to the Present* (Cambridge, 1955), 30; Samuel E. Morison and Henry S. Commager, *The Growth of the American Republic* (2 vols., New York, 1950), II, 38–43.

[29] Robert E. Riegel and David F. Long, *The American Story: Volume One: Youth* (New York, 1955); Harry J. Carman and Harold Syrett, *A History of the American People* (2 vols., New York, 1952), II, 20–31.

[30] Thomas A. Bailey, *The American Pageant: A History of the Republic* (Boston, 1956), 467–74.

of many Radical defenders of the Negro voter. It is equally proper to bear in mind the frankly racial motives of some of the Radicals' opponents. A glance at source materials of the sixties, for example, shows that many so-called conservatives opposed the Radical program for the South not because they were devoted to states' rights, or agrarianism, or the Constitution, or the Democratic party alone, but plainly and simply because they thought it was sinful to give so-called Africans the right to share in governments framed by a clearly superior Anglo-Saxon race. In combing the Civil War files of such northern Democratic papers as the New York *World,* Chicago *Times,* and Cincinnati *Enquirer,* one finds diatribes against "niggers" and the "Republican niggerocracy" quite as fulsome as anything ever concocted by today's racists.[31] Instincts of decency as much as anything else prompt the suppression of such material, but silence on the subject covers up some of the ignobler motives of men who are now and then lauded as brave opponents of "Radical tyranny." It is hardly correct to judge "Radicals" by their worst motives and "Redeemers" only by their best.

Negro historians, from the venerable days of George Williams to the modern times of John Hope Franklin, Rayford W. Logan, and others, have had, perforce, to recognize a conflict between the status conservatism of a dominant white race and the aspirations of the Negro people. Reviewers sometimes tend to patronize their works as restricted by adherence to a minority point of view. But white historians, naturally enough, write from a majority point of view which is sometimes confused with objectivity—and which leads even the fairest of them on occasion into unrecognized value judgments. Take, for example, the simple matter of suffrage. Many textbooks deprecate the enfranchisement of freedmen almost immediately after emancipation. While by no means "naturally" inferior, they argue, the victims of slavery were as yet too ignorant and irresponsible to be trusted with political power. The statement is true in part, but the historian who demands intelligence and responsibility as prerequisites for the ballot is, wittingly or not, making the Federalist and Whig case against universal suffrage. Unique as was the experience in slavery, it would be difficult to prove that the freedman was inherently less ready to vote than the illiterate backwoodsman or the freshly-arrived immigrant. Yet the same historian who has doubts about the freedman as voter often votes in earlier chapters *for* the Jacksonians and *against* the Know-Nothings. It would be a good thing, in fact, if more historians examined critically the libertarian and equalitarian assumptions, both romantic and ration-

---

[31] Abundant documentation of this statement is available in the newspapers mentioned. For a brief sample drawn from the news columns only, see Bernard A. Weisberger, *Reporters for the Union* (Boston, 1953), 265–70.

alistic, which have governed our experiment in democracy, but the examination ought to extend to all groups, localities, and periods, and not merely to Reconstruction Negroes. The members of the James Ford Rhodes school of historians were more consistent in this regard. Often they *did* distrust the immigrant as a voter, and if they supported universal suffrage, it sometimes seemed to be on the ground that illiterate Anglo-Saxons were by nature better citizens than men of lesser breeds without a "genius for self-government." Their views should not be perpetuated nowadays by mixing them with the base alloy of hypocrisy. It would be better to discuss the Negro vote in terms of public resistance to it and of what parties gained by it—in terms of motive and expediency—rather than by Olympian judgments on how "good" a voter the Negro made. Evaluations of the political records of entire groups of citizens are at best difficult, and at worst dangerous.

Historians are not obliged, of course, to support the Negro's case unreservedly wherever it appears. They ought, nonetheless, to walk humbly when talking of the American Negro as slave, freedman, voter, or worker. He is known to us almost exclusively through the writings of white men, who, whether well-intentioned or not, were interested parties to a conflict.[32] Conflicts may be solved peaceably, but not wished away. The conflict between white Southerners' determination to be the architects of their own society and black Southerners' desire for a place of dignity in that society did not disappear in 1877. It was "solved" by Northern acquiescence in the subordination of the Southern Negro. Paul Buck's well-known "road to reunion" was paved with the broken ambitions of the freedmen.[33] If Reconstruction is to be correctly branded as a failure, it is just to point out that its aftermath

---

[32] One basic historiographical problem, in fact, revolves around the question of whether "the Negro" revealed by the documents is the true image of himself or the man whom whites want him to be. One may hope that not all Negroes feel like the grandfather in Ralph Ellison's *Invisible Man* (New York, 1952), whose dying words were: "Son . . . I never told you, but our life is a war and I have been a traitor all my born days, a spy in the enemy's country ever since I gave up my gun back in the Reconstruction" (13–14). But considering the Negro's position in American society, one may also wonder if there is not a certain applicability to him in words used by a president of the Southern Historical Association to describe white ex-Confederates in Reconstruction: "Southerners were being forced, like the peoples in any conquered and occupied country, to resort to deception, violence, and intrigue. Double standards and non-moral attitudes were inevitable results." Avery Craven, "The Price of Union," *Journal of Southern History*, XVIII (February 1952), 11.

[33] This fact is underscored by contrasting the optimistic and conciliatory statements reported in *Roads to Reunion* (Boston, 1937) with the unpleasant facts noted in Rayford W. Logan, *The Negro in American Life and Thought: The Nadir, 1877–1901* (New York, 1954).

also represented a great failure of democracy.   But American historians do not, to judge by their works, like the word "failure" any
better than the word "conflict."   Neither fits the textbook myths of
underlying unity, of unceasing progress, of all problems ultimately
coming out right, somehow, in the pendulum swings of time.   In the
case of the knotty race problem, however, only a hardheaded approach
to distasteful truths will yield real understanding.

Secondly, it is time for a fresh look at the "abnormal corruption" of
Reconstruction, which has long colored the period's image.   True, it is
now often palliated by comparison with the general fraudulence of the
Grant era—the grafting of a Tweed, the gaudy robberies of the Erie
gang, the copious cheats practiced by the appointees and favorites of
the Hero of Appomattox.   Yet this does not get at the *basic* historical
question.   Where does "corruption" begin and "lawful business" end
in our society, which has encouraged unlimited gainfulness and freedom from restraint as legitimate goals, and insisted meanwhile that
these characteristics can readily be combined with public virtue and
civic responsibility.   Tocqueville, acute as usual, saw the catch.   "When
the taste for physical gratifications" among a democratic people out-
grew their wisdom and experience, he prophesied in warning of
dangers to democratic states, some men would "lose all self-restraint. . . .
In their intense and exclusive anxiety to make a fortune they [would]
lose sight of the close connection that exists between the private fortune of each . . . and the prosperity of all."[34]   From the beginning, the
United States has liberally rewarded enterprise and industry—one
form of the pursuit of private fortune—and assumed that the public
prosperity would flourish in consequence.   But with unerring period-
icity some businessmen have run so far and so fast in their quest
that they have found even our few legal safeguards of the public weal
in their way.   Then they have tried to evade, hurdle, or destroy them,
producing, in consequence, what is called "fraud."

Let the judicious historian of Reconstruction consider the widespread land frauds involved in the sale of portions of the public domain
in the old Northwest.   Let him recall the fragrant Yazoo scandals, and
reflect on Joseph G. Baldwin's description of the Southwest of Jackson's
day:—"What country could boast more largely of its crimes?   What
more splendid role of felonies! . . . What more magnificent operations in
the land-offices! . . . And in INDIAN affairs!—the very mention is suggestive of the poetry of theft—the romance of a wild and weird larceny!"[35]   Let those who read Reconstruction history recall the banking

---

[34] Alexis de Tocqueville, *Democracy in America,* tr. by Henry Reeve, revised
by Francis Bowen, ed. by Phillips Bradley (2 vols., New York, 1945), II, 140–41.
[35] Joseph G. Baldwin, *The Flush Times of Alabama and Mississippi* (New York,
1853), 238.

swindles and internal improvement bubbles and repudiations of the period just before 1837, and then, skipping ahead five or six decades, dwell on the state house gangs and municipal rings with whom the Progressives did battle.   Let all American scholars contemplate the Harding regime, and then ponder soberly our own society, with its expense-account millionaires, its depletion allowances, its licensing scandals, its much-advertised union corruption, its much *less* well-advertised business corruption and tax evasion, its paid "amateur" university athletes, its call girls hired to "entertain" key "accounts," and its numerous other evidences of the conflicts that can arise between "good business" and "good morals."   In the face of all this, can the Reconstruction legislatures which showered the resources of their states on promoters and developers be properly called "abnormal"?   What manner of historical "abnormality" is it which recurs every twenty years or so, if not oftener?

This is not to suggest that students of the national past should now turn to the writing of a running record entitled *Main Currents in American Larceny*. The matter is not that simple. Yet it has been made so; our use of the word "corruption" in connection with Reconstruction and other periods supports the faith that our institutions are fundamentally whole and sweet, and that only when "dishonest men" get control of them are the times out of joint. We could do with a rereading of Lincoln Steffens. And we could do more good by asking ourselves questions than by condemning rascals. Is this cycle of so-called "corruption" and "purification" inherent in our marriage, during the last century, of the acquisitive mentality and the liberal state?   Did we thus, to borrow from Shaw's definition of marriage, combine "the maximum of temptation with the maximum of opportunity"?

Certainly the "carpetbaggers," for example, deserve a fresh look. Remarkably few of them are well-known to history. Mostly they were young men winging into undeveloped territory in search of profitable opportunities, with a light load of moral as well as of personal baggage. Such enterprise was praised when it carried "civilization" into the West, where only aborigines were dispossessed of their birthright. It was condemned in the South when it resulted in the impoverishment of disfranchised whites. Yet was not the "carpetbagger" as much a product of nineteenth-century America's values of "get" and "build" and "hustle" as was, say, the frontiersman? Or the industrial tycoon? Or the "Bourbon" who took over where the "carpetbagger" left off— without bothering to plow back some of the loot into vote-getting social services as the "carpetbagger" had done? There is no need to rehabilitate the "carpetbagger"—although it may be unjust to leave him in outer darkness when some historians are telling us once more that his counterparts in Northern business circles were creative capitalists.

But chroniclers of America will do American democracy better service if they examine it with true impartiality and do not dismiss its contradictions as merely accidental, or as the work of powers of darkness.

A third error in compiling the Reconstruction record has been its treatment as an almost isolated episode in federal-state relations. The national fetish of Constitution-worship is partly to blame here. "Constitutional history" is not valid as a study of inviolable principles, but rather as an examination of how men adapt their principles to the actual shifts of power within a political system. Thus, to talk of Reconstruction's "constitutionality" is not very useful except as theoretical exercise. The real question is one of just how the Constitution itself was reconstructed. Historians ought to beware of the snare which entangled Andrew Johnson. Some of his supporters have praised his "realism" in contrast to the alleged Radical bemusement with the "abstraction" of Negro equality. Yet it was Johnson and some other "conservatives" who believed that the victors, after the bloodiest civil war of modern history, would restore the defeated enemy to a share in national power immediately—and out of respect for a compact whose interpretation had been one of the very causes of the war. This is a high order of abstraction! Yet it was fundamentally American. Even the Radicals showed a surprising concern for the maintenance of the forms of the federal system, whatever the realities, and for the appearances of constitutionalism. Otherwise why did this "united" and "vindictive" group not choose to protect "its" national program by simply occupying and running the South as conquered territory for a dozen years, as some suggested?[36] Why, otherwise, were they so ready to undertake the bothersome (and ultimately unworkable) business of building Republican machines in the defeated states and then readmitting them?

The perspective of the present day should give us, as historians, a clearer view. We can see that throughout the modern world a massive centralization of power and a corresponding decline in localism and provincialism were in process. We need to spend less time in praising the Jeffersonian dream and more in analyzing the forces that eroded it. In 1787 the state governments were the nurseries of national statesmen. Today they are often enough, in Harry Ashmore's phrase, "the happy hunting grounds of the interests," and a state legislator is frequently

---

[36] Such a policy would have appeared logical to twentieth-century nationalism. Even John W. Burgess, no friend to the racial policies of Radicalism, defended the Wade-Davis bill, considered the idea of restoring the South to territorial status to be "sound political science," and considered the theory of Congressional (as opposed to Presidential) reconstruction "in the right, logically, morally, and legally." John W. Burgess, *Reconstruction and the Constitution, 1866–1876* (New York, 1902), 17–18, 60, 111.

"a small-town lawyer who makes no secret of the fact that he has accepted a part-time job that pays little . . . in order to run errands for his clients."[37] We need to know the extent to which this transition has taken place and how it came about. Yet there are few state studies that analyze problems and forces as probingly as those of Shugg on Louisiana, Hartz on Pennsylvania, or the Handlins on Massachusetts, to name three outstanding examples.[38] There are many "narrative" state histories—many of them monuments to local patriotism—designed to serve the needs of required courses in state history at public universities, courses too often thrust upon the most defenseless member of the department. This creates a fundamental weakness, for good history of the United States must rest on sound historical knowledge of each of them. A sound beginning would be the study of Reconstruction as an episode in the decline and fall of the states, and not as a conspiracy to overthrow a wise and good constitutional arrangement.

A fourth barrier to the writing of a sound, modern history of Reconstruction lies in the fact that historians as a group are too often bounded, when dealing with economic and social matters, by obsolete, unsophisticated, and intellectually isolated viewpoints. A few examples will readily illustrate this point. Reconstruction is still frequently taught as the story of how "the North" attempted to remold "the South." But the sectional approach so well employed by historians of a past generation has exhausted most of its utility. Beyond a certain point, the theory of sectionalism fails to explain similarities of pattern clearly visible in "North," "South," and "West," and what is more, it stumbles over the widespread cultural and economic differences among regions *within* each section. Nowadays, the use of a purely sectional analysis is a triumph of mere habit over critical thought.

Also noticeable is a lack of refinement in economic as well as geographical thought. Textbooks cling yet to the well-known view—once a "radical revision" in itself—that the Civil War and Reconstruction sealed the triumph of "industry" over "agriculture," the process christened by Charles A. Beard as the "second American revolution."[39]

---

[37] Harry Ashmore, *An Epitaph for Dixie* (New York, 1958), 111.

[38] Roger Shugg, *Origins of Class Struggle in Louisiana; a Social History of White Farmers and Laborers During Slavery and After, 1840–1875* (Baton Rouge, 1939); Louis Hartz, *Economic Policy and Democratic Thought: Pennsylvania, 1776–1860* (Cambridge, 1948); Oscar and Mary F. Handlin, *Commonwealth; a Study of the Role of Government in the American Economy: Massachusetts, 1774–1861* (New York, 1947). The selection of these three works is not meant to imply that they are our only valuable state histories, but to illustrate the type of analysis too rarely undertaken.

[39] Charles A. and Mary Beard, *The Rise of American Civilization* (2 vols. in one, New York, 1930), II, 52–121. It is interesting to note how "revisionists" are themselves revised. Both Beard and Howard K. Beale (in *The Critical Year;*

Yet this conflict cannot be neatly packaged. Richard Hofstadter reminds readers in an article lately published that Americans in sentimental championship of the yeoman as the staunch foe of Mammon, only pay tribute to "the fancied innocence of their origins," and Henry Nash Smith has dealt elaborately with a national image of the farming West which he calls "the myth of the garden."[40] The facts are less picturesque. The American farmer, perennially in search of a cash crop, had never, in Parrington's words, "been a land-loving peasant, rooted to the soil and thriving only in daily contact with familiar acres. He had long been half middle-class, accounting unearned increment the most profitable crop, and buying and selling land as if it were calico."[41] In him we can see already outlines of today's businessman-farmer, private plane, automatic feeder, and all. As for the agrarian South in 1860, it was neither the "feudal" empire of Marxist historians (who have been as obtuse as anyone about Reconstruction), nor yet the physiocratic paradise envisioned by Jefferson, Nathaniel Macon, or John Taylor. Its prosperous planters with their wide holdings and great labor gangs were farmer-capitalists, curiously modern in some ways as they were archaic in others. Reconstruction's real economic story is in the emergence of a new *kind* of agrarian-industrial capitalism in the South, and the need of history is for studies of how this came about, to what end, and to whose advantage—not for lamentations on the disappearance of a fancied Arcadian way of life.

A last example of overly restricted outlooks among historians is in the charge that Reconstruction made the South a victim of colonialism.[42]

---

a *Study of Andrew Johnson and Reconstruction,* New York, 1930) assumed the triumph of "business" to be evident in the Radical plan of Reconstruction. Yet this view is undergoing new scrutiny. In a recent article on the money question, Irwin Unger shows an abundance of evidence to support his contention that it is "clearly not valid to speak of a single business attitude toward the money question after the Civil War." "Business Men and Specie Resumption," *Political Science Quarterly,* LXXIV (March 1959), 46–70. Stanley Coben, in "Northeastern Business and Radical Reconstruction: A Re-examination," *Mississippi Valley Historical Review,* XLVI (June 1959), 67–90, concludes from an examination of tariff and currency debates that "factors other than the economic interests of the Northeast must be used to explain the motivation and aims of Radical Reconstruction."

[40] Richard Hofstadter, "The Myth of the Happy Yeoman," *American Heritage,* VII (April 1956), 43; Henry Nash Smith, *Virgin Land: The American West as Symbol and Myth* (Cambridge, 1950), 123–260, but especially 123–33.

[41] Vernon L. Parrington, *Main Currents in American Thought* (3 vols., New York, 1930), III, 26.

[42] Thus Coulter declares that Reconstruction "riveted tighter upon the South a colonial status under which it had long suffered," *South during Reconstruction,* I, while Walter P. Webb made this complaint the basis of an entire book, *Divided We Stand; the Crisis of a Frontierless Democracy* (New York, 1937).

This is a valuable insight, but its value is diminished sharply by the failure to take cognizance of comparable world developments. "Colonialism" is a complex term, describing a relationship which brings about vast changes in class structure, local leadership, resource exploitation, social mobility, and even religious belief in both colony and mother country. Few writers who employ "colonialism" as a key to Reconstruction show much familiarity with the best comparative studies of the subject by European historians, or by economists, sociologists, and geographers. Rather, they applaud or, more often, condemn on the basis of emotional reactions aroused by the word itself.

Finally, the historical profession is not likely to revise its notions concerning Reconstruction or any other phase of the American experience unless it subjects itself to the same discriminating analysis which it applies to the documents of history. Historians themselves work from implicit assumptions, measurable in the light of sociology and psychology, and it is a legitimate duty of scholars to examine those assumptions. It is surely no disparagement to the historians of the generation of Rhodes, Burgess, Dunning, and Fleming to point out that their background predisposed them towards a dim view of so-called "Black Reconstruction." The success of Rhodes in the coal business is well known. Dunning was the son of a New Jersey manufacturer. Burgess was trained to be a lawyer and studied abroad, an option not open to the lesser classes of mankind in the years just after the Civil War. Fleming's father had been a "well-to-do farmer" in Alabama before the war ruined him. It might be noted, too, that the authors of at least five of the "standard" monographs on Reconstruction in individual states—Garner, Hamilton, Lonn, Ramsdell, and Staples—had reached the age of twenty-one by 1901.[43] These are in no sense submitted as hostile suggestions. These men and women were fair-minded and thorough. We who write history today will do well to be as scrupulous within our own limitations. What is more, these students of sixty years ago unearthed materials which must form the basis of any future judgments on Reconstruction. Yet they *did* come from an "old-stock" background; they *were* the children of small property-owners and professional men, and in entering academic life they were themselves joining a genteel profession; they *were* taught, in the formative years of adolescence, to believe that Civil Service, a low public debt, stout constitutions, and Anglo-Saxon leadership were the pillars of a great and enduring republic which was

---

[43] Biographical data and dates of birth are from the *Dictionary of American Biography* and its two supplements and from the 1942 and 1951 editions of the *Directory of American Scholars*. Information on Thompson, Fertig, Ficklen, and Eckenrode, not available at the time of this writing, might increase the list of writers on Reconstruction in individual states who were born before 1880.

naturally perfect, though it might sometimes be tainted by the work of wicked plutocrats or ignorant foreign voters.[44] We need not wonder that these men and their students identified themselves with the displaced and respectable leaders of the "white South," and not with the adventurers, social climbers, and black and white laborers who wielded power for what must have seemed, retrospectively, a brief and unpleasant hour. But we ought to recognize that the Reconstruction story which they left arose in part out of identification with a supposed natural aristocracy of ownership and talent.

These observations are only the framework of an answer to the question of why Reconstruction represents a challenge not met by academic historians. Underlying the problem is the fact that Reconstruction confronts American writers of history with things which they prefer, like other Americans, to ignore—brute power and its manipulation, class conflict, race antagonism. Yet these things make it an essentially modern period. Reconstruction cannot be properly "gotten at" by the well-worn roads of agrarianism, sectionalism, or constitutional analysis. It cannot be approached without perhaps requiring of American historians that they yield up some of their marvelous ability to read unity, progress, and patriotism into every page of the American record—that they face problems which all their piety and wit cannot dismiss or solve with credit to all. Yet those who teach and write the American story cannot be a mere priesthood of patriotism, unless they wish to invite the dominion of the second-rate. If they do not confront tragedies, paradoxes, tidal forces in the culture—if they do not show the forces eroding the compromises of the post-Civil War period and illustrate the frustrating complexity of the problems now awakened again—then Reconstruction will have added the historical guild to the list of its "victims."

JOHN HOPE FRANKLIN

The Act of March 2, 1867, was specific about the qualifications of those who were to have a voice in the new program of reconstruction. Constitutions were to be written by delegates "to be elected by the male citizens of the state, twenty-one years old and upward, of whatever race, color, or previous condition, who have been resident in said state for one year . . . except such as may be disfranchised for participation in the rebellion or for felony at common law." It was no easy

---

[44] Hofstadter has sharply etched a similar group mentality in his analysis of the Progressives in *The Age of Reform; from Bryan to F. D. R.* (New York, 1955). SOURCE: John Hope Franklin, *Reconstruction: After the Civil War* (Chicago: University of Chicago Press, 1961), pp. 85–103. Copyright © 1961 by the University of Chicago.

task to administer satisfactorily these provisions of the Act. The commanding generals in the Southern military districts were hard pressed to find competent and qualified registrars to enrol the electorate. They used Union army officers and Freedmen's Bureau agents; and a few of them used some Negroes. Travel into remote areas was difficult, and in some instances weeks elapsed before registrations were received, compiled, and made ready for elections.

Some of the commanding generals felt a deep responsibility to provide a little political education for those voters who had never had the experience or the opportunity to participate in politics. Several of them gave explicit instructions to registration officials to provide the freedmen with adequate information regarding their political rights. Freedmen's Bureau officers and agents engaged by the generals to work in the registration program helped the new voters understand their rights and duties. When Bureau officials had no political literature of their own to distribute, they disseminated materials prepared by the Union League, which was, as we shall see, easily the most active organization in the political education of the Negro.

When the criteria for becoming electors were applied to the people of the South, three groups qualified. One group was the vast majority of Negroes whose loyalty to the Union was unquestioned and who merely had to prove that they were not felons and had lived in the state one year. Another was the Northerners who had taken up residence in the South. If they met the residence requirements, they were enrolled. Finally, there were the native Southerners who qualified to take the "ironclad oath," and who were scrutinized with the greatest care. The rank and file among these groups was to be the center of the controversy that raged over the ensuing decade. Out of these groups were to come the leaders who bore the majority responsibility for both the good and the evils flowing from the difficult task of rebuilding the South.

The entrance of Negroes into the political arena was the most revolutionary aspect of the reconstruction program. Out of a population of approximately four million, some 700,000 qualified as voters, but the most of them were without the qualifications to participate effectively in a democracy. In this they were not unlike the large number of Americans who were enfranchised during the age of Jackson or the large number of immigrants who were being voted in herds by political bosses in New York, Boston, and other American cities at this time. They were the first to admit their deficiencies. Beverly Nash, an unlettered former slave sitting in the South Carolina convention, expressed the views of many when he said: "I believe, my friends and fellow-citizens, we are not prepared for this suffrage. But we can learn. Give a man tools and let him commence to use them, and in time he will learn a trade. So it is with voting. We may not understand it at the start, but in time we shall learn to do our duty."

Like Nash most of the Negroes were illiterate. A slave existence could hardly be expected to prepare one for the responsibilities of citizenship, especially when there were laws, as there were in all slave states, banning the teaching of slaves. Even if Negroes were free, as were more than 200,000 in the slave states before the war, laws forbade their being taught to read and write. Indeed, when they came out of slavery many Negroes did not know their own names; many did not even have family names. It goes without saying that a considerable number had not the vaguest notion of what registering and voting meant.

None of this is surprising. It had been only two years since emancipation from a system that for more than two centuries had denied slaves most rights as human beings. And it must be remembered that in these two years the former Confederates, in power all over the South, did nothing to promote the social and political education of the former slaves. What is surprising is that there were some—and no paltry number—who in 1867 were able to assume the responsibilities of citizens and leaders.

Among South Carolina's Negro leaders was state treasurer Francis L. Cardozo, educated at Glasgow and London, who had been a minister in New Haven and, after the war, was principal of a Negro school in Charleston. Robert B. Elliott, born in Massachusetts, trained at Eton College in England, and elected to Congress in 1870, was urbane and articulate. J. J. Wright, a state supreme court justice, had studied at the University of Pennsylvania and had been a respected member of the Pennsylvania bar before moving to South Carolina after the war. Congressman James Rapier's white father sent him to school in Canada, and when he returned to his native Alabama after the war he had not only an ample formal education but a world of experience gained from travel and work in the North. Florida's secretary of state, Jonathan C. Gibbs, graduated from Dartmouth College and had been a Presbyterian minister for several years when reconstruction began. Among the Negro leaders of North Carolina James W. Hood, assistant superintendent of public instruction, and James H. Harris, an important figure in the 1868 constitutional convention, were educated, respectively, in Pennsylvania and Ohio. Many others, among them Henry M. Turner of the Georgia legislature, Hiram Revels, United States senator from Mississippi, and Richard H. Gleaves, member of Congress from South Carolina, had much more than the rudiments of a formal education when they entered upon their official duties.

Significant among Negro leaders were those who were almost wholly self-educated. Robert Smalls of South Carolina pursued his studies diligently until he had mastered the rudiments. Later he went to the United States House of Representatives. In Mississippi, John Roy Lynch regularly took time off from his duties in a photographer's studio to gaze across the alley into a white schoolroom, where he kept up with the class until he had mastered the courses taught there. When he became speaker of the Mississippi house and later a member of Congress, he relied on this earlier training. Before Jefferson Long went into Congress from Georgia, he had educated himself and had become a merchant tailor in Macon. There were numerous other self-educated Negro leaders, including John Carraway and Peyton Finley of Alabama, James O'Hara and A. H. Galloway of North Carolina, and James W. Bland and Lewis Lindsay of Virginia. From this educated element came the articulate, responsible Negroes who contributed substantially to the writing of the new constitutions and the establishment of the new governments in the former slave states.

Most of the Negro leaders were ministers. A fair number taught school. Some were employees of the Freedmen's Bureau or another federal agency. Here and there one found a Negro who had been trained in the law. There were, of course, farmers; and there were some artisans engaged in a variety of occupations. The economic interests and aspirations of the Negro leaders varied widely. It would be wrong to assume that they had no economic interests or that they had no views regarding the economic future of the South.

One of the really remarkable features of the Negro leadership was the small amount of vindictiveness in their words and their actions. There was no bully, no swagger, as they took their places in the state and federal governments traditionally occupied by the white planters of the South. The spirit of conciliation pervaded most of the public utterances the Negroes made. In his first speech in the South Carolina convention Beverly Nash asserted that the Southern white man was the "true friend of the black man." Pointing to the banner containing the words "United we stand, divided we fall," Nash said, "If you could see the scroll of the society that banner represents, you would see the white man and the black man standing with their arms locked together, as the type of friendship and union which we desire."

Negroes generally wished to see political disabilities removed from the whites. In South Carolina several Negroes presented a resolution asking Congress to remove all such disabilities, and it was passed. In Louisiana the Negroes requested that former Confederates be permitted to vote but, for the time being, not to hold office. In Alabama James T. Rapier, a Negro delegate to the constitutional convention, successfully sponsored a resolution asking Congress to remove the political disabilities of those who might aid in reconstruction. In Mississippi a Democratic paper, the Jackson *Clarion*, admitted that in their general conduct Negroes "have shown consideration for the feelings of the whites. . . . In other words, the colored people had manifested no disposition to rule or dominate the whites, and the only Color Line which had existed, grew out of the unwise policy which had previously been pursued by the Democratic Party in its efforts to prevent the enjoyment by the newly-emancipated race of the rights and privileges to which they were entitled, under the Constitution and laws of the country." In South Carolina Beverly Nash declared that in public affairs "we must unite with our white fellow-citizens. They tell us that they have been disfranchised, yet we tell the North that we shall never let the halls of Congress be silent until we remove that disability."

Negroes attempted no revolution in the social relations of the races in the South. Francis B. Simkins in his "New Viewpoints of Southern Reconstruction" has accurately observed that "the defiance of the traditional caste division occasionally expressed in an official reception or in an act of the legislature was not reflected generally in common social relations." Negroes, as a rule, conceded to the insistence of whites that they were a race apart; and they made little or no attempt to invade social privacies. They did not even attempt to destroy white supremacy except where such supremacy rejected Negroes altogether as human beings, and there was almost nowhere any serious consideration given to providing legal approbation of interracial marriages. While Negroes sought equality as human beings, they manifested no desire to involve themselves in the purely social relations of whites as individuals or as groups. "It is false, it is a wholesale falsehood to say that we wish to force ourselves upon white people," declared the near-white P. B. S. Pinchback of Louisiana.

Nor did any considerable number of Negroes seek to effect an economic revolution in the South. Henry McNeal Turner, the fearless Negro leader who was almost universally disliked by white Georgians, did what he could to assist the whites in recovering their economic strength. In the Georgia convention he secured the passage of two resolutions that indicated a remarkable willingness to stabilize the economic life of the white community. One sought to prevent the sale of property whose owners were unable to pay their taxes; the other provided for the relief of banks. In South Carolina Negro leaders such as Robert DeLarge and Francis Cardozo supported relief measures with the full knowledge that whites would benefit as much as Negroes.

The movement of Northerners into the South after the Civil War is a part of the exciting drama of the migrations that had seen the continent populated from ocean to ocean and had taken Americans, new and old, wherever opportunity beckoned. The movement into the South was greatly stimulated by the favorable observations of scores of thousands of Union soldiers who had seen action on Southern battle-fields. Some were mustered out of the army while still in the South and, despite some Southern feelings of hostility against them, decided to adopt the South as their home. Others, back in their Northern homes, waited only for the first opportunity to return to the South. By the fall of 1866, for example, more than five thousand Union soldiers had settled in Louisiana alone. The movement was also stimulated by the large number of industrialists and investors who saw in the under-developed South an important new economic frontier. Those committed to the view that the South's recovery from the war would be accom-panied by an era of unparalleled expansion began to move into the region, bringing with them their own resources, and often the resources of others, with which to build railroads and factories and to purchase farm land and other properties.

Many federal agents—some from the Department of the Treasury, others from the Freedmen's Bureau—settled in the South and called it home. Northern teachers, men and women, braved numerous indignities at the hands of hostile whites in order to teach Negroes, and they cast their lot with the South. There were those from the North, moreover, who saw new political opportunities in the South. They hoped to use the newly enfranchised element and the problems arising out of reconstruction to achieve political power and economic gain. For them the South was a "happy hunting ground" that they could not resist. As to any frontier, there went to the South the adven-turers, those who wanted to "get rich quick," and ne'er-do-wells who were fully prepared to embrace *any* cause, including Radical Recon-struction, that would benefit them.

These were the people who have been called "carpetbaggers" for the last ninety years. This opprobrious term, used as early as 1846 to describe any suspicious stranger, was applied indiscriminately to all Northerners in the South during reconstruction. It has generally im-plied that as a group they had nothing in the way of worldly posses-sions and were thoroughly unprincipled in their determination to fleece and exploit the South until their carpetbags fairly bulged with the possessions of Southerners and they were forced to acquire new coffers in which to place their ill-gotten gains. They have been de-scribed as a group at work on a grand master plan to Africanize the country. One historian described them as "gangs of itinerant adven-turers, vagrant interlopers" who were "too depraved, dissolute, dis-honest and degraded to get the lowest of places in the states they had just left." These descriptions fall far short of the mark. They impugn the integrity and good intentions of thousands whose motives were otherwise. Even more important, perhaps, is the fact that such descrip-tions show no understanding of the variety and complexity of the motives underlying the migrations and no appreciation for the economic and political relationships that grew out of such motives.

There is no evidence that even the considerable number of Negro migrants from the North were interested in "Africanizing" the country. Indeed the term was an extravagance, a flourish—like "Negro rule"—used to express disgust. The other common descriptions are equally inaccurate. As Thomas Conway pointed out a few months after the war, many Northerners, including the teacher, preacher, merchant, husbandman, mechanic, laborer, and discharged Union soldier, were ready to move South. He had persuaded Northern men to take $3,000,000 into the South to purchase land, make loans, and advances on crops. Their only fears were whether there was sufficient law and order to maintain security for their investments. But they went South, and they continued to go all during the reconstruction period. In November, 1865, Sidney Andrews observed that already several Massachusetts men were in business in Charleston; and he estimated that at least half the stores on the principal streets of the city were run by Northern men.

The careers of Captain H. S. Chamberlain and General John T. Wilder, both of Ohio, illustrate the kind of activities in which numerous so-called carpetbaggers were engaged. When Chamberlain was mustered out of the Union army in Knoxville, Tennessee, in 1865, he at once entered the iron and coal business in Knoxville and is regarded by some as the real founder of the modern iron industry south of the Ohio. In 1867 Chamberlain joined with General Wilder, late of Wilder's Lightning Brigade of Ohio, to organize the Roane Iron Company, which bought large tracts of coal and iron land and engaged extensively in the operation of coke works, iron mines, and furnaces. Together they became involved in many industrial and financial ventures, including the Dixie Portland Cement Company, the Brookside Cotton Mills of Knoxville, and the First National Bank of Chattanooga.

That all so-called carpetbaggers were not simply Radicals with no consideration for the welfare and development of the South can be seen also in the life of Willard Warner, planter, politician, and iron manufacturer. Born in Granville, Ohio, and educated at Marietta College, Warner served in the Union army and went to the Ohio senate in 1865. Two years later he moved to Alabama, and with his ample resources engaged in cotton planting for several years. He became active in Republican politics and served in the United States Senate from 1868 to 1871. Then he organized the Tecumseh Iron Company and served as president and manager until 1873. For this venture more than $100,000 was supplied by his Northern associates. Later he moved to Tennessee, where he had extensive investments and blast furnaces.

The overthrow of reconstruction seems not to have affected this "carpet-bagger," for as late as 1900 the Conservatives (the Democrats) in his adopted state elected him to the Tennessee legislature.

If recent historians have reviled Northerners who settled in the South after the Civil War, their Southern contemporaries were inclined to be grateful to them for their contributions to Southern development. Clinton A. Cilley, born in New Hampshire and a Harvard graduate, settled in North Carolina in 1866. After a career in the law, including several years as a judge of the Lenoir Superior Court, he was called in 1900 "one of North Carolina's ablest lawyers and finest citizens." General Wilder, the iron manufacturer, was very popular among Southerners, including former Confederates. During the Spanish-American War the governor of Tennessee named the training camp near Knoxville "Camp Wilder," in honor of the carpetbagger from Ohio. Lieutenant B. H. True of the 136th New York Volunteers, who settled in Georgia in 1865, was consistently popular with his new neighbors; they not only supported his newspaper, the *Appeal and Advertiser,* but elected him, as the "celebrated farmer from Morgan County," to the State Agricultural Society.

The interest of such men and groups of men in the political future of the South was real. With so much at stake in the way of investments and with full appreciation of the economic potential of the South they could not be indifferent to the uncertain political winds that were blowing across their adopted home. Their interest transformed itself into a strong desire to attain certain specific political goals for the South. One was the achievement and maintenance of law and order. They had seen enough hostility and lawlessness in many Southern communities to cause considerable uneasiness about the safety of their investments. They wanted governments that would insure this safety; and if they could facilitate the establishment of such governments, they would certainly do so. Another was the maintenance of a close alliance between government and the business community. They had seen the importance of such an alliance in numerous developments in Washington during the war and in the effective service that several state governments in the North had rendered the business community. Favorable banking and insurance laws, tax exemptions or rebates, land grants and other assistance to railroads were among the favors the government could and would, under certain desirable circumstances, grant to business and industry. If at all possible, Northerners would see that this was done in the South.

Finally, most Northerners in the South were convinced that their goals could best be attained through a vigorous, well-organized Republican party throughout the South. This was, after all, the party responsible for the intimate relationship between government and

business on the national level and in several Northern state governments. They knew that there was little chance of luring the former
Confederates into the Republican party and that the Democratic party
would oppose at every turn whatever Republicans attempted to do.
Southern Democrats tended to equate Republicans with abolitionists
and thus to regard them as the destroyers of the South's cherished
economic and social system. Northern Republicans had to look to
others in the South for political support.

A Republican in the South did not have to belong to the Thaddeus
Stevens–Charles Sumner wing of the party to reach the conclusion
that Negro suffrage was not only desirable but imperative. For the
conclusion was inescapable that the party's strength would come from
Negroes and from whatever support they could secure from loyal
native Southerners. They did all they could to promote the enfranchisement of the Negro and draw him into the Republican party. This
did not mean, however, that the so-called carpetbaggers were interested
in "Africanizing" the South. Even when they undertook to "North-
ernize" the South, there was no revolution in the general social relations
between Negroes and whites. B. H. True, a New Yorker living in Georgia, said that he was as friendly toward the Negro as anyone, "but there
is an antagonism which we all have against the race; that I cannot get
rid of; I do not believe any man can." Had these Radicals been radical
on social questions, they would have opposed the laws against inter-
marriage that were enacted during the Radical regime. They would
also have stood for one system of public schools open to all races, but
their infrequent expressions in favor of such a system were feeble
indeed. These matters—unlike Negro suffrage—were not among their
primary interests, and they gave them scant attention.

It was only natural that Northerners in the South could wield political influence and exercise power far out of proportion to their numbers. They were the best prepared to step into the vacuum created by
the disfranchisement of the former Confederates. They had training
and experience in political and economic matters that neither Negroes
nor loyal native Southerners had. They clearly knew what their interests
were and how best they could be secured. Finally they had the support
of the powerful, victorious party that was in control of affairs in Washington. While their influence in the South was not always decisive
or even critical, it was invariably a factor in the determination of
affairs, present and future, in the Southern states.

No group of postwar Southern leaders has been reviled or castigated
—or misunderstood—more than loyal native Southerners, commonly
known as "scalawags." The term came in all likelihood from Scalloway,
a district in the Shetland Islands where small, runty cattle and horses
were bred. It was used in western New York before the Civil War in

referring to a "mean fellow, a scape grace." In the South the term was used by the opponents of reconstruction to describe those they regarded as the lowest, meanest element in society. These were the Southerners who could swear that they had never voluntarily given aid, countenance, counsel, or encouragement to persons in rebellion and had exercised or attempted to exercise the functions of no office under the Confederacy. They were largely men who had opposed secession. The votes against secession in some state legislatures, together with the known sentiment against such drastic action, indicates that a considerable number of Southerners dragged their feet or refused to have any part in the Confederate cause. Many had for years smarted under a system that gave every advantage to the planter class, to which very few of them belonged. They bitterly resented the course of action, pursued by the planter class, which had led to a war that, from their point of view, became more and more a "poor man's fight."

It is impossible to determine how many so-called scalawags were qualified to participate in reconstruction under the terms of the several acts of Congress. Likewise it is impossible to determine the extent to which those who took the "ironclad oath" were eligible to do so. After June, 1867, those who took the oath were, as President Johnson had indicated to the commanding generals, judges of their own honesty. Since the machinery as well as the personnel of registration was of questionable efficiency, it is entirely possible that many who were clearly not eligible registered anyway. There were some eligibles who refused to register, and many who were not eligible advised the loyal Southerners to have no part in the Radical regime. Others advised the eligibles to register and then defeat the Radical effort by voting against it. "If we are to wear manacles," said Governor Perry of South Carolina, "let them be put on by our tyrants, not ourselves."

But there were those in the South who counseled loyal Southerners to participate in the new reconstruction program and then to restrain any excessive or revolutionary tendencies that might militate against the best interests of the South. The fact that Negroes were to participate did not degrade white Southerners or diminish their influence unless they purposely abandoned the field to Negroes. The New Orleans *Picayune* told its readers that promptness in registering and voting would convince the North "that we mean to take care of our own affairs." The Savannah *News* gave similar advice when it declared that Georgia expected every man to do his duty and register without delay to show his reverence for his "noble commonwealth." The Charleston *Daily Courier* echoed the same view: "That you should register is an imperative duty which each man owes to himself, to his community and to his state."

A curious assortment of native Southerners thus became eligible to participate in Radical Reconstruction. And the number increased as the President granted individual pardons or issued new proclamations of amnesty. It became increasingly difficult to make a distinction between the views of the loyal Southerners and the views of those whose citizenship was being restored. On political and social questions they ranged from the radicalism of James W. Hunnicut of Virginia, who stood for the full legal and social equality of Negroes and whites, to the conservatism of Milton Candler, a Georgia senator who claimed that Negroes were not citizens and therefore were not eligible to hold office. Certainly the majority of these loyal Southerners could not be described as Radicals in the sense of embracing policies and programs for Negroes set forth by the Radicals in Congress. Often they advocated segregation of Negroes and whites in educational and other institutions. Often they spoke as vigorously for the rights of the South as did any former Confederate. Their primary interest was in supporting a party that would build the South on a broader base than the plantation aristocracy of ante-bellum days. They found it expedient to do business with Negroes and so-called carpetbaggers; but often they returned to the Democratic party as it gained sufficient strength to be a factor in Southern politics.

These were the people who were called scalawags by their adversaries. They hardly deserved the name, nor did they deserve the numerous other opprobrious labels pinned on them by hostile critics. Wade Hampton called them "the mean, lousy and filthy kind that are not fit for butchers or dogs." Another called them "scaly, scabby runts in a herd of cattle." Even the historians have joined in the verbal assault on these loyal native Southerners. One describes scalawags as "vile, blatant, vindicative, unprincipled." Perhaps during the period of their ascendancy the scalawags committed many offenses against the social order; for the graft and corruption they must take at least a part of the blame. But their most serious offense was to have been loyal to the Union during the Civil War or to have declared that they had been loyal and thereby to have enjoyed full citizenship during the period of Radical Reconstruction.

It is extremely difficult to determine the strength of the three groups that dominated the South during Radical Reconstruction. There was constant fluctuation in the show of strength, particularly among the native Southerners and the Northerners living in the South. And there was constant defection, with Negroes dropping out of the picture under Ku Klux Klan or other pressures, with Northerners leaving or going over to the Conservatives, as the opponents of Radical Reconstruction were called, and with "loyal" Southerners deviating from or deserting the Radical cause altogether. The best that one can do is look at the comparative numerical strength of the three groups and draw some inferences from the observation. A likely time for such a comparison is 1867–68, when the several state conventions wrote the new constitutions required by the Reconstruction Acts (see table).

MEMBERSHIP OF STATE CONVENTIONS, 1867–68

STATE	NEGRO	White			TOTAL	Percentage		
						Negro	White	
		Native	North-ern	Total			Native	North-ern
Alabama	18	59	31	90	108	17	55	28
Arkansas	8	35	23	58	66	13	52	35
Florida	18	12	15	27	45	40	27	33
Georgia	33	128	9	137	170	19	74	7
Louisiana	49	*	*	49	98	50	*	*
Mississippi	17	29	54	83	100	17	29	54
North Carolina	15	100	18	118	133	11	75	14
South Carolina	76	27	21	48	124	61	22	17
Virginia	25	33	47	80	105	24	31	45
Texas	9	*	*	81	90	10	*	*

* Further breakdown unavailable.

The figures in the table illustrate several significant points. In the first place, except for South Carolina, Negroes enjoyed no numerical domination in the conventions. The only other state in which they were nearly a majority was Louisiana, where by agreement they were to constitute 50 per cent of the delegates. Thus "Negro rule," as reconstruction has been erroneously described, had an inauspicious beginning and, indeed, was never to materialize. Second, the so-called carpetbaggers were in the minority in every state except Mississippi. Many were so preoccupied with personal undertakings, or with setting up schools and churches, that they had no time for public service. Their position, however, was adequately represented by those new settlers who did find time to serve. Finally, the native whites had a larger numerical representation in the conventions than is usually recognized. Dominating several conventions, such as those in Alabama, Georgia, and North Carolina, and having substantial numbers in others, they were prepared to play a significant part in the deliberations and in the administration of affairs in their states.

Although leadership in the South came from these three groups, at least in the early days of congressional reconstruction, it does not follow

95616

that the leaders invariably worked together in promoting a Radical program. Their motives, values, and goals were not the same and their effort to work together was often strained because of these differences. Far from entering into any conspiracy to degrade and destroy the Southern way of life, they frequently worked at cross purposes. At times the position of the Negro leaders approached that of the crusading abolitionists. Meanwhile, the so-called carpetbaggers frequently preoccupied themselves with building up the alliance between the business community and the Republican-controlled state government. All too often, moreover, the loyal Southerners talked and acted like the conservative former Confederates whom they presumably opposed. Co-operation was at best loose and irregular, forced at times only by the threat of their common destruction. It was under these circumstances that the three groups of leaders forged a program for the reconstruction of the Southern states. How such a program actually emerged is one of the fascinating chapters in American history.

3

Business Men and Specie Resumption
IRWIN UNGER

In the foreshortened view that we take of the past, we tend to wrap it up in serviceable themes and periods. Both serve the same cause, that of defining the past in terms that make it an intelligible and meaningful prelude to the present. A notable example of this is the way we have hitherto regarded the men and events of the decades immediately following the Civil War. We have attached to them convenient labels and significances, by which they clearly articulate the demise of an older, agrarian order and the birth of a newer, industrial one.

A more accurate presentation of the postwar decades has recently been offered by Irwin Unger, of New York University, in The Greenback Era:

SOURCE: *Political Science Quarterly*, LXXIV (March, 1959), 46–70. Reprinted by permission.

A Social and Political History of American Finance, 1865–1879 *(1964).* *The volume, for which Professor Unger received a Pulitzer prize, is the product not only of a remarkably thorough canvassing of sources but also of a sophisticated mastery of the historical discipline. It is a significant study for several reasons. First, it restores to a proper balance our perspective of the years from 1865 to 1880, by reminding us that national politics concerned itself with issues other than that of Reconstruction, and indeed with some that were then considered no less important. Second, it calls into serious question one of the most important and widespread interpretations of the era, that of Charles A. Beard, disputing his thesis that the era saw the capture of the national government by the "business interests" and that the nation's postwar history can be seen as a clear and simple contest between two great economic groups, business and agriculture. On the contrary, submits Unger, the financial history of Reconstruction discloses a complex pluralistic society, one that contained a variety of interests and evolved through the interplay of a number of forces. Third, the Civil War may not have been the great watershed of the nation's history that we have hitherto presumed it to be. From his own close analysis of the greenback era, Unger sees significant lines of continuity running from the years before the war through and beyond the Civil War period. In terms of ideas and institutions, patterns of social organization and leadership, he concludes, "much remained of the old America."*

In the essay reprinted below, Unger takes up the subject that is also central to his book: the views of businessmen in the postwar era on the issue of national financial policy, and particularly on the issue of specie resumption. He addresses himself to such questions as the following: How valid is Charles Beard's portrait of the postwar era as one in which the Northeastern business men controlled the government and ran it to their own advantage? In what ways, and for what reasons, were businessmen in general divided over the issue of specie resumption? How did the more dynamic groups differ from those that were more stable? How did business attitudes toward specie resumption change over the decade and a half following Appomattox, and why?

The debate over specie resumption was a most important one, reflecting and summarizing as it did the debate over national policy. As Unger puts it: "In the decade and a half following Appomattox, national finance absorbed more of the country's intellectual and political energy than any other public question except Reconstruction. The debate over paper money, debt repayment, the national banks, and silver remonetization reflected the ambitions, aspirations, and frustrations of the most active and vigorous men of the republic and set the terms of American political conflict for the remainder of the century." (The Greenback Era, *Princeton: Princeton University Press, p. 3.)*

For some years it has been fashionable in American historiography to find the key to the era after the Civil War in the struggle between business and agriculture. A number of distinguished historians, drawing their inspiration from the seminal work of Charles A. Beard, have pictured the war itself as a "Second American Revolution," in the course of which the "triumphant business man" of the Northeast wrested control of the national government from the agrarian South and West and enacted a legislative program designed to provide a hospitable setting for the growth of American business enterprise.

A major item in this program—and the focus of the present essay—was the return to specie payments in 1879. After a "long bitter struggle" in which, to quote Beard, "the agrarian section" succumbed to the "investing section," the fiat greenback currency issued during the war was made redeemable in gold. In 1875 Congress passed the Resumption Act, providing for the return to specie four years later. On January 1, 1879, successful resumption was achieved, and the "captains of business enterprises and the financiers heaved a sigh of relief."

It is clear that a large part of the opposition to resumption was indeed western in origin. But close examination of the contemporary business press, trade association reports, and the letters of business men and politicians reveals that much of this hostility stems from western business men and that, in fact, business men in general were deeply divided over the Reconstruction currency issue, with important groups in both East and West distinctly unfriendly to "sound money."

One primary division over the money issue was that between seaboard merchants and those of the interior. Men engaged in foreign trade operations saw the paper régime as a constant threat to profits. Importers of dry goods, notions, wines, hardware, and the other foreign products which America consumed in the Gilded Age paid for their wares in bills of exchange on England or some other specie standard nation, or, occasionally, in specie itself. The importer then sold these goods in the United States for legal tender greenbacks. If in the interval between the purchase of goods abroad and their sale at home the price of gold measured in paper greenbacks were to rise, the importer might realize a large profit, since domestic prices of imported goods moved with the gold price. With a decline, prices offered might no longer cover the merchant's own cost in gold or exchange. So unsettling was this régime to importers, declared a New York Chamber of Commerce report in 1867, that many "prudent men will not willingly embark their money . . . in ventures to distant markets . . . with the possibility of a fall [in gold] ere their return can be brought to market." In the export trade, merchants' and brokers' commissions were equally at the mercy of the fluctuating gold-paper ratio which made the shipping of American staples "almost as uncertain as a ticket in a lottery." To guard against these vicissitudes merchants and brokers engaged in hedging operations on the gold exchange, which had appeared shortly after specie suspension. Although partially protected against loss, the merchants objected to the necessity of becoming gold gamblers, in this way obliged to keep a closer watch on the fluctuations of the gold premium than on their primary commercial concerns, and through the greenback period the traders of the port cities were among the most intransigent sound money men.

Repeatedly between 1865 and 1879 the seaboard trade associations, particularly the New York Chamber of Commerce and the Boston and Philadelphia Boards of Trade, made known their antipathy to irredeemable greenback circulation. Scarcely a year passed without each of these bodies remonstrating with Congress against continuing the deplorable paper standard which, in the words of the New York Chamber, had subjected the merchants to countless "inconveniences, losses, and evils." During these same years the National Board of Trade, composed of northern commercial associations, annually adopted sound money resolutions.

But while trade uncertainties might incline most eastern seaport merchants to resumption, among the eastern commercial men as among other categories of business men, there were numerous dissenters from the prevailing group orthodoxy. Individual foreign traders sometimes preferred the windfall gains that accompanied a rising gold premium to the "legitimate" profits of trade. Many importers, John Murray Forbes pointed out, would resist any move that threatened to depress gold. "Even men sound in theory" who had experienced the boon of a rising gold premium would find reason, he warned, for postponing resumption "till *they* have got out."

Among merchants of the interior, "sound finance" was considerably less popular than among the foreign traders. While western trade associations at times endorsed resumption, the commercial men of Chicago, Cincinnati, St. Louis and other western trading centers often disagreed with their eastern counterparts on the subject of the national finances. The merchants of the port cities may have suffered inconveniences under the greenback standard, Westerners conceded, but at all events they were adequately supplied with credit and banking facilities. By contrast, in the distribution of national banks and national bank currency after 1864, Westerners pointed out, their section had been distinctly shortchanged, with New York and New England taking the largest share of the $300 million of bank circulation authorized. Until the 1870's the original authorization remained fixed, and this limit placed a rigid ceiling on bank expansion, subjecting the West, it was charged, to a chronic credit shortage. Since domestic commerce was exempt from the vexing trade fluctuations that bedeviled foreign trade under the paper standard, it is easy to understand why western merchants often resisted resumption and frequently endorsed a form of inflation through "free banking"—the free entry into the banking system of any capitalist who qualified under the law.

Financial differences between East and West were often graphically displayed during the currency discussions of contemporary mercantile organizations. At the 1868 National Commercial Convention western attempts to carry a free banking resolution were resisted by eastern merchants who, demanding "above all . . . a sound measure of value," attacked the proposal as irresponsible and dangerous. Merchants of the interior cities called attention to the high interest rates and the difficulties of procuring credit in the nation's newer regions. There were important differences between foreign and internal commerce that delegates must not forget, a member of the Chicago Board of Trade pointed out. "These gentlemen on the sea board base all their calculations on gold to bring them to par with foreign countries. We claim that . . . domestic commerce may be worthy of consideration as well." The West could be relied on not to repudiate the national debt, but it did demand some kind of monetary relief. "If we can get a free banking law," the Chicago delegate concluded, "we will take that." Despite the Westerners' earnest efforts, however, on this occasion the free banking proposal was killed by a decisive majority of eastern delegates. Similarly, at the annual National Board of Trade convention in 1873, attempts to force the Board to endorse immediate resumption met intense western opposition, and, when it appeared that soft money men might actually carry the convention for expansion, the well-organized conservatives hurriedly forced an adjournment.

A similar East-West division could be found among the financial men. At first, however, Treasury Secretary Hugh McCulloch's rigorous greenback contraction, inaugurated in 1865–66 as preliminary to resumption, received an apparently unanimous ovation from the bankers. But it was McCulloch's misfortune that contraction coincided with a recession beginning in mid-1866, and thereafter western bankers, overextended and vulnerable, rapidly reversed themselves. "The only true and safe policy at the present time," pronounced an Ohio financier early in 1868, was "neither contraction nor expansion but to *let the currency alone.*" "*Time* and patience," another wrote Senator John Sherman, were needed "to get back to a specie basis."

West of Ohio the financial men were not content merely to complain. In Iowa the National Bankers Association was actively engaged in undermining the Treasury's contraction policy. H. M. Kingman, Cashier of the First National Bank of Dubuque, wrote in late 1866 of "the efforts making against the old fogy notions of Sec. McCulloch in the matter of returning to specie payts. by retiring legal tenders." The

Iowa bankers tried to get William Allison, member of Congress from the Dubuque district, to manage the anti-contraction campaign. Allison, a holder of national bank stock himself, Kingman noted, had the "views of his constituents at heart" in the matter of the currency.

The recruiting of Allison was apparently part of a concerted drive launched by western bankers to have McCulloch's contraction power withdrawn. Sometime during 1866 these western financiers retained the Merchants' Union Law Company, a firm of professional lobbyists, to help defend their interests in Washington. The firm solicited contributions for fighting further monetary curtailment and other legislation inimical to the banking interests, and circulated a printed petition which charged that "further reduction of the volume of currency at present would prove highly injurious to the banking, manufacturing and mercantile interests of the country." So importunate were their demands that they provoked one member of Congress—John Wentworth of Illinois—into the unusual step of denouncing their petition on the floor of the House as organized special pleading. This group was probably the same "bankers' lobby" that later in the year was reported to have joined with the whiskey lobby in an attempt to oust McCulloch from the Treasury.

The money issue divided the manufacturers as well as the bankers and commercial men, but here the significant division of opinion lay between the stable and the more dynamic business elements rather than between East and West. For the first decade of the post-war greenback period, leaders in iron and steel manufacturing, an industry undergoing rapid growth and profound technological change, were among the more determined foes of "forced resumption." McCulloch's earliest contraction moves had wrung anguished cries from the ironmen. The Secretary was denounced as an impractical and dangerous theorist who expected to achieve specie payments by a "few legislative *'whereases* and *be it enacteds.'*" Manufacturing was "sweating under a load of taxation which some years ago was *unimaginable*," complained one iron manufacturer; why not wait then until tariff and internal revenue rates were adjusted to more advantageous levels before placing the great burden of contraction on the producing interests? McCulloch's "*species* of experiment," protested another in 1866, was destroying the nation's heavy industry. "The plain state of the case is that the *Industrial* interests, which build up the wealth and revenue of the country, are paralyzed by the *uncertainty* which prevails in regard to his . . . proceedings. What we want is *rest*, breathing time . . . to develop our resources—*dig out* our coal and *iron* and manufacture our iron into rails and machinery."

The ironmasters deplored not only the price deflation under McCulloch's remorseless contraction, but also the accompanying fall of the gold premium which, they believed, served to reduce the cost of competing foreign iron. Even before passage of the Contraction Act the ironmen denounced McCulloch's deflationary funding operations for reviving iron importations from England. By forcing down the gold premium, a delegation from the Iron and Steel Association informed the Secretary in March 1866, he had admitted a flood of foreign pig and fabricated iron and had "come close to destroying the American iron industry."

In their excited reaction to increasing European competition the iron manufacturers made the charge—a cliché of post-war tariff polemics —that foreign gold was behind McCulloch's deflation program. "The contraction and resumption policy," asserted Joseph Wharton of the Bethlehem Iron Company, "was probably urged upon McCulloch by our English enemies. . . . Nothing more in the interest of those . . . enemies and more deadly to the soldiers and champions of the nation who are in mine, mill and farm desperately fighting for her independence could be devised" than a hasty return to specie.

In time this doctrine of the gold premium as an additional tariff levy became a fixed prop of the currency controversy. In 1868 the American Industrial League—a high tariff pressure group composed largely of Pennsylvania ironmasters—made it part of its credo, and thereafter derided bullionist principles as "the bugaboo of the financial nursery, effective to frighten children but of little account in the light of mature experience." The League carried on a running battle with the low tariff, sound money men, and helped establish a pattern linking protection with expansionist financial views, so that by the mid-seventies the inflationist agitation was frequently ascribed to manufacturers who wished to secure "a virtual increase of the impost on foreign products which come into competition with their own."

Following repeal of the Contraction Act in February 1868, the ironmen came out openly for positive monetary expansion. But the ironmasters did not consider themselves radical on the financial question. Never during the greenback period did any substantial body of iron manufacturers approve of the notorious Ohio Idea, the scheme advanced by George Pendleton in 1867 to pay the federal debt in greenbacks. *Iron Age,* the industry's leading trade publication, called Pendleton by the harsh epithet of "repudiator," and commended McCulloch for his courage in resisting paper redemption. The Industrial League in 1868 pronounced "that at all costs to individuals or classes the public faith with the national creditors must be kept unbroken."

Although hostile to "repudiation" the ironmasters, like the western merchants, objected to the shortage of banking and credit facilities in their districts and the resulting exorbitant rates they were frequently forced to pay for credit. Eber Ward of Detroit, pioneer producer of

Bessemer steel, told a Congressional committee in 1874 of the "great increase of business" which had "largely outgrown the amount of currency that the Government [had] furnished." Interest rates were, consequently, high, making it almost impossible to make a profit producing iron and steel in the West. The editor of the *American Manufacturer*, published at Pittsburgh, scolded the proponents of "contraction and forced resumption" for their blindness to the "real condition of matters in the West." If these "theorists" were compelled to manage an iron foundry in the western states for a year or two they would understand what difficulties were involved "in making a profit when interest rates were from eighteen to thirty per cent on good security." The ironmen of Pennsylvania professed to see similar conditions in their own neighborhood. With a population equal to that of New England, the nation's leading iron and steel producing state had only one-eighth that region's circulation, asserted Henry C. Carey, for many years chief apologist of the nation's iron manufacturers. The commercial states had "established a monoply of money power without a parallel in the world"; and while interest rates were low in New England and New York, they ranged from 10 to 30 per cent elsewhere.

Like western merchants who confronted much the same set of conditions, the iron manufacturers championed free banking as the safe method of expanding the currency. In the sixties Daniel Morrell, president of the mammoth Cambria Iron Works, was one of the leading proponents in Congress of repealing the bank circulation limit. In the following decade free banking became something of an obsession with the ironmasters. During the months following the 1873 panic, while Congress searched anxiously for a financial restorative, the ironmen insisted on a moderate greenback expansion coupled with free banking. Even before Congress convened, the American Iron and Steel Association called for a "financial system adequate to the largely increased and increasing business needs of the country." In the middle of the session, the Union Meeting of American Iron Masters adopted resolutions calling on Congress to lift the bank note ceiling and increase the greenback issue to its original $400 million.

In the months following the panic the industry's trade publications were also active in urging bank expansion. "That we need more currency is the universal testimony of all but the money lenders, who reap the harvest of usurious gains when money is stringent," declared *Iron Age* in October 1873. Ten years before, Congress had fixed a bank note limit which, with the growth of industry, had become grossly inadequate for the nation's needs. The law must be changed lest a rigid circulation become a straitjacket for American manufacturing. In the fall of 1873, *Iron Age* editor John Williams plumped for free banking, but accepted the greenback expansion bill which Congress passed in April 1874. Grant's veto of this measure—the so-called Inflation Bill—cut off that avenue of expansion and Williams soon returned to the safer free banking camp.

The other organs of the iron and steel industry, including *The American Manufacturer* and the *Industrial Bulletin*—the latter the publication of the Industrial League—took up the inflationist cause during the crisis of 1873–1874. "Currency is but a tool," explained an *American Manufacturer* editorial shortly after the collapse, "an agent to perform a certain work, viz., exchange and barter, and each community should have the right to decide how much will answer its needs." The *Industrial Bulletin* eulogized expansionist Senator Simon Cameron of Pennsylvania, who had brought the currency question "down out of the clouds into the region of fact and common sense," and derided a much-lauded sound money address of Missouri's Carl Schurz as "the sort of special plea that a lawyer who had a bad cause might make." The *Bulletin* had not a "particle of confidence" in the hard money philosophers who believed "that when perfectly solvent business men need money they should not be able to get it."

Through most of the greenback period the ironmasters remained antagonistic to tight money. Abhorring the "repudiation" doctrines of western agrarians, they stood for moderate, controlled expansion guided by the increasing business needs of the growing nation. "The country needs more money, and there should be an orderly method of freely getting it," was Congressman Daniel Morrell's succinct summary of the ironmaster's position during the decade following Appomattox.

In the less dynamic areas of American manufacturing, hard money sentiment predominated. By the 1860's, the textile industry of New England was firmly established, with its period of most rapid expansion already past. New England's banking resources were more than adequate for the industry's needs, and the Yankee cotton manufacturers did not feel the same credit pinch that made other business men easy prey to soft money doctrines. Moreover, the ability of the cotton manufacturers to undersell foreign competitors in the United States reduced the attractions of the tariff effect produced by the gold premium. In fact, the cotton men were often more disturbed by the postwar loss of foreign markets, which they ascribed to inflated American prices, than they were by British competition.

Some of the most ardent supporters of McCulloch's contractions were to be found within the ranks of the New England textile men. William Gray of the Atlantic Cotton Mills was prominent among the business men urging McCulloch not to falter in his unpopular deflation policy. Edward Atkinson, a cotton manufacturer as well as an economic popularizer and reformer who looked upon "the financial question as almost as vital as the question of reconstruction," was one of the most active and effective assailants of financial deviation through the greenback period. At the 1868 National Commercial Convention it was Atkinson who rallied the forces which defeated the free banking resolutions of the western merchants. Between 1868 and 1879 the Brookline reformer and his circle of "radical" business men waged a veritable crusade against monetary heresy. Atkinson himself published at least eight articles and pamphlets in the sound money cause before 1880, and during the late 1860's joined with such members of the eastern intelligentsia as Charles Francis Adams, Jr., Edwin L. Godkin of the *Nation,* Charles Eliot Norton of the *North American Review,* and Professor Francis Lieber of Columbia College to form an "Economic Club" which distributed sound money tracts and broadsides to business men, editors and prominent politicians. Later, during the Congressional session that followed the panic of 1873, Atkinson was a leading figure in the massive propaganda campaign mounted against the Inflation Bill.

Among the more conventional textile men, Amos A. Lawrence of the prominent Massachusetts industrial dynasty was another outspoken antagonist of the paper standard. Like Gray, Lawrence defended the Contraction Act, which, though it had admittedly produced some business distress, had also come "near bringing us back to specie." With that measure repealed, he noted, the whole painful process of contraction would sooner or later have to be repeated. Lawrence detested the greenbacks and believed it would be the "greatest blessing" if one fifth of "that filthy currency were destroyed by fire." It is not, then, surprising that he judged harshly the rare financial heterodoxy of his fellow textile manufacturers. Such a man as Senator William Sprague, the millionaire cotton magnate of Rhode Island, who had made mild inflationist pronouncements in Congress, was in Lawrence's eyes a rank opportunist. The Spragues, he pointed out, were "the greatest speculators among the whole body of manufacturers in New England" and feared contraction would ruin them.

Lawrence was not the only sound money man who used the label "speculator" to disparage anti-resumption business men, and in these years there was, indeed, much irresponsible gambling by business men on the fluctuating gold-paper ratios. One blatant case of such speculation involving Charles Speer, a Pittsburgh banker, vividly illustrates the extent to which immediate circumstances often governed the currency attitudes of business men. Early in 1867, Speer, who was Assistant Cashier of the First National Bank of Pittsburgh, became involved in specie manipulations and soon was "in on $20,000 gold." Shortly thereafter he suffered serious losses following a sharp break in the gold premium, and by early November he was thinking seriously of selling out. But Speer continued to hope for a rise and at the end of the month he wrote his friend Chauncey F. Black, son of Judge Jeremiah S. Black, expecting to pick up some inside information of Washington affairs that might help him decide on his future course. Was Congress likely to agitate the currency question at the current session? he asked his friend. Was there a chance that the Pendleton scheme might be adopted? What about the rumors that McCulloch might be dismissed? Any of these contingencies, or indeed any move that raised the threat of inflation, would advance gold. If none of these developments could be expected in the near future, Speer would sell out, take his losses, and "wait for a better time to go in."

The gold gambler was, perhaps, a special case, but in a broad sense much of the business of the buoyant post-war era was speculative. These were the years of the "Great Barbecue," when bold and often unscrupulous business adventurers were appropriating the nation's untapped resources and transforming its undeveloped regions into a great industrial and agricultural empire. To the promoters of the new western railroads, mines, and timber lands, falling price levels spelled ruin, and they often looked benignly on currency expansion. "Talk about basing the currency on gold," observed Colonel Beriah Sellers, the literary prototype of the post-war businessman-speculator,[1] "you might as well base it on pork. Gold is only one product. Base it on everything. You've got to do something for the West. . . . We must have improvements." The Colonel's views, if not his particular exuberance, might have been echoed by almost any of the ambitious promoters of the Gilded Age.

In many ways Jay Cooke, the prominent Philadelphia banker, typifies such post-war business promoters. Cooke had been the Treasury's chief bond agent during the war and felt strongly about repaying the bondholders "faithfully" in gold. He was quick to detect and denounce the slightest hint of repudiation, and feared that an uncontrolled inflation would destroy federal credit. In 1866 his brother, Henry D. Cooke, helped lobby the Contraction Act through Congress. But shortly thereafter Cooke had become involved in numerous promotional business ventures, ranging from life insurance to coal, iron, and timber land speculations, and had begun to develop the interest in western railroads that was later to prove his undoing. The Philadelphian not only came to deplore contraction but, like other promoters during these years, was soon proclaiming the virtues of a "currency expansion *moderate* but keeping pace with the new habits and enlarged area of Country." In a letter of 1869, he asked:

---

[1] This, of course, was the colorful figure of Mark Twain's and Charles Dudley Warner's *The Gilded Age*.

Why should this Grand and Glorious Country be stunted and dwarfed— its activities chilled and its very life blood curdled by these miserable "hard coin" theories—the musty theories of a by gone age—These men who are urging on premature resumption know nothing of the great & growing west which would grow twice as fast if it was not cramped for the means necessary to build Rail-Roads and improve farms and convey the produce to market.

Cooke was only one of a large contingent of investors who permitted their stake in a growing America to influence their view of national finances. The career of Thomas Ewing, Jr., illustrates even more vividly the relationship between inflationist convictions and promotional business activities, and also sheds considerable light on the origins of political greenbackism. Ewing, a brevet Major-General during the Civil War, was the son of a Whig Senator of the Jacksonian era who was later a cabinet member under Harrison, Tyler and Taylor successively. After the war, the young Ewing tried his hand at law in Washington, but returned to Ohio in 1870, where he soon became a prominent figure in the state Democratic party. At about the same time, the General and his brothers Charles and Hugh developed sizable interests in central Ohio coal and iron lands, began to invest in the Chesapeake and Ohio Railroad, and embarked on the manufacture of rails to supply the demands of the burgeoning railroad network.

The panic of 1873 and the long business decline that followed were a heavy blow to the Ewing enterprises. The Chesapeake and Ohio defaulted soon after September 1873, and in the following months the family partners were hard pressed to preserve their other investments. During the remainder of the decade, while the Ewings fought a losing battle to escape bankruptcy, like other business men, they held the "infernal" Resumption Act of January 1875 responsible for much of their distress. The resumption measure, passed by a strict party vote in the Republican-dominated Forty-third Congress, had, the Ewings believed, paralyzed all business activity and made it impossible for the family to recoup its losses. "If that . . . law were repealed or amended," the General pointed out to his brother Charles in 1877, the family "coal and iron lands would sell at once."

Through the late seventies Ewing led the Ohio Democracy in a succession of political contests which superficially resemble the Ohio greenbackism of the previous decade. But unlike the Pendletonians of the sixties Ewing did not speak primarily to the state's agrarian masses. While many of his followers actively cultivated the labor vote, Ewing directed his appeals to Ohio business men, who, like himself, were disturbed by the imminence of resumption.

Ewing's speeches in the hard-fought 1875 gubernatorial contest in Ohio disclose the antipathy that he and other western business promoters felt toward the resumption legislation of 1875. "The business men of the country," Ewing declared in an address at Findlay, were "thoroughly satisfied with the greenbacks—they have never asked redemption in coin." Under the paper system the nation's manufacturers and commerce had "prospered beyond all precedent, and prospered most when it [the greenback issue] was relatively most abundant." It was not the laborers, farmers, or "producing capitalists" who demanded contraction and specie payments; it was the security holders, "not the workers but the drones of the hive," who hoped to profit by depressing all prices and values. The Republicans asserted that only debtors would suffer by contraction. But who were these debtors? They were "largely active men, who combine their energies and talent with the capital of non-producers to carry on the work of production and exchange." These "active men" needed credit but could not afford to borrow, knowing that in addition to the normal interest rate some 17 per cent would be added by the "difference between greenbacks now and gold on the first of January 1879."

Ewing brought his anti-resumption views to Congress in 1877, and, appointed to second place on the House Banking and Currency Committee, the Ohioan immediately became a leader of the anti-resumption forces. Under Ewing's management the Democratic House voted to repeal the Resumption Act in November 1877, only to see the motion buried in the Republican Senate.

Ewing's campaign for repeal continued as long as he had hope of salvaging the family fortunes. In 1879, although the nation had already returned to specie, he ran for the governorship of Ohio on a repeal platform. His defeat coincided with the virtual liquidation of the family's business investments, and shortly thereafter Ewing retired from politics to practice law in New York City.

It would be a mistake to suggest a perfectly stable pattern of business opinion on the Reconstruction financial question. The influence of the 1866–1868 recession in transforming the views of western financial men has already been noted, and other shifts of opinion closely related to the business cycle were to occur. During the boom period of the early seventies, for example, business groups hitherto committed to sound finance defended the paper standard with regularity. In 1870, though three previous conventions had adopted strong pro-resumption resolutions, the National Board of Trade session was, for the first time, unfriendly to immediate resumption. Even eastern merchants and financial men, obviously content with the new era of prosperity, urged caution in tampering with the nation's paper currency system. "The labor of man applied to the soil and attention to economy in his expenditure," not legislation, asserted George Buzby of the Philadelphia Commercial Exchange, would bring the nation to hard money. Banker

George Opdyke of the New York Chamber of Commerce pointed out how the country, with little interference in money matters from Congress, had enjoyed a season of "at least average commercial prosperity," and "a rapid strengthening of the resources of the country." The return to specie would be accomplished "more certainly by letting well enough alone than attempting to intervene."

Perhaps the most graphic expression of the altered climate of commercial opinion at the 1870 meeting appears in the remarks of Simeon B. Chittenden, a prominent Brooklyn merchant. At the previous Board convention Chittenden had endorsed resumption. But prosperity had seriously corroded his sound money scruples. Had Congress resumed immediately after Appomattox, he now reflected, "we should not have had the great development of railroads which have come as an incident to our paper money and which may yet prove . . . that a great war and paper money may possibly be a great blessing." Chittenden was not comfortable with his new principles. He could not be certain, he remarked uneasily, that good times were a product of inflation. Still, history would probably show "that the magnificent development of our country was an incident of the great rebellion and of the prodigious amount of paper money which consequently was circulated through the country."

A small majority of the convention, composed largely of the Philadelphia, Pittsburgh, New York and Louisville delegations, rejected a vigorous pro-resumption resolution but the Board made its gesture toward orthodoxy by adopting a weak endorsement of specie payments in principle. By 1874, however, financial disaster had destroyed the happy vision of American business borne along on a swelling greenback tide and the eastern merchants were once again back in the sound money fold.

That political and ideological factors were also capable of altering business opinion is revealed by the abrupt shift of the ironmasters' financial views beginning in mid-1875. This change apparently was related to the hard-fought gubernatorial contests of that year in Ohio and Pennsylvania. A number of Ewing's followers in the 1875 Ohio campaign engaged in blatant rabble-rousing in appealing for the labor vote, and their excesses deeply offended editor John Williams of *Iron Age*. There was a time, Williams explained during the height of the campaign, when the financial debate had been confined to men of intelligence and education. But that was no longer true. It had become a political recreation, with the "people taking sides . . . without any clearer idea of the consequences of extreme legislation upon either side than is gained from partisan and disingenuous discussion in the political newspapers and upon the stump." After the Ohio election Williams noted that "a success [for the inflationists] . . . would have . . .

created an uncertainty as to the future legislation of Congress on the currency question. . . . While a majority of our manufacturers and businessmen do not favor any experimental financial legislation, and are averse to a sudden contraction, they believe that the whole policy of the government should point steadily to resumption."

The *American Manufacturer,* which spoke for the trans-Allegheny iron interests, from a very explicit soft money position in the early seventies, had become evasive by 1876. "We disdain being committed to any of the [monetary] theories afloat," announced a July editorial. In publishing the 1876 platform of the inflationist Independent party the journal described itself as "non-committal upon the doctrines of the platform." By early 1877 the *Manufacturer,* now resigned to resumption, was demonstrating the feasibility of specie payments as soon as the nation developed a favorable trade balance.

The year 1875, which marked the about-face of the editorial policy of *Iron Age,* also witnessed an abrupt shift in the financial attitudes of the Industrial League. In the gubernatorial campaign of that year the Pennsylvania Democracy, hoping to capitalize on the apparent strength of anti-resumption opinion, took over entire the platform of the Ewing Democracy in Ohio. Like their western brethren the Pennsylvanians were soon waging their state campaign by appealing to discontented labor as well as to disaffected business men. Disturbed by the "radical" tenor of inflationist harangues, the League's Executive Committee, consisting of ironmaster Joseph Wharton, William Sellers, a prominent machine tool manufacturer, and publisher-historian Henry Charles Lea, issued a manifesto which reversed the currency position the League had taken since its organization. The Democrats' monetary notions were "revolutionary" and "intrinsically in the highest degree unsound," this declaration announced. "Sooner or later the country must return to the standard of value that no nation can change, and all schemes which promise relief by postponing the inevitable are worse than futile and must render the restoration destructive which otherwise should be beneficial."

Despite the defections to sound money, many business men continued to resist specie payment until the very end of the greenback period. The early resumption moves of Treasury Secretary John Sherman in 1877 produced serious alarm "almost approaching a panic" among the bankers and commercial men of Indianapolis. William Allison, now senior Senator from Iowa, wrote Sherman in June that western railroads were in "bad condition" with "heavy floating debts held by the banks." If the Treasury's resumption policy precipitated a panic it would "break some of our larger railroad corporations." Allison pleaded with Sherman in the name of the railroads to desist from locking up gold and currency for resumption purposes during the all-important fall harvest season. Individual western business men and

Entrepreneurial Liberty and the
Fourteenth Amendment
JOHN P. ROCHE

It is a commonplace that law and its interpretation are part of a larger social process. Roscoe Pound, the famous dean of the Harvard Law School, believed that jurisprudence is sociological. And James Willard Hurst, of the Wisconsin Law School, has noted that "the most creative, driving, and powerful pressures upon our law emerged from the social setting." Felix Frankfurter, too, set jurisprudence in a wider context: "The process of constitutional interpretation compels the translation of policy into judgment, and the controlling conceptions of justices are their 'idealized political picture' of the existing social order." It may be true, as Finley Peter Dunne's Mr. Dooley tartly pointed out, that the Supreme Court follows the election returns. But it is surely beyond doubt that the Court has remade the Constitution to the conditions of each successive age. In this sense the Court, as Henry Steele Commager brilliantly perceived, has long been sitting as a continuous constitutional convention. And in this sense, too, ours has been a government of men, not laws, one that substantiates Charles Evans Hughes's comment (made before he became Chief Justice of the Supreme Court) that "the Constitution is what the judges say it is."

These observations will help us understand the significant thesis that John P. Roche poses in the following article: that the Supreme Court, during the late nineteenth and early twentieth centuries, made the doctrine of entrepreneurial liberty central to American constitutional law and that, far from espousing a laissez-faire *economy, the Court adapted the Constitution to the needs of the great private governments of big business. Roche has taught at Brandeis University and served as special consultant to President Johnson, acting as liaison between the administration and the American intellectual community. He has been a longtime student of American political institutions. His many publications include:* The Dynamics of Democratic Government *(with Murray S. Stedman, Jr., 1954),* Courts and Rights: The

SOURCE: *Labor History*, IV (Winter, 1963) 3–31. Reprinted by permission.

American Judiciary in Action *(1961), and* The Quest for the Dream: The Development of Civil Rights and Human Relations in America *(1963).*

Professor Roche's thesis is a provocative one, and encourages a whole series of relevant questions. In what major ways has the Supreme Court's interpretation of the Constitution changed since 1789? How far have the modifications expressed an overall continuity of premises and values regarding American life? What factors have been responsible for these changing interpretations? What factors, in particular, were responsible for the formulation and vitality of "the doctrine of entrepreneurial liberty"? To what extent has American constitutional interpretation been attributable to specific key individuals who have sat on the Supreme Court—such men, for example, as Marshall, Story, Taney, Field, Holmes, Brandeis, and Warren? If the Constitution was formulated to express the desire of Americans for social transformation, how much has it since served as a brake on social progress? To put this somewhat differently: Can an instrument devised in the eighteenth century remain sufficiently valid and utile in meeting twentieth-century problems? In what way do the Constitution and its interpretation express the American social myth? And what is the relevance of the American Constitution, and of the social institutions and ideas that it expresses, to the world of the late twentieth century, with its many new nations and new constitutions?

The questions that Professor Roche's essay evoke could be extended. However numerous, they lead us back to the premise we began with, one which Carl Becker, so keen a student of American political ideas, memorably expressed: "Looked at in this gray light, constitutions are seen to be documents historically conditioned, the imperfect and temporary products of time and place. Whatever the intention of their framers may have been, their meaning is determined by the ingenuity of judges, God helping them, to luff and fill before the shifting winds of social opinion."

In the last quarter of the nineteenth century and well on into the twentieth, so the legend runs, the United States was dominated by a "conservative," "individualist," *laissez-faire* elite which succeeded in rewriting the Constitution and notably the Fourteenth Amendment to impose its ideology upon the nation. This notion has a certain superficial persuasiveness, but regrettably it is hardly sustained by a close analysis of the history of the period. There was clearly an elite of businessmen, but it was neither ruggedly individualistic, in terms of classic liberal economic thought, nor "conservative," in any acceptable definition of that much-abused term. On the contrary, this elite lived at the public trough, was nourished by state protection, and devoted most of its time and energies to evading Adam Smith's individualistic injunctions. In ideological terms, it was totally opportunistic: It demanded and applauded vigorous state action in behalf of its key values, and denounced state intervention in behalf of its enemies. The Constitution was not, in short, adapted to the needs of *laissez-faire* "conservatism"— which is a respectable, internally consistent system of political economy —but to the exigent needs of the great private governments. The "Robber Barons" had no ideology, they had interests. They had no theory of the state, but they knew what they wanted from it. Their key value, entrepreneurial liberty, might require a strong state one day (to combat trade unions) and a weak state the next (which would not pass wage and hour legislation), and this inconsistency troubled them not. If some scribe wanted to make them into "industrial statesmen," or "pillars of conservatism," that was merely one of the eccentricities of the division of labor.

Nowhere does this opportunism, this absence of theoretical consistency or of any concern for consistency, appear more clearly than in the adaptation of the Fourteenth Amendment, especially the due process clause, to the needs of private government. Central to the power of private governments in the American "Age of Enterprise" was the doctrine that private agreements between parties attained a sacred status, that such contracts were on a higher level of legitimacy than the police power of the state. To put it another way, the sanctity of contract put inter-"personal" (corporations, it should be noted, qualified as "persons") relationships largely beyond the authority of the political sovereign. From a different perspective the question was, to what extent is the authority of the community limited by private arrangements among its citizens; that is, by "liberty of contract"?

The argument began early in the history of the Republic. The framers of the Constitution included, without discussion, a proviso that no state could "impair the obligation of a contract." It is impossible to know what they had in mind, but in all probability the stipulation was aimed at state legal tender laws, such as that in Rhode Island, which had required creditors to accept depreciated paper currency in payment of debts incurred in specie. While on its face the limitation was absolute, it is inconceivable that the authors of the Constitution intended to put private agreements wholly beyond the reach of the state's police power. Like many other provisions of the Constitution, it was agreed to in haste to be interpreted by later generations in leisure.

In the early Supreme Court cases, the Justices established the basic positions which, in differing contexts, have survived to our own time. John Marshall on one side asserted the vested rights view that contracts are made in heaven, that is, they have their roots in the natural law and are superior to the civil law. Marshall was far too shrewd to claim that all interpersonal agreements were inviolable contracts; by employing his favorite device—circular logic—he explained that a law forbidding usury did not impair contractual obligations because an arrangement to pay excessive interest was not, in the first place properly speaking, a "contract." Q.E.D. The opposing view, that contracts are conceived in the womb of the civil law rather than in a natural law never-never land, was vigorously asserted by Justice William Johnson. Contracts, he argued, were always formulated and executed within the jurisdiction of the state police power. True, the legislature did not have unlimited authority to modify or abrogate agreements, but it could establish rules and standards binding on private parties. These rules and regulations could even be applied retrospectively—to contracts made before they were encountered—if it could be shown that the contracting parties *should have known* that the legislature had reserved power in this area.

This is an extremely complex, even metaphysical doctrine. If, for example, X, a brewer, signed a twenty-year contract to supply Y, an innkeeper, with beer and after five years the state instituted prohibition, was the contract voided? From the natural-law viewpoint, the contract cannot be impaired by such a statute, and as the prohibition movement swept across the United States in the mid-nineteenth century many liquor manufacturers hopefully fortified themselves with long-term contracts with a view to putting their business beyond the reach of the police power. But from the civil-law position, no private arrangements can bind the sovereign; therefore when X and Y made their contract, they did so with the knowledge that it was subject to later legislative modification. To put it another way, all contracts are enacted in a contingent universe, and this contingency is an implicit premise in the private agreement. Once the Taney Court added to this proposition the corollary that all doubts are resolved in favor of the public, the contract clause of the Constitution (Art. I, Sec. 10) went into hibernation as a significant limit on public policy.

With this hasty summary in mind, let us direct our attention to the revival of the concept of contract which in the last years of the nineteenth and first quarter of the twentieth centuries became the fundamental buttress of private government. This resurgence took place under two main headings. First, the concept of contract was broadened to include the substantive right to pursue a calling, both on an individual and on a corporate level. Second, the right to make contractual arrangements to exercise one's calling became a "property" right protected from state infringement by the due process clause of the Fourteenth Amendment. As Justice Field argued in a classic formulation of this position, his dissent in the *Slaughterhouse Cases* (1873), a butcher has a natural right to exercise his trade—contract for his services—and a state law which deprives him of his freedom to make his own arrangements (contracts) has expropriated his property rights in his enterprise. Field was even prepared to argue that such a statute constituted slavery in violation of the Thirteenth Amendment!

In effect, the old Marshallian interpretation of the contract appeared in a new guise, a far broader and more sophisticated one than the Chief Justice had ever envisioned. Instead of giving natural law attributes to contracts only, Field and his followers widened the protection to encompass the *right to enter into contracts,* that is, to the prerogative of doing business on one's own terms, which I have designated entrepreneurial liberty. And on his own West Coast Circuit, where he was boss, Justice Field implemented his convictions in what was known as "Ninth Circuit Law." Relying on a technicality which prevented Supreme Court review of *habeas corpus* decisions, Field and his judicial associates established as constitutional law in the Ninth Circuit the proposition that the rights to pursue legitimate callings, to make and enforce contracts, and to do business free from extraordinary legislative control were incorporated in the due process and equal protection clauses of the Fourteenth Amendment. In this backdoor fashion, natural entrepreneurial rights entered the Constitution.

While Field never denied the existence of the police power, his whole position was based on the proposition that in any conflict between private *economic* rights and public authority the burden of proof rested on the state. The state, in other words, had to demonstrate to the satisfaction of the Court that its regulations were justified. In the absence of strong historical or contextual proof of legitimacy, Field almost automatically voted "No!," but it was possible on occasion— *e.g., Barbier* v. *Connolly* (1885), *Soon Hing* v. *Crowley* (1885)—to convince him that the police power had been legitimately exercised. Yet in the area of non-economic rights (rights of Negroes, for example, to equal political treatment) he gave the police power its head.

This is not the place for a discussion of the rapid spread of Justice Field's—and Justice Bradley's—dissenting views in the *Slaughterhouse Cases.* Needless to say, the conception that there was constitutional protection for the right to follow one's calling—and that the contractual arrangements made in pursuing business goals were largely immune to public authority—became the ideological *point d'appui* for the corporations in their struggle against regulation. State judges were particularly susceptible to this line of argument, and in New York, Pennsylvania, West Virginia, and many other states the divine right of contract supplied the rationale for voiding state regulatory legislation. Contracts were the instruments by which men implemented their property rights in their economic capacities; thus legislatively to prohibit paying miners in company script, when they had agreed to this form of remuneration in their employment contracts, was to deprive the *miners* of their "property right" to make their own economic decisions. The average miner never really appreciated this judicial concern for his integrity; from his worm's-eye view a contract with the coal company was hardly the outcome of bargaining between equals. But the judges persisted in protecting him from his own base instincts, which would have led him to become a "ward of the state"—a fate worse than death.

This judicial altruism deserves emphasis. There is no necessity to believe that the judges were insincere when they protected the furious farmers from "serfdom" by striking down legislative enactments designed to curb railroad shipping practices, or when they rescued the industrial worker from "slavery" by asserting freedom of contract in his behalf. Just as in the *Income Tax Cases* (1895) communism was seen as the logical consequence of a graduated tax, so serfdom and slavery were seen as the natural end results of dependence on the state. This was the era when, under the Social Darwinist aegis, that evil abstraction The State was first loosed in the land. The conflict of the age was seen as one between The Individual and The State, and the consequences of Statism (the triumph of the weak over the strong in Spencerian terms) would be decadence and dictatorship.

The logic of this position was absurd in its own terms. As a contemporary critic like Lester F. Ward pointed out (to an empty house), if the weak succeeded in beating the strong by ganging up against them, according to the syllogism of Social Darwinism, they became the "fittest." In other words, if one argues that Nature awards the prize to the "fittest" and that the "fittest" are those who emerge on top of the pile, then the workers or farmers who successfully club down the industrial magnates with the state as their weapon deserve the Darwinian accolade. The logic of Social Darwinism was that the winner takes all; no ground rules were prescribed. What the state, and later the federal judges, did in the name of impartiality was strip the weak of their capacity for collective action. In the event that the workers did persuade the state legislature to act in their behalf, a judge would hastily blow the whistle, cancel the victory, and in the name of fair play return power to the opposition. Or, to change the analogy, the courts effectively sent the workers and the farmers into the boxing ring with the injunction that if they used their best punch on the corporations, it would be ruled a foul.

Moreover, this judicial posture completely overlooked the extent to which the great private governments were in point of fact "wards of the state." Hothouse conditions were established for industrial growth by the protective tariff which in essence gave these tariff-protected industries the power to tax the American consumer. On a different level, state and federal judges were always ready to rush to the aid of a corporation which was having difficulties with a labor union—even if it was necessary, as in the *Debs Case*, to improvise a legal foundation for such intervention. Indeed, the Debs imprisonment and the Pullman Strike which led to it provide an excellent example of the extent to which the federal government would aid a private government in distress.

In May 1894, trouble broke out in the feudal demesne of George Pullman, the company town of Pullman on the outskirts of Chicago. Workers who protested against wage cuts were thrown out of their "homes"; Pullman refused even to discuss the matter, and his employees *en masse* joined Eugene Debs' American Railway Union (A.R.U.) and struck. Debs, who had led the A.R.U. to a sensational victory over the Great Northern Railroad in 1893, realized that the strike had to be handled with great care—any violence or disorder would provide the federal government with an excuse to intervene as it had in 1877. With great care and tactical brilliance, Debs masterminded a spectacular "functional revolution" against the private government of George Pullman: On June 26 the word went out along the lines to boycott the "Palace Cars" without interrupting other rail transportation. Suddenly, all over the West Pullman cars appeared quietly resting on sidings—the workers simply shunted them out of trains and left them behind.

This tactic unsettled the railroads, who could hardly claim that shunting Pullman cars out of trains was "revolutionary violence," and they hastily devised a counter-tactic: They attached the United States' mail cars to the Pullmans. This hardly deterred the workers, who cut the Palace Cars out of any location in the train, so the managers took the next step: *They* refused to run any trains not made up to *their* specifications, *i.e.*, they declared war on the "public" and tied up the railroads. Knowing the close connection between the General Managers' Association and Attorney General Richard Olney, Debs had been particularly careful not to interrupt mail service; now it was stopped by the Managers themselves, though of course they assigned the blame to the A.R.U.

The national government moved into action on July 2, 1894, when at Olney's instruction an injunction was requested from the United States District Court in Chicago forbidding any interference with rail traffic into that city. Although there was no federal statute governing the matter, the Court took jurisdiction on the grounds that the strike was holding up the mails and was an unlawful restraint on interstate commerce. At this point, violence did break out—aimed at preventing the enforcement of the decree—and the next day, over the objections of the Governor of Illinois, John P. Altgeld, federal troops were moved into Chicago to break the strike. Concurrently Debs and other leaders of the A.R.U. were arrested on a shotgun indictment charging them with violations of the Sherman Anti-Trust Law and contempt of court.

We can not linger with the details, which have been chronicled at length by several historians. The important point for our purposes here is the flimsy legal basis on which federal intervention was founded. There simply was no federal law authorizing the Debs injunction, and it supposedly had been determined as far back as 1812 (*United States* v. *Hudson and Goodwin*) that the national government had no common-law jurisdiction; that is, that the federal authorities could not exercise punitive sanctions without statutory authority. But the Supreme Court was equal to the occasion: Justice Brewer for a unanimous Court held that the absence of specific authority was inconsequential since the "obligations which [the federal government] is under to promote the interest of all, and to prevent the wrongdoing of one resulting in injury to the general welfare, is often of itself sufficient to give it standing in court. . . ." *In re Debs* (1895). The implication of this startling and revolutionary holding was that the federal government had an inherent power to protect the "general welfare"—a view which conservatives would later denounce as unconstitutional and communistic, but which they welcomed in 1895 when it justified the imprisonment of "Dictator Debs."

Mr. George Pullman and the General Managers' Association were obviously "wards of the state." Their right to engage in business on their own terms, allegedly founded in higher law, rested in fact on the coercive power of the government: on the injunction, which the Managers' Association significantly called a "gatling gun on paper"; and on the actual gatling guns of United States troops. But while we can, armed with the clarity of hindsight, make this assertion, the fact remains that the myth of rugged individualism dominated the constitutional ethos, seemingly unharmed, even untouched, by the corrosion of contrary data. Let us now turn to an examination of the Supreme Court's application of this dogma of entrepreneurial liberty to three areas of political economy: labor relations, rate regulation, and social legislation.

The trade union movement in both the United States and Great Britain began life with a common-law bar sinister emblazoned on its shield; it was considered as a conspiracy in restraint of trade liable to criminal prosecution, civil suit for damages, or both. While by the end of the nineteenth century trade unions in the United States were no longer automatically illegal conspiracies, in any attempt to exercise economic power they were subject to an almost infinite number of legal harassments. The long-range goal of union organizations has always been job control; that is, the power to require union membership as a condition of employment. With this, of course, goes the right of the union to recognition by management as the bargaining agent (or agents, there can be more than one union involved) for the employees. Few nineteenth century employers were willing to accept unionization, and when the unions attempted to attain their ends by striking, they found the weight of legal precedent an almost insuperable barrier to success. I have mentioned above the fiction of equilibrium which was important in trade union litigation; here let us concentrate on a few Supreme Court decisions which exemplified the judicial approach towards industrial relations. These cases, it should be noted, are those which used "liberty of contract" as the rationale of decision—rather than those resting on the commerce power and Sherman Act.

In the wake of the Pullman strike, President Cleveland appointed a special commission to investigate railroad problems. When this body reported to the President in November 1894, it recommended, *inter alia,* that Congress take action to protect the railway workers' right to organize unions, and a bill was subsequently introduced by Congressman Erdman of Pennsylvania which included such a provision. A ferocious legislative battle ensued—the Senate killed two House versions in 1895 and 1897—but finally in 1898 President McKinley signed the Railway Labor Act establishing the Railway Labor Board, mediation machinery, and a provision (Section 10) banning the "yellow dog" contract, the blacklist, and dismissal for union membership. All this enactment accomplished was the legitimatizing of unionism on interstate railroads—essentially it superseded the feudal law of the private railroad government which had made union activity a capital offense in economic terms. In other words, it gave the railroad unions *right of access,* but no more.

It was one thing to have such a law on the books, quite another to get it enforced. Despite widespread violations, it was not until 1907 that the first test case reached the Supreme Court (two others had aborted *en route*). William Adair, the chief of operations of the Louisville and Nashville Railroad, had been indicted for firing O. B. Coppage on the ground that the latter had, in violation of his contract, joined the Brotherhood of Locomotive Firemen. The railroad claimed that Section 10 of the Erdman Act was unconstitutional: first, it was not properly within Congressional authority under the commerce power to regulate labor relations; and, second, assuming it could be founded on the commerce power, the provision was a violation of the due process clause of the Fifth Amendment as an infringement of "liberty of contract." Our concern here is with the second of these allegations.

In *Adair* v. *United States* (1908), the Supreme Court sustained the railroad view by a vote of six to two. Writing for the majority, Justice Harlan first of all declared Section 10 to be a violation of the Fifth Amendment, and then for good measure he added that the power to regulate labor contracts was *not* encompassed in the commerce power.

Section 10, Harlan held, was "an invasion of the personal liberty, as well as of the right of property, guaranteed by" the due process clause of the Fifth Amendment. The Louisville and Nashville Railroad thus had the right "to prescribe the terms upon which the services of Coppage would be accepted, and it was the right of Coppage to become or not, as he chose, an employee of the railroad company upon the terms offered to him." In other words, the Louisville and Nashville Railroad and Coppage "have equality of right, and any legislation that disturbs that equality is an arbitrary interference with the liberty of contract which no government can legally justify in a free land."

Justice Oliver Wendell Holmes, Jr., who as we shall see shortly was himself anything but flexible in his approach to the mythology of the common law, dissented on the ground that the Erdman Act was a legitimate exercise of the commerce power and that "the section (10) is, in substance, a very limited interference with freedom of contract" well within the power of Congress. Justice McKenna also dissented, confining himself almost wholly to the question of the commerce clause.

If the due process clause of the Fifth Amendment could be construed as banning legislative efforts to end the "yellow dog" contract on the national level, it logically followed that the equivalent provision of the Fourteenth Amendment could similarly undermine state efforts to the same end. And so the Court held in 1915 by a six to three division (*Coppage* v. *Kansas*). Justice Pitney, who replaced Harlan in 1912, continued Harlan's views but added to them a pious patina which the bluff old Kentucky Unionist never employed. In some ways the Pitney opinion in *Coppage* v. *Kansas* sounds like a caricature of the "rugged individualist" viewpoint written by an enemy. The right freely to enter into contracts, said the Justice, "is as essential to the laborer as to the capitalist, to the poor as to the rich." Unfortunately perhaps "wherever the right of private property exists, there must and will be inequalities of fortune; and thus it naturally happens that parties negotiating about a contract are not equally hampered by circumstances." Translated into English, Pitney's cloudy legalese amounts to the statement that the poor man's right to negotiate from weakness is as essential to him as the rich man's right to negotiate from strength.

To ensure that his point was appreciated on the appropriate philosophical level, Pitney then turned to cosmology for what might be called the ontological proof of the validity of the "yellow dog" contract:

> And, since *it is self-evident* that, unless all things are held in common, some persons must have more property than others, *it is from the nature of things* impossible to uphold freedom of contract and the right of private property without at the same time recognizing as legitimate those inequalities of fortune that are the necessary result of the exercise of those rights. (Italics added.)

Holmes dissented tersely; one suspects that he may have been slightly nauseated. The old warrior believed firmly that the first law of life was struggle, but he despised metaphysical efforts to demonstrate that the winners in the battle of life had received some Divine afflatus. Justice Day, joined by Hughes, also dissented, pointing out at some length that the Kansas statute under attack was "intended to promote the same liberty of action for the employee as the employer confessedly [through employer groups such as the General Managers' Association] enjoys. The law should be as zealous to protect the constitutional liberty of the employee as it is to guard that of the employer."

The third, and last, case for discussion here took the principles enounced in *Adair* and *Coppage* to their logical conclusion. The long legal struggle began in 1906 when the United Mine Workers of America (U.M.W.) struck the Hitchman Coal and Coke Company in the West Virginia panhandle. The strike was defeated and in its aftermath the company set up its own "union" which required as a condition of employment that the miners sign a "disloyalty oath" to the U.M.W. in which they promised, under penalty of dismissal, never to affiliate with that Union. In 1907 the U.M.W. began its campaign to recapture the allegiance of the miners, and the company went to court. Without going into the intricate legal details, the company asked for and received an injunction prohibiting the U.M.W. from attempting to organize its workers—such an effort, even though it was peaceful, amounted to a conspiracy to induce breach of contract. Indeed, Judge Dayton forbade the Union from employing "argument, reason and persuasion" with the Hitchman workers; he actually barred union organizers from "talking to" the men.

This "temporary" injunction was in effect until 1912, when Judge Dayton finally got around to a decision on the merits. (In injunctive proceedings, there are various stages: in the first, a preliminary injunction can be issued on an *ex parte* basis—that is, one party, threatened by immediate damage, can get a freeze order; in the second, which is an adversary proceeding, both parties present argument and the judge decides whether or not there is an adequate case for continuing the freeze; in the third, if the preliminary injunction has been made temporary at the second state, the judge holds a full trial on the merits and reaches a final determination.) To the surprise of no one, Judge Dayton made the injunction permanent—which meant that any efforts to unionize Hitchman would be punishable as contempt of court. However, the Union was pleased and startled when, two years later (the organizers had now been barred from the mines for seven years), the Court of Appeals over-ruled Judge Dayton at every point. Hitchman promptly appealed to the Supreme Court.

The Supreme Court, in 1917 (*Hitchman Coal & Coke Co.* v. *Mitchell*), split six to three in favor of the Company. Justice Pitney for the Court had no difficulty fitting the Hitchman situation into his cosmology: If the "yellow dog" contract had Divine sanction, then it was self-evident in the nature of things that the Union's efforts were sacrilegious. The injunction was sustained and the labor movement was effectively barred from ever attempting to organize workers who had signed "yellow dog" contracts—any effort to this end would automatically fall into the category of a conspiracy to achieve an illegal end, breach of contract. The right of union organizers even to freedom of speech was held to be subordinate to the sanctity of contractual obligations.

Justice Brandeis wrote a sharp dissent for himself, Justice Holmes, and Justice Clarke. In essence, Brandeis denied every contention of the majority: The U.M.W. was a legal body employing legal means to achieve a legal end. While he did not question the validity of the "yellow dog" contract, Brandeis pointed out that dismissal was a consequence of joining a union, not of talking about or preparing to join the union. Brandeis' views were warmly greeted by the unions as well as by progressives generally, but the employers had the majority and set to work with it.

In tactical terms, the opinion of the Court enshrined the injunction as the primary weapon against unionization. And it was a devastating weapon. In the first place, as we have seen in *Hitchman,* the procedures were such that, once a temporary injunction had been granted, years might pass before final determination of the issues. Throughout this period the injunction remained in force, undermining any sustained organizing campaign. If the union organizers decided to ignore the injunction and go ahead with their drive (even today, with all the conveniences of the National Labor Relations Acts, a unionization campaign calls for sustained, continuous effort), they were promptly arrested for contempt of court. Under the Clayton Act of 1914, they had the right to a jury trial; but jury or no jury, they went out of circulation in the sense that their work for the union ceased. In managerial circles the injunction was rated higher than a regiment of national guardsmen. In psychological terms, the onus for "breaking the law" was always on the unions; a refusal to obey even the most openly bitter anti-labor judge left the unionists under these circumstances in "defiance of the Constitution."

When the Supreme Court incorporated what I have called the dogma of entrepreneurial freedom into the Fourteenth Amendment, it crippled the efforts of the trade unions to organize. In a different sector of the economy this potent concept was at work undermining the efforts of state and local governments to regulate the rates charged by utilities, railroads, and similar corporations. Probably no area of public law is more complex than that concerned with the determination of "reasonable" rates, and we shall not get involved in the substantive problems.

Our concern is rather with the antecedent question: Who shall have the power to evaluate the "reasonableness" of rates? What might be called the administrative school of thought, which was on the rise in the years we are discussing, asserted that the determination of rates was a legislative-administrative problem, one which could be handled intelligently only by a body of experts acting under state authority. In this tradition various states established railroad or public utility commissions with rate-fixing powers. The other school of thought asserted that only a judicial body could exercise jurisdiction over "reasonableness," that historically the concept of a "reasonable return" was a common law derivative, that for the legislature to meddle in the area was a violation of the separation of powers, and thus of due process of law.

All utilities are inherently quasi-public in character, and under the old rules of the common law they were subjected to a special degree of control by the sovereign. A railroad, for example, was given a public charter, trolleys operated on the streets by franchise, gas companies ran their pipes with public assent. No one has a natural or civil right to build a railroad any more than he can convert his suburban backyard into a stone quarry or an airport. Throughout the middle years of the nineteenth century the police power was dominant over the assertion of vested rights, and in 1877 the Supreme Court, in the so-called *Granger Cases,* appeared to give the states the green light for vigorous regulation of "businesses affected with a public interest." The *Granger Cases* are fascinating reading; the first, *Munn* v. *Illinois,* is characteristically quoted in case books, but there were eight cases decided *en masse* (with Justice Field in bitter opposition) which effectively undercut every line of attack that corporations could launch against the police power, at least in the constitutional sense. In the leading case, Illinois was permitted to establish maximum storage rates for grain elevators; in the remaining cases a wide range of legislative railroad regulation was approved, including freight and passenger rates. Chief Justice Waite flatly and virtually without discussion rejected the contention that the states could not regulate interstate railroads; he suggested that if various citizens did not like the substance of the regulations, they should go into politics and get the legislature to change its laws. These decisions, barked Field in dissent, "practically destroy all the guarantees of the Constitution and of the common law . . . for the protection of the railroad companies." The nub of the controversy was the locus of authority to define "reasonable" rates: The corporations asserted that only by a judicial proceeding could this be done—a judge, or a judge and jury, would then decide in a specific case whether the company had overcharged. The states, with the Court's agreement, felt that the evaluation of fair and reasonable rate structures was within the jurisdiction of the legislature—either directly or through delegation to a commission.

From the corporate viewpoint, there were several lines of possible assault on the *Granger* decisions. For the railroads, in particular, the claim could be made that state regulation was an intrusion into Congress' power over interstate commerce. In the absence of any commerce power issue, the corporations could keep chewing away at the police power on several grounds and hope that one or another Justice would be converted, or that new judges coming on the bench would accept their views. There was always hope that the Contract clause could be revived; Justice Field was constantly recommending the useful potentialities of the Fourteenth Amendment; and there were even odd-ball decisions such as Justice Miller's in *Loan Association* v. *Topeka* (1875), which suggested that the Court could find a basis in natural law for frustrating "robbery" carried on under the auspices of the police power. Moreover, the vital statistics of the Court were morbidly reassuring: In the decade following the *Granger Cases* (1877), five new Justices were appointed to the Court, all from legal and professional backgrounds which suggested they would take seriously the threat to property rights.

With this transformation of the Court in mind, let us turn to the famous case of *Chicago, Milwaukee & St. Paul Railway Co.* v. *Minnesota* (1890) in which the Supreme Court began the retreat from the *Granger Cases.* Minnesota had set up a railroad commission charged by the legislature with ensuring that the roads exacted only "equal and reasonable rates," and this commission had ordered the Chicago, Milwaukee & St. Paul to lower its charges for hauling milk. Writing for the six-judge majority, Justice Blatchford neatly side-stepped *Munn* v. *Illinois,* holding that the determination of a "reasonable" rate could not be delegated to a non-judicial body such as a commission. "The question of the reasonableness of a rate of charge for transportation [he asserted] is eminently a question for judicial decision." In essence, Blatchford announced that no administrative (and by implication, legislative—legislatures do not operate "under the forms" supplied "by the wisdom of successive ages for the investigation judicially" of controversial issues) determination of a rate schedule could ever be final. He issued an invitation to any railroad or utility grieved by legal rate schedules to take the issue of "reasonableness" to court. Perhaps caught up by the spirit of the age, the Justice declared a judicial corner on "reasonableness," and would permit no unsanctified legislative body to infringe the monopoly.

Four years later Justice Brewer—Field's nephew, if possible a stronger supporter of entrepreneurial freedom than his uncle—filled in the gaps in Blatchford's argument. Under review was a schedule of rates prepared, *after notice and hearings,* by the Texas Railroad Commission which were challenged as "unreasonable" by a railroad bond-holder. Conceding that the Court could not itself go into the rate-making business, Brewer made it perfectly clear that the Justices knew "unreasonable" rates when they saw them. A railroad had a constitutional right to charge enough to defray expenses and make some return to its investors: "justice demands that every one should receive some compensation for the use of his money or property, if it be possible without prejudice to the rights of others." Brewer was a bit vague on the constitutional basis of this right to make a profit, but he seems to have tucked it into the Equal Protection clause of the Fourteenth Amendment: "The equal protection of the laws—the spirit of common justice—forbids that one class [railroad bondholders] should by law be compelled to suffer loss that others [shippers] may make gain."

If one recalls the fantastic financial operations of the railways in the nineteenth and early twentieth century, the problem comes into better focus. The common prank of the financiers was over-capitalization—a railroad with a cash value of a million dollars would be capitalized at two million, bonds would be issued calling for 4 or 5 per cent return, and rates would be fixed at a level which would, hopefully, bring this or better. In California in the 1870s, the Southern Pacific Railroad was bitterly contesting its valuation for tax purposes at $16,500 per mile as confiscatory, but was capitalized at $43,500 per mile! Now the question arises: Which figure should be used to compute a "reasonable" rate? If the railroad commission employs the net value of the property, the rates necessary to provide a "fair return" will be considerably below those which would be derived from using the capitalized value of the property. Assuming that a 5 per cent return is considered "reasonable," and we continue the fictitious example above of the one million dollar railroad capitalized at two millions, a fair rate in the first instance would bring in $50,000 a year, in the second, $100,000. In practical terms, freight and passenger charges would have to be doubled to sustain the two million rate-base.

Turn this proposition around and another dimension, basic to the cases under discussion, becomes obvious. A railroad, overcapitalized let us say by 50 per cent—a fifteen million dollar indebtedness on a ten million cash outlay—in order to stay solvent must pay its bondholders a total of $600,000 a year, assuming a 4 per cent coupon. But a state railroad commission, after careful assessment of the net value of the actual assets of the line, fixes a rate schedule which cannot earn more than $450,000 in profits. Has the commission acted "unreasonably"? The answer to this question is not founded on legal doctrine, but on economic and political presuppositions. If a judge adopts the ruthless view of classic *laissez-faire* economics, he will doubtless hold that the investor has the job of anticipating future risks and acting accordingly, that it is not the task of the judiciary to rescue bondholders from the penalties of economic stupidity. If the judge believes that it is the function of the state to protect the public from extortion, he will unquestionably accept the decision of the railroad commission as binding on the corporation.

However, to return to the main line of the argument, if the judge believes that the well-being of the investor and the liberty of action of the entrepreneur are the key social and economic values, he will defend the corporation's inflated rate-base against both economic rationality and the police power. It was this course which the Supreme Court took in the 1890s and early decades of this century. As time went by, the judicial weapon became more precise: indeed, in 1930 the Court was able to state, *ex cathedra*, that a Baltimore trolley company had a constitutional right to a return of 7.44 per cent on the value of its property! Presumably 7.43 per cent would have been a deprivation of due process.

What is important to note is that the Court assumed, without any justification, that the restrictions of due process on the state's police power were identical with the restrictions on its power of eminent domain. Once this analogy was established, the fight was over—the conclusions were subsumed in the premises. Now it is quite clear that the state acting under its power of eminent domain must reimburse the citizen fair value for his property. If a house is condemned to make room for a superhighway, its owner is entitled to full reimbursement of his investment. *But the police power does not proceed on the same basis.* One may have paid a thousand dollars for an ounce of the best heroin, but if it is seized by the state there will be no compensation. Nor do prohibition laws respect a man's property right in alcoholic beverages. The only due process a heroin pusher or a bootlegger can expect is procedural: He has the right to a fair trial in criminal court. He has no right to a 7.44 per cent return on his investment.

Thus if one begins with the assumption that the state of Texas, or Minnesota, in establishing regulations governing railroad rates, was limiting the corrupt endeavors of corporate officials and protecting the public from institutionalized embezzlement and extortion, the Supreme Court's decisions amounted to a protection of criminal behavior. Indeed, this was the way many agrarian radicals and urban progressives interpreted the work of the Court. However, from the viewpoint of Justice Field, Justice Brewer, or the seven other Justices who *unanimously* concurred in the Texas holding discussed above (*Reagan* v. *Farmers' Loan and Trust Co.*, 1894), this criticism was a form of blasphemy. And it should be reiterated that they were honest, dedicated men—dedicated to the proposition that entrepreneurial rights were a mundane manifestation of natural law, and to its Siamese twin which holds that those who would lay profane hands on corporate prerogatives were the harbingers of socialistic serfdom.

Before the Court could with confidence invoke a precise fraction such as 7.44 per cent, there had to be a formula. As Robert L. Hale pointed out many years ago, the process of formulation was rather peculiar. The Court in fact began with the "right" answer, and then had to work backwards to the "right" question. The answer as we have seen was that a utility had the right to a "fair return" or a "reasonable return" on its investment. But what was to be the rate-base, the foundation on which any hypothetical "fair return" would be computed? In 1899 the question for this answer was formulated by Justice Harlan in *Smythe* v. *Ames.*

This is not the place to investigate the chaos which for half a century developed in the wake of the "rule of *Smythe* v. *Ames*"; nor are we here concerned with the circular logic which sustained it (earning power is a key consideration in "value"; thus to diminish the earning power by rate restrictions is automatically to reduce the "value"). Its importance lay in the enormous freedom it gave to public utilities and the almost infinite number of roadblocks it put in the way of effective state regulation. No matter how much work a group of utility experts had put into the determination of a rate-scale based on a "fair value," once this schedule had been promulgated by a regulatory commission, an inevitable trip was taken to the federal court. There the whole question was argued *de novo* with the Supreme Court reserving the right to throw out any set of regulations that did not insure a "reasonable" return on "fair value" as violative of the due process clause of the Fourteenth Amendment. And while this argument was, of course, conducted in precise legal terminology, it was in essence an elaborate exercise in constitutional mysticism. As Justice Stone, discussing one component of Harlan's formula, observed many years later: "In assuming the task of determining judicially the present fair replacement value of the vast properties of public utilities, courts have been projected into the most speculative undertaking imposed upon them in the entire history of English jurisprudence."

The constitutional dogma of entrepreneurial liberty thus simultaneously crippled the power of the trade unions to achieve recognition and bargaining status and undermined the authority of the state over public utilities. In both instances, the natural right to conduct business on one's own terms was incorporated into the Fourteenth Amendment. Let us now turn to the third dogmatic manifestation: the employment of "liberty of contract" as a weapon against social legislation. It would be wise at this point to re-emphasize a definitional matter which is relevant here, serving to distinguish this category of legislative interference from the one just examined. No public utility could ever, even in the view of a judge as committed to entrepreneurial liberty as Stephen J. Field, justify in legal terms full freedom from special regulation. These "quasi-public" enterprises—railroads, turnpikes, traction companies, gas and water distributors—were designated as businesses "affected with a public interest" and were theoretically far more subordinate to the police power than "private" undertakings. The category of businesses "affected with a public interest" was, however, not simple to define. In the *Granger Cases,* Chief Justice Waite ducked the definitional issue by suggesting that it lay within the jurisdiction of the state legislature; Field retorted that to do so would leave the entire business world at the mercy of meddling legislation, that it would permit legislative interference on a self-validating basis and effectively destroy the line between "quasi-public" and private enterprise.

In his dissent in the *Munn Case,* Field argued that the state of Illinois had no right to regulate the charges of an admittedly monopolistic combine of grain elevator operators. This monopoly, he declared, was an outgrowth of their entrepreneurial talent, not of state action; therefore there was nothing "quasi-public" about their actions. He was infuriated by the Chief Justice's statement that property "becomes clothed with a public interest when it is used in such a manner as to be of public consequence and affect the community at large." Logically Field's argument was sound—Waite's definition was circular—but for the time being he had to bide his time and merely register his protests in choleric dissents. And it should be added, just to maintain the right atmosphere of ambiguity, that the Chief Justice was forced to hedge his bet: in 1886 (*Stone* v. *Farmers' Loan & Trust Co.*) while sustaining the actions of Mississippi's railroad commission, he added by way of dictum that "it is not to be inferred that this [regulatory power] is itself without limit. This power to regulate is not a power to destroy, and limitation is not the equivalent of confiscation." In short, Waite too had to admit that there were situations where the legislative power could be checked by judicial application of the Fourteenth Amendment.

While the Court was undergoing the personnel shift discussed earlier, the drums of reform were beating throughout the land. Under pressure from Populists and urban progressives, state legislatures began to enact social legislation designed to ameliorate some of the worst evils of corporate power and industrial squalor. In most instances these statutes had to run the gauntlet of due process in the state courts before they entered the federal forum. While I have not, for reasons of space, devoted coverage to decisions of the inferior federal or state courts, it would be wise at this point to note that the precepts of entrepreneurial liberty gained support on the state judicial level before they did in the federal jurisdiction. The vehicle for this judicial offensive was the due process clause of state constitutions. The courts of

Illinois, New York, and Pennsylvania were particularly vigorous in their exposition of the Field-Bradley gloss on due process as set out in the *Slaughterhouse Cases* (1873).

Let us examine one extremely significant New York decision, *In re Jacobs* (1885), for the path that it broke, a path which the United States Supreme Court took in several later decisions. The *Tenement House Cigar Case*, as it was called, arose from a New York statute of 1884. Trimmed to the essentials, this law prohibited the manufacture of cigars or other tobacco products on the dwelling floors of tenements (four or more family habitations) in cities of more than 500,000 population (Brooklyn and New York). Like many other pieces of social legislation then and now, it was passed on an *ad hoc* basis, by cigar-smoking legislators, and a cigar-smoking Governor, Grover Cleveland, after a newspaper exposé of the filthy conditions of cigar manufacture. Cigars were then made by hand and the wrapper was sealed by the cigarmaker in a primitive and unhygienic fashion—he licked it with his tongue. As the legislators learned of the squalid environment and the high disease rate of tenement dwellers (tuberculosis was endemic), they rushed to protect the public health from this menace.

An obscure cigarmaker named Peter Jacobs violated the law, was arrested and convicted, appealed, and then vanished from history. At this point in the process, the poverty-stricken defendant turned the matter over to the highest-priced lawyer in New York, William M. Evarts. Evarts took his responsibilities to the cigarmakers seriously, and presented to the New York Supreme Court a brief arguing that the state law violated the due process clause of the New York Constitution by arbitrarily depriving tenement-house cigarmakers of their livelihood. The Supreme Court agreed with Evarts, and the State appealed to the Court of Appeals (New York's highest tribunal). Here Evarts rang all the changes on entrepreneurial freedom, invoking due process, freedom of contract, and even natural law. He denied that the statute was a health measure; on the contrary, it was a discriminatory piece of class legislation *disguised as a health measure.* Carried away by his compassion for the small entrepreneur, Evarts even saw the evil hand of monopolistic capital behind the bill: it would place "the whole industry under the domination of organized capital and combination on the one hand, and lays it open on the other to unrestrained domination of trade unions."

Not only did the Court of Appeals accept Evarts' contentions, but Judge Earl virtually wrote his decision from Evarts' brief—which in turn plagiarized extensively from the earlier dissents of Justices Field and Bradley. Speaking for a unanimous Court, Earl agreed that the law arbitrarily deprived the cigarmakers of their property rights in their calling and of liberty as well. The Court gave short shrift to the allegation that this was a health measure—there was no evidence that manufacturing cigars was bad for the health—and added:

> Under the mere guise of police regulations, personal rights and private property cannot be arbitrarily invaded, and the determination of the legislature is not final or conclusive. If it passes an act ostensibly for the public health, and thereby destroys or takes away the property of the citizen, or interferes with his personal liberty, then it is for the courts to scrutinize the act and see whether it really relates to and is convenient and appropriate to promote the public health.

To show that it meant business, the same Court six months later uncovered another arbitrary interference with property rights disguised as a health measure—this time an act prohibiting the manufacture of butter substitutes.

Both the late Benjamin R. Twiss and Clyde E. Jacobs have discussed at length the spread of the dogma of entrepreneurial liberty in the state courts and there is no need, or room, here to recapitulate their findings. It is an index of the extent of this phenomenon in the state jurisdiction that when the first important case came before the United States Supreme Court in 1898 (*Holden* v. *Hardy*) those opposing the statute involved pointed out that in fourteen states similar enactments had been declared unconstitutional! *In re Jacobs* became one of the most extensively cited cases in legal history.

In 1897, in a case of little significance here (*Allgeyer* v. *Louisiana*), the Supreme Court squarely affirmed the doctrine of liberty of contract and voided a state insurance regulation which impinged on this "property" right. Then in 1898 came the first big test in the area of "social legislation," *Holden* v. *Hardy*. A Utah statute of 1896 penalized any employer who required more than an eight-hour day of underground miners or smelter workers. Holden violated the law and upon arrest filed a petition for *habeas corpus*. He claimed that since the statute was unconstitutional, he was illegally imprisoned and, getting no succor from the Utah courts, appealed to the Supreme Court. The Utah enactment, he asserted, was a regulation of hours of employment disguised as a health measure; it was an arbitrary infringement on entrepreneurial liberty which hid under the cloak of the police power. But, despite the pressure which had built up in the state and lower federal courts, the Supreme Court sustained the eight-hour law, though on a very narrow basis. Writing for the seven-Justice majority, Justice Brown held that traditionally the states had special police jurisdiction over dangerous employments and that the Utah law fell into this category. The problem, Brown suggested, was at root factual; that is, the Court had the task of examining the facts in any specific case and determining whether "there are reasonable grounds for believing that [special health regulation for an industry] is supported by the facts

. . . or whether [legislative] action be a mere excuse for an unjust discrimination, or the oppression, or spoilation of a particular class." In short, Justice Brown accepted the premise of *In re Jacobs,* but denied its applicability to the matter *sub judice.*

Justices Rufus Wheeler Peckham and David Brewer dissented without opinion, but it is not difficult to project their views. Brewer we have already identified as Stephen Field's nephew and a fanatical fighter for entrepreneurial freedom of action; Peckham was a graduate of the reactionary New York Court of Appeals. And although the Court's opinion in *Holden* v. *Hardy* had rejected their view of the merits, it had endorsed their presuppositions. Underground miners were a hard test of their principle; they had to accept Holmes' view that hard cases make bad law and await a better opportunity. One was shortly forthcoming.

In 1897, following another series of newspaper articles exposing the foul conditions in bakeries, the New York legislature passed a statute which was designed to deal comprehensively with the problems of the baking industry. Although a health measure in form, in substance it was more; after the success of the Utah eight-hour law (which had been promoted by the Western Federation of Miners), the trade unions decided to press for regulation of working hours as part of the "health" package—similarly the Cigarmakers Union had supported the statute voided in *In re Jacobs.* In addition to requiring bakeries to install sanitary equipment and follow (from our view in the middle of the twentieth century) minimal health standards—"Every such bakery shall be provided with a proper wash room and water closet . . . apart from the bakeroom"[1]—the enactment stated that "no employee shall be required or permitted to work . . . more than sixty hours in one week, or more than ten hours in any one day."

The New York courts sustained the act as a valid exercise of the state's power and Lochner appealed to the Supreme Court. The decks were cleared and the Court was confronted with the one key issue: Was the New York statute a "health" law? In the light of Justice Brown's remarks in *Holden* v. *Hardy,* both sides presented briefs designed to base their cases on the "facts." Indeed Julius Mayer, for the State, submitted what later became known as a "Brandeis Brief": an elaborate study of the vital statistics of bakers to demonstrate that special measures were justified to protect the health of this category of workers. Bakers, he urged, were like underground miners or smelter operators, engaged in a "dangerous trade"; thus *Holden* v. *Hardy* was binding.

Justice Peckham wrote the opinion of the Court for the five-judge majority. Precisely speaking, he held that the New York law was not a "health" measure but an unconstitutional violation of liberty of con-

---

[1] The statute is cited in *Lochner* v. *New York,* 198 U.S. 45, 110 (1905).

tract. Broadly construed, and his language was such as to encourage broad construction, he denounced all efforts to limit entrepreneurial freedom in the name of the public health and welfare. His opinion, in fact, was little less than a tirade against "social legislation"; he was determined not to permit the camel's nose under the tent:

> If this statute be valid, and if, therefore, a proper case is made out in which to deny the right of an individual, *sui juris* [legally competent], as employer or employee, to make contracts for the labor of the latter . . . there would seem to be no length to which legislation of this nature might not go.

Disregarding any statistics to the contrary, Peckham then announced that there could be "fair doubt that the trade of the baker" was particularly unhealthy—it was healthier than some, and less healthy than others. With some sardonic cruelty he pointed out that "very likely physicians would not recommend the exercise of that or of any other trade as a remedy for ill health," and that "it might safely be affirmed that almost all occupations more or less affect the health . . . labor, even in any department, may possibly carry with it the seeds of unhealthiness." Thus if the state law was upheld, "No trade, no occupation, no mode of earning one's living could escape this all pervading power, and the acts of the legislative in limiting the hours of labor in all employments would be valid, although such limitations might seriously cripple the ability of the laborer to support himself and his family."

It is a great temptation to quote at length from this incredible holding —which in truth reads like a Marxist parody of capitalist principles— but the tone, the temper, and the law have all been conveyed by these excerpts. One final matter deserving notice is Peckham's general bull of excommunication; after listing a number of state court decisions invalidating "social legislation," he concluded: "It is impossible for us to shut our eyes to the fact that many of the laws of this character, while passed under what is claimed to be the police power for the purpose of protecting the public health or welfare, are, in reality, passed from other [and by implication unconstitutional] motives." This was nothing less than an invitation to aggrieved entrepreneurs to bring their legislative woes to the Supreme Court for principled redress.

Justice Harlan wrote a dissent which was joined by White and Day in which, drawing from the New York brief, he argued that the facts indicated that baking was a dangerous trade and consequently the rule of *Holden* v. *Hardy* should be determining. Separately dissenting, Oliver Wendell Holmes wrote one of his classic little feuilletons in which he seemingly rejected the judicial function as viewed by *both* Peckham and Harlan. "The Fourteenth Amendment," he noted caustically, "does not enact Mr. Herbert Spencer's Social Statics" and the job of the Court was not to prescribe a political economy for the people, one way or the other: "I strongly believe that my agreement or disagreement [with the principles of "social legislation"] has nothing to do with the right of a majority to embody their opinions in law." Holmes succinctly, with his usual flair for epigrammatic prose, concluded:

> [A Constitution] is made for people of fundamentally differing views, and the accident of our finding certain opinions natural and familiar, or novel, and even shocking, ought not to conclude our judgment upon the question whether statutes embodying them conflict with the Constitution of the United States.

> Géneral propositions [*e.g.,* liberty of contract] do not decide concrete cases. The decisions will depend on a judgment or intuition more subtle than any articulate premise. . . . Every opinion tends to become a law. I think that the word "liberty," in the 14th Amendment, is perverted when it is held to prevent the natural outcome of a dominant opinion, *unless it can be said that a rational and fair man necessarily would admit that the statute proposed would infringe fundamental principles as they have been understood by the traditions of our people and our law.* (Italics added.)

This dissent has been widely hailed as a rejection of the theory that the Court should intervene to substitute its views on economic or political policy for those of a state legislature, or Congress. Careful reading of the section I have italicized indicates, however, that Holmes too hedged his bet. He did not deny that there might be circumstances when the Court should reject state regulations as violative of due process. In fact, in Holmes' thirty years on the Court, the Justices declared state action to be in violation of the Fourteenth Amendment 174 times, and Holmes only dissented in forty-three. In other words, Holmes was not opposed to judicial oversight *per se*, but he was ready to give the wisdom of the legislature far greater weight than most of his colleagues. To some extent he identified legal theory with autobiography: who is his "rational and fair man" if not a wise and sceptical old historian of the common law who has looked death in the face in battle, and recognizes with the Preacher that "all is Vanity"?

For years Populists, progressives, and Socialists had been demanding that the Supreme Court's authority be circumscribed—William Jennings Bryan had made a campaign issue of the Court's power in 1896—but the *Lochner Case* also led enlightened conservatives into the ranks of the critics. Even Charles Warren, a constitutional scholar as eminent for his vehement endorsement of judicial review as for his meticulous historical work, was unable to find a good word for Peckham's holding, and the latter was denounced in season and out by the ever-swelling group of distinguished intellectuals, lawyers, and social workers who were spearheading the drive for social legislation.

However, *Lochner* was law and Peckham's views went forth as an authoritative pronouncement on the meaning of due process—even though the shift of one judge could lead to a different determination of similar matters in later litigation. The New York Court of Appeals, in particular, took the words of its alumnus seriously: if *Lochner* was a caricature of myopic entrepreneurial principles, the New York decisions in *People* v. *Williams* (1907) and *Ives* v. *South Buffalo Railway Co.* (1911) were caricatures of a caricature. In the former case, a New York law prescribing a ten-hour day and prohibiting night work for women *only* was voided, and in the latter, a very moderate (by later standards) Workmen's Compensation Law was invalidated; both enactments were unconstitutional limitations on entrepreneurial freedom. Whatever may have been the legal niceties (*Holden* v. *Hardy* was, of course, still good law for relevant categories of employment), *Lochner* appeared to be a virtually impregnable barrier to the enactment of effective factory legislation.

There was one hopeful sign, but it was hard to know its portent. In 1908 (*Muller* v. *Oregon*), the Supreme Court unexpectedly sustained an Oregon statute which forbade employers to contract for more than a ten-hour day with women factory workers. The unanimous Court, without in any way undermining or challenging the validity of *Lochner* v. *New York,* revived *Holden* v. *Hardy* and held it applicable. Women, said Justice Brewer, are different—as everyone knows—and the Court takes "judicial cognizance of all matters of general knowledge." In the brief presented for Oregon, Louis D. Brandeis had set forth at elaborate length historical and contemporary evidence that women were entitled to special protection (the first "Brandeis Brief"): since there were two perfectly good precedents, one (*Holden* v. *Hardy*) which would validate the statute, and the other (*Lochner* v. *New York*) which would invalidate it, Brandeis concentrated on a factual presentation to lead the Court into the right category. The extent of his success can be gauged by the unanimity of the Justices and by the fact that Brewer wrote the opinion—though Paul Freund has suggested that Brewer always exhibited "marked sympathy for womenkind," which may have provided a special feature in this case. At any rate, for whatever it may be worth, the Supreme Court did assert as a constitutional principle that women were different, thus providing some foothold for social legislation.

To conclude this analysis, we can summarize by stating that in the period from roughly 1890 to World War I a new principle became entrenched in American constitutional law: the doctrine of entrepreneurial liberty. Essentially this doctrine was a break with the common law and the common law premise of the overriding interest of the community, or police power. The right to use one's property, to exercise one's calling, was given a natural-law foundation—in a philosophically vulgar fashion—over and above the authority of the society to enforce the common weal. The consequence of this doctrine was not a *laissez-faire* universe, but one dominated by private governments which demanded (and to a great extent received) freedom for their activities and restraints on the actions of their competitors, *e.g.,* trade unions, regulatory commissions, or reform legislatures. In historical terms, "free enterprise" thus involved two concomitant propositions: freedom of the entrepreneur to follow his calling, and a governmental, constitutional protection of the entrepreneur from his institutional enemies, public and private. We can get the full flavor of the *Zeitgeist* by concluding with the entrepreneurial benediction pronounced in July, 1902, by George F. Baer, President of the Reading Railroad:

> The rights and interests of the laboring man will be protected and cared for —not by the labor agitators, but by the Christian men to whom God in His infinite wisdom has given the control of the property interests of the country, . . .

5

The Election of 1896: Outcome and Significance
PAUL W. GLAD

From a distant perspective, it would appear that American political history is dull. We have long since known, and we have been abetted in the knowledge by foreign observers, that ours is a politics of mediocrity. It proceeds from universally accepted principles, rigidly framed by an American consensus. It rests not on dialogue but on bickering, and because the area of profound political differences is limited, the intensity of the bickering is great. If, in our politics, we do not so much discuss as wrangle, one of the

SOURCE: Paul W. Glad, *McKinley, Bryan, and the People* (Philadelphia: J. B. Lippincott, 1964), pp. 195–209. Copyright © 1964 by Paul W. Glad. Reprinted by permission.

principal reasons is that we are a people of roughly homogeneous interests, concurring in an ideology which insists on the interests we share rather than those which could divide us.

A cursory review of our presidents would seem to support these comments. A few great figures command our retrospect—Jefferson, Jackson, Lincoln, Wilson, both Roosevelts—rising like majestic peaks from a terrain that is otherwise flat and monotonous. The great ones have summoned us to change the practices of a business society to meet moral imperatives, the others have accepted the practices as their own morality; the great ones have led the nation, the others have been at best good followers. In the study of our nation's politics, presidential elections elicit greater interest than presidents. The quadrennial appeal to the electorate is more often than not a greater drama than its principals and its theme add up to. It is one of the great rituals of modern democracy, an act of secular faith, in which, to lend meaning to the drama, differences of approach are translated into differences of principles and superficial divergences made to appear fundamental.

But how far are these observations true of the election of 1896? Charged with tremendous meaning in its day, it appears hardly less significant even in retrospect. Among the younger historians who are helping us gain a fresh view of the election, two deserve special mention: Robert H. Wiebe of Northwestern University and Paul W. Glad of the University of Wisconsin. Wiebe's **The Search for Order,** *1877–1920 (1967) is a book of unusual and profound intelligence, one which invites comparison with the best of recent European historical writing. Wiebe's theme is the transformation of America from a society of island communities, with personal, informal ways, into one of centralized authority and bureaucracy, with formal, impersonal rules. The transformation expressed itself as a running contest between the men in power—the leaders of America's rising urban-industrial system —and the champions of the community. In 1896, the differences between the contenders seemed sharper, more dramatic than ever: ". . . a decade's accumulated bitterness ultimately flowed into a single national election." Trapped within their respective demonologies, the contenders saw their opponents in the self-persuading terms of terror and frenzy: to the Republicans, the Democrats were Jacobins, who had declared war against civilization; to the Democrats, the Republicans were conspirators, to be crushed by a holy crusade. The election's outcome marked the triumph of centralized power, operating through national institutions, over the communities.*

Professor Glad's **McKinley, Bryan, and the People** *(1964), from which the selection below is reprinted, is a first-rate study of the election of 1896. Glad's theme, which complements Wiebe's, is that the election articulated the running conflict of two myths: an older agrarian myth, which saw the farmer as a hero and the country towns as a locus of morality, and a newer urban myth, which lionized the self-made man and saw the industrial city as the locus of possibility and the better life. In the following selection, the*

concluding section of his book, Glad explores McKinley's election—the fac-
tors which brought it about and its larger significance. Glad's analysis of the
nature of the popular vote and of its relevance to voting patterns as they
had been defined in earlier elections is especially noteworthy. Here Glad
is summarizing important recent studies of late nineteenth-century political
trends by several younger historians, including Samuel P. Hays of the Uni-
versity of Pittsburgh, J. Rogers Hollingsworth of the University of Wis-
consin, and Samuel T. McSeveney of Brooklyn College.

Seen in perspective, the election of 1896 is one particular element in a
larger process. The student will naturally wish to inquire about the process.
How valid, for example, are our initial observations about the dullness and
mediocrity of American politics, and why? In what way has the European
political process been more concerned with fundamental issues, more sig-
nificantly an instrument for considering and resolving basic social problems?
If the election of 1896 was more significant than others, what convergence
of factors made it so? Which have been the other critical elections in
American history, what central issues were considered, and how were they
handled? How effective is the American presidential election, coming with
mechanical regularity at four-year intervals, in sounding out national
sentiment when larger issues are to be decided? To what extent is the elec-
tion a referendum on issues, to what extent a decision based on personalities?
What has been the nature of our presidential candidates—their personal
interests, their party connections, their outlook on national issues, their
intellectual caliber, their effectiveness in addressing themselves to the
central problems of their day? In answering these questions, the student
will surely wish to seek significant clues not only in such dramatic moments
of the American past as the election of 1896 but also in the urgent decisions
that are being made right now.

How had it been done? A reporter had asked Mark Hanna that question earlier in the day. The manager had come down to Canton from
Cleveland in the afternoon to spend an hour or so with the Major in
his library. Jaunty and exuberant, Hanna had responded with confidence. "I have kept them moving, kept them moving all the while. I
have not given them a moment's rest." He said that the Democratic
National Committee had planned to center its campaign on Michigan,
Minnesota, and Indiana, the middle western states where they thought
they had the best chance. The Republican organization, without relax-
ing its efforts in the Middle West, had met the threat by diversionary
tactics in the states of the upper South. "I have kept the ball moving
in the outlying states at such a lively pace as to require all the energies
of our friends, the enemy, to be shown in them," said Hanna. "I have
run the campaign as nearly as possible on business principles, and of
course I shall be glad if my efforts meet with the approbation of my

party." Republicans cheerfully granted their approval as GOP news-papers proclaimed a landslide victory.

Those who had supported the Democratic ticket could not, of course, accept Hanna's analysis. "The battle is over and we have lost!" wrote Arthur Sewall to Bryan. "You have made a noble fight for the principles of our party, but with the press, pulpit and money power against us, the odds were too great." He thought that six months had been too short a time properly to educate the people on the issues. But principles can never die, and Sewall looked forward to victory in four years. John Peter Altgeld was "satisfied that there never again can be the same con-centration of adverse conditions and forces that existed this year." He was convinced that another assault on the "fortified strongholds of plutocracy and corruption" would batter them down and drive the money power from the land. A month after the election Altgeld wrote Chairman Jones expressing the belief that "there were fully 100,000 fraudulent votes counted in Illinois this fall," and that "the states of Indiana, Kentucky and California were stolen."

The charges of fraud were coupled with charges of coercion. Mira-beau Towns, Chairman of the Bryan-Sewall Club of Brooklyn, was only one of many who wrote Bryan about tyrannical measures which had been employed against him. "Social ostracism, bank intimidation, employers bulldozing employees and newspaper scurrility and abuse, all combined to one end, had a powerful influence upon the weak and vacillating members of the community." Towns believed that the mid-summer advance in the price of wheat had also had a decisive influence. But even this was not enough fully to account for the defeat of the De-mocracy. As an easterner, Towns was well aware of the political capital Republicans had made of some of Bryan's radical support. Altgeld, in particular, had been portrayed as the evil influence behind the ticket, and while no one could question his great talents, "his prominence injured our case."

From a Populist viewpoint the failure in November could be attrib-uted to the difficulties of working harmoniously with Democrats. "We ought never to make this kind of campaign again," wrote George F. Washburn, Chairman of the People's party headquarters in Chicago. "The populists cannot continue as an annex or ally, working at cross purposes. We must be merged into one main army, equally recognized and respected." That other members of his party would agree to merge except under Populist leadership may be doubted. "I fear the two ele-ments of our party which have been contending for supremacy, will clash in the near future," commented H. E. Taubeneck. "I am more discouraged over that than any other one thing." Unquestionably divisions in the Bryan camp worked to his disadvantage, and the bolt-of-gold Democrats did not help matters.

Populists could argue with some justification that they had provided Bryan's most effective support. Yet their discussion of reorganizing under new leadership to advance old causes enunciated in the Omaha platform had a hollow ring. It was Ignatius Donnelly who perhaps best expressed the mood of Populists after the election. "Alas and Alack!" he wrote in his diary after watching the discouraging returns come in. "It seems useless to contend against the money power. Every election marks another step downward into the abyss, from which there will be no return save by fire and sword." Bryan's defeat moved him deeply and stirred doubts about some of his profoundest convictions. "The people are too shallow and too corrupt to conduct a republic," Donnelly wrote on, pouring out his feelings. "It will need a god come to earth with divine power, to save them. And are they worth saving? Will they stay saved?" Unlike Altgeld, he believed the times had never been more favorable or conditions more promising. "We had a splendid candidate and he had made a gigantic campaign; the elements of reform were fairly united; and the depression of business universal, and yet in spite of it all the bankrupt millions voted to keep the yoke on their own necks! I tremble for the future." Then came a wail of anguish: "Will the long lane never have a turning? Will the sun of triumph never rise? I fear not."

If Populists could not hope for better things, however, Democrats were persuaded that they could. They began to play with election figures; and the more they juggled the returns, the more convinced they became that victory would be achieved in 1900. Bryan published a collection of campaign documents, observations, and reminiscences which he entitled, significantly, *The First Battle*. In that work he pointed out that his vote of some 6,500,000 had nearly equaled the combined Democratic and Populist vote in 1892 and had exceeded by almost a million Cleveland's popular vote in 1892. Bryan calculated that his popular vote in the states he carried was 2,427,172, or 829,712 more than the Democratic vote in those states in 1892 and 59,647 more than the vote for both Cleveland and Weaver. In the states which went to McKinley, Bryan's figures indicated that his popular vote was 4,019,294, or 56,069 more than the vote for Cleveland and 214,474 less than the vote for both Cleveland and Weaver. Bryan's vote fell below Cleveland's vote in Alabama, Connecticut, Delaware, Georgia, Louisiana, Maine, Maryland, Massachusetts, New Hampshire, New Jersey, New York, Pennsylvania, Rhode Island, Vermont, Virginia, and Wisconsin. In all other states he ran ahead of the man who sat in the White House from 1893 to 1897.

Bryan did not, however, deal only in facts. He was much too intrigued with what might have been. McKinley's plurality, he observed, was less than the plurality provided by three states: Pennsylvania,

New York, and Massachusetts. But what wonders might be accomplished through artful manipulation Bryan was to show when he took a careful look at six closely contested states. He figured that a change of 962 votes in California, 1,059 in Oregon, 142 in Kentucky, 9,002 in Indiana, 2,826 in North Dakota, and 5,445 in West Virginia would have brought him a total of 224 electoral votes and the election. "This calculation," he explained, "is made to show how narrow was the defeat of bimetallism and what is possible for the future." He might have added that the gold Democratic vote in California and Kentucky would have given him those two states.

If McKinley's victory was not as overwhelming as his managers made it out to be, neither was it as close as Bryan would have had it appear. A more impartial analysis than either provided shows that it was neither a landslide nor a hairline victory. Other generalizations can be derived from the accompanying tables. New England, as everyone knew it would, gave McKinley a large majority. He polled more than two-thirds of the votes cast there. Of the three Middle Atlantic States, Cleveland had carried New York and New Jersey in 1892. Bryan lost all three by a combined total of more than 650,000 popular votes. In the five states of the Old Northwest—the crucial section—McKinley polled 2,018,508 votes to Bryan's 1,650,210, and he secured the electoral votes of all five. Cleveland had done much better: Indiana, Illinois, and Wisconsin had given him 51 electoral votes, and he had added 5 more from Michigan and 1 from Ohio.

In the states bordering the northeastern quarter of the country (those Hanna referred to as the "outlying states") McKinley won some important victories. He captured Delaware, Maryland, West Virginia, Iowa, Minnesota, North Dakota, and all but 1 electoral vote in Kentucky. Of those states, only Iowa and Minnesota had voted for Harrison as opposed to Cleveland. McKinley's triumphs in the border and West North Central States could not be described as crushing or overwhelming, but except in Kentucky they were relatively safe ones. They provided him with 54 valuable electoral votes. He could afford to let Bryan sweep the rest of the country, although he did in fact win majorities in Oregon and California.

Just as significant as conclusions that might be drawn from comparing Bryan's showing with that of Cleveland is the long-range trend which the election of 1896 points up. Traditionally, the GOP had been strong in western states, and the South had been solidly Democratic; in the Northeast and the Middle West the parties had been in equilibrium. Elections had gone to Republicans or Democrats as the northeastern quarter of the nation had veered toward one party or the other. One of the most far-reaching political realignments in American history began in 1894, however, when Republicans won heavy majorities throughout most of the country. Until 1912 they were to retain control over every one of the fourteen northeastern states, along with Delaware, Maryland, West Virginia, Iowa, Minnesota, North Dakota, Oregon, and California. In other words, they continued to hold until the election of Woodrow Wilson every state, except Kentucky, that went to McKinley in 1896. Thus for a period of almost twenty years (and they were years of more than passing importance) the GOP dominated that section of the country where industrialization and urbanization were most highly developed. After Wilson there was of course another period of Republican supremacy which lasted until 1932.

Outside the solid South, which was obviously a special case, no such long-range party hegemony is discernible in the states that voted for Bryan. Utah went solidly Republican in the presidential elections after 1896. Kansas, South Dakota, Wyoming, and Washington gave their electoral votes to Republican candidates in 1900, 1904, and 1908. Bryan's own state voted Republican in 1900 and 1904. The GOP captured Missouri, Montana, and Idaho in 1904 and 1908. And the silver states of Colorado and Nevada went Republican in 1904. The South's consistent record in voting the Democratic ticket had, as in other periods, little to do with anything but a desire to maintain white supremacy.

Analysis of electoral votes and popular votes by states and sections obviously does not disclose everything one might wish to know about voting patterns in 1896. What, for example, was the difference between farm votes and city votes within those states and sections? William Diamond provided an answer to that question in a study published in 1941. By his definition "all agglomerated populations of 45,000 or more" were called "urban." Of the thirty-two states with such concentrations, twenty went to McKinley and twelve to Bryan. The twenty McKinley states contained sixty-five cities, but there were only seventeen cities in the twelve Bryan states. Ten Bryan states had no urban population at all; three McKinley states had none.

"In the nation as a whole," noted Diamond, "Bryan polled a considerably smaller percentage of the votes of cities than he did of rural sections." This generalization is true of states carried by Bryan as well as of states that went to McKinley. Yet there were some significant differences between the urban vote of Republican states and the urban vote of Democratic states. Relative to his rural vote, Bryan fared better in the cities of northeastern sections and of mineral areas than he did in the cities of southern and western agricultural regions. Cities in New England and in the Mountain States actually gave him a larger percentage of their vote than did the surrounding countryside. Rounding off Diamond's figures, $33\frac{1}{2}$ per cent of the urban and $24\frac{1}{2}$ per cent of the rural vote of New England went to Bryan. In the Mountain states

STATE	Repub-lican	Democrat Populist	National Democrat	Prohibi-tion	Socialist Labor	TOTAL
Alabama	54,737	131,226	6,464	2,147	....	194,574
Arkansas	37,512	110,103	....	893	....	148,508
California	146,688	144,618	2,006	2,573	1,611	297,496
Colorado	26,279	161,269	1	2,110	160	189,819
Connecticut	110,297	56,740	4,336	1,806	1,223	174,402
Delaware	16,883	13,425	887	353	....	31,548
Florida	11,288	32,736	1,778	654	....	46,456
Georgia	60,107	94,733	2,809	5,613	....	163,262
Idaho	6,314	23,135	....	172	....	29,621
Illinois	607,130	464,523	6,390	9,818	1,147	1,089,008
Indiana	323,754	305,573	2,145	5,323	329	637,124
Iowa	289,293	223,741	4,586	3,544	453	521,617
Kansas	159,345	172,915	1,209	2,318	....	335,787
Kentucky	218,171	217,890	5,114	4,781	....	445,956
Louisiana	22,037	77,175	1,834	....	....	101,046
Maine	80,461	34,587	1,867	1,589	....	118,504
Maryland	136,978	104,746	2,507	6,058	588	250,877
Massachusetts	278,976	121,385	11,809	3,060	2,137	417,367
Michigan	293,582	237,268	6,968	6,846	294	544,958
Minnesota	193,503	139,735	....	4,348	954	338,540
Mississippi	5,123	63,793	1,071	485	....	70,472
Missouri	239,333	313,576	2,363	2,462	595	558,329
Montana	10,494	42,537	....	186	....	53,217
Nebraska	103,064	115,999	2,885	2,040	186	224,174
Nevada	1,938	8,376	....	....	....	10,314
New Hampshire	57,444	21,650	3,420	825	228	83,567
New Jersey	221,371	133,695	6,378	5,617	3,986	371,047
New York	819,838	551,513	18,972	16,086	17,731	1,424,140
North Carolina	155,243	174,488	578	681	....	330,990
North Dakota	26,335	20,686	....	358	....	47,379
Ohio	525,991	477,497	1,858	7,784	1,165	1,014,295
Oregon	48,779	46,739	977	919	....	97,414
Pennsylvania	728,300	433,228	11,000	20,147	1,683	1,194,358
Rhode Island	37,437	14,459	1,166	1,161	558	54,781
South Carolina	9,313	58,801	824	....	....	68,938
South Dakota	41,042	41,225	....	683	....	82,950
Tennessee	149,703	168,847	2,106	3,140	....	323,796
Texas	158,894	361,224	4,853	1,722	....	526,693
Utah	13,491	64,607	21	....	....	78,119
Vermont	51,127	10,640	1,331	733	....	63,831
Virginia	135,388	154,985	2,127	2,344	115	294,959
Washington	39,153	51,646	1,668	1,116	....	93,583
West Virginia	105,379	94,488	678	1,223	....	201,768
Wisconsin	268,051	165,349	4,553	7,799	1,311	447,063
Wyoming	10,072	10,375	....	159	....	20,606
Total	7,035,638	6,467,946	131,529	141,676	36,454	13,813,243

SOURCE: House Document 960, *Statistical Abstract of the United States, 1912,* 62d Cong., 3rd Sess., p. 729.

Electoral Votes and States	For President		For Vice President		
	McKinley	Bryan	Hobart	Sewall	Watson
11 Alabama	..	11	..	11	..
8 Arkansas	..	8	..	5	3
9 California	8	1	8	1	..
4 Colorado	..	4	..	4	..
6 Connecticut	6	..	6	..	..
3 Delaware	3	..	3	..	..
4 Florida	..	4	..	4	..
13 Georgia	..	13	..	13	..
3 Idaho	..	3	..	3	..
24 Illinois	24	..	24	..	..
15 Indiana	15	..	15	..	..
13 Iowa	13	..	13	..	..
10 Kansas	..	10	..	10	..
13 Kentucky	12	1	12	1	..
8 Louisiana	..	8	..	4	4
6 Maine	6	..	6	..	..
8 Maryland	8	..	8	..	..
15 Massachusetts	15	..	15	..	..
14 Michigan	14	..	14	..	..
9 Minnesota	9	..	9	..	..
9 Mississippi	..	9	..	9	..
17 Missouri	..	17	..	13	4
3 Montana	..	3	..	2	1
8 Nebraska	..	8	..	4	4
3 Nevada	..	3	..	3	..
4 New Hampshire	4	..	4	..	..
10 New Jersey	10	..	10	..	..
36 New York	36	..	36	..	..
11 North Carolina	..	11	..	6	5
3 North Dakota	3	..	3	..	..
23 Ohio	23	..	23	..	..
4 Oregon	4	..	4	..	..
32 Pennsylvania	32	..	32	..	..
4 Rhode Island	4	..	4	..	..
9 South Carolina	..	9	..	9	..
4 South Dakota	..	4	..	2	2
12 Tennessee	..	12	..	12	..
15 Texas	..	15	..	15	..
3 Utah	..	3	..	2	1
4 Vermont	4	..	4	..	..
12 Virginia	..	12	..	12	..
4 Washington	..	4	..	2	2
6 West Virginia	6	..	6	..	..
12 Wisconsin	12	..	12	..	..
3 Wyoming	..	3	..	2	1
447	271	176	271	149	27

Source: *Congressional Record*, vol. XXIX, pt. 2, 54th Cong., 2d Sess., p. 1694.

he polled 87 per cent of the urban vote and 80 per cent of the rural. Those were the only sections where his percentage of the urban vote was greater than his percentage of the rural vote.

In the Middle Atlantic states Bryan secured slightly more than 37 per cent of the urban vote and 37⅔ per cent of the rural vote, while in the East North Central states his percentages were 42½ and 44⅔. Cities of New York, however, voted more like those of New England than they did like those of Pennsylvania. Seven of New York's eight cities gave Bryan a higher percentage of votes than did rural portions of the state. Five of the eight cities in Pennsylvania—including the three largest, Philadelphia, Pittsburgh, and Allegheny—gave strong support to McKinley.

"For the remainder of the nation," Diamond observed, "whether one moves westward into the main field of action of the Populists or southward into traditionally Democratic territory, the rural sections of the great majority of the states voted more heavily for Bryan than did the cities located in those states . . . ." Milwaukee, Peoria, and Fort Wayne were alone among cities of the east north central region in giving Bryan a larger percentage of the vote than he received from neighboring rural populations. The silver-tongued orator carried Missouri, Kansas, and Nebraska. But St. Joseph, St. Louis, Omaha, and the two Kansas Cities all gave majorities to McKinley. Nowhere in the nation was the difference between city and country so great as in the South. In that section Bryan received more than 59 per cent of the rural vote but less than 44½ per cent of the urban vote. He lost Kentucky in part because Louisville gave McKinley a heavy majority. Out on the Pacific Coast Portland followed the Louisville pattern.

Totals for the entire country indicate that Bryan secured 40.61 per cent of the urban vote and 48.34 per cent of the rural vote. Of course the urban vote is itself made up of many different elements. Big businessmen and small businessmen, managers and mechanics, skilled workers and unskilled workers, professionals and preachers, ethnic groups and native American groups all contribute to the urban vote. Much investigation must be carried on before anyone can say with certainty which of those groups, if any, were most inclined to cast ballots for McKinley in 1896. Yet discounting the charges of coercion and intimidation, and lacking complete evidence, historians are no doubt justified in concluding that Bryan's program simply did not attract enough votes from urban labor. Bryan necessarily argued economic theory. Anyone who has grappled with the silver issue—or who has tried to explain it to students—can readily understand that McKinley had much the easier task when he could bypass theories and assert that silver meant wages paid in fifty-three-cent dollars.

If workers were in general persuaded by Republican arguments, ethnic groups should also have found them convincing. Immigrants probably had difficulty in following Bryan's reasoning, especially when he cast his discussion of the silver question in Jeffersonian or Jacksonian terms. Obviously ethnic groups did not have identical interests, and they were divided in their political loyalties. Bloc voting tended to split the so-called foreign vote even though there were some changes over previous years. According to a careful study of election returns in Chicago, Bryan carried traditionally Democratic Irish and Polish precincts, while McKinley won in Italian, German, and Swedish precincts. Both parties directed appeals, often in the native tongue, to specific ethnic groups. Nevertheless bloc voting can easily be overemphasized; the overriding issues were economic, not ethnic. The depression and the way in which Republicans played upon the prosperity theme help to explain why the Democratic candidate of 1896 received a smaller percentage of the immigrant vote than did the Democratic candidate of 1892.

Bryan's support, then, was primarily rural. But here too it should be pointed out that there was really no such thing as a farm vote per se. Diamond's statistics indicate that, in the various sections, Bryan received from 33.47 to 46.04 per cent of the urban vote. On the other hand his vote in rural areas varied from 24.44 to 59.08 per cent, a much wider range than in the cities. The sectional differences among farmers may be attributed to a number of factors: the degree to which agriculture was diversified, the proportion of farm ownership and tenancy, or the size and distribution of debts and mortgages. Whatever influences may have been in operation Bryan made a poor showing in some agricultural regions. New England farmers gave him a smaller percentage of their ballots than he received from any other rural area. And in the Old Northwest, where one might well argue that he lost the election, he received less than 45 per cent of the rural vote, certainly not a figure he could point to with pride. In Minnesota, one of the states where Democrats thought they had a good chance, Bryan's 40.65 per cent of the farm vote was actually less than his percentage of the urban vote.

If all farmers and workers had agreed on objectives and had considered Bryan's election the only means of achieving them, Ignatius Donnelly would have been right when he said that the American people voted to keep the yoke on their necks. But only masochists would vote for the yoke, and nobody ever won an election by appealing to masochists. The fact is that farmers and workers could not concur on objectives, and failing to unite on goals they failed to unite in support of Bryan or anyone else. The one thing on which all farmers and workers could agree was the truism that they would be better off under conditions of full employment and general economic prosperity. The Republican candidate was widely hailed as the advance agent of prosperity, and he succeeded in persuading voters that the epithet fit.

"The effect of the election was magical in its restoration of commercial confidence," reported *The Review of Reviews* in December. "Buying and selling were immediately resumed, and the demand for goods of all kinds led to the opening of hundreds of factories which had been shut down for a considerable time." The announcement of recovery was premature, but the President-elect came to be regarded as a major economic prophet even before his inauguration. Production curves and indices of business activity began to rise during the summer of 1897. They continued to rise throughout his years in office, and the full dinner pail became McKinley's symbol. By 1900 people wondered what all the shouting had been about.

Bryan tried to explain. Principles were eternal. What was true in 1896 would always be true, and he refused to budge from the position he had taken. He insisted that the Democracy write a silver plank into its platform in 1900. Many thought at the time that he was both stubborn and fatuous; many more have continued to think so ever since. But that does not mean he was wrong. On the contrary, he always maintained that he had been right. He had pleaded for an increase in the money supply through the free coinage of silver. Even though a free coinage law was never passed, money stock did increase rapidly after 1896. Its growth was interrupted only once during the period of Republican ascendency which began with McKinley's election. New gold discoveries in Alaska, Australia, and South Africa, as well as the cyanide process, helped to bring about that result. World output of gold increased from an average of some 5 or 6 million ounces annually to 22 million ounces by 1910.

During the campaign of 1900 Bryan contended that not enough gold had yet been released to produce the desired result and that free coinage would still be beneficial. Not until 1907, seven years after Congress had passed a gold standard act, did he concede that free silver was no longer necessary. Whatever justification he might have had for insisting that he had been right in principle, his continued appeals for silver fell on skeptical ears. Compared with McKinley, Bryan sounded like a faker. He seemed even more foolish and misguided than Grover Cleveland. From that day to this Republicans have been prone to characterize the Democratic party as the party of economic vagaries and fiscal irresponsibility.

Although Bryan emphasized silver as the paramount issue in 1896, his harp had more than one string. From the beginning of his active political career he argued that parties had a responsibility to frame issues and explain them to the people. A new issue—the issue of imperialism—arose during the McKinley years. Industrialists and administration men began to assert with increasing conviction that, as Theodore C. Search, President of the National Association of Manufacturers, put it, "Manufacturers have found the capacity of the home market insufficient to absorb their normal output, and the only avenue of relief has presented itself in an enlarged export trade." The belief that industrialization had proceeded faster than the power of the home market to consume provided a motive for McKinley's program of expansion. To his mind, military victories in the Spanish-American War justified acquisition of Puerto Rico, Guam, and the Philippines. But beyond that, establishing control over the islands was essentially a move toward finding new markets overseas. The Open Door policy in China grew out of the same considerations. Imperialists applauded McKinley's line of action, whether they recognized its economic implications or not; it was a mark of the nation's greatness and a sure sign of its future importance in world affairs.

Bryan, on the other hand, fought the new interpretation of manifest destiny with all the eloquence at his command. Instead of developing markets overseas, he proposed to raise general American purchasing power to the point where American production could be absorbed in markets at home. During the debate over imperialism he played the part of opposition leader, a role he assumed naturally after 1896. A persistent critic of both foreign and domestic policies which the national government pursued during the years of Republican ascendency, he was to serve his country well. Long after McKinley lay dead at the hands of a demented assassin, Bryan was a force of major importance in American politics.

Having won fame and a loyal following in 1896, he used both in urging a variety of causes and reforms: tariff reform, an income tax, trust regulation, a guarantee of bank deposits, abandonment of the injunction as a weapon in labor disputes, reform of rules in the House of Representatives, the direct election of senators, woman suffrage, the initiative, referendum, and recall, direct primaries, and international arbitration. In 1906 he also came out for government ownership of railroads, although he soon abandoned the idea on grounds that the American people were not yet ready for it. Later on he began to agitate for prohibition. For the most part he was consistent in his demands and at the same time acutely conscious of a need to adapt programs and policies to fluctuating conditions. He was in some measure responsible for the successes of the progressive period. One may well argue that his contribution was as important as any he might have made had he been elected in 1896, or in 1900 when he ran again, or in 1908 when he was defeated for the third and last time.

Part of the importance of the election of 1896—and perhaps the chief reason for its fascination—lies in the insight into American politics which it affords. Seers of the time commonly saw signs that pointed to revolution, or at the very least to radical innovations. The depression of the nineties increased the intensity of labor unrest and agrarian discontent. Some welcomed the indications of upheaval, while others feared them. But politics and parties functioned in such a way as to thwart a revolutionary thrust. The sword of radicalism was broken before it could strike a blow. The limited character of Bryan's monetary reforms assured the continuity of American political and economic development regardless of the outcome at the polls.

To conservatives, then, the election of 1896 provides an outstanding example of what one of them has called "the genius of American politics." This "genius" involves nothing more and nothing less than a capacity to consider and dispose of concrete issues without resorting to doctrinaire and revolutionary extremes. Never dogmatic, it has taken the American experience as its guide. Thus it has sometimes found expression in myths which that experience has appeared to validate. So it was with the myth of the self-made man and the myth of the yeo-man which shaped the thinking of McKinley and Bryan.

To those of more radical temperament, the election demonstrates what they feel is becoming increasingly obvious in the second half of the twentieth century: that parties and political institutions are struc-turally inadequate and that they are incapable of responding to chang-ing economic and social needs. Among other things, critics have pointed to shortcomings of legislative processes, to conflicts of interest between state and national governments, to weaknesses in the instru-ments of economic control, to crippling disagreements over the role of the national government in areas of social welfare, education, and civil rights. Back in the 1890's, many Populists shared Bryan's belief in the agrarian myth; many workers entertained thoughts of becoming self-made men. But the truly radical thinkers, those for whom Henry Demarest Lloyd spoke, recognized the myths for what they were and sought to face the economic realities of that period.

Both Bryan and McKinley, each in his own way, took the side of the conservatives. Perhaps they sensed that radicalism might itself produce rigidities which could prevent all hope of realizing the American dream. But that is unlikely, for neither one contemplated reaching a final utopia. Certainly they could not have foreseen that in the frustra-tion of defeat some of the most disappointed of Populists would create a terrifying mystique based on nativism, negrophobia, and growing convictions that honest folk were victims of a nefarious conspiracy.

While acceptance of traditional myths influenced Bryan and McKin-ley in their perception of realities, it did not necessarily make them blind to fundamental questions. William Jennings Bryan went to the heart of the political struggle of the nineties in his "Cross of Gold" speech: "changing conditions make new issues; . . . the principles upon which Democracy rests are as everlasting as the hills, but . . . they must be applied to new conditions as they arise." He was touching on what would become the central problem facing Americans in the twentieth century, the problem of advancing and applying democratic principles in a period when social, economic, and technological changes were more rapid and far-reaching than ever before.

THE EMERGENCE OF AN INDUSTRIAL ECONOMY

6

The Beginnings of "Big Business" in American Industry

ALFRED D. CHANDLER, JR.

In today's world, the feature of American life that commands attention is that ours is a capitalist economy. It is, moreover, one that is dominated by big business. The productivity, in goods and services, of any one of our major industrial corporations exceeds that of many a small nation. While American public policy has, at times, sought to temper the excesses of our industrial giants, its guiding assumption has been that they play a role of great significance in our economic development and that they have shared a mutuality of interests with the nation at large. Thus, Charles Wilson, Secretary of Defense in the Eisenhower administration and formerly president of General Motors, was uttering what appeared to be axiomatic (however much he may have offended some liberal sentiment) when he said that "what's good for General Motors is good for the country." Scholars have increasingly recognized the contributions that our major corporations have made to American economic growth; and they have, in recent years, been devoting extensive study to the rise of big business in America and, in particular, to certain firms that served as models for big business organization.

This explains the importance of the following essay by Alfred D. Chandler, Jr., who has taught at M.I.T. and the Johns Hopkins University, and who is a leading authority on American economic history. In seeking to understand the rise of big business in the United States during the late nineteenth century, Professor Chandler poses several questions for considera-

SOURCE: *Business History Review*, XXXIII (Spring, 1959), 1–31. Reprinted by permission.

tion. *In what major ways was American industry transformed at that time? What changes, in particular, occurred in the consumers' goods industries, and why did vertical integration proceed the way it did? What changes occurred in the producers' goods industries, and why did integration proceed one way in the extractive industries and another in the finished producers' goods industries? In what respects were the basic innovations in big business—new forms of organization and methods of marketing—the product of the new nationwide, urban market? From the larger perspective of our economic development, how do these innovations differ from those of earlier and later periods, for what reasons, and with what consequences?*

The problem he considers in the essay—the nature and process of industrial innovation—Professor Chandler has pursued at great length, primarily focusing on the twentieth century, in a very valuable monograph, Strategy and Structure: Chapters in the History of the Industrial Enterprise *(1962). Three themes stand out in both the monograph and the essay: first, that to understand industrial history one must also understand industrial management, organization, and sociology. Chandler stresses the basic institutional patterns that define the emergence of the modern industrial corporation: the formation of a bureaucracy, the growth of departmentalization, and the differentiation of economic and administrative functions. Second, industrial forms and larger economic conditions were interacting forces in the evolution of American business. If it is true enough that external conditions shaped the organization of big business, it is also true that the resultant organization became a governing condition of further industrial development. Third, in the main, however, the changing market has been the single most important factor in determining the changing structure and strategy of American industrial enterprise.*

Stressing the theme that ours is a market economy, Professor Chandler brings us back to our initial observation that the role of big business has been a central one in American capitalist growth. In this fact, above all, he finds the key to our industrial history and in effect to the distinguishing feature of American economic life in today's world of multifarious economic ideas and institutions.

CRITERIA FOR SELECTION AND ANALYSIS

The historian, by the very nature of his task, must be concerned with change. What made for change? Why did it come when it did, and in the way it did? These are characteristically historians' questions. For the student of American business history, these basic questions can be put a little more precisely. What in the American past has given businessmen the opportunity or created the need for them to change what they were doing or the way they were doing it? In other words, what stimulated them to develop new products, new markets, new sources of raw materials, new ways of procuring, processing, or marketing the goods they handled? What encouraged them to find new methods of financing, new ways of managing or organizing their businesses? What turned them to altering their relations with their working force, their customers and competitors, and with the larger American public?

The question of what constitutes the dynamic factors in American business history, dynamic in the sense of stimulating change and innovation, can be more clearly defined if the country's land, natural resources, and cultural patterns are taken as given. Land and resources were the raw materials with which the businessmen had to work, and the cultural attitudes and values helped set the legal and ethical rules of the game they had to play. Within this cultural and geographic environment a number of historical developments appear to have stimulated change. These provide a framework around which historical data can be compiled and analyzed.

The following major dynamic forces have been visible in the American business economy since 1815: the western expansion of population; the construction and initial operation of the national railroad network; the development of a national and increasingly urban market; the application of two new sources of power, the internal combustion engine and electricity, to industry and transportation; and the systematic application of the natural and physical sciences, particularly chemistry and physics, to industry through the institutionalizing of research and development activities.

The first, the westward expansion, appears to have provided the primary impetus, except possibly in New England, to business innovation in the years from 1815 to about 1850; the building of the railroads appears to have been the major factor from the 1850's to the late 1870's; the growth of the national and urban market from the 1880's until a little after 1900; the coming of electricity and the internal combustion engine from the early 1900's to the 1920's; and, finally, the growth of systematic and institutionalized research and development since the 1920's.

These five factors are essentially aspects of fundamental population changes and technological advances. There were, of course, other factors that encouraged business innovation and change. The coming of the new machines and mechanical devices may have been a more important stimulant to innovation in New England than the growth of her markets and sources of supply in the expanding South and West. Wars usually precipitated change. The business cycle, flow of capital, government policy and legislation all played a significant part in business innovation. But such political and financial developments appear to have intensified or delayed the more basic changes encouraged initially by fundamental population shifts and technological achievements.

The purpose of making such a list is, however, not to argue that one development was more dynamic than the other. Nor are these five factors to be considered as "causes" for change; nor are they "theses" to be argued as representing reality, nor "theories" to provide an overall explanation of change or possibly of predicting change. They are, rather, a framework on which historical information can be tied and inter-related. They provide a consistent basis upon which meaningful questions can be asked of the data.

This framework and these questions are, it should be emphasized, concerned only with fundamental changes and innovation in the business economy. They do not deal with the day-to-day activities to which businessmen must devote nearly all of their time. They are not concerned with the continuous adaptation to the constant variations of the market, sources of supply, availability of capital, and technological developments. Nor do they consider why some businesses and businessmen responded quickly and creatively to the basic population and technological changes and others did not. But an understanding of the continuous response and adjustment would seem to require first an awareness of the meaning of the more fundamental or "discontinuous" changes.

Since historical compilation and analysis must be selective, it is impossible to undertake any historical study without some criteria either implicit or explicit for selection. Further study and analysis, by indicating the defects of this approach and framework, will suggest more satisfactory ones. In the process, an analysis and interpretation of change in the American business past should come a little nearer to reality.

The purpose of this article then is, by using the framework of basic, dynamic forces, to look a little more closely at the years that witnessed the beginnings of big business in American industry. What types of changes came during these years in the ways of marketing, purchasing, processing, and the forms of business organization? Why did these changes come when they did in the way they did? Was the growth of the national market a major prerequisite for such innovation and change? If not, what then was? How did these innovations relate to the growth of the railroad network or the coming of electricity and the internal combustion engine?

In addition to secondary works on this period, the data used in seeking answers to these questions have been annual and other corporation reports, government documents, articles in periodicals, histories, and biographies concerning the 50 largest industrial companies in the country in 1909. Nearly all these companies, listed in Table I, had their beginnings in the last years of the nineteenth century.

MAJOR CHANGES IN AMERICAN INDUSTRY
AT THE END OF THE NINETEENTH CENTURY

Between the depression of the 1870's and the beginning of the twentieth century, American industry underwent a significant transformation. In the 1870's, the major industries serviced an agrarian economy. Except for a few companies equipping the rapidly expanding railroad network, the leading industrial firms processed agricultural products and provided farmers with food and clothing. These firms tended to be small, and bought their raw materials and sold their finished goods locally. Where they manufactured for a market more than a few miles away from the factory, they bought and sold through commissioned agents who handled the business of several other similar firms.

By the beginning of the twentieth century, many more companies were making producers' goods, to be used in industry rather than on the farm or by the ultimate consumer. Most of the major industries had become dominated by a few large enterprises. These great industrial corporations no longer purchased and sold through agents, but had their own nationwide buying and marketing organizations. Many, primarily those in the extractive industries, had come to control their own raw materials. In other words, the business economy had become industrial. Major industries were dominated by a few firms that had become great, vertically integrated, centralized enterprises.

In the terms of the economist and sociologist a significant sector of American industry had become bureaucratic, in the sense that business decisions were made within large hierarchical structures. Externally, oligopoly was prevalent, the decision-makers being as much concerned with the actions of the few other large firms in the industry as with over-all changes in markets, sources of supplies, and technological improvements.

These basic changes came only after the railroads had created a national market. The railroad network, in turn, had grown swiftly primarily because of the near desperate requirements for efficient transportation created by the movement of population westward after 1815. Except for the Atlantic seaboard between Boston and Washington, the construction of the American railroads was stimulated almost wholly by the demand for better transportation to move crops, to bring farmers supplies, and to open up new territories to commercial agriculture.

By greatly expanding the scope of the agrarian economy, the railroads quickened the growth of the older commercial centers, such as New York, Philadelphia, Cincinnati, Cleveland, and St. Louis, and helped create new cities like Chicago, Indianapolis, Atlanta, Kansas City, Dallas, and the Twin Cities. This rapid urban expansion intensified the demand for the products of the older consumer goods industries —particularly those which processed the crops of the farmer and planter into food, stimulants, and clothing.

At the same time, railroad construction developed the first large market in this country for producers' goods. Except for the making of relatively few textile machines, steamboat engines, and ordnance, the iron and nonferrous manufacturers had before 1850 concentrated on providing metals and simple tools for merchants and farmers. Even textile machinery was usually made by the cloth manufacturers themselves. However, by 1860, only a decade after beginning America's first major railroad construction boom, railroad companies had already replaced the blacksmiths as the primary market for iron products, and had become far and away the most important market for the heavy engineering industries. By then, too, the locomotive was competing with the Connecticut brass industry as a major consumer of copper. More than this, the railroads, with their huge capital outlay, their fixed operating costs, the large size of their labor and management force, and the technical complexity of their operations, pioneered in the new ways of oligopolistic competition and large-scale, professionalized, bureaucratized management.

The new nationwide market created by the construction of the railroad network became an increasingly urban one. From 1850 on, if not before, urban areas were growing more rapidly than rural ones. In the four decades from 1840 to 1880 the proportion of urban population rose from 11 per cent to 28 per cent of the total population, or about 4 per cent a decade. In the two decades from 1880 to 1900 it grew from 28 per cent to 40 per cent or an increase of 6 per cent a decade. Was this new urban and national market, then, the primary stimulant for business innovation and change, and for the coming of big business to American industry?

CHANGES IN THE CONSUMERS' GOODS INDUSTRIES

The industries first to become dominated by great business enterprises were those making consumer goods, the majority of which were processed from products grown on the farm and sold in the urban markets. Consolidation and centralization in the consumers' goods industries were well under way by 1893. The unit that appeared was one which integrated within a single business organization the major economic processes: production or purchasing of raw materials, manufacturing, distribution, and finance.

Such vertically integrated organizations came in two quite different ways. Where the product tended to be somewhat new in kind and especially fitted for the urban market, its makers created their businesses by first building large marketing and then purchasing organizations. This technique appears to have been true of the manufacturers or distributors of fresh meat, cigarettes, high-grade flour, bananas, harvesters, sewing machines, and typewriters. Where the products were established staple items, horizontal combination tended to precede vertical integration. In the sugar, salt, leather, whiskey, glucose, starch, biscuit, kerosene, fertilizer, and rubber industries a large number of small manufacturers first combined into large business units and then created their marketing and buying organizations. For a number of reasons the makers of the newer types of products found the older outlets less satisfactory and felt more of a need for direct marketing than did the manufacturers of the long-established goods.

The story of the changes and the possible reasons behind them can be more clearly understood by examining briefly the experience of a few innovating firms. First, consider the experience of companies that grew large through the creation of a nationwide marketing and distributing organization. Here the story of Gustavus F. Swift and his brother Edwin is a significant one. Gustavus F. Swift, an Easterner, came relatively late to the Chicago meat-packing business. Possibly because he was from Massachusetts, he appreciated the potential market for fresh western meat in the eastern cities. For after the Civil War, Boston, New York, Philadelphia, and other cities were rapidly outrunning their local meat supply. At the same time, great herds of cattle were gathering on the western plains. Swift saw the possibilities of connecting the new market with the new source of supply by the use of the refrigerated railroad car. In 1878, shortly after his first experimental shipment of refrigerated meat, he formed a partnership with his younger brother, Edwin, to market fresh western meat in the eastern cities.

For the next decade, Swift struggled hard to carry out his plans, the essence of which was the creation, during the 1880's, of the nationwide distributing and marketing organization built around a network of branch houses. Each "house" had its storage plant and its own marketing organization. The latter included outlets in major towns and cities, often managed by Swift's own salaried representatives. In marketing the product, Swift had to break down, through advertising and other means, the prejudices against eating meat killed more than a thousand miles away and many weeks earlier. At the same time he had to combat boycotts of local butchers and the concerted efforts of the National Butchers' Protective Association to prevent the sale of his meat in the urban markets.

To make effective use of the branch house network, the company soon began to market products other than beef. The "full line" soon came to include lamb, mutton, pork, and, some time later, poultry, eggs, and dairy products. The growing distributing organization soon demanded an increase in supply. So between 1888 and 1892, the Swifts set up meat-packing establishments in Kansas City, Omaha, and St. Louis, and, after the depression of the 1890's, three more in St. Joseph, St. Paul, and Ft. Worth. At the same time, the company systematized the buying of its cattle and other products at the stockyards. In the 1890's, too, Swift began a concerted effort to make more profitable use of by-products.

Before the end of the 1890's, then, Swift had effectively fashioned a great, vertically integrated organization. The major departments— marketing, processing, purchasing, and accounting—were all tightly controlled from the central office in Chicago. A report of the Commissioner of Corporations published in 1905 makes clear the reason for such control:

> Differences in quality of animals and of their products are so great that the closest supervision of the Central Office is necessary to enforce the exercise of skill and sound judgement on the part of the agents who buy the stock, and the agents who sell the meat. With this object, the branches of the Selling and Accounting Department of those packing companies which have charge of the purchasing, killing, and dressing and selling of fresh meat, are organized in the most extensive and thorough manner. The Central Office is in constant telegraphic correspondence with the distributing houses, with a view to adjusting the supply of meat and the price as nearly as possible to the demand.

As this statement suggests, the other meat packers followed Swift's example. To compete effectively, Armour, Morris, Cudahy, and Schwarzschild & Sulzberger had to build up similar integrated organizations. Those that did not follow the Swift model were destined to remain small local companies. Thus by the middle of the 1890's, the meat-packing industry, with the rapid growth of these great vertically integrated firms had become oligopolistic (the "Big Five" had the major share of the market) and bureaucratic; each of the five had its many departments and several levels of management.

This story has parallels in other industries processing agricultural products. In tobacco, James B. Duke was the first to appreciate the growing market for the cigarette, a new product which was sold almost wholly in the cities. However, after he had applied machinery to the manufacture of cigarettes, production soon outran supply. Duke then concentrated on expanding the market through extensive advertising and the creation of a national and then worldwide selling organization. In 1884, he left Durham, North Carolina, for New York City, where he set up factories, sales, and administrative offices. New York was closer to his major urban markets, and was the more logical place to manage an international advertising campaign than Durham. While he was building his marketing department, Duke was also creating the network of warehouses and buyers in the tobacco-growing areas of the country.

In 1890, he merged his company with five smaller competitors in the cigarette business to form the American Tobacco Company. By 1895 the activities of these firms had been consolidated into the manufacturing, marketing, purchasing, and finance departments of the single operating structure Duke had earlier fashioned. Duke next undertook development of a full line by handling all types of smoking and chewing tobacco. By the end of the century, his company completely dominated the tobacco business. Only two other firms, R. J. Reynolds & Company and P. Lorillard & Company had been able to build up comparable vertically integrated organizations. When they merged with American Tobacco they continued to retain their separate operating organizations. When the 1911 antitrust decree split these and other units off from the American company, the tobacco industry had become, like the meat-packing business, oligopolistic, and its dominant firms bureaucratic.

What Duke and Swift did for their industries, James S. Bell of the Washburn-Crosby Company did during these same years in the making and selling of high-grade flour to the urban bakeries and housewives, and Andrew J. Preston achieved in growing, transporting, and selling another new product for the urban market, the banana. Like Swift and Duke, both these men made their major innovations in marketing, and then went on to create large-scale, departmentalized, vertically integrated structures.

The innovators in new consumer durables followed much the same pattern. Both Cyrus McCormick, pioneer harvester manufacturer, and William Clark, the business brains of the Singer Sewing Machine Company, first sold through commissioned agents. Clark soon discovered that salaried men, working out of branch offices, could more effectively and at less cost display, demonstrate, and service sewing machines than could the agents. Just as important, the branch offices were able to provide the customer with essential credit. McCormick, while retaining the dealer to handle the final sales, came to appreciate the need for a strong selling and distributing organization, with warehouses, servicing facilities, and a large salaried force, to stand behind the dealer. So in the years following the Civil War, both McCormick and Singer Sewing Machine Company concentrated on building up national and then worldwide marketing departments. As they purchased their raw materials from a few industrial companies rather than from a mass of farmers, their purchasing departments were smaller, and required less attention than those in the firms processing farmers' products. But the net result was the creation of a very similar type of organization.

In those industries making more standard goods, the creation of marketing organizations usually followed large-scale combinations of a number of small manufacturing firms. For these small firms, the coming of the railroad had in many cases enlarged their markets but simultaneously brought them for the first time into competition with many other companies. Most of these firms appear to have expanded production in order to take advantage of the new markets. As a result, their industries became plagued with overproduction and excess capacity; that is, continued production at full capacity threatened to drop prices below the cost of production. So in the 1880's and early 1890's, many small manufacturers in the leather, sugar, salt, distilling and other corn products, linseed and cotton oil, biscuit, petroleum, fertilizer and rubber boot and glove industries, joined in large horizontal combinations.

In most of these industries, combination was followed by consolidation and vertical integration, and the pattern was comparatively consistent. First, the new combinations concentrated their manufacturing activities in locations more advantageously situated to meet the new growing urban demands. Next they systematized and standardized their manufacturing processes. Then, except in the case of sugar and corn products (glucose and starch), the combinations began to build large distributing and smaller purchasing departments. In so doing, many dropped their initial efforts to buy out competitors or to drive them out of business by price-cutting. Instead they concentrated on the creation of a more efficient flow from the producers of their raw materials to the ultimate consumer, and of the development and maintenance of markets through brand names and advertising. Since the large majority of these combinations began as regional groupings, most industries came to have more than one great firm. Only oil, sugar, and corn products remained long dominated by a single company. By World War I, partly because of the dissolutions under the Sherman Act, these industries had also become oligopolistic, and their leading firms vertically integrated.

Specific illustrations help to make these generalizations more precise. The best-known is the story of the oil industry, but equally illustrative is the experience of the leading distilling, baking, and rubber companies.

The first permanent combination in the whiskey industry came in 1887 when a large number of Midwestern distillers, operating more than 80 small plants, formed the Distillers' and Cattle Feeders' Trust. Like other trusts, it adopted the more satisfactory legal form of a holding company shortly after New Jersey in 1889 passed the general incorporation law for holding companies. The major efforts of the Distillers Company were, first, to concentrate production in a relatively few plants. By 1895 only 21 were operating. The managers maintained that the large volume per plant permitted by such concentration would mean lower costs, and also that the location of few plants more advantageously in relation to supply and marketing would still reduce expenses further. However, the company kept the price of whiskey up, and since the cost of setting up a distillery was small, it soon had competition from small local plants. The company's answer was to purchase the new competitors and to cut prices. This strategy proved so expensive that the enterprise was unable to survive the depression of the 1890's.

Shortly before going into receivership in 1896, the Distillers Company had begun to think more about marketing. In 1895, it had planned to spend a million dollars to build up a distributing and selling organization in the urban East—the company's largest market. In 1898, through the purchase of the Standard Distilling & Distributing Company and the Spirits Distributing Company, it did acquire a marketing organization based in New York City. In 1903, the marketing and manufacturing units were combined into a single operating organization under the direction of the Distillers Securities Company. At the same time, the company's president announced plans to concentrate on the development of brand names and specialties, particularly through advertising and packaging. By the early years of the twentieth century, then, the Distillers Company had become a vertically integrated, departmentalized, centralized operating organization, competing in the modern manner, more through advertising and product differentiation than price.

The experience of the biscuit industry is even more explicit. The National Biscuit Company came into being in 1898 as a merger of three regional combinations: the New York Biscuit Company formed in 1890, the American Biscuit and Manufacturing Company, and the United States Biscuit Company founded a little later. Its initial objective was to control price and production, but as in the case of the Distillers Company, this strategy proved too expensive. The Annual Report for 1901 suggests why National Biscuit shifted its basic policies:

> This Company is four years old and it may be of interest to shortly review its history. . . . When the Company started, it was an aggregation of plants. It is now an organized business. When we look back over the four years, we find that a radical change has been wrought in our methods of business. In the past, the managers of large merchandising corporations have found it necessary, for success, to control or limit competition. So when this company started, it was thought that we must control competition, and that to

do this we must either fight competition or buy it. The first meant a ruinous war of prices, and a great loss of profit; the second, a constantly increasing capitalization. Experience soon proved to us that, instead of bringing success, either of those courses, if persevered in, must bring disaster. This led us to reflect whether it was necessary to control competition . . . we soon satisfied ourselves that within the Company itself we must look for success.

We turned our attention and bent our energies to improving the internal management of our business, to getting full benefit from purchasing our raw materials in large quantities, to economizing the expenses of manufacture, to systematizing and rendering more effective our selling department; and above all things and before all things to improve the quality of our goods and the condition in which they should reach the customer.

It became the settled policy of this Company to buy out no competition. . . .

In concentrating on distribution, the company first changed its policy from selling in bulk to wholesalers to marketing small packages to retailers. It developed the various "Uneeda Biscuit" brands, which immediately became popular. "The next point," the same Annual Report continued, "was to reach the customer. Thinking we had something that the customer wanted, we had to advise the customer of its existence. We did this by extensive advertising." This new packaging and advertising not only quickly created a profitable business, but also required the building of a sizable marketing organization. Since flour could be quickly and easily purchased in quantity from large milling firms, the purchasing requirements were less complex, and so the company needed a smaller purchasing organization. On the other hand, it spent much energy after 1901 in improving plant layout and manufacturing processes in order to cut production costs and to improve and standardize quality. Throughout the first decade of its history, National Biscuit continued the policy of "centralizing" manufacturing operations, particularly in its great New York and Chicago plants.

In the rubber boot, shoe, and glove industries, the story is much the same. Expansion of manufacturing facilities and increasing competition as early as 1874, led to the formation, by several leading firms, of the Associated Rubber Shoe Companies—an organization for setting price and production schedules through its board of directors. This company continued until 1886. Its successor, the Rubber Boot and Shoe Company, which lasted only a year, attempted, besides controlling prices and production, to handle marketing, which had always been done by commissioned agents. After five years of uncontrolled competition, four of the five firms that had organized the selling company again combined, this time with the assistance of a large rubber importer, Charles A. Flint. The resulting United States Rubber Company came, by 1898, to control 75 per cent of the nation's rubber boot, shoe, and glove output.

At first the new company remained a decentralized holding company. Each constituent company retained its corporate identity with much freedom of action including the purchasing of raw materials and the selling of finished products, which was done, as before, through jobbers. The central office's concern was primarily with controlling price and production schedules. Very soon, however, the company began, in the words of the 1896 Annual Report, a policy of "perfecting consolidation of purchasing, selling, and manufacturing." This was to be accomplished in four ways. First, as the 1895 Annual Report had pointed out, the managers agreed "so far as practicable, to consolidate the purchasing of all supplies of raw materials for the various manufacturies into one single buying agency, believing that the purchase of large quantities of goods can be made at more advantageous figures than the buying of small isolated lots." The second new "general policy" was "to undertake to reduce the number of brands of goods manufactured, and to consolidate the manufacturing of the remaining brands in those factories which have demonstrated superior facilities for production or advantageous labor conditions. This course was for the purpose of utilizing the most efficient instruments of production and closing those that were inefficient and unprofitable." The third policy was to consolidate sales through the formation of a "Selling Department," which was to handle all goods made by the constituent companies in order to achieve "economy in the distribution expense." Selling was now to be handled by a central office in the New York City headquarters, with branch offices throughout the United States and Europe. Of the three great new departments, actually manufacturing was the slowest to be fully consolidated and centralized. Finally, the treasurer's office at headquarters began to obtain accurate data on profit and loss through the institution of uniform, centralized cost accounting.

Thus United States Rubber, National Biscuit, and the Distillers Securities Company soon came to have organizational structures paralleling those of Swift and American Tobacco. By the first decade of the twentieth century, the leading firms in many consumers' goods industries had become departmentalized and centralized. This was the organizational concomitant to vertical integration. Each major function, manufacturing, sales, purchasing, and finance, became managed by a single and separate department head, usually a vice president, who, assisted by a director or a manager, had full authority and responsibility for the activities of his unit. These departmental chiefs, with the president, coordinated and evaluated the work of the different functional units, and made policy for the company as a whole. In coordinating, appraising, and policy-making, the president and the vice presidents in charge of departments came to rely more and more on the accounting and statistical information, usually provided by the finance department, on costs, output, purchases, and sales.

CHANGES IN THE PRODUCERS' GOODS INDUSTRIES

Bureaucracy and oligopoly came to the producers' goods industries somewhat later than to those making products for the mass market. Until the depression of the 1890's, most of the combinations and consolidations had been in the consumers' goods industries. After that, the major changes came in those industries selling to other businesses and industrialists. The reason for the time difference seems to be that the city took a little longer to become a major market for producers' goods. Throughout the 1880's, railroad construction and operation continued to take the larger share of the output of steel, copper, power machinery, explosives, and other heavy industries. Then in the 1890's, as railroad construction declined the rapidly growing American cities became the primary market. The insatiable demand for urban lighting, communication, heat, power, transportation, water, sewerage, and other services directly and indirectly took ever growing quantities of electric lighting apparatus, telephones, copper wire, newsprint, streetcars, coal, and iron, steel, copper, and lead piping, structures and fixtures; while the constantly expanding urban construction created new calls on the power machinery and explosives as well as the metals industries. Carnegie's decision in 1887 to shift the Homestead Works, the nation's largest and most modern steel plant, from rails to structures, symbolized the coming change in the market.

Also the new combinations and consolidations in the consumers' goods industries increased the demand for producers' products in the urban areas. Standard Oil, American Tobacco, Swift and other meat packers, McCormick's Harvesting Machinery and other farm implement firms, American Sugar, Singer Sewing Machine, and many other great consumer goods companies concentrated their production in or near major cities, particularly New York and Chicago.

The changes after 1897 differed from the earlier ones not only in types of industries in which they occurred but also in the way they were promoted and financed. Combinations and vertical integration in the consumer goods industries before 1897 had been almost all engineered and financed by the manufacturers themselves, so the stock control remained in the hands of the industrialists. After 1897, however, outside funds and often outside promoters, who were usually Wall Street financiers, played an increasingly significant role in industrial combination and consolidation. The change reflected a new attitude of investor and financier who controlled capital toward the value of industrial securities. Before the depression of the 1890's investment and speculation had been overwhelmingly in railroad stocks and bonds. The institutionalizing of the American security market in Wall Street had come, in fact, as a response to the needs for financing the first great railroad boom in the 1850's.

The railroads, however, had made a poor showing financially in the middle years of the 1890's when one-third of the nation's trackage went through receivership and financial reorganization. The dividend records of some of the new large industrial corporations, on the other hand, proved unexpectedly satisfactory. Moreover, railroad construction was slowing, and the major financial and administrative reorganizations of the 1890's had pretty well stabilized the industry. So there was less demand for investment bankers and brokers to market new issues of railroad securities.

Industrials were obviously the coming field, and by 1898 there was a rush in Wall Street to get in on this new business. The sudden availability of funds stimulated, and undoubtedly overstimulated, industrial combination. Many of the mergers in the years after 1897 came more from the desire of financiers for promotional profits, and because combination had become the thing to do, and less from the special needs and opportunities in the several industries. Moreover, as the financiers and promoters began to provide funds for mergers and expansion, they began to acquire, for the first time, the same type of control over industrial corporations that they had enjoyed in railroads since the 1850's.

The changes in the producers' goods industries were essentially like those in the consumer goods firms before the depression. Only after 1897 the changes came more rapidly, partly because of Wall Street pressures; and the differences that did develop between the two types of industries reflected the basic differences in the nature of their businesses. Like the companies making consumer goods, those manufacturing items for producers set up nationwide and often worldwide marketing and distributing organizations, consolidated production into a relatively few large plants and fashioned purchasing departments. Because they had fewer customers, their sales departments tended to be smaller than those in firms selling to the mass market. On the other hand, they were more concerned with obtaining control over the sources of their supply than were most of the consumer goods companies.

Here a distinction can be made between the manufacturers who made semi-finished products from raw materials taken from the ground, and those who made finished goods from semi-finished products. The former, producing a uniform product for a few large industrial customers, developed only small sales departments and concentrated on obtaining control of raw materials, and often of the means of transporting such materials from mine to market. The latter, selling a larger variety of products and ones that often required servicing and financing, had much larger marketing and distributing organizations. These makers of finished goods, except for a brief period around 1900, rarely attempted to control their raw materials or their semi-finished steel and other metal supplies. They did, however, in the years after 1900, begin to buy or set up plants making parts and components that went into the construction of their finished products.

Except in steel, integration usually followed combination in the producers' goods industries. And for both makers of semi-finished and finished goods, integration became more of a defensive strategy than it was in the consumers' goods industries processing agricultural products. In the latter the manufacturers had an assured supply of raw materials from the output of the nation's millions of farms. In the former, on the other hand, they had to consider the threatening possibility of an outsider obtaining complete control of raw materials or supplies.

By the early twentieth century nearly all the companies making semi-finished product goods controlled the mining of their own raw materials. The industries in which they operated can, therefore, be considered as extractive. This was also true of two consumers' goods industries: oil and fertilizer. The experience of these two provides a good introduction to the motives for integration and the role it played in the coming of "big business" in steel, copper, paper, explosives and other businesses producing semi-finished goods.

In both the oil and fertilizer industries, control over raw materials came well after combination and consolidation of groups of small manufacturing firms. The Standard Oil Trust, after its formation in 1882, consolidated its manufacturing activities and then created a domestic marketing organization. Only in the late 1880's, when the new Indiana field began to be developed and the older Pennsylvania ones began to decline, did the Trust consider going into the production of crude oil. Both Allan Nevins in his biography of John D. Rockefeller and the Hidys in their history of Standard Oil agree that the need to be assured of a steady supply of crude oil was the major reason for the move into production. Other reasons, the Hidys indicate, were a fear that the producers might combine and so control supplies, and the desire of the pipeline subsidiaries to keep their facilities operating at full capacity. Although neither Nevins nor the Hidys suggest that the desire to obtain a more efficient flow of oil from the well to the distributor was a motive for this integration, both describe the committees and staff units that were formed at the central office at 26 Broadway to assure more effective coordination between production, refining, and marketing.

What little evidence there is suggests somewhat the same story in the fertilizer industry. Shortly after its organization in the mid-1890's, the Virginia-Carolina Chemical Company, a merger of many small southern fertilizer firms, began, apparently for the same defensive reasons, to purchase phosphate mines. Quickly its major competitor, the American Agricultural Chemical Company, a similar combination of small northeastern companies formed in 1893, responded by making its own purchases of mines. As the latter company explained in a later annual report: "The growth of the business, as well as the fact that available phosphate properties were being fast taken up, indicated that it was the part of wisdom to make additional provision for the future, and accordingly . . . available phosphate properties were purchased, and the necessary plants were erected and equipped, so the company now has in hand a supply of phosphate rock which will satisfy its growing demand for 60 years and upwards." However, neither of these companies appeared to have set up organizational devices to guide the flow of materials from mine to plant to market; nor did the managers of a third large integrated fertilizer company, the International Agricultural Corporation, formed in 1909.

Defensive motives were certainly significant in the changes in the steel industry. Here the story can be most briefly described by focusing on the history of the industry's leader, the Carnegie Steel Company. That company's chairman, Henry C. Frick, had in the early 1890's consolidated and rationalized the several Carnegie manufacturing properties in and about Pittsburgh into an integrated whole. At the same time, he systematized and departmentalized its purchasing, engineering, and marketing activities. The fashioning of a sales department became more necessary since the shift from rails to structures had enlarged the number of the company's customers.

Then in 1896 the Carnegie company made a massive purchase of ore lands when it joined with Henry W. Oliver to buy out the Rockefeller holdings in the Mesabi Range. As Allan Nevins points out, the depression of the 1890's had worked a rapid transformation in the recently discovered Mesabi region. By 1896, the ore fields had become dominated by three great interests: the Oliver Mining Company, the Minnesota Mining Company, and Rockefeller's Consolidated Iron Mines. A fourth, James J. Hill's Great Northern Railroad, was just entering the field. Frick's purchases, therefore, gave the Carnegie company an assured supply of cheap ore, as well as providing it with a fleet of ore ships. Next, Frick and Carnegie bought and rebuilt a railroad from Lake Erie to Pittsburgh to carry the new supplies to the mills.

Yet the steel company's managers did little to coordinate systematically the mining, shipping, and manufacturing units in their industrial empire. These activities did not become departments controlled from one central office but remained completely separate companies under independent managements, whose contact with one another was through negotiated contracts. This was the same sort of relation that existed between the Frick Coke Company and Carnegie Steel from the time Frick had joined Carnegie in 1889. If the Carnegie company's strategy had been to provide a more effective flow of materials as well as to assure itself of not being caught without a supply of ore and the means to transport it, then Frick and Carnegie would have created some sort of central coordinating office.

The steel industry responded quickly to the Carnegie purchases. In 1898, Chicago's Illinois Steel Company, with capital supplied by J. P. Morgan & Company, joined the Lorain Steel Company (with plants on Lake Erie and in Johnstown, Pennsylvania) to purchase the Minnesota Mining Company, a fleet of ore boats, and railroads in the Mesabi and Chicago areas. Again, little attempt was made to coordinate mining and shipping with manufacturing and marketing. In the same year, many iron and steel firms in Ohio and Pennsylvania merged to form the Republic and National Steel Companies. Shortly thereafter, a similar combination in the Sault Sainte Marie area became the Consolidated Lake Superior Company. These three new mergers began at once to set up their marketing organizations and to obtain control by lease and purchase of raw materials and transportation facilities. In 1900, several small firms making high-grade steel did much the same thing by the formation of the Crucible Steel Company of America. In these same years, the larger, established steel companies, like Lackawanna, Cambria, and Jones & Laughlin obtained control of more supplies of ore, coke, and limestone and simultaneously reorganized their manufacturing and marketing organizations. Like Carnegie and Federal, they at first made little effort to bring their mining and coke operations under the direct control of the central office.

In copper, defensive motives for integration appear to have been somewhat less significant. In the 1890's, mining, smelting and refining were combined on a large scale. During the 'eighties the railroad had opened up many western mining areas, particularly in Montana and Arizona; a little later the new electrical and telephone businesses greatly increased the demand for copper. Mining firms like Anaconda, Calumet & Hecla, and Phelps Dodge moved into smelting and refining, while the Guggenheims' Philadelphia Smelting & Refining Company began to buy mining properties. In the copper industry, the high cost of ore shipment meant that smelting and—after the introduction of the electrolytic process in the early 1890's—even refining could be done more cheaply close to the mines. Of the large copper firms, only Calumet & Hecla and the Guggenheims set up refineries in the East before 1898, and both made use of direct water transportation.

After 1898, several large mergers occurred in the nonferrous metals industries. Nearly all were initially promoted by eastern financiers.

Of these, the most important were Amalgamated Copper, engineered by H. H. Rogers of Standard Oil and Marcus Daly of Anaconda, the American Smelting and Refining Company which the Guggenheims came to control, and United Copper promoted by F. Augustus Heinze. United Copper remained little more than a holding company. Amalgamated set up a subsidiary to operate a large refinery at Perth Amboy and another, the United Metals Selling Company, with headquarters in New York City, to market the products of its mining and processing subsidiaries. The holding company's central offices in New York remained small and apparently did comparatively little to coordinate the activities of its several operating companies. The Guggenheims formed a much tighter organization with direct headquarters control of the company's mining, shipping, smelting and marketing departments. On the whole, there appears to have been somewhat closer coordination between mining and processing in the large copper than in the major steel companies.

Lowering of costs through more effective coordination appears to have been a major motive for consolidation and combination in three other businesses whose raw materials came from the ground: explosives, paper, and coal. The mergers that created the Pittsburgh Coal Company in 1899 and greatly enlarged the Consolidation Coal Company in 1903 were followed by a reorganization and consolidation of mining properties and then by the creation of large marketing departments which operated throughout most of the country. The merger of close to 30 paper companies, forming the International Paper Company in 1899, was followed first by consolidation and reorganization of the manufacturing plants, next by the formation of a national marketing organization with headquarters in New York City, and then by the purchase of large tracts of timber in Maine and Canada. These three activities were departmentalized under vice presidents and controlled from the New York office. In all these cases, the central office was responsible for the flow of materials from mine or forest to the customer or retailer.

The explosives industries underwent a comparable sweeping change in 1902 and 1903. Since the 1870's, price and production schedules had been decided by the industry's Gunpowder Trade Association, and almost from its beginning, that Association had been controlled by one firm, the E. I. DuPont de Nemours & Company. However, the member concerns had retained their own corporate identities and managements. In 1902, the DuPonts bought out a large number of these independent companies through exchanges of stock, and then consolidated them into a single centralized organization. In the process, plants were shut down, others enlarged, and new ones built. A nationwide selling organization was created, and centralized accounting, purchasing, engineering and traffic departments formed.

Once the new organization was completed, then the company's executives obtained control of their raw materials through the purchase of nitrate mines and deposits in Chile.

Except possibly in paper, the control of price and production does not appear to have been a major motive for the initial combinations in the extractive industries making producers' goods. In steel before 1901, and in nonferrous metals and coal, there were several combinations, but none acquired as much as 20 per cent of the market. Nor is there any evidence that the creators of the different mergers, while they were forming their organizations, were arranging with one another to set over-all price and production schedules. In explosives, control of competition could not have been a significant reason for the 1902 changes since the DuPont company had enjoyed such control since the 1870's. In coal and explosives, and possibly in copper, the major motive for combination, consolidation, and the integration of supply with the manufacturing and marketing processes seems to have been an expectation of lowered costs through the creation of a national distributing organization, the consolidation of manufacturing activities, and the effective coordination of the different industrial processes by one central office. In steel and possibly copper, the desire for an assured supply of raw materials appears to have been more significant in encouraging combination and integration.

Control of price and production was, on the other hand, much more of an obvious motive for combination and resulting consolidation in the industries manufacturing finished products or machinery from the semi-finished materials produced by the extractive firms. Concern over supply, however, was also a cause for change, for after 1898 the users of steel, copper, coal, and other semi-finished materials felt threatened by the growing number of combinations among their suppliers. In any case, between 1898 and 1900 there was a wave of mergers in these industries, largely Wall Street financed, which led to the formation of American Tin Plate, American Wire & Steel, American Steel Hoop, National Tube, American Bridge, American Sheet Metal, Shelby Steel Tube, American Can, National Enameling & Stamping Company and a number of other combinations among steel-fabricating firms. At the same time, there were many amalgamations in the power machinery and implement businesses, such as American Car & Foundry, American Locomotive, Allis-Chalmers, International Steam Pump, and International Harvester. The largest combination among the copper users, the American Brass Company, came a little later, in 1903, after the Guggenheims, Rogers, and Heinze had completed the major copper mergers.

Nearly all these combinations quickly consolidated their constituent companies into a single operating organization. Manufacturing facilities were unified and systematized, over-all accounting procedures instituted, and national and often worldwide distributing organizations formed. Many set up central traffic and purchasing departments; some even began to assure themselves control over supply by building up their own rolling mills and blast furnaces. As American Wire & Steel and National Tube began to make their own steel, they cancelled contracts with Carnegie and other semi-finished steel producers. This development, in turn, led Carnegie to develop plans for fabricating his own finished products.

The resulting threat of overcapacity and price-cutting led to the formation of the United States Steel Corporation. This giant merger, which included Carnegie, Federal and National Steel, and the first six of the fabricating companies listed above, continued on as a combination. Although the activities of the various subsidiaries were re-formed and redefined, there was no consolidation. United States Steel remained a holding company only, and the central office at 72 Broadway did comparatively little to coordinate the operations of its many subsidiary companies.

After 1901, the fabricators and the machinery manufacturers made little attempt to produce their own steel or copper. Nor did the makers of semi-finished products try, for some years to come, to do their own fabricating. Possibly the metal users realized that even with the formation of United States Steel they were fairly certain of alternative sources of supply. Also they may have found that once they had combined they had enough bargaining power to assure themselves of a supply of steel and other materials more cheaply than they could make it themselves.

While such firms no longer sought to control their basic materials, many, particularly the machinery makers like General Electric, Westinghouse, American Car & Foundry, International Harvester and, a little later, General Motors, began to purchase or set up subsidiaries or departments to make parts and components. Here again the motive was essentially defensive. Since much of their manufacturing had now become mainly assembly, they wanted to be sure to have a supply of parts available at all times. The lack of a vital part could temporarily shut down a plant. However, they expected to take only a portion of the output; a major share was sold to outsiders. One outstanding exception to this pattern was Henry Ford. He came to control his raw materials as well as his parts and components, and rarely sold such parts to outside companies. But Ford's insistence on having a completely integrated organization from mine to market, concentrated largely in one huge plant, proved to be one of the most costly mistakes in American business history.

Control of parts and accessory units led to a diversification of the types of products these manufacturing companies made and sold. Such diversification brought, over time, important changes in business organization. Even more significant for stimulating product diversification was the new "full line" strategy adopted by a number of these recently consolidated concerns. Such a policy, initiated largely to help assure the maximum use of the new departments, encouraged technological as well as organizational change.

Pioneers in developing "full lines" in the producers' goods industries were two great electrical companies: General Electric and Westinghouse. Unlike almost any other of the leading American industrial companies in 1900, these two had begun as research and development rather than manufacturing organizations. Because of their origins, they had the skilled personnel and the necessary equipment to move, in the mid-1890's, from making lighting equipment alone to manufacturing many lines of electric traction and power machinery products. Allis-Chalmers, International Steam Pump, and American Locomotive began, shortly after their formation and subsequent consolidations, to develop new lines using electric and gasoline engines. International Harvester, building up a number of farm implement lines, also started to experiment with the use of the gasoline engine for machinery on the farm. In this same first decade of the twentieth century, rubber, explosives, and chemical companies began to turn to industrial chemistry in their search to develop broader lines of products.

Continuing diversification came, however, largely in industries where science, particularly chemistry and physics, could be most easily applied. And it was in these industries, and in those which were directly affected by the coming of two new sources of power, electricity and the internal combustion engine, that the major innovations in American industry came after 1900. The chemical, automotive, power machinery, rubber, and petroleum industries led the way to the development of new processes and products, new ways of internal organization and new techniques of external competition as the new century unfolded. The metals industries and those processing agricultural goods have, on the other hand, changed relatively little since the beginning of the century. In these industries, the same firms make much the same products, use much the same processes, and compete in much the the same manner in the 1950's as they did in the 1900's. For them the greatest period of change came in the last decade of the nineteenth century.

CONCLUSION: THE BASIC INNOVATIONS

The middle of the first decade of the new century might be said to mark the end of an era. By 1903, the great merger movement was almost over, and by then the metals industries and those processing agricultural products had developed patterns of internal organization and external competition which were to remain. In those years, too, leading chemical, electrical, rubber, power machinery and implement companies had initiated their "full line" policy, and had instituted the earliest formal research and development departments created in this country. In this decade also, electricity was becoming for the first time a significant source of industrial power, and the automobile was just beginning to revolutionize American transportation. From 1903 on, the new generators of power and the new technologies appear to have become the dominant stimuli to innovation in American industry, and such innovations were primarily those which created new products and processes. Changes in organizational methods and marketing techniques were largely responses to technological advances.

This seems much less true of the changes during the 20 to 25 years before 1903. In that period, the basic innovations were more in the creation of new forms of organization and new ways of marketing. The great modern corporation, carrying on the major industrial processes, namely, purchasing, and often production of materials and parts, manufacturing, marketing, and finance—all within the same organizational structure—had its beginnings in that period. Such organizations hardly existed, outside of the railroads, before the 1880's. By 1900 they had become the basic business unit in American industry.

Each of these major processes became managed by a corporate department, and all were coordinated and supervised from a central office. Of the departments, marketing was the most significant. The creation of nationwide distributing and selling organizations was the initial step in the growth of many large consumer goods companies. Mergers in both the consumer and producer goods industries were almost always followed by the formation of a centralized sales department.

The consolidation of plants under a single manufacturing department usually accompanied or followed the formation of a national marketing organization. The creation of such a manufacturing department normally meant the concentration of production in fewer and larger plants, and such consolidation probably lowered unit costs and increased output per worker. The creation of such a department in turn led to the setting up of central traffic, purchasing, and often engineering organizations. Large-scale buying, more rational routing of raw materials and finished products, more systematic plant lay-out, and plant location in relation to materials and markets probably lowered costs still further. Certainly the creators of these organizations believed that it did. In the extractive and machinery industries integration went one step further. Here the motives for controlling raw materials or parts and components were defensive as well as designed to cut costs through providing a more efficient flow of materials from mine to market.

These great national industrial organizations required a large market to provide the volume necessary to support the increased overhead costs. Also, to be profitable, they needed careful coordination between the different functional departments. This coordination required a steady flow of accurate data on costs, sales, and all purchasing, manufacturing, and marketing activities. As a result, the comptroller's office became an increasingly important department. In fact, one of the first moves after a combination by merger or purchase was to institute more effective and detailed accounting procedures. Also, the leading entrepreneurs of the period, men like Rockefeller, Carnegie, Swift, Duke, Preston, Clark, and the DuPonts, had to become, as had the railroad executives of an earlier generation, experts in reading and interpreting business statistics.

Consolidation and departmentalization meant that the leading industrial corporations became operating rather than holding companies, in the sense that the officers and managers of the companies were directly concerned with operating activities. In fact, of the 50 companies with the largest assets in 1909, only United States Steel, Amalgamated Copper, and one or two other copper companies remained purely holding companies. In most others, the central office included the heads of the major functional departments, usually the president, vice presidents, and sometimes a chairman of the board and one or two representatives of financial interests, These men made major policy and administrative decisions and evaluated the performance of the departments and the corporation as a whole. In the extractive industries a few companies, like Standard Oil (N.J.) and some of the metals companies, were partly holding and partly operating companies. At Standard Oil nearly all important decisions were made in the central headquarters, at 26 Broadway, which housed not only the presidents of the subsidiaries but the powerful policy formulating and coordinating committees. But in some of the metals companies, the subsidiaries producing and transporting raw materials retained a large degree of autonomy.

The coming of the large vertically integrated, centralized, functionally departmentalized industrial organization altered the internal and external situations in which and about which business decisions were made. Information about markets, supplies, and operating performance as well as suggestions for action often had to come up through the several levels of the departmental hierarchies, while decisions and suggestions based on this data had to be transmitted down the same ladder for implementation. Executives on each level became increasingly specialists in one function—in sales, production, purchasing, or finance —and most remained in one department and so handled one function only for the major part of their business careers. Only he who climbed to the very top of the departmental ladder had a chance to see his own company as a single operating unit. Where a company's markets, sources of raw materials, and manufacturing processes remained relatively stable, as was true in the metals industries and in those processing agricultural goods, the nature of the business executive's work became increasingly routine and administrative.

When the internal situation had become bureaucratic, the external one tended to be oligopolistic. Vertical integration by one manufacturer forced others to follow. Thus, in a very short time, many American industries became dominated by a few large firms, with the smaller ones handling local and more specialized aspects of the business. Occasionally industries like oil, tobacco, and sugar, came to be controlled by one company, but in most cases legal action by the federal government in the years after 1900 turned monopolistic industries into oligopolistic ones.

Costs, rather than interfirm competition, began to determine prices. With better information on costs, supplies, and market conditions, the companies were able to determine price quite accurately on the basis of the desired return on investment. The managers of the different major companies had little to gain by cutting prices below an acceptable profit margin. On the other hand, if one firm set its prices excessively high, the other firms could increase their share of the market by selling at a lower price and still maintain a profit. They would, however, rarely cut to the point where this margin was eliminated. As a result, after 1900, price leadership, price umbrellas, and other evidences of oligopolistic competition became common in many American industries. To increase their share of the market and to improve their profit position, the large corporations therefore concerned themselves less with price and concentrated more on obtaining new customers by advertising, brand names, and product differentiations; on cutting costs through further improvement and integration of the manufacturing, marketing, and buying processes; and on developing more diversified lines of products.

The coming of the large vertically integrated corporation changed more than just the practices of American industrialists and their industries. The effect on the merchant, particularly the wholesaler, and on the financier, especially the investment banker, has been suggested here. The relation between the growth of these great industrial units and the rise of labor unions has often been pointed out. Certainly the regulation of the large corporation became one of the major political issues of these years, and the devices created to carry out such a regulation were significant innovations in American constitutional, legal, and political institutions. But an examination of such effects is beyond the scope of this paper.

One question remains to be reviewed. Why did the vertically integrated corporation come when it did, and in the way it did? The creation by nearly all the large firms of nationwide selling and distributing organizations indicates the importance of the national market. It was necessary that the market be an increasingly urban one. The city took the largest share of the goods manufactured by the processors of agricultural products. The city, too, with its demands for construction materials, lighting, heating and many other facilities, provided the major market for the metals and other producers' goods industries after railroad construction slowed. Without the rapidly growing urban market there would have been little need and little opportunity for the coming of big business in American industry. And such a market could hardly have existed before the completion of a nationwide railroad network.

What other reasons might there have been for the swift growth of the great industrial corporation? What about foreign markets? In some industries, particularly oil, the overseas trade may have been an important factor. However, in most businesses the domestic customers took the lion's share of the output, and in nearly all of them the move abroad appears to have come after the creation of the large corporation, and after such corporations had fashioned their domestic marketing organization.

What about the investor looking for profitable investments, and the promoter seeking new promotions? Financiers and promoters certainly had an impact on the changes after 1897, but again they seem primarily to have taken advantage of what had already proved successful. The industrialists themselves, rather than the financiers, initiated most of the major changes in business organization. Availability of capital and cooperation with the financier figured much less prominently in these industrial combinations and consolidations than had been the case with the earlier construction of the railroads and with the financing of the Civil War.

What about technological changes? Actually, except for electricity, the major innovations in the metals industries seem to have come before or after the years under study here. Most of the technological improvements in the agricultural processing industries appear to have been made to meet the demands of the new urban market. The great technological innovations that accompanied the development of electricity, the internal combustion engine, and industrial chemistry did have their beginning in these years, and were, indeed, to have a fundamental impact on the American business economy. Yet this impact was not to be really felt until after 1900.

What about entrepreneurial talent? Certainly the best-known entrepreneurs of this period were those who helped to create the large industrial corporation. If, as Joseph A. Schumpeter suggests, "the defining characteristic [of the entrepreneur and his function] is simply

THE FIFTY LARGEST INDUSTRIALS
(Numbers indicate relative size according to 1909 assets)

Consumers' Goods Companies

Agricultural Processing	*Extractive*	*Manufacturing*
3. Am. Tobacco	2. Standard Oil	4. Int'l. Harvester
8. Armour & Co.	26. Va.-Carolina Chem.	10. U.S. Rubber
9. American Sugar	35. American Agri. Chem.	12. Singer Mfg. Co.
13. Swift & Co.		
30. Nat'l. Biscuit		
33. Distillers' Securities		
50. United Fruit		

Producers' Goods Companies

Agricultural Processing	*Extractive*	*Manufacturing*
6. Central Leather	1. U.S. Steel	7. Pullman
18. Corn Products Co.	5. Amalgamated	15. Gen. Elec.
21. Am. Woolens	(Anaconda) Copper	16. Am. Car & Foundry
	11. Am. Smelting &	19. Am. Can
	Refining	22. Westinghouse
	14. Pittsburgh Coal	24. DuPont
	17. Colo. Fuel & Iron	29. Am. Locomotive
	20. Lackawanna	36. Allis-Chalmers
	23. Consolidation Coal	44. Int. Steam Pump
	25. Republic Steel	46. Western Electric
	27. Int'l. Paper	
	28. Bethlehem Steel	
	31. Cambria Steel	
	33. Associated Oil	
	34. Calumet & Hecla	
	37. Crucible Steel	
	38. Lake Superior Corp.	
	39. U.S. Smelting & Ref.	
	40. United Copper	
	41. National Lead	
	42. Phelps Dodge	
	43. Lehigh Coal	
	45. Jones & Laughlin	
	48. Am. Writing Paper	
	49. Copper Range	

the doing of new things, and doing things that are already done, in a new way (innovation)," Rockefeller, Carnegie, Frick, Swift, Duke, Mc-Cormick, the DuPonts, the Guggenheims, Coffin of General Electric, Preston of United Fruit, and Clark of Singer Sewing Machine were all major innovators of their time. And their innovations were not in technology, but rather in organization and in marketing. "Doing a new thing," is, to Schumpeter, a "creative response" to a new situation, and the situation to which these innovators responded appears to have been the rise of the national urban market.

There must be an emphasis here on the words "seem" and "appear." The framework used is a preliminary one and the data itself, based on readily available printed material rather than on business records, is hardly as detailed or accurate as could be desired. More data, more precise and explicit questions, and other types and ranges of questions will modify the generalizations suggested here. For the moment, however, I would like to suggest, if only to encourage the raising of questions and the further compilation and analysis of data, that *the* major innovation in the American economy between the 1880's and the turn of the century was the creation of the great corporations in American industry. This innovation, as I have tried to show, was a response to the growth of a national and increasingly urban market that was created by the building of a national railroad network—the dynamic force in the economy in the quarter century before 1880. After 1900 the newly modified methods of interfirm and intrafirm administration remained relatively unchanged (as did the location of major markets and sources of raw materials) except in those industries directly affected by new sources of power and the systematic application of science to industry. In the twentieth century electricity, the internal combustion engine, and systematic, institutionalized research and development took the place of the national urban market as the dynamic factor in the American industrial economy.

The Robber Baron Concept
in American History
HAL BRIDGES

Divide and Ruin
EDWARD C. KIRKLAND

In the drama of the American past, no act is more significant than the rapid emergence of big business during the late nineteenth century and no role more central than that of the business leaders and the business community. The roles, however, have been differently assayed by successive generations of historians, each of which has tended to appraise what the business leaders did on the basis of its own experience and its own perspective of the American past. By and large, the businessmen have come off as villains of the piece. It was commonplace, until the 1950's, to represent the great revolution in railroads, steel, oil, and finance, after the Civil War, as the ruthless achievement of "robber barons." In the morality play which history is often made out to be, the character of business appeared with simple and unmitigated traits: it has been represented as black, parasitical, unscrupulous, and untrustworthy.

The following essays by Hal Bridges and Edward C. Kirkland undertake to explain and correct this stereotype of our late nineteenth-century business leaders. Professor of History at the University of California (at Riverside), Hal Bridges has closely explored a notable member of the "robber baron" generation in Iron Millionaire: The Life of Charlemagne Tower *(1952). In the essay below, Professor Bridges traces the growth of the robber-baron*

SOURCE: *Business History Review*, XXXII (Spring, 1958), 1–13. Reprinted by permission.

concept, indicating who its principal exponents were and why some of them came to accept it. He indicates too how the robber-baron concept has, of recent years, been substantially revised.

Kirkland, who has taught at Brown University and Bowdoin College and who served as Pitt Professor of American Institutions at Cambridge University, is one of our principal writers of American economic history. He is the author of such significant studies as Men, Cities, and Transportation: A Study in New England History (2 volumes, 1948), Business in the Gilded Age (1952), Dream and Thought in the Business Community, 1860–1900 (1956), and Industry Comes of Age: Business, Labor, and Public Policy, 1860–1900 (1961), as well as a scholarly and popular History of American Economic Life. He has also been president of the Economic History Association and of the Mississippi Valley Historical Association. It was in the latter connection that he delivered the following address. In it, his purpose, like that of Professor Bridges, is to examine the principles governing American business thought and action during the late nineteenth century. From his study of these principles, Professor Kirkland arrives at conclusions which he applies to the study of history.

Both essays point up the need for fair-mindedness and definition in understanding the generation of so-called robber barons. Both essays also emphasize, of course, the changing climate of historical opinion in our own time. It is perhaps inevitable, in an age when the question of our role in world politics is also a question of the productivity of our economic system, that we are concerned with knowing something about the age when our system took giant strides in industrialization and about the men who helped it take those strides. Our view of their achievement and their ethic is no longer hostile. The muckraking tone has left our historical estimates of them. American scholars are looking more favorably at the business leaders and the business community of the post-Civil War decades.

But in our appraisal of the "robber barons," mere condemnation has not been supplanted by mere espousal. We are tending to see them as men of a particular age, displaying the virtues and shortcomings of the values they shared with their contemporaries. As Thomas C. Cochran puts it, for example, "the great industrialists were necessarily men of their time and culture," and "there is no indication that their aims or ethics differed from the rest of society." As social Darwinists, many of them believed that success, however achieved, led inevitably to social progress. In Robert Wiebe's view, the business leaders of the late nineteenth century were "trapped by their present, scurrying where they appeared to stalk." They were men of specific purpose rather than broad vision, tacticians rather than strategists, above all men who, without real awareness or perception, were extending local institutions to meet national needs and who were trying "to master an impersonal world through the customs of a personal society." (The Search for Order, 1877–1920, ch. 2, passim.)

Plus comprendre, *then, has not meant* tout pardonner.   *Historical understanding has moved to a new perspective of our changing morality play of the American past, in which the "robber barons" are hardly heroes, yet, for that matter, neither are they simply villains; they appear to be, to some degree certainly, not merely victimizers but victims.   The newer historiography is indicating, too, that a moral gauge alone may not give us the entire measure of the "robber barons."   We are seeing them more as instruments of their age than as its molders, more as puppets than as puppeteers. They are, in this perspective, like Thomas Hardy personages, stumbling through a destiny whose dimensions and sway they can only dimly perceive.*

HAL BRIDGES

Widespread in American historical writing is the idea that business leaders in the United States from about 1865 to 1900 were, on the whole, a set of avaricious rascals who habitually cheated and robbed investors and consumers, corrupted government, fought ruthlessly among themselves, and in general carried on predatory activities comparable to those of the robber barons of medieval Europe. Such at any rate appears to be the content of the idea when put into plain language. As actually used by historians, the concept tends to become more suggestive than precise. In this study it will be referred to as the idea of the robber barons, and an effort will be made to trace the broad outlines of its historical development after the Civil War, to point out historical interpretations at variance with it, and to appraise its value for present-day historians.

In the post-Civil War era, some relatively early expressions of the idea of the robber barons can be found. In 1869 E. L. Godkin in *The Nation* denounced Cornelius Vanderbilt's extortionate ways and called the Commodore "a lineal successor of the mediaeval baron that we read about. . . ."[1]   In the early seventies the Grangers adopted resolutions comparing American railroad corporations to oppressive "feudal barons of the Middle Ages."[2]   In the eighties and nineties cries of robbery came from Greenbackers and Populists. Matthew Josephson states that he drew the title of his book *The Robber Barons* from "the folklore of the Kansas Greenbackers and Populists of the 1880's."[3]

---

[1] "The Vanderbilt Memorial," *The Nation*, Vol. IX (Nov. 18, 1869), pp. 431–432; quoted in Edward C. Kirkland, *Business in the Gilded Age: The Conservatives' Balance Sheet* (Madison, Wisconsin, 1952), p. 37.

[2] Charles Francis Adams, Jr., *Railroads: Their Origin and Problems* (New York, 1893), pp. 128–129.

[3] Allan Nevins and Matthew Josephson, "Should American History Be Rewritten?" *The Saturday Review*, Vol. XXXVII (Feb. 6, 1954), p. 10. H. D. Lloyd in "The Political Economy of Seventy-Three Million Dollars," *The Atlantic Monthly,*

With the publication in 1894 of Henry Demarest Lloyd's *Wealth against Commonwealth*, the idea of the robber barons gained new importance for American intellectuals. Lloyd, an independently wealthy journalist, was an Emersonian religious thinker and a social reformer who almost but never quite joined the Socialist party.[4] The impassioned rhetoric of his book was aimed not only at the Standard Oil monopoly but at an even bigger target—business, the capitalistic system as it then existed. "Business," he wrote, "colors the modern world as war reddened the ancient world." And, anticipating somewhat a later theme of Thorstein Veblen, he declared that if civilization was destroyed it would not be by Macaulay's "barbarians from below" but by "barbarians . . . from above," the "great money-makers" who now exercised "power kings do not know." Among these moneyed barbarians were the rulers of Standard Oil. The record of the Standard corporation, which Lloyd set forth in detail, illustrated his thesis that "Monopoly is Business at the end of its journey."[5]

Allan Nevins has called *Wealth against Commonwealth* propaganda rather than history; Chester M. Destler has defended the book as essentially accurate, and the most recent study of the rise of the Standard monopoly supports Nevins' judgment.[6] But if there is controversy over Lloyd's accuracy, there is general agreement that his book strongly influenced public opinion. More, probably, than *Chapters of Erie, and Other Essays,* or *Progress and Poverty,* or such relatively mild novels as *The Gilded Age, Looking Backward,* and *A Traveler from Altruria,* it served to fasten a robber baron portrait of the postwar businessmen into the American mind.

This portrait was etched more deeply as the century waned and Populism broadened into Progressivism. The intellectual preoccupa-

---

Vol. L (1882), pp. 69–81, compared Jay Gould to an assassin. Inspired by this article, Carl Schurz referred to contemporary business leaders as "the robber barons" in a Phi Beta Kappa oration at Harvard University. Also, in *The Chicago Tribune* "of the early eighties" Lloyd's editorials "made repeated comparisons between the great railroad magnates and the nobility of the Medieval Rhine." See Chester M. Destler, "Entrepreneurial Leadership Among the 'Robber Barons': A Trial Balance," *The Tasks of Economic History* (Supplemental Issue of *The Journal of Economic History*), Vol. VI (1946), p. 28, n. 1.

[4] Daniel Aaron, *Men of Good Hope: A Story of American Progressives* (New York, 1951), pp. 150, 158, 169.

[5] Henry Demarest Lloyd, *Wealth against Commonwealth* (New York, 1902 ed.), pp. 509, 510, 6 [sic].

[6] For the Nevins-Destler debate over Lloyd's accuracy see Chester McA. Destler, "Wealth against Commonwealth, 1894 and 1944," *American Historical Review,* Vol. L (Oct., 1944), pp. 49–69, and Allan Nevins, Letter to the Editor, *American Historical Review,* (April, 1945), pp. 676–689. Ralph W. Hidy and Muriel E. Hidy, *Pioneering in Big Business, 1882–1911* (New York, 1955), p. 644, supports Nevins' judgment.

tions of the Progressive Era—the national debate over controlling the trusts, the muckrakers' revelations, Socialist agitation, and the novels of big business by naturalists like Frank Norris and Theodore Dreiser— created a climate of suspicion and hostility toward American business leaders. Business chicane was held up to the public by a host of writers, including Lincoln Steffens, whose *Shame of the Cities* exposed corrupt politics and corporate privilege more fully than had James Bryce's *American Commonwealth;* Gustavus Myers, whose Socialist *History of the Great American Fortunes* was to become a source book for future writers of robber baron history; Thorstein Veblen, who began in the *Theory of the Leisure Class* and the *Theory of Business Enterprise* a series of attacks on predatory businessmen; E. A. Ross, whose *Sin and Society* denounced corporate amorality; and Ida Tarbell, who retraced Lloyd's steps more thoroughly and objectively in her *History of the Standard Oil Company.*

Two eminent American historians whose work reflected the Progressive ideology were Vernon Louis Parrington and Charles A. Beard. Both made zestful use of the idea of the robber barons. Parrington, whose Progressive cast of mind was reinforced by a Jeffersonian agrarian bias against businessmen, seems to have accepted the idea with little reservation, though he expressed it in maritime metaphors. When in the last volume of his *Main Currents in American Thought* he presents his "Figures of Earth," the outstanding personages of the Gilded Age, he discusses "ruthless, predatory" business leaders, "the raw materials of a race of capitalistic buccaneers." Within the space of three more sentences he remarks that "Pirate and priest issued from the common source. . . ." And again in the next sentence, "The romantic age of Captain Kidd was come again. . . ." Plainly this master of metaphors loved to take his figures of earth to sea aboard a pirate ship; and it is perhaps not unfair to say that few if any of his metaphors, either in his description of the Gilded Age or in his artistic narrative of the Progressive Era, convey other than a predatory image of the American businessman.[7]

To the mind of Charles Beard, historical patterns were not so clearcut. His analysis of post-Civil War business leaders in *The Rise of American Civilization,* written with Mary Beard, emphasized the historical importance of the businessman in successive civilizations from ancient times to modern America. The Beards not only pointed out the creative results of American business expansion, but held Ida Tarbell "partly responsible for the distorted view" of the Standard Oil Com-

---

[7] Vernon Louis Parrington, *Main Currents in American Thought* (New York, 1930 ed.), Vol. III, pp. 10–12, 405–413.

pany to be found "in the popular mind." Her history they dismissed as "a drama with heroes and villains, rather than a cold and disinterested summary by an impartial student." And yet, for all their interest in objectivity, the Beards made extended use of the idea of the robber barons. Phrases like "barons of business," and "the new capitalist baronage" run through a narrative that presents a generally negative analysis of the methods and motives of business consolidation. The following passage is typical: "If the barons of capitalism did not themselves put on armor and vanquish the possessors of desirable goods in mortal combat . . . they did sometimes hire strong-arm men. . . . Usually, however, they employed less stereotyped means to attain their ends; namely, stock manipulation, injunctions, intimidation, rate cutting, rebates, secret agreements, and similar pacific measures."[8]

Why did Beard and Parrington so freely employ the idea of the robber barons? The answer to this question, to the extent that it can be provided, would seem also to help us understand the meaning and uses of the idea for Progressive writers in general, and for the many latter-day historians who have been influenced by Beard and Parrington.[9] A number of factors must be considered.

First, it seems proper to place both Beard and Parrington within the general category of Richard Hofstadter's discontented professoriat of the Progressive Era, those members of a rising academic profession who were critical of American business civilization, resentful of being controlled by boards of trustees dominated by conservative businessmen, and troubled by academic-freedom cases.[10] Parrington and Beard knew from personal experience how conservative pressure could affect college faculties. In 1908 Parrington lost his position as professor of English at the University of Oklahoma during the controversy that arose when President David R. Boyd of the university was replaced by a political supporter of the governor of the state, C. N. Haskell, who was soon to be accused of improper affiliations with the Standard Oil

---

[8] Charles A. Beard and Mary R. Beard, *The Rise of American Civilization* (New York, 1934 ed.), Vol. II, pp. 166–210; for quoted portions see pp. 187, 201.

[9] Richard Hofstadter has called attention to the Progressive bent of Beard and Parrington and their wide appeal to other writers. See his "Charles Beard and the Constitution," in Howard K. Beale, ed., *Charles A. Beard: An Appraisal* (Lexington, Kentucky, 1954), p. 88. That there is high professional regard for *Main Currents* and *The Rise of American Civilization* is clearly shown in John Walton Caughey, "Historians' Choice: Results of a Poll on Recently Published American History and Biography," *Mississippi Valley Historical Review*, Vol. XXXIX (Sept., 1952), p. 299.

[10] Richard Hofstadter, *The Age of Reform: from Bryan to F. D. R.* (New York, 1955), pp. 154–155.

Company.[11]   In 1917 Beard resigned from Columbia University after he became convinced that conservative trustees were trying to purge the faculty of liberals on the pretext that they were disloyal Americans. Max Lerner has described this resignation as basically "a protest against business control of university educational policy." Such unpleasant experiences may well have influenced Parrington and Beard toward a readier acceptance of what Hofstadter and Walter Metzger call the "potent academic stereotype" of "the businessman as a malefactor."[12]

Another probable influence upon Beard and Parrington is the Progressive concept of reality. The Progressives, according to Hofstadter, conceived of reality as something akin to what the muckrakers revealed. Basically it was "rough and sordid . . . hidden, neglected, and . . . off-stage . . . essentially a stream of external and material events. . . ."[13] The relation of the robber baron idea to this kind of reality is obvious. When Beard and Parrington wrote of the rough, sordid, hidden and off-stage methods by which a Jay Gould manipulated railroads, they could sincerely feel that they were describing the basic reality of business in Gould's time. Parrington also reflects the fascination with brute strength that Alfred Kazin has emphasized as a facet of the Progressive mind. His business leaders of the seventies were vital, "primitive souls . . .

---

[11] Parrington called this controversy a "political cyclone." George Harvey Genzmer, "Vernon Louis Parrington," Dictionary of American Biography, Vol. XIV (1934), ed. by Dumas Malone, p. 253. Along with President Boyd, some dozen members of the Oklahoma faculty were fired. The controversy arising from these dismissals and the accusations of improper relationships with Standard Oil that led in the fall of 1908 to Governor Haskell's resignation as treasurer of the Democratic National Committee can be followed in a series of unsigned editorial articles in The Outlook, Vol. XC (1908), Sept. 5, pp. 15–17, Oct. 3, pp. 233, 235–237, 242–244, 249–251, Oct. 17, pp. 325–326. It might also be noted that Parrington's good friend and colleague at the University of Washington, J. Allen Smith, was fired from Marietta College for publishing liberal monetary views and supporting William Jennings Bryan in the election of 1896. Richard Hofstadter and Walter P. Metzger, The Development of Academic Freedom in the United States (New York, 1955), pp. 423–424.

[12] Investigations by the trustees and summary dismissals of faculty members preceded Beard's resignation. See Charles A. Beard, "A Statement," The New Republic, Vol. XIII (Dec. 29, 1917), pp. 249–250. Lerner's interpretation can be found in his Ideas Are Weapons: The History and Uses of Ideas (New York, 1939), p. 158. Additional details are given in Hofstadter and Metzger, Academic Freedom, pp. 501–502. The reference to the academic stereotype of the businessman is on page 420 of this work; in Chapter IX, "Academic Freedom and Big Business," Hofstadter and Metzger show how the stereotype developed in the Populist and Progressive Eras, and how it does not always fit the facts of academic-freedom cases prior to the First World War.

[13] Hofstadter, "Charles Beard and   e Constitution," p. 87.

never feeble . . . never given to puling or whining," men of the bold buccaneer or robber baron breed.[14]

Also pertinent to this inquiry is the Marxian economic approach to history that has influenced Beard and Parrington and other Progressive writers, [15] and indeed the entire American historical profession, which has made much fruitful use of economic interpretation while rejecting other aspects of Marxism. The idea of the robber barons fits nicely into economic interpretation: the very imagery of it tends to exclude non-economic analysis. Moreover, the idea affords a convenient means of classifying a lot of individualistic businessmen, plus an opportunity for interesting, colorful writing. The business buccaneers, though wicked, were "picturesque in their rascality."[16] Nor, finally, should it be forgotten that at the time *Main Currents* and *The Rise of American Civilization* were written historians knew relatively little about post-Civil War business expansion, aside from the more sensational and sordid events. The Beards, in fact, carefully pointed out that the methods that brought about this expansion had "never been subjected to scientific analysis."[17]

Readily available to other writers, then, in the history of Parrington and Beard, the idea of the robber barons flourished in the debunking twenties and took on fresh vitality in the thirties. During the Great Depression, businessmen were more suspect than ever. Intellectuals quoted the Brookings Institution on America's wasted capacity to produce, Keynes on the "secular stagnation" of capitalism, and Berle and Means on the future dangers of corporate growth. Businessmen were blamed for America's entry into the First World War, and also, after a brief NRA honeymoon, for the continuing depression. Some former Progressives, and young intellectuals who might once have been Progressive, embraced Communism.[18]

The nation was in a mood receptive to a number of new books that embodied the idea of the robber barons, such as Lewis Corey's *The House of Morgan,* Frederick Lewis Allen's *The Lords of Creation,* and Josephson's *The Robber Barons.* Josephson, who dedicated his book to Charles and Mary Beard, traveled further down the road of Marxian

---

[14] Alfred Kazin, *On Native Grounds: An Interpretation of Modern American Prose Literature* (New York, 1942), p. 93; Parrington, *Main Currents,* Vol. III, p. 12.

[15] Hofstadter, "Charles Beard and the Constitution," pp. 81–82.

[16] Parrington, *Main Currents,* Vol. III, p. 12.

[17] C. A. and Mary Beard, *The Rise of American Civilization,* Vol. II, p. 198.

[18] A. D. H. Kaplan, *Big Enterprise in a Competitive System* (Washington D.C., 1954), pp. 27–29; Eric F. Goldman, *Rendezvous with Destiny* (New York, 1953), pp. 353–367; Aaron, *Men of Good Hope,* pp. 295–297.

determinism than the Beards had gone. His barons, though touched with an aura of glamor, were essentially grim, amoral figures, furthering the Marxian process of expropriation and consolidation of property. Their activities were making the masses of workers dissatisfied with the old business system and "the fearful sabotage practiced by capital upon the energy and intelligence of human society."[19] In the stricken nation of the thirties, epitomized in John Dos Passos' *U.S.A.,* Josephson's book read convincingly enough. Perhaps more than any other single volume it served to disseminate the phrase, "the robber barons," through American historical writing. It was, in a sense, the culmination of the idea expressed in its title.

Now let us consider some views of American business leaders that, taken all together, might be termed the revisionist approach to the idea of the robber barons. Edward C. Kirkland has called attention to Charles Francis Adams, Jr., E. L. Godkin, and Andrew Carnegie as conservatives of the Gilded Age whose "conclusions that the business order of their day was not all evil, loss, and hypocrisy should contribute to a more balanced judgment of the era."[20] Adams considered the robber baron metaphor, as applied by the Grangers to railroad corporations, "a grotesque absurdity."[21] However, it should be noted that in 1869, the year he wrote "Chapters of Erie," Adams remarked in a private letter that Daniel Drew, Cornelius Vanderbilt and Jay Gould made "the old robber barons" appear like "children in the art of thieving. . . ."[22] Actually Adams seems to have entertained toward the American business world ambivalent attitudes that reflect his personal aspirations and experiences as railroad reformer, railroad president, and victim of Jay Gould.[23]

If Adams did not wholly accept the idea of the robber barons, neither did a major American historian, Frederick Jackson Turner. Turner was certainly no apologist foɪ industrial wrongdoing, yet his complex approach to the past led him to see aspects of American industrial expansion that did not fit into the robber baron mold. In an essay first

---

[19] Matthew Josephson, *The Robber Barons: The Great American Capitalists 1861–1901* (New York, 1934). The quoted portion is from p. 453.

[20] Kirkland, *Business in the Gilded Age,* p. 59.

[21] Adams, *Railroads,* pp. 128–129; Kirkland, *Business in the Gilded Age,* p. 12.

[22] Joseph Dorfman, *The Economic Mind in American Civilization,* Vol. III, 1865–1918 (New York, 1949), p. 23.

[23] In his autobiography, Adams set forth his often quoted view of American big businessmen as "mere money-getters . . . essentially unattractive and uninteresting," but also confessed that as his life's achievement he "would like to have accumulated—and ample and frequent opportunity for so doing was offered me—one of those vast fortunes of the present day, rising up into the tens and scores of millions . . ." so that he could have donated a fortune to Harvard. *Charles Francis Adams 1835–1915: An Autobiography* (Boston, 1916), pp. 190, 210.

published in 1926 he distinguished Western builders of new industry from Eastern speculative investors in old enterprises, and characterized John D. Rockefeller, Cyrus McCormick, J. O. Armour, and Jay Cooke, among others, as creative sons of Middle Western pioneers.[24] Earlier, at a time when trust-busting ideas were in the air, he had stressed the complexities involved in historical analysis of the two decades of industrial expansion from 1890 to 1910. The occasion was his presidential address of 1910 to the American Historical Association. He noted that the two decades in question were "peculiarly the era when competitive individualism" in America changed into monopoly, but quoted E. H. Harriman to the effect that industrial combination and expansion were in keeping with the speculative pioneer spirit that had developed the nation. He then pointed out that American ideals and moral standards were changing. The squatter ideal of "individual freedom to compete unrestrictedly for the resources of a continent" was yielding to an increasing use of government in order that Americans might preserve another ideal—democracy. Violations of land laws that were formerly condoned by the public and defended in Congress now resulted in jail sentences. "That our great industrial enterprises developed in the midst of these changing ideals," Turner concluded, "is important to recall when we write the history of their activity."[25]

In this same address Turner reminded his fellow historians that among the "complex of forces" molding the past were individual leaders, who were shaped by their own creative genius and by the psychology, moral tendencies, and ideals of their time and place.[26] His words, which thirty-nine years later would be echoed by historians seeking greater understanding of American business leaders,[27] might well serve as a general criterion for biographical writing, and biographers who have studied American businessmen in this spirit have produced works that seriously challenge the idea of the robber barons. A number of nonrobber baron biographies appeared in the antibusiness

---

[24] Frederick Jackson Turner, *The Significance of Sections in American History* (New York, 1932), pp. 262–264. Compare the strong emphasis on the creative achievement of post-Civil War industrial capitalists in Louis M. Hacker, *The Triumph of American Capitalism* (New York, 1940), pp. 427–435.

[25] Frederick Jackson Turner, *The Frontier in American History* (New York, 1920), pp. 317–321, 328.

[26] *Ibid.*, p. 322.

[27] There is a striking similarity between the approach to the past advocated here by Turner and the modern methods for understanding business leaders that are set forth, much more fully, of course, and in more technical language, in *Change and the Entrepreneur: Postulates and Patterns for Entrepreneurial History* [Research Center in Entrepreneurial History, Harvard University], (Cambridge, Massachusetts, 1949), pp. 108–175.

thirties, contrasting markedly with the general tenor of popular thought. Among these were works by John T. Flynn, Burton J. Hendrick, William T. Hutchinson, Allan Nevins, and Henrietta M. Larson.[28] All wrote with varying degrees of sympathy, and re-created business leaders too multisided to be dismissed simply as predatory money seekers. In each business career examined, negative and positive means and ends seemed inseparably bound together. With this duality in mind, N. S. B. Gras in his introduction to Larson's *Jay Cooke* declared that businessmen are generally "above the average in creative work" and complained that a "recent national pastime" had been to judge them without studying them.[29]

The dual nature of business careers was one of several theses advanced in Allan Nevins' *John D. Rockefeller*, which appeared in 1940. Nevins as early as 1927 had published a balanced account of post-Civil War business, and in 1934 had demurred at Josephson's sweeping use of the robber baron metaphor.[30] In the Rockefeller biography, he followed the English economist Alfred Marshall in ascribing the Standard Oil Trust to "a combination of exceptional constructive ability and astute destructive strategy." He held that Rockefeller and his associates had often used methods that were morally wrong as well as unlawful, but like Charles R. Van Hise he argued that the kind of monopoly control they effected was a natural and even inevitable response to the cutthroat competition of the times, in Europe as well as in the United States. Like Turner, he stressed the changing business ethics of Rockefeller's era. And like Joseph Schumpeter he drew attention to the complexity of the motives of entrepreneurs. The chief motive of leaders like Rockefeller, Nevins asserted, was not greed but "competitive achievement, self-expression, and the imposition of their wills on a given environment." Schumpeter had distinguished entrepreneurial activities in which financial gain was secondary, and "economic action becomes akin to sport." Nevins wrote: "In business . . . Americans of the nine-

---

[28] John T. Flynn, *God's Gold: The Story of Rockefeller and His Times* (New York, 1932); Burton J. Hendrick, *The Life of Andrew Carnegie* (Garden City, New York, 1932), 2 vols.; William T. Hutchinson, *Cyrus Hall McCormick: Harvest, 1856–1884* (New York, 1935); Allan Nevins, *Abram S. Hewitt: With Some Account of Peter Cooper* (New York 1935); Henrietta M. Larson, *Jay Cooke: Private Banker* (Cambridge, Mass., 1936).

[29] Larson, *Jay Cooke*, p. xiv.

[30] *The Emergence of Modern America 1865–1878* (New York, 1927), pp. 42, 397–400; review of *The Robber Barons* in *The Saturday Review of Literature*, Vol. X (March 3, 1934), p. 522. But in *Grover Cleveland: A Study in Courage* (New York, 1933), p. 607, Nevins in summarizing the social unrest of the nineties mentioned only the sordid side of the Standard Oil record and favorably described Lloyd's *Wealth against Commonwealth* as a "searching exposure" and the parent of later muckraking literature.

teenth century found the Great Game." This analysis contrasts somewhat with that of Werner Sombart, who conceded that entrepreneurs
have nonacquisitive motives, but argued that since profit is the measure
of capitalistic success all other motives in capitalistic enterprise become
"subordinate to profit making."[31]

When Nevins in 1953 published a second biography of Rockefeller,
he adhered essentially to his earlier interpretation, but advanced a more
elaborate hypothesis of business leadership after the Civil War. The
constructive aspects of this leadership were in the long run, he declared,
more important than the destructive. American historians should follow the English example and correct their national industrial history—
too long based mainly on legislative investigations of business chicane
—to show the constructive side. America's industrial revolution had
"cost less than Germany's, much less than England's, and infinitely
less than Russia's." Further, and most important, the rapid expansion
of American industry after the Civil War had come just in time to insure
victory for "the free world" in the two World Wars. But had better ways
been available for building national industrial strength? Nevins did
not inquire. His broad hypothesis, which of course did not escape
challenge, probably represents the culmination to date of the revisionist
approach to the idea of the robber barons.[32]

Yet business history of all types, biographical and otherwise, offers
numerous other studies of a nonrobber baron nature, some of them
quite recent. James Blaine Hedges, Richard C. Overton, Edward C.
Kirkland, and Thomas C. Cochran, among others, have emphasized the
constructive work of certain railroad leaders of the Gilded Age.[33]
Fritz Redlich has redefined Schumpeter's "entrepreneur" as "creative
entrepreneur" and analyzed the creative achievement of American

---

[31] Allan Nevins, *John D. Rockefeller: The Heroic Age of American Enterprise*
(New York, 1940), Vol. I, pp. 603–622, Vol. II, pp. 707–714; Charles R. Van Hise,
Concentration and Control: A Solution of the Trust Problem in the United States
(New York, 1912); Joseph A. Schumpeter, *The Theory of Economic Development*,
trans. Redvers Opie (Cambridge, Mass., 1934), p. 93; Werner Sombart, "Capi-
talism," *Encyclopedia of the Social Sciences*, ed. by Edwin R. A. Seligman and
Alvin Johnson, Vol. III (1930), p. 200.

[32] Allan Nevins, *Study in Power: John D. Rockefeller* (New York, 1953), Vol. I,
p. viii, Vol. II, pp. 426–436. See also Allan Nevins, "New Lamps for Old in
History," *The American Archivist*, Vol. XVII (Jan., 1954), pp. 3–12. Josephson
opposes this hypothesis in Nevins and Josephson, "Should American History
Be Rewritten?", pp. 9–10, 44–46.

[33] James Blaine Hedges, *Henry Villard and the Railways of the Northwest* (New
Haven, 1930); Richard C. Overton, *Burlington West: A Colonization History of the
Burlington Railroad* (Cambridge, Mass., 1941); Edward Chase Kirkland, *Men,
Cities and Transportation: A Study in New England History 1820–1900*, 2 vols.
(Cambridge, Mass., 1948); Thomas C. Cochran, *Railroad Leaders 1845–1890: The
Business Mind in Action* (Cambridge, Mass., 1953).

business leaders in banking and the iron and steel industry.[34]   Ralph and Muriel Hidy, restudying the rise of the Standard Oil monopoly, have portrayed Rockefeller as only one member of a business team that mistakenly tried to apply previously learned small business mores to giant industry, and responded somewhat involuntarily to the "prods and pressures" of a changing political and legal climate.[35]   Other writers have produced biographies of secondary business leaders who were not robber barons,[36] while statistical studies have thrown new light on the American business elite.[37]

The American business mind is a fruitful field of present-day investigation for entrepreneurial historians who utilize the concepts of social role, social sanctions, and cultural codes of conduct.   Notably, Thomas Cochran has demonstrated that Social Darwinism and the Gospel of Wealth are, though certainly important, not the whole story of the business mind, and that certain American railroad leaders of the period 1845–1890 could be influenced quite as often by their view of their proper social role in a given situation as by predatory motives.[38]

Thus, although historians like Josephson and Destler continue vigorously to defend the idea of the robber barons,[39] the current trend in American historiography is away from this concept.   Michael Kraus has written that the idea is fading, the 1954 report of the Committee on Historiography of the Social Science Research Council views it skepti-

---

[34] Fritz Redlich, *History of American Business Leaders: A Series of Studies,* Vol. I, *Theory, Iron and Steel, Iron Ore Mining* (Ann Arbor, Michigan, 1940), Vol. II, *The Molding of American Banking: Men and Ideas, Part I, 1781–1840* (New York, 1947), *Part II, 1840–1910* (New York, 1951).

[35] Hidy and Hidy, *Pioneering in Big Business,* pp. xxviii, 3–8, 201–232, 715–717.

[36] For example, Hal Bridges, *Iron Millionaire: Life of Charlemagne Tower* (Philadelphia, 1952); Philip Dorf, *The Builder: A Biography of Ezra Cornell* (New York, 1952).

[37] For example, Francis W. Gregory and Irene D. Neu, "The American Industrial Elite in the 1870's: Their Social Origins," in William Miller, ed., *Men in Business: Essays in the History of Entrepreneurship* (Cambridge, Mass., 1952), pp. 193–211.   See also Sidney Ratner, ed., *New Light on the History of Great American Fortunes: American Millionaires of 1892 and 1902* (New York, 1953), in which Ratner in his introduction criticizes various statistical studies of American business leaders.

[38] Cochran, *Railroad Leaders,* pp. 1–16, 92–93, 172, 182–183, 200–228.   For another interesting approach to the business mind of the Gilded Age see Edward C. Kirkland, "Divide and Ruin," *Missippi Valley Historical Review,* Vol. XLIII (June, 1956), pp. 3–17.   See also, by Kirkland, *Dream and Thought in the Business Community, 1860–1900* (Ithaca, N.Y., 1956).

[39] Josephson, "Should American History Be Rewritten?", pp. 9–10, 44–46; Destler, "Entrepreneurial Leadership," pp. 28, 38, and "The Opposition of American Businessmen to Social Control During the 'Gilded Age,'" *Mississippi Valley Historical Review,* Vol. XXXIX (March, 1953), pp. 641–672.

cally, Thomas Cochran calls it legend.[40]   All this may be in part a manifestation of present-day conservatism, but this writer regards it primarily as the logical reaction of historians to the cumulative evidence contained in the studies that have been designated here as the revisionist approach to the idea of the robber barons.   Of course the revisionist views are not flawless.   As a summary critique of them it can be said that the naturalness or inevitability of monopoly at any time in the United States is a moot question;[41] that both Turner and Nevins have been accused of ignoring important aspects of the American economy;[42] that all biographers are open to the charge of being too sympathetic toward their subjects; and that the company records with which business historians work make it difficult for them to avoid a board-of-directors bias.   Yet when all discounts have been made for possible error, there does seem to be enough truth left in the revisionist views to reveal the inadequacy of the idea of the robber barons.   In an emotional, romanticized way, this concept sums up the business activities of Jay Gould and his kind and expresses the predatory side of the careers of many other business leaders of the post-Civil War era.   But it grants insufficient recognition to the creative aspects of such careers or to business leaders of habitually high moral standards.   It tends to deny to business leaders through thirty-five years of American life that basic capacity for doing good as well as evil which historians freely concede to other members of the human race.   Born apparently of a desire for denunciation rather than objective analysis, the idea of the robber barons seems destined to fall into increasing disuse, as historians seek to apply ever more precise thinking to the complex American past.

EDWARD C. KIRKLAND

In order to dispel at once any mystery inherent in the title, this essay is primarily about the business generation of the "robber barons."   I propose to explore not so much what the businessman of that era thought as the scheme of thought with which he chose to approach the

---

[40] Michael Kraus, *The Writing of American History* (Norman, Okla., 1953), p. 337; *The Social Sciences in Historical Study: A Report of the Committee on Historiography Bulletin 64* (New York, 1954), p. 154; Thomas C. Cochran, "The Legend of the Robber Barons," *The Pennsylvania Magazine of History and Biography,* Vol. LXXIV (July, 1950), pp. 307–321.

[41] Vigorous arguments against the inevitability of monopoly are presented in Walter Adams and Horace M. Gray, *Monopoly in America: The Government as Promoter* (New York, 1955).

[42] On Turner see for example Louis M. Hacker, "Sections—Or Classes?" *The Nation,* Vol. CXXXVII (July 26, 1933), pp. 108–110.   On Nevins see for example Lewis Galantière, "John D.: An Academy Portrait," *The New Republic,* Vol. CIII (Dec. 9, 1940), pp. 795–797.   ·

problems of his day. Since this is the Mississippi Valley Historical Association, I shall at least be gracious enough to start my remarks in the West. Charles Elliott Perkins, president of the Chicago, Burlington and Quincy Railroad, provides my text. In 1885 he wrote in one of his frequent memoranda (for this was the manner in which he liked to express himself): "The question of political economy is not, What is noble? What is good? What is generous? What are the teachings of the Gospel? —But what, if anything, is it expedient for society, for government, to do about the production, distribution, and consumption of property, of wealth?" It is true, he continued, that "heroic example and noble obligation" are essential for a nation. "But these are individual, not governmental qualities. There is nothing noble, or generous, or heroic, or christian in a rich man's involuntary submission to taxation for the benefit of those who are less rich, if society shall deem it expedient to tax him for that object. . . . This is what some of the more recent writers call the old political economy, the economic law of Adam Smith, which they denounce as too cold and heartless for a Christian People."

The utterance was exceptional in its precision and force, but its ideas were commonplace among businessmen of that generation. Not only did they exalt the individual in the economic sphere, but they attempted to divide the individual into functions or compartments, which should as a matter of right and expediency have no relation to each other. In short, economic activity stood apart from the spheres of moral and personal considerations.

Businessmen demonstrated the application of this formula in labor policy. To the assertion of reformers and labor spokesmen that labor was entitled to a "living" wage, one which entitled the laborer to a "decent" or "respectable living," Perkins replied: "To say that a man is entitled to wages sufficient to maintain his family respectably is meaningless. What is the measure? Who is to decide what is enough to keep a man and his family respectable? Shall the laborer fix his own compensation and *somebody* be found to employ him? You may say society is morally bound to see that no honest man who is willing to work shall starve, and it may be admitted that it is better to give such men work than to give money without work. But that is public charity in either case, because if you do work which is not needed for the sake of giving employment, that is not *business*. It is easy to say that a man ought to be 'decently' paid, or 'well paid,' or 'reasonably' paid. But what is decent, or good, or reasonable pay? Is it what a man wants? Suppose two men apply for work. One says, 'I am careful, frugal, have an economical wife, can get along respectably on a dollar and a half a day,

SOURCE: *Mississippi Valley Historical Review*, XLIII (June, 1956), 3–17. Reprinted by permission.

and am ready to go to work at that.' The other says, 'I am more frugal than number one. I can get along respectably on a dollar a day and am ready to go to work at that.' Both being equally capable of doing the job, which shall be taken?" The answer, according to the principles of political economy here defined, is obvious.

This response of the business community to the interrelation of wages and human considerations was automatically extended to cognate matters of labor welfare—pensions, relief societies, payments for injuries. The objections to these devices were numerous. They relieved the men of the care and responsibility for themselves, and care and responsibility were developmental. "The fact that some men are unfortunate does not change the rule. If a man put his hand over the fire, by accident or misfortune, he is burnt just as much as if he put it there intentionally." The one way to deal with these matters was to deal with them through the economic relation, the way of wages. Make the latter large enough so that men who chose to do so could take care of themselves, including emergencies. "No man can decide for another what he shall give away from motives of sympathy," wrote Perkins. "Stockholders employ agents to conduct their business affairs. If such gratuities (payment for injuries) are given, it must be for business policy or business expediency and not charity." Perkins denied that this attitude regarded men as commodities. "Of course men are not commodities . . . but their labor, when offered for sale, is just as much a commodity as the thing it produces, and all sympathy which leads people to think otherwise is doing more harm than good, like unwise charity." The capitalist not only divided himself, he divided the laborer as well.

Lest these be regarded as the self-interested rationalizations of employers, perhaps we should resort to academic economists to learn what they, in their detachment, thought on the matter. Arthur Lapham Perry of Williams College, author of one of the most widely used early texts in economic theory and a devout Christian as well, wrote of the wage contract: "When A hires B to work in his factory, this new relation is economical, not moral. . . . What is the economical relation? This. A desires the personal service of B in his factory purely for his pecuniary benefit, and assumes his own ability to make all the calculations requisite for determining how much he can (profitably to himself) offer B for his service; and B, who knows all about his own skill . . . wants to sell his service to A for the sake of the pecuniary return or wages. There is no obligation resting upon either. Man to man, each in his own right. There is no benevolence in the heart of either, so far as this matter goes. Benevolence is now an impertinence. It is a question of honest gain in broad daylight. Benevolence is blessed in its own sphere, but there is no call for it here and now. . . . The less either (A or B) thinks and talks and acts about the other in all the other relations of life,

the better hope of good success to both in this relation. Church relations and social relations and political relations are all of consequence
in themselves; but when any of these begin to get mixed up with labor-
relations, there is soon a muss and a mess."

In the circumstances, it was natural that the businessman should
have a dubious approach to the agencies, political and religious, which
were trying to introduce into business affairs values and considerations
which the businessmen thought had nothing to do with business. The
laws of trade, sometimes vulgarized as "business principles," governed
and should govern production, distribution, and consumption; statute
laws, passed by legislatures and Congress, could have no bearing and
no influence in this area. If they did, they acted only to distort and delay
matters. The great tide of natural law would sooner or later break
through and assert itself. Consequently businessmen, as a matter of
principle, sought to stand outside the political process. Early in the
1880's, Henry Varnum Poor, the railroad expert and organizer of
manuals, reached the heart of the matter: "Railroad Men form no
political party. They are of all shades of parties. There is no possibility
that they should be combined for any political object. They reject instead of craving political influence. They are as free from sinister political bias as our farmers, merchants, or manufacturers."

A few years later, when Lyman J. Gage, president of the First National Bank of Chicago and one of the most perceptive businessmen of
that city, addressed the American Bankers' Association, he admitted
that the general attitude of his hearers was that they should have no
concern with politics or government and that the businessman thought
of himself as "a business man, pure and simple." Certainly the historians who picture the businessman of this period in politics up to his
last dollar would deny the justice of either adjective. But an illustration
of the possible validity of the businessman's attitude was provided by
Charles Francis Adams, Jr. As railroad commissioner of Massachusetts
through the 1870's he was the advocate of general rather than special
legislation for the railroads: general legislation would take railroad
officials and the railroad lobby out of the legislature. In the 1880's, as
president of the Union Pacific, his consuming objective was the passage by Congress "of such laws as will once and for all separate the government from the management of this or any other railroad corporation." And in the same strain, Edwin L. Godkin of the *Nation* argued for
free trade to protect Congress against the lobby of manufacturers.
"The way to arm them against temptation is to leave them as little as
possible to sell of the things which capitalists are eager to buy."

Godkin was getting at the separation of business and politics
through the back door. While individuals like Gage were urging participation by businessmen in the political process to do away with the

"demagogue" and the "political trickster," the *Nation* was arguing that businessmen abjure membership in legislatures because, too "practical minded," they could not look at public issues comprehensively and they did not understand the interests of others. "Practical men will not make good laws; it demands theories." Whatever the favored approach to the matter of division, a New England banker, Henry Lee Higginson, expressed the business wish most pithily: "Let us ask Congress to do their work in their own way and let us [businessmen] do ours in our way."

The businessman on the whole was also sure that religion and business should be separated. Partly this was a result of a historic estrangement. Edward Atkinson, Boston cotton capitalist and a Unitarian—and perhaps not, therefore, a religious person—informed his readers: "For nearly fifty years I have been engaged in the practical work of this life, occupied in the functions of life which the priest in almost all churches and under all the various phases of religion has been apt to disparage and to hold in slight repute." Whether or not the antagonism between clergyman and businessman was historically inescapable, the growth of the social gospel after the Civil War and the liveliness of "ethical economists," the allies of its pastors, were sure to stimulate a reaction in the business community. The outlook of this new group was of course the exact opposite of that of the business community; it sought to introduce morals and values into economic operations, "to apply Christianity," as the phrase of one of its leaders, Washington Gladden, put it, to substitute for the word individual the concept social, as in "social justice," "social Christianity," "social gospel."

One answer of the business spokesman was that such an objective was not the business of Christianity. The business of religion was the "old theological gospel," not the "gospel of social endeavor," the saving of souls and instruction in morals, not the "industrial millennium." On matters traditionally religious, clerics were scientific experts. "When Dr. Lyman Beecher took the charge of a group of 'anxious inquirers' out of the hands of Judge Gould at Litchfield, he did so as a professional man, just as a physician would have taken a case of typhoid out of the hands of an apothecary, and the church saw clearly the overwhelming necessity of the judge's deposition." But in matters of business and political economy, clergymen were not experts but amateurs. Andrew Carnegie announced: "Ecclesiastics . . . their attention being chiefly fixed upon the other world . . . seldom shine as advisers upon affairs pertaining to this." Generally he refused to include among his philanthropies gifts to churches. He made one exception—church organs. The reason for this exceptional generosity —he gave 8,000—he explained, "You can't always trust what the pulpit says but you can always depend upon what the organ says." Carnegie's anticlericalism and rationalism were well known. But on this point John D. Rockefeller, who generally suffered Baptist clergymen gladly, agreed: "I have sometimes been tempted to say that our clergymen could gain by knowing the essentials of business life better. . . . People who have had much to do with ministers and those who hold confidential positions in our churches have at times had surprising experiences in meeting what is sometimes practised in the way of ecclesiastical business, because these good men have had so little of business training in the work-a-day world."

So much for the true theory of the relationship between economics and religion. Departure from this theory of separation was bound to be damaging in practical affairs. A few surmises to the effect that the agitation of preachers and their lay readers, the "ethical economists," might in some way have been responsible for the Haymarket bomb outrage stiffened into certainty in the next decade. Both groups were blamed in a general way for the discontent of the 1890's and were held directly responsible for the Pullman outbursts. As Godkin wrote Charles Eliot Norton, "The labor craze fanned and promoted by 'ethical' professors and clergymen ended in the Chicago riots." Beyond the evil of particular circumstances, the social gospel weakened the qualities of character which the business world so highly esteemed. In a discussion of the morals of the future, Godkin grieved that public admiration was no longer given to "the just, austere, proud, and truthful man," but to the man of "brotherly kindness." Humanity had become more important than honesty. Whether because clerical criticism of business practices embraced a wider area or because its persistence was getting under the businessman's skin, the resentment of the latter seemed to increase as time went by. In the end Charles Elliott Perkins was reminding Henry Lee Higginson, "Without such mitigation by business of his [the workingman's] circumstances, no other kind of assistance is of the slightest use to a man—one who is hungry and cold can think of nothing else—no gospel touches him." Whatever the soundness of this observation in a historical sense, it would seem to cast some doubt on the business theory that religion and business could occupy separate spheres. Anyway, religion apparently should not bite the hand that fed it.

Just why so many members of the business community thought it feasible to isolate their various interests one from another is a problem. So pervasive an influence has been assigned in this era to phrenology that I am tempted to find here another reflection of its importance. "The mind," wrote Orson Fowler, one of the high priests of the phrenological movement, "is a plurality of innate and independent faculties

—a congregate of distinct and separate powers." But probably any parallelism between the ideas of the business community and phrenology is whimsey. Somewhat more plausible is the idea that the businessman divided his interest into separate compartments because this was the correct way of logically arriving at sound conclusions. Perkins was fond of resorting to John Locke's dictum: "The greatest part of true knowledge lies in the distinct perception of things in themselves distinct." Rigorously applied, this aphorism should have restrained the habit of arguing by analogy so prevalent with Perkins and other businessmen. In their hands the statement really had another purpose. It was a method for reducing problems to their essentials, for stripping away irrelevancies. Since that business generation was confronted with the complex problems attendant upon rapid change, they had to use every device of exacting analysis to find the answers. "There is a great difference," wrote Perkins, "in attitudes and rules of conduct for an individual employer of small numbers of men and a corporation employing 10–20 thousand." The "distinct perception of things in themselves distinct" was one way of discovering the differences in these attitudes and rules.

Be that as it may, the decision to operate under the aegis of a "distinct perception of things in themselves distinct" was impossible. Chauncey M. Depew in an address before the New York State Chamber of Commerce found it was not easy for rich men to be philanthropists when they had acquired wealth under conditions which "dry up generous impulses and make the possessor hard, cold, and unsympathetic." Charles Elliott Perkins found in practice that the businessman was indivisible. Fighting his employees who had struck for higher wages in 1888, Perkins elected to stand on the high ground of principle. Faced with a delegation of workers, he wrote on a slip of paper which he passed to an associate, "As an officer, I can't sympathize with the men, but as an individual, I do sympathize with them."

Few incidents were more instructive of the impossibility of the program of a "distinct perception of things in themselves distinct" than the experience of Charles Francis Adams, Jr., when he was president of the Union Pacific. Here was a man of principle and honesty, a civil service reformer, and one who believed that it was advantageous for railroads and the state to have little to do with each other. Yet since the government had originally given the Union Pacific a land grant and financial assistance, and since representatives from the western states, especially Iowa, frequently voiced the anti-railroad feeling of their constituencies in Congress, Adams had to maintain a *de facto* office of the railroad in Washington, although "it will not do to have it suggested that we have a lobby on the spot." Nonetheless Adams and the Union Pacific's counsel, Moorfield Storey, were always going to the capital and in emergencies Adams sent General Grenville M. Dodge thither "to fix things up."

This concentrated mobilization did not work. As Adams wrote: "This gang of operators in Washington are certainly a most ingenious set of fellows. They every now and then put in a bit of work which I cannot but look upon with admiration. It is very much to me as if I were obliged to watch a set of burglars who were breaking into my vault, and unable to prevent their operations, yet from time to time deeply impressed with the skill with which the rascals went to work." Though he professed an inability to do anything about these raids, Adams was later offering to do favors in behalf of certain bills desired by the Iowa congressmen if they would vote for his, authorizing "employments to aid in procuring the passage" of legislation, and finally he was writing Dodge in Washington in a personal letter: "I wish you would see if you can do anything to expedite the matter. If you cannot do it in one way, do it in another. Anyhow let it be done. I know you are quite equal to the occasion. Simply advise me what has been done, I will remit to you." Whatever these confidences add up to, they at least reveal the pathetic, and in this case somewhat ludicrous, fate of a man bent on separating business and government. He was caught in the toils. In a later letter Adams attempted an explanation. He confided to Dodge, "Of course we do not wish to meddle in politics except in self-defense."

The policy with which the businessmen chose to approach their own problems and the problems of their day was not only impossible; it was ruinous on every score. In the field of labor relations there was bound to be an increasing degree of impersonalization as the scale of business and the size of labor forces was enlarged. The deliberate attempt to add a designed indifference and apartness to this inherent tendency simply made matters worse. Even if the relationship between employer and employee were economic and not one of benevolence, this did not mean that the employees liked it that way. Though they complained about wages and hours, a recurrent lament of the workers was that employers thought of men not as individuals but as part of the machines, that employees were known by number, not by name, and came into contact only with superintendents. The old friendly feelings were gone and society was crystallizing into classes. "Labor unions," said one of their partisans proudly, suggest remedies implying "something more than 'business principles'; they imply the subordination of what are regarded as 'business principles' to morality." In the final analysis the history of labor organization and of labor-management strife in the late decades of the nineteenth century revealed the folly of the business attitude.

The history of national legislation in the same period does not point to so sharp a failure. In spite of the common interpretation that the legislation after the Civil War was business oriented, actually business strategy in this area was directed to retaining advantages which it had won accidentally—say the tariff and the national banks during the Civil War—and to securing the veto or repeal of legislation it did not desire, such as the issue of legal tenders or the repeal of the Sherman Silver Purchase Act. A systematic reading of a business-minded journal, like the *Commercial and Financial Chronicle,* gives the impression of one long shriek on the political retreat. Commenting upon the congressional year 1874, the *Chronicle* sighed: "The season has not been a favorable one for financial wisdom, and any proposed law which does not carry with it the certainty of positive injury is regarded to a certain extent as a safety valve, by standing in the place of some other provision which would be still less propitious." For business *vis-à-vis* public legislation, these years were one long holding operation. The exhortations of Lyman Gage, toward the end of the period, advising the businessmen to organize as citizens and shopkeepers, not into "a political machine—that would be as unwise as it would be impossible, but if I could, I would make it an avenue through which should be poured in many streams over all the people the healthful influences of a better knowledge of the true laws of our politico-social-economic life," confessed the disadvantage of separating business from government.

Whether the ability of businessmen to take the church or leave it alone was equally ruinous for them, many would say was impossible to tell. It is not given to historians to see beyond the grave, nor has any arrangement yet devised bestowed infallibility in location theory upon Protestant clergymen, particularly the social gospel variety. Be that as it may, many men of the cloth were quite certain that here the theory of divide led, as it did elsewhere, to ruin. When J. P. Morgan died in 1913, an Episcopalian divine in Philadelphia preached a sermon, "Has J. P. Morgan gone to heaven? If not, why not?" and found that he had not, partly because he was neither Christian nor democrat; and somewhat more modestly the *United Mine Workers Journal* suggested an investigating committee to determine the dead financier's whereabouts. When John D. Rockefeller died in 1937, it was the labor press and spokesmen, rather than the pastors, who speculated whether the oil king had gone to heaven or hell and seemed to lean toward the latter destination. In view of the dearth of answers on the other side of this eternal question "Whither Bound?" here as elsewhere to divide was to ruin.

My exposition of the disadvantage of dividing his personality and his character, as the businessman sought to do, is in a sense a parable. In my estimation that experience carries a lesson for historians as historians. In the narrower field of writing about business and business-men, it seems to me to be ruinous to accept the businessman's habit of division and to apply it to him. This is the defect, to my way of thinking, in much business history writing. While it is only redressing the balance to focus such narratives upon the entrepreneurial decision, written in terms of business documents, such procedure, without atten-tion to the social and political context, ruins the picture. To segregate the criticism of a big business in separate, topical chapters near the end of a volume is a somewhat less obvious road to ruin. Such distortions are not necessarily committed only by the supporters of business enter-prise as it was. The foes of business who focus upon only one aspect of what they criticize, who select opinions without attention to the whole life of the businessman and his achievements, can easily make a monster or caricature out of Stephen J. Field or William Graham Sumner, apologists for business freedom.

Nor need the caution "divide and ruin" be applied only to historians who wrote about business. It has relevance, I believe, to all practicing historians in the field of American history. I say practicing historians, for it is to this common man in the history field and to his difficulties that I wish to address my peroration. As long as I can remember, as an individual historian I have been exhorted and often scolded by presidents of historical associations, by the authors of numbered bulle-tins financed by foundations, and by sages emerging from the self-contemplation and intercommunion of committees and institutes, to do something: for example, either to embrace the contributions of other social sciences, to realize I cannot be objective because I have a frame of reference, or perhaps to acknowledge that I am studying or teaching something that does not exist, for there is no such thing as history or historical fact. Without wishing either to disparage or to deride these contributions—for I believe all intellectual activity to be commendable—I take consolation for my philistine attitude from the fact that few historians in their day-to-day work apparently pay much attention to these formulations, theses, and ultimatums; that is to say, I rarely hear these matters discussed informally among historians and even more rarely discover books written in accord with these whole-some prescriptions. Perhaps the reason is a failure of "communica-tion," to borrow a word from the inventory of verbiage which this thought has accumulated.

While waiting upon the results of a study—an all-expense tour financed by one of our foundations that likes to grant its money to projects working along the frontiers of knowledge—I would like to hazard a guess as to why this body of preachment has had, compara-tively, so little influence upon historians. One reason is because some of the assertions clearly are not true. For instance, the average historian, like other human beings, knows things happen to him and have happened to him. Equipped with this common experience, he quite rightly regards debates as to whether there is such a thing as history or a historical fact as simply for the stratosphere and the metaphysician. He proceeds on the sound assumption that he is studying and teaching something. The other reason for the negligible influence of thinking about history and of talk about historiography is that it has little bearing upon what the average practicing historian thinks is his job or duty. Throughout his apprenticeship and afterwards, he is engaged in trying, with the materials he has at hand, to become an honest observer and a trained diagnostician of what has taken place. This is an absorbing and exacting mission. I know that in the case of an American historian, the task does not generally involve the mastery of those recondite skills—epigraphy, and paleography, and the like—which our brethren in European history have to have at their finger tips, and perhaps can be accomplished without the knowledge of any other language than English. Furthermore the problems of longtime-spans, with which President Lynn Thorndike dealt in his witty and erudite address before the American Historical Association last December, are not so frequently ours.

No matter how often we have been patronized because we deal with matters which are not unknown or mysterious or remote enough to be quite civilized or cultured, I believe we have a greater problem in becoming skilled and honest observers than our colleagues in European history. However partisan they may later become, they can at least approach ancient Tuscany or the medieval fair with relative detachment. If we are to secure a comparably serene view of our subject matter, we have to wrench ourselves out of our cultural environment and heritage and cut the political, economic, and social threads tying us to what we are talking about. Such a task, if it is to be bravely performed, requires dedication and discipline. On the whole the practitioners of American history, to their credit, have not taken the easy way of stretching out on the frame-of-reference theory and saying that as long as they acknowledge they are doing so, the affirmation explains and justifies their omissions and commissions. Seeking to be expert observers, they have sought to transcend rather than to accept their personal limitations.

In the attainment of such balance and freedom, it is essential to apply the same standards of judgment and appraisal to all groups and to all individuals: to realize, for instance, that success is no more a reason for denying a man or a cause a hearing than failure is a reason for granting it; to discard the sentimentalism that associates truth with one social class and error with another; to acknowledge that trade unions as well as corporations may use power arbitrarily. Since I have been talking about businessmen, perhaps I had better resort for the last time to a quotation from Charles Elliott Perkins. He was writing to a judge who had declared that we could not find truth unless we had the broadest sympathy with and care for the individual and the community. Perkins disagreed. He granted that "so far as sympathy is an attribute of the human mind, we must take it into account in trying to discover what individuals will as a rule do under given conditions. But I can't agree we cannot discover the truth 'if we go at it in cold blood.' The cooler we keep the better. The trouble is, as old John Locke points out in his Essay on the Understanding, that most people have too much sympathy either with their own preconceived ideas or with one side or the other of a controversy. To be a good judge you must not care *what* the truth is—only to find it, and the more you care what it is, the less likely you are to find it."

Surely a presidential address as old-fashioned as this should not conclude with a quotation from business. If it is to be true throughout to the context of the nineteenth century, where it belongs, it should include a bit of verse and a bit of Latin. I can kill two birds with one stone by acknowledging that about all I recall from my reading of Vergil's *Aeneid* is the line

Tros Tyriusque mihi nullo discrimine agetur

which my classics teacher, in order to communicate with a bunch of average high-school seniors, told us might be translated:

Democrats and Republicans I treat alike.

Fellow members of the Mississippi Valley Historical Association: Let us be on our guard lest, by dividing our standards, we ruin not only ourselves as practicing historians but also the heritage of American history which we are under obligation to honor, to explore, and to transmit.

The Knights of Labor and
the Trade Unions, 1878–1886
GERALD N. GROB

The powerful forces that were transforming American business after the Civil War inevitably transformed the nature and problems of American labor. The major factors were the fabulous growth of industry, the advent of steel, the almost universal spread of the factory system, the vast increase in population and in the size of the laboring force, the revolution in transportation and communication, and the great extension of markets. As these forces gathered momentum, workers had to find new answers to the question of securing and improving their position. How were they to respond to the challenge of the new industrial order? Were they to adopt as their goal the reordering of society or were they to address themselves rather to the more immediate issues of wages, hours, and other working conditions? What form of organization would be most effective in achieving their goals?

One of the most dramatic episodes in the story of labor's response to the new industrial order, and one which epitomized the difficult choices that labor had to make, was the struggle between the Knights of Labor and the trade unions during the 1880's. It is this struggle which is the subject of the following essay by Professor Gerald N. Grob of Clark University, who has written of the ideological conflict in the American labor movement during the period 1865–1900 in his recent study, **Workers and Utopia** *(1961). He is also the author of* **The State and the Mentally Ill: A History of Worcester State Hospital in Massachusetts, 1830–1920** *(1966), for which he won the American Association for State and Local History Manuscript Award for 1965. In the essay below, Professor Grob subjects some of the more salient labor developments of the 1880's to fresh and thought-provoking analysis. In tracing the organizational differences between the Knights of Labor and the trade unions he reveals the essential differences in their approaches to unionism and to society.*

SOURCE: *The Journal of Economic History,* XVIII (June, 1958), 176–92. Reprinted by permission of the publisher and author.

The way America met the problems of the 1880's ought to be regarded as part of the larger way in which labor, both in America and in other advanced industrial societies, has responded to the advent of modern enterprise during the nineteenth and twentieth centuries. Almost universally, labor faced the choice of seeking a basic reform of society or of concentrating on the improvement of working conditions within the framework of the existing industrial order. The choice it would make depended obviously on a variety of factors: the degree to which industrialization had already proceeded; the political influence, including the extent of enfranchisement, of the working classes; the amount of freedom accorded unions by law; the prevailing conditions of work; the size and power of the unions; and the relation of labor's demands to the existing social structure as well as to the demands of other classes. Seen in this light, there is much in the Knights of Labor program that is reminiscent of the program of Robert Owen and of the Chartists in England and of Fourier, Proudhon, and Louis Blanc in France; there is also much in the trade-union approach that seems similar to that of the new unionism in mid-Victorian England.

The advances of labor in all of Western society during the past century, it would appear, have been made not by the triumph of larger plans for reforming society but by the piecemeal gains achieved through pressures on both management and political parties. These gains were achieved within the premises of established order. But there is a qualitative change which a prolonged series of quantitative changes produces. It may therefore be fair to ask whether labor has not, in the final analysis, made over industrial society by accepting it.

The year 1886 was destined to be a crucial one in the history of the American labor movement. The eight-hour crusade, the numerous strikes, the Haymarket bomb, the entrance of workingmen into the political arena at the state and national levels, and the mushroom growth of labor organizations all contributed to the agitation and excitement of the year. Yet the importance of these events was overshadowed by a development that was to have such far-reaching implications that it would determine the future of the labor movement for the succeeding half century. That development was the declaration of war by the trade unions against the reform unionism of the Knights of Labor.

The struggle between the Knights and the other unions represented a clash of two fundamentally opposing ideologies. The Knights of Labor, on the one hand, grew out of the reform and humanitarian movements of ante-bellum America, and was the direct descendant, through the National Labor Union, of the labor reform tradition of the Jacksonian era. Banking on the leveling influence of technological change, its leaders sought to organize the entire producing class into a single irresistible coalition that would work toward the abolition of the wage system and the establishment of a new society. "We do not believe," a high official of the Knights remarked, "that the emancipation of labor will come with increased wages and a reduction in the hours of labor; we must go deeper than that, and this matter will not be settled until the wage system is abolished." The leaders of the Knights therefore emphasized education and cooperation, and they bitterly opposed their constituents' participation in such affairs as the Southwest and stockyards strikes of 1886, as well as the very popular eight-hour movement of that same year.

The reform ideology of the Knights, in turn, had an important impact upon the development of its structure, which followed a heterogeneous rather than a homogeneous pattern. Minimizing the utility of organization along trade lines, the Order emphasized instead the grouping of all workers, regardless of craft, into a single body. Highest priority therefore was given to the mixed local assembly, which included all workers irrespective of their trade or degree of skill. Neither a trade, plant, nor industrial union, the mixed assembly could never be more than a study or debating group. Including many diverse elements (even employers), it could not adapt itself to meet the problems of a specific industry or trade. The mixed assembly might agitate for reform or participate in politics, but it could never become the collective bargaining representative of its members.

Given the predominance of the mixed over the trade local, the structure of the Knights inevitably developed along geographical rather than jurisdictional lines, and the district assembly, which included mixed as well as trade locals, became the most characteristic form of organization. The highest governmental body of the Knights—the General Assembly—was not intended as a medium for collective bargaining. Indeed, its very inclusiveness precluded such a possibility.

The trade unions, on the other hand, rejected the broad reform goals of the Knights, emphasizing instead higher wages, shorter hours, and job control. Such objectives were clearly incompatible with an organizational structure such as that developed by the Knights. Eschewing the multitrade local that had been so prevalent during the 1860's and was being perpetuated by the Order, the trade unions began to stress the craft-industrial form of organization both at the local and national levels. A relative scarcity of labor, together with a rapidly expanding economy, had created a favorable environment for the trade unions. Gambling on the hope that the rise of a national market made organization along trade rather than geographical lines more effective, union leaders chose to concentrate upon the task of organizing the workers along trade lines into unions designed for collective bargaining rather than social reform.

Therefore, given the inherent differences in ideology and structure, the conflict between the Knights and the trade unions was, if not inevitable, certainly not an unexpected or surprising development. Undoubtedly the antagonistic personalities of partisans on both sides hastened an open rift. Yet the hostilities between the Knights and the trade unions cannot be explained solely in terms of personalities, for the conflict was not simply a struggle for power between two rivals. It was a clash between two fundamentally different ideologies—with the future of the labor movement at stake.

I

The contest between trade unionists and reformers for control of the labor movement developed on two planes. Commencing first as an internal struggle within the Knights, it eventually expanded and soon involved the national unions. Within the Knights the struggle revolved around the unresolved question as to which form of organization best met working-class necessities. On the surface the issue of mixed versus trade locals was simply a structural problem. In reality, however, the differences between the two forms indicated the existence of a fundamental cleavage in ultimate objectives, for the mixed assembly could be utilized only for reform or political purposes, while the trade assembly was generally a collective bargaining organization.

Although the national leadership of the Knights regarded the mixed assembly as the ideal type of unit, a large proportion of its local assemblies were trade rather than mixed. The first local, composed of garment cutters, was strictly craft, and remained so to the end. Most of the other locals that followed were also trade assemblies. On January 1, 1882, according to the *Journal of United Labor,* there were 27 working districts and over 400 local assemblies. Of the latter, 318 were trade and only 116 were mixed. Thirteen additional districts, not functioning, had 53 trade and 87 mixed locals, attesting to the relative instability of the mixed form of organization. Of the 135 locals attached directly to the General Assembly, 67 were trade and 68 were mixed.

Despite the wide latitude given them to organize trade local assemblies, the trade element within the Knights nevertheless found it difficult to function efficiently. Local trade assemblies, no matter how inclusive in their particular area, were often ineffective when operating in a market that was regional or national rather than local in character. So long as employers could find a ready supply of nonunion labor elsewhere, efforts at collective bargaining by locals would be ineffective. The only solution lay in national organization, and the trade exponents within the Knights pressed for national and regional trade districts that would transcend the limited geographical area normally encompassed by the local or district assembly.

The General Assembly, therefore, meeting in January 1879, author-ized the establishment of autonomous national trade districts within the framework of the Knights. But only nine months later the Assembly completely reversed itself by declaring that trade locals were "con-trary to the spirit and genius of the Order," and it returned exclusive jurisdiction over all locals to the district assembly of their area.

In December 1881, however, the Federation of Organized Trades and Labor Unions, predecessor of the American Federation of Labor (A.F. of L.), held its first convention. Of the 107 delegates present, no less than 50 came from the Knights.

The following September the General Assembly heard the secretary of the Knights warn that trade sentiment was growing rapidly. "Many Trades Unions have also written me," he remarked, "stating that they were seriously meditating the propriety of coming over to us in a body, freely expressing the opinion that their proper place was in our Order." To prevent any mass exodus from the Order to the rival Federation, and also to recruit members from the trade unions, the General Assem-bly enacted legislation authorizing and encouraging the formation of national and regional trade districts. This move was reaffirmed and even extended at the meetings of the General Assembly in 1884 and 1886.

While permissible, at least in theory, the establishment of trade districts was not a simple matter. The basic philosophy of the Knights militated against organization along craft lines, and the establishment of autonomous trade units within the framework of the Order aroused strong opposition. "I do not favor the establishment of any more Na-tional Trade Districts," Terence V. Powderly, head of the Knights from 1879 to 1893, told the General Assembly in 1885, "they are a step back-ward." Other reform unionists, echoing Powderly's sentiments, charged that trade districts violated the fundamental principles of the Knights. Holding tenaciously to their reform concepts, the leaders of the Knights were insistent in their demands that organization should not proceed along trade lines.

Applicants for trade districts therefore could not always be certain that charters would be granted them, even though they had met all the formal requirements. In some cases charters were granted without any questions. Window Glass Workers' Local Assembly (L.A.) 300 was chartered as a national trade district at a time when such districts were contrary to the laws of the Knights, and the telegraphers were organized nationally in 1882 as District Assembly (D.A.) 45. For a while these two were the only national districts, although before 1886 there were two district assemblies composed of miners, five of shoemakers, three of railroad employees, and one each of printers, plumbers, leather workers, government employees, and streetcar employees. Between

1883 and 1885 the General Assembly went on record as favoring the establishment of trade districts of shoemakers, plate-glass workers, and plumbers. On the other hand, after sanctioning the formation of builders' districts in 1882, it refused the following year to permit these districts to be represented on the General Executive Board. Even while passing legislation authorizing trade districts, the General Assembly refused to allow woodworkers, cigarmakers, and carpenters to organize trade districts. Furthermore, it passed a resolution stating that no charter for a trade district would be granted unless the applicants could demonstrate to the satisfaction of the General Executive Board that the craft could not be effectively organized under the system of mixed or territorial districts. The attitude of the board, however, was often conditioned by the antitrade unionism of its officers. In 1886, for example, it refused to sanction the request of five building trade locals that they be permitted to withdraw from D.A. 66 and organize their own district. At the same time it empowered a New Hampshire local to change from a trade to a mixed assembly.

Trade units, generally speaking, were authorized usually in efforts to attract workers to join the Knights. Thus the International Trunkmakers Union came into the Order as a trade district. Once inside, however, workers found it considerably more difficult to secure trade charters. After affiliating in 1882, to cite one case, the plumbers later left the Knights when they encountered difficulty in obtaining a charter for a national trade district, and they established the International Association of Journeymen Plumbers, Steam Fitters, and Gas Fitters.

The hostility of the national leadership of the Knights was not the sole obstacle to the formation of trade units. Mixed and territorial districts, which were first in the field and were already established as functioning organizations, were also antagonistic toward trade districts. If the latter were formed, not only would a mixed district suffer a loss of membership to a trade district, but it would also surrender its absolute jurisdiction over a given territorial area, since the autonomous trade district would exercise control over the entire craft in that area.

The General Assembly and the General Executive Board often supported the mixed and territorial districts in disputes with trade districts. Frequently the district's consent was a prerequisite to secession and the establishment of a trade district. This consent was not easily obtained. In 1886 D.A. 30 of Massachusetts turned down an application by four of its locals for permission to withdraw and form a national trade assembly of rubber workers. While the General Assembly supported a district court decision that members of trade locals could not be compelled to join mixed locals, the General Executive Board refused to force trade members of mixed locals to transfer to trade assemblies.

Even after obtaining a charter, trade districts encountered difficulties with the mixed district in their areas. Dual jurisdiction often led to friction, though in theory the system of mixed and trade districts appeared perfectly harmonious and compatible. For example, D.A. 64 of New York City, composed of workers in the printing and publishing business, became embroiled in a rivalry with D.A. 49 (mixed). In 1883 D.A. 64 failed to get exclusive jurisdiction over all workers in the trade. Soon afterward D.A. 49 charged that the printers were accepting locals not of their trade, and that these locals had also withdrawn from D.A. 49 without permission. An investigation by the secretary of the General Executive Board disclosed that D.A. 64 had been initiating lithographers, typefounders, pressmen, and feeders in order to strengthen itself as a bargaining unit, and that it had not engaged in raiding forays against D.A. 49. Although the Board upheld D.A. 64, the decision did not resolve the rivalry, and the two districts continued their feud.

With the single exception of L.A. 300, trade districts did not enjoy any appreciable measure of success between 1878 and 1885. The far-reaching reform goals of the Knights and its structural inclusiveness left the advocates of trade organization in the position of a perpetual minority. The expansion of the Knights into the more sparsely populated regions of the South and West, moreover, further diminished trade influence, since the mixed assembly was dominant in rural areas. Lacking a majority, the trade members were unable to establish a central strike fund or concentrate on collective bargaining, and they found that their immediate goals were being subordinated to and sacrificed for more utopian objectives.

II

The struggle between trade unionists and reformers within the Knights, however, was completely overshadowed by the rupture of relations in 1886 between the Knights and the national unions. The latter, stronger and more cohesive than the trade districts of the Order, were better able to take the lead in the conflict between reform and trade unionism. Disillusioned with labor reformism, the trade unions acted upon the premise that the traditional programs of the past were no longer suitable to the changing environment, and they led the assault against the Knights of Labor in 1886.

During the early 1880's, however, it was by no means evident that the Knights and the national unions were predestined to clash. The Federation of Organized Trades and Labor Unions permitted district assemblies of the Knights to be represented at its annual conventions, and many trade union leaders also belonged to the Order. Local unions and assemblies often cooperated in joint boycotts, and expressions of friendliness by the national unions toward Powderly and other officials of the Knights were not uncommon. The International Typographical Union expressed appreciation in 1882 for the aid given it by the Knights in a number of cities, and then went on to adopt resolutions recommending cooperation with other labor organizations and permitting its members to join any body that would further the interests of the craft in their particular locality. In other words, the national unions regarded the Knights as a valuable economic ally.

In turn, the Knights vehemently denied having any hostile designs upon the trade unions, and in a number of prominent cases before 1885 it acted accordingly. Nevertheless, with its structural inclusiveness and reform ideology, it was perhaps inevitable that the Order, in its efforts to bring all workingmen into a single organization, would undercut trade union organizational efforts. Thus the General Assembly authorized a committee in 1883 to confer with union representatives in the hope of incorporating all the trade unions within the Knights.

In the absence of any national or international union, the absorption of local unions by the Knights in the form of trade assemblies created no friction. Indeed, isolated local unions were eager to affiliate with such a powerful national organization. By 1886, therefore, the Knights claimed nearly eleven hundred local assemblies, many of which undoubtedly represented local trade unions having no parent national union.

When, however, the Knights began to organize workingmen in trades already having national organizations, friction was quick to arise. The trouble that followed the Order's expansion into the realm of the trade unions was not simply a jurisdictional rivalry between similar organizations. As discussed above, the Order and the national unions had opposing conceptions of the legitimate functions of the labor movement, which in turn had led to different structural forms. The expansion of the Order's mixed units thus served to undermine the economic functions of the trade unions, since the heterogeneous character of the former prevented them from exercising any appreciable degree of economic power. Furthermore, the structural diversity of the Knights caused trouble when its trade assemblies sought to perform tasks that logically fell within the purview of the trade unions. The national unions, moreover, took the position that geographical trade assemblies were inadequate to meet the challenge of a nationalized economy, and in fact were little better than mixed district assemblies. In defense, union officials generally refused to consent to a mutual recognition of working cards, and they demanded that the Knights cease interfering in trade affairs.

The Knights, however, did not heed the warnings of the national unions, and its organizers continued their sporadic work in trades having national unions. "Every week," John Swinton reported in 1885, "Trade Unions are turned into Local Assemblies, or Assemblies are organized out of Trade Unions." As early as 1881 a district leader attempted to capture a typographical union local, and by 1884 there were over forty local assemblies of printers in the Knights. The overzealous activities of the Order's organizers also led to trouble with the Bricklayers and Masons International Union.

The trade unions continuously charged that the Order had accepted scabs and unfair workers. It is probable that the unions greatly exaggerated this grievance, but there is little doubt that the existence of two labor organizations, each purporting to accomplish different ends, created a disciplinary problem. Intraunion disagreements frequently concluded with one party seceding and joining the Order as a local assembly. Thus the trade unions found that the Knights were attracting dissidents who normally might have remained in the union.

Despite the proselytizing activities of the Knights, there was no general conflict with the other unions before July 1885. At this time the membership of the Order was slightly over 100,000, and examples of clashes with the trade unions were generally the exception rather than the rule. When differences did arise, the trade unions often made conciliatory efforts at peaceful adjustment. Thus the convention of the International Typographical Union agreed in 1884 to its president's suggestion that he confer with Powderly in order to iron out existing grievances, although it refused to sanction a proposed amalgamation with the Order.

In only one major case—that involving the Cigar Makers International Union—did the differences between a national union and the Knights erupt in open hostilities before 1886. Historians, placing much emphasis upon this particular conflict, have credited Adolph Strasser and Samuel Gompers, the leaders of the Cigar Makers, with the dual responsibility of helping to precipitate the internecine war between the national unions and the Knights, and then founding the A.F. of L. as a rival national federation.

While the national unions generally supported the Cigar Makers in its struggle with the Knights, it is improbable that sympathy for the Cigar Makers would have led to a fight with the Order. Undoubtedly Strasser and Gompers exerted great efforts to induce the unions to lend them support. The fact is also incontrovertible that both were determined, forceful, and sometimes ruthless men. Nevertheless, their efforts would have been useless unless a solid basis of discontent had already existed. In other words, for the unions to break with the Knights, there must have been more compelling reasons than simply the activities of two individuals.

III

To understand the conflict that split the labor movement, the rapid growth of the Knights after 1885 must be examined. In the twelve months between July 1885 and June 1886 the Order's membership increased from 100,000 to over 700,000. This growth, at least in part, came about at the expense of the other unions. In many cases workers abandoned their trade unions to join the Knights. The Journeymen Tailors National Union found that many of its locals had transferred to the Knights, resulting in a considerable loss of membership. A vice-president of the Amalgamated Association of Iron and Steel Workers complained in 1886 that some sublodges in his area had been disbanded because of inroads by the Order. Further difficulty was caused by overzealous organizers who made determined efforts to transform trade unions into local assemblies. In February 1886 the secretary of the Journeymen Bakers National Union protested against such activities. "We never knew," responded the secretary-treasurer of the Knights, "that the K. of L. was proscribed from bringing into its fold all branches of honorable toil."

The Knights, in other words, had adopted an organizational policy diametrically different from that of the trade unions. The traditional concept of organization held by the A. F. of L. (the representative of the trade unions) required that federal labor unions (local units including workers of all trades having no separate unions of their own) be splintered into separate homogeneous craft units as soon as there were enough workers in that locality to form such bodies. The aim of such a policy was to develop the collective bargaining potentialities of the various trades. The Knights, on the other hand, sought to reverse this strategy and proceed in the opposite direction, and it encouraged the combining of trade units into mixed assemblies, which at most were reform or political units. Beneath the structural and organizational differences of the two groups, therefore, lay opposing goals.

To what extent did the Knights encroach upon the domain of the trade unions? Peter J. McGuire of the Carpenters claimed that between 150 and 160 trade unions, including the Molders, Boiler-Makers, Bakers, Miners, Typographical, and Granite Cutters, had grievances against the Order. Only in the case of the Bricklayers and Masons International Union, however, is the evidence fairly complete. In response to a survey conducted in the summer of 1886, the union's secretary received eighty-seven replies. Eight locals reported the existence of bricklayers and masons assemblies within their jurisdiction, four claimed the Knights were working for subunion wages, and three asserted the Knights were working longer hours. "But there are a large number of such men scattered throughout the country who belong to mixed assemblies," the secretary reported—and herein lay the union's major grievance. The complaints of the Bricklayers and Masons were echoed by most of the other major national unions.

In general, the national unions were fearful of the Knights for two closely related reasons. The mixed assembly, in the first place, was incompatible with trade union goals. In theory both structural forms could exist side by side, each pursuing its own ends. Thus the mixed assembly could concentrate on reform and politics, while the trade unions could develop their collective bargaining functions. The *modus vivendi*, however, presupposed that workers could belong simultaneously to both trade unions and mixed assemblies. At a time when the labor movement's primary problem was to organize and stay organized, such an assumption was unwarranted, and trade union leaders recognized the mutual hostility of the mixed assembly and trade union.

In the second place, trade union officials opposed the chartering of trade assemblies within the Knights for the reason that these units had proved incapable of developing collective bargaining and other union institutions. Furthermore, the geographical and regional organization of the Knights meant that there was little hope for the mature evolution of the national trade assembly. Since local trade assemblies were often ineffective when operating in an environment marked by a nationalized economy and the geographical mobility of labor, trade union leaders argued that these units were attempting to perform functions that logically belonged to the national unions, and in the long run tended to undermine the standards of membership and employment that the unions had struggled so fiercely to establish.

By the spring of 1886 relations between the trade unions and the Knights had so deteriorated that a collision appeared imminent. Five prominent unionists therefore called for a meeting of union leaders to arrange a settlement of differences, while at the same time Powderly summoned the General Assembly in a special session to consider, among other things, the troubles with the trade unions. The conference of trade union officials then appointed a committee of five to draw up a plan of settlement. Under the moderating influence of McGuire, who played the leading role, the committee drew up a "treaty," which it submitted to the General Executive Board of the Knights on May 25, 1886.

By the terms of this treaty the Knights would refrain from organizing any trade having a national organization, and also would revoke the charter of any existing trade assembly having a parent union. In the second place, any workers guilty of ignoring trade union wage scales, scabbing, or any other offense against a union, would be ineligible for membership in the Order. Third, any organizer who tampered with or interfered in the internal affairs of trade unions would have his commission revoked. Finally, local and district assemblies were not to interfere while trade unions engaged in strikes or lockouts, and the Knights would not be permitted to issue any label or trade-mark where a national union had already done so.

On the surface it appears surprising that the trade unions, which claimed to represent about 350,000 workers (although their actual membership was about 160,000), would present such a document to an organization having 700,000 members. Yet the treaty was neither a bargaining offer nor a declaration of war. It was rather the logical outcome of the duality that had pervaded the labor movement since the Civil War. Under its terms the labor movement would be divided into two separate and distinct compartments. The Knights of Labor, on the one hand, would continue its efforts to abolish the wage system, reform society, and educate the working class. The national unions, on the other hand, would be left paramount in the economic field, and the Order would no longer be permitted to exercise any control over wages, hours, working conditions, or the process of collective bargaining. In other words, trade unionism and reform unionism had come to a parting of the ways.

In one sense the treaty was an expression of the fear of the skilled workers that they were being subordinated to the interests of the unskilled. Yet the polarization implied in such an interpretation should not be exaggerated, for it cannot be said that the Knights themselves represented the unskilled workers. The Order was not an industrial union, nor did it emphasize collective bargaining. It was rather a heterogeneous mass that subordinated the economic functions of labor organizations to its primary goal of reforming society. The mixed assembly, while including workers of all trades and callings, was in no sense an industrial union, since it was not organized either by industry or factory. Moreover, the trade unions had never excluded the unskilled from the labor movement; they simply maintained that organization along craft lines was historically correct. "In truth," remarked Gompers, "the trade union is nothing more or less than the organization of wage earners engaged in a given employment, whether skilled or unskilled, for the purpose of attaining the best possible reward, [and] the best attainable conditions for the workers in that trade or calling."

The General Assembly of the Knights, in turn, submitted its own proposals to the union committee. Its terms included protection against unfair workers, a mutual exchange of working cards, and the holding of a joint conference before either organization presented wages and hours demands to employers. Clearly the Assembly's position was in fundamental disagreement with that of the trade unions. The latter had demanded unitary control over the economic field, while the Knights had demanded equal jurisdiction over membership and working standards. Thus neither side evinced willingness to compromise over basic issues.

Although failing to conclude a settlement with the trade unions, the special session of the General Assembly did not close the door to further negotiations. For the time being, therefore, the conflict remained in abeyance. While matters were pending, however, the Knights made a determined effort to end friction by intensifying its campaign to bring the national unions under its control. The national unions, however, recognized that the structure of the Knights was incompatible with trade union objectives, and the policy of the Order was only partially successful. Some of the smaller unions, including the Seamen's Benevolent Union, the Eastern Glass Bottle Blowers' League, and the Western Green Bottle Blowers' Association, joined the Knights. The American Flint Glass Workers Union, on the other hand, refused to go along with the other glassworkers because of an earlier dispute with the Order. In New York City the Knights made a determined but unsuccessful attempt to capture the German shoemakers and the Associated Jewelers. Most of the larger and more important unions emphatically rejected the Order's overtures. The members of the Amalgamated Association of Iron and Steel Workers overwhelmingly defeated a referendum on the subject, while a similar poll conducted by the secretary of the Bricklayers and Masons resulted in the same conclusion. The Iron Molders' convention turned down the merger proposal by a vote of 114 to 27. Furthermore, the Typographical Union, the Carpenters, the Plumbers and Gas Fitters, the coal miners, and the Stationary Engineers all rejected the invitation to join the Knights.

At the regular meeting of the General Assembly in October 1886 further negotiations between the trade unions and the Knights again ended in failure. The action by the Assembly in ordering all workers holding cards in both the Knights and the Cigar Makers International Union to leave the latter under pain of expulsion was interpreted by both sides as constituting a final break and an open declaration of war. The trade union committee therefore issued a call on November 10, 1886, for all unions to send representatives to a convention in Columbus, Ohio, on December 8, to form an "American Federation or Alliance of all National and International Trade Unions." Out of this meeting came the A.F. of L. Completely dominated by the national unions, the December convention excluded assemblies of the Knights from membership, and then proceeded to establish the new organization on a firm foundation.

Thus by the end of 1886 the die had been cast, and the Knights and national unions prepared for war. Why had all negotiations failed? Undoubtedly the intractability of leaders on both sides contributed to the difficulties, but there were also those who had made sincere efforts to head off the impending conflict. The trade unions, furthermore, had encountered jurisdictional rivalries with the Knights, but this has been an endemic problem of the labor movement, and one which has not always had an unhappy ending.

The conflict between the Knights and the trade unions, then, had a much broader significance than the negotiations between them indicated, and represented the culmination of decades of historical development. The Knights, growing out of the humanitarian and reform crusades of ante-bellum America, emphasized the abolition of the wage system and the reorganization of society. To achieve this purpose it insisted on the prime importance of the mixed assembly, which would serve as the nucleus of an organization dedicated to reform. The trade unions, on the other hand, accepted their environment, and sought to take advantage of the relative scarcity of labor and the rising scale of production. Hence they emphasized the collective bargaining functions of labor organizations, thus tacitly accepting the workers' wage status.

Perhaps grounds for compromise did exist, but neither side was prone to make any concessions. The national unions, by insisting upon strict trade autonomy as a *sine qua non* of settlement, were in effect demanding that the Knights should virtually abandon any pretense at being a bona fide labor organization. It is true that the unions could have organized as national autonomous trade districts if the Knights had been ready to grant permission. The leaders of the Knights, however, were unwilling to permit their organization to be transformed into what the A.F. of L. ultimately became. Indeed, after 1886 many national trade districts left the Order because of their inability to function within the framework of that body. The national unions, moreover, were not encouraged by the experiences of trade districts within the Knights before 1886. Finally, there was the simple element of power, and both the trade unions and the Knights, as established organizations, were adamant in their refusal to surrender any part of it.

Between reform and trade unionism, therefore, existed a gulf that the leaders of the 1880's were unable to bridge. By 1886 this chasm had widened to such a degree that cooperation between the two seemed virtually impossible and war seemed to be the only solution. Reform and trade unionism had at last come to a parting of the ways, and upon the outcome of the ensuing struggle hinged the destiny of the American labor movement.

CHANGING PATTERNS OF
LIFE AND THOUGHT

10

Race Relations in the Postwar South
C. VANN WOODWARD

Of all the problems confronting American society in the postwar decades, one of the most significant was that of the status of the Negro. How would the Civil War amendments—the Thirteenth, Fourteenth, and Fifteenth—be translated into reality, and with what social and economic consequences? Because the bulk of the Negro population was concentrated in the South, the problem was immediately a Southern one. But its solution depended on how well the South would fare in the altered political and economic circumstances of the nation at large. To say, therefore, that the South lost the favored position it had enjoyed before the war in national politics and that its economy assumed a colonial subservience to that of the industrial Northeast is also to explain, to a large degree, why great tensions built up within Southern society. Inevitably, these tensions were reflected in its approach to the Negro problem. By 1900, the South had formulated its solution. Every state of the old Confederacy had begun to impose upon the Negro an ever-extending dominion of "Jim Crow" laws, keeping his activities scrupulously segregated from those of the white population and binding him and his fellows in a caste of social inferiority.

Just why and how the South took the course of segregation is the subject of a superb little book entitled The Strange Career of Jim Crow *(1955, 1966), by Professor C. Vann Woodward of Yale University. Professor Wood-*

SOURCE: *The Progressive*, December, 1962, pp. 12–16. The original title of the article was "The South in Perspective." Reprinted by permission of *The Progressive*.

ward is clearly a member of the small company of the master historians of our own age. His writings, which are concerned primarily with Southern history in the late nineteenth and early twentieth centuries, also include Tom Watson: Agrarian Rebel *(1938),* Reunion and Reaction: The Compromise of 1877 and the End of Reconstruction *(1951),* Origins of the New South, 1877–1913 *(1951), and* The Burden of Southern History *(1960). In each of them, Professor Woodward comes to grips with fundamental issues. Since he sees the historical process as a complex one that is not susceptible of facile explanations, he assumes an attitude of moderation and understanding, and artfully keeps his analysis, charged though it often is with contemporary significance, from becoming a tract for the times or a sounding-board for his own convictions.*

In The Strange Career of Jim Crow, *Professor Woodward canvasses the history of the Southern system of rigid Negro segregation, from its beginnings in the late nineteenth century, through its ascendancy in the first decades of the twentieth, to its weakening and erosion in the forties and fifties. Throwing light upon some cloudy conceptions, he shows that the Supreme Court decision of May, 1954, was not a sharp break with earlier pronouncements on Negro civil rights but was rather part of an era of New Reconstruction, reflecting a general decline, already in process, of the whole pattern of segregation. Particularly revealing are his comments on the South's struggle with the problem of race relations after the so-called "Redemption" of the 1870's, by means of which the carpetbaggers' regime was overthrown. For a few decades, Professor Woodward explains, the South explored other alternatives than "Jim Crow." Many vital groups, including conservative leaders, Populist reformers, and liberals in general, actively and often effectively pursued a course of politics and social relations which included Negroes as well as whites. But they ended in failure.*

Why they failed is Woodward's particular concern in the essay below, in which he suggests and undertakes to answer the following questions. How did Southern racial relations and attitudes during the ante-bellum period differ from those of the rest of the Western world? For what reasons? What were the nature and substance of Southern race relations during the postwar decades? What conditions restrained the South from instituting a system of legal race segregation during these decades rather than a little later? Why were these restraints removed? In what way, and for what reasons, did the South march "into the progressive movement under the banner of white supremacy"? Why did racial tensions decline during the 1930's and 1940's?

The story of Jim Crow is integral to the story of America, and thus poses for us some difficult and often troubling questions. Why, for example, did a nation so committed to institutions of liberty paradoxically commit a substantial minority to a permanently inferior status? The status of the Negro in American history may, indeed, serve as a criterion for measuring the actual realization of each of the whole complex of values—such as equality, social mobility, and ethnic plurality—that are regarded as central to the American heritage. To what extent, one might further inquire, has the Negro problem since the Civil War been that of an immiscible immigrant minority in what, for other groups, has proven an ethnic melting pot? How did the position of the Negro under slavery compare with his position under the rule of segregation? To what extent did the North, during the period that this rule was developing in the South, adhere to similar practices of segregation, and thus in fact similarly reduce the Negro to an inferior status? Why? What have been the changing anthropological attitudes toward the Negro? What larger cultural developments explain these changing views? (One would, in this connection, need only to compare the presentation of the slave in Ulrich B. Phillips's **American Negro Slavery,** *which appeared in 1918, with that in Kenneth M. Stampp's* **The Peculiar Institution,** *which appeared in 1956.)*

The American dilemma continues to be the one that Gunnar Myrdal anatomized so graphically over two decades ago. How shall a nation so committed to principle as ours live with two principles so utterly at war with each other: equality and racism? How shall we achieve social stability if the basic fact of our republic is the struggle between the doctrine of democracy and the doctrine of color? Woodward, writing in 1962, sought to explain how Southern attitudes to race had evolved. Almost a decade later we can see that the Negro Revolution became the dominant fact of our lives at the time when citizens in the North and in the West were asked to abide by the program of race relations their leaders had formulated for the South. The painful irony of our racial attitudes today is that in the process of trying to convert the South to the American tenet of equality, the rest of America is more consciously adopting the Southern tenet of racism. If the South is becoming American, at least in this respect America is also becoming Southern.

In the powerful tension between the realization of equality and the eradication of racism, militancy of black leadership has increased. Negro insistence that white America admit black people to the American republic of equality reverberates everywhere in our civic lives. The Negro's quest for equality is the principal force affecting our major cities. The frustrations of that quest explain why the program of the Negro Revolution has changed from integration to black power. It signifies that the perennial conflict between privilege and disadvantage, wealth and poverty, equality and inferiority has been reduced in America to one between white and black. These are our days of crisis and passion. The question that lies implacably athwart the republic's path is whether we shall be able to resolve the problem of our race relations in a manner consistent with American ideals, or whether we shall make Jim Crow the essential condition of black-white relations and give the principle of racism a new vitality and a universal dominion. Woodward's article, concerning the way the South pursued its tortured course of race relations in the post-Civil War decades, is immediately relevant to this question. What Southern white leaders did at that time carries for us a momentous lesson, if we are at all ready or able to learn it.

The one-hundredth anniversary of the Emancipation Proclamation inevitably draws fresh attention to the South, the historical theater for the drama of emancipation. It is there that the large majority of the liberated Negro slaves and their descendants have labored to achieve the full status of freedom and fulfill the old promise of equality. Until lately their progress has been slow; they still have far to go to attain their goals and achieve the full constitutional rights promised them a hundred years ago.

Whatever other factors may have brought the Negro to his present status, the white man's rule in the South bears a heavy share of responsibility, as attested by the Southern record—denial of equal justice before the law; disfranchisement; disbarment from jury service; exclusion from public office; infringement of political rights of all kinds; denial of equal opportunity in public and private employment, of equal pay for equal work, of equal education.

The white man's responsibility for the frustration of the Negro's hopes is spelled out most elaborately in the system of segregation. Far more explicitly than the surreptitious and extra-legal discrimination, such as the stuffed ballot box, the doctored jurors list, or the sly literacy test, the Jim Crow system openly proclaimed the white man's determination to keep the Negro "in his place." This intention could be read not only in the Jim Crow statutes; it glared out from thousands of conspicuously posted signs—*"White"* and *"Colored"*—that marked off the color line. Schools, hospitals, prisons, parks, welfare establishments, every public institution proclaimed the rigid rule of separation. Just as conspicuous and harsh was the enforcement of segregation in private business establishments, in trains, buses, streetcars, hotels, theaters, and playing fields. There it was, for all the world to see.

In recent years some of those signs have been taken down, some of the Jim Crow laws have disappeared from the books, and still others are slated to go. Some attitudes have softened. A "New Negro" and a new generation of whites have opened the choked channels of communication and established new contacts: both have begun, if only covertly and brokenly, to talk and think together. The more hopeful believe that the long ice age of race relations in the South might be approaching an end, and that the great thaw has at last begun.

This may be a valid belief, and there is certainly some truth in it. But the resistance, if no longer so "massive," is still powerful. Progress continues to be halting, and there would seem to be few signs of acceleration. The hope for fulfillment of the various Supreme Court orders against segregation by the centennial anniversary of the Emancipation Proclamation, making 1963 a Jubilee Year, has long been doomed to disappointment.

But even if the most hopeful prognosis were acceptable, even if the great thaw were upon us and the Jubilee Year at hand, it would still be appropriate at this time to ask an accounting of the South. Why has it taken so long to begin? When, if ever, is full compliance with the law to be expected? And beyond that, what manner of people is it who can cling so tenaciously to nineteenth century attitudes well past the middle of the twentieth century? I do not propose to excuse or explain away the faults and guilts of Southern white people. My purpose is rather to place their record in the historical perspective that the past century affords and to derive a degree of understanding from the process.

A century ago, Southern whites were given a momentous assignment by history, a role that was not to be required of the dominant white throughout the western world until our own time. This was the imposed obligation of abandoning the racial assumptions of a lifetime and uprooting dogmas deeply embedded in regional culture. These assumptions and dogmas were sustained by a Western culture built on the idea that white men, Europeans and Americans, were destined to rule the earth. The natural corollary of this idea was that colored people were inferior to white people; that, being inferior, they were in some degree subordinate to the white will, and that, being subordinate, they were destined to serve white interests.

While they shared most of these racial attitudes, the great majority of Europeans and Americans lived beyond personal contact with Africans and Asians, and before the middle of the nineteenth century they had repudiated slavery as an acceptable form of colored subordination, though they by no means repudiated subordination of the colored in other forms. Unlike the majority of Western whites, the U.S. Southern whites lived in the presence of large numbers of colored people, and continued to hold nine-tenths of them as chattel long after slavery was repudiated by most of the Western world. The South's ideology was an anachronism well before the middle of the nineteenth century, but Southerners clung to their dogmas all the more desperately and fiercely because of the intellectual isolation in which they found themselves.

While slave revolts sometimes preceded and abetted liberation, slavery was abolished by other nations and their colonies without revolution and civil war. Peaceful emancipation was accomplished by the English, Dutch, Danish, Spanish, and Portuguese people in the New World, and while the French suffered some violence, it was not drawn-out. The United States was the only Western nation in which slavery was abolished at the cost of a prolonged and bloody civil war that ended in a crushing and catastrophic defeat of the slaveholders.

The defeat not only freed the slaves but destroyed a social order and a ruling class. Losses had to be reckoned not merely in money, but in blood and pride and prestige and inner security, and they were not confined to a slaveholding minority but shared by a whole people. In the mind of the South this historic trauma has been lodged for a century, fatefully associated with the accompanying experience of emancipation. On the rational level, the South "accepted" both defeat and emancipation and proclaimed the acceptance repeatedly. But on a deeper level, acceptance was blocked off and rejected, and the rejection was pushed below the threshold of consciousness, beyond the reach of rational appeal.

Hard on defeat came the experience of Reconstruction, with all the attendant shocks of military rule, rebel disfranchisement, Negro enfranchisement, and social upheaval. The majority of Southern whites did not accept this sequel of defeat on any plane, conscious or otherwise. They yielded only temporarily to superior force, and as soon as they were able—by ruse or craft or force—they overturned the entire enterprise. In the process, however, the hated symbols of humiliation —Federal bayonets, martial law, carpetbaggers, and disfranchisement of Southern whites—were fatefully associated in the disturbed mind of the South with the more laudable social objectives of Reconstruction, including equal justice, civil rights, political equality, public education, and racial democracy for the Negro.

Thus the real and fancied humiliations of Reconstruction were combined with the traumatic shame of defeat to crystallize the rejection of emancipation and civil rights for Negroes and to constitute for decades to come a barrier to a rational approach to all questions of race relations. More than that, they constituted a defense against criticism, an evasion of responsibility, and a release from guilt. The Civil War legacy for the South was, in the words of Robert Penn Warren, "The Great Alibi."

The low point of race relations in the South and the extremes of race policy, however, did not coincide with either of the traumatic experiences of military defeat or Reconstruction, nor was it reached in the period immediately following. The low point came still later, probably not until the twentieth century. But when twentieth century racial extremists undertook a defense of their policies, they invented the theory that the rigid and harsh policies of exclusion and proscription and segregation were actually of ancient origin, brought to perfection in slavery days, and sanctioned by centuries of usage. Their defenders maintained that such practices were the inevitable consequence of the association of two races of different characteristics and cultural attainments. Reconstruction, according to this theory, only served to prove how hopeless it was to change or abolish ancient customs and folkways by legislation and idealistic reform. Seen in this light, the whole episode of Reconstruction constituted a brief and unfortunate interruption of the "normal" relations between the two races. Furthermore, the overthrow of Reconstruction was pictured as a restoration of normal conditions, a return to sanity—a return, therefore, to the Jim Crow system.

The facts were quite different. In reality, there was no such tradition to which the South could return. Segregation, in any modern sense of the word, was not only unnecessary under slavery, it was impracticable as well. Segregation on a racial basis was incompatible with the efficient management, the round-the-clock policing, and on-the-job supervision which "the peculiar institution" required. Slavery itself was quite sufficient to define the Negro's inferior status. On the other hand, in the Northern states which had abolished slavery, quite an elaborate and thoroughgoing system of segregation had been established before 1860 to define the status that slavery had once defined for the Negro. In the free states before the Civil War, according to historian Leon Litwack, in virtually every phase of existence, "Negroes found themselves systematically separated from whites." This was not true in the South nor was it to be for a generation to come.

The end of slavery brought a readjustment in racial relations, but not so drastic a readjustment as is generally attributed to Reconstruction. The efforts of the Radicals to establish racial equality and civil rights for the freedmen were frustrated not only by resistance in the South but by insufficient support in the North. Their experiments with integration in the schools were rare, successful only in New Orleans, and even there only temporarily. In three significant fields—the military services, the new public schools, and the churches—Reconstruction actually fostered segregation. Withdrawal of Negroes from the churches, however, was voluntary. It was a means used by Negroes to gain control over some of their most important institutions.

Yet it was not the overthrow of Reconstruction which ushered in the era of Jim Crow. That was not to come until near the end of the nineteenth century. The last quarter of the century, however, was no golden age of race relations. On the contrary, it was a period of race conflict and violence, brutality and exploitation, and it was then that the crime of lynching reached its peak. Moreover, the fanatical advocates of segregation, disfranchisement, and racial ostracism were already at work. But for nearly two decades after the end of Reconstruction, the zealots were held in check and their harsh demands for ostracizing the Negro and separating the races were denied.

The explanation is not simple. The Negro still bore the stigma of slavery so plainly, in his speech, his manners, and his person, that segregation was still unnecessary to set him apart as an inferior in status. He so rarely had the economic means for enjoying such things as hotels, theaters, decent housing, amusements, and restaurants— or even trains and steamboats—that there was no pressing incentive to exclude him. The few Negroes who did have the means often used such facilities without hindrance or segregation. But the great majority were impoverished sharecroppers and farm hands who never had the opportunity to test such rights.

There were still other restraints that held extremists and segregationists in check. One of these was that the Negro continued to vote in most parts of the South for many years after Reconstruction. Until 1901, except for one term, there was always at least one Negro Congressman from the South. The conservative rulers who dominated politics in this period, solicited or bought or coerced Negro votes for their own purposes, and, in effect, entered into a curious alliance with the Negro, based on an attitude toward him which was a heritage of plantation paternalism. Conservatives openly regarded Negroes as inferiors, but felt so secure in their own status they saw no reason to ostracize, segregate, or humiliate them.

There was also a temporary barrier to racism constructed by Southern radicals, the Populists of the Nineties. A party of agrarian reform, the Populists challenged the conservative claim of Negro support with an appeal of their own. Avoiding the patronizing approach that both the Radical Republicans and the conservative Democrats adopted toward Negroes, the Populists appealed to them from a platform of common economic interests and grievances, and with the promise of political and civil rights. In spite of traditional antagonisms, they succeeded in temporarily patching together a political reconciliation of normally irreconcilables with which to wage a fight for mutual rights against the conservatives.

Toward the end of the century, the delicate balance of forces in the South and North that had held back the triumph of intolerance broke down. Hatred, jealousy, fear, and fanaticism had long been present in the South. What unleashed them upon society was the almost simultaneous collapse or decline of the numerous restraints that had hitherto combined to hold the forces of racial extremism in check. These included not only the internal restraints imposed by the prestige and influence of the Southern conservatives and the interracial alliance formed by the Southern radicals, but also the external restraints of Northern opinion, the liberal press, the U. S. Supreme Court, and Federal law.

The conservative rulers of the Southern states in the Nineties found themselves under heavy attack and their regime in jeopardy, principally because of the unpopularity of their business policies among the depressed farmers. In their frantic efforts to protect their power by stopping the revolt led by the Populists, the conservatives lost their heads and sought to reenact the triumph of the Seventies by which they had overthrown the carpetbaggers and gained control of the South. Persuading themselves that the crisis of the Nineties was as desperate as that of the Seventies, they resorted to the same expedients of fraud, intimidation, and violence, and used the propaganda of race to unify white support. Alarmed by the success the Populists were enjoying with their appeal to the Negro vote, the conservatives revived the cry of "white supremacy." In doing so they were appealing to the very forces of fanaticism and racism they had sought to restrain.

These tactics were successful in crushing the Populist revolt, but the methods the conservatives used made a mockery of their old plea for moderation and fair play in race relations. Conservative spokesmen would continue to protest from time to time against racial injustice, but they had undermined their own moral authority and influence on race policy, and they would never again be listened to with the same respect.

The Populist experiment in interracial harmony and political alliance, precarious at best and handicapped from the start by suspicion and prejudice, was another casualty of the political and economic crisis of the period. When it became apparent that their opponents would stop at nothing to divide the racial alliance and would steal the Negro votes when they could not buy them, the bi-racial partnership of Populism began to dissolve; it broke up in bitterness and frustration. Some of the Populists understood that the Negro was merely one of the hapless victims rather than the author of the party's downfall. But for the majority it came much easier to blame the Negro, to make him the scapegoat, and to vent upon him all the pent-up bitterness and frustration they felt against the real offenders who contrived to escape their wrath. After the collapse of Populism, agrarian discontent among Southern whites was a seed-bed rather than an antidote for racist propaganda.

The removal of internal checks went far toward making the Negro a victim of racial aggression, but his adversaries were also encouraged by the relaxation of those restraints which Northern opinion had imposed for the protection of freedmen. The Northern liberal retreat on the race issue dated from the Liberal Republican revolt against President Ulysses S. Grant's Administration in 1872. Liberal acquiescence in the Compromise of 1877, when Carl Schurz and Frederick Douglass joined President Rutherford B. Hayes's Administration, meant that liberals agreed to leave the freedman to the custody of the conservative redeemers on the promise that they would protect his constitutional rights. When the promise was forgotten and the Negro's rights were violated, little protest was heard from the liberals. Former abolitionists and pre-Civil War champions of the slave grew acquiescent or silent.

Mugwumps and Liberals of the East were attracted to the cause of sectional reconciliation between North and South. Since the Negro was the symbol of sectional antagonism, they often deplored further agitation in his behalf and took an indulgent attitude toward the less extreme racial policies of the South. In the pages of *Harper's, Scribner's, Century,* the *North American Review,* and the *Atlantic Monthly* in the closing decades of the nineteenth century can be found all the shibboleths of white supremacy. The Negro usually was pictured as innately inferior, shiftless, and hopelessly unfit for the responsibilities of civilization. Such concessions were eagerly seized upon, reprinted, and played up by the Southern press. They helped confirm the view that the South had little to fear from Northern critics, and while they doubtless did much to foster the reconciliation of the estranged North and South, they did so at the expense of the Negro.

A significant shift in leadership among Negroes themselves tended to encourage the impression of vanishing resistance. Negro opinion itself had long ceased to be a significant deterrent to white aggression. But the rise of Booker T. Washington and his almost unrivaled leadership of American Negroes from 1895 until his death in 1915 was interpreted by many whites as an invitation to further assaults on the Negro. It is certain that Washington did not intend his "Atlanta Compromise" to constitute such an invitation. But in proposing the retirement of the mass of Negroes from the political life of the South and in stressing the humble industrial role his race was destined to play, he would seem to have encouraged an impression of submissiveness on the part of the Negro.

In the meantime, the U.S. Supreme Court was also engaged in a policy of reconciliation, but reconciliation between state and Federal jurisdiction, as well as between North and South, both achieved, again, at the expense of the Negro. On the highest Federal judicial authority the South was informed that the law of the land offered no substantial impediment to the policies of white supremacy. The Court drastically curtailed the power of the Federal government to intervene in the states to protect the right of Negroes, and to all intents and purposes nullified the Fourteenth and Fifteenth Amendments as they affected the freedmen. In two decisions especially, both handed down in the Nineties, the Supreme Court paved the way for the curtailment of Negro rights, disfranchisement, and a full-blown system of segregation. In *Plessy v. Ferguson,* decided in 1896, the Court formally subscribed to the doctrine that "legislation is powerless to eradicate racial instincts" and laid down the "separate but equal" rule in defense of segregation which was to be the law of the land until 1954. Then, in 1898, in the case of *Wil-*

liams v. Mississippi, the Supreme Court completed the opening of the
legal road to disfranchisement by giving its approval to the Mississippi
plans for depriving Negroes of the vote.

The historical development that completed the merging of Southern
and national racial outlook, however, was America's plunge into imperialism in 1898.   American adventures in the Pacific and Caribbean
rather suddenly and unexpectedly brought under the jurisdiction of
the United States some eight million colored people in addition to
those within its continental borders. *The Nation* described them as "a
varied assortment of inferior races which, of course, could not be allowed to vote."   Their presence had obvious implications for the
Negro's status. "If the stronger and cleverer race," asked the *Atlantic
Monthly,* "is free to impose its will upon 'new-caught, sullen peoples'
on the other side of the globe, why not in South Carolina and Mississippi?"   The New York *Times* remarked in an editorial of May, 1900,
that "Northern men . . . no longer denounce the suppression of the
Negro vote [in the South] as it used to be denounced in Reconstruction
days.   The necessity of it under the supreme law of self-preservation
is candidly recognized."   Within the South itself leaders of the white
supremacy movement thoroughly grasped and gladly expounded the
implications of the new imperialism for their domestic policies.   Thus
the twentieth century dawned upon a new era of harmony between
white people, North and South, on race.

With a sense of acceptance and unity with the national temper such
as it had not enjoyed since the Jacksonian period, the South marched
into the progressive movement under the banner of white supremacy.
The rise of progressivism coincided with the crest of the wave of racism and merged with it in the South—and sometimes outside the South
—to such an extent that the two movements were often indistinguish-
able. Their leaders were frequently identical. In fact, the typical Southern reformer rode to power on a platform designed to deprive the Negro
of his vote.

The strong contingent of Southern progressives which promoted
Woodrow Wilson's campaign for the Presidential nomination, managed his race for election, and filled high offices in his administration,
carried to Washington its racial policies as well as its reform bills.
These Southern progressives left their stamp on the Wilsonian New
Freedom in the form of segregation, downgrading, and dismissal of
Negro employees in the Washington bureaus. President Wilson himself defended segregation in the Federal government as "distinctly
to the advantage of the colored people themselves."

In the years following World War 1, the impulses of racism surged
powerfully through the North and West. A wave of race riots and
lynchings without precedent in American history swept across the

country in 1919, and violence flared in all sections. The new Ku Klux Klan, which reached its crest in the mid-Twenties, attracted a following outside the South even larger than within. Under its direction racial aggression was organized on a nationwide scale.

During the Thirties, tension between the races eased perceptibly. Lynchings declined rapidly and almost disappeared. In the South, for the first time, both races joined the same political party, and that party appeared to be honestly trying to improve the lot of the colored man as well as that of the white man. The New Deal scored modest gains for both races. At the same time, however, the wall of segregation remained unyielding—in fact, its defenses were virtually unchallenged. Southern segregationists could count themselves New Dealers in good standing almost as readily as their fathers had been accepted as good Wilsonians. The paradoxical combination of racism and progressivism was still generally respectable in political circles. On the surface, the sense of unity and approval within the nation that the South had gained by 1900 was still enjoyed without serious disturbance four decades later.

In the Forties, however, the South's sense of security was abruptly shattered by a barrage of agitation for Negro rights and an avalanche of demands, denunciations, and opprobrium descending from above the Mason-Dixon line. As inevitable and belated as this movement was, it nevertheless caught the South unprepared. The North was impatient with the South's reaction. What right had the South to be surprised and shocked at reasonable demands for rights that had been promised the Negro a century ago? Was not a hundred years enough time, after all, to adjust to the law of the land and the claims of conscience?

The true perspective on the South's contemporary reaction, however, is not revealed by the entire century since emancipation. The significant period is rather the half century after the nation repudiated or abandoned its Civil War promises of Negro rights and racial equality. That was the period when civil rights for Negroes became a dead letter, when disfranchisement enjoyed Federal approval and support, when *Plessy v. Ferguson* was the law of the land, when progressivism was for whites only, and when racism was a national creed and not a regional peculiarity.

11

Origins of Immigration Restriction, 1882–1897: A Social Analysis

JOHN HIGHAM

America is a nation of immigrants. The unrestricted flow of Europeans to our shores has been a central feature of our history from the time of the settlement at Jamestown until very recently. The migration of millions across the Atlantic is an epic odyssey of privation, of hopes, and of participation in building a new civilization. A student of American history is naturally concerned with understanding the nature and impact of this migration. Why did the Europeans come? To what extent did they realize their hopes in coming? Why and how were they accepted? What was their role in shaping American ideas and institutions? It is clear, certainly, that in becoming a part of America they could not but remake what America had been. And yet, paradoxically, they reinforced what America had been, for they gave ever new tone to its ethnic diversity, to the openness of its ways, to the multiplicity of its religions and mores, to the myth of its promises and possibilities.

Considerably less dramatic a feature of our story than the mass exodus from Europe, but perhaps no less important for the future, is the fact that the mass exodus is over. Beginning in 1921, acts were passed which put an end to America's traditional policy of welcoming immigrants. Nativist groups, working in a climate of social duress, succeeded in having quantitative and qualitative controls imposed on incoming foreigners: quantitatively, by reducing the number permitted annually to the merest fraction of what it had been before; qualitatively, by giving the preponderance in the sharply reduced quotas to Britons and Germans rather than to southern and eastern Europeans. Nativism was, however, not new to the American scene, nor was the attempt to keep out the foreigner. Whenever it appeared, nativism bespoke the ambivalence of Americans with regard to the national purpose. In a nation offering opportunity to all, many of those who had had the op-

SOURCE: *Mississippi Valley Historical Review*, XXXIX (June, 1952), 77–88. Reprinted by permission.

portunity wished to keep it for themselves. In a nation given to the making of brave new worlds, many of those who had already made their worlds questioned and feared the worlds their successors would make. The success of the nativists and their cohorts during the 1920's was the culmination of earlier efforts on their part, particularly during the late 1880's and 1890's, when the movement to restrict immigration had assumed the proportions of a crusade.

This movement is the particular concern of Professor John Higham of the University of Michigan. A scholar of first-rate ability, Higham has specialized in American ethnic history and in the study of American historical writing. He is the author, with Leonard Krieger and Felix Gilbert, of History *(1965), a highly valuable study of the American professional historian and his role in the growth of American historical scholarship; he has also edited* The Reconstruction of American History *(1962), a collection of essays that deal with currently changing interpretations of central aspects of the American past. His most important work,* Strangers in the Land *(1955, 1963), is a study of patterns of American nativism during the period from 1860 to 1925. "It deals," says Higham, "with the American people. Nativism as a habit of mind illustrates darkly some of the large contours of the American past; it has mirrored our national anxieties and marked out the bounds of our tolerance." In the essay below, he explores the nativist upsurge of the late nineteenth century and its relevance to certain larger changes in American society. The essay is a model of critical analysis. It has the virtue, too, of challenging some established views concerning the origins of the restriction movement. Professor Higham's basic purpose is to discover what was responsible for this movement. He analyzes the importance of each of four contemporary factors: the varied attempts at reform, the advent of the "new immigration," the vast increase in the size and importance of the Roman Catholic Church, and the social and economic dislocations of the new urban and industrial order.*

What Professor Higham discusses has relevance to our own times, and his treatment of the subject suggests further questions in this connection. What, for example, has become of nativism since the end of unrestricted immigration? Has nativism been adopted by the recent immigrant in an attempt to become more loyal than the loyal citizen, more American than his compatriot? Has it thus been transmuted into a national ideal, a shared value for all immigrant groups? Has it in its transmutation made Americanism a cult of formal loyalty, with days of ritual to proclaim both being American and being loyal? To what extent does this development explain why the United States, alone among the Western democracies, has agencies (such as the House Committee on Un-American Activities) entrusted with eliminating what they deem to be un-national elements in civic life? To what extent was the regime of McCarthyism during the 1950's likewise one of nativism? If social tensions were in large measure responsible for the sacrifice of one of our pivotal ideals, that of unqualified welcome to the immigrant, what impact will present and future social tensions have upon our other pivotal ideals? To what extent have those who formulated our restriction policy realized their goals? What have been the larger consequences of this policy: in terms of the welfare of American society, the world's view of America and of America's role in world affairs, the contribution to American development of the thousands and hundreds of thousands who might have sought to live among us but were turned away?

In 1965, United States immigration policy was somewhat modified, in the respect that the national origins quotas imposed by the Immigration Act of 1924 were eliminated. But the larger policy of restriction was continued for immigrants coming here from outside the Western hemisphere, and, for the first time, an annual limit of 120,000 was set for individuals coming from within the Western hemisphere. If America has been a nation of immigrants, what will it become now that it is not? It is probable that ethnic distinctions will become less sharp, a condition which would further the homogenizing of values already begun by mass cities, mass advertising and sales, mass entertainment, mass literature, and mass arts. It is not clear that this change will mean a certain gain. The cultural diversity and play of alternate ideas and institutions which have been a central feature of our history because of our open door to immigrants will begin to pass from the scene. The concept of America and American will be a different one from that which it has been for three centuries.

At no period in American national history has immigration from Europe been so strongly encouraged and so fervently blessed as in the 1860's and early 1870's. During these years the federal government, two thirds of the states, and innumerable business organizations raided Europe's manpower. Exuberant patriots rejoiced at the trans-Atlantic influx, and few indeed opposed it. Yet a very few years saw a very great change. A campaign to reduce immigration replaced the campaign to increase it; friendliness turned into fright. Beginning with the law of 1882, which established federal supervision of immigration and excluded certain groups unable to support themselves, the restriction movement blossomed into a formidable and even violent crusade in the late eighties and nineties. It reached its crest in the winter of 1896–1897, when only the stubbornness of Grover Cleveland prevented the enactment of a drastic test to stop the entry of illiterates. Thereafter the drive subsided abruptly, but it left a legacy of tensions, policies, and ideas which a later generation abundantly exploited.

To explain the formative stage in the restriction of European immigration, one might employ several methods. Most broadly, one might attempt a cultural approach, appraising the clash of native and immigrant folkways and illuminating the American experience by contrast with the traditions and behaviors of other nations. Most specifically, one might examine the tangled interlocking of particular events and ideas within the restriction movement. The second procedure could profitably direct attention to struggles for partisan political advantage, to the activities of important individuals, or to the appearance of new antiforeign concepts. The present essay follows a course somewhere between these two general methods, less adventurous perhaps than the first, less precise than the second. The object here is to establish—in summary fashion—the connections between the nativist upsurge and certain large, concurrent changes in American society. This stressing of the functional context neither does justice to the weight of persistent traditions nor does it clarify the totality of immediate circumstance. But whatever may have been the cultural heritages behind immigration restriction, they were catalyzed by a new social situation. And whatever political maneuvers or intellectual ferment may have contributed, they worked within a framework of social change.

Of the general mutations in late nineteenth-century America, four had a special relevance to the rise of the restriction movement. The first of these to play a measurable part in the organized campaign was the development of a confused but many-pronged reform movement aimed at solving the problems of an urban, industrial society. A second transformation came with the so-called "new immigration," the flow of peasant and ghetto peoples from Italy, Austria-Hungary, the Balkans, and Russia, which began increasing rapidly in the early 1880's. Thirdly, the Roman Catholic Church experienced an unusual surge of strength and activity during the same years. Finally, the period from 1885 to 1897 was one of drastic social and economic dislocations—an epoch in which anger and misery raised a frightening challenge to the historic promise of a fluid society. Each of these factors entered into the making and shaping of the immigration restriction movement. In one aspect it was a reform effort, in another an expression of ethnic antipathy. In still another, it represented a response to anti-Catholic sentiment. And it was also a reaction to fears and frustrations generated by class conflict and economic collapse. None of these causes operated independently, but they had diverse and unequal impacts and deserve separate consideration.

The first general immigration law in 1882 demonstrated the early influence of humanitarian and reform impulses in launching the restriction movement. For many years relief agencies in eastern cities had been more or less constantly concerned at the strain which impoverished and disorganized immigrants imposed upon their own financial resources and upon the life of the community. The charity groups had more philanthropic than reformist zeal, but many of them did hope for social improvement through public action. They began to lobby for federal supervision and regulation of immigration in 1876, after the Supreme Court forbade the states to collect an immigrant welfare fund from shipowners. Six years later the charity officials won their fight, although the statute was less restrictive than they had hoped it might be.

The emergence of other groups with broader conceptions of social responsibility and a larger interest in public control quickened the restriction movement. To various types of reformers, restriction seemed a relatively easy and painless way of invoking national authority to combat corruption, squalor, and injustice. Was not the immigrant a demoralized tool of privilege? Edmund James said so as early as 1883, and the progressive-minded economists who joined him in founding the American Economic Association offered a prize of $150 for the best essay on "The Evil Effects of Unrestricted Immigration." Following Josiah Strong, many spokesmen of the Social Gospel took a similar view. The rising municipal reform movement felt a special alarm over the boss-ridden immigrant vote and produced in Abram S. Hewitt the most colorful nativist of the 1880's.

While middle-class critics of laissez faire lent dignity to restriction-ism, organized labor put pressure behind it. Through the Knights of Labor unionization was recovering in the early eighties from the debacle of the previous decade; but unemployment and immigration were increasing too. Vaguely class-conscious in outlook, the Knights held corporate wealth responsible for the tightening job market. Accordingly, they opened an assault, not on immigration itself, but on the importation of European labor by American employers. This attack led to the second step in federal restriction, the contract labor law of 1885, which expressed the Knights' conviction that undesirable immi-gration was almost entirely provoked by scheming capitalists. Other unions drew the same distinction between voluntary and induced immigration. For seven years after 1885 the principal labor spokesmen rebuffed all pleas for a general limitation on immigration. The Ameri-can Federation of Labor rejected the literacy test as late as 1896. They did so partly because of an idealistic belief in the international soli-darity of the working class and partly because an extremely large proportion of union members were themselves foreign-born. These factors limited the role of organized labor in the early restriction move-ment more than historians have usually believed.

Neither middle-class nor working-class reformers had a prepon-derant effect on the nativist crusade as a whole, but their attitudes point to another of its aspects. Very often the arguments for restriction as a technique of social improvement revealed a sharp contempt for the new immigration from southern and eastern Europe. Many reformers were also race-conscious. Indeed, the first concentrated attack on the new immigrants came from labor leaders during the campaign for the contract labor law.   Since employers apparently introduced the first appreciable Slovakian and Italian settlements into the mining and industrial centers of western Pennsylvania in the early eighties, union officials concluded that this new immigration was an entirely unnatural one—a product of corporate greed. In this context hatred of the strange newcomers seemed very natural.   Identifying southern Europeans with contract labor, the unions fell to reviling the people along with the system.   In the next few years this ethnic animosity infected a number of liberal intellectuals.   The economist Edward Bemis concocted the idea of a literacy test in 1887 as a means of discriminating against southern and eastern Europeans.

By 1890 abhorrence of the new immigration was spreading to wider circles.   Exactly why many Americans singled out these peoples for special dislike is not entirely clear.   For one thing, their very newness meant that they had fewer powerful friends and less influence than longer established groups; it also meant that they could provide a target for both the old immigration and the old stock. For another thing, the new immigrants submitted to particularly primitive living conditions—a fact which, in itself, affronted the competitive, material values of the period. Thus the Italians, who had a lower standard of living than any of the other prominent nationalities, also experienced more prejudice than any of the others.   Some West Coast nativists thought that the Italians were no less degraded than the Chinese.

Whatever the reasons for the particular distrust of the new immigration, we should not overestimate this aspect of the late nineteenth-century restriction movement.   Antipathy to southern and eastern Europeans did channel support to the plan for a literacy test, but that antipathy did not dominate the movement as a whole. If it had done so, one might expect to find a close correlation between the size of the new immigration and the intensity of xenophobia.   The two trends arose simultaneously in the 1880's, but they soon parted company. From 1893 through 1895 immigration from southern and eastern Europe decreased sharply while the campaign for restriction surged ahead with increasing power.   Not until the turn of the century did the new immigration begin to skyrocket, yet this was the very time when opposition died to a whisper.   Furthermore, restrictionists often showed little discrimination in choosing adversaries. An extensive examination of congressional debates and hearings, magazine articles, newspaper editorials, and the publications of nativist and other organizations indicates that a general dislike of *all foreigners* was much more pervasive than the specific dislike of the new nationalities. Actually, the new immigration stands out in hindsight more sharply than it did at the time.   As late as 1900, 74 per cent of the European-born population of the United States derived from accustomed sources.   With vast numbers of old immigrants still conspicuous and partially unassimilated, antiforeignism prevailed over ethnic distinctions.

Clearly, other factors entered into the making of this generalized antiforeign sentiment. Some of it arose out of a third change in the American scene—a revival of religious conflict. With the meeting of the Third Plenary Council in 1884, the Roman Catholic Church in the United States entered upon one of its most vigorous decades, a period which brought twenty new dioceses, many parochial schools, the establishment of the Catholic University of America, and the appointment of the first Apostolic Delegate to the United States. Also, the Council's decrees strengthened the Catholic school policy and led to new pressure for state aid to parochial education. These advances touched off a wave of Protestant hysteria. The few existing nativist societies expanded rapidly in the late eighties, and many new ones appeared. Like similar Protestant groups in earlier periods, these organizations were antiforeign as well as anti-Catholic. Since the Roman hierarchy followed the leadership of the Vatican, anti-Catholic crusaders regarded the Church as alien and subversive. Since it recruited members chiefly from immigration, most religious nativists joined the restriction movement. Another connection between anti-Catholic and antiforeign fears arose out of the condition of municipal politics; in the eyes of alarmed Protestants the growing power of Irish Catholics in city government seemed an additional reason to slam the national gates. During this period Protestant agitators paid backhanded tribute to the importance of the Irish in ecclesiastical and political affairs by continuing to hurl more abuse at them than at any other nationality. It is significant that the American Protective Association, which absorbed most of the other anti-Catholic societies in the early nineties, showed almost no interest in the new immigration and had little part in the campaign for the literacy test.

This fact in itself suggests that the impact of anti-Catholicism on the restriction movement was hardly decisive. The passion of midwestern Protestants, who armed to meet a rumored papal uprising in 1893, soon spent itself in empty fury. The immigration restriction bill introduced by William A. Linton, chief A.P.A. spokesman in Congress, never got out of committee. The A.P.A. itself began to decline in 1894, two years before the restriction movement reached its crest. Indeed, anti-Catholicism throughout this period lacked the respectability which it had previously enjoyed. No outstanding political leader identified himself with it, as Rutherford B. Hayes had done in 1875, and even many Protestant ministers urged a reduction of immigration without mentioning its denominational character.

Xenophobia in late nineteenth-century America had a more potent source than religion or racism or reform. In its larger aspect it issued from a crisis in the whole American social order. From the mid-eighties to the mid-nineties a society already uneasy at the emergence of the first great trusts felt the shock of fierce industrial unrest. Americans had long believed that their land of mobility and opportunity was immune to the class conflicts of Europe. The railroad strikes of 1877 passed too quickly to do serious damage to their faith. But the labor upheaval that began in 1885 ushered in a decade of massive and recurrent discontent. Alarmed at these new class antagonisms, unwilling to recognize them as indigenous, and unready to deal with them as such, many Americans surrendered to the conviction that they came from abroad. The equation between immigration and unrest seemed confirmed by the riot which occurred in Haymarket Square in Chicago in 1886. Coming as it did at the height of the huge eight-hour strikes, the bombing at Chicago struck panic from coast to coast over the threat of foreign-born anarchists. No other single incident did so much to provoke restriction sentiment. For years the memory of Haymarket and the dread of imported anarchy haunted the American consciousness. No general stereotype of the immigrant prevailed more widely than that of a lawless creature, given over to violence and disorder. Scores of conservative politicians, newspaper editors, educators, popular writers, and Protestant clergymen labeled the immigrant as peculiarly susceptible to anarchism. Many blamed all of the major strikes of the period on foreign influence, and the composition of the trade unions gave specious credibility to the charge.

In short, fears for social stability and the projection of those fears upon the immigrant became almost a common denominator of the restriction movement. Of all major restrictionist groups, only organized labor did not connect immigration with unrest; and even here a patrician organization like the Order of Railway Conductors, which favored cooperation with management, denounced immigration as the chief cause of current labor troubles. Middle-class reformers saw the immigrant as both an author of revolution and an agent of reaction. Opponents of Catholicism and of the new immigration often reacted in a similar way. The A.P.A. and other Protestant societies deplored the use of the strike and proposed antiforeign measures as a solution to class conflict. The first full-length anti-Semitic tract written in the United States, the work of a Greek immigrant in 1888, described the strike as a peculiarly Jewish idea and John D. Rockefeller as a representative of the Jewish monopoly. At a more august social level the fear of the foreign-bred discontent contributed powerfully to the mushroom growth of hereditary patriotic societies in the early nineties. Many of the new societies followed the lead of the Sons of the American Revolution in dedicating themselves to saving the country from insurrectionary immigrants. The same concern contributed powerfully to a shift of business opinion toward a restrictionist position. By the late 1880's large numbers of American business leaders were turning to immigration restriction as a weapon against strikes, lawlessness, and other disorders.

The specter of unrest would not have looked so frightening to Americans if they had preserved intact their old confidence in the capacity of their civilization to liberate men automatically from the restraints of fixed class and enforced poverty. But changes in American conditions seemed now to narrow the horizon of opportunity and compound the menace of discontent. The year after Haymarket the agricultural frontier collapsed. Simultaneously, alarm over the dwindling of the public domain became widespread. Here was another reason for reducing immigration. As early as 1883 Henry George warned that the immigrant tide was becoming dangerous because the safety valve of western land was closing. After 1886 many newspapers expressed similar fears. In the midst of more concrete troubles, western farmers shared in the general anxiety over pressure of immigration on the remaining land supply. Then in 1893 economic distress spread throughout the whole country. In the next three years the contraction of employment and business activity added an urgency to the nation's claustrophobia. While restriction proposals as harsh as total prohibition received a hearing, an organized campaign for the literacy test developed. To this plan Congress gave its first and overwhelming approval in 1896.

Then suddenly the fears and frustrations of the Cleveland period dissolved, and the restriction crusade faded with them. Beginning in 1897 a tide of prosperity washed over the country's domestic troubles; soon the intoxication of war and imperialism added further impetus to the revival of national self-confidence. As the tensions of the nineties relaxed, much of the interest in restricting immigration disappeared.

The downfall of nativism at the close of the century emphasizes again its function as an outlet for the baffled discontents of the preceding years. For the social historian those discontents supply the central key to the origins of immigration restriction. But surely this key will not unlock the whole problem. A balanced view will encompass the many-sidedness and complexity of the situation from which restriction arose. It grew in a climate of social crisis, but its roots extended into reform, into religion, and into immigration itself.

12

American Protestantism
Since the Civil War:
From Denominationalism to Americanism
SIDNEY E. MEAD

It is a commonplace of the philosophy of history that the diversified activities of a society in any particular age are integrally related and that a dominant tendency pervades them all. For this reason it may be suggested that the remolding of economic life in late nineteenth-century America had a close relevance to the course taken by religious institutions and ideas. But what indeed was the relevance? Did religion become pervasively secular and material? Were the precepts of Christ overridden by the precepts of big business? And what became of the Protestant ethos in the politics of the post-Civil War decades?

A challenging answer is afforded by the following essay by Sidney E. Mead, Professor of American Church History at the Claremont Graduate School in California. Professor Mead has taught at the University of Chicago and was also president of the Meadville Technological School in Chicago. The essay below was the third in a series of four delivered as the Charles R. Walgreen Foundation Lectures on "The Shape of Protestantism in America" at the University of Chicago in October, 1954; the series, which appeared in separate issues of The Journal of Religion, *has been incorporated in Mead's* The Lively Experiment: The Shaping of Christianity in America *(1963). In this third lecture, Professor Mead analyzes Protestant thought during the late nineteenth century, making the interesting suggestion that it combined two different forms of belief. He carefully answers a few basic questions that derive from this suggestion. What were the principal components of Protestant ideology during the late nineteenth century? What factors explain the ideological amalgamation of Protestant orthodoxy*

SOURCE: *The Journal of Religion,* XXXVI (January, 1956), 1–15. Copyright 1956 by the University of Chicago Press. Reprinted by permission of the University of Chicago Press and the author.

and the secular premises of American society? How does Protestant thought support the idea of progress, or the acquisitive society, or the American idea of destiny?

Professor Mead's thesis is certainly thoughtful and stimulating, raising as it does some important questions about Protestant ideology not merely in the age of big business but also throughout the course of American history. Did not late nineteenth-century Protestantism also witness the rise and growth of the social gospel, which, as its historian Charles Howard Hopkins has described it, "involved a criticism of conventional Protestantism, a progressive theology and social philosophy, and an active program of propagandism and reform"? Would not, moreover, the very great popularity of the Christian novels of such writers as Edward Payson Roe, Lew Wallace, Charles Monroe Sheldon, and Henry Sienkiewicz, with their parables of virtue and their apotheosis of the righteous way, suggest, at the very least, that the precepts of the new industrialism were far from being uniformly or uncritically accepted? Was it something unique for the Protestant thought of this age to approve of secular values and developments? Or has not Protestantism, as the religion of lay groups in society (princely or bourgeois), generally approved of the secular order? Has it not been the tendency of Protestant ideology, as we have long known from the studies of Max Weber and R. H. Tawney, to sanctify the acquisitive society and to view the pursuit of God and of wealth as mutually consistent?

In pursuing Professor Mead's suggestions one would certainly wish to examine their meaning for the present. What are the premises of Protestant thought today? To what extent do they still represent a syncretism of religious orthodoxy and secular rationalism? To what extent, moreover, do they embrace or reject the course and values of American society? Here is a critical point of inquiry, for if, as Professor Mead suggests, Protestantism after the Civil War became identified with Americanism, was Americanism, conversely, also identified with Protestantism? Is it today? What are the major developments in contemporary American religion? To what extent has the cold war been a religious war? In its ideological struggle with the "godlessness" of the Communist world, has the American world stood on the side of the godly? In what sense, with what doctrines, by what means? The answers to these questions will afford the student a significant insight into the history of his own times.

By the decade 1850–60 denominationalism was generally accepted in the United States and was assumed to be the proper organizational embodiment of the Christianity of the self-consciously evangelical Protestant churches. Such general acceptance of this form suggests the general prevalence of a state of mind or outlook which I attempted to define in an article on "Denominationalism" published in *Church History* in December, 1954. The argument of the present article is that dur-

ing the second half of the nineteenth century there occurred a virtual
identification of the outlook of this denominational Protestantism with
"Americanism" or "the American way of life" and that we are still
living with some of the results of this ideological amalgamation of
evangelical Protestantism with Americanism.

It is a commonplace that in the period roughly from 1870 to 1900
evangelical Protestant Christianity largely dominated the American
culture, setting the prevailing mores and the moral standards by which
personal and public, individual and group, conduct was judged. As
H. Paul Douglass put it, "despite multiplying sectarian differences,
Protestantism's prevalence tended to create a Protestant cultural type.
. . . It was a triumph of religion still on a communal level." Indeed,
down to the present, a "rebel" in America has to rebel against *these*
standards in order to acquire the name.

To the free churches, inasmuch as Christian humility permitted, such
dominance was a sound source of pride and a basis for self-approbation,
for it demonstrated their success in meeting the terms implied in their
original acceptance of the fact of separation of church and state. With
religious freedom, these churches had given up coercive power and had
assumed the responsibility collectively to define and inculcate in the
population the basic beliefs necessary for the being and the well-being
of the democratic society, while armed only with persuasive power.
Their dominance seemed to demonstrate that they could do this effectively. Then with the Civil War the North became dominant, and "to
Protestants of the Northern States, the years of the Civil War furnished
the supreme vindication" of their way. The free churches seemed to
have been tried and found adequate, and it is little wonder that, in
spite of theological differences and multiplying sectarian divisions,
"in its most characteristic pronouncements American Protestantism
substantially approved the church-state status quo."

What was not so obvious at the time was that the United States, in
effect, had two religions, or at least two different forms of the same religion, and that the prevailing Protestant ideology represented a
syncretistic mingling of the two. The first was the religion of the denominations, which was commonly articulated in the terms of scholastic Protestant orthodoxy and almost universally practiced in terms of
the experimental religion of pietistic revivalism. This defines for our
purposes Protestant "evangelicalism."

The second was the religion of the democratic society and nation.
This was rooted in the rationalism of the Enlightenment (to go no
farther back) and was articulated in terms of the destiny of America,
under God, to be fulfilled by perfecting the democratic way of life for
the example and betterment of all mankind. This was a calling taken as
seriously as every Christian saint or administrator took his peculiar

vocation. Said one of its high priests in 1826: "We stand the latest, and, if we fail, probably the last experiment of self-government by the people."

This religion was almost universally practiced in terms of the burgeoning middle-class society and its "free-enterprise" system, the most persuasive argument for which was the plain fact that it worked to the economic and general material betterment of men, until Andrew Carnegie, in summarizing his version of its beneficent effects, could say that such "is the true Gospel concerning Wealth, obedience to which is destined some day to solve the problem of the Rich and the Poor, and to bring 'Peace on earth, among men Good-Will.'"

The primary concern in this article is to deal with the high degree of amalgamation of the two faiths during the decades following the Civil War, giving some attention to the ideological content of the resulting syncretistic view. It is necessary, first, to give some explanation of the situation which enabled the ideological amalgamation of such diverse and even logically inconsistent elements at the time. I suggest three roots of this situation.

The first root was the widespread triumph of pietistic revivalism in the denominations during and following the Revolutionary epoch, at the time when essentially rationalistic assumptions and thinking were largely determining the legal and political structures of the new nation. This meant, aside from a genial lack of concern for logical consistency, a widespread tendency to equate "spreading scriptural holiness over the land" through revivals with "reforming the nation." Assuming, perhaps, that "spreading scriptural holiness" in their fashion was seeking first the Kingdom of God, it was not difficult also to assume that all things else, such as social and political reformation, would be added thereto.

The second root was the almost universal reaction in the free churches against the whole ethos of the Enlightenment that took place at the same time. This threw the emerging denominations back upon scholastic Protestant orthodoxy for their intellectual structure and professed theology and created in them a mood to articulate and defend it stubbornly and uncompromisingly. This, in turn, created a basic and continuing dichotomy, for the emerging civilization continued to be informed by the spirit and ideas of the Enlightenment moving toward the whole world-view of modern science.

The third root was the often noted lack of intellectual interests and structure of the pietistic Protestantism which came to dominance. Pietistic sentiment, with its emphasis on personal religious experience, elaborated its own version of Pascal's "The heart has its reasons, which reason does not know" into a more or less systematic excuse for giving up the intellectual wrestle with the modern age. Nor was pietism in this respect confined to the uneducated revivalists on the geographical frontier and the ignoramuses on the social and intellectual fringes of all places. Horace Bushnell's distinguished theological career began when, during a revival in Yale College in 1831, he finally burst out:

> O men! what shall I do with these arrant doubts I have been nursing for years? When the preacher touches the Trinity and when logic shatters it all to pieces, I am all at the four winds. But I am glad I have a heart as well as a head. My heart wants the Father; my heart wants the Son; my heart wants the Holy Ghost—and one just as much as the other. My heart says the Bible has a Trinity for me, and I mean to hold by my heart. I am glad a man can do it when there is no other mooring.

Thereafter, aided and instructed somewhat by Samuel Taylor Coleridge, he spun out over a long period of years his own reflections on the Christianity of the heart that was secure from the "speculations of philosophers and literati"—indeed, even from "the manner of the theologians"—all of whom were thought to have an exaggerated regard for intellectual structure and logical consistency. A fitting end-result of this view was Lyman Abbott's glorying in the fact that, at Plymouth Church, "we do not ask what men believe" as a condition of membership.

It is unnecessary to dwell upon the point that such a view made religion almost impervious to the "acids of modernity" which were already eating away the faith of many; gave systematic theology a security largely untroubled by the problem of its relationship to the emerging scientific world view; and placed the question of the Christian's role as a businessman and citizen in the democratic society beyond the ken of practical theology. Meanwhile, what C. H. Hopkins called "a smug preoccupation with the salvation and perfection of the individual" largely pervaded the revivalistic denominations, tending to focus their attention on the personal vices and morals of individuals, until such personal habits as smoking, drinking, dancing, and Sunday observance became the outstanding indexes to Christian character. From the midst of this period came Daniel Dorchester's exultation that "under Protestantism, religion became purely a personal thing, passing out from under the exclusive control of the sacraments, the arbitrary sway of assumed prerogatives, into irrepressible conflicts with individual lusts and worldly influences."

Francis Wayland had foreseen something like this outcome as early as 1842 and was very unhappy about it. Looking around, he noted that

> one man asserts that his religion has nothing to do with the regulation of his passions, another that it has nothing to do with his business, and another that it has nothing to do with his politics. Thus while the man professes a religion which obliges him to serve God in everything, he declares that

whenever obedience would interfere with his cherished vices, he will not serve God at all.

He was grieved to observe that "the pulpit has failed to meet such sentiments at the very threshold, with its stern and uncompromising rebuke." The root of the difficulty in the churches, he thought—sensing the meaning of pietistic revivalism—is that "men are told how they must feel, but they are not told how they must act, and the result, in many cases ensues, that a man's belief has but a transient and uncertain effect upon his practice."

But since men, if not given instruction and guidance in such matters as citizenship and conduct in business by ministers and theologians in their churches, will nevertheless be instructed and guided by some prevailing code, the effectual abdication of the Protestant churches left the way open for the sway of the ideas and ideals of the emerging acquisitive society.

Hence the dichotomy noted and stated so well by the two Randalls, between the professed beliefs of the denominations and the "moral and social ideals and attitudes, . . . the whole way of living" which they "approved and consecrated." On the side of the latter, they came "to terms with the forces of the modern age," but "on the side of beliefs" not only did they "not come to terms with the intellectual currents of Western society" but they were "involved in a profound intellectual reaction against just such an attempt at modernism" as was implied therein. A not unexpected result was that when, in 1897, George A. Gordon surveyed the scene with critical eye, he concluded that "the theological problem for to-day" is the almost complete "absence of a theology giving intellectual form and justification to the better sentiment of the time." For example, he added, "among almost all our effective preachers the sympathies are modern; but in the greater number the theology is either ancient or nonexistent. In either case, the mass of prevailing emotion and practical activity has no corresponding body of ideas with it." Hence "the scheme entertained is usually some decrepit modification of the Calvinistic kind . . . while the purposes, sentiments, and practical outlooks are all of this new and greater day."

However, as the nineteenth century had moved into the balmy days of the Victorian age, the democratic society with its "free-enterprise" system proved obviously beneficial in terms that could be made tangible and measured in incomes and material goods. As this happened, activistic American Protestants lost their sense of estrangement from the society, began to see that it was profoundly Christian and to bless and defend it in a jargon strangely compounded out of the language of traditional Christian theology, the prevalent common-sense philosophy, and laissez faire economics. This compounding was made easier by the teaching of such men as Bushnell and his disciples that the form of expression in words was relatively unimportant, thus sanctifying a studied ambiguity.

In the context of this general interpretation of developments, it is not too difficult to understand why an aura of religious consecration came to surround the acceptance and promulgation of the syncretistic point of view. Especially important in this regard was the matter of religious freedom—how it was originally conceived and by whom. In the first place, it was the rationalists who made sense out of it theoretically and, on the basis of their theory, worked out the legal and political forms for the separation of church and state. In the second place, the churches accepted religious freedom and separation in practice, although there was little obvious theoretical justification for it in the classical Protestant theology which they professed. In effect, then, they accepted it in practice as a good thing, but on the rationalists' theoretical terms. The prevalence of pietistic sentiment at the time enabled this theoretical ambiguity to go largely unquestioned. Nevertheless, the rationalists' theory had far-reaching and devastating implications so far as the free churches were concerned. Most important was the implication that only what the religious "sects" held and taught in common (the rationalists' "essentials of every religion") was relevant to the public welfare of the new commonwealth. For the obverse side of this was that what each group held peculiar to itself, and hence what gave it its only reason for separate existence, was irrelevant to the general welfare of the whole commonwealth. No wonder that a sense of irrelevance has always haunted the most sectarian religious leaders in America. Further, the basic competition between the religious groups inherent in the system of religious freedom has always augmented the sectarian emphases, while at the same time such emphases on peculiarities undercut the sense of relevance to the life of the whole commonwealth.

This dilemma has troubled some religious leaders in America from the beginning. It is revealed, for example, in the typical insistence of Professor Bela Bates Edwards in 1848 that "perfect religious liberty does not imply that the government of the country is not a Christian government." But the most he could assert positively was that there is a "real, though indirect, connection between the State and Christianity." What, then, is the nature of this indirect connection? Tocqueville thought that he saw it. While supposing that there was some "direct influence of religion upon politics in the United States," he concluded that "its indirect influence" was "still more considerable," and added:

> The sects which exist in the United States are innumerable. They all differ in respect to the worship which is due from man to his Creator; but they all agree in respect to the duties which are due from man to man. Each

sect adores the Deity in its own peculiar manner; but all the sects preach the same moral law in the name of God.

To be sure, he sensed that the situation involved a kind of compartmentalization, and what he said of Roman Catholics might equally be applied to the Protestant groups. Their priests in America, he thought,

> have divided the intellectual world into two parts: in the one they place the doctrines of revealed religion, which command their assent; in the other they leave those truths, which they believe to have been freely left open to the researches of political inquiry. Thus the Catholics of the United States are at the same time the most faithful believers and the most zealous citizens.

The same kind of compartmentalization was exhibited by John Leland, the Baptist elder and perennial democrat, who on the matter of religious freedom spoke, on the one hand, "as a religionist" and, on the other hand, "as a statesman," coming to separate conclusions in each that would be hard to reconcile theoretically.

It is suggested that Christianity was made relevant to the public welfare at the expense of cherishing unresolved theoretical difficulties in its mind. And so long as these remain unresolved, discussions of the sects' relation to the general welfare are likely to generate more heat than light. Hence, for example, the common fervency of the insistence upon the dogma of "real, but indirect connection," which, I take it, has usually meant what Tocqueville noted, that the religious denominations in common inculcate the same basic moral standards which are the foundation of the Republic. This it is that makes their work relevant to the general welfare of the democracy. And this comes close at least to tacit acceptance of the rationalists' view of the matter.

Meanwhile, the whole grand dream of American destiny, under God, instrumented through the democratic way, while its tangled roots drew nourishment from many different soils in past centuries, was nevertheless profoundly Protestant Christian in origins and conception. Hence the "democratic faith" had always a positive and apparently independently legitimate place in the religious affections of the people. And this the free churches, in order to make themselves relevant, have always been under pressures to accept on faith and to sanctify.

Grant all this, plus the prevalence of a fuzzy and amorphous intellectual structure in the religious groups, and the way is left open for the uncritical adoption of whatever standards do actually prevail in the society. Hence, as noted, the American denominations have successively loaned themselves to the sanctification of current existing expressions of the American way of life.

John Herman Randall, Jr., by taking a more theoretical route as befits a philosopher, arrives at the similar conclusion that "Protestantism left the way open for the assimilation of any pattern of values that might seem good in the light of men's actual social experience . . . and has thus tended to become largely an emotional force in support of the reigning secular social ideals." However, it is not quite fair to conclude further, as he does, that Protestantism has offered "*no* opposition to any ideal deeply felt" and "no independent guidance and wisdom," although the denominations have always exhibited a surprising lack of ability to launch a cogent criticism of their culture, and during the period we are discussing such criticism was almost non-existent. "The most significant feature of the New Theology" of the period, as W. S. Hudson makes clear, "was its lack of normative content," which made it "compatible with every conceivable social attitude." It is not to be wondered at that when, during a later period of trouble, businessmen looked to their churches for guidance, they complained that they received back only the echoes of their own voices.

But whatever historical explanations are accepted as most plausible, there remains the general agreement that, at the time Protestantism in America achieved its greatest dominance of the culture, it had also achieved an almost complete ideological and emotional identification with the burgeoning bourgeois society and its free-enterprise system, so that "in 1876 Protestantism presented a massive, almost unbroken front in its defense of the social status quo."

Furthermore, Protestants, in effect, looked at the new world they had created, were proud of its creator, and, like Jehovah before them, pronounced it very good. A widespread complacency, a smug self-satisfaction with things as they were (or as they were supposed to be) settled upon them as soot settles on Chicago. This complacency, while a bit incredible to the mid-twentieth century, is not too difficult to understand historically. To do so, it is necessary to keep in mind the almost universal prevalence of a providential view of history— which itself is no mean evidence for the cultural dominance of the denominations. Late in 1864 Horace Bushnell proclaimed:

> We associate God and religion with all that we are fighting for. . . . Our cause, we love to think, is especially God's and so we are connecting all most sacred impressions with our government itself, weaving in a woof of holy feeling among all the fibres of our constitutional polity and government. . . . The whole shaping of the fabric is Providential. God, God is in it, every where . . . every drum-beat is a hymn, the cannon thunder God, the electric silence, darting victory along the wires, is the inaudible greeting of God's favoring work and purpose.

Granted this sentiment, it was natural that the outcome of the Civil War should suggest to those of the North that "the sword of victory had been wielded by the arm of Providence," while many in the South tended humbly to submit "to the inscrutable ways of the same Power," as the young South Carolinian interviewed by John Trowbridge, who had concluded, "I think it was in the decrees of God Almighty that slavery was to be abolished in this way, and I don't murmur."

However, the ways of Providence were not to all as inscrutable as to Abraham Lincoln, who, after plumbing the awful depths of the war's events, spoke of the altogether righteous judgments on both North and South of the "Almighty" who "has His own purposes" in history—purposes which might not fully coincide with the desires of either side. On this basis, Lincoln concluded in humility that it behooved finite men to proceed "with malice toward none, with charity for all."

There was little of such humility in the heart and hardly a hint of such somber mystery tinging the thought of the Rev. Henry Ward Beecher—that magnificent weathervane of respectable opinion and on some issues an aboriginal Brooklyn Dodger—when in May, 1963, he addressed the anniversary meeting of the American Home Missionary Society in Chicago. "See," he exulted, "how wonderfully God, in his good providence, is preparing us for the work." For "while the South is draining itself dry of its resources . . . the Northern States are growing rich by war." And "what does this mean but this—that God is storing us with that wealth by which we are to be prepared to meet the exigencies which war shall bring upon us."

And what "exigencies" are to be brought upon us? Beecher expressed no doubts:

> We are to have the charge of this continent. The South has been proved, and has been found wanting. She is not worthy to bear rule. She has lost the scepter in our national government; she is to lose the scepter in the States themselves; and this continent is to be from this time forth governed by Northern men, with Northern ideas, and with a Northern gospel.

And the reasons are clear: "this continent is to be cared for by the North simply because the North has been true to the cause of Christ in . . . a sufficient measure to secure her own safety; and the nation is to be given to us because we have the bosom by which to nourish it."

Instructed by such worthy religious leaders, it is not to be wondered at if the final victory was widely interpreted as a vindication of the righteousness of the cause of the victors. And this in turn easily merged with a vindication of what the victorious North was rapidly becoming —an industrialized civilization under "business" control. For, to quote a well-known textbook, "the Northern victory meant that certain forces and interests, long held in check by the combination of the agricultural South and West, could now have free and full play. . . . Finance and industrialism could move forward to completion without effective opposition."

From here it was but another short step to the enshrinement of the political instrument which, in the hands of Providence, had guided the Union to victory over slavery and disunion. By 1865 a writer in the Methodist *New York Christian Advocate* had already proclaimed that "we find the political parties of the day so made out, that it may . . . be determined on which side an orderly and intelligent Protestant will be found, and on which the profane, the dissolute and the Romanist." The Republican party, said Henry Wilson, contained "more of moral and intellectual worth than was ever embodied in any political organization in any land. . . . [It was] created by no man . . . [but] brought into being by Almighty God himself." This, of course, meant enshrinement of what the party became soon after Lincoln's death, when "it allied itself with the forces of corporate industry, a greater concentration of power in politics and economic life than the slaveholders had ever dreamed of possessing."

But if Americans were religious and idealistic, they were also pragmatic. If it appears that they too simply saw the smiles of beneficent Providence in the trinity of Northernism, business, and the Republican party, it must also be remembered that the system appeared to work— to produce tangible fruits in the great and obvious material prosperity that o'erspread the land like a flood and promised, eventually at least, to saturate all levels of society. Thousands of inventions, garnered up and universally applied by free and daring enterprises, revolutionized transportation, communication, agriculture, and industry, while the prevailing system seemingly distributed the benefits more widely and equitably than any had before it. It was these practical, tangible results that provided the most persuasive argument for "the American way of life" and tended to dampen all critical, as well as carping, voices in whatever realm as "un-American." Further, as time passed, a rather definite and complete ideological structure—constituting an explanation and defense—was compounded out of conservative laissez faire economic theory, the "common-sense" philosophy of the schools, and the pietistic orthodoxy of the churches.

The foundation of the whole structure was the idea of "progress." It was belief in progress that made tolerable the very rapid changes to which people were being subjected, as well as some of the less desirable aspects of what was happening. The idea of progress was compounded of the Christian doctrine of Providence and the scientific idea of evolution and was summed up in the slick phrase popularized by John Fiske and Lyman Abbott: "Evolution is God's way of doing things." So, for example, it could be proclaimed as late as 1928 that "the fact of human progress is seen to be part of the inevitable evolutionary process; and religious faith seeks in the cosmos which produced us and which carries us along the evidence of the activities of God."

To those standing on such a teleological escalator, change held no terrors. And undesirable features of the passing scene might be endured with patience bred of the knowledge that they would inevitably be transcended, since, as Henry Ward Beecher assured a Yale audience, "Man is made to start and not to stop; to go on, and on, and up, and onward . . . and ending in the glorious liberty of the sons of God." Meanwhile, as John Bascom had said, "death is of little moment, if it plays into a higher life. The insects that feed the bird meet their destination. The savages that are trodden out of a stronger race are in the line of progress." And "We—we as interpreters—are not to bring higher and impossible motives and feelings into a lower field."

That such sentiments were not restricted to the eggheads and/or the well-to-do is suggested by the popularity of some of the so-called "sentimental" gospel songs that the so-called "common people" sang in the churches:

> He leadeth me; O blessed thought!
> O words with heavenly comfort fraught!
> Whate'er I do, where'er I be,
> Still 'tis God's hand that leadeth me.

And when bleak failure seemed to encompass them and cankerous despair threatened to eat away the soul, they still sang,

> We wonder why the test
> When we try to do our best.
> But we'll understand it better by and by.

The understanding at the time was aided by the enunciation of a constellation of basic principles or doctrines which together gave content and structure to the idea of progress by explaining its practical workings in human society. One of the most complete statements of these doctrines was achieved by Andrew Carnegie in his article called "Wealth," which appeared in the June, 1889, issue of the *North American Review* and was described by the editor as one of the finest articles he had ever published.

Carnegie eschewed airy speculation and proposed to speak of "the foundations upon which society is based" and of the laws upon which "civilization itself depends"—the laws which "are the highest results of human experience" and "the soil in which society so far has produced the best fruit." And, he added as an anathema, "Objections to the foundations upon which society is based are not in order."

First was the familiar law of "the sacredness of property"—or the right of every individual to have and to hold and be protected by the government of the society in the possession of whatever property he could get.

Second were the twin laws of competition and the accumulation of wealth. The competition is for property, and these laws explain the way in which property gets distributed in a society. All men enter into the competition. But it is recognized that men differ in inherent aptitudes or talents in relationship to it. For example, some men are gifted with a "talent of organization and management" which "invariably secures" for them "enormous rewards, no matter where or under what laws or conditions." Ergo, "it is a law, as certain as any of the other named, that men possessed of this peculiar talent for affairs, under the free play of economic forces, must, of necessity, soon be in receipt of more revenue than can be judiciously expended upon themselves." In brief, "it is inevitable that their income must exceed their expenditures, and that they must accumulate wealth." The wealthy man may be regarded as the victim of circumstances over which he has no control.

Carnegie was realist enough to recognize that "society pays" a great price "for the law of competition," which, indeed, "may be sometimes hard for the individual." Nevertheless, "the advantages of this law are also greater still," for not only has it produced "our wonderful material development, which brings improved conditions in its train," but "it is best for the race, because it insures the survival of the fittest in every department." This suggests a rather clear and universal, not to say comforting, criterion for judging who are the "fittest" in the society.

The Right Reverend William Lawrence of Massachusetts propounded his ecclesiastical version of the agnostic's sentiments in an article published in January, 1901. Sniffing "a certain distrust on the part of our people as to the effect of material prosperity on their morality," he suggested that it would be well to "revise our inferences from history, experience, and the Bible" and shed that "subtle hypocrisy which has beset the Christian through the ages, bemoaning the deceitfulness of riches and, at the same time working with all his might to earn a competence, and a fortune if he can." Having rid himself of such false inferences and hypocrisy, man may now recognize the two great guiding principles for his life. The first is that it is "his divine mission" to "conquer Nature, open up her resources, and harness them to his service." The second is that, "in the long run, it is only to the man of morality that wealth comes" for "Godliness [in God's Universe] is in league with riches." This being the case, the good Bishop added, "we return with an easier mind and clearer conscience to the problem of our twenty-five billion dollars in a decade," confident that "material prosperity is in the long run favorable to morality."

Third was the law or rule of stewardship, which followed upon the views of the sacredness of property and the laws of competition and accumulation. In brief, the use and disposition of the property, as well as its mere possession, are sacred to the man who accumulates it. God gave it to him by endowing him with certain talents, and he is responsible for it *to God* alone, and certainly not to the unfit or the lesser fit in the community.

"We start," said Carnegie, "with a condition of affairs under which the best interests of the race are promoted, but which inevitably gives wealth to the few." And "thus far . . . the situation can be surveyed and pronounced good." Therefore, the "only question with which we have to deal," he continued, is "What is the proper mode of administering wealth after the laws upon which civilization is founded have thrown it into the hands of the few?" There were, he thought, but three possibilities. "The few" might leave it to their families, they might bequeath it "for public purposes," or they might administer it during their lives. He ruled out the first two as irresponsible, even coming to the radical conclusion that the state might well confiscate through inheritance taxes at least half of fortunes so left.

The true duty of "the man of Wealth" is to live modestly and unostentatiously, "provide moderately for the legitimate wants of those dependent upon him," and, beyond that,

> to consider all surplus revenues which come to him simply as trust funds, which he is . . . strictly bound as a matter of duty to administer in the manner which, in his judgment, is best calculated to produce the most beneficial results for the community . . . thus becoming the mere agent and trustee for his poorer brethren, bringing to their service his superior wisdom, experience, and ability to administer, doing for them better than they would or could do for themselves.

The main rule to be followed is "to help those who will help themselves" and to eschew the "indiscriminate charity" which presents "one of the most serious obstacles to the improvement of our race," by encouraging "the slothful, the drunken, the unworthy."

Such stewardship was taken seriously by many wealthy men of the day and produced in them an honest and consecrated devotion to their sacred duties which only the sneering souls of the mean in mind could belittle. In 1856 John P. Crozer was somewhat awed to note that "wealth flows in from all sources." And this, he added, made him feel "as often before, in making up my yearly accounts, oppressed with the responsibility of my stewardship. I am, indeed, perplexed how I shall use, as I ought to, the great and increasing wealth which God has bestowed upon me." "I love to make money almost as well as a miser," he wrote but added, "I love to give it away for charitable purposes." But he realized, as he searched his soul, "I . . . must set a guard over myself, lest the good designed be lost in the luxury of giving." For excuses are so easily framed, and the heart of man is so deceitful, that one can easily reason himself into the belief that, all things considered, he has done pretty well. I find such a process of reasoning in my own mind; but calm reflection tells me that I have not done well. I am a very unprofitable servant to so good a Master; and as he has made me the steward of a large estate, it becomes me "to lend to the Lord" freely of my substance.

And, still troubled, he prayed with real humility, "O my Lord, if it is thy righteous pleasure, direct me clearly and decisively to some path of duty and usefulness, apart from the absorbing influence of wealth and worldly mindedness."

Later, of course, when such devoted men were harassed by the rise of the unfit and strikes rocked their companies, this paternalistic conception of stewardship would show another face, as when George F. Baer, president of the Philadelphia and Reading Railway, wrote in 1902 to an inquirer:

> I beg of you not to be discouraged. The rights and interests of the laboring man will be protected and cared for—not by the labor agitators, but by the Christian men to whom God in His infinite wisdom has given control of the property interests of the country, and upon the successful Management of which so much depends.

Meanwhile, as intimated previously, Protestantism—at least in the "respectable" churches—effused a benign sanctity over all. The older "people's" churches were rapidly becoming "middle class," at least in mentality and leadership. As A. M. Schlesinger, Sr., says, even the Baptists "abandoned their contempt for wealth," as God gave gold in abundance to some of their more worthy members. And even in 1866 a writer in the Methodist *Christian Advocate* was pleased to note that "by virtue of the habits which religion inculcates and cherishes, our Church members have as a body risen in the social scale, and thus become socially removed from the great body out of which most of them originally gathered." And he added with a hint of smugness, "this tendency of things is natural and universal, and in its results unavoidable; perhaps we might add, also, not undesirable."

At the same time, American scholars, many of them ministers turned professors, worked out, as Henry Mays says, "a school of political economy which might well be labeled clerical laissez faire." And in this area, perhaps, the ideological amalgamation of which we have spoken is best and most clearly illustrated. Said the Rev. John McVicker of Columbia: "That science and religion eventually teach the same lesson, is a necessary consequence of the unity of truth, but it is seldom that this view is so satisfactorily displayed as in their searches of Political Economy."

But Americans, in spite of the long century of relative peace and stability in the world following 1814 and their almost complete freedom from embroilment in European affairs, which permitted them to work out their own problems with a minimum of outside interference, were never complete isolationists ideologically. From this they were saved by the strong sense of destiny under God, which pervaded their thinking from the beginning. By 1825 Francis Wayland, Jr., a Baptist minister, had already proclaimed sentiments that should have raised eyebrows in Europe: "What nation will be second in the new order of things, is yet to be decided; but the providence of God has already announced, that, if true to ourselves, we shall be inevitably first."

The keynote of the American idea of destiny was struck by John Winthrop in his address "Written on Boarde the Arrabella" in 1630. He said:

> The worke wee haue in hand is by a mutall consent through a speciall overruleing providence, and a more than an ordinary approbation of the Churches of Christ to seeke out a place of Cohabitation and Consorteshipp vnder a due forme of Government both ciull and ecclesiasticall.

If we are faithful to our covenant with him, Winthrop continued,

> we shall finde that the god of Israell is among vs . . . when hee shall make vs a prayse and glory, that men shall say of succeeding plantacions: the Lord make it like that of New England: for wee must Consider that wee shall be as a Citty vpon a Hill, the eies of all people are vpon vs.

Thenceforth throughout American history this strong sense of particular calling, of destiny under God, has remained a constant part of the ideological structure of the nation. Clothed in various languages in various times and places, the theme has remained the same, although God, like Alice's Cheshire cat, has sometimes threatened gradually to disappear completely or, at most, to remain only as a disembodied and sentimental smile.

Perhaps the version of destiny intimated by Winthrop in his reference to the "Citty vpon a Hill" with "the eies of all people . . . vpon vs" has been most commonly dominant—namely, that American destiny is to be fulfilled merely by setting an example for all to follow. Thus in the *Discourse* quoted earlier, Francis Wayland, Jr., held that "our power resides in the force of our example. It is by exhibiting to other nations the practical excellence of a government of law, that they will learn its nature and advantages, and will in due time achieve their own emancipation." Already, he thought, "our country has given to the world the first ocular demonstration, not only of the practicability, but also of the unrivalled superiority of a popular form of government."

William R. Williams in 1846 more obviously wove the strands of evangelical Christianity into those of American destiny: "Our Heavenly Father has made us a national epistle to other lands," he wrote.

See that you read a full and impressive comment to all lands, of the power of Christian principle, and of the expansive and self-sustaining energies of the gospel, when left unfettered by national endowments, and secular alliances. The evangelical character of our land is to tell upon the plans and destinies of other nations.

It is small wonder that Americans down to the present commonly find it hard to understand why the nations of the world do not automatically adopt the fine way of life which their country so completely and beautifully exemplifies.

It was the idea of destiny which in the period we are discussing, as in all periods before and since, added "the inducements of philanthropy to those of patriotism" in the American mind and broadened the idea of progress and its laws to include all of humanity. America's destiny came to be seen as her call to spread the amazing benefits of the American democratic faith and its free-enterprise system throughout the world, gradually transforming the world into its own image. The idea of destiny lay back of and tempered Bishop Lawrence's belief that "Godliness is in league with riches." So, he concluded, "we have learned how to win wealth: we are learning how to use and spend it." But wealth and character go together. "Without wealth, character is liable to narrow and harden. Without character, wealth will destroy." Therefore,

the call of to-day is . . . for the uplift of character,—the support of industry, education, art, and every means of culture; the encouragement of the higher life; and, above all, the deepening of the religious faith of the people; the re-kindling of the spirit that, clothed with her material forces, the greater personality of this Nation may fulfill her divine destiny.

But, by the time he wrote in 1901, the United States, fresh from its first venture in imperialistic war, was already beginning to be impressed by the meaning and possibilities of the physical power which destiny had placed in its hands and the idea had been hatched that the power as well as the wealth was given by divine appointment to be used.

Josiah Strong, erstwhile Congregational pastor in Cheyenne and at the time secretary of that denomination's Home Missionary Society, sounded the Christian version of this view in his very popular book, *Our Country,* first published in 1885.

The Anglo-Saxon race—and in America all immigrants soon became Anglo-Saxon—is the representative of two closely related ideas, "Civil Liberty" and "pure spiritual Christianity." Hence, he concluded, "it is chiefly to the English and American peoples that we must look for the evangelization of the world," for there is no doubt that these two ideas are necessary if "all men" are to "be lifted up into the light of the highest Christian civilization." Hence it is obvious that "the Anglo-Saxon . . . is divinely commissioned to be, in a peculiar sense, his brother's keeper."

And when we of this generation add to this fact the equally obvious fact of the Anglo-Saxon's "rapidly increasing strength in modern times . . . we have well-nigh a demonstration of his destiny." For "does it not look as if God were not only preparing in our Anglo-Saxon civilization the die with which to stamp the peoples of the earth, but as if he were also massing behind that die the mighty power with which to press it?"

The English, however, may be discounted, and the Americans "may reasonably expect to develop the highest type of Anglo-Saxon civilization." For it follows from the fact that "human progress follows a law of development" that "our civilization should be the noblest; for we are 'The heirs of all the ages in the foremost files of time.' "

Thus, he explained, "God, with infinite wisdom and skill, is training the Anglo-Saxon race for an hour sure to come"—the hour of *"final competition of races."* And, he modestly concluded, "can anyone doubt that the result of this competition of races will be the 'survival of the fittest'?" Planting his feet firmly on the escalator, he proclaimed the present knowledge that the "inferior tribes were only precursors of a superior race, voices in the wilderness crying: 'Prepare ye the way of the Lord!' "

So this eminent Congregational leader, having to his own satisfaction plumbed at last the depths of inscrutable Providence, knew that "God has two hands. Not only is he preparing in our civilization the die with which to stamp the nations, but, by what Southey called the 'timing of Providence,' he is preparing mankind to receive our impress."

With such well-nigh infallible religious guides abroad in the land, it is small wonder that a mere junior Senator, Albert J. Beveridge, of Indiana, was prepared to defend annexation of the Philippines on January 9, 1900, with the words:

> We will not renounce our part in the mission of the race, trustee, under God, of the civilization of the world. . . . He has made us the master organizers of the world to establish system where chaos reigns. . . . He has made us adept in government that we may administer government among savage and senile peoples. . . . And of all our race, He has marked the American people as His chosen Nation to finally lead in the regeneration of the world. This is the divine mission of America, and it holds for us all the profit, all the glory, all the happiness possible to man. We are trustees of the world's progress, guardians of its righteous peace. The judgment of the Master is upon us: "Ye have been faithful over a few things; I will make you ruler over many things."

Finally, "exhibiting a nugget of gold, he cried: 'I picked this up on the ground in one of these islands. There are thousands of others lying about.'"

But already the worm was beginning to turn—and a Christian note of profounder depth was struck by Senator George F. Hoar, who rose merely to say: "The Devil taketh him up into an extremely high mountain and showeth him all the kingdoms of the world and the glory of them and saith unto him, 'All these things will be thine if thou wilt fall down and worship me.'"

We have noted, then, that the bulk of American Protestantism achieved during this period a working ideological harmony with the modes of the modern industrialized civilization, the free-enterprise system, and the burgeoning imperialism. Professor W. S. Hudson, treating the more purely theological aspects of this development in a most discerning book on *The Great Tradition of the American Churches,* makes good his claim that "the New Theology was essentially a culture religion." The doctrines of the "gospel of wealth" in the context of the idea of destiny under God gave a satisfactory explanation of the facts of human life as experienced in the United States. It should never be forgotten that at this time the observational order coincided in high degree with the conceptual order and that such coincidence defines social stability.

This it was that created an atmosphere in which those actually in control—the only people that really mattered—could live at ease in the vast expanding new Zion. This was Edith Wharton's "age of innocence," Henry S. Canby's "age of confidence"; and its flower was a host of middle-class "fathers" of the type pictured by Clarence Day. Perhaps its outstanding characteristic was complacency, based on the feeling that God was in his heaven and all was right with the world. Surveying the period in retrospect, we may agree with Whitehead that "the prosperous middle classes, who ruled the nineteenth century, placed an excessive value upon placidity of existence" and that this is hardly a sufficient basis for an enduring culture.

Looking backward today from a world which promises to be somewhat different from that Utopia which Edward Bellamy anticipated in 1888, it seems obvious enough to us that the outward harmony was achieved by overlooking certain incongruous elements in the situation that had troubled only such gloomy and lonesome prophets as Nathaniel Hawthorne, Herman Melville, Walt Whitman, and Henry Adams. Hence the world that seemed so fine and stable to Carnegie and Bishop Lawrence, to Crozer and Henry Ward Beecher, to Josiah Strong and Russell Conwell—to all the "fathers" of Day's type—was about to explode. The period of cultural triumph of the denominations merged—not with a whimper, but with a bang—into the period of upheaval and crisis.

But these denominations, however much their normative theology might be eroded, their historical sense blunted, and their Christianity identified with the current forms of the American way of life, still bore latent within them a sense of continuity with the Christian past—with the prophets of the Old Testament God of judgment; with the Nazarene and his Sermon on the Mount; with the Christian church through the ages—and here was a basis for perspective on the immediate scene. Hence the crisis itself carried within it the possibility of religious renewal and theological reconstruction, rooted in the view that, from a Christian standpoint, the whole ideology of the complacent period rested on an idolatry made possible because the dominant churches had largely forgotten to preach and had failed to inculcate belief in the First Commandment.

13

The Genteel Reformers
RICHARD HOFSTADTER

In the Western world, the nineteenth century marked the transition from aristocracy to democracy. The transition was so profound in Europe that its American counterpart has tended to be ignored. Tocqueville reduced the American idea to democracy in order to delineate it more sharply vis-à-vis the European. But if the demarcation between aristocracy and democracy was not at all as clearly defined in America as it was in Europe, the presence of an aristocracy was, as Tocqueville himself recognized, a fact of American life; and the challenge to it by the expanding forces of democracy was a salient condition of our nineteenth-century history.

The role corresponding to that played by European aristocracy was played in America by a social and intellectual elite. Because the class was not

SOURCE: Richard Hofstadter, *Anti-Intellectualism in American Life* (New York: Alfred A. Knopf, Inc., 1963), pp. 172–91, 196. Copyright © 1962, 1963 by Richard Hofstadter. Another version of this selection appeared under the title "Idealists and Professors and Sore-Heads: The Genteel Reformers" in *The Columbia University Forum*, V (Spring, 1962), 5–11. Reprinted by permission of Alfred A. Knopf, Inc.

legally constituted as such, and did not necessarily inherit its position by birth, its identity was harder to sustain and its character and composition have been difficult to define. But its role has been a pervasive one in American history, and its goals—the purification of national politics and the greater achievement of national purpose—have persisted from one era to the next. Indeed, reform in American history may, in one significant respect, be seen as the attempt of the "aristocracy" to lead the nation back to an earlier, remembered morality from which the politics of democracy had caused it to stray. The social composition of our aristocratic elite has varied but the elite itself has regularly appeared: as the Puritan leadership of the seventeenth century, the Founding Fathers of the Revolutionary age, the New England reformers of the Jacksonian era, the "genteel reformers" of the Gilded Age, the Progressive spokesmen of the early twentieth century.

Historians have paid increasing attention to this social-intellectual elite in recent years. Among the interesting studies that deal with its nature and role are Stanley Elkins and Eric McKitrick, "The Founding Fathers: Young Men of the Revolution" (Political Science Quarterly, *June 1961: this essay may be found in Volume I); Sidney Aronson,* Status and Kinship in the Higher Civil Service *(1964); David Donald, "Toward a Reconsideration of the Abolitionists" (in* Lincoln Reconsidered, *1956); Stow Persons, "The Origins of the Gentry" (in* Essays on History and Literature, *edited by R. H. Bremner, 1966), and George E. Mowry's several books on the Progressives.*

"Aristocratic" elites both in the United States and Great Britain perennially feared the consequences of the politics of democracy. They felt that the appeal to numbers might vitiate the appeal to discretion, that policy might be dictated by the self-interest of the "masses" rather than the disinterestedness of the "classes." The fear resonated variously in nineteenth-century English and American literature: in James Fenimore Cooper's American Democrat, Walt Whitman's Democratic Vistas, Walter Bagehot's English Constitution, John Stuart Mill's On Liberty, *to cite some familiar examples. The anxiety that ran through this literature was that the higher goals of national policy would be abased by political leaders in their quest for popular majorities, and that what the people, in their several interests, might consider to be good for themselves, would very often not be good for the nation as a whole.*

Inevitably, the aristocratic-intellectual elite and the democratic politicians clashed over the ends and means of politics. Responding to charges that they were self-seeking and coarse, the politicians often questioned the practical competence and acumen of their opponents. Their attack on the intellectual elite was particularly acerbic during the Gilded Age, and it is this subject that concerns Richard Hofstadter in the essay reprinted below. DeWitt Clinton Professor of American History at Columbia University, Hofstadter is the author of several highly significant books. These include

The American Political Tradition (1948), The Age of Reform (1955), for which he won the Pulitzer prize in history, and Anti-Intellectualism in American Life (1963), for which he received the Pulitzer prize in general nonfiction and from which the following essay has been taken. In each of his major works Hofstadter has sought to show the differences between the myth of the American past and the actual fact of it and to explore those strains in American life that have run against the intent of the American idea. He has reiterated his basic theme not so much to reprove Americans for their failures as to remind them of their ideals. His essay on the "Genteel Reformers" of the Gilded Age is a footnote to his larger argument that American political culture has much that is questionable and gross, and that it is indeed often so emotional as to become irrational.

The gentleman-scholar of the Gilded Age stood outside looking in on the exercise of power; and in calling for reform, he remembered an earlier age in which he had held power in his own hands. The politicians' view of the "genteel reformers" presented in Hofstadter's essay is surely a suggestive one, posing a number of questions. What are the larger implications of the view that the "genteel reformers" were hardly masculine? What indeed have been the changing concepts of masculinity in America, and what have the changes signified? How far has the course of American thought witnessed the transformation of the concept of virtue from being manly to being male, from celebrating moral restraint to celebrating sexual indulgence? Who are today's social or intellectual elite? If the scholarly class in America is disaffected today, how much of the reason is due to the fact that scholars serve merely as experts but not as functionaries, that they are asked merely to advise, not to rule? From a larger perspective Hofstadter's account reminds us that the democratization of American politics has beset us with serious problems and that perhaps the most serious of them is that our social and intellectual elite does not have the power to guide public policy.

By mid-century, the gentlemen had been reduced to a marginal role in both elective and appointive offices in the United States, and had been substantially alienated from American politics. For a time the Civil War submerged their discontents. The war was one of those major crises that suspend cultural criticism. It was a cause, a distraction, a task that urgently had to be done, and, on the whole, Northerners of the patrician class rallied to the support of their country without asking whether the political culture they proposed to save was worth saving. Lincoln, as they came to know him, was reassuring, and he pleased them by appointing men of learning and letters to diplomatic posts— Charles Francis Adams, Sr., John Bigelow, George William Curtis, William Dean Howells, and John Lothrop Motley. If American democratic culture could produce such a man, it was possible that they, after all, had underestimated it.

But when the war was over, the failure of the system seemed only to have been dramatized. Hundreds of thousands of lives had been lost to redeem the political failures of the pre-war generation, and during the terrible fiasco of Reconstruction, it became clear that beyond the minimal goal of saving the Union nothing had been accomplished and nothing learned. The new generation of entrepreneurs was more voracious than the old, and politics appeared to have been abandoned to bloody-shirt demagogy, to dispensing the public domain to railroad barons, and to the tariff swindle. The idealistic Republican Party of 1865 had become the party of men like Benjamin F. Butler and Ben Wade, and the creature of the scandalmakers of the Grant administration.

Many reformers saw how the tide of events was running as early as 1868, when Richard Henry Dana, Jr., tried to oust Benjamin F. Butler from his Massachusetts Congressional seat. For them the issue was sharply drawn: in the Bay State, the heart and center of the Brahmin class and the moral and intellectual wellspring of the patrician type, one of their own kind was now trying to remove from the political scene the man who had become the pre-eminent symbol of candid cynicism in politics. This was, *The New York Times* thought, "a contest between the intelligent, sober-minded, reflective men of the district, and the unthinking, reckless, boisterous don't-care-a-damnative portion of the community."[1] It proved also to be a contest between a tiny minority and the overwhelming majority of the immigrants and workers, marked by the almost classic ineptitude of Dana's electioneering techniques.[2] The dismal prospects of men of Dana's kind were harshly clarified by the election; Dana got less than ten per cent of the votes.

The humiliation of Dana was the first of a series of shocks. The reformers' friends were faring badly. Motley, on the strength of a rumor, was forced out of his diplomatic post by Andrew Johnson; reappointed by Grant, he was ditched once again because Grant wanted to strike through him at Sumner. Judge Ebenezer R. Hoar's nomination for the Supreme Court was rejected mainly because the politicians didn't like him. ("What could you expect," asked Simon Cameron, "from a man

---

[1] *The New York Times*, October 24, 1868. For years Butler used the Brahmins' hatred of him as a political asset. A supporter in 1884 declared that he won elections because "all the snobs and all the dilettantes hate him, and Harvard College won't make him a doctor of laws." H. C. Thomas: *Return of the Democratic Party to Power in 1884* (New York, 1919), p. 139.

[2] It was in this campaign that Butler, driving a wedge between Dana and working-class constituencies, accused Dana of wearing white gloves. Dana admitted that he did at times wear white gloves and clean clothes, but assured his audience, the workingmen of Lynn, that when he spent two years before the mast as a young sailor, "I was as dirty as any of you." Benjamin F. Butler: *Butler's Book* (Boston, 1892), pp. 921-2.

who had snubbed seventy Senators?") The able economist, David A. Wells, was cut out of his office as special revenue agent because of his free-trade views. Jacob Dolson Cox, a leading advocate of civil-service reform, felt impelled by lack of presidential support to resign as Grant's Secretary of the Interior. By 1870, Henry Adams, explaining why he had left Washington to teach at Harvard, wrote: "All my friends have been or are on the point of being driven out of the government and I should have been left without any allies or sources of information."[3]

The young men who had hoped that the party of Lincoln and Grant might bring about a reform no longer had any illusions. As the grim shape of the new America emerged out of the smoke of the war, there emerged with it a peculiar American underground of frustrated aristocrats, a type of genteel reformer whose very existence dramatized the alienation of education and intellect from significant political and economic power. The dominant idea of the genteel reformers was public service; their chief issue, civil-service reform; their theoretical spokesman, E. L. Godkin of the *Nation;* their most successful political hero, Grover Cleveland. Their towering literary monument proved to be that masterpiece in the artistry of self-pity, Henry Adams's *Education.*

The historian, looking back upon the genteel reformers and realizing how many grave social issues they barely touched upon and how many they did not touch at all, may be inclined to feel that their blood ran thin, and to welcome the appearance among them in later days of such a bold and distracted figure as John Jay Chapman. But this class represented the majority of the politically active educated men of the community; and the place of mind in American politics, if mind was to have any place at all, rested mainly upon their fortunes. This they understood themselves; it was what Lowell meant when he begged Godkin to protest in the *Nation* against "the queer notion of the Republican Party that they can get along without their brains"—and Charles Eliot Norton when he made his pathetic if rather parochial plaint that "the *Nation* & Harvard & Yale College seem to me almost the only solid barriers against the invasion of modern barbarism & vulgarity."[4]

The reform type was not national or representative. As a rule, the genteel reformers were born in the Northeast—mainly in Massachusetts, Connecticut, New York, and Pennsylvania—although a scattered few lived in those parts of the Middle West which had been colonized by Yankees and New Yorkers. Morally and intellectually these men

[3] Adams to C. M. Gaskell, October 25, 1870, in W. C. Ford, ed.: *Letters of Henry Adams* (Boston, 1930), p. 196.

[4] J. R. Lowell to Godkin, December 20, 1871, in Rollo Ogden, ed.: *Life and Letters of Edwin Lawrence Godkin* (New York, 1907), Vol. II, p. 87; C. E. Norton to Godkin, November 3, 1871, in Ari Hoogenboom: *Outlawing the Spoils* (Urbana, Illinois, 1961), p. 99.

were the heirs of New England, and for the most part its heirs by descent. They carried on the philosophical concerns of Unitarianism and transcendentalism, the moral animus of Puritanism, the crusading heritage of the free-soil movement, the New England reverence for education and intellectualism, the Yankee passion for public duty and civic reform.

They struck the Yankee note, one must add, of self-confidence and self-righteousness; most of the genteel reformers were certain of their own moral purity. "Each generation of citizens," declared the publisher George Haven Putnam, describing them in his autobiography, "produces a group of men who are free from self-seeking and who, recognizing their obligations to the community, are prepared to give their work and their capacities for doing what may be in their power for the service of their fellow-men."[5] This capacity for disinterested service was founded upon financial security and firm family traditions. The genteel reformers were not usually very rich, but they were almost invariably well-to-do. Hardly any were self-made men from obscure or poverty-stricken homes; they were the sons of established merchants and manufacturers, lawyers, clergymen, physicians, educators, editors, journalists, and publishers, and they had followed their fathers into business and the professions. Their education was far above the ordinary: at a time when college diplomas were still rare, there were among them an impressive number with B.A.'s, and most of those who lacked B.A.'s had law degrees. Several were historians, antiquarians, and collectors; others wrote poetry, fiction, or criticism. A high proportion of the college men had gone to Harvard or Yale, or to such outposts of the New England educational tradition as Amherst, Brown, Williams, Dartmouth, and Oberlin. Those whose religious affiliations can be determined belonged (aside from a few independents and skeptics) to the upper-class denominations, and especially those most affected by the New England tradition or those which appealed to mercantile patricians—Congregationalists, Unitarians, and Episcopalians.[6]

Politically and morally, as Henry Adams so poignantly demonstrated, the genteel reformers were homeless. They had few friends and

---

[5] George Haven Putnam: *Memories of a Publisher* (New York, 1915), p. 112.

[6] My generalizations about the reformers are based on an analysis of factors in the careers of 191 men in an unpublished master's essay at Columbia University written by James Stuart McLachlan: *The Genteel Reformers: 1865–1884* (1958). His conclusions are similar to those in Ari Hoogenboom's analysis of civil-service reformers, op. cit., pp. 190–7. Cf. his essay, "An Analysis of Civil Service Reformers," *The Historian*, Vol. XXIII (November, 1960), pp. 54–78. Paul P. Van Riper emphasizes the prior abolitionist sympathies of these reformers, and their preoccupation with individual liberty and political morality; *History of the United States Civil Service* (Evanston, Ill., 1958).

no allies. Almost everywhere in American life—in business as well as in politics—an ingenuous but coarse and ruthless type of person had taken over control of affairs, a type Adams found in possession when he returned to Washington from England after the Civil War:[7]

> In time one came to recognize the type in other men [than Grant], with differences and variations, as normal; men whose energies were the greater, the less they wasted on thought; men who sprang from the soil to power; apt to be distrustful of themselves and of others; shy; jealous, sometimes vindictive; more or less dull in outward appearance, always needing stimulants; but for whom action was the highest stimulant—the instinct of fight. Such men were forces of nature, energies of the prime, like the *Pteraspis*, but they made short work of scholars. They had commanded thousands of such and saw no more in them than in others. The fact was certain; it crushed argument and intellect at once.

Wherever men of cultivation looked, they found themselves facing hostile forces and an alien mentality. They resented the new plutocracy which overshadowed them in business and in public affairs—a plutocracy they considered as dangerous socially as it was personally vulgar and ostentatious; for it consisted of those tycoons about whom Charles Francis Adams, Jr., said that after years of association he had not met one that he would ever care to meet again, or one that could be "associated in my mind with the idea of humor, thought or refinement."[8] No less vulgar were the politicians—"lewd fellows of the baser sort," Godkin called them[9]—who compounded their vulgarity with inefficiency, ignorance, and corruption. Henry Adams had not long returned to Washington when a Cabinet officer told him how pointless it was to show patience in dealing with Congressmen: "You can't use tact with a Congressman! A Congressman is a hog! You must take a stick and hit him on the snout!" Everyone in Boston, New England, and New York agreed in warning Adams that "Washington was no place for a respectable young man," and he could see for himself that the place had no tone, no society, no social medium through which the ideas of men of discernment and refinement could influence affairs.[10]

> Society seemed hardly more at home than he. Both Executive and Congress held it aloof. No one in society seemed to have the ear of anybody in

---

[7] *The Education of Henry Adams* (New York: Modern Library edition; 1931), p. 265.

[8] Charles Francis Adams: *An Autobiography* (Boston, 1916), p. 190.

[9] E. L. Godkin: "The Main Question," *Nation,* Vol. IX (October 14, 1869), p. 308.

[10] Adams: *Education,* pp. 261, 296, 320. Cf. James Bryce: "Why the Best Men Do Not Go into Politics," *The American Commonwealth* (New York, 1897), Vol. II, chapter 57.

Government. No one in Government knew any reason for consulting any one in society. The world had ceased to be wholly political, but politics had become less social. A survivor of the Civil War—like George Bancroft, or John Hay—tried to keep footing, but without brilliant success. They were free to do or say what they liked, but no one took much notice of anything said or done.

The genteel reformers were as much alienated from the general public as they were from the main centers of power in the business corporations and the political machines. They had too much at stake in society to campaign for radical changes and too much disdain for other varieties of reformers to make political allies. The discontented farmers, with their cranky enthusiasms and their monetary panaceas, inspired in them only distaste. Snobbishness and gentility, as well as class interest, estranged them from the working class and the immigrants. Charles Francis Adams, Jr., expressed a feeling common to his class when he said: "I don't associate with the laborers on my place"; and he was no doubt doubly right when he added that such association would not be "agreeable to either of us."[11]   As for the immigrants, the reformers considered their role in the misgovernment of cities to be one of the chief sources of the strength of the bosses. Reformers were sometimes skeptical about the merits of unrestricted democracy and universal manhood suffrage, and toyed with the thought of education tests or poll taxes that would disfranchise the most ignorant in the electorate.[12]

Thus estranged from major social interests which had different needs from their own, the genteel reformers were barred from useful political alliances and condemned to political ineffectuality. They had to content themselves with the hope that occasionally they could get their way by acting "on the limited number of cultivated minds,"[13] by appealing, as James Ford Rhodes put it, to men of "property and intelligence."

---

[11] *Autobiography*, pp. 15–16.

[12] See "The Government of our Great Cities," *Nation*, Vol. III (October 18, 1866), pp. 312–13; *North American Review*, Vol. CIII (October, 1866), pp. 413–65; Arthur F. Beringause: *Brooks Adams* (New York, 1955), pp. 60, 67; Barbara M. Solomon: *Ancestors and Immigrants* (Cambridge, Mass., 1956). On the outlook of the reformers, see Geoffrey T. Blodgett's sensitive account of "The Mind of the Boston Mugwump," *Mississippi Valley Historical Review*, Vol. XLVIII (March, 1962), pp. 614–34.

[13] Adams to Gaskell, quoted in Ernest Samuels: *The Young Henry Adams* (Cambridge, Mass., 1948), p. 182. Cf. Putnam's view: "It was our hope that as the youngsters came out of college from year to year with the kind of knowledge of the history of economics that would be given to them by professors like William Graham Sumner of Yale, we should gradually secure a larger hold on public opinion, and through the influence of leaders bring the mass of the voters to an understanding of their own business interests." Putnam: op cit., pp. 42–3.

"We want a government," said Carl Schurz in 1874, "which the best people of this country will be proud of."[14] What they were really asking for was leadership by an educated and civic-minded elite—in a country which had no use for elites of any kind, much less for an educated one. "The best people" were outsiders. Their social position seemed a liability; their education certainly was. In 1888 James Russell Lowell complained that "in the opinion of some of our leading politicians and many of our newspapers, men of scholarly minds are *ipso facto* debarred from forming any judgment on public affairs; or if they should be so unscrupulous as to do so . . . they must at least refrain from communicating it to their fellow-citizens."[15]

Aware that their public following was too small to admit of a frontal attack on any major citadel of politics or administration, the genteel reformers were driven to adopt a strategy of independency. The margin of strength between the two major parties was frequently so narrow that, by threatening to bolt, a strong faction of independents might win an influence out of proportion to their numbers.[16] For a short time, the reformers seemed to be poised tantalizingly on the fringes of real influence. At first, they thought they might have some say in the Grant administration, and when Grant disappointed them, most of them took part in the ill-fated bolt of the liberal Republicans in 1872. Then they were courted so carefully by Hayes that their expectations were aroused, only to be disappointed again. For the most part, they had to content themselves with limited victories, like the reform of the post office and the New York Customs House, or the occasional appointment of such men as Hamilton Fish, E. R. Hoar, William M. Evarts, Carl Schurz, or Wayne MacVeagh, to Cabinet posts. Their happiest moment came in the election of 1884, when they convinced themselves that the Mugwump bolt from the Republican Party had swung the state of New York from Blaine to Cleveland, and with it the election. But their outstanding legislative success was in civil-service reform, with the passage of the Pendleton Act in 1883. This deserves special attention, for civil-service reform, the class issue of the gentleman, was a touchstone of American political culture.

---

[14] Quoted in Eric Goldman: *Rendezvous with Destiny* (New York, 1952), p. 24. One advocate of civil-service reform pointed out that in "the early days of the Republic" all public servants from cabinet officers down to subordinate members "were generally selected from well-known families," and argued that civil-service reform would reintroduce this practice. Julius Bing: "Civil Service of the United States," *North American Review*, Vol. CV (October, 1867), pp. 480–1.

[15] "The Place of the Independent in Politics," *Writings*, Vol. VI (Cambridge, Mass., 1890), p. 190.

[16] On the strategy of independency, see James Russell Lowell: "The Place of the Independent in Politics," pp. 190 ff.; and E. McClung Fleming: *R. R. Bowker, Militant Liberal* (New York, 1952), pp. 103–8.

The central idea of the reformers—the idea which they all agreed upon and which excited their deepest concern—was the improvement of the civil service, without which they believed no other reform could be successfully carried out.[17] The ideal of civil-service reform brought into direct opposition the credo of the professional politicians, who put their faith in party organization and party rewards and the practices of rotation in office, and the ideals of the reformers, who wanted competence, efficiency, and economy in the public service, open competition for jobs on the basis of merit, and security of tenure. The reformers looked to various models for their proposals—to the American military services, to bureaucratic systems in Prussia or even China; but principally this English-oriented intellectual class looked for inspiration to England, where civil-service reorganization had been under way since the publication of the Northcote-Trevelyan Report in 1854.

The English civil-service reformers had designed their proposals in full awareness of the organic relation of the civil service to the class structure and to the educational system. They had planned a civil service which, as Gladstone observed, would give the gentlemanly classes "command over all the higher posts" and allot to members of the lower classes the positions that could be filled by persons with more practical and less expensive training.[18] The scheme owed much to the influence of Lord Macaulay, who conceived of "a public service confined in its upper reaches to gentlemen of breeding and culture selected by a literary competition." The higher posts would be filled by gentlemen who had received a rigorous classical training at one of the ancient universities, the lower posts by candidates with a less exalted education —and within each category recruitment by competitive examination would guarantee the merit of those chosen. By 1877, Sir Charles Trevelyan, one of the leading reformers, reported to an American friend that the British changes had been not only successful but popular. "Large as the number of persons who profited by the former system of patronage were," he observed,

> those who were left out in the cold were still larger, and these included some
> of the best classes of our population—busy professional persons of every
> kind, lawyers, ministers of religion of every persuasion, schoolmasters,
> farmers, shopkeepers, etc. These rapidly took in the idea of the new institu-
> tion, and they gladly accepted it as a valuable additional privilege.

Moreover, Sir Charles remarked, the same change that had increased the efficiency of the civil and military services "has given a marvellous stimulus to education." Formerly, upper-class boys who intended to go

---

[17] On the centrality of this reform, see Paul P. Van Riper: op. cit., pp. 83–4.

[18] See J. Donald Kingsley: *Representative Bureaucracy: An Interpretation of the British Civil Service* (Yellow Springs, Ohio, 1944), pp. 68–71 and *passim*.

into public service had had no inducement to exert themselves because they were certain to get an appointment. Now they knew that their future depended in some good measure upon their own energies, and "a new spirit of activity has supervened. The opening of the civil and military services, in its influence upon national education, is equivalent to a hundred thousand scholarships and exhibitions of the most valuable kind. . . ."[19]

The appeal of the British reformers to their American counterparts is quite understandable. The concern of the leading American reformers was not, for the most part, self-interested, in so far as most jobs that would be opened in the American civil service, if competitive examinations were adopted, would not be of sufficient rank to attract them.[20] But it was humiliating to know that by the canons of the society in which they lived they were not preferred for office and could not help their friends.[21] What was mainly at issue for them was a cultural and political ideal, a projection of their own standards of purity and excellence into governmental practice. It was the "national character" which was at stake. The principles of freedom and competitive superiority which they had learned in their college courses in classical economics and had applied to the tariff question ought to be applied to public office: open competition on the basis of merit should be the civil-service analogue of fair competition in industry.[22] But to the professional politicians the means of determining merit—the competitive examination— seemed to have about it the aura of the school, and it instantly aroused

---

[19] Sir Charles Trevelyan to Dorman B. Eaton, August 20, 1877, in Dorman B. Eaton: *Civil Service in Great Britain: A History of Abuses and Reforms and Their Bearing upon American Politics* (New York, 1880), pp. 430–2.

[20] No doubt many reformers hoped wistfully that the kind of recognition Lincoln had given to literary men might be resumed, but such posts were above and outside the civil-service system. Characteristically, the reformers aspired to elective rather than appointive office. About half of the leading reformers held office at one time or another, but chiefly in elective positions. A few went to Congress, but most of their elected offices were in state legislatures. McLachlan: op. cit., p. 25.

[21] Consider the implications of Henry Adams's letter to Charles Francis Adams, Jr., April 29, 1869: "I can't get you an office. The only members of this Government that I have met are mere acquaintances, not friends, and I fancy no request of mine would be likely to call out a gush of sympathy. [David Ames] Wells has just about as much influence as I have. He can't even protect his own clerks. Judge Hoar has his hands full, and does not interfere with his colleagues. . . ." *Letters,* p. 157.

[22] There was an assumption on the part of some that social standing would count, however, in the competition for jobs. Carl Schurz once proposed that "mere inquiries concerning the character, antecedents, social standing, and general ability [of a candidate] may be substituted for formal examination." Hoogenboom: op. cit., p. 115.

their hostility to intellect, education, and training. It was, as they began to say, a "schoolmaster's test." Touching the professions directly on a sensitive nerve, the issue brought forth a violent reaction which opened the floodgates of anti-intellectualist demagogy. The professionals denounced the idea of a civil service based upon examinations and providing secure tenure as aristocratic and imitative of British, Prussian, and Chinese bureaucracies; as deferential to monarchical institutions, and a threat to republicanism; and as militaristic because it took as one of its models the examination requirements that had been instituted in the armed services. From the first, the distrust of trained intellect was invoked. When a bill calling for civil-service reform was introduced in 1868 by Representative Thomas A. Jenckes of Rhode Island, it was denounced in the House by John A. Logan of Illinois in these terms:[23]

> This bill is the opening wedge to an aristocracy in this country. . . . It will lead us to the point where there will be two national schools in this country —one for the military and the other for civil education. These schools will monopolize all avenues of approach to the Government. Unless a man can pass one or another of these schools and be enrolled upon their lists he cannot receive employment under this Government, no matter how great may be his capacity, how indisputable may be his qualifications. When once he does pass his school and fixes himself for life his next care will be to get his children there also. In these schools the scholars will soon come to believe that they are the only persons qualified to administer the Government, and soon come to resolve that the Government shall be administered by them and by none others.

It became clear, as the debate over civil service developed, that the professionals feared the demand for competence and the requirements of literacy and intelligence as a threat to the principles upon which the machines were based, and with this threat before them, there was almost no limit to the demagogy they would exert in behalf of the spoils principle. A Congressman from Indiana held up the frightening prospect that a graduate of, say, Washington College in Virginia, of which Robert E. Lee was president, would do better on a competitive examination than a disabled soldier of some "common school or workshop of the West, who lost a limb at the battle of Chickamauga." The people, he said, "are not quite ready to permit the students of rebel colleges, upon competitive examinations and scholastic attainments, to super-

---

[23] *Congressional Globe,* 40th Congress, 3rd session, p. 265 (January 8, 1869). It is suggestive that competitive civil service, so often criticized in the United States as undemocratic, was at times assailed in Britain as excessively democratic, and as throwing the aristocracy on the defensive in the competition for posts. Kingsley: op. cit., p. 62. Others felt that this would only raise the morale and tone of the class of gentlemen. Cf. Asa Briggs: *Victorian People* (London, 1954), pp. 116–21, 170–1.

sede the disabled and patriotic soldiers of the Republic, who with fewer educational advantages but larger practical experience are much better fitted for the position."[24]

In similar terms, Senator Matthew H. Carpenter of Wisconsin declaimed that during the Civil War,[25]

> when the fate of the nation was trembling in the balance, and our gallant youths were breasting the storm of war, the sons of less patriotic citizens were enjoying the advantages of a college course. And now, when our maimed soldiers have returned, and apply for a Federal office, the duties of which they are perfectly competent to discharge, they are to be rejected to give place to those who were cramming themselves with facts and principles from the books, while they were bleeding for their country, because they do not know the fluctuations of the tide at the Cape of Good Hope, how near the moon ever approaches the earth, or the names of the principal rivers emptying into the Caspian Sea.

Suggesting that "admission into the kingdom of heaven does not depend upon the result of a competitive examination," the senator rang the changes on the contrast between formal education and practical intelligence: "The dunce who has been crammed up to a diploma at Yale, and comes fresh from his cramming, will be preferred in all civil appointments to the ablest, most successful, and most upright business man of the country, who either did not enjoy the benefit of early education, or from whose mind, long engrossed in practical pursuits, the details and niceties of academic knowledge have faded away as the headlands disappear when the mariner bids his native land goodnight."

Such comments were not confined to Northerners who were waving the bloody shirt. Representative McKee of Mississippi objected that

---

[24] *Congressional Globe,* 42nd Congress, 2nd session, p. 1103 (February 17, 1872). This form of competition with college-trained men also troubled the veterans' organizations. See Wallace E. Davies: *Patriotism on Parade* (Cambridge, Mass., 1955), pp. 247, 285–6, 311.

[25] *Congressional Globe,* 42nd Congress, 2nd session, p. 458 (January 18, 1872). Many local bosses, of course, were as troubled as the Congressmen about the effect of competitive examinations on their procedures. "I suppose," objected the Boston boss, Patrick Macguire, apropos a Massachusetts civil-service law, "that if any one of my boys wants to have a position in any of the departments of Boston, to start with I shall have to send him to Harvard College. It is necessary that he should graduate with the highest honors, and I suppose that the youths who are now studying there can look forward to the brilliant career that waits for them in our metropolis when they should have been educated up to the proper point where they are able to handle the pick-axe and the shovel, and all others who don't have the good fortune to be well educated must stand aside and look for positions elsewhere." Quoted in Lucius B. Swift: *Civil Service Reform* (n.p., 1885), p. 10.

educational criteria would make it almost impossible for the less educated sections of the country to capitalize on their old privileges under the geographic criterion for appointment. His complaint, quite candidly put, was that if competence were to be required he would be unable to get jobs for his Mississippi constituents. "Suppose," he said, "some wild mustang girl from New Mexico comes here for a position, and it may be that she does not know whether the Gulf stream runs north or south, or perhaps she thinks it stands on end, and she may answer that the 'Japan current' is closely allied to the English gooseberry, yet although competent for the minor position she seeks, she is sent back home rejected, and the place is given to some spectacled school ma'am who probably has not half as much native sense as the New Mexican."[26] McKee complained:

> I had a constituent here who knew more than your whole civil service board. He was brought up here from Mississippi and they found him incompetent for the lowest grade of clerkship; and yet he is now cashier or teller of one of the largest banks on the Pacific slope. And they gave the appointment to a spectacled pedagogue from Maine, who, as far as business capacity and common sense was concerned, was not fit to be clerk to a bootblack. [Laughter.] That is the way it has been all along.

For a long time the opponents of civil service succeeded in creating in the public mind a conception of civil-service reform which had very little to do with reality but which appealed formidably to egalitarian sentiments, machine cupidity, and anti-intellectualism. E. L. Godkin once remarked that when reform agitation first appeared, it was greeted as simply another of "the thousand visionary attempts to regenerate society with which a certain class of literary men is supposed to beguile its leisure." In the inner political circles, between 1868 and 1878, it was known, with much mingled disgust and amusement, as "snivel service reform." "The reformers were sometimes spoken of as a species of millennarians, and others as weak-minded people, who looked at political society as a sort of Sunday-school which could be managed by mild exhortation and cheap prizes, and whom it was the business of practical men to humor in so far as it could be done harmlessly, but not to argue with."[27] The professional politicians succeeded in persuading themselves that civil-service reform meant favoritism to the college-educated; that it would restrict job-holding to a hereditary college-educated aristocracy; and that all kinds of unreasonable and esoteric questions would be asked on civil-service examinations. (R. R. Bowker pro-

---

[26] *Congressional Globe,* 42nd Congress, 3rd session, p. 1631 (February 22, 1873).

[27] E. L. Godkin: "The Civil Service Reform Controversy," *North American Review,* Vol. CXXXIV (April, 1882), pp. 382–3.

tested that "a great deal of nonsense [is] talked and written about asking a man who had to clean streets questions about ancient history, astronomy, and Sanskrit.") The idea of a literate competitive examination filled the anti-reformers with horror, a horror doubtless shared by many potential job applicants. "Henceforth," declared one of the more articular opponents of reform,[28]

> entrance into the civil service is to be through the narrow portal of competitive examination, practically limiting entry to the graduates of colleges, thus admitting a Pierce and excluding a Lincoln; the favored few thus admitted remaining for life; exempt, likewise, from vicissitudes; advancing, likewise, in a regular gradation, higher and higher; a class separate from the rest of the community, and bound together by a common interest and a common subordination to one man, he also the commander-in-chief of the Army— the President of the United States.

In vain did reformers protest that there was nothing undemocratic about tests open equally to all applicants, especially since the American educational system itself was so democratic, even at the upper levels.[29] In vain did they reprint the texts of examinations which already existed in order to show that potential clerks were not expected to be members of the American Philosophical Society or graduates of the Ivy League colleges. In vain did they produce statistics showing that, for instance, in the New York Customs House, where the competitive examination system had been used before 1881, only a very modest proportion of candidates examined or appointed were college graduates.[30] The grim specter of the educated civil servant haunted the professionals to the very end. Even after President Garfield's assassination, when public sentiment for civil-service reform rapidly mounted, his successor, Chester A. Arthur, professed to Congress his anxiety that civil-service examinations would exalt "mere intellectual proficiency" above other qualities and that experienced men would be at a disadvantage in competing with immature college youths.[31] Senator George H. Pendleton, steering the civil-service reform bill through Congress, found it necessary to reassure the Senate that the system of examinations did not present only "a scholastic test" unfairly favoring the college-bred.[32] Had it not been for the fortuitous shooting of Garfield, it is likely that the

---

[28] William M. Dickson: "The New Political Machine," *North American Review*, Vol. CXXXIV (January 1, 1882), p. 42.

[29] Andrew D. White: "Do the Spoils Belong to the Victor?" *North American Review*, Vol. CXXXIV (February, 1882), p. 129–30.

[30] Godkin: "The Civil Service Reform Controversy," p. 393.

[31] J. R. Richardson: *Messages and Papers of the Presidents*, Vol. X, pp. 46, 48–9.

[32] *Congressional Record*, 47th Congress, 2nd session, pp. 207–8 (December 12, 1882).

reforms embodied in the Pendleton Act would have been delayed for almost a generation.

In the attacks made by the reformers on the professional politicians, one finds a few essential words recurring: *ignorant, vulgar, selfish, corrupt.* To counter such language, the politicians had to have an adequate and appealing answer. It was not merely the conduct of the public debate which was at stake but also their need to salve their own genuine feelings of outrage. Where rapport with the public was concerned, the politicians, of course, had a signal advantage. But if the debate itself were to be accepted in the terms set by the reformers, the politicians would suffer considerably. Like all men living at the fringes of politics, and thus freed of the burdens of decision and responsibility, the reformers found it much easier than the professionals to keep their boasted purity. Most of the reform leaders were men from established families, with at least moderate wealth and secure independent vocations of their own, and not directly dependent upon politics for their livelihood; it was easier for them than for the professionals to maintain the atmosphere of disinterestedness that they felt vital to the public service. Besides, they *were* in fact better educated and more cultivated men.

The politicians and bosses found their answer in crying down the superior education and culture of their critics as political liabilities, and in questioning their adequacy for the difficult and dirty work of day-to-day politics. As the politicians put it, they, the bosses and party workers, had to function in the bitter world of reality in which the common people also had to live and earn their living. This was not the sphere of morals and ideals, of education and culture: it was the hard, masculine sphere of business and politics. The reformers, they said, claimed to be unselfish; but if this was true at all, it was true only because they were alien commentators upon an area of life in which they did not have to work and for which in fact they were unfit. In the hard-driving, competitive, ruthless, materialistic world of the Gilded Age, to be unselfish suggested not purity but a lack of self, a lack of capacity for grappling with reality, a lack of assertion, of masculinity.

Invoking a well-established preconception of the American male, the politicians argued that culture is impractical and men of culture are ineffectual, that culture is feminine and cultivated men tend to be effeminate. Secretly hungry for office and power themselves, and yet lacking in the requisite understanding of practical necessities, the reformers took out their resentment upon those who had succeeded. They were no better than carping and hypocritical censors of office-holders and power-wielders. They were, as James G. Blaine once put it, "conceited, foolish, vain, without knowledge . . . of men. . . . They are noisy but not numerous, pharisaical but not practical, ambitious but not wise, pretentious but not powerful."[33]

The clash between reformers and politicians created in the minds of the professionals a stereotype of the educated man in politics that has never died. It is charmingly illustrated in the sayings, recorded (and perhaps dressed up) by a reporter around the turn of the century, of a candid practitioner of metropolitan politics, George Washington Plunkitt of Tammany Hall. If Tammany leaders were "all bookworms and college professors," Plunkitt declared,[34]

> Tammany might win an election once in four thousand years. Most of the leaders are plain American citizens, of the people and near to the people, and they have all the education they need to whip the dudes who part their name in the middle.... As for the common people of the district, I am at home with them at all times. When I go among them, I don't try to show off my grammar, or talk about the Constitution, or how many volts there is in electricity or make it appear in any way that I am better educated than they are. They wouldn't stand for that sort of thing.

Again:[35]

> Some young men think they can learn how to be successful in politics from books, and they cram their heads with all sorts of college rot. They couldn't make a bigger mistake. Now, understand me, I ain't sayin' nothin' against colleges. I guess they have to exist as long as there's bookworms, and I suppose they do some good in certain ways, but they don't count in politics. In fact, a young man who has gone through the college course is handicapped at the outset. He may succeed in politics, but the chances are 100 to 1 against him.

---

[33] Gail Hamilton: *Biography of James G. Blaine* (Norwich, 1895), p. 491. For a testy attack on literary men and reformers in politics, and their patronizing attitude toward professionals, see Senator Joseph R. Hawley: *Congressional Record,* 47th Congress, 2nd session, p. 242 (December 13, 1882).

[34] William L. Riordon: *Plunkitt of Tammany Hall* (1905; ed. New York, 1948), pp. 60–1. One is reminded here of the techniques of the delightful Brooklyn Democratic leader Peter McGuiness. Challenged for the leadership of his district during the early 1920's by a college graduate who maintained that the community should have a man of culture and refinement as its leader, McGuiness dealt with the newcomer "with a line that is a favorite of connoisseurs of political strategy. At the next meeting McGuiness addressed, he stood silent for a moment, glaring down at the crowd of shirtsleeved laborers and housewives in Hoover aprons until he had their attention. Then he bellowed, 'All of yez that went to Yales or Cornells raise your right hands. . . . The Yales and Cornells can vote for him. The rest of yez vote for me.'" Richard Rovere: "The Big Hello," in *The American Establishment* (New York, 1962), p. 36.

[35] Ibid., p. 10.

It was not enough for the politicians to say that the reformers were hypocritical and impractical. Their cultivation and fastidious manners were taken as evidence that these "namby-pamby, goody-goody gentlemen" who "sip cold tea"[36] were deficient in masculinity. They were on occasion denounced as "political hermaphrodites" (an easy transition from their uncertain location as to political party to an uncertain location as to sex). The waspish Senator Ingalls of Kansas, furious at their lack of party loyalty, once denounced them as "the third sex"—"effeminate without being either masculine or feminine; unable either to beget or bear; possessing neither fecundity nor virility; endowed with the contempt of men and the derision of women, and doomed to sterility, isolation, and extinction."[37]

From the moment the reformers appeared as an organized force in the Liberal Republican movement of 1872, they were denounced by Roscoe Conkling, one of the most flamboyant of the spoilsmen, as a "convention of idealists and professors and sore-heads."[38] Conkling also produced one of the classics of American invective, and spelled out the implications of the charge of deficient masculinity. Conkling's victim was George William Curtis, once a student at the German universities, editor of *Harper's* and a prominent reformer, the friend of such men as Bryant, Lowell, and Sumner, and one of the most prominent advocates of a more aggressive role in politics for educated men. The occasion was the New York State Republican Convention of 1877, at which a battle between bosses and reformers over the party organization came to a head. When Conkling's moment came, he asked: "Who are these men who, in newspapers and elsewhere, are cracking their whips over Republicans and playing school-master to the Republican party and its conscience and convictions?" "Some of them are the man-milliners, the dilettanti and carpet knights of politics," he went on— and the term man-milliners, a reference to the fashion articles that Curtis's magazine had recently started to publish, evoked howls of derisive laughter. After denouncing the reformers for parading "their own thin veneering of superior purity," and ridiculing their alleged treachery and hypocrisy, their "rancid, canting self-righteousness," he

---

[36] A letter to *The New York Times*, June 17, 1880, quoted by R. R. Bowker: *Nation*, Vol. XXXI (July 1, 1880), p. 10.

[37] *Congressional Record*, 49th Congress, 1st session, p. 2786 (March 26, 1886). "They have two recognized functions," the senator said of the third sex. "They sing falsetto, and they are usually selected as the guardians of the seraglios of Oriental despots."

[38] Matthew Josephson: *The Politicos* (New York, 1938), p. 163. Conkling's words are reminiscent of those of the businessman who objected to economic reformers as "philanthropists, professors, and Lady Millionaires." Edward C. Kirkland: *Dream and Thought in the Business Community* (Ithaca, 1956), p. 26.

closed with the remark: "They forget that parties are not built by de-
portment, or by ladies' magazines, or by gush. . . ."[39]

What Plunkitt later suggested when he referred to "dudes that part
their name in the middle" Conkling here made as clear as it was ad-
missible to do.   The cultivated character and precise manners of the
reformers suggested that they were effeminate.   Culture suggested
feminity; and the editorship of a ladies' magazine proved it in Curtis's
case.   The more recent attacks by Senator McCarthy and others upon the
Eastern and English-oriented prep-school personnel of the State Department, associated with charges of homosexuality, are not an altogether novel element in the history of American invective.   That the
term "man-milliners" was understood in this light by many contemporaries is suggested by the fact that though the New York *Tribune*
reported Conkling's speech in full, with the offending word, Conkling's
nephew dropped "man-milliners" from his account of this incident in
the biography of his uncle and substituted asterisks as though he were
omitting an unmistakable obscenity.[40]

What the politician relied upon, as the basis for an unspoken agreement about the improper character of the reformers, was the feeling,
then accepted by practically all men and by most women, that to be
active in political life was a male prerogative, in the sense that women
were excluded from it, and further, that capacity for an effective role
in politics was practically a test of masculinity.   To be active in politics
was a man's business, whereas to be engaged in reform movements
(at least in America) meant constant association with aggressive, reforming, moralizing women—witness the case of the abolitionists.
The common male idea, so often heard in the debate over woman suffrage, was that women would soil and unsex themselves if they entered
the inevitably dirty male world of political activity, about which Senator Ingalls once said that its purification was "an iridescent dream."

If women invaded politics, they would become masculine, just as
men became feminine when they espoused reform.   Horace Bushnell
suggested that if women got the vote and kept it for hundreds of years,
"the very look and temperament of women will be altered."   The
appearance of women would be sharp, their bodies wiry, their voices
shrill, their actions angular and abrupt, and full of self-assertion, will,

---

[39] Alfred R. Conkling: *Life and Letters of Roscoe Conkling* (New York, 1889),
pp. 540–1; for the full account of the incident see pp. 538–49.

[40] See also the attack on Curtis in the Elmira *Advertiser*, October 6, 1877, as
reported in Thomas Collier Platt's *Autobiography* (New York, 1910), pp. 93–5.
Here "a smart boy named Curtis, who parted his hair in the middle like a girl"
and lived in an exclusively feminine environment, ran afoul of a masculine
redhead named Conkling, who beat him up, to the indignation of Curtis's
maiden aunts and all the female neighbors.

boldness, and eagerness for place and power. It could also be expected that in this nightmare of female assertion women would actually "change type physiologically, they will become taller and more brawny, and get bigger hands and feet, and a heavier weight of brain," and would very likely become "thinner, sharp-featured, lank and dry, just as all disappointed, over-instigated natures always are." [41]

In compensation for their political disability, women were always conceded to embody a far greater moral purity than men (though this purity was held to be of a frailer variety);[42] and it was conventionally said that they would make it effective in the world through their role as wives and mothers. So long as they stayed out of politics, the realm of ideals and of purity belonged to them. By the same token, the realm of reality and of dirty dealings, in so far as it must exist, belonged to men; and the reformers who felt that they were bringing purer and more disinterested personal ideas into politics were accused by their opponents of trying to womanize politics, and to mix the spheres of the sexes. Just as women unsexed themselves by entering politics, so reformers unsexed themselves by introducing female standards— i.e., morality—into political life. The old byword for reformers—"long-haired men and short-haired women"—aptly expressed this popular feeling.

The notion that the demand for women's suffrage was perversely unsexing, even dehumanizing, was one of the central themes of Henry James's *The Bostonians*. Like Bushnell, James feared that the male world would be undone by the perverse aggressiveness of women and of feminine principles. His Southern hero, Basil Ransom, bursts out:[43]

> The whole generation is womanized; the masculine tone is passing out of the world; it's a feminine, a nervous, hysterical, chattering, canting age, an age of hollow phrases and false delicacy and exaggerated solicitudes and coddled sensibilities, which, if we don't look out, will usher in the reign of mediocrity, of the feeblest and flattest and the most pretentious that has ever been. The masculine character, the ability to dare and endure, to know

---

[41] Horace Bushnell: *Women's Suffrage: the Reform against Nature* (New York, 1869), pp. 135–6. Cf. p. 56: "The claim of a beard would not be a more radical revolt against nature."

[42] Cf. Bushnell: "We also know that women often show a strange facility of debasement and moral abandonment, when they have once given way consentingly. Men go down by a descent—*facilis descensus*—women by a precipitation. Perhaps the reason is, in part, that more is expected of women and that again because there is more expectancy of truth and sacrifice in the semi-christly, subject state of women than is likely to be looked for in the forward, self-asserting headship of men." Ibid., p. 142.

[43] *The Bostonians* (1886; ed. London, 1952), p. 289.

and yet not fear reality, to look the world in the face and take it for what it is—a very queer and partly very base mixture—that is what I want to preserve, or rather, as I may say, recover. . . .

The world that James had in mind as having already been deprived of its masculine character was not, surely, the world of Jim Fisk, Carnegie, Rockefeller, or the railroad barons, nor the world of the Tweed Ring or Roscoe Conkling; rather it was the world of the cultivated man, whose learning had once been linked with masculine firmness to the life of action and assertion, the Eastern society, epitomized by Boston, which in all America James knew best. There seemed to be an almost painful need in this society for the kind of man who could join the sphere of ideas and moral scruples with the virile qualities of action and assertion.

Whether or not the reformers fully realized it, the stigma of effeminacy and ineffectuality became a handicap to them, a token of their insulation from the main currents of American politics. One of the first to meet this challenge was Theodore Roosevelt. A recruit from the same social and educational strata as the reform leaders, he decided at an early age that the deficiencies charged against them were real, and that if reform was to get anywhere, their type must be replaced by a new and more vigorous kind of leader from the same class. . . .

A citified, commercial civilization, bedeviled by serious depression and troubled for the first time by the fear of decadence, greeted Roosevelt as the harbinger of a new and more vigorous and masculine generation. Roosevelt paved the way for Progressivism by helping to restore prestige to educated patricians who were interested in reform, by reinvesting their type with the male virtues. American men, impelled to feel tough and hard, could respond to this kind of idealism and reform without fearing that they had unmanned themselves. In Roosevelt one finds the archetype of what has become a common American political image: the aspiring politician, suspected of having too gentle an upbringing, too much idealism, or too many intellectual interests, can pass muster if he can point to a record of active military service; if that is lacking, having made the football team may do.

But Roosevelt had accomplished more than the negative service of dispelling the image of the gentleman scholar as effeminate and ineffectual in politics. He had begun to show that this type of man had a useful part to play. In the generation he and his contemporaries were replacing, men of intellect had laid claim to leadership too much on the ground that their social standing and their mental and moral qualities entitled them to it. T. R. and his generation were more disposed to rest their claim on the ground that they performed a distinct and necessary function in the national scheme of things. For them, the role of the scholar in politics was founded upon his possession of certain serviceable skills that were becoming increasingly important to the positive functions of government. The era of the frustrated gentleman-reformer in politics was coming to a close. With the emergence of the Progressive generation, the era of the scholar as expert was about to begin.

14

The Magazine Revolution and Popular Ideas in the Nineties
FRANK LUTHER MOTT

It is perhaps too much to say that in a nation's reading habits may be found its history. But in the newspapers, periodicals, and general literature of a state and an age the student of the past can, by careful probing, discover a portrait of liveliness that belies the statement that "there is nothing so dead as yesterday's newspaper." He can, for example, establish the sociology of reading, the inclination of certain classes toward particular types of literature. From the nature and currency of the publications he canvasses, the student can establish the values of a society, the pattern of change and continuity in its institutions, the interplay between its literature and its historical development.

The door which popular literature opens into history is, in essence, the theme of the following essay on "The Magazine Revolution and Popular Ideas in the Nineties" by Frank Luther Mott, late Dean of the School of Journalism of the University of Missouri. Professor Mott edited several newspapers, wrote a number of books on different aspects of the history of journalism, and was the author of an outstanding History of American Magazines *(5 volumes, 1930–68), for which, in 1939, he received the Pulitzer prize in history. In the essay which follows, Professor Mott explores the four principal areas of concern which dominated the new ten-cent magazine of the 1890's, and relates those areas to broader tendencies in the American scene.*

SOURCE: *The Proceedings of the American Antiquarian Society*, LXIV (April, 1954), 195–214. Reprinted by permission.

One would naturally wish to apply to other periods of our history the suggestions for an understanding of the 1890's that are contained in this essay. For gaining some acquaintance with those other periods, one could not do better than to consult Professor Mott's History of American Magazines. *Most absorbing, certainly, would be an excursion into the values and institutions of our own age by the route of our most popular publications. What should we discover? That we are status-seekers? Overly preoccupied with sex? Worshippers of the "almighty dollar"? Mentally stereotyped by the impact of our television sets? Fearful of the Soviet challenge? Or the reverse of all of these? To what extent would our areas of interest be similar to those of the 1890's? Whatever answers we find, we may be sure that in our popular literature we shall come upon a lively image of the sense of direction and purpose, the hopes and frustrations, the articulated self-consciousness, the social ways and ideas—in sum, the history—of our nation of more than two hundred million people in the 1960's and 1970's.*

Low-priced periodicals were not uncommon from the very beginning of American magazine history, but the ten-cent magazine of the eighteen-nineties was something different. The sudden and overwhelming popularity of such magazines as *McClure's*, the *Cosmopolitan*, and *Munsey's* was more than a movement or a trend or an episode. It upset the established order; it was a revolution in our magazine publishing and reading.

This revolution took place within the framework of the technology, economics, and culture of that decade. The main technological change contributing to the production of the ten-cent magazine was the adaptation of photography to the engraving of printing plates by the half-tone process, which made it possible to produce beautiful illustrations at a tenth of the cost of that which was obtained from woodcuts. The chief economic factor was the Hard Times of the early nineties, which made the people count their pennies, and welcome attractive general magazines which sold for a dime instead of the thirty-five or twenty-five cents they were accustomed to pay. On the cultural side, perhaps the one thing that contributed most to the prosperity of the ten-cent magazine was the remarkably aggressive drive for self-improvement which characterized middle-class society in this decade.

But statements of this kind tend to over-simplify the matter. These things made the way easier for the ten-cent magazine, certainly, but there were many other elements in the picture which interacted with the growth of the cheap magazines. The increase of national advertising, for example, was a tremendous aid to these periodicals; but, on the other hand, the great circulations which the cheap magazines built up made that increase possible. In fact, there were action and reaction and interaction wherever the ten-cent magazine functioned—and this to a far greater extent than had ever been the case with the more expensive monthly or quarterly.

The noble old thirty-five cent magazine had always to aim at the educated and moneyed audience, and naturally it was inclined to be aristocratic in tastes and in political and social attitudes. One must speak in general terms, for there were differences in this ivory-tower aspect of the older magazines—differences, for example, between the *Knickerbocker, Graham's, Harper's,* the *Atlantic,* the *Galaxy,* the *Century,* and *Scribner's*—but as long as the price was kept at thirty-five and twenty-five cents, it can be said that the general literary magazine maintained a certain degree of aloofness as an observer of the passing scene, as well as an esthetic level above that of hoi polloi.

But attend, if you please, to what happens when the magazine descends from the tower of ivory. Mingling with the crowd in the marketplace, it is concerned with the common life of the people, not as picturesque elements, but as matters for understanding and improvement. It becomes a reformer. The entertainment it offers is not always that of cultivated refinement, but it is responsive to popular taste. It enters into an exciting game of give-and-take with the newspapers. It not only becomes a spokesman for popular ideas, but it develops in many cases into an integral part of popular movements.

It is the role which the leading ten-cent magazines played in relation to certain social developments of the nineties that it is proposed to discuss in this essay. The first of these developments is one already referred to—the directed and organized passion for self-improvement, the mass movement toward adult education. To realize the nature and extent of the interplay between the magazines and the agencies for such education, we have to understand, on the one side, what the new ten-cent monthlies were like—the spirit and impact of them—and, on the other, the earnestness and strength of the desire for culture on the part of large groups of the population, and the forms which their quest developed.

Perhaps the best way to suggest the popular appeal of the ten-cent magazine is to summarize in a few words the leading types of content in *McClure's,* which was the best of them. It contained the finest popular fiction of the times, by writers of established literary reputation, as Stevenson, Kipling, Hardy, Zangwill, Conan Doyle, Stephen Crane, O. Henry, and so on. But more important was the nonfiction, with the great Tarbell lives of Napoleon and Lincoln and the exciting articles about new developments in science and transportation by Cleveland Moffett and Henry J. W. Dam. Then there were the great railroading articles and stories by Cy Warman and Herbert Hamblen. Wild animals, exploration, and the search for the North Pole, and later the Klondike discoveries were prominent, with articles by the explorers themselves. But the largest element in S. S. McClure's pattern for a magazine was the exploitation of human personalities. The great Tarbell series, with their portraits; the "Human Documents" department, and many richly illustrated serial biographies and individual profiles and character sketches—these were the essential stuff of the magazine. And remember that all this was accompanied by copious illustration, brilliant and well printed. And finally, text, typography, and illustration combined in a liveliness and freshness of presentation which, however, avoided flippancy.

William Archer, writing of the ten-cent magazines in an English review, spoke of their "extraordinarily vital and stimulating quality," and added: "There is nothing quite like them in the literature of the world—no periodicals which combine such width of popular appeal with such seriousness of aim and thoroughness of workmanship."

Now let us confront these magazines with the culture hunger of hundreds òf thousands of middle-class adults who felt keenly the difference between ten cents and thirty-five cents in a time of financial stringency. The development of American book publishing and, even more clearly, the growth of lending libraries throughout the country, testify to the increase of reading among the people in the nineties. More spectacular was the flowering of great home-study organizations of many kinds.

The Chautauqua Literary and Scientific Circle in 1892 numbered a hundred thousand adults who pursued its prescribed courses of reading and held regular discussion meetings. At least twice a month Father, carrying two folding chairs, and Mother, with the books for current study under her arms, would wend their way to some central private home, there to spend the evening talking with others of the home-town group about the history and culture of some ancient or modern civilization. The C. L. S. C. was an extraordinary movement, by which more than three-quarters of a million adults, over a third of a century, pursued one or more annual courses of reading, chiefly in the humanities. Editor Albert Shaw, in the *Review of Reviews,* called it "the greatest popular educational movement of modern times."

But there were many other such movements: the country was full of them. The Bay View Reading Circle grew from small beginnings at Flint, Michigan, to large proportions. Women's clubs experienced a record-breaking development in the nineties and became a familiar element in American life, and most of them were study clubs in the fields of literature, art, travel, etc. Browning clubs were active and numerous; and there were many independent study groups of men and women, meeting once a month or oftener through the winter, devoted to Shakespeare, current literature and events, local history, and so on. Correspondence Schools scored their first successes in this period.

University Extension, with its lecture courses, institutes, summer sessions, etc., was active at the beginning of the nineties at Johns Hopkins and the universities of Chicago, Wisconsin, Minnesota, and the State of New York. Herbert B. Adams, the chief founder of the American Historical Association, was a leader in this great movement, which was to prove more permanent than most of the others mentioned here. Adams once wrote in a magazine article that University Extension was "the Salvation Army of education."

Now, the passion for information and culture which was the basis for all these organizations welcomed *McClure's* and similar magazines with delight. Self-culture enthusiasts still respected the *Atlantic*, the *Century*, *Harper's*, and *Scribner's*; but they bought *McClure's* and the *Cosmopolitan*. They also bought many other magazines, for the boom in periodical publication started by the ten-centers and aided by the boom in adult education, as well as the expansion of the latter nineties in industry and money and ideas and nearly everything else, made a great era for new magazines. Of these, many catered to the avid desire for information—like the *Review of Reviews*, *Our Day*, *Our Times*, *Self Culture*, *The World To-Day*, *The Progress of the World*, *Current Literature*, and the *Eclectic Magazine*—to name only some leaders among the monthly compends of information and current events. Among the weeklies of this class were the *Literary Digest*, *Public Opinion*, the *Living Age*, the *Pathfinder*, *The Great Round World*, and two shorter-lived journals called by the comprehensive titles, *Knowledge* and *Information*. The former was "A Supplement to the Encyclopedias," and *Current Encyclopedia* was a digest of the Werner *Britannica*. Buffalo was the home of a magazine called *Queries*, which printed long quizzes in various fields and offered prizes for the most correct answers. Many magazines printed quizzes in their back pages, but these were usually related to their own contents.

The C. L. S. C. had its own excellent magazine called the *Chautauquan*, and the Bay View Reading Circle had its *Bay View Magazine*. *Progress*, of Chicago, existed chiefly for its home-study lessons. Such general reviews as the *Arena* and the *Forum* formed their own study clubs, with country-wide organization and prescribed programs. John Brisben Walker's *Cosmopolitan*, however, did more than that. It set up a Correspondence University on a grand scale which was too successful; it was swamped by the tremendous number of students who enrolled at too low a fee. We might extend the catalog of examples of this relationship between the magazines and the adult self-improvement and home-study of the decade, but these will be enough to demonstrate that here was an impressive phenomenon in the development of magazines in the nineties.

Another field in which the ten-cent magazines acted as stimuli with a fairly obvious collective response, and in which again there were many elements and agencies at work with reciprocal action, was that of the Interests of the Young Man. It is probable that the original ten-cent magazines were not precisely aware that they were challenging youth; but editors like McClure, Munsey, and Walker, and the staff writers they drew into their circle, had youthful minds themselves, and their natural intercourse was with youth. The emphasis they all placed on the successful careers of great men, whether in the past or the present; the new discoveries in science and industry, with emphasis on the romance of transportation; and the features and stories about exploration, travel, and adventure—all this set a rich table for youth.

Indeed, any magazine which closely followed the currents of its times, as the ten-cent monthlies did from the first, was bound to challenge youth, for it was a period in which the ideas and aspirations of youth were paramount—a forward-looking, ambitious, hopeful period. This was true especially of the later nineties. The amazing growth of industry and production in general, the new prosperity, the short and triumphant War with Spain, the discovery of gold in the Klondike, the fever for Expansion, the realization of new world power, the progress of the gospel of Manifest Destiny: these were the inspiring factors of fin-de-siècle optimism. It was a mounting fever as the Twentieth Century—the century of unlimited opportunity—approached. "Success" was the device on Youth's banner, the watchword of the new century. Edward Bok wrote in the *Cosmopolitan* as early as 1894 that in the United States "every success is possible, and a man may make of himself just what he may choose." Eventually some of the more dignified and expensive reviews were swept into this collective mass attitude, and one of the most remarkable contributions to its literature was written by Walter Hines Page in launching his magazine *The World's Work* on the eve of the new century. A few lines of this pronunciamento may be quoted:

> The United States is become the richest of all countries. . . . Our commercial supremacy is inevitable . . . The perfection of method and mechanism [in the organization of industry] has changed social ideals and intelligent points of view. It is, in fact, changing the character of man.

Even if the changes which were abroad in the land were not as fundamental as that, they did affect the magazines in many ways. Nearly all the periodicals were ringing joyous changes on the success bells at the turn of the century. Thus Theodore Roosevelt wrote on "Character and Success" for the *Outlook* of March 31, 1900; the reformer B. O. Flower wrote on "Successful Men of the Ages" in his *Arena* for September, 1901; John Holme, the printer-artist, wrote on "Successful Personalities" for the *Cosmopolitan* of November, 1900; "Why One Man Succeeds and His Brother Fails" was a *Ladies' Home Journal* topic in February, 1901, and so on. Ray Stannard Baker, in an article entitled "The New Prosperity" in *McClure's*, pointed out that the year 1899 had been the most successful in the history of the country. President Schurman, of Cornell University, declared in *World's Work* that "the opportunities for young men under the present system of combinations of capital are greater than ever before in the history of the world." Opportunity, youth, success! Such was the magic formula.

The newsstands were crowded with success magazines of many kinds. Some carried the charmed words in their titles: *Young Men's Journal, Opportunity, Successful American, Successward.* In 1897 Orison Swett Marden, the American Samuel Smiles, began his magazine entitled *Success,* which, for a short time in the new century, was not only to preach but to exemplify the theme of its title.

The most important magazine development in this field, while it did not directly involve the ten-cent general monthly, was closely related to the revolution in magazine publishing which occurred in the nineties. The amazing achievement of Cyrus H. K. Curtis with the *Ladies' Home Journal* at ten cents had been one of the guideposts to success which had influenced McClure, Munsey, and Walker in their decision to set that price for their magazines. The *Journal's* circulation kept well ahead of that of any of the general monthlies selling for ten cents through the nineties. When Curtis rather casually bought the bankrupt *Saturday Evening Post* in 1897, he at first made it a kind of weekly *Ladies' Home Journal;* but soon, with the advice and the aggressive editorial direction of George Horace Lorimer, he made it a young man's periodical, at five cents a copy, featuring articles on success in business, discussions of public affairs from the young man's point of view, something about sports and college education, and fiction emphasizing the romance in these topics. The *Post* was full of the Manifest Destiny doctrine. A signed editorial by Maurice Thompson concluded:

> We are revelling in mighty exertion; the waiting world knows not the tremendous reserve of our power. It is exhilarating to feel the nation's muscles expand and harden. Here is a return of the heroic form and force. . . . Patriotism is but another name for growth; it is but a mode of motion toward the consummation of national stature, a part of the sweep upward and onward to that "far-off divine event to which the whole creation moves."

The young and handsome Albert J. Beveridge, spokesman of this gospel in the United States Senate, soon became a leading contributor; Beveridge fitted the *Post,* and the *Post* fitted Beverage. On January 9,

1900, the brilliant young orator from Indiana arose in the Senate and uttered the words that have sometimes been recognized as a classic statement of doctrine:

> Of all our race, God has marked the American people as His chosen Nation to finally lead in the regeneration of the world. This is the divine mission of America, and it holds for us all the profit, all the glory, all the happiness possible to man. We are trustees of the world's progress, guardians of its righteous peace.

It was under the inspiration of such splendid periods in his oratory, but even more under the influence of his frequent contributions to the *Saturday Evening Post,* that many young men came to hold Beveridge as paragon and model.

Though it was indeed a young man's era, and the air was full of inspiration and challenge to youth, the young man sometimes wondered if the trusts, of which he heard more and more, might not tend to reduce opportunities for ambitious beginners. In its second number, *The World's Work* printed an article by Henry Harrison Lewis which carried as its title the query, "Are Young Men's Chances Less?" The author concluded that "there is always room at the top"; but in the next number the editor confessed that though the good old slogan stated a truth, it was "a sort of misleading truth." In fact, the growth of the trusts was alarming, the revelations of slum conditions in the great cities were shocking, the growth of labor unions threatened industrial peace, the farmer was ever the victim of economic injustice.

And so the third area in which the ten-cent group of magazines was active in its inter-relations was that of economic and social reform. For although the latter nineties were a time of "expansionism," of tremendous American self-confidence, of hope and youthful ambition, and of T.R. and the strenuous life, they were also years of comparative heedlessness and ignorance of the world at large, of growing consciousness of social and economic diseases, and of William Jennings Bryan and Eugene Debs. When one reads the files of the fifty leading magazines of the period, one is struck, to be sure, by the vast emphasis on American successful achievement; but one is often even more impressed, especially toward the end of the decade, by the steadily mounting voices of protest and the multiplying programs for reform.

The fact is that the growth of the trusts was alarming to many observers and had furnished campaign issues ever since 1888. Moreover, revelations of shocking conditions in the slums and of poverty and injustice on the farm while the number of millionaires mounted indicated the increasing gap between the rich and poor. The growth of labor unions threatened industrial peace. Socialism gained converts on all levels. And so, to all the self-confidence, the boasts of success, and the youthful ambition, there was a steady and increasing counter-point of dissent and criticism and revolt. It is in this area of exposé and reform that the ten-cent magazines developed a varied set of interests, with actions and reactions.

It is doubtful, however, if any one of the leaders of the cheap-magazine revolution of the nineties possessed what might be called a highly sensitive social conscience. What they did have (McClure especially) was a sensitive perception of what was in the wind—a highly cultivated feeling for whatever was both significant and inter-esting in social, political, and scientific matters. There was, therefore, some probing of abuses by these leaders in the nineties; and when the voices of unrest grew louder at the turn of the century, it was McClure who stumbled upon the "muckraking" formula which, in the next few years, was to enlist the efforts of many sincere reformatory writers and not a few opportunistic scribblers, to do much good and some harm, to make some magazines very prosperous and to wreck others. Yet one should beware of the conclusion that McClure's discovery of a magazine technique of exposure was quite accidental. It came, after all, out of McClure's own characteristic editorial methods, such as locating sensitive and important areas for investigation, studying problems by on-the-spot editors who talked with persons intimately concerned, and publishing one well written and realistic article right on the heels of another.

But the "muckraking" movement was the climax of hundreds of articles in scores of magazines throughout the nineties. It is true that it was the monthlies which had got their start in the ten-cent revolution of the mid-nineties which eventually exploited "muckraking" in the exciting ten years which began with 1903—*McClure's, Munsey's, Cos-mopolitan, Hearst's, Everybody's, Hampton's, Metropolitan,* to mention only the leading monthlies of the movement—but the criticism and data of exposure had built up all through the nineties strong feelings of indignation and outrage in many quarters through articles in a great variety of periodicals.

Warnings of the dangers involved in the growth of trusts, for exam-ple, had been common in such magazines as the *Arena, Twentieth Cen-tury,* and the *North American Review,* and not uncommon in many others. Said the New York *Saturday Globe* as early as 1889: "A thorough examination of the nature, history, and methods of trusts is the most timely of all topics." And ten years later Professor Ernest A. Smith, of Allegheny College, pointing out in the *Chautauquan* an increase of no less than fifty per cent in the capital stock and bonded debt of trusts in only the first two months of 1899, observed: "The tremendous rush for forming new enterprises in this year is of a nature to demand con-sideration, even if it has not, as one writer has put it, created as much

excitement as the blowing up of the *Maine.*" The excitement grew, as the trusts became a political issue in the national campaign of 1900, and the next year *Life* was revising the Catechism:
"Who made the world, Charles?"
"God made the world in 4004 B.C., but it was reorganized in 1901 by James J. Hill, J. Pierpont Morgan, and John D. Rockefeller."
Combinations of wealth were not more alarming, however, than the sufferings of the poor, especially in the slums of the great cities. The magazines gave major attention, all through the nineties, to the varied problems posed by the stupendous growth of large metropolitan centers. Great size was in itself a danger to the society of a city, in the view of some. Percy Stickney Grant, the radical New York preacher, wrote for *Everybody's* about these "social ulcers":

> They swell and fester on the surface of human population, which is healthy only in its sparser distribution. They are full of filth, poverty, and vice. They graduate thieves, murderers, and pandars as naturally as universities graduate scholars. This is not the worst: cities not only produce vice and crime; they also consume virtue. More horrible than a disease, they appear like diabolical personalities which subsist upon the strength, health, virtue, and noble aspiration produced in the country. A city is a Moloch; the fagots of its fires are human bodies and souls.

If this seems extreme, what of Edwin Lawrence Godkin's statement in the *North American Review:* "The most serious question which faces the modern world today is the government of great cities under universal suffrage." In the same journal, Chief Inspector Thomas Byrnes titled an article about New York lodging houses "Nurseries of Crime." Such things led naturally to Lincoln Steffens' "muckraking" series in *McClure's,* "The Shame of the Cities."
Encouraging was the growth of the new science of sociology, and its step-sister, the new profession of Social Service. These movements were not founded upon romantic ideas, oratory, or wishful thinking, but on sound investigative procedures. The *American Journal of Sociology* and the *Annals of the Academy of Political and Social Science* were two of the most significant of the learned journals of the time, and attracted much attention outside academic fields. *Charities* and *Charities Review,* later consolidated into a journal called *Survey,* published much about housing for the poor. *Municipal Affairs,* a review begun in 1897, thought the tremendous national interest in the problems of the city pointed to a "Civic Renaissance." Albert Shaw, editor of the *Review of Reviews,* was a specialist on municipal questions.
Most of the journals just mentioned were almost as much interested in the plight of the farmer as in that of the city dweller. The *Arena,* one of the most reformatory magazines of the nineties, printed much about

economic injustice to the farmer; and it made Hamlin Garland a kind of contributing editor of both fiction and articles on the subject. The sale of farm mortgages, said *Belford's Magazine,* of Chicago, was "a terrible traffic. The mortgages that are sold are really written in blood. They represent the sweat and tears of an utterly hopeless struggle." By the end of the decade, however, land prices rose sharply; and a boom time set in for the farmer and for farm papers.

But the most controversial of the reform movements was that of the organization of labor, with its issues dealing with strikes, the fixed wage, the closed shop, arbitration of disputes, etc. The magazines were, in general, by no means in full sympathy with labor activities. As a rule, they accepted the unions and admitted that they had brought some benefits to the workers; but they were greatly concerned with abuses of labor leadership and management, opposed to the fixed wage, and even more militant against the closed shop. The *Arena* was exceptional in presenting sympathetic studies of the big strikes and defending unionism. Many national unions started their own journals, and the *American Federationist* began in 1894 with Samuel Gompers as editor. Louis F. Post's *The Public* was a good weekly review with strong labor leanings which began in Chicago in 1898. But more typical of the majority was an editorial in the *Saturday Evening Post* shortly after Edwin Markham's poem "The Man With the Hoe" had made a great popular impression. It pointed out that after all, somebody had to perform hard labor, and why get sentimental about his lot? "It may be," philosophized the editorial writer, from his easy chair,

> that those who engender discontent in the hearts of laboring men are worse than the heartless taskmasters. . . . Love, brotherhood, charity, fellowship, humane liberality we can all cultivate; but we can never obliterate the Man With the Hoe until the necessity of the labor-product, of which he is the representative sign, shall cease to exist.

Reform movements of all kinds were active, despite the *American Fabian's* complaint that the prosperous years at the close of the decade made hard times for reform papers! The fact seems to be that what Henry Frank, in the *Arena,* called "an irresistible tide of moral and reformatory thought, sweeping over all the lands of Christendom" characterized all of the final decade of the Nineteenth Century and the first of the Twentieth. Prohibition, divorce, prison reform, and even spelling reform were discussed in leading magazines. The *Journal of the American Medical Association* contained a terrific indictment of the tobacco habit in its number for April 1, 1899, and it was by no means intended as an April Fool joke. Crusades against war, child labor, immigration, and vivisection; and in favor of woman suffrage, religious liberalism, and direct legislation—all these were common. There were several periodicals which served the Bellamy "Nationalist" clubs and Henry George's single-tax cause. It seems rather extraordinary that even conservative reviews gave space to sympathetic presentations of Socialism.

A fourth field in which the ten-cent magazines of the nineties were important, through both direct and reciprocal action, was that of national advertising. It was in the great ten-cent magazines of the nineties that such advertising made its first extensive and spectacular showing, so that *McClure's,* for instance, carried a hundred and fifty pages of "ads" in its number for December, 1895, and ten years later occasionally two hundred pages of them. These figures are to be compared with the ten or a dozen pages of advertising, chiefly of books and other periodicals, which the standard magazines carried in the seventies and early eighties.

It was suggested at the beginning of this paper that the unprecedented extent of the circulations of the ten-cent magazines made this increase of advertising possible. This was unquestionably the case; but, as in every other area of magazine activity which has been considered, there were other factors which reacted with those offered by the growth of the cheap general magazine to produce the observed results. In this instance it was a change in the marketing process which played into the hands of the publishers of the booming ten-centers— a change that grew out of the expanding industrial and fiscal economy of the latter eighties.

Until about 1885 the channel of the marketing process went from manufacturer to jobber to retailer to consumer with much regularity. Advertising, which was aimed (except in trade papers) to reach the consumer, was pretty much limited to the third and fourth stations on this channel; that is, it was performed by the retailer to stimulate the final objective of the whole process—purchase by the consumer. And since the retailer's market was a local one, the newspapers, with their close-to-home circulations, were used for advertising, rather than the nationally or regionally distributed magazines. The marketing-advertising situation thus described is subject to some important exceptions, however. It had been demonstrated long before that consumer advertising by the manufacturer could, in some few fields, create such a demand that retailers would require large quantities of the advertised article from the jobbers; and jobbers, passing the demand back, would turn the manufacturer's advertising dollar into many profit dollars. This was so well recognized in the fields of proprietary medicines and cosmetics that new remedies, soaps, etc., commonly had to be backed by advertising to get themselves established in any large way. Important additions to manufacturer's (national) advertising in the sixties and seventies were sewing machines, pianos, and organs. Book publishers were among the earliest national advertisers, and periodicals themselves took much space, usually on an exchange basis. Farm papers and mail-order journals also made exceptions to the standard marketing-advertising formula.

Indeed, exceptions increased to such an extent in the eighties that it was not surprising to anyone when, with the industrial expansion of the latter eighties, accompanied by the appearance of many new products on the market, national advertising became more and more general. It then came to include such foods as Baker's Cocoa, Royal Baking Powder, Quaker Oats, etc.; such apparel items as W. L. Douglas $3 Shoes, Bay State $3 Pants, Cluett Shirts and Collars, and R & G Corsets; as well as many other things like Sapolio, Pears' Soap, and Scott's Emulsion. All these products and many more were advertised in monthly and weekly magazines and newspapers by their manufacturers in the system which was called by local newspapers "foreign" advertising, but which came increasingly to be known as national, as opposed to local, advertising.

Though the extension of this national marketing effort was not surprising when it came to pass gradually in the late eighties and early nineties, it appeared as an amazing phenomenon in the ten-cent magazines. It then came in as a kind of tidal wave of a returning prosperity and an extraordinary expansion of business of all kinds, making use of larger circulations than had ever before been known, exploiting more articles and devices and equipment for more comfortable, healthful, happy living than readers had ever known or imagined. Thus national advertising entered on the prologue to a golden age.

Many readers found the advertising half of the fat ten-cent magazines quite as interesting as the text half. It was not necessary to mix the "ad" pages confusingly with the text to get them read; they were read anyway. Readers of the nineties were not sated with such announcements; moreover, as one looks those "ads" over today, one finds a certain charm and simplicity in them which later advertising does not quite match. Publishers, seeing what their own pages did for the products of others, used advertising widely to promote their own magazines. Curtis built *Ladies' Home Journal* circulation, and later that of the *Saturday Evening Post,* largely through newspaper advertising. Munsey promoted his *Magazine* in its early months and years as a ten-cent monthly, through copious space in the newspapers; and his example was followed by other publishers. *Printer's Ink,* "the little schoolmaster of advertising," recorded all this advertising history, and itself grew fat and prosperous.

The advertising which flooded into the magazines in the nineties was varied in character. There were the camera "ads," led by those of the Eastman Kodak Company, with their slogan, "You press the button; we do the rest." Phonograph "ads" came later, with the Victrola's "His Master's Voice" picture. Bicycle advertising by many manufacturers was copious: in the March, 1896, number of the *Cosmopolitan* appeared the announcements of no less than thirty-eight makers of bicycles. Foods—especially breakfast cereals, canned beans, pickles, and crackers—were widely advertised. A dozen kinds of soap were made known to readers through trademark pictures and slogans. Bathtubs, too, were pictured and extolled.

All this made the magazines prosperous, and profits from the resultant sales made the manufacturers rich; but the real beneficiaries of the whole system were the readers. Many things which were advertised were useless, and some harmful; but in general this aid to the cheap and rapid distribution of bathtubs and cosmetics and pianos and books and typewriters and phonographs was a great social and economic service. The advertising of the nineties, with all its hideous faults (some of which it was mending through the efforts of publishers and agents) was in many cases pointing the way to better standards of living and the pursuit of happiness. Even soaps doubtless made their contribution to contemporary civilization: certainly Henry Ward Beecher, writing a testimonial for Pears' Soap, thought so:

> If cleanliness is next to Godliness, soap must be considered as a means of Grace, and a clergyman who recommends moral things should be willing to recommend soap. I am told that my commendation of Pears' Soap has opened for it a large sale in the United States. I am willing to stand by every word in favor of it that I have ever uttered. A man must be fastidious indeed who is not satisfied with it.

How important the influence of Sapolio, with its gospel of Spotless Town, or of the Lackawanna Railroad's talk about clean travel, may have been at the turn of the century, it would be hard to tell; but it may be found pleasant at the close of this essay to note brief quotations from the advertising of those two concerns. It was the period of "jingles" in "ads"—a device not unlike the singing radio commercials of a later time. Sapolio, presenting an amusing picture of the dapper Mayor of Spotless Town, has him speak his piece thus:

> I am the Mayor of Spotless Town,
> The brightest man for miles around.
> The shining light of wisdom can
> Reflect from such a polished man,
> And so I say to high and low:
> The brightest use Sapolio.

The Lackawanna Railroad, making a bid for passenger business on its line between Buffalo and New York, featured the fact that it used anthracite instead of bituminous coal for its locomotives. Let us hope that it had some influence in banishing the old coal-soot-laden passenger coaches with its verses about the dainty Phoebe Snow:

> Says Phoebe Snow,
> About to go
> Upon a trip to Buffalo:
> My gown stays white
> From morn till night
> Upon the Road of Anthracite.

It would, of course, be impossible to measure or even estimate the impact of the cheap general illustrated magazines on the society and economy of the eighteen-nineties, or to define the scope of their influence; but this discussion of four areas in which they sustained various important relationships may illustrate their close integration with the life of the period.

THE ERA OF PROGRESSIVISM AND WAR, 1900–1920

15

The Politics of Reform in Municipal Government in the Progressive Era
SAMUEL P. HAYS

From one significant perspective, American history has been a history of recurrent reform. In a general way, we may venture to say that reform has been generated by glaring discrepancies between prevailing institutions and changing social needs and values. But to realize all that the generalization means, we should have to answer carefully, for each reform movement we are studying, the several questions which it clearly invites. What discrepancies had arisen between social institutions and needs, and for what reasons? What ideals did the reformers invoke when they proposed reforms? To what extent were their ideals the same as those of earlier generations, to what extent different? Was the reformers' concept of reform essentially one of restoration or one of innovation? Did they appeal to group interests or to a larger, disinterested, communal morality? What were the social origins of the reformers? Did they have a particular class identity? Was their program a true statement of their intent or a device to achieve aims which they could not publicly express?

During the past two decades, no other reform movement—with the possible exception of the Jacksonian period—has commanded so much attention as that of the Progressive era. It emerged as a focus of historical study both because the papers of important Progressives became increasingly available and because Progressivism was regarded as an immediate pre-

SOURCE: *Pacific Northwest Quarterly*, LV (October, 1964), 157–69. Reprinted by permission.

cursor of the reform movements of our own age. The prevailing view of Progressive reform, the so-called Mowry-Hofstadter thesis, belonged to a consensual orientation toward the American past that was current during the 1950's. The premises of this view were that the Progressives were basically conservative: they belonged to the upper middle class; they felt they had lost control, status, and prestige to the new rich and to labor; they opposed class control and class consciousness; they saw life in moral terms; and they sought the restoration of earlier values.

In recent years, this thesis has been more and more questioned, both by those who accept it in essence but would extend the ranks of the Progressives to include other groups of reformers and by those who feel that the thesis is essentially incorrect. Figuring conspicuously in the latter group is Samuel P. Hays of the University of Pittsburgh, whose essay is reprinted below. A highly intelligent writer on American life during the late nineteenth and early twentieth centuries, as he has shown in **The Response to Industrialism, 1885–1914** *(1957) and* **Conservation and the Gospel of Efficiency** *(1959), Professor Hays is also an advocate of the use of behavioral science in historical research. It is precisely this kind of use that he evidences in the following article, in which he shows that a historian must study not only the rhetoric of reformers but also their political practices, and that Progressivism arose out of "competition for supremacy between two systems of decision-making."*

In refuting the Mowry-Hofstadter thesis and in presenting yet another perspective of the Progressive era, Hays inevitably encourages questions about what he is proposing. How far are the two theses—that of his predecessors and his own—mutually exclusive? The first stresses the Progressives' morality and hopes for realizing the promise of American life, but embraces fully their concern with power. The second stresses political control, but takes great pains to explain the ideology and rhetoric of Progressivism. In pressing the argument that Progressivism was an upperclass rather than a middle-class movement, is not Hays perhaps extending the membership of the first class too broadly and compressing too much the membership of the second? One should recall, for example, that Mowry identified the California Progressives as "fortunate sons of the upper middle class." And when Hays makes professionals central to the municipal reform movement, is he not admitting through the back door the social group he ejected through the front?

It is fair, moreover, to question Hays's insistence on divorcing the ideological struggle from the real one, as well as his view of the ideology of reform as a tactic for achieving power. Is not the rhetoric of democracy its own reality? Could not democratic ideals be appealed to, for introducing innovations into municipal government and for making it efficient? In saying that the corrupt politics of the Progressive era is to be understood in terms of power rather than of morals, is not Hays making a rather specious distinction between the two, one whereby he can better dispute the historiography of his predecessors? Whatever its cause, is not public corruption as much a moral issue as it is an issue of power? And is not Hays's approach one where plus comprendre *tends to become* tout pardonner? *Disquieting too is Hays's assertion that not only later "liberal" historians but also contemporaries of the Progressive movement failed to understand truly the deeper dynamics of a process which only now are we beginning to perceive correctly. And by his invidious use of the word "liberal" in characterizing earlier interpretations of the Progressive movement, what does Hays mean to imply? He does not say.*

The questions we are putting to Professor Hays are their own evidence that he has formulated a challenging thesis. Moreover, his new interpretation of the Progressive era testifies both to our specific and continuing interest in the early twentieth century and to our preoccupation with American reform movements in general. The fact is that the American nation was conceived in more than liberty: it was also conceived in reform. A study of American ideology and American politics must begin with this understanding.

In order to achieve a more complete understanding of social change in the Progressive Era, historians must now undertake a deeper analysis of the practices of economic, political, and social groups. Political ideology alone is no longer satisfactory evidence to describe social patterns because generalizations based upon it, which tend to divide political groups into the moral and the immoral, the rational and the irrational, the efficient and the inefficient, do not square with political practice. Behind this contemporary rhetoric concerning the nature of reform lay patterns of political behavior which were at variance with it. Since an extensive gap separated ideology and practice, we can no longer take the former as an accurate description of the latter, but must reconstruct social behavior from other types of evidence.

Reform in urban government provides one of the most striking examples of this problem of analysis. The demand for change in municipal affairs, whether in terms of over-all reform, such as the commission and city-manager plans, or of more piecemeal modifications, such as the development of city-wide school boards, deeply involved reform ideology. Reformers loudly proclaimed a new structure of municipal government as more moral, more rational, and more efficient and, because it was so, self-evidently more desirable. But precisely because of this emphasis, there seemed to be no need to analyze the political forces behind change. Because the goals of reform were good, its causes were obvious; rather than being the product of particular people and particular ideas in particular situations, they were deeply imbedded in the universal impulses and truths of "progress." Consequently, historians have rarely tried to determine precisely who the municipal reformers were or what they did, but instead have relied on reform ideology as an accurate description of reform practice.

The reform ideology which became the basis of historical analysis is well known. It appears in classic form in Lincoln Steffens' *Shame of the Cities*. The urban political struggle of the Progressive Era, so the argument goes, involved a conflict between public impulses for "good government" against a corrupt alliance of "machine politicians" and "special interests."

During the rapid urbanization of the late nineteenth century, the latter had been free to aggrandize themselves, especially through franchise grants, at the expense of the public. Their power lay primarily in their ability to manipulate the political process, by bribery and corruption, for their own ends. Against such arrangements there gradually arose a public protest, a demand by the public for honest government, for officials who would act for the public rather than for themselves. To accomplish their goals, reformers sought basic modifications in the political system, both in the structure of government and in the manner of selecting public officials. These changes, successful in city after city, enabled the "public interest" to triumph.[1]

Recently, George Mowry, Alfred Chandler, Jr., and Richard Hofstadter have modified this analysis by emphasizing the fact that the impulse for reform did not come from the working class.[2] This might have been suspected from the rather strained efforts of National Municipal League writers in the "Era of Reform" to go out of their way to demonstrate working-class support for commission and city-manager governments.[3] We now know that they clutched at straws, and often erroneously, in order to prove to themselves as well as to the public that municipal reform was a mass movement.

The Mowry-Chandler-Hofstadter writings have further modified older views by asserting that reform in general and municipal reform in particular sprang from a distinctively middle-class movement. This has now become the prevailing view. Its popularity is surprising not only because it is based upon faulty logic and extremely limited evidence, but also because it, too, emphasizes the analysis of ideology rather than practice and fails to contribute much to the understanding of who distinctively were involved in reform and why.

---

[1] See, for example, Clifford W. Patton, *Battle for Municipal Reform* (Washington, D. C., 1940), and Frank Mann Stewart, *A Half-Century of Municipal Reform* (Berkeley, 1950).

[2] George E. Mowry, *The California Progressives* (Berkeley and Los Angeles, 1951), 86–104; Richard Hofstadter, *The Age of Reform* (New York, 1955), 131–269; Alfred D. Chandler, Jr., "The Origins of Progressive Leadership," in Elting Morrison *et al.*, ed., *Letters of Theodore Roosevelt* (Cambridge, 1951–54), VIII, Appendix III, 1462–64.

[3] Harry A. Toulmin, *The City Manager* (New York, 1915), 156–68; Clinton R. Woodruff, *City Government by Commission* (New York, 1911), 243–53.

Ostensibly, the "middle-class" theory of reform is based upon a new type of behavioral evidence, the collective biography, in studies by Mowry of California Progressive party leaders, by Chandler of a nation-wide group of that party's leading figures, and by Hofstadter of four professions—ministers, lawyers, teachers, editors. These studies demonstrate the middle-class nature of reform, but they fail to determine if reformers were distinctively middle class, specifically if they differed from their opponents. One study of 300 political leaders in the state of Iowa, for example, discovered that Progressive party, Old Guard, and Cummins Republicans were all substantially alike, the Progressives differing only in that they were slightly younger than the others and had less political experience.[4] If its opponents were also middle class, then one cannot describe Progressive reform as a phenomenon, the special nature of which can be explained in terms of middle-class characteristics. One cannot explain the distinctive behavior of people in terms of characteristics which are not distinctive to them.

Hofstadter's evidence concerning professional men fails in yet another way to determine the peculiar characteristics of reformers. For he describes ministers, lawyers, teachers, and editors without determining who within these professions became reformers and who did not. Two analytical distinctions might be made. Ministers involved in municipal reform, it appears, came not from all segments of religion, but peculiarly from upper-class churches. They enjoyed the highest prestige and salaries in the religious community and had no reason to feel a loss of "status," as Hofstadter argues. Their role in reform arose from the class character of their religious organizations rather than from the mere fact of their occupation as ministers.[5] Professional men involved in reform (many of whom—engineers, architects, and doctors—Hofstadter did not examine at all) seem to have come especially from the more advanced segments of their professions, from those who sought to apply their specialized knowledge to a wider range of public affairs.[6] Their role in reform is related not to their attempt to defend earlier patterns of culture, but to the working out of the inner dynamics of professionalization in modern society.

---

[4] Eli Daniel Potts, "A Comparative Study of the Leadership of Republican Factions in Iowa, 1904–1914," M.A. thesis (State University of Iowa, 1956). Another satisfactory comparative analysis is contained in William T. Kerr, Jr., "The Progressives of Washington, 1910–12," PNQ, Vol. 55 (1964), 16–27.

[5] Based upon a study of eleven ministers involved in municipal reform in Pittsburgh, who represented exclusively the upper-class Presbyterian and Episcopal churches.

[6] Based upon a study of professional men involved in municipal reform in Pittsburgh, comprising eighty-three doctors, twelve architects, twenty-five educators, and thirteen engineers.

The weakness of the "middle-class" theory of reform stems from the fact that it rests primarily upon ideological evidence, not on a thorough-going description of political practice. Although the studies of Mowry, Chandler, and Hofstadter ostensibly derive from behavioral evidence, they actually derive largely from the extensive expressions of middle-ground ideological position, of the reformers' own descriptions of their contemporary society, and of their expressed fears of both the lower and the upper classes, of the fright of being ground between the millstones of labor and capital.[7]

Such evidence, though it accurately portrays what people thought, does not accurately describe what they did. The great majority of Americans look upon themselves as "middle class" and subscribe to a middle-ground ideology, even though in practice they belong to a great variety of distinct social classes. Such ideologies are not rationalizations or deliberate attempts to deceive. They are natural phenomena of human behavior. But the historian should be especially sensitive to their role so that he will not take evidence of political ideology as an accurate representation of political practice.

In the following account I will summarize evidence in both secondary and primary works concerning the political practices in which municipal reformers were involved. Such an analysis logically can be broken down into three parts, each one corresponding to a step in the traditional argument. First, what was the source of reform? Did it lie in the general public rather than in particular groups? Was it middle class, working class, or perhaps of other composition? Second, what was the reform target of attack? Were reformers primarily interested in ousting the corrupt individual, the political or business leader who made private arrangements at the expense of the public, or were they interested in something else? Third, what political innovations did reformers bring about? Did they seek to expand popular participation in the governmental process?

There is now sufficient evidence to determine the validity of these specific elements of the more general argument. Some of it has been available for several decades; some has appeared more recently; some is presented here for the first time. All of it adds up to the conclusion that reform in municipal government involved a political development far different from what we have assumed in the past.

Available evidence indicates that the source of support for reform in municipal government did not come from the lower or middle classes, but from the upper class. The leading business groups in each city and professional men closely allied with them initiated and dominated

---

[7] See especially Mowry, *The California Progressives.*

municipal movements. Leonard White, in his study of the city manager published in 1927, wrote:

> The opposition to bad government usually comes to a head in the local chamber of commerce. Business men finally acquire the conviction that the growth of their city is being seriously impaired by the failures of city officials to perform their duties efficiently. Looking about for a remedy, they are captivated by the resemblance of the city-manager plan to their corporate form of business organization.[8]

In the 1930's White directed a number of studies of the origin of city-manager government. The resulting reports invariably begin with such statements as, "the Chamber of Commerce spearheaded the movement," or commission government in this city was a "businessmen's government."[9] Of thirty-two cases of city-manager government in Oklahoma examined by Jewell C. Phillips, twenty-nine were initiated either by chambers of commerce or by community committees dominated by businessmen.[10] More recently James Weinstein has presented almost irrefutable evidence that the business community, represented largely by chambers of commerce, was the overwhelming force behind both commission and city-manager movements.[11]

Dominant elements of the business community played a prominent role in another crucial aspect of municipal reform: the Municipal Research Bureau movement.[12] Especially in the larger cities, where they had less success in shaping the structure of government, reformers established centers to conduct research in municipal affairs as a springboard for influence.

The first such organization, the Bureau of Municipal Research of New York City, was founded in 1906; it was financed largely through the efforts of Andrew Carnegie and John D. Rockefeller. An investment banker provided the crucial support in Philadelphia, where a Bureau was founded in 1908. A group of wealthy Chicagoans in 1910 established the Bureau of Public Efficiency, a research agency. John H. Pat-

---

[8] Leonard White, *The City Manager* (Chicago, 1927), ix–x.

[9] Harold A. Stone et al., *City Manager Government in Nine Cities* (Chicago, 1940); Frederick C. Mosher et al., *City Manager Government in Seven Cities* (Chicago, 1940); Harold A. Stone et al., *City Manager Government in the United States* (Chicago, 1940). Cities covered by these studies include: Austin, Texas; Charlotte, North Carolina; Dallas, Texas; Dayton, Ohio; Fredericksburg, Virginia; Jackson, Michigan; Janesville, Wisconsin; Kingsport, Tennessee; Lynchburg, Virginia; Rochester, New York; San Diego, California.

[10] Jewell Cass Phillips, *Operation of the Council-Manager Plan of Government in Oklahoma Cities* (Philadelphia, 1935), 31–39.

[11] James Weinstein, "Organized Business and the City Commission and Manager Movements," *Journal of Southern History*, XXVIII (1962), 166–82.

[12] Norman N. Gill, *Municipal Research Bureaus* (Washington, 1944).

terson of the National Cash Register Company, the leading figure in Dayton municipal reform, financed the Dayton Bureau, founded in 1912. And George Eastman was the driving force behind both the Bureau of Municipal Research and city-manager government in Rochester. In smaller cities data about city government was collected by interested individuals in a more informal way or by chambers of commerce, but in larger cities the task required special support, and prominent businessmen supplied it.

The character of municipal reform is demonstrated more precisely by a brief examination of the movements in Des Moines and Pittsburgh. The Des Moines Commercial Club inaugurated and carefully controlled the drive for the commission form of government.[13] In January, 1906, the Club held a so-called "mass meeting" of business and professional men to secure an enabling act from the state legislature. P. C. Kenyon, president of the Club, selected a Committee of 300, composed principally of business and professional men, to draw up a specific proposal. After the legislature approved their plan, the same committee managed the campaign which persuaded the electorate to accept the commission form of government by a narrow margin in June, 1907.

In this election the lower-income wards of the city opposed the change, the upper-income wards supported it strongly, and the middle-income wards were more evenly divided. In order to control the new government, the Committee of 300, now expanded to 530, sought to determine the nomination and election of the five new commissioners, and to this end they selected an avowedly businessman's slate. Their plans backfired when the voters swept into office a slate of anticommission candidates who now controlled the new commission government.

Proponents of the commission form of government in Des Moines spoke frequently in the name of the "people." But their more explicit statements emphasized their intent that the new plan be a "business system" of government, run by businessmen. The slate of candidates for commissioner endorsed by advocates of the plan was known as the "businessman's ticket." J. W. Hill, president of the committees of 300 and 530, bluntly declared: "The professional politician must be ousted and in his place capable business men chosen to conduct the affairs of the city." I. M. Earle, general counsel of the Bankers Life Association and a prominent figure in the movement, put the point more precisely: "When the plan was adopted it was the intention to get businessmen to run it."

---

[13] This account of the movement for commission government in Des Moines is derived from items in the Des Moines *Register* during the years from 1905 through 1908.

Although reformers used the ideology of popular government, they in no sense meant that all segments of society should be involved equally in municipal decision-making. They meant that their concept of the city's welfare would be best achieved if the business community controlled city government. As one businessman told a labor audience, the businessman's slate represented labor "better than you do yourself."

The composition of the municipal reform movement in Pittsburgh demonstrates its upper-class and professional sources.[14] Here the two principal reform organizations were the Civic Club and the Voters' League. The 745 members of these two organizations came primarily from the upper class. Sixty-five per cent appeared in upper-class directories which contained the names of only 2 per cent of the city's families. Furthermore, many who were not listed in these directories lived in upper-class areas. These reformers, it should be stressed, comprised not an old but a new upper class. Few came from earlier industrial and mercantile families. Most of them had risen to social position from wealth created after 1870 in the iron, steel, electrical equipment, and other industries, and they lived in the newer rather than the older fashionable areas.

Almost half (48 per cent) of the reformers were professional men: doctors, lawyers, ministers, directors of libraries and museums, engineers, architects, private and public school teachers, and college professors. Some of these belonged to the upper class as well, especially the lawyers, ministers, and private school teachers. But for the most part their interest in reform stemmed from the inherent dynamics of their professions rather than from their class connections. They came from the more advanced segments of their organizations, from those in the forefront of the acquisition and application of knowledge. They were not the older professional men, seeking to preserve the past against change; they were in the vanguard of professional life, actively seeking to apply expertise more widely to public affairs.

Pittsburgh reformers included a large segment of businessmen; 52 per cent were bankers and corporation officials or their wives. Among them were the presidents of fourteen large banks and officials of Westinghouse, Pittsburgh Plate Glass, U.S. Steel and its component parts (such as Carnegie Steel, American Bridge, and National Tube),

---

[14] Biographical data constitutes the main source of evidence for this study of Pittsburgh reform leaders. It was found in city directories, social registers, directories of corporate directors, biographical compilations, reports of boards of education, settlement houses, welfare organizations, and similar types of material. Especially valuable was the clipping file maintained at the Carnegie Library of Pittsburgh.

Jones and Laughlin, lesser steel companies (such as Crucible, Pittsburgh, Superior, Lockhart, and H. K. Porter), the H. J. Heinz Company, and the Pittsburgh Coal Company, as well as officials of the Pennsylvania Railroad and the Pittsburgh and Lake Erie. These men were not small businessmen; they directed the most powerful banking and industrial organizations of the city. They represented not the old business community, but industries which had developed and grown primarily within the past fifty years and which had come to dominate the city's economic life.

These business, professional, and upper-class groups who dominated municipal reform movements were all involved in the rationalization and systematization of modern life; they wished a form of government which would be more consistent with the objectives inherent in those developments. The most important single feature of their perspective was the rapid expansion of the geographical scope of affairs which they wished to influence and manipulate, a scope which was no longer limited and narrow, no longer within the confines of pedestrian communities, but was now broad and city-wide, covering the whole range of activities of the metropolitan area.

The migration of the upper class from central to outlying areas created a geographical distance between its residential communities and its economic institutions. To protect the latter required involvement both in local ward affairs and in the larger city government as well. Moreover, upper-class cultural institutions, such as museums, libraries, and symphony orchestras, required an active interest in the larger municipal context from which these institutions drew much of their clientele.

Professional groups, broadening the scope of affairs which they sought to study, measure, or manipulate, also sought to influence the public health, the educational system, or the physical arrangements of the entire city. Their concerns were limitless, not bounded by geography, but as expansive as the professional imagination. Finally, the new industrial community greatly broadened its perspective in governmental affairs because of its new recognition of the way in which factors throughout the city affected business growth. The increasing size and scope of industry, the greater stake in more varied and geographically dispersed facets of city life, the effect of floods on many business concerns, the need to promote traffic flows to and from work for both blue-collar and managerial employees—all contributed to this larger interest. The geographically larger private perspectives of upper-class, professional, and business groups gave rise to a geographically larger public perspective.

These reformers were dissatisfied with existing systems of municipal government. They did not oppose corruption per se—although there was plenty of that. They objected to the structure of government which enabled local and particularistic interests to dominate. Prior to the reforms of the Progressive Era, city government consisted primarily of confederations of local wards, each of which was represented on the city's legislative body. Each ward frequently had its own elementary schools and ward-elected school boards which administered them.

These particularistic interests were the focus of a decentralized political life. City councilmen were local leaders. They spoke for their local areas, the economic interests of their inhabitants, their residential concerns, their educational, recreational, and religious interests—i.e., for those aspects of community life which mattered most to those they represented. They rolled logs in the city council to provide streets, sewers, and other public works for their local areas. They defended the community's cultural practices, its distinctive languages or national customs, its liberal attitude toward liquor, and its saloons and dance halls which served as centers of community life. One observer described this process of representation in Seattle:

> The residents of the hill-tops and the suburbs may not fully appreciate the faithfulness of certain downtown ward councilmen to the interests of their constituents. . . . The people of the state would rise in arms against a senator or representative in Congress who deliberately misrepresented their wishes and imperilled their interests, though he might plead a higher regard for national good. Yet people in other parts of the city seem to forget that under the old system the ward elected councilmen with the idea of procuring service of special benefit to that ward.[15]

In short, pre-reform officials spoke for their constituencies, inevitably their own wards which had elected them, rather than for other sections or groups of the city.

The ward system of government especially gave representation in city affairs to lower- and middle-class groups. Most elected ward officials were from these groups, and they, in turn, constituted the major opposition to reforms in municipal government. In Pittsburgh, for example, immediately prior to the changes in both the city council and the school board in 1911 in which city-wide representation replaced ward representation, only 24 per cent of the 387 members of those bodies represented the same managerial, professional, and banker occupations which dominated the membership of the Civic Club and the Voters' League. The great majority (67 per cent) were small businessmen—grocers, saloonkeepers, livery-stable proprietors, owners of small hotels, druggists—white-collar workers such as clerks and bookkeepers, and skilled and unskilled workmen.[16]

---

[15] *Town Crier* (Seattle), Feb. 18, 1911, p. 13.
[16] Information derived from same sources as cited in footnote 14.

This decentralized system of urban growth and the institutions which arose from it reformers now opposed. Social, professional, and economic life had developed not only in the local wards in a small community context, but also on a larger scale had become highly integrated and organized, giving rise to a superstructure of social organization which lay far above that of ward life and which was sharply divorced from it in both personal contacts and perspective.

By the late nineteenth century, those involved in these larger institutions found that the decentralized system of political life limited their larger objectives. The movement for reform in municipal government, therefore, constituted an attempt by upper-class, advanced professional, and large business groups to take formal political power from the previously dominant lower- and middle-class elements so that they might advance their own conceptions of desirable public policy. These two groups came from entirely different urban worlds, and the political system fashioned by one was no longer acceptable to the other.

Lower- and middle-class groups not only dominated the pre-reform governments, but vigorously opposed reform. It is significant that none of the occupational groups among them, for example, small businessmen or white-collar workers, skilled or unskilled artisans, had important representation in reform organizations thus far examined. The case studies of city-manager government undertaken in the 1930's under the direction of Leonard White detailed in city after city the particular opposition of labor. In their analysis of Jackson, Michigan, the authors of these studies wrote:

> The *Square Deal*, oldest Labor paper in the state, has been consistently against manager government, perhaps largely because labor has felt that with a decentralized government elected on a ward basis it was more likely to have some voice and to receive its share of privileges.[17]

In Janesville, Wisconsin, the small shopkeepers and workingmen on the west and south sides, heavily Catholic and often Irish, opposed the commission plan in 1911 and 1912 and the city-manager plan when adopted in 1923.[18] "In Dallas there is hardly a trace of class consciousness in the Marxian sense," one investigator declared, "yet in city elections the division has been to a great extent along class lines."[19] The commission and city-manager elections were no exceptions. To these authors it seemed a logical reaction, rather than an embarrassing fact that had to be swept away, that workingmen should have opposed municipal reform.[20]

[17] Stone *et al.*, *Nine Cities*, 212.
[18] *Ibid.*, 3–13.
[19] *Ibid.*, 329.
[20] Stone *et al.*, *City Manager Government*, 26, 237–41, for analysis of opposition to city-manager government.

In Des Moines, working-class representatives, who in previous years might have been council members, were conspicuously absent from the "businessman's slate." Workingmen acceptable to reformers could not be found. A workingman's slate of candidates, therefore, appeared to challenge the reform slate. Organized labor, and especially the mineworkers, took the lead; one of their number, Wesley Ash, a deputy sheriff and union member, made "an astonishing run" in the primary, coming in second among a field of more than twenty candidates.[21] In fact, the strength of anticommission candidates in the primary so alarmed reformers that they frantically sought to appease labor.

The day before the final election they modified their platform to pledge both an eight-hour day and an "American standard of wages." They attempted to persuade the voters that their slate consisted of men who represented labor because they had "begun at the bottom of the ladder and made a good climb toward success by their own unaided efforts."[22] But their tactics failed. In the election on March 30, 1908, voters swept into office the entire "opposition" slate. The business and professional community had succeeded in changing the form of government, but not in securing its control. A cartoon in the leading reform newspaper illustrated their disappointment; John Q. Public sat dejectedly and muttered, "Aw, What's the Use?"

The most visible opposition to reform and the most readily available target of reform attack was the so-called "machine," for through the "machine" many different ward communities as well as lower- and middle-income groups joined effectively to influence the central city government. Their private occupational and social life did not naturally involve these groups in larger city-wide activities in the same way as the upper class was involved; hence they lacked access to privately organized economic and social power on which they could construct political power. The "machine" filled this organizational gap.

Yet it should never be forgotten that the social and economic institutions in the wards themselves provided the "machine's" sustaining support and gave it larger significance. When reformers attacked the "machine" as the most visible institutional element of the ward system, they attacked the entire ward form of political organization and the political power of lower- and middle-income groups which lay behind it.

Reformers often gave the impression that they opposed merely the corrupt politician and his "machine." But in a more fundamental way they looked upon the deficiencies of pre-reform political leaders in terms not of their personal shortcomings, but of the limitations in-

---

[21] Des Moines *Register and Leader,* March 17, 1908.
[22] *Ibid.,* March 30, March 28, 1908.

herent in their occupational, institutional, and class positions. In 1911 the Voters' League of Pittsburgh wrote in its pamphlet analyzing the qualifications of candidates that "a man's occupation ought to give a strong indication of his qualifications for membership on a school board."[23]   Certain occupations inherently disqualified a man from serving:

> Employment as ordinary laborer and in the lowest class of mill work would naturally lead to the conclusion that such men did not have sufficient education or business training to act as school directors. . . . Objection might also be made to small shopkeepers, clerks, workmen at many trades, who by lack of educational advantages and business training, could not, no matter how honest, be expected to administer properly the affairs of an educational system, requiring special knowledge, and where millions are spent each year.

These, of course, were precisely the groups which did dominate Pittsburgh government prior to reform.   The League deplored the fact that school boards contained only a small number of "men prominent throughout the city in business life . . . in professional occupations . . . holding positions as managers, secretaries, auditors, superintendents and foremen" and exhorted these classes to participate more actively as candidates for office.

Reformers, therefore, wished not simply to replace bad men with good; they proposed to change the occupational and class origins of decision-makers.   Toward this end they sought innovations in the formal machinery of government which would concentrate political power by sharply centralizing the processes of decision-making rather than distribute it through more popular participation in public affairs. According to the liberal view of the Progressive Era, the major political innovations of reform involved the equalization of political power through the primary, the direct election of public officials, and the initiative, referendum, and recall.   These measures played a large role in the political ideology of the time and were frequently incorporated into new municipal charters.   But they provided at best only an occasional and often incidental process of decision-making.   Far more important in continuous, sustained, day-to-day processes of government were those innovations which centralized decision-making in the hands of fewer and fewer people.

The systematization of municipal government took place on both the executive and the legislative levels.   The strong-mayor and city-manager types became the most widely used examples of the former.   In the first

---

[23] Voters' Civic League of Allegheny County, "Bulletin of the Voters' Civic League of Allegheny County Concerning the Public School System of Pittsburgh," Feb. 14, 1911, pp. 2–3.

decade of the twentieth century, the commission plan had considerable appeal, but its distribution of administrative responsibility among five people gave rise to a demand for a form with more centralized executive power; consequently, the city-manager or the commission-manager variant often replaced it.[24]

A far more pervasive and significant change, however, lay in the centralization of the system of representation, the shift from ward to city-wide election of councils and school boards. Governing bodies so selected, reformers argued, would give less attention to local and particularistic matters and more to affairs of city-wide scope. This shift, an invariable feature of both commission and city-manager plans, was often adopted by itself. In Pittsburgh, for example, the new charter of 1911 provided as the major innovation that a council of twenty-seven, each member elected from a separate ward, be replaced by a council of nine, each elected by the city as a whole.

Cities displayed wide variations in this innovation. Some regrouped wards into larger units but kept the principle of areas of representation smaller than the entire city. Some combined a majority of councilmen elected by wards with additional ones elected at large. All such innovations, however, constituted steps toward the centralization of the system of representation.

Liberal historians have not appreciated the extent to which municipal reform in the Progressive Era involved a debate over the system of representation. The ward form of representation was universally condemned on the grounds that it gave too much influence to the separate units and not enough attention to the larger problems of the city. Harry A. Toulmin, whose book, *The City Manager*, was published by the National Municipal League, stated the case:

> The spirit of sectionalism had dominated the political life of every city. Ward pitted against ward, alderman against alderman, and legislation only effected by "log-rolling" extravagant measures into operation, mulcting the city, but gratifying the greed of constituents, has too long stung the conscience of decent citizenship. This constant treaty-making of factionalism has been no less than a curse. The city manager plan proposes the commendable thing of abolishing wards. The plan is not unique in this for it has been common to many forms of commission government. . . .[25]

---

[24] In the decade 1911 to 1920, 43 per cent of the municipal charters adopted in eleven home rule states involved the commission form and 35 per cent the city-manager form; in the following decade the figures stood at 6 per cent and 71 per cent respectively. The adoption of city-manager charters reached a peak in the years 1918 through 1923 and declined sharply after 1933. See Leonard D. White, "The Future of Public Administration," *Public Management*, XV (1933), 12.

[25] Toulmin, *The City Manager*, 42.

Such a system should be supplanted, the argument usually went, with city-wide representation in which elected officials could consider the city "as a unit." "The new officers are elected," wrote Toulmin, "each to represent all the people. Their duties are so defined that they must administer the corporate business in its entirety, not as a hodge-podge of associated localities."

Behind the debate over the method of representation, however, lay a debate over who should be represented, over whose views of public policy should prevail. Many reform leaders often explicitly, if not implicitly, expressed fear that lower- and middle-income groups had too much influence in decision-making. One Galveston leader, for example, complained about the movement for initiative, referendum, and recall:

> We have in our city a very large number of negroes employed on the docks; we also have a very large number of unskilled white laborers; this city also has more barrooms, according to its population, than any other city in Texas. Under these circumstances it would be extremely difficult to maintain a satisfactory city government where all ordinances must be submitted back to the voters of the city for their ratification and approval.[26]

At the National Municipal League convention of 1907, Rear Admiral F. E. Chadwick (USN Ret.), a leader in the Newport, Rhode Island, movement for municipal reform, spoke to this question even more directly:

> Our present system has excluded in large degree the representation of those who have the city's well-being most at heart. It has brought, in municipalities . . . a government established by the least educated, the least interested class of citizens.
>
> It stands to reason that a man paying $5,000 taxes in a town is more interested in the well-being and development of his town than the man who pays no taxes. . . . It equally stands to reason that the man of the $5,000 tax should be assured a representation in the committee which lays the tax and spends the money which he contributes. . . . Shall we be truly democratic and give the property owner a fair show or shall we develop a tyranny of ignorance which shall crush him.[27]

Municipal reformers thus debated frequently the question of who should be represented as well as the question of what method of representation should be employed.

---

[26] Woodruff, *City Government*, 315. The Galveston commission plan did not contain provisions for the initiative, referendum, or recall, and Galveston commercial groups which had fathered the commission plan opposed movements to include them. In 1911 Governor Colquitt of Texas vetoed a charter bill for Texarkana because it contained such provisions; he maintained that they were "undemocratic" and unnecessary to the success of commission government. *Ibid.*, 314–15.

[27] *Ibid.*, 207–208.

That these two questions were intimately connected was revealed in other reform proposals for representation, proposals which were rarely taken seriously. One suggestion was that a class system of representation be substituted for ward representation. For example, in 1908 one of the prominent candidates for commissioner in Des Moines proposed that the city council be composed of representatives of five classes: educational and ministerial organizations, manufacturers and jobbers, public utility corporations, retail merchants including liquor men, and the Des Moines Trades and Labor Assembly. Such a system would have greatly reduced the influence in the council of both middle- and lower-class groups. The proposal revealed the basic problem confronting business and professional leaders: how to reduce the influence in government of the majority of voters among middle- and lower-income groups.[28]

A growing imbalance between population and representation sharpened the desire of reformers to change from ward to city-wide elections. Despite shifts in population within most cities, neither ward district lines nor the apportionment of city council and school board seats changed frequently. Consequently, older areas of the city, with wards that were small in geographical size and held declining populations (usually lower- and middle-class in composition), continued to be overrepresented, and newer upper-class areas, where population was growing, became increasingly underrepresented. This intensified the reformers' conviction that the structure of government must be changed to give them the voice they needed to make their views on public policy prevail.[29]

It is not insignificant that in some cities (by no means a majority) municipal reform came about outside of the urban electoral process. The original commission government in Galveston was appointed rather than elected. "The failure of previous attempts to secure an efficient city government through the local electorate made the business men of Galveston willing to put the conduct of the city's affairs in the hands of a commission dominated by state-appointed officials."[30] Only in 1903 did the courts force Galveston to elect the members of the commission, an innovation which one writer described as "an abandonment of the commission idea," and which led to the decline of the influence of the business community in the commission government.[31]

In 1911 Pittsburgh voters were not permitted to approve either the

---

[28] Des Moines *Register and Leader,* Jan. 15, 1908.

[29] Voters' Civic League of Allegheny County, "Report on the Voters' League in the Redistricting of the Wards of the City of Pittsburgh" (Pittsburgh, n.d.).

[30] Horace E. Deming, "The Government of American Cities," in Woodruff, *City Government,* 167.

[31] *Ibid.,* 168.

new city charter or the new school board plan, both of which provided for city-wide representation; they were a result of state legislative enactment. The governor appointed the first members of the new city council, but thereafter they were elected. The judges of the court of common pleas, however, and not the voters, selected members of the new school board.

The composition of the new city council and new school board in Pittsburgh, both of which were inaugurated in 1911, revealed the degree to which the shift from ward to city-wide representation produced a change in group representation.[32] Members of the upper class, the advanced professional men, and the large business groups dominated both. Of the fifteen members of the Pittsburgh Board of Education appointed in 1911 and the nine members of the new city council, none were small businessmen or white-collar workers. Each body contained only one person who could remotely be classified as a blue-collar worker; each of these men filled a position specifically but unofficially designed as reserved for a "representative of labor," and each was an official of the Amalgamated Association of Iron, Steel, and Tin Workers. Six of the nine members of the new city council were prominent businessmen, and all six were listed in upper-class directories. Two others were doctors closely associated with the upper class in both professional and social life. The fifteen members of the Board of Education included ten businessmen with city-wide interests, one doctor associated with the upper class, and three women previously active in upper-class public welfare.

Lower- and middle-class elements felt that the new city governments did not represent them.[33] The studies carried out under the direction of Leonard White contain numerous expressions of the way in which the change in the structure of government produced not only a change in the geographical scope of representation, but also in the groups represented. "It is not the policies of the manager or the council they oppose," one researcher declared, "as much as the lack of representation for their economic level and social groups."[34] And another wrote:

> There had been nothing unapproachable about the old ward aldermen. Every voter had a neighbor on the common council who was interested in serving him. The new councilmen, however, made an unfavorable impres-

---

[32] Information derived from same sources as cited in footnote 14.

[33] W. R. Hopkins, city manager of Cleveland, indicated the degree to which the new type of government was more responsive to the business community: "It is undoubtedly easier for a city manager to insist upon acting in accordance with the business interests of the city than it is for a mayor to do the same thing." Quoted in White, *The City Manager*, 13.

[34] Stone *et al.*, *Nine Cities*, 20.

sion on the less well-to-do voters. . . . Election at large made a change that, however desirable in other ways, left the voters in the poorer wards with a feeling that they had been deprived of their share of political importance.[35]

The success of the drive for centralization of administration and representation varied with the size of the city. In the smaller cities, business, professional, and elite groups could easily exercise a dominant influence. Their close ties readily enabled them to shape informal political power which they could transform into formal political power. After the mid-1890's the widespread organization of chambers of commerce provided a base for political action to reform municipal government, resulting in a host of small-city commission and city-manager innovations. In the larger, more heterogeneous cities, whose subcommunities were more dispersed, such community-wide action was extremely difficult. Few commission or city-manager proposals materialized here. Mayors became stronger, and steps were taken toward centralization of representation, but the ward system or some modified version usually persisted. Reformers in large cities often had to rest content with their Municipal Research Bureaus through which they could exert political influence from outside the municipal government.

A central element in the analysis of municipal reform in the Progressive Era is governmental corruption. Should it be understood in moral or political terms? Was it a product of evil men or of particular socio-political circumstances? Reform historians have adopted the former view. Selfish and evil men arose to take advantage of a political arrangement whereby unsystematic government offered many opportunities for personal gain at public expense. The system thrived until the "better elements," "men of intelligence and civic responsibility," or "right-thinking people" ousted the culprits and fashioned a political force which produced decisions in the "public interest." In this scheme of things, corruption in public affairs grew out of individual personal failings and a deficient governmental structure which would not hold those predispositions in check, rather than from the peculiar nature of social forces. The contestants involved were morally defined: evil men who must be driven from power, and good men who must be activated to secure control of municipal affairs.

Public corruption, however, involves political even more than moral considerations. It arises more out of the particular distribution of political power than of personal morality. For corruption is a device to exercise control and influence outside the legal channels of decision-making when those channels are not readily responsive. Most generally, corruption stems from an inconsistency between control of the

---

[35] *Ibid.*, 225.

instruments of formal governmental power and the exercise of informal influence in the community. If powerful groups are denied access to formal power in legitimate ways, they seek access through procedures which the community considers illegitimate. Corrupt government, therefore, does not reflect the genius of evil men, but rather the lack of acceptable means for those who exercise power in the private community to wield the same influence in governmental affairs. It can be understood in the Progressive Era not simply by the preponderance of evil men over good, but by the peculiar nature of the distribution of political power.

The political corruption of the "Era of Reform" arose from the inaccessibility of municipal government to those who were rising in power and influence. Municipal government in the United States developed in the nineteenth century within a context of universal manhood suffrage which decentralized political control. Because all men, whatever their economic, social, or cultural conditions, could vote, leaders who reflected a wide variety of community interests and who represented the views of people of every circumstance arose to guide and direct municipal affairs. Since the majority of urban voters were workingmen or immigrants, the views of those groups carried great and often decisive weight in governmental affairs. Thus, as Herbert Gutman has shown, during strikes in the 1870's city officials were usually friendly to workingmen and refused to use police power to protect strikebreakers.[36]

Ward representation on city councils was an integral part of grassroots influence, for it enabled diverse urban communities, invariably identified with particular geographical areas of the city, to express their views more clearly through councilmen peculiarly receptive to their concerns. There was a direct, reciprocal flow of power between wards and the center of city affairs in which voters felt a relatively close connection with public matters and city leaders gave special attention to their needs.

Within this political system the community's business leaders grew in influence and power as industrialism advanced, only to find that their economic position did not readily admit them to the formal machinery of government. Thus, during strikes, they had to rely on either their own private police, Pinkertons, or the state militia to enforce their use of strikebreakers. They frequently found that city officials did not accept their views of what was best for the city and what direction municipal policies should take. They had developed a common out-

---

[36] Herbert Gutman, "An Iron Workers' Strike in the Ohio Valley, 1873–74," *Ohio Historical Quarterly*, LXVIII (1959), 353–70; "Trouble on the Railroads, 1873–1874: Prelude to the 1877 Crisis," *Labor History*, II (Spring, 1961), 215–36.

look, closely related to their economic activities, that the city's economic expansion should become the prime concern of municipal government, and yet they found that this view had to compete with even more influential views of public policy. They found that political tendencies which arose from universal manhood suffrage and ward representation were not always friendly to their political conceptions and goals and had produced a political system over which they had little control, despite the fact that their economic ventures were the core of the city's prosperity and the hope for future urban growth.

Under such circumstances, businessmen sought other methods of influencing municipal affairs. They did not restrict themselves to the channels of popular election and representation, but frequently applied direct influence—if not verbal persuasion, then bribery and corruption. Thereby arose the graft which Lincoln Steffens recounted in his *Shame of the Cities*. Utilities were only the largest of those business groups and individuals who requested special favors, and the franchises they sought were only the most sensational of the prizes which included such items as favorable tax assessments and rates, the vacating of streets wanted for factory expansion, or permission to operate amid antiliquor and other laws regulating personal behavior. The relationships between business and formal government became a maze of accommodations, a set of political arrangements which grew up because effective power had few legitimate means of accomplishing its ends.

Steffens and subsequent liberal historians, however, misread the significance of these arrangements, emphasizing their personal rather than their more fundamental institutional elements. To them corruption involved personal arrangements between powerful business leaders and powerful "machine" politicians. Just as they did not fully appreciate the significance of the search for political influence by the rising business community as a whole, so they did not see fully the role of the "ward politician." They stressed the argument that the political leader manipulated voters to his own personal ends, that he used constituents rather than reflected their views.

A different approach is now taking root, namely, that the urban political organization was an integral part of community life, expressing its needs and its goals. As Oscar Handlin has said, for example, the "machine" not only fulfilled specific wants, but provided one of the few avenues to success and public recognition available to the immigrant.[37] The political leader's arrangements with businessmen, therefore, were not simply personal agreements between conniving individuals; they were far-reaching accommodations between powerful sets of institutions in industrial America.

---

[37] Oscar Handlin, *The Uprooted* (Boston, 1951), 209–17.

These accommodations, however, proved to be burdensome and unsatisfactory to the business community and to the upper third of socio-economic groups in general. They were expensive; they were wasteful; they were uncertain. Toward the end of the nineteenth century, therefore, business and professional men sought more direct control over municipal government in order to exercise political influence more effectively. They realized their goals in the early twentieth century in the new commission and city-manager forms of government and in the shift from ward to city-wide representation.

These innovations did not always accomplish the objectives that the business community desired because other forces could and often did adjust to the change in governmental structure and reëstablish their influence. But businessmen hoped that reform would enable them to increase their political power, and most frequently it did. In most cases the innovations which were introduced between 1901, when Galveston adopted a commission form of government, and the Great Depression, and especially the city-manager form which reached a height of popularity in the mid-1920's, served as vehicles whereby business and professional leaders moved directly into the inner circles of government, brought into one political system their own power and the formal machinery of government, and dominated municipal affairs for two decades.

Municipal reform in the early twentieth century involves a paradox: the ideology of an extension of political control and the practice of its concentration. While reformers maintained that their movement rested on a wave of popular demands, called their gatherings of business and professional leaders "mass meetings," described their reforms as "part of a world-wide trend toward popular government," and proclaimed an ideology of a popular upheaval against a selfish few, they were in practice shaping the structure of municipal government so that political power would no longer be broadly distributed, but would in fact be more centralized in the hands of a relatively small segment of the population. The paradox became even sharper when new city charters included provisions for the initiative, referendum, and recall. How does the historian cope with this paradox? Does it represent deliberate deception or simply political strategy? Or does it reflect a phenomenon which should be understood rather than explained away?

The expansion of popular involvement in decision-making was frequently a political tactic, not a political system to be established permanently, but a device to secure immediate political victory. The prohibitionist advocacy of the referendum, one of the most extensive sources of support for such a measure,. came from the belief that the referendum would provide the opportunity to outlaw liquor more rapidly. The Anti-Saloon League, therefore, urged local option. But the League was not consistent. Towns which were wet, when faced with a county-wide local-option decision to outlaw liquor, demanded town or township local option to reinstate it. The League objected to this as not the proper application of the referendum idea.

Again, "Progressive" reformers often espoused the direct primary when fighting for nominations for their candidates within the party, but once in control they often became cool to it because it might result in their own defeat. By the same token, many municipal reformers attached the initiative, referendum, and recall to municipal charters often as a device to appease voters who opposed the centralization of representation and executive authority. But, by requiring a high percentage of voters to sign petitions—often 25 to 30 per cent—these innovations could be and were rendered relatively harmless.

More fundamentally, however, the distinction between ideology and practice in municipal reform arose from the different roles which each played. The ideology of democratization of decision-making was negative rather than positive; it served as an instrument of attack against the existing political system rather than as a guide to alternative action. Those who wished to destroy the "machine" and to eliminate party competition in local government widely utilized the theory that these political instruments thwarted public impulses, and thereby shaped the tone of their attack.

But there is little evidence that the ideology represented a faith in a purely democratic system of decision-making or that reformers actually wished, in practice, to substitute direct democracy as a continuing system of sustained decision-making in place of the old. It was used to destroy the political institutions of the lower and middle classes and the political power which those institutions gave rise to, rather than to provide a clear-cut guide for alternative action.[38]

The guide to alternative action lay in the model of the business enterprise. In describing new conditions which they wished to create, reformers drew on the analogy of the "efficient business enterprise," criticizing current practices with the argument that "no business could conduct its affairs that way and remain in business," and calling upon business practices as the guides to improvement. As one student remarked:

---

[38] Clinton Rodgers Woodruff of the National Municipal League even argued that the initiative, referendum, and recall were rarely used. "Their value lies in their existence rather than in their use." Woodruff, *City Government*, 314. It seems apparent that the most widely used of these devices, the referendum, was popularized by legislative bodies when they could not agree or did not want to take responsibility for a decision and sought to pass that responsibility to the general public, rather than because of a faith in the wisdom of popular will.

The folklore of the business elite came by gradual transition to be the symbols of governmental reformers. Efficiency, system, orderliness, budgets, economy, saving, were all injected into the efforts of reformers who sought to remodel municipal government in terms of the great impersonality of corporate enterprise.[39]

Clinton Rodgers Woodruff of the National Municipal League explained that the commission form was "a simple, direct, businesslike way of administering the business affairs of the city . . . an application to city administration of that type of business organization which has been so common and so successful in the field of commerce and industry."[40] The centralization of decision-making which developed in the business corporation was now applied in municipal reform.

The model of the efficient business enterprise, then, rather than the New England town meeting, provided the positive inspiration for the municipal reformer. In giving concrete shape to this model in the strong-mayor, commission, and city-manager plans, reformers engaged in the elaboration of the process of rationalization and systematization inherent in modern science and technology. For in many areas of society, industrialization brought a gradual shift upward in the location of decision-making and the geographical extension of the scope of the area affected by decisions.

Experts in business, in government, and in the professions measured, studied, analyzed, and manipulated ever wider realms of human life, and devices which they used to control such affairs constituted the most fundamental and far-reaching innovations in decision-making in modern America, whether in formal government or in the informal exercise of power in private life. Reformers in the Progressive Era played a major role in shaping this new system. While they expressed an ideology of restoring a previous order, they in fact helped to bring forth a system drastically new.[41]

The drama of reform lay in the competition for supremacy between two systems of decision-making. One system, based upon ward representation and growing out of the practices and ideas of representative government, involved wide latitude for the expression of grassroots impulses and their involvement in the political process. The other grew out of the rationalization of life which came with science and technology, in which decision arose from expert analysis and

---

[39] J. B. Shannon, "County Consolidation," *Annals of the American Academy of Political and Social Science*, Vol. 207 (January, 1940), 168.

[40] Woodruff, *City Government*, 29–30.

[41] Several recent studies emphasize various aspects of this movement. See, for example, Loren Baritz, *Servants of Power* (Middletown, 1960); Raymond E. Callahan, *Education and the Cult of Efficiency* (Chicago, 1962); Samuel P. Hays, *Conservation and the Gospel of Efficiency* (Cambridge, 1959); Dwight Waldo, *The Administrative State* (New York, 1948), 3–61.

flowed from fewer and smaller centers outward to the rest of society. Those who espoused the former looked with fear upon the loss of influence which the latter involved, and those who espoused the latter looked only with disdain upon the wastefulness and inefficiency of the former.

The Progressive Era witnessed rapid strides toward a more centralized system and a relative decline for a more decentralized system. This development constituted an accommodation of forces outside the business community to the political trends within business and professional life rather than vice versa. It involved a tendency for the decision-making processes inherent in science and technology to prevail over those inherent in representative government.

Reformers in the Progressive Era and liberal historians since then misread the nature of the movement to change municipal government because they concentrated upon dramatic and sensational episodes and ignored the analysis of more fundamental political structure, of the persistent relationships of influence and power which grew out of the community's social, ideological, economic, and cultural activities. The reconstruction of these patterns of human relationships and of the changes in them is the historian's most crucial task, for they constitute the central context of historical development. History consists not of erratic and spasmodic fluctuations, of a series of random thoughts and actions, but of patterns of activity and change in which people hold thoughts and actions in common and in which there are close connections between sequences of events. These contexts give rise to a structure of human relationships which pervade all areas of life; for the political historian the most important of these is the structure of the distribution of power and influence.

The structure of political relationships, however, cannot be adequately understood if we concentrate on evidence concerning ideology rather than practice. For it is becoming increasingly clear that ideological evidence is no safe guide to the understanding of practice, that what people thought and said about their society is not necessarily an accurate representation of what they did. The current task of the historian of the Progressive Era is to quit taking the reformers' own description of political practice at its face value and to utilize a wide variety of new types of evidence to reconstruct political practice in its own terms. This is not to argue that ideology is either important or unimportant. It is merely to state that ideological evidence is not appropriate to the discovery of the nature of political practice.

Only by maintaining this clear distinction can the historian successfully investigate the structure of political life in the Progressive Era. And only then can he begin to cope with the most fundamental problem of all: the relationship between political ideology and political practice. For each of these facets of political life must be understood in its own terms, through its own historical record. Each involves a distinct set of historical phenomena. The relationship between them for the Progressive Era is not now clear; it has not been investigated. But it cannot be explored until the conceptual distinction is made clear and evidence tapped which is pertinent to each. Because the nature of political practice has so long been distorted by the use of ideological evidence, the most pressing task is for its investigation through new types of evidence appropriate to it. The reconstruction of the movement for municipal reform can constitute a major step forward toward that goal.

16

Uses of Power
JOHN M. BLUM

The presidency of Theodore Roosevelt illustrates two important points about history: that it moves by accident no less than by design, and that in its movement the role played by the individual is a considerable one. Nominated for vice-president on the Republican ticket in 1900, and to no small degree because some party leaders wanted to get rid of him as governor of New York, Roosevelt became president in September, 1901, upon the assassination of McKinley. Once in office, he demonstrated in short order that the presidential role was defined ultimately by the individual who was playing it. Taking over from McKinley, Roosevelt extended it vastly. He conducted American foreign affairs with vigor and audacity. He established his authority over the leaders of the Republican party. He amplified the president's control of the Congress. Most important, he turned forcefully and decisively to meet the challenge of the new industrial order: to master the pull of forces within it and to resolve the great social problems it had engendered. He proceeded with a full and conscious set of convictions about how

SOURCE: John M. Blum, *The Republican Roosevelt* (Cambridge, Mass.: Harvard University Press, 1954), pp. 106–24. Copyright 1954 by the President and Fellows of Harvard College. Reprinted by permission of the publishers.

the challenge was to be met and, in particular, about what his own part was to be in meeting it.

How he proceeded is the theme of the following chapter from The Republican Roosevelt *(1954), by Professor John Morton Blum of Yale University. Professor Blum is one of the most capable and sophisticated biographers among the coterie of historians in our major universities who are concentrating their efforts on the major political leaders of the twentieth century. He has produced a number of first-rate books as associate editor (with Elting E. Morison):* The Letters of Theodore Roosevelt *(8 volumes, 1951–54); and as author:* Joe Tumulty and the Wilson Era *(1951),* Woodrow Wilson and the Politics of Morality *(1956), and* From the Morgenthau Diaries *(3 volumes, 1959–67).*

In the essay which follows, Professor Blum answers the root questions about Roosevelt's approach, as president, to the new industrial order. What, in Roosevelt's view, were the valid purposes and instrumentalities of governmental power? How did he use power to resolve the problems as well as to coordinate the interests of agriculture, labor, and business? With what success? What were the inadequacies of Roosevelt's larger scheme for the uses of power?

Professor Blum's perceptive essay encourages further thought about the way different American presidents have met the problem of reordering society to accommodate new circumstances. To what extent have they succeeded? How have their respective programs related to the American political tradition? One would, in answering the first question, have to define the terms and criteria that enter into an evaluation of each president's program and of his success in carrying it through. Clearly, for example, the changing estimate of Theodore Roosevelt's achievement by different historians is not entirely a product of new facts about him that they have uncovered. Their estimate, certainly, is as much a product of their own values as of his. As to the second question: one would do well, in classifying a president's approach to the problem of social order as either liberal or conservative, to define quite closely the meaning of these terms. They are used perhaps too broadly and too confusedly. One has, for example, to face up to the paradox that in our political tradition liberalism has been essentially conservative and conservatism has been essentially liberal. Adherents to both political philosophies have subscribed to a broadly common set of principles and have approached these principles pragmatically.

Theodore Roosevelt's program and achievement raise questions concerning the program and achievement of other presidents, who, like himself, were confronted with new conditions and had to use their power to meet them. What were these conditions at other critical points in the American past: in the ages of Washington, Jackson, Lincoln, and Franklin Delano Roosevelt? How did each of these presidents meet them? What were their respective philosophies regarding the nature of the social problems of their times, the role of the president in resolving them, and the purposes and instruments of power?

Is it fair to say, citing the example of Theodore Roosevelt's time, that the greater the power exercised by forces either inside or outside a society, the greater has been the governmental power needed to order and control those forces? Seen in this context, what has been the tendency since Theodore Roosevelt's presidency insofar as the extent and use of governmental power are concerned? Have there been any checks or limits placed upon this power?

Finally, what programs for American social development have been proposed by political leaders today to accommodate the newer domestic and foreign circumstances of our times? What are the nature and extent of the power they have used or plan to use? It is urgent that we consider these questions. For the central issue before us is whether or not the American society which our political leaders propose, and, by their use of power, seek to realize, will be able to meet the challenge of the new world in which we live.

"The word happiness," Lionel Trilling has proposed, "stands at the very center" of liberal thought.[1] It is a word which Theodore Roosevelt used rarely when speaking of himself and almost never when referring to other people. This was not an accident. Roosevelt concerned himself not with happiness but with hard work, duty, power, order. These conditions he valued not as prerequisites for some ultimate happiness but as ends in themselves. All interrelated, they blanketed myriad specifics. Hard work involved, among other things, an identity with task, whether the mining of coal or the writing of history; it was a part of duty and a preliminary of order. Duty demanded a like service to the nation, productive labor, and devoted attention to family. It demanded also physical and intellectual courage, honesty, and constancy. These qualities can produce frightening obstacles to personal happiness. There is a story that Roosevelt, more than two years after the death of his first wife, while contemplating his second marriage, for three days paced in a small guest room of a friend's home, pounding one fist into the other palm, expostulating the while to himself: "I have no constancy. I have no constancy." Not even in love was Roosevelt a liberal.

Roosevelt's politics, certainly, pertained not at all to happiness. There was none of Bentham, none of Mill in his public pronouncements or his private letters. Like those more reflective men, Roosevelt had a good deal of difficulty in defining his beliefs, but manifestly he believed in power and in order. With power he sought to impose order; only with order, he contended, could there be morality.

[1] Lionel Trilling, *The Liberal Imagination* (New York, 1950), p. xii.

Because after his fortieth year Roosevelt experienced no major change of thought, all this, inherent in his early thinking, contained the substance of his behavior as President. But during his Presidency he came better to understand himself, and with this new understanding he formalized, candidly and rather consistently, the principles that underlay his purpose. Distinct long before Herbert Croly wrote his *Promise of American Life,* these principles in 1912 provided Roosevelt with a rationalization, indeed with some motivation, for his devastating departure from the Republican party. Consequently they merit analysis not only in themselves but also as a measure of the conduct of the man.

Roosevelt began with power. Attaining it, he appreciated the chase and the reward. "There inheres in the Presidency," he observed, "more power than in any other office in any great republic or constitutional monarchy of modern times . . ." "I believe," he added, "in a strong executive; I believe in power . . ." This conclusion Roosevelt fortified with Hegelian conviction. The animal energy of that "bore as big as a buffalo" that so distressed Henry Adams provided the very force on which Roosevelt unerringly relied. Heroes, he knew, were not made by epigrams. His audiences of "townspeople, . . . of rough-coated, hardheaded, gaunt, sinewy farmers . . . their wives and daughters and . . . children . . . ," he sensed, "for all the superficial differences between us, down at bottom" had "the same ideals . . ." "I am always sure of reaching them," he confided to John Hay, "in speeches which many of my Harvard friends would think not only homely, but commonplace." "The people who believed in me and trusted me and followed me . . . ," Roosevelt asserted, felt that "I was the man of all others whom they wished to see President." Such confidence sustained heroic moods.

Every executive officer, in particular the President, Roosevelt maintained, "was a steward of the people bound actively and affirmatively to do all he could for the people . . ." He held therefore that, unless specifically forbidden by the Constitution or by law, the President had "to do anything that the needs of the nation demanded . . ." "Under this interpretation of executive power," he recalled, "I did and caused to be done many things not previously done . . . I did not usurp power, but I did greatly broaden the use of executive power." To this interpretation, Roosevelt confessed, his temperament compelled him. So, of course, did his profession; elected or appointed, the bureaucrat would exalt his valleys. Realizing this, the second Charles Francis Adams feared a regulatory bureaucracy as much as he despised the competitive confusion it was intended to stabilize. Not so Roosevelt. He broadened power precisely for the purpose of establishing order.

Throughout his life, Roosevelt displayed a morbid fear of social violence which, he seemed to feel, lay ominously on the margin of normal political life. He convinced himself that William Jennings Bryan,

Eugene V. Debs, the Socialist leader, and Big Bill Haywood of the Industrial Workers of the World had inherited the mission of Marat and Robespierre. This was not just campaign hyperbole. In season and out, with wearing repetition he discovered the Jacobin in each dissenter of his time. To their evil he apposed a twin, the evil of those "malefactors of great wealth" who on lower Broadway held their court of Louis XVI. Unleashed, the energies of these extremes could in conflict wreck society. They had therefore to be curtailed.

To modulate the threatening conflict Roosevelt in part relied upon that indefinite composite which he called national character. He meant by this not only personal morality but also the conglutinations that history prepared, the accepted traditions of political and social behavior by which people imposed order on themselves. Yet these traditions, he recognized, depended heavily upon material conditions which in the twentieth century were changing rapidly. The change Roosevelt welcomed; he foresaw more strength than danger in the new industrialism. But it demanded, he realized, concomitant political changes whose contours tradition could not draw.

If self-imposed order was in his time no longer to be anticipated, it had to be provided from above. This called for strong, disinterested government equipped to define, particularly for a powerful executive prepared to enforce, the revised rules under which the America of immense corporations, of enormous cities, of large associations of labor and farmers could in orderly manner resolve its conflicts. Definition and enforcement were needed at once, for within the lifetime of Roosevelt's older contemporaries social relations had changed "far more rapidly than in the preceding two centuries." The ensuing weaknesses in traditional political behavior strained the fabric of personal morality. In the United States of 1908, the President remarked in his perceptive last annual message to Congress, "the chief breakdown is in dealing with the new relations that arise from the mutualism, the interdependence of our time. Every new social relation begets a new type of wrong-doing—of sin, to use an oldfashioned word—and many years always elapse before society is able to turn this sin into crime which can be effectively punished at law."

Through mutualism itself Roosevelt hoped to stabilize social arrangements. His recommendations were designed first to create a political environment favorable to social and economic combinations which, he believed, the nation needed, and second, ordinarily through responsible administrative agencies, to prescribe the rules for the operation of those combinations. American industry afforded a salubrious example of "the far-reaching, beneficent work" which combination had already accomplished. In steel alone a Spencerian progression from the simple heterogeneous to the complex homogeneous suggested the almost limitless possibilities of power and productivity. Such a progression, Roosevelt believed, neither should nor could be arrested. But it had to be disciplined. Combinations in industry, susceptible as they were to the temptations of unbridled power, had to be made responsible through government to the whole people. They had, furthermore, to be balanced by other, also responsible combinations, voluntarily formed to promote the efficiency of less well organized parts of society. "This is an era," Roosevelt preached, "of federation and combination . . ."

"A simple and poor society," he later postulated, "can exist as a democracy on a basis of sheer individualism. But a rich and complex industrial society cannot so exist; for some individuals, and especially those artificial individuals called corporations, become so very big that the ordinary individual . . . cannot deal with them on terms of equality. It therefore becomes necessary for these ordinary individuals to combine in their turn, first in order to act in their collective capacity through that biggest of all combinations called the government, and second, to act, also in their own self-defense, through private combinations, such as farmers' associations and trade-unions."

Attempting as he did to apply this doctrine to agriculture, labor and industry, Roosevelt envisioned an equilibrium of consolidated interests over which government would preside. To the farmer his purpose appealed least. Roosevelt was, after all, primarily an eastern, urban man. He had never fully understood the dreadful anxieties that underlay the agrarian movements of the 1890's or the deficiencies in national banking and credit arrangements that aggravated farm finance. He developed his program, furthermore, at a time when agricultural prosperity tended to obscure even for farmers the continuing weaknesses of their situation. Nevertheless, much of his advice was sound.

"Farmers must learn," Roosevelt proposed, "the vital need of cooperation with one another. Next to this comes cooperation with the government, and the government can best give its aid through associations of farmers rather than through the individual farmer . . . It is greatly to be wished . . . that associations of farmers could be organized, primarily for business purposes, but also with social ends in view . . . The people of our farming regions must be able to combine among themselves, as the most efficient means of protecting their industry from the highly organized interests which now surround them on every side. A vast field is open for work by co-operative associations of farmers in dealing with the relation of the farm to transportation and to the distribution and manufacture of raw materials. It is only through such combination that American farmers can develop to the full their economic and social power."

Through the Department of Agriculture, within the restrictive limits of its budget and authority, Roosevelt promoted farm co-operatives. To the recommendations of farm associations about changes in national transportation policy he gave a sympathetic hearing. "To ascertain what are the general, economic, social, educational, and sanitary conditions of the open country, and what, if anything, the farmers themselves can do to help themselves, and how the Government can help them," he appointed in 1908 the Country Life Commission. The report of this commission, although ignored by a Congress which refused even to appropriate funds for its printing, was a landmark in national thinking about the melioration of almost every aspect of rural life. To it, as to Roosevelt's own counsel, federal administrations later profitably returned.

Roosevelt intended that farm life should become increasingly institutionalized. While he urged this, he expected the farmers voluntarily to form their own organizations. Still the most individualistic-minded of Americans, they proceeded slowly. He could not command them, as he advised them, to exploit more fully the bicycle and the telephone; he could not force them to emulate the marketing coöperatives of Denmark. Consequently the immediate results of his advice were negligible. When he acted himself, however, instead of simply urging them to act, he accomplished more. His employment of the strength of the government, especially of his office, imposed upon the country a conservation policy from which the farmers, however much they disliked it at the time, ultimately benefited.

Roosevelt sponsored conservation not so much to preserve a domain for agriculture as to preserve and enhance the strength of the whole nation. He was inspired not by farmers and ranchers but by intellectuals and interested commercial groups. Nevertheless, in effect his policy organized an essential element of prosperous rural existence. This it did directly through the irrigation act which compelled its beneficiaries to mutualism. Indirectly, Roosevelt's public power policy, resisting uncontrolled exploitation of water power sites, began to reserve control of power for the federal government. Through government agencies, interests of agriculture could be consolidated and advanced. By "planned and orderly development"—"essential to the best use of every natural resource"—these agencies could define and attain objectives which farmers' organizations, even if they had had the perspicacity to define, lacked the authority to attain. The varied purposes of his power policy, the need to restrain the haphazard and selfish methods of private direction, and the inadequacies of voluntary associations alike persuaded the President that for orderly development order had to be established from above.

Much more favorably than did the farmers, American labor responded to Roosevelt's doctrine of federation and combination. Agrarian spokesmen at the turn of the century, still anti-monopolists in their orientation, proposed to solve the trust problem by disintegrating

industrial combinations.   The representatives of organized labor, on
the contrary, intended to live with big business by bargaining with it.
The general secretary of the United Garment Workers, the head of the
United Mine Workers, and the president of the American Federation
of Labor, among others, accepting the consolidation of industry as inevitable and salutary, sought to lead labor to comparable consolidations
and to persuade government to protect the processes of combination
and negotiation.   Roosevelt spoke, therefore, to a receptive audience
when he maintained that labor should reap "the benefits of organization," that wageworkers had "an entire right to organize" and "a legal
right . . . to refuse to work in company with men who decline to join
their organizations."

Repeatedly Roosevelt acted upon this principle. He drew upon the
advice of the leaders of the railroad brotherhoods and the American
Federation of Labor in fashioning his recommendations to Congress
for legislation to govern the hours and working conditions of women
and children, to extend the eight-hour day, to provide for comprehensive employers' liability, and to improve railroad safety precautions.[2]
During the most celebrated strike of his term in office, his intercession
defended the right of the anthracite miners to bargain collectively.
Continually he endeavored to restrict the use of injunctions, the most
formidable weapon against labor.   The court's order prohibiting boycotting in the Buck's Case he criticized severely; he ordered the Justice
Department to assist an iron molders' local whose strike had been en-
joined. There must, Roosevelt insisted, "be no . . . abuse of the injunctive power as is implied in forbidding laboring men to strive for their
own betterment in peaceful and lawful ways; nor must the injunction
be used merely to aid some big corporation . . . a preliminary injunction
in a labor case, if granted without adequate proof . . . may often settle
the dispute . . . and therefore if improperly granted may do irreparable
wrong . . . I earnestly commend . . . that some way may be devised
which will limit the abuse of injunctions and protect those rights which
from time to time it unwarrantably invades."

---

[2] Roosevelt also agreed with Gompers and other craft union leaders who
argued that mass immigration from the Orient and from southern and eastern
Europe impaired labor's ability to organize. These immigrants—the labor
unionizers held—willing to work for low wages, unfamiliar with American
ways, were difficult if not impossible to organize. To protect American
labor they therefore advocated the restriction of immigration, first of Asiatics,
later also of Europeans. Roosevelt's attitudes toward immigration restriction
were at most times close to those of labor leaders, not so much because they
influenced him as because he shared their prejudices, as did so many Americans. Although he praised some unions for their work in Americanization, he
generally failed to understand that the craft unions could not organize immigrant labor largely because they would not try.

Encouraged to bargain, allowed to strike, the union was to consolidate the interests of labor. This had value for Roosevelt insofar as it promoted efficiency and order. But some unions, like the syndicalist Industrial Workers of the World, cultivated violence; some labor leaders, like the socialist Debs, defending these unions, seemed to Roosevelt to court revolution. To handle such cases, he believed it "wrong altogether to prohibit the use of injunctions," for "there must be no hesitation in dealing with disorder."

The measure of order, difficult at best, Roosevelt would not leave to the judiciary. During and immediately after his tenure, the courts granted injunctions indiscriminately and nullified much of the labor legislation he considered necessary and just. Underwriting as they did the status quo, they prevented the very changes upon which, he felt, a new social equilibrium depended. It was judicial interpretation of labor law that motivated Roosevelt finally to propose the recall of judicial decisions, a system which referred the interpretation of the needs of society to a momentary majority of the people. Conversely, Roosevelt was impatient with the legal impediments to silencing a Debs or a Haywood. Order for him was order. If a man incited violence, if he only endeavored to incite violence, indeed if he merely defended the prerogative of another man to incite violence, Roosevelt yearned at once to stamp him underfoot.

In dealing with radical newspapers and with the syndicalist Western Federation of Miners, Roosevelt, assuming the prerogatives of a steward of the people, decreed from his high office dicta of order with which many peaceable men could not conscientiously agree. By the same standard, while President he initiated a criminal libel suit—a suit presuming an offense against the United States—against a publisher who had criticized him, and he kept in prison without legal sanction a petty criminal who had violated not a law but his concept of the right. Such lawless uses of power, however meritorious or moral their intent, undermined the traditional principles of restraint upon which American order had been built. This created a danger that labor leaders recognized. They had too often been the victims of arbitrary power— ordinarily industrial rather than political—to trust completely any man who proposed himself to decide when their contests were safe and when they were not.

Labor had other reservations about Roosevelt. Just short of the full meaning of his preachments he stopped. On the issue of injunctions, he retreated in 1908 when the Republican National Convention did. Bryan, Brandeis and for a while Woodrow Wilson made no such forced marches. Furthermore, Roosevelt's doctrine of consolidation did not quite possess him. He would consolidate for order and also to establish the prescriptions for morality. But in the end he measured morality by the individual. "The chief factor in the success of each man—," he asserted, "wageworker, farmer, and capitalist alike—must ever be the sum total of his own individual qualities and abilities. Second only to this comes the power of acting in combination or association with others." He judged on this basis that the "legal right" of wageworkers "to refuse to work in company with men who decline to join their organizations" might or might not, "according to circumstances," be a "moral right." There fell the union shop. Roosevelt reserved to himself definition of the moral right. He sustained the open shop in the Government Printing Office because he did not consider the circumstances a proper legal or moral basis for unionization. Where could he or his successor be expected next to draw the line?

The farmers could at once agree with Roosevelt about the primacy of individual qualities. The industrialist, protected by the legal fiction that a corporation—whatever its size—was an individual, could accept this dictum. Not so the labor leader. If the union did not contain every interested individual, its position relative to management suffered, and its victories benefited neutral noncontributors. This for labor leaders was a question not of morality but of money and of power. The President's ambivalence confused their issue.

In Roosevelt's program the farm community found discomforting unfamiliarity; about it union labor entertained anxious doubts. Businessmen were more enthusiastic, for from industry and transportation Roosevelt took his model. With accelerating tempo for two generations men of business had made consolidation their instrument not only of profits but also, more significantly, of order. Abandoning the insecurity and debilitation of competition, the enterprising in rails, steel, oil, copper, tobacco, sugar, salt—the list seems endless—had, after strife, in each industry organized stable structures. Their own achievement they admired. It was, they testified at symposiums on trusts, to congressional committees, in essays, memoirs and commencement addresses, the necessary and efficient way of business life, perhaps the only way of any life. With few exceptions they wished to have their institutions left alone. Here only did Roosevelt disagree. Because the consolidations were capable of doing much that was bad as well as much that was good, they had to be supervised. But they were not to be destroyed. "In curbing and regulating the combinations of capital which are . . . injurious . . . ," he instructed Congress in his second annual message, "we must be careful not to stop the great enterprises which have legitimately reduced the cost of production, not to abandon the place which our country has won in the leadership of the international industrial world . . ."

Again and again during his Presidency Roosevelt made the distinction between size and behavior that characterized his speeches of 1912 on the regulation of industry. For the orderly system of control in which he believed he first shaped his railroad policy. In developing that policy, he announced his preference for supervised pooling as an efficient regulatory device. Enlarging his thesis, he asserted late in 1911 that "nothing of importance is gained by breaking up a huge inter-State and international industrial organization *which has not offended otherwise than by its size* . . . Those who would seek to restore the days of unlimited and uncontrolled competition . . . are attempting not only the impossible, but what, if possible, would be undesirable." "Business cannot be successfully conducted," he wrote in the same article, "in accordance with the practices and theories of sixty years ago unless we abolish steam, electricity, big cities, and, in short, not only all modern business and modern industrial conditions, but all the modern conditions of our civilization." This statement recognized association-alism as being as much a part of modern life as were the physical conditions that compelled it. Roosevelt also realized that, just as government could best supply a "planned and orderly development" of natural resources, so was oligopoly distinguished by its ability to provide experts to plan and to allocate from profits adequate resources to implement their plans—by its ability, therefore, to keep order without stultification.

But business had "to be controlled in the interest of the general public" and this could be accomplished in only one way—"by giving adequate power of control to the one sovereignty capable of exercising such power—the National Government." As an initial means for this control Roosevelt led Congress to establish the Bureau of Corporations. In his long struggle for the Hepburn Act he went considerably further. He next concluded and soon specifically proposed that "what is needed is the creation of a Federal administrative body with full power to do for ordinary inter-State industrial business carried on on a large scale what the Inter-State Commerce Commission now does for inter-State transportation business."

After leaving the Presidency, in the columns of *The Outlook* Roosevelt elaborated his plan. He would "regulate big corporations in thoroughgoing and effective fashion, so as to help legitimate business as an incident to thoroughly and completely safeguarding the interests of the people as a whole." The antitrust law, designed and interpreted "to restore business to the competitive conditions of the middle of the last century," could not "meet the whole situation." Size did indeed "make a corporation fraught with potential menace to the community," but the community could "exercise through its administrative . . . officers a strict supervision . . . to see that it does not go wrong," "to insure . . . business skill being exercised in the interest of the public . . ."

Criticizing the suit initiated by the Taft Administration against the United States Steel Corporation, and deploring the vagueness of the Supreme Court's "rule of reason" in the Standard Oil and tobacco cases, Roosevelt explained how "continuous administrative action" might operate. The commission to regulate corporations was to have the power to regulate the issue of securities, thereby to prevent overcapitalization; to compel publicity of accounts, thereby to reveal the detailed techniques of business procedures; and to investigate any business activity. If investigation disclosed the existence of monopoly —of a consolidation that could control the prices and productivity of an industry—the commission was to have two alternatives. If unethical practices had produced monopoly—Roosevelt cited the oil and tobacco industries as examples of this—the monopoly should be dissolved under the Sherman Act. If, however, the monopoly resulted from natural growth—Roosevelt had in mind the United States Steel Corporation and the International Harvester Company—the commission was to control it by setting maximum prices for its products, just as the I.C.C. set maximum freight rates. This was not all. Believing that administrative control should "indirectly or directly extend to . . . all questions connected with . . . [the] treatment of . . . employees," he proposed that the commission should have authority over hours, wages, and other conditions of labor.

Within each industry, then, consolidation was to establish order; acting in the public interest, the federal executive was to insure equity in this order. This fitted the grand scheme. It also offered to farm and labor groups, through the presumed disinterestedness of government, a countervailing force against the most advanced and, at that time, least controlled social group. By consolidation and administration Roosevelt would punish sin and achieve stability. To discipline consolidation, to make possible administration, his first requisite was power. The cycle was complete.

The question remains of how well this arrangement could be expected to function. Even a sampling of evidence suggests that it raised problems as large as those it presumed to solve. There was, for one, the problem of the natural growth of industrial combinations. Roosevelt considered it, in general terms, desirable. He believed, clearly, that an administrative agency could better judge what was natural growth than could the courts. Furthermore, as his relations with his Attorneys General and his directions to the chairman of the Interstate Commerce Commission indicate, he had considerable confidence in his own capacity to make administrative decisions pertinent to transportation and industry. How then explain the suit against the Northern Securities Company? The defendants in that case had by forming a holding company combined into a potentially efficient regional system the basic units of railway transportation in the Northwest. Railways had for decades been consolidating, naturally enough in the logic of railroad economics. The Northern Securities combination restored financial order among the rivals it merged and seemed capable of becoming a useful part of an orderly, integrated transportation network. Yet in 1902 Roosevelt proceeded against it. One suspects that he would have done so even if the I.C.C. at that time had had the authority to set maximum rates.

Two major considerations apparently motivated Roosevelt. First, the farmers of the Northwest and their local political representatives wanted the holding company dissolved. It was good politics for Roosevelt to attack it. Second, as Roosevelt recalled in his autobiography, "the absolutely vital question" of "whether the government had power to control [corporations] . . . at all . . . had not yet been decided . . . A decision of the Supreme Court [in the E. C. Knight case] had, with seeming definiteness, settled that the National Government had not the power." "This decision," Roosevelt continued, alluding to his prosecution of the Northern Securities Company, "I caused to be annulled . . ." He attacked to establish the government's power, for the while his power; he selected a corporation indisputably engaged in interstate commerce; he deliberately chose to charge a hill made vulnerable by popular opinion. Particularly when used by a man who has and loves power, such criteria may become terrifying.

This possibility Roosevelt intended partially to avoid by his reliance upon experts. Presumably the specialists who were to staff a regulatory commission would be restrained by the data they commanded. Unhappily this need not be the case. Emanating in large degree from the organizations to be controlled, the data explored by administrative commissions can often capture them. In such a pass, regulation may approach consent, and stability become stultification. Nor do experts, any more than other men, live by data alone. Besides common colds and ulcers, they develop loyalties and habits. In government, as in business or in education, administrators become to some extent victims of their institutions. For many of them, lines of authority and procedure come to have an attraction of their own, an attraction that frequently induces a soporific insistence on inert routine, a fatal disinclination to innovation, sometimes to formalized action beyond the shuffling of bureaucratic dust.

Furthermore, even meaningful, objective data and personal energy and imagination do not necessarily make regulation by administration what Roosevelt thought it might be. He seemed to presume that politics would stop at the commission's water line. In a sense this is true. Railroads petitioning the I.C.C. may in that process be at once all

Federalists, all Republicans. But in another sense it is not true. The conflicting interests whose reconciliation politics must effect continue to conflict before the tribunals of administration. In a contest behind closed doors among spokesmen of management, labor and government, the adroit politician will ordinarily prevail.

The possibility remains that the problems of competition, consolidation and control can be resolved more equitably—though perhaps with more waste—in the open environments provided by the legislative or the adversary process. If it is hard to find good congressmen and judges, so it is hard to find good commissioners. And whatever the deficiencies of parliaments and courts, they concern themselves with concrete rules of conduct, written for all to see, by which behavior can be measured. These rules pertain, moreover, not only to citizens and corporations, but also to their public servants.

The conclusion imperiously suggests itself that Roosevelt did not want to be controlled, that he did not want to be inhibited by a body of law, whether or not it was properly interpreted, nor delayed by the impedance of legislatures. He proposed to govern. Basically this was also the desire of the leaders of American industry and finance. Relentless agents of consolidation, they imposed and administered orders of their own. Many of them were willing in the interest of industrial peace to go a long way in condoning combinations formed by union labor. With the leaders of these newer orders they were then prepared, man to man, to bargain. Some of them foresaw that in the society they molded, big government might have to provide balance. Most of them, however, as was the case with Morgan when Roosevelt moved against the Northern Securities Company, thought that they could bargain, man to man, with government. Here they miscalculated. Their rule began to fade when Roosevelt began to make of government a superior rather than a negotiating power.

Yet intellectually and emotionally he was always more one of them than was he an agrarian reformer or a partner of little business and of labor—a Bryan or a La Follette or a Brandeis. Perhaps with a sense of this affinity to men of business, Roosevelt called himself a conservative; and with reference to his difference—to his insistence that the governing was the government's—he added that a true conservative was a progressive. This was the position also of George W. Perkins, who for a time personified articulate finance; of Frank Munsey, consolidator of journalism, like Perkins a Bull Mooser; of Herbert Croly, who promised to American life little that Roosevelt had not already offered; of Brooks Adams, who would have arrested the disintegration of a democracy he never understood by consolidation, conservation, and administration—the very trinity of Roosevelt. To champion consolidation as a means to order, to believe in administration and to practice it well, this was the creed of a business elite in the early century and of that conservative intelligentsia they helped to inspire.

It rested upon a feeling about power that J. Pierpont Morgan, prodded by a congressional committee, disclosed, a feeling to which Roosevelt thoroughly subscribed. Morgan saw nothing wrong about the scope of his power, for he maintained that his morality controlled it. He also arranged that the specialists in his house helped exercise it. Roosevelt made a like claim and like arrangements. Yet Morgan was neither virtuous nor successful in his ventures with the New Haven railroad, and Roosevelt was just as vulnerable to failures of the soul and errors of the flesh. In a nation democratic by intent, Morgan's responsibility to a limited number of investors made his power less acceptable than did Roosevelt's responsibility to the whole electorate, but if their power was relatively responsible, it was in both cases absolutely corruptible.

To his great credit and doubtless greater pain, Roosevelt, understanding this, surrendered his power. Explaining his decision not to be a candidate in 1908, Roosevelt wrote: "I don't think that any harm comes from the concentration of power in one man's hands, provided the holder does not keep it for more than a certain, definite time, and then returns to the people from whom he sprang." This decision was a large achievement of restraint. Roosevelt could certainly have had the Republican nomination and would probably have won the election. The temptations to continue were enormous. Nevertheless he declined. This strength of character supported strongly the claims he made to the use of power; yet it was not enough.

Suppose only that Roosevelt was human and fallible—he need not have been paranoid or depraved, fallibility is here enough—and he claimed too much. Four years or eight years or twelve years, the number of terms is unimportant, may be in the history of this nation a brief and placid time or a tempestuous eternity. Roosevelt, it happened, ruled in a time of relative quiet. Even then he made mistakes. He made perhaps his worst mistakes, though he endeavored to be moral and informed, when his power was least restrained—mistakes possibly more of principle than of policy, but mistakes about which Americans since have often been ashamed: the episode in Panama for one, or the criminal libel suit against Pulitzer for his misinterpretation of that episode. During the last years of his life, after his power was gone, Roosevelt exhibited the characteristics that least became him, prejudices of mind and traits of personality that he had subdued while he felt the responsibilities of office. In office in time of turmoil he might not have conquered them. So too with any man. But Roosevelt especially may have benefited from the limits on Presidential power which men who understood the problem in 1787 created. When he had to proceed with sensitivity for the constitutional balances to his power, the will of Congress and of the courts—or, indeed, for the institutional balances within his party—Roosevelt's performance was noteworthy. Then he demonstrated perception, knowledge, principle of a kind, energy tempered with restraint.

Consolidation, administration, stability—for these he used his power, but they turned on power itself, and power, while it must be, must not be all. This Roosevelt's foreign policy . . . also suggested. Coming back to the beginning, perhaps power particularly must not be all when it promises hard work, duty, order, morality—even welfare —but never mentions happiness. There was strength in Roosevelt's structure and potential for contentment, but in chancing very little, his order risked too much. The wonder is, intrepid though he was, that he never really knew this.

17

The South and the "New Freedom": An Interpretation
ARTHUR S. LINK

Woodrow Wilson stands clearly in the line of our great political leaders. But just where does he stand? And what, indeed, do we mean by a great political leader? What is the role a great leader plays in the American democratic process? Does he articulate great causes? Does he march in the van of important movements? Or is he molded by events rather than being their molder? Is the essence of the great leader that he is, paradoxically, the great follower? And how are we to form an estimate of his greatness? What criteria shall we use? One need only appose Woodrow Wilson to Theodore Roosevelt to understand the difficulty of defining what makes a great leader great. These men, it would seem, were substantially different in their

SOURCE: *The American Scholar*, XX (Summer, 1951), 314–24. Copyright 1951 by the United Chapters of Phi Beta Kappa. Reprinted by permission of the publishers and author.

personal qualities, their views of the presidency, their philosophies of government, and the nature of their achievement. And yet, it is clear, both were great political leaders.

Some very helpful and revealing suggestions concerning Woodrow Wilson's leadership and achievement are offered in the following essay by Arthur S. Link, Professor of History at Princeton University. The foremost Wilson scholar of our times, Professor Link is engaged in a large-scale biography of the American president, of which five volumes, covering Wilson's career up to America's entry into World War I, have thus far been published. Among Professor Link's many other writings is his **Woodrow Wilson and the Progressive Era, 1910–1917** *(1954), an important contribution to the New American Nation Series. Professor Link is also editor of the Wilson papers, which are being published under the sponsorship of the Woodrow Wilson Foundation; four volumes, covering the years from 1856 to 1885, have thus far appeared (1966–68). In the essay that follows, Link analyzes one of Wilson's principal achievements: his program of domestic reform.*

Historians have long been aware of the fact that Wilson's campaign in 1912 proposed a liberal philosophy which he called the New Freedom and that when he took office several acts of a basically progressive nature were passed. What historians have not adequately understood was the nature of the New Freedom, the nature of the progressive program that was enacted during the first Wilson administration, the relevance of the philosophy to the program, and the role of Wilson in translating the former into the latter. These points Professor Link undertakes to explain in his essay, in which he makes it quite clear that the New Freedom was one thing and the progressive program enacted under Wilson quite another. He also makes it clear that the transformation of the philosophy into the program was a fascinating process of political chemistry.

It is important for us to study Woodrow Wilson, as an aid to understanding the role of the leader in a democracy as well as the democratic process itself. What qualities, we should like to know, does democracy require for leadership? Does the leader represent the collective will? How well has the patrician fared as leader? The scholar? The businessman? To what extent is a great leader a man of morality, to what extent a man of practical purpose? Is it fair to say that Wilson succeeded insofar as he reduced principle to politics and failed insofar as he tried to reduce politics to principle? And how far would this explain the degree of success or failure of other major presidents, such as Jefferson and Lincoln, who, cast in a role similar to Wilson's, had a moral lesson to teach to the world of practical politics?

A study of Woodrow Wilson is important also because the lesson he was trying to teach is one which, since his day, we have ever more desperately been trying to learn. The lesson has to do with the principles of international

*organization and with America's part in insuring their fulfillment. If the
estimate that historians have set on Wilson has undergone considerable
change since his own day, much of it is to be attributed to the changing
sentiments of each successive decade about the validity of his plans for a
new international order and about the way he sought to realize those plans.
Historians today tend, in the main, to see Wilson's role as a double one, as
the prophet of the world order and world peace, and as the statesman who
sought to realize his prophecy. If they explain, decry, or lament the failure
of the statesman, they embrace the vision of the prophet. As Arthur Link
puts it in* Wilson the Diplomatist *(Baltimore: The Johns Hopkins Press,
1957), it is the great political leader as prophet "who survives in history,
in the hopes and aspirations of mankind and in whatever ideals of international service that the American people still cherish. One thing is certain,
now that men have the power to sear virtually the entire face of the earth:
The prophet of 1919 was right in his larger vision; the challenge that
he raised then is today no less real and no less urgent than it was in his
own time."*

The election of Woodrow Wilson and Democratic majorities in the
House and Senate in 1912 confronted the Democrats of the South with
their most serious challenge since before the Civil War. They had come
to power more because of the disruption of the Republican party than
because their party now represented the majority opinion of the
country, and the future of the Democratic party for many years to come
would depend upon their performance during the next two years. But
the question whether they were not too much rent by personal factionalism and too sectionally conscious to govern in the national interest
remained yet to be answered.

Southern Democrats in 1913 controlled practically all important congressional committees; they had a large majority in the Democratic
caucuses in both houses; they had a president apparently responsive to
their wishes, and they had a goodly representation in the cabinet.
Judged by all superficial appearances, at least, the South was "in the
saddle." These, however, were only the outward signs of control. The
fact that Southerners happened to be chairmen of certain committees
may or may not be important. The important question is whether
they used the power they possessed to achieve political and economic
objectives that the South especially desired, and whether they helped
to shape the character of Wilsonian reform.

Wilson came to the presidency in 1913 with a clear conception of
what the Democratic party should do to right the wrongs that special
privilege had allegedly perpetrated through the Republican party. He
would have the Democrats revise the tariff to eliminate all features of
special privilege to domestic industries, bring the national banks into

effective cooperation and control, and work out a new code for business in order to restore competition and make impossible the misuse of power by the giant corporations. This was the sum and substance of the "New Freedom." The political and economic millennium was to be achieved by these simple expedients, all of which were based upon the assumption implicit in Wilson's campaign addresses of 1912, namely, that the limits of federal authority under the Constitution would not permit, and wise statesmanship would not desire, the extension of federal authority directly into business operations or the use of that authority to change the social and economic relationships then existing among the various interest groups.

Wilson originally conceived of the New Freedom as the political means of implementing the doctrines of laissez-faire, by removing all kinds of special class legislation. It was, therefore, a program intended to meet the needs primarily of the business community. There was nothing in it for the farmers or laborers directly, although these groups presumably would benefit from lower tariff rates and the restoration of competition in business. But Wilson had no more idea of legislating to advance the interests of these particular groups than he did of granting subsidies to American manufacturers. It can be said, in brief, that the Wilsonian program had the one supreme objective of taking the government out of the business of subsidizing and directly regulating economic activity and of taking the country back to some mythical age when there was a perfect natural identification of economic interests.

The most significant fact about the first Wilson administration is that the New Freedom, as it was originally conceived by its author, survived for only a few months. It required only short contact with reality to convince Wilson that his elaborate doctrines of 1912 were inadequate to deal with such great concentrations of economic power as existed at the time. More important as a factor in moving him away from his laissez-faire position, however, were certain powerful political forces over which Wilson and his administration had no control and which, as it were, seized control of administration policy and pushed it far beyond the bounds that Wilson and his advisers had originally thought desirable. In effect, what occurred from 1913 to 1917 was that Wilson adopted many of the assumptions and almost the whole platform of Theodore Roosevelt's New Nationalism.

The metamorphosis in the Wilsonian program is the key to understanding the first Wilson administration. The Southern contribution toward bringing the administration to an advanced position with regard to the exercise of federal authority was considerable, but the character of this contribution was different from what has been generally assumed. The Southern Democrats in Congress were divided roughly into two factions. First, there was what might be called the administration faction, consisting mainly of committee chairmen like Oscar W. Underwood and Carter Glass, who, by and large, represented a political tradition and constituencies whose interests were more or less divergent from those of the more numerous Southern group. Members of the administration faction were for the most part conservatives, although most of them had no fundamental political principles, were loyal party men, and would follow Wilson's lead. Secondly, there was a larger faction that represented more accurately the political traditions and economic interests of the South — the spokesmen for the agrarian interests of the South, men like Claude Kitchin, Otis Wingo, James K. Vardaman and Robert L. Henry.

The Southern Agrarians of the Wilson period were the direct inheritors and now the prime articulators in the Democratic party of the philosophy underlying the Agrarian crusade — namely, that it was government's duty to intervene directly in economic affairs in order to benefit submerged or politically impotent economic interests. As it turned out, the existence and power of the Southern Agrarian group had important consequences for the Democratic party, the Wilson administration, and the nation. Whereas the administration faction usually followed the regular party line, the Southern Agrarians were often far to the left of it; and in the end they helped to make Wilson an advanced progressive and helped to commit his administration to a broad program of welfare legislation.

The program of the Southern Agrarians was aimed at benefiting the farmers almost exclusively. Although this had been true also of the Democratic program in 1896, Bryan and progressive Democrats in the North and West had moved beyond the almost pure agrarianism of 1896. There was a growing concern for the plight of submerged groups from about 1890 to 1913 and a consequent rise of a great movement for social justice. This phase of progressivism had not been totally absent in the South, but the Southern states were still overwhelmingly rural, and most Southerners had no conception of the grave social and economic problems raised by industrialization and urbanization.

Hence Southern progressives were more concerned with strengthening the political and economic position of the farmers, through regulation of railroads and corporations, a low tariff, the direct primary, and the like, than with tenement reforms, minimum wage legislation, or workmen's compensation legislation. But the important point about the Southern Agrarian program is not that it was limited in scope, but that its advocates were an important element in the Democratic party and that they were now in a position to give voice to their own demands.

The brief period when the philosophy of the New Freedom had any real authority was the few months in 1913 when the Underwood tariff bill was under discussion in Congress. There was little disagreement among Democratic congressmen, progressive or conservative, over the provisions of the bill, except for minor differences on the wool and sugar schedules. There was a much greater difference of opinion between the conservatives and the agrarian radicals, however, on the question of the reorganization of the banking system and the control of the money supply. It was here that the Southern Agrarians, acting with their colleagues from the West, first helped to move their party away from laissez-faire toward a dynamic concept of government.

In line with his New Freedom principles Wilson was inclined to favor the banking and monetary system proposed by the National Monetary Commission, one providing for a reserve association or associations owned and controlled by the bankers themselves. The original Glass bill, which had the tentative endorsement of the administration, provided for such an arrangement. But even before the federal reserve bill emerged from the House Banking Committee, there occurred a momentous struggle within the party councils that was not ended until the Agrarian leaders had won all their important demands. Secretary of State Bryan and Louis D. Brandeis persuaded the President that a banking bill which did not provide for exclusive governmental control, on the top level, was not only unwise but also would never be approved by the House caucus. This was true, incidentally, regardless of the position Bryan might have taken in the controversy.

Wilson was won over by the persuasive arguments of Bryan and Brandeis and the threats of the radicals. Thus the Glass bill, as it finally emerged from the House committee, provided for a decentralized reserve system, for government issue of federal-reserve currency, and for an overall supervision and limited control of the new system by a central reserve board composed exclusively of presidential appointees. It marked, to all practical purposes, the demise of the New Freedom and the beginning of the rise to dominance of the progressives in the Wilson administration.

Bryan and the Western Democrats were now satisfied, but not the Southern Agrarian leaders. In spite of the radical changes that had been effected, the new banking system still would operate exclusively for the benefit of the business community. Here was the rub, as far as the Southern radicals were concerned. After tariff reform had been accomplished, their main objective was the establishment of a system by which farmers could obtain easier and cheaper credit. When the Glass bill was published, and the Southern Agrarians discovered that it included no provision for agricultural credit, they rose in rebellion and declared that they would help the Republicans defeat the measure if the administration did not concede their demands. The fight between the administration forces and the Southern Agrarians was bitter, and for a time threatened to defeat banking reform altogether. Suffice it to say that, in spite of the ridicule of the Eastern press and in spite of the opposition of the administration and of Wilson's spokesmen in the House, the Federal Reserve Bill as finally passed by Congress contained ample provisions for short-term agricultural credit. And this was true because Wilson realized that he must give in to the demands of the Southerners.

The philosophic foundations of the New Freedom were dealt another heavy blow during the formulation of an antitrust policy by administration leaders. It was Wilson's original idea that all that was required was to define precisely what constituted an unfair trade practice or illegal restraint of trade, so as to remove all element of doubt from the laws. The enforcement of the antitrust laws would be delegated, as before, to the Justice Department and the courts. Some of the Southern radicals proposed more drastic remedies, such as prescribing by law the percentage of the total production of a field of industry which one corporation would be allowed to control, or a high excess profits tax which would increase in direct proportion to the size of the industry; but they made no determined fight for these proposals. Wilson, therefore, gave the job of drawing up the measure to Representative Clayton of Georgia, chairman of the Judiciary Committee, and the bill that came out of his committee was simply a synthesis of current ideas, most of which were already embodied in the laws of many states. In addition, Representative Covington of Kentucky drew up at Wilson's request a bill providing for an interstate trade commission, which was to be an enlarged Bureau of Corporations and without any real authority over business practices.

Thus far Wilson had proceeded in line with his New Freedom concepts. At this point, however, an important turn in administration policy occurred. Brandeis, George L. Rublee, and Representative Stevens of New Hampshire visited the President and persuaded him to change the character of his antitrust program entirely. Under their direction, the Clayton bill was rewritten so as to provide for greater flexibility in defining an unfair trade practice and, more important, the interstate commerce commission was reconstituted as the Federal Trade Commission and given apparently vast authority over the day-to-day operations of the business world. The Covington bill had provided for nothing more than an investigatory body to serve as an adjunct of the Justice Department. In the revised bill, the Commission was established as an independent regulatory agency, empowered to supervise business practices and to issue cease and desist orders when it found that corporations were engaging in unfair practices. This last change marked the complete adoption by the Wilson administration of Roosevelt's program for the regulation of business.

The Southern leaders in Congress had nothing to do with bringing about this profound change in Wilson's antitrust policy. The Southern and Western Agrarian radicals, acting with a small Labor bloc in the House, worked hard, however, to have a provision inserted in the Clayton bill exempting farm and labor unions from the operation and application of the antitrust laws. This had been one of the major objectives of the American Federation of Labor since 1906 and had been given Democratic approval in the platforms of 1908 and 1912. Although Wilson was rapidly abandoning his New Freedom assumptions, he was not yet ready to go so far as to approve what was obviously legislation in the interest of particular classes. Since the first days of his administration he had resisted bitterly this move, and a bill specifically exempting farm and labor unions from antitrust prosecutions, which had been passed by the House in the previous session, was blocked by administration pressure. When the Clayton bill was under discussion in the House committee, however, the Agrarian and Labor bloc declared that they would guarantee its defeat unless Wilson gave in to their demands.

Thus faced with another major revolt within his party, Wilson resolved his dilemma by resorting, it must be admitted, to one of the most artful dodges in the history of American politics. The famous labor provisions of the Clayton bill were drawn by Representative E. Y. Webb of North Carolina, who had succeeded Clayton as chairman of the Judiciary Committee, and represented Wilson's attitude perfectly. On the face of it, the new provision did indeed seem to give the exemption and immunity from antitrust prosecutions that the farm and labor spokesmen were demanding. Actually, this was not the case at all. Farm and labor organizations were not to be construed by the courts as being, *per se,* combinations in restraint of trade, but they were in no way freed from the threat of prosecution if they violated the antitrust laws.

Wilson had completed his program of domestic reform by the fall of 1914. In his letters and public statements at the time, he made it clear that he thought everything had been done that was necessary to clear away special privilege and put all classes on an equal footing. Under the operation of the beneficent new laws, Wilson was sure that the nation would enjoy a long period of prosperity and economic freedom. As we have seen, he had been forced partially to abandon his earlier position and to make important concessions in order to get his program across. He was reconciled to the concessions he had been compelled to make, but he was absolutely determined to draw the line at the point it had reached by the fall of 1914.

In fact, a pronounced reaction against progressive policies had set in among Wilson and his advisers during the spring of 1914, and relations between the President and progressive leaders became exceedingly strained at this time. The following year, 1915, was practically barren of progressive accomplishments, except for the La Follette's Seamen's Act, which the administration had opposed and which Wilson almost vetoed. There were, however, several great political forces at work which were so strong that Wilson would be compelled to accommodate his program to satisfy their demands. One was the well-organized Agrarian movement for the establishment of a federal system of long-term rural credits. Another was the movement in behalf of federal social legislation, which was rapidly gaining momentum during this period. Another was the movement for women's suffrage, which was becoming so powerful that it would soon be dangerous for any politician to oppose it. Finally, there was the fact that the Progressive party was obviously disintegrating after 1914 and that the only hope the Democrats had of obtaining a national majority in 1916 was in winning a large minority of the former Bull Moosers to the Democratic side.

Wilson resisted this movement to extend the intervention of the federal government into the fields mentioned here as long as he could do so safely. Then, when it became evident that the Democrats could win the election of 1916 only by adopting the New Nationalism, lock, stock and barrel, Wilson capitulated and supported the very demands he had so long opposed, as strongly as if he had been their originator. We do not have the space to discuss this last and most important phase of Wilsonian reform in any detail, except to consider the extent to which the Southern leaders contributed to the administration's final, complete surrender to the New Nationalism.

The main objective of the Southern Agrarian progressives after 1914 was the adoption of a federal rural credits bill. The first nation-wide movement for long-term federal rural credit facilities had been inaugurated by the Southern Commercial Congress in 1913, and during the next year or two there was widespread discussion of the subject all over the country. In the spring of 1914 a joint subcommittee drew up the bill which was finally passed in 1916 and which would have passed in 1914 had not Wilson let it be known that he would veto the bill if Congress enacted it. Both Wilson and the Agrarian leaders proclaimed themselves advocates of a rural credits measure. What, therefore, was the root of the difference between them? Wilson would not agree to the establishment of a system involving direct subsidies or financial support by the government, and Wilson, Secretary of Agriculture Houston, and Carter Glass were insistent that the government should do no more than provide for the structure of a rural credits system, with capital and management to be provided by private sources. The Agrarian spokesmen, on the other hand, contended that any system which was not operated and financed by the government was bound to fail. But as this involved the direct intervention by the government in behalf of a special class, Wilson was absolutely adamant against it. The result was an impasse, with both sides holding out stubbornly for their own proposals until 1916, when Wilson accepted the Agrarian proposal for reasons of political expediency.

It was, in fact, in agricultural legislation that the Southern Agrarians had the greatest influence in the shaping of the later Wilsonian program. Their greatest contribution was undoubtedly the forcing of the Rural Credits Act of 1916, but they were also able to obtain the adoption of the Lever Warehouse Act in 1914, the Smith-Lever Act for rural extension work of the same year, the Smith-Hughes Act for vocational education, and the program of federal subsidies for highway improvement in 1916.

Southern influence was practically negligible, however, in the formulation of the remaining great social and economic legislation of 1916—the federal Workmen's Compensation Act, the Child Labor Law, the Adamson Act, and the act establishing the Federal Tariff Commission. But there still remain three other areas of legislation in which the influence of the Southern Agrarians was decisive and which merit notice here.

The first involved the question of what sort of military and naval bills Congress should enact in 1916. On this controversial subject the Southern progressives joined with radicals throughout the country in resisting the administration's designs greatly to increase the navy and to establish a large volunteer army. They were not successful in blocking the movement for a large navy, because the pressure here was too great. But they were signally successful in blocking Wilson's plans for military preparedness, indeed, in emasculating them.

The second field of legislation in which Southern progressive influence was decisive was the area of federal fiscal policy. Before the outbreak of the World War, Wilson and McAdoo were able to keep a firm grip on the formulation of tax policies, and their influence was conservative indeed. The tax structure that the Republicans had erected and which was weighted so heavily in favor of the upper classes was left practically undisturbed by the Wilson administration. An income tax provision was included in the Underwood Tariff Law, to make up the anticipated deficit resulting from the lower duties, but the rates were very low and the administration was quick to make it clear that it had no intention of using the income tax to effect a redistribution of wealth.

The outbreak of the war in Europe in the summer of 1914 caused a temporary disarrangement of the finances of the United States and resulted in a sharp decline in imports, which meant that the administration was faced with an alarming decline in revenues. To meet this emergency, McAdoo proposed a series of new excise taxes and a tax on freight shipments, such as had been applied during the Spanish-American War. The Southern and Western Agrarians rebelled at the administration's emergency tax program, claiming that it would throw the whole burden of carrying the country through the crisis on the masses and demanding instead an increase in the income tax. They were successful in eliminating the tax on freight shipments and in getting most of the new taxes put on alcoholic beverages and other luxuries. Even so, they did not like the emergency tax law and vowed that they would continue to fight all such consumption taxes.

With the opening of Congress in December, 1915, the Southern progressives found themselves virtually in control of the House Ways and Means Committee. Long before the new session convened, a majority of the committee declared in writing to the new chairman, Claude Kitchin of North Carolina, their determination to overhaul the tax structure and make it more democratic. The result was that during the winter and spring of 1916 the control of federal tax policy was literally taken out of the hands of the administration leaders and assumed by these Southern Agrarians and their Western allies. It was obvious by this time that some kind of preparedness measures would be adopted, and that either the government would have to find new sources of revenue or else resort to borrowing. The Republicans proposed a bond issue; the administration proposed new consumption and excise and increased income taxes. The Ways and Means Committee, however, replied with one of the most startling and significant tax bills in the history of the country. The Southern Agrarians, who had bitterly resisted the preparedness movement, saw now that new defense measures were inevitable; but they were determined that the people of the East, who had been most vociferous in support of preparedness, should pay for it. Kitchin said as much in fact, before the House caucus when he explained the new tax bill, which greatly increased the income tax, levied the first federal inheritance tax in our history, and placed an excess profits tax on munitions manufacturers.

The last area in which Southern influence was decisive in determining the policies of the Wilson administration was the federal government's policy toward Negroes. Here the Southern contribution was definitely retrogressive and proved that it was impossible for white Southerners of all shades of opinion to get much beyond the rationale of slavery. Suffice it to say that Wilson practically sacrificed the Negroes on the altar of political expediency, by allowing segregation in the government departments, dismissal and downgrading of Negro civil servants in the South, and the like, in order to win Southern support for his program.

Yet in spite of this and other blind spots in the Southern progressive program, it must be concluded that the contributions of the Southern Agrarians were undoubtedly in many ways decisive in moving the Wilson administration away from a static laissez-faire program, to which it was originally dedicated, toward a dynamic, positive program of federal action. Although their program was limited in scope and motivated largely by class interests, the Southern progressives could claim as much credit as could several other major groups for the amazing metamorphosis in Democratic policy that occurred from 1913 to 1916. That is the real significance of their contribution.

18

National Interest and American Intervention, 1917: An Historiographical Appraisal
DANIEL M. SMITH

Why has the United States been waging war in Asia? War marks a point of crisis in any nation; in one that is democratic, it compels a solemn referendum on national purpose and on the conduct of national affairs. At least two principles govern the conduct of American politics, in times of both peace and war: one is a sense of practicality, befitting a nation of Poor Richards looking for the main chance, and the second is a sense of ideals, befitting a nation of Puritans, whose city on a hill has the eye of all people upon it. Which principle is foremost for us in this most recent war we have been fighting in Asia? What has motivated our actions in previous wars? How far are the two principles separable? How much do our ideals inform and express our practicality, how much does practicality shape and govern our ideals?

SOURCE: *The Journal of American History*, LII (June, 1965), 5–24. Reprinted by permission.

The questions are relevant to all the wars we have fought, but they are particularly relevant to those we have fought since 1917, when we entered World War I. Having hitherto confined ourselves to a policy of territorial—basically continental—expansion, we then became a more active participant in world affairs. Having previously enjoyed the advantage of great national power, we then, in the face of challenge, felt called upon to take up its responsibilities. The American orbit had run, inevitably and irreversibly, across the European. But in entering the war, which of the two principles of our politics had moved us: the ideal or the practical? And if both, then in what proportions, and with what relevance to each other? In our entry into the war, what in particular was the role of Woodrow Wilson? From what premises had he proceeded? Was he a lofty idealist, or was he no less a hard politician? Who were his principal advisers, and how far had they shaped his policies?

These questions have confronted all historians who, during the past half century, have probed into the reasons why we entered World War I. In the past decade and a half the subject has attracted considerable attention, because of the increasing availability of the personal manuscript sources dealing with the period, because the centenary celebration of Wilson's birth raised the debate over his policies anew, and because the continuing threat of the cold war has kept alive for us the question of how to wage diplomacy instead of war. It is to this recent discussion among historians concerning our entry into World War I that Daniel M. Smith, of the University of Colorado, addresses himself in the essay reprinted below. Professor Smith's several works attest both to his expertness in American diplomatic history and to his special command of the problem of our involvement in World War I: Robert Lansing and American Neutrality, 1914–1917 (1958), Major Problems in American Diplomatic History (1964), and The Great Departure: The United States and World War I, 1914–1920 (1965). In the following essay, Smith applies his own close knowledge of the subject to a careful analysis of what some of its foremost students—Robert E. Osgood, Edward H. Buehrig, Arthur S. Link, and Ernest R. May—have been writing.

If history does not repeat itself, it surely continues itself. If we cannot in our war today find exact instruction for what we are doing, we can at least find the dimensions in which to place it. We can try, through the past, to gain a meaningful perspective on why a great power goes to war and on how far, in a presidential democracy, the war expresses presidential leadership and democratic polity. Our experience in World War I marked for us, as Smith has elsewhere phrased it, a great departure from an earlier world and an irrevocable step "into the more dangerous and challenging world of the twentieth century." That departure and step merit our closest study because they are immediately related to the wars we have fought since World War I, including the Asian wars we have been fighting in recent years.

In the two decades since 1945 several significant studies have been published on American involvement in World War I. These works have advanced beyond the revisionist debates of the 1930s to a more balanced consideration of economic, psychological, and political factors. Also they study the causes of hostilities within the context of developments in the principal European belligerent countries. An important aspect has been the investigation of considerations of the national interests in the decision of the United States to enter the great conflict in 1917.[1] The purpose of this essay is to examine these recent studies, with an especial concentration on the theme of the national interest and its influence on American foreign policy makers.

In 1950 Richard W. Leopold published a stimulating article on the historiography of the American involvement in World War I.[2] He pointed out that scholars had not achieved a consensus on the problem and that a general study had not been published since 1938. Until then the historical debate that began almost with President Woodrow Wilson's war message could be categorized into two schools. One was the "submarine" school, best represented by Charles Seymour, which contended that the nation had entered the war primarily because of violations of neutral rights and international law and morality by the ruthless German submarine campaigns. Another school comprised the unneutrality group, with Charles C. Tansill as the latest spokesman,

---

[1] Only a few of the reviews in the major historical journals of the works examined in this paper commented to an appreciable extent on the emergence of the national interest theme. Ernest R. May, *Mississippi Valley Historical Review*, XLIII (June 1956), 147–48, pointed out that Edward H. Buehrig's study was important as a contribution to a more realistic appraisal of Wilsonian diplomacy; Julius W. Pratt, *American Historical Review*, LXIV (July 1959), 1023–24, called the Smith study of Lansing a "partial answer" to the role of balance-of-power concepts in the 1917 intervention; and Richard L. Watson, Jr., *ibid.*, 973–75, gave the best review from that point of view to the May volume.

[2] Richard W. Leopold, "The Problem of American Intervention, 1917: An Historical Retrospect," *World Politics*, II (1950), 405–25. Richard L. Watson, Jr., in "Woodrow Wilson and His Interpreters, 1947–1957," *Mississippi Valley Historical Review*, XLIV (Sept. 1957), 207–36, examines recent literature, and especially the Wilson centennial outpouring, on the domestic and foreign policies of the Wilson administration. Ernest R. May, in two short articles, makes perceptive comments on the major currents of interpretation on American involvement in 1898, 1917, and 1941. He describes himself, Arthur S. Link, and others as moving away from earlier "What went wrong" approaches to a Rankean "What happened" emphasis. See May, "Emergence to World Power," John Higham, ed., *The Reconstruction of American History* (New York, 1962), 180–96; and *American Intervention: 1917 and 1941* (Service Center for Teachers of History, Pamphlet 30, 1960).

that emphasized the patent American unneutrality in favor of the Allied Powers.[3]

During World War II, Leopold noted, a new interpretation emerged that the basic motive for intervention in 1917 had been to protect the nation's security against the menace of possible German victory and a disturbance to the balance of power, and to preserve Anglo-American domination of the North Atlantic. In 1943 Walter Lippmann maintained that the submarine issue had been merely the formal occasion for war, while "the substantial and compelling reason . . . was that the cutting of the Atlantic communications meant the starvation of Britain and, therefore, the conquest of Western Europe by imperial Germany."[4] While acknowledging that Wilson officially had justified hostilities on the basis of submarine violations of American neutral rights, Lippmann contended that this would not have sufficed as a rationalization if most Americans had not realized, intuitively or consciously, that a German victory would imperil American security. In another wartime book the newspaperman Forest Davis advanced a similar explanation.[5] As Leopold observed, however, scholars remained skeptical of these interpretations that seemed to project the fears of 1941 into the 1917 era, and at most viewed them as insights requiring extensive research and study. Diplomatic historian Thomas A. Bailey, for example, commented that there had been no rushing into war to redress the power balance and save the Allies in 1917, as seemingly they were winning; only after it was in the war did America realize the dire Allied plight.[6]

---

[3] Charles Callan Tansill, *America Goes to War* (Boston, 1938); Charles Seymour, *American Diplomacy During the World War* (Baltimore, 1934) and *American Neutrality, 1914–1917* (New Haven, 1935). Tansill ignored the issue of American security and global aspects of the war. He disclaimed having a particular thesis to offer. Seymour dismissed political and economic factors as peripheral and attributed the war entry primarily to outraged sentiment at submarine warfare and a determination to protect American lives and property on the high seas. Harley Notter, *The Origins of the Foreign Policy of Woodrow Wilson* (Baltimore, 1937), 642–43, 647, 650, concluded that by 1917 Wilson viewed Germany as a danger to the peace and security of America and the world, but that the United States entered the war only because of intolerable violations of its neutral rights. A slim volume by Samuel R. Spencer, Jr., *The Decision for War, 1917* (Rindge, N.H., 1953), adhered to the submarine thesis while stressing the *Laconia* sinking and release of the Zimmermann telegram in Feb. 1917 as events in the transition to full hostilities. Also see Barbara W. Tuchman, *The Zimmermann Telegram* (New York, 1958).

[4] Walter Lippmann, *U. S. Foreign Policy: Shield of the Republic* (Boston, 1943), 33–37.

[5] Forest Davis, *The Atlantic System: The Story of Anglo-American Control of the Seas* (New York, 1941), 240–46.

[6] See Thomas A. Bailey, *Woodrow Wilson and the Lost Peace* (New York,

The diplomat and historian, George F. Kennan, published in 1950 a volume of essays on recent American diplomacy in which he recognized that there had been high American officials in World War I cognizant of the need to preserve a favorable balance of power against the disturbing possibility of a German triumph. Kennan concluded, however, that such a realistic approach had not been shared by the great majority of citizens; instead, the nation plunged into war on the narrow grounds of defending neutral rights and then turned the struggle into a moralistic-legalistic crusade to remold the world order.[7] The more detailed study, *Ideals and Self-Interest in American Foreign Relations*, published in 1953 by Robert Endicott Osgood, in general substantiated that interpretation.[8]

Osgood acknowledged the plausibility of the Lippmann thesis and in his study, based on printed materials, he recorded similar views held by a number of Americans in 1914–1917.[9] As a *New Republic* editor Lippmann had written several articles[10] contending that American security was involved in the continuation of the existing balance of power, as had the American diplomat Lewis Einstein in 1913 and 1914.[11] Other prominent Americans publicly advanced arguments that vital national interests would be threatened by a German victory. Theodore Roosevelt mixed with such views a type of belligerent moralism that advocated hostilities in 1916 in order to uphold national honor and save civilization from the new barbarians.[12]

Several of Wilson's advisers, Osgood wrote, analyzed the meaning

---

1944), 12–13, and *A Diplomatic History of the American People* (6th ed., New York, 1958), 594n. Richard W. Van Alstyne, *American Diplomacy in Action* (rev. ed., Stanford, 1947), 225–56, 289, conceded, on the other hand, that while the majority of citizens had not been aware of balance of power arguments, some persons including high officials had been influenced by such considerations.

[7] George F. Kennan, *American Diplomacy, 1900–1950* (Chicago, 1951), 64–66, 70–74. Also see Edward Mead Earle, "A Half-Century of American Foreign Policy: Our Stake in Europe, 1898–1914," *Political Science Quarterly*, LXIV (June 1949), 168–88.

[8] Robert Endicott Osgood, *Ideals and Self-Interest in American Foreign Relations* (Chicago, 1953). Approximately one third of this study is devoted to the Wilson period.

[9] *Ibid.*, 115–34.

[10] Walter Lippmann, *Annals of the American Academy of Political and Social Science*, LXVI (1916), 60–70; *Stakes of Diplomacy* (New York, 1915), preface; and *New Republic*, X (Feb. 17, 1917), 59–61.

[11] Lewis Einstein, "The United States and Anglo-German Rivalry," and "The War and American Policy," *National Review*, LX (Jan. 1913), 736–50 and LXIV (Nov. 1914), 357–76.

[12] Osgood, *Ideals and Self-Interest*, 135–53. Also see Howard K. Beale, *Theodore Roosevelt and the Rise of America to World Power* (Baltimore, 1956).

of the war to America from a balance-of-power view. The list included Colonel Edward M. House; Robert Lansing, Counselor and then Secretary of State in mid-1915; the ambassador to Britain, Walter Hines Page; and James W. Gerard, ambassador to Germany. These men envisioned a German conquest in Europe as a threat to American security in the western hemisphere and analyzed the war in terms of the national interest in Anglo-American naval predominance in the Atlantic. Yet such considerations, though increasing their willingness to support neutrality policies favorable to the Allies, did little more than quicken events which led the United States into the war. That was because the advisers did not really expect Germany to win and therefore their recommendations to the President did not advocate intervention on the grounds of an endangered security. Events did not seem to pose the clear alternative of fighting Germany or confronting a nearly certain later attack by that power, so it was easier to follow the line of submarine violations of honor and morality and to enter the war on that popular basis.[13] In any case, Osgood concluded, it would be difficult to prove that these advisers had any appreciable influence on the idealistic Wilson, for the President was in nearly complete control of foreign affairs and was unusually independent of counselors.[14]

Osgood thus seemed reluctant to accept the implications of his own findings, that presidential assistants had taken a realistic approach toward the European war. Furthermore, Osgood tended to concentrate on the question of immediate security. These advisers saw the national interest in a broader sense as embracing not only security but economic interests and a favorable postwar position. Osgood's own reasoning strongly suggests that House, Lansing, and others might not have recommended to Wilson considerations of honor, morality, and ideology as justifications for belligerency if they had not viewed Germany as a menace to broadly defined national interests. Later studies also have revealed that Wilson was capable of a more realistic approach to the war and that he was far more receptive to advice and dependent on counselors than previously assumed.

Osgood and Kennan undoubtedly have been correct that there was little evidence of popular apprehensions of a direct German threat in 1914–1917. Much evidence exists, however, that an influential minority viewed imperial Germany askance. Since 1898 American military and naval leaders increasingly envisioned Germany as offering a threat to American security in the western hemisphere. The Navy General Board in 1901 recommended purchase of the Danish West Indies because "In view of the isthmian canal and the German settlements in

---

[13] Osgood, *Ideals and Self-Interest,* 154–71.
[14] *Ibid.,* 172–75.

South America, every additional acquisition by the United States in the West Indies is of value."[15] In testimony before the House Naval Affairs Committee in 1914, Admiral Charles Vreeland justified naval expansion as needed to cope with Germany and Japan.[16] A Navy General Board estimate of 1910, recirculated in February 1915, concluded that only Germany, driven by population pressures and rivalries in Latin America and the Far East, could undertake singlehandedly war on the United States and was therefore the most probable potential enemy.[17] The War Department also had defensive war plans drawn with Germany as the theoretical opponent.[18] A lengthy War College paper, 1909–1910, by Captain Paul B. Malone, described Germany as the most serious economic competitor of the United States, in contact and conflict with America both in Latin America and China. Although the author did not flatly predict hostilities he commented that, in the past, war had been the virtually inevitable result of such conflicting interests.[19]

The historian Alfred Vagts has attempted to explain the fact that navalists in Germany and the United States, from the late 1890s to 1914, viewed each other as a probable opponent on the grounds that each needed an excuse to justify large naval expansion programs.[20] He

---

[15] General Board No. 187, 31-01, Vol. I, 374. Report of Nov. 12, 1901, Naval War Records Office (Arlington, Virginia). Unclassified. Rumors of German endeavors to acquire the Galapagos Islands caused the Navy and War departments on several occasions to object to the State Department on the grounds of proximity to the Panama Canal; similar objections were made against possible German acquisition of Haiti's Mole St. Nicholas, in 1910 and 1912. See correspondence of April 25, 28, 1911, State Department File Number 822.014G/177, 178; Aug. 25, 1910, June 27, 1912, *ibid.*, 838.802/5, 12 (National Archives).

[16] Harold and Margaret Sprout, *The Rise of American Naval Power, 1776–1918* (Princeton, 1942), 311–13. The Navy League centered its none too successful propaganda before 1914 for a more powerful navy on the German menace to the Monroe Doctrine. See Armin Rappaport, *The Navy League of the United States* (Detroit, 1962), 31–66.

[17] War Portfolio No. 1, Atlantic Station—approved by the General Board, Oct. 19, 1910 and reissued in Feb. 1915, Naval War Records Office.

[18] No. 9433, War Materials Division (National Archives). Still classified as confidential in 1960.

[19] "The Military Geography of the Atlantic Seaboard, Considered with Reference to an Invading Force," War College Division, General Staff, 6916–1, War Materials Division.

[20] Alfred Vagts, "Hopes and Fears of an American-German War, 1870–1915," *Political Science Quarterly*, LIV (Dec. 1939), 514–35, and LV (March 1940), 53–76. Fritz T. Epstein, "Germany and the United States: Basic Patterns of Conflict and Understanding," G. L. Anderson, ed., *Issues and Conflict* (Lawrence, Kansas, 1959), 284–314, concludes that German-American friction prior to 1914 reflected psychological differences rather than actual clashes of interest.

concluded that actual commercial competition between the two states was small and that each power lacked coaling stations and naval cruising range for an attack on the other. Talk of rivalry in both countries primarily reflected the propaganda efforts of big navy advocates. No doubt a degree of validity must be accorded Vagts' interpretation, but the evidence indicates that the apprehensions were genuine and were shared by many leading civilians. On the other hand, apparently there were no official interchanges in the 1910–1917 period between the two defense departments and State in regard to American national interests in the outcome of a general Europe war. Officials in all three departments apparently shared similar appraisals of the situation, and perhaps informally discussed it, but no effort was made to plan and coordinate policy to cope with the danger.[21]

The decade before World War I witnessed a slowly maturing conviction among informed Americans that Germany was a potential enemy and Great Britain a natural ally of the United States. Editorials in the New York *Times* envisioned Germany as hostile, thus requiring an American navy of at least comparable size, and repeatedly expressed confidence in an enduring Anglo-American community of interest.[22] From 1898 the American periodical press also occasionally printed articles expressing distrust of Germany's expansionist tendencies. *Munsey's Magazine* in 1901 featured a comparison of the German and American navies and called for greater naval preparations to cooperate with Great Britain in meeting the German challenge in the western hemisphere.[23] Articles from English journals on the theme of German naval threats to the United States were reprinted in American publications.[24] Comparisons of the American and German navies were drawn

---

[21] Based on the author's perusal of State-Navy files in the National Archives, and on a recent article by Fred Greene, "The Military View of American National Policy, 1904–1940," *American Historical Review*, LXVI (1961), 354–77. Greene points out that the army and navy staffs often complained of lack of policy guidance from the State Department before 1940 and were compelled to try to define basic national interests themselves as guidelines for defense plans. J. A. S. Grenville, in "Diplomacy and War Plans in the United States, 1890–1917," *Transactions of the Royal Society*, 5th Series, XI (London, 1961), 1–21, notes that American strategic war plans, revised in 1915 and 1916, were defensive in character and were designed not to cope with the current war but to meet the threat of the victor after the war in Europe was over. Also see Ernest R. May, "The Development of Political-Military Consultation in the United States," *Political Science Quarterly*, LXX (June 1955), 161–80.

[22] New York *Times*, July 17, Aug. 20, 26, 1898; Feb. 18, 1899.

[23] Walter S. Meriwether, "Our Navy and Germany's," *Munsey's Magazine*, XXIV (March 1901), 856–73.

[24] See *American Monthly Review of Reviews*, XIX (Jan. 1899), 86–88; *Living Age*, CCXXIX (June 1, 1901), 583–86; *ibid.*, CCLXXVIII (July 12, 1913), 67–81.

and parity was strongly recommended.[25] A 1909 article in *The Independent* by Amos S. Hershey, professor of Political Science and International Law at Indiana University, depicted Germany as menacing both world peace and American interests in the Far East and Latin America. To meet that danger Hershey advocated a defensive Anglo-American alliance. He wrote prophetically: "the people of the United States could hardly remain neutral in a war between Germany and Great Britain which might possibly end in German naval supremacy. . . . A blockade of the British Isles by German cruisers and submarine mines, or the loss involved in the danger to contraband trade would be severely felt in this country."[26]

Understandably, the general conflagration which began in 1914 increased the conviction of a number of Americans that Germany was in fact a menace and that American interests could best be secured through an Allied triumph.[27] In the 1916 annual volume of the American Academy of Political and Social Science well-known scholars and pundits presented several papers that emphasized that United States security was involved in the preservation of British sea power.[28] To help focus the widespread interest in 1916 in the preparedness question, the editors of *The Independent* printed an outline of pro and con arguments, prepared by Preston William Slosson, entitled: "Resolved: That the United States should enter the Great War on the side of the Entente Allies." The affirmative side asserted among other arguments that a Teutonic victory would endanger the future security of the American people.[29]

These references to public opinion do not indicate that a majority of citizens in 1917 supported intervention on the grounds of vital national concerns. However, the evidence does reveal that for over a decade a number of educated and informed persons were exposed repeatedly to warnings that Germany challenged the security and the economic welfare of the nation. The existence of these attitudes probably made it

---

[25] *Harper's Weekly*, XLVII (March 14, 1903), 428–29; New York *Times*, Feb. 20, 1905; W. G. Fitz-Gerald, "Does Germany Menace the World's Peace?", *North American Review*, CLXXXIV (April 19, 1907), 853–60.

[26] Amos S. Hershey, "Germany—The Main Obstacle to the World's Peace," *Independent*, LXVI (May 20, 1909), 1071–76. For a similar analysis by a well-known English journalist, writing for *Fortnightly Review*, see Sydney Brooks, Great Britain, Germany and the United States," reprinted in *Living Age*, CCLXII (July 31, 1909), 259–66.

[27] For example, see New York *Times* editorials of Oct. 14, 19, 1914, Nov. 29, 1916, and letters Oct. 16, 18, Nov. 10, 1914.

[28] See articles by S. N. Patten, George Louis Beer, and Walter Lippmann, in *Annals of the American Academy of Political and Social Science*, LXVI (1916), 1–11, 60–70, 71–91. Dissenting views were also voiced.

[29] *Independent*, LXXXVI (May 8, 1916), 228

inestimably easier to condemn Germany on moral and ideological grounds after 1914 and facilitated eventual war entry on the basis of a defense of neutral rights.

Edward H. Buehrig, as Osgood a political scientist, made an important contribution to the "national interest" school in a subtle study entitled *Woodrow Wilson and the Balance of Power*.[30] Based largely on printed sources and a few manuscript collections, the volume explained the American intervention in the war in 1917 as resulting from the German challenge to Britain's position as the dominant sea power. If Americans had been accustomed to viewing foreign relations in terms of practical power issues the ultimate war entry possibly might have been based squarely on considerations of security and economic connections. As it was, Germany and the United States were soon entrapped in complicated questions of neutral rights and drifted into war because of different attitudes toward British control of the seas. The United States accepted the British role as beneficial to its interests; Germany felt compelled to challenge it with every available weapon. Consequently, even though a bilateral German-American war was highly improbable, an Anglo-German struggle which threatened to alter drastically Britain's position posed serious questions to America's trans-Atlantic connections and created tensions culminating in war.[31]

The submarine issue was a point of departure for an evolving American policy toward the war. Without it, of course, German-American relations would have been smoother. American neutrality was in practice favorable to the Allies, but Germany decided to use fully the submarine weapon in 1917 because it alone seemed to promise victory. Probably no other course by the United States, short of cooperation with Germany to challenge the British blockade in order to renew substantial American trade with the Central Powers, could have averted unrestricted U-boat warfare. Germany naturally resented the American munitions trade with the Allies but, except as a moral justification, it played no important role in German decisions. What really was sought was to reverse British control of the seas and markets. To have satisfied the Berlin government by effecting a major change in neutral trade would have harmed important American economic interests and would have meant a disturbing replacement of British power with German.[32]

Wilson in 1915 adopted the policy of holding Germany fully accountable for losses of American lives and ships by submarine attacks around the British Isles in order to defend the traditional American concept of

---

[30] *Woodrow Wilson and the Balance of Power* (Bloomington, 1955).
[31] *Ibid.*, viii-ix, 16–17.
[32] *Ibid.*, 79–84, 90, 102–5.

neutral rights and "freedom of the seas." He chose to uphold international law, and thereby to defend a conception of the national interest, for Americans had long believed that the nation's security was
closely connected with the preservation of the world legal structure.
In speeches advocating defensive military preparations in 1916, Wilson
clearly developed that theme: the United States had to defend legal
principles and support the international community. Germany's lawless methods of warfare affected American security, the President implied, dependent as it was on maintenance of national honor and rights
and the preservation of the structure of international law and morality.[33]

When the *Sussex* controversy in 1916 made imminent the prospect of
entering the war over the submarine issue, Wilson turned to diplomatic
intervention in hopes of avoiding hostilities. The House-Grey Memorandum, negotiated earlier by Colonel House with British Foreign
Secretary Sir Edward Grey, provided that at a time propitious for the
Allies Wilson was to propose a conference to terminate the war; if
Germany declined or rejected a "reasonable" peace, the United States
"probably" would enter the struggle on the Allied side. The refusal of
Britain and France to invoke the plan, which Wilson had hoped would
end the war before America should be forced in, compelled the President to seek other means for mediation.[34]

In May 1916 President Wilson addressed the League to Enforce
Peace and advocated a universal association of nations that would accord with America's national interest by preserving world free trade
and access to markets ("freedom of the seas") and would protect all
nations through territorial guarantees. This global organization, said
Wilson, could prevent future wars by substitution of conferences for
force, and the United States could facilitate the transition by making it
known that its power would be thrown onto the international scales
in behalf of peaceful means of adjustment. Buehrig analyzed the address as revealing not only Wilsonian idealism but also his interest in
maintaining a stable world balance of power. Clear indications that the
British government would not aid in promoting a negotiated peace
caused Wilson in late 1916 to turn to other avenues for peace.[35] Wilson
moved beyond considerations of a balance of power to a community
of power when in December 1916 he requested statements of belligerent
war aims and early in 1917 appealed for "peace without victory." The
President thereby completed a shift from the initial policy of defense of
maritime neutral rights to mediation efforts and a just peace on which
to build a new community of nations. When Germany subsequently
launched unrestricted submarine warfare and abolished not only all

---

[33] *Ibid.*, 106–8, 117–21, 149.
[34] *Ibid.*, 172–73, 228, 230–35.
[35] *Ibid.*, 238–46.

neutral rights but also made clear the determination to dictate a conqueror's peace, Wilson took the nation into war. He had no real choice, Buehrig concluded, either from the standpoint of maritime legal rights or of future world peace and stability.[36]

In Buehrig's view, Wilson in shaping American policy lacked neither astuteness nor an appreciation of balance-of-power concepts. The idealistic element in his policy finally received the major emphasis, over realistic considerations, because the President's temperament so required. The need to adjust policies to the requirements of an American public not trained to appraise world affairs in practical terms was also a probable factor.[37]

The Buehrig study has made at least two important contributions. In contrast to Osgood he defined the American concept of the national interests as comprising not only immediate but long-term security, economic interest in freedom of the seas, and the desire for world order and safety through preservation of an international regime of law. Buehrig also has carefully analyzed the elements of Wilsonian policies and thereby detected, along with idealistic elements, indications of a realistic consciousness of the balance of power and concrete American interests involved in the war.[38]

In an early volume in the New American Nation series, *Woodrow Wilson and the Progressive Era,* Arthur S. Link subscribed to the "submarine" school in interpreting the entry of the United States into World War I.[39] He recognized that House and Lansing had viewed realistically the European struggle, but he maintained that the two advisers "had only an incidental influence" on the President. In the ulti-

---

[36] *Ibid.,* 260–66.

[37] *Ibid.,* 274–75.

[38] Buehrig noted that Robert Lansing held balance-of-power concepts about the war, but he asked to what degree this was submerged by an ideological view of the struggle. *Ibid.,* 135–37. That question was answered, at least partially, by Daniel M. Smith's *Robert Lansing and American Neutrality, 1914–1917* (Berkeley, 1958), and "Robert Lansing and the Formulation of American Neutrality Policies, 1914–1915," *Mississippi Valley Historical Review,* XLIII (June 1956), 59–81. Lansing, on the basis of his private diaries, was depicted by Smith as combining ideological considerations with a concern for the nation's economic and security interests in the war, and to have concluded in July 1915 that on both grounds a German victory should be prevented, by an American intervention if necessary. Smith shows that Lansing helped shape the basic neutrality policies in the early months of the war and thereafter was a strong advocate of a firm approach toward the submarine issue. Lansing rarely spoke directly to Wilson of security interests, apparently because of an appreciation of the President's psychology, but he did to Colonel House. He also recommended measures to Wilson based on concrete economic considerations, and he couched other suggestions in idealistic terminology.

[39] Arthur S. Link, *Woodrow Wilson and the Progressive Era, 1910–1917* (New York, 1954).

mate analysis it was Wilson who, influenced by public opinion, had determined the American course. To mid-1916 Wilson had followed a neutrality course benevolent toward the Allies because of his moralistic appraisal of the war, German violations of international law, and the apparent greater readiness of Great Britain to make a reasonable peace. When he became convinced that the Allies in fact did not desire a fair settlement but sought, as Germany, a conclusive victory, he moved toward a genuinely impartial position. If Germany had not violated the *Sussex* pledge by unrestricted submarine warfare early in 1917, there would have been no war between the two countries. Considerations of finance, economic ties, ideology, or security were not involved in the presidential decision. War finally came because the submarine assaults on American lives and shipping left Wilson no feasible alternative.[40]

As he continued his multi-volume study of Wilson, Link seemed to modify his views of the causes of American intervention. In 1957 his Albert Shaw Lectures on Diplomatic History were published as *Wilson the Diplomatist*.[41] The interpretation generally followed that of the earlier volume: a genuinely neutral America adjusted to British measures, but the U-boat campaigns were opposed for legal and moral reasons.[42] By early 1917, however, after failure of efforts to halt the war short of total victory for either side and thereby to preclude American involvement and establish the basis for a stable postwar world, Wilson apparently decided to effect a diplomatic withdrawal. Continuation of the war, he foresaw, would cause further deterioration of neutral rights. The President seemingly was willing to retreat on strict accountability and perhaps would have accepted a new U-boat campaign against armed merchantmen or all belligerent vessels except passenger liners. The German decision to attack all shipping, neutrals included, forced Wilson to break diplomatic relations.[43]

Link thus considered the submarine issue to have been the immediate cause of hostilities, but he concluded that the agonized Wilson reluctantly accepted full hostilities in 1917, as opposed to armed neutrality or a limited naval war, only because of other factors. One of the most important of these, though supported by little direct evidence, was Wilson's "apparent fear that the threat of a German victory imperiled the balance of power and all his hopes for future reconstruction of the world community."[44] Wilson seems not to have apprehended a serious German danger to the United States nor did he seek to preserve the old

---

[40] *Ibid.*, 279–81.
[41] *Wilson the Diplomatist: A Look at His Major Foreign Policies* (Baltimore, 1957).
[42] *Ibid.*, 32–35, 40–54.
[43] *Ibid.*, 70, 80–82.
[44] *Ibid.*, 88.

balance of power. Yet the Allies appeared to be on the verge of losing the war and that would mean German conquest and the end of Wilsonian hopes for a new world order. He remarked to Colonel House that Germany seemed to be a madman who required restraining—and he apparently thought that only through American armed intervention could a Central Power victory be avoided and American prestige among the Allies enhanced so that a just peace could be achieved. The President undoubtedly also was affected in the war decision by an aroused American public and by the reiterated counsel of his close advisers.[45]

In the preface of the third volume in the Link biography, *Wilson: The Struggle for Neutrality*,[46] the author expressed the hope that in this study of the first fifteen months of neutrality he had purged his mind of preconceived interpretations and could let the men and events speak for themselves. He would appear to have succeeded admirably in this exhaustively researched volume. Realistic appraisals of the war by House and Lansing had an important effect on Wilson's mind. House, as Lansing, was favorably inclined toward the Allies and feared the militaristic and expansionist tendencies of Germany. As a result, the Colonel advised Wilson to acquiesce in Allied war measures and to oppose those of Germany. Yet House did not want a sweeping Allied victory, only one sufficient to check Teutonic ambitions and still leave Germany powerful enough to block Russian imperialism.[47] President Wilson, after initial sympathy for the Allies, achieved a large degree of impartiality on the question of war guilt. As the war continued, Wilson was increasingly persuaded that the greatest opportunity for a just and lasting peace would come from an indecisive conclusion of the war. As he told a newspaperman, however, while "I cannot regard this [a sweeping Allied triumph] as the ideal solution, at the same time I cannot see now that it would hurt greatly the interests of the United States if either France or Russia or Great Britain should finally dictate the [peace] settlement."[48] Wilson thus indicated, by the close of 1914, a realistic view that the preferable result of the war would be a deadlock which would preserve the existing power structure and facilitate a just peace, but that American interests would not be adversely affected by a decisive Allied triumph. As far as American policy was concerned,

---

[45] *Ibid.*, 89–90.

[46] Arthur S. Link, *Wilson: The Struggle for Neutrality, 1914–1915* (Princeton, 1960). An excellent first chapter discusses American public opinion and the role of belligerent propaganda. Link finds invalid the assumptions of many writers that most Americans were irrationally pro-Ally and that German propaganda was generally inept and ineffective.

[47] *Ibid.*, 45–48.

[48] *Ibid.*, 49–56.

however, both moral and practical considerations required maintenance of neutrality.

The fourth volume in Link's series, *Wilson: Confusions and Crises*, necessarily lacks the unifying themes present in the earlier volumes. Among other topics, domestic and foreign, it narrates America's relations with the belligerents through the *Sussex* crisis. The section on the House-Grey Memorandum, based on heretofore unexploited sources including French materials which the author could not directly quote or cite, is particularly valuable. Link depicts the divergence of motives behind the scheme: House, believing that intervention in the war was almost inevitable, was prepared to go far in assuring the Allies of American backing, whereas the President apparently contemplated only peaceful mediation. He believes Grey did not take his "understanding" with the Colonel very seriously, as he doubted the possibility of American intervention, and was aware that the Allied governments were averse to a negotiated peace and sought a decisive triumph over the Central Powers.[49]

These interpretations reveal that Link is constantly reevaluating the materials as he continues his biography of Wilson. Wilson is now seen as not only the moralist and idealist, but also as aware of balance-of-power arguments, responsive to the advice of realistically-inclined counselors, and to a considerable degree framing the American course on the basis of practical considerations of the national interest. Completion of the biography and the concluding judgment of Link can only be awaited with great interest.

The centennial of Wilson's birth in 1956 occasioned a number of commemorative essays and books. Osgood and Buehrig restated their evaluations of Wilsonian neutrality;[50] Charles Seymour reiterated the submarine thesis,[51] and William L. Langer concurred.[52] Two short and unfootnoted but well-researched biographies were published by

---

[49] Arthur S. Link, *Wilson: Confusions and Crises, 1915–1916* (Princeton, 1964), 111–13, 130, 138–40.

[50] Edward H. Buehrig, "Idealism and Statecraft," *Confluence*, V (Oct. 1956), 252–63; Robert E. Osgood, "Woodrow Wilson, Collective Security, and the Lessons of History," *ibid.* (Jan. 1957), 341–54.

[51] Charles Seymour, "Woodrow Wilson in Perspective," *Foreign Affairs*, XXXIV (Jan. 1956), 175–86. In an article, "The House-Bernstorff Conversations in Perspective," A. O. Sarkissian, ed., *Studies in Diplomatic History and Historiography in Honour of G. P. Gooch* (London, 1961), 90–106, Seymour acknowledged that House had some fears of a German threat to American security and that his pro-British sentiments affected his interest in mediation schemes. Seymour credited the protracted and confidential House-Bernstorff negotiations in 1915–1916 with helping to postpone war until the final crisis in 1917.

[52] William L. Langer, "From Isolation to Mediation," Arthur P. Dudden, ed., *Woodrow Wilson and the World of Today* (Philadelphia, 1957), 22–46.

John A. Garraty and John M. Blum. Garraty described American neutrality as decidedly pro-Ally, because of Wilson's biases, but the President's views and emotions precluded him from either accepting a German victory or intervening in the war. Wilson eventually lost much of his faith in the Allies and attempted to mediate in late 1916, but was forced into the conflict by the submarine issue.[53] Blum believed that Wilson lacked a realistic appraisal of the war's meaning for American interests and that the country entered the conflict only because of unrestricted U-boat warfare.[54] A generally persuasive and solidly-based psychological study, *Wilson and Colonel House,* was published by Alexander L. and Juliette L. George, that pointed out that while Wilson undoubtedly was familiar with the balance-of-power concept, his psychological aversion to frank considerations of power and self-interest made it difficult for him to frame policies clearly based on such grounds.[55] Two years after the centennial, Arthur Walworth published a two-volume biography of Wilson that, while well-researched, hewed to the Seymour interpretation and made little new contribution to understanding the causes of involvement.[56]

The first extensive exploration of the formulation of German policy toward the United States appeared in Karl E. Birnbaum's *Peace Moves and U-Boat Warfare.*[57] His book, concentrating on the *Sussex* crisis and after, does not focus on American policy making but it does have important implications for American diplomatic historians. He found that not only did German policy oscillate between peace moves and intensification of submarine warfare, but that a third course was also pursued of trying to manage issues with the United States so that even full underseas warfare would not lead to hostilities.

In the *Lusitania* and *Arabic* crises full compliance with Wilson's demands was precluded by official skepticism of the President's impartiality and by German public opinion, which was embittered at the American war trade and hopeful of the power of submarine warfare.[58]

---

[53] John A. Garraty, *Woodrow Wilson: A Great Life in Brief* (New York, 1956), 96–97, 99, 112, 116–17.

[54] John Morton Blum, *Woodrow Wilson and the Politics of Morality* (Boston, 1956), 96, 100, 129.

[55] Alexander L. and Juliette L. George, *Woodrow Wilson and Colonel House: A Personality Study* (New York, 1956), 159–60.

[56] Arthur Walworth, *Woodrow Wilson* (2 vols., New York, 1958). For an interesting survey of modern American foreign policy by a French scholar, see Jean-Baptiste Duroselle (trans. by Nancy Lyman Roelker), *From Wilson to Roosevelt: Foreign Policy of the United States, 1913–1945* (Cambridge, 1963). Duroselle attributes involvement to Wilson's desire to establish a just peace and a stable and progressive postwar world society.

[57] Karl E. Birnbaum, *Peace Moves and U-Boat Warfare* (Stockholm, 1958).

[58] *Ibid.,* 28–32, 36–37, 39.

As 1915 ended, Chancellor Theobald von Bethmann-Hollweg came under great military and public pressures for full underseas warfare. Bethmann, deeply fearful of the dire consequences of hostilities with America, was hampered in resistance by the weakness of Kaiser Wilhelm II and by his own lack of energy and will.[59] The *Sussex* pledge, therefore, was only a temporary triumph over the U-boat enthusiasts.[60]

The Chancellor initiated a peace move in late 1916 in the hope of either forcing a general peace conference or of creating an atmosphere of reasonableness that would prevent hostilities with the United States when more drastic submarine warfare began. The overture failed and when Wilson asked on December 18 for a statement of belligerent war goals, the Berlin government gave it an evasive, negative reply because both the military and civilian officials distrusted the President's motives and suspected collusion with the Allies. Unfortunately, in Birnbaum's view, the quick reply to Wilson's overture doomed the policy of trying to create a rapport sufficiently strong to avoid hostilities over a new underseas campaign. This was the final failure of Germany's American policy.[61] At the decisive conferences at Pless on January 9, 1917, the military and naval leaders unanimously insisted on unrestricted underseas warfare as the best hope for victory, whereas the Chancellor merely recited his past objections before deferring to the military view. Birnbaum believes that even at this date a more vigorous objection by Bethmann, analyzing the probable results of unrestricted warfare and the effects of an American entry, might have swayed the Kaiser and have postponed the decision at least long enough to try to cushion its impact on Wilson.

German vacillation between peace efforts and the submarine panacea finally broke down in a decision for the latter because of doubts over Wilson's neutrality and goals, and the growing primacy of the shortsighted military voice within the German government. Although the author disavowed in the preface any intention of answering the question of whether German-American hostilities were avoidable, in his conclusions he attributed considerable weight to German skepticism of Wilson engendered by the pro-Ally nature of American neutrality and the different attitudes of Washington toward Allied as opposed to German infractions of international law.[62] In that sense Birnbaum suggests a partial answer to the question if a more impartial American neutrality would not have strengthened the hands of German moderates in resisting pressures for unrestricted U-boat warfare.

---

[59] *Ibid.*, 51–53, 58–61.
[60] *Ibid.*, 78–79, 86.
[61] *Ibid.*, 270.
[62] *Ibid.*, 31, 336–38.

The latest one-volume study of the neutrality period is Ernest R. May's *World War and American Isolation.*[63] Utilizing multi-archival research in Europe and the United States, May has examined the evolution of policies from the British and German perspectives as well as the American. He pointed out that in both Great Britain and Germany questions of policy toward neutral America were intertwined in domestic politics. In comparison with the Birnbaum study, May developed in greater detail the story of domestic German political pressures on foreign policy.

British Foreign Secretary Grey successfully shaped the English course in the first six months of the war by proceeding cautiously and considerately in applying maritime measures so that Anglo-American friendship would be preserved and strengthened. Even when Grey had lost the ability to control events because of mounting public pressures in England for a more drastic blockade, he had helped establish a moral basis of friendship capable of surviving a more trying period.[64]

In Germany Bethmann "fought long and hard against reckless opponents, only in the end to fail."[65] May thus gave a more favorable appraisal than did Birnbaum and Link, who portrayed the Chancellor in less flattering terms as failing to make a serious effort either to comprehend Wilson's peace objectives in 1916, to develop a reasonable German peace move, or to subject Admiralty claims for the submarine to close scrutiny and refutation.[66] May depicted the harried Chancellor as convinced that the submarine could not defeat England and that war with the United States would be disastrous for Germany. He could not force abandonment of the U-boat weapon, however, because of the fanatical attitude of the navy admirals, the submarine enthusiasm of the German public, and the pressures of the conservative political parties and press. Caught in a dilemma, complicated by reliance on the vacillating Kaiser, the Chancellor temporized and delayed, making enough concessions to the United States to avoid war in the *Lusitania, Arabic,* and *Sussex* crises and yet endeavoring to permit the navalists use of the submarine just short of that point. At best, therefore, Bethmann could only postpone a decision for war with America.[67] By the fall of 1916 the new supreme army command of Field Marshal Paul von Hindenburg and

---

[63] *The World War and American Isolation, 1914–1917* (Cambridge, 1959).

[64] *Ibid.,* 18–19, 21–25, 32–33. May has concluded that American economic retaliation in late 1916 would not have been fatal to Britain, which by then had developed alternative sources of munitions supplies. *Ibid.,* 321–22.

[65] *Ibid.,* [vii].

[66] Link, *Wilson the Diplomatist,* 79–80. In *The Struggle for Neutrality,* 399, 401–03, 553, Link portrayed Bethmann more favorably as compelled by his precarious position to temporize in regard to U-boat warfare.

[67] May, *World War and American Isolation,* 197–205.

General Erich F. W. Ludendorff had come to dominate Wilhelm, and Bethmann could no longer control the Reichstag. Hence when the army leaders joined the admirals in insistence on unrestricted underseas warfare as the one reliable hope for victory, the Chancellor was compelled to acquiesce. Any other course would have meant his immediate political demise.[68]

In concurrence with Buehrig and other writers, May described American neutrality as generally benevolent toward the Allies. Yet permission of belligerent loans and the arms trade were not deliberately unneutral but merely reflected America's view of international law and its trade interests. Legal and moral factors also were involved in the different American policies toward the British blockade and the submarine zone, but "the central difference in the two cases was a matter of national interest and not of either law or morality." Wilson could be satisfied that he had complied with the requirements of international law and morality and had served the national interests.[69]

May agreed with previous writers that House and Lansing viewed a triumphant Germany as a future threat to American security. House repeatedly warned Wilson in late 1914 and after that Germany would never forgive America for its pro-Ally attitude and if it won the war would hold the United States accountable and might challenge the Monroe Doctrine in South America. The Colonel did not desire a smashing Allied victory, however, for that would leave Russia free to expand.[70] As for Wilson, May stated that "He does appear, however, to have shared the view of Lansing and House that Germany was an enemy. He hoped that she might be too exhausted by the European war to turn immediately upon the United States, but he was not sanguine."[71] Wilson in late 1915 admitted to House that a victorious Germany might well take the western hemisphere as its next target, and his speeches for military preparedness in 1916 revealed a deep apprehension for the future security of the Americas. The President differed from these advisers primarily in his emotional attachment to peace. Consequently, although Wilson accepted the judgments of House and Lansing for a

---

[68] *Ibid.*, 288–89, 413–15.

[69] *Ibid.*, 45–53. Although Link, in the earlier volumes, described American neutrality to 1916 as benevolent but legally neutral toward the Allies, in *The Struggle for Neutrality*, 687, 691–92, he emphasizes the essential impartiality of American policies. Wilson acquiesced in Allied maritime measures, as required by trade, sympathy, and neutrality, but he also sought an adjustment to German submarine warfare by narrowing an initial condemnation of the U-boat as a weapon to mere insistence on the safety of American lives aboard belligerent liners. Thus the Oct. 21, 1915 protest to Britain was "fair warning" not to expect a benevolent neutrality. Neither side could reasonably complain that Wilson was against it.

[70] May, *World War and American Isolation*, 77–78.

[71] *Ibid.*, 169.

firm policy toward Germany, caution and pacifist inclinations caused him to follow a course of patience and delay, hoping for a "miraculous deliverance" from his dilemma. Additionally, Wilson's caution re-flected his consciousness of the divided state of American public opinion, military weaknesses of the United States, and the hope of playing a role of peacemaker in the European war.[72]

Ruthless use of the submarine was the only kind of German action that could have engendered German-American hostility, as Germany lacked other means to affect directly American interests. Wilson could have accepted German underseas warfare in early 1915, just as he had British actions, but he instead chose to condemn it. Other alternatives were rejected apparently because the U-boat campaign violated inter-national law and morality, and because it endangered important Ameri-can economic interests in the war trade with the Allies.[73] After the *Lusi-tania* crisis American national prestige was fully committed to the strict accountability policy and diplomatic flexibility was greatly circum-scribed. If only moral principles and economic interests had been in-volved, some possibility of compromise would have remained; what prevented Wilson and his advisers from considering such, however, was apprehension that prestige would be lost by a retreat or a compro-mise. House conceived of prestige in reference to the diplomatic influ-ence of the American government. Lansing saw it also as closely connected to domestic public confidence in the administration, while Wilson thought of prestige as affecting national pride and involving moral purposes.[74] To the American leaders the concept of national interests thus included not only security but legal, economic, and pres-tige factors as well.

The unrestricted submarine campaign in 1917 caused Wilson to respond with a decision for war apparently in large part because of his concern for the nation's prestige and moral influence as a great power. Acceptance of the new U-boat war would have been a surrender in the light of past American declarations and seemed impossible to Wilson, not so much now on the grounds of immediate economic or security considerations, but because of the damaging blow American prestige and influence would have suffered. Each succeeding crisis with Ger-many had seen American prestige more deeply committed; and the submarine issue had become a symbol of Wilson's dedication to uphold international law and the rights of humanity.[75] Full belligerency, rather than armed neutrality, was chosen because of the President's growing

---

[72] *Ibid.,* 167–78.

[73] *Ibid.,* 137–42. Contrary to Link, May viewed the Feb. 10, 1915 strict ac-countability note as initially intended to cover loss of American lives on bellig-erent as well as American merchant ships.

[74] *Ibid.,* 156–59.

[75] *Ibid.,* 426–27.

distrust of Germany, his desire to unite the American people, and his belief that the nation's role in the war would be limited militarily. May concluded that Wilson had held balance-of-power ideas but that they were subsidiary to his idealistic desire for a just and lasting world peace. Although Wilson has been criticized by some historians for not taking the nation into war to protect its security, May believes it difficult to find fault with Wilson's statesmanship. Not perceiving an immediate danger to America from a German victory in the war, Wilson realistically coped with the only endangered national interests, economic and prestige, and idealistically sought to promote world peace through a new international order.[76]

The problem of the role of the national interests in the neutrality period receives at least a partial answer in the studies by Buehrig, Link, and May. The evidence that Wilson was more realistic than portrayed in the past, and that he was aware of and held to some degree balance of power and national interest concepts, is too extensive to be dismissed as a mere selection of isolated statements from the larger corpus of Wilsonian materials. Contrary to previous interpretations, the works of Buehrig, Link's recent volumes, and May reveal that Wilson often was influenced by his realistic counselors, and that he shared much of their evaluations of the meaning of the European war. Secretary Lansing had the clearest conviction that American security would be menaced by a German victory and might require intervention to avert that possibility. House and Wilson generally believed that the outcome of the war most favorable to American and world interests would be a peace short of total victory for either side. May pointed out that both the Colonel and Wilson foresaw that a victorious Germany would probably threaten the position of the United States in South America. Yet as Buehrig, Link, and May agree, balance of power and other considerations caused Wilson and House in 1915 and 1916 to try to mediate the war and thus to avoid American involvement and to preserve the exist-

---

[76] *Ibid.*, 433–37. Richard W. Leopold, *The Growth of American Foreign Policy* (New York, 1962), has usefully synthesized recent scholarship on the neutrality era. He views Wilson's acquiescence in the Allied maritime system as necessitated by America's economic and other national interests, and by the impossibility of maintaining an absolutely impartial neutrality when challenged by conditions of modern warfare (pp. 299, 303). The President, despite some evidence of pro-Ally feelings and balance-of-power concerns, "steered a course which was dictated solely by what he thought . . . to be best for America" (p. 311). The resultant economic ties with the Allies did not make war inevitable; only the German declaration of unrestricted submarine warfare, based on hopes of victory and not on resentment of America's role, left no alternative but entry into the war (pp. 303, 336). See also Leopold's "The Emergence of America as a World Power: Some Second Thoughts," John Braeman and others, eds., *Change and Continuity in Twentieth-Century America* (Columbus, 1964).

ing equipoise. When the President finally did take the nation into the conflict in 1917, it was not because he feared an immediate German menace to American security.

How, then, were concepts of the national interest involved in the American war entry? Buehrig saw the answer in a Wilsonian balance of power concern being transformed into reliance on a community of power concept to protect American interests and preserve a just future peace. The unrestricted submarine announcement of 1917 precipitated war because of past policy stands, and because Germany was seen as a menace to the new world order envisioned by Wilson. Link portrayed Wilson as driven into acceptance of full hostilities over the submarine issue because of fear of a German victory endangering the balance of power and precluding realization of his idealistic and moralistic hopes for world reconstruction. May placed the emphasis on the prestige factor, which in a sense combined both national interests (security, economic, and diplomatic influence) and moralistic ideas of national honor and duty.

The more simplistic explanations of American involvement in the European war, current in the 1920s and 1930s, whether on the narrow grounds of a defense of legal neutral rights or of unneutral economic ties with the Allies, no longer suffice. The Buehrig, Link, and May studies make that conclusion abundantly clear. Just as clearly, the hypothesis that the United States went to war in 1917 to protect its security against an immediate German threat lacks persuasiveness. It appears that a complex of factors, including legitimate economic interests, some fear of a German victory and long-term threat to the western hemisphere, moral and legal reactions to the submarine, a very sensitive awareness of the involvement of American prestige, and especially Wilson's determination to promote a just and enduring postwar system, underlay American policies and the war entry in 1917. Defined as meaning more than immediate security needs, the authors reviewed agreed that the concept of involved American national interests had a large place in Wilsonian policies and war entry. At least as important, however, if not more so, were moral and idealistic factors.

A Study in Nativism:
The American Red Scare of 1919–20
STANLEY COBEN

John Higham's **Strangers in the Land,** *which appeared in 1955, is a first-rate study of American nativism during the period 1860–1925. The principal components of nativism, Higham found, have been nationalism and ethnic prejudice. These sentiments expressed themselves in American life in three principal ways: as anti-Catholicism, as fear of foreign radicals, and as a claim for the superiority of the Anglo-Saxon "race" to which the white Protestant majority belonged. During four periods of major national crisis, nativism boiled up as a dominant force in American politics: in the late 1790's, in the 1850's, in the decade from 1886 to 1896, and in the era of World War I. But nativism, says Higham, has been more than a phenomenon of crisis or of crackpots; it has characterized the American people. It has been a habit of mind which "illuminates darkly some of the large contours of the American past; it has mirrored our national anxieties and marked out the bounds of our tolerance."*

In the essay reprinted below, Stanley Coben, of the University of California (at Los Angeles), concentrates his attention on the nature and causes of the Red Scare of 1919–20. Coben is the author and editor of several notable volumes. His interest in the Red Scare derives naturally enough from his biography of A. Mitchell Palmer, who was Attorney General of the United States at the time and whose conduct of the famous (or infamous) "Palmer Raids" was a planned and self-interested attempt to root out foreign radicals and gain the Democratic nomination for president. In the following article, Coben uses concepts from cultural anthropology and social psychology to reach a deeper perception of American nativism as it was expressed by the Red Scare. In doing so, he leans heavily on Anthony F. C. Wallace's ideas about societal disruption and "revitalization movements."

Coben's application of cultural anthropology to a study of the Red Scare offers us refreshing insights not only into the phenomenon of nativism but

SOURCE: *Political Science Quarterly,* LXXIX (March, 1964), 52–75. Reprinted by permission.

also into the relevance of the phenomenon to the larger course of American life and thought. It also raises important questions. What social function does nativism fulfill? Can the American nation be validly compared with other cultural groups? Is it not fair to suggest that our culture is more a loose agglomeration of value-clusters rather than a single tightly knit system of values and that our nativism, accordingly, is more complex and less susceptible of the kind of analysis that Coben's application to it of primitive, more homogeneous cultural patterns would seem to suggest? May it not be postulated that the function that nativism has to serve—and therefore its vitality, indeed its virulence—is in inverse proportion to the uniformities and homogeneities of a particular culture? Would this not in fact explain why American nativism has been an especially tenacious variety?

How far can we accept the suggestion that American nativism is the recourse of persons troubled by severe inner turmoil themselves, who use the "nation" to protect themselves as individuals? This presupposes a direct relation between the individual's needs and his use of the nation in meeting them. But are there not intermediary groups in American life—such as the Irish Catholics, urban Jewish, white Protestant, Negro—to which the individual more immediately belongs and which may serve to protect him against anxiety and psychic turmoil?

If nativism has, as Higham suggests, boiled over during four distinct periods in our history, does not the fact of its occasional intensification suggest conversely that nativism is integral to American culture? Is it not endemic to a nation without natives? Has not the threat to the American value system been perpetual, a constant invasion by fleets of ever new immigrants? Has not American nativism been the perennially proclaimed and enforced attempt at imposing a national identity upon a nation of foreigners? Has not an insistence on patriotism, the key ingredient of nativism, been a continuing aspect of American life? And if patriotism is, as Edmund Burke called it, the last refuge of the scoundrel, has it not been the natural habitat of the American?

From the perspective of cultural anthropology, we can gain a broader view of American cultural identity. The student of our history would do well to note that it is an identity we also express in our historiography and that, in this sense, our historians are tribal bards writing tribal legends. The multifarious ways of a folk uniquely characterize the folk, while yet performing the basic functions that folkways universally perform. If American nativism is part of the construct of our values, and a continuing force today, how is it articulated and with what meaning? May we not venture that it has, in its most significant and recent aspect, taken the form of a white fear of the Negro's claim to full equality, and that the "Negro Revolution" has stirred up precisely those deeper fears—about race and radicalism, in-groups and out—on which an only slightly transformed nativism has been currently thriving?

At a victory loan pageant in the District of Columbia on May 6, 1919, a man refused to rise for the playing of "The Star-Spangled Banner." As soon as the national anthem was completed an enraged sailor fired three shots into the unpatriotic spectator's back. When the man fell, the *Washington Post* reported, "the crowd burst into cheering and handclapping." In February of the same year, a jury in Hammond, Indiana, took two minutes to acquit the assassin of an alien who yelled, "To Hell with the United States." Early in 1920, a clothing store salesman in Waterbury, Connecticut, was sentenced to six months in jail for having remarked to a customer that Lenin was "the brainiest," or "one of the brainiest" of the world's political leaders.[1] Dramatic episodes like these, or the better known Centralia Massacre, Palmer Raids, or May Day riots, were not everyday occurrences, even at the height of the Red Scare. But the fanatical one hundred per cent Americanism reflected by the Washington crowd, the Hammond jury, and the Waterbury judge pervaded a large part of our society between early 1919 and mid-1920.

Recently, social scientists have produced illuminating evidence about the causes of eruptions like that of 1919–20. They have attempted to identify experimentally the individuals most responsive to nativistic appeals, to explain their susceptibility, and to propose general theories of nativistic and related movements. These studies suggest a fuller, more coherent picture of nativistic upheavals and their causes than we now possess, and they provide the framework for this attempt to reinterpret the Red Scare.

Psychological experiments indicate that a great many Americans— at least several million—are always ready to participate in a "red scare." These people permanently hold attitudes which characterized the nativists of 1919–20: hostility toward certain minority groups, especially radicals and recent immigrants, fanatical patriotism, and a belief that internal enemies seriously threaten national security.[2]

---

[1] *Washington Post,* May 7, 1919; Mark Sullivan, *Our Times, The United States 1900–1925* (New York, 1935), VI, 169; *The Nation,* CX (April 17, 1920), 510–11. The most complete account of the Red Scare is Robert K. Murray, *Red Scare, A Study in National Hysteria* (Minneapolis, 1955). But see the critical review of Murray's book by John M. Blum in *Mississippi Valley Historical Review,* XLII (1955), 145. Blum comments that Murray failed to explain "the susceptibility of the American people and of their elite to the 'national hysteria.' . . . About hysteria, after all, psychology and social psychology in particular have had considerable to say." John Higham places the postwar movement in historical perspective in his superb *Strangers in the Land, Patterns of American Nativism, 1860–1925* (New Brunswick, 1955), especially Chaps. 8 and 9.

[2] On the incidence of prejudice against minorities in the Unites States, see Gordon W. Allport and Bernard M. Kramer, "Some Roots of Prejudice,"

In one of the most comprehensive of these experiments, psychologists Nancy C. Morse and Floyd H. Allport tested seven hypotheses about the causes of prejudice and found that one, national involvement or patriotism, proved to be "by far the most important factor" associated with prejudice. Other widely held theories about prejudice —status rivalry, frustration-aggression, and scapegoat hypotheses, for example—were found to be of only secondary importance.[3] Summarizing the results of this and a number of other psychological experiments, Gordon W. Allport, a pioneer in the scientific study of prejudice, concluded that in a large proportion of cases the prejudiced person is attempting to defend himself against severe inner turmoil by enforcing order in his external life. Any disturbance in the social *status quo* threatens the precarious psychic equilibrium of this type of individual, who, according to Allport, seeks "an island of institutional safety and security. The nation is the island he selects . . . It has the definiteness he needs."

Allport pointed out that many apprehensive and frustrated people are not especially prejudiced. What is important, he found,

> is the way fear and frustration are handled. The institutionalistic way— especially the nationalistic—seems to be the nub of the matter. What happens is that the prejudiced person defines 'nation' to fit his needs. The nation is first of all a protection (the chief protection) of him as an individual. It is his in-group. He sees no contradiction in ruling out of its benefit orbit those whom he regards as threatening intruders and enemies (namely, American minorities). What is more, the nation stands for the status quo. It is a conservative agent; within it are all the devices for safe living that he approves. His nationalism is a form of conservatism.[4]

Journal of Psychology, XXII (1946), 9–39; Morris Janowitz and Dwaine Marvick, "Authoritarianism and Political Behavior," *Public Opinion Quarterly*, XVII (1953), 185–201; Bruno Bettelheim and Morris Janowitz, *Dynamics of Prejudice, A Psychological and Sociological Study of Veterans* (New York, 1950), 16, 26, and *passim*.

[3] Nancy C. Morse and F. H. Allport, "The Causation of Anti-Semitism: An Investigation of Seven Hypotheses," *Journal of Psychology*, XXXIV (1952), 197–233. For further experimental evidence indicating that prejudiced individuals are more anxious, neurotic, or intolerant of ambiguity than those with more "liberal" attitudes, Anthony Davids, "Some Personality and Intellectual Correlates to Intolerance of Ambiguity," *Journal of Abnormal and Social Psychology*, LI (1955), 415–20; Ross Stagner and Clyde S. Congdon, "Another Failure to Demonstrate Displacement of Aggression," *Journal of Abnormal and Social Psychology*, LI (1955), 695–96; Dean Peabody, "Attitude Content and Agreement Set in Scales of Authoritarianism, Dogmatism, Anti-Semitism and Economic Conservatism," *Journal of Abnormal and Social Psychology*, LXIII (1961), 1–11.

[4] Gordon W. Allport, *The Nature of Prejudice* (Cambridge, 1955), 406; see Boyd C. Shafer, *Nationalism, Myth and Reality* (New York, 1955), 181.

Substantial evidence, then, suggests that millions of Americans are both extraordinarily fearful of social change and prejudiced against those minority groups which they perceive as "threatening intruders." Societal disruption, especially if it can easily be connected with the "intruders," not only will intensify the hostility of highly prejudiced individuals, but also will provoke many others, whose antagonism in more stable times had been mild or incipient, into the extreme group.

A number of anthropologists have come to conclusions about the roots of nativism which complement these psychological studies. Since the late nineteenth century, anthropologists have been studying the religious and nativistic cults of American Indian tribes and of Melanesian and Papuan groups in the South Pacific. Recently, several anthropologists have attempted to synthesize their findings and have shown striking parallels in the cultural conditions out of which these movements arose.[5] In every case, severe societal disruption preceded the outbreak of widespread nativistic cult behavior. According to Anthony F. C. Wallace, who has gone farthest toward constructing a general theory of cult formation, when the disruption has proceeded so far that many members of a society find it difficult or impossible to fulfill their physical and psychological needs, or to relieve severe anxiety through the ordinary culturally approved methods, the society will be susceptible to what Wallace has termed a "revitalization movement." This is a convulsive attempt to change or revivify important cultural beliefs and values, and frequently to eliminate alien influences. Such movements promise and often provide participants with better means

---

[5] See, especially, the works of Anthony F. C. Wallace: "Revitalization Movements," *American Anthropologist*, LVIII (1956), 264–81; "Handsome Lake and the Great Revival in the West," *American Quarterly*, IV (1952), 149–65; "Stress and Rapid Personality Change," *International Record of Medicine and General Practice Clinics*, CLXIX (1956), 761–73; "New Religions Among the Delaware Indians, 1600–1900," *Southwest Journal of Anthropology*, XII (1956), 1–21. Also, Michael M. Ames, "Reaction to Stress: A Comparative Study of Nativism," *Davidson Journal of Anthropology*, III (1957), 16–30; C. S. Belshaw, "The Significance of Modern Cults in Melanesian Development," *Australian Outlook*, IV (1950), 116–25; Raymond Firth, "The Theory of 'Cargo' Cults: A Note on Tikopia," *Man*, LV (1955), 130–32; Lawrence Krader, "A Nativistic Movement in Western Siberia," *American Anthropologist*, LVIII (1956), 282–92; Ralph Linton, "Nativistic Movements," *American Anthropologist*, XLV (1943), 220–43; Margaret Mead, *New Lives for Old* (New York, 1956); Peter Worsley, *The Trumpet Shall Sound* (London, 1957). Several sociologists and psychologists have come to conclusions about the causes of these movements that are similar in important respects to Wallace's, although less comprehensive. See Leon Festinger, *A Theory of Cognitive Dissonance* (New York, 1957); Hadley Cantril, *The Psychology of Social Movements* (New York, 1941), especially pp. 3–4, Chaps. 5, 8, and 9; Hans H. Toch, "Crisis Situations and Ideological Revaluation," *Public Opinion Quarterly*, XIX (1955), 53–67.

of dealing with their changed circumstances, thus reducing their very high level of internal stress.[6]

American Indian tribes, for example, experienced a series of such convulsions as the tide of white settlers rolled west. The Indians were pushed onto reservations and provided with Indian agents, missionaries, and physicians, who took over many of the functions hitherto assumed by chiefs and medicine men. Indian craftsmen (and craftswomen) were replaced by dealers in the white man's implements. Most hunters and warriors also lost their vocations and consequently their self-respect. What an anthropologist wrote of one tribe was true of many others: "From cultural maturity as Pawnees they were reduced to cultural infancy as civilized men."[7]

One of the last major religious upheavals among the Indians was the Ghost Dance cult which spread from Nevada through Oregon and northern California in the 1870's, and a similar movement among the Rocky Mountain and western plains Indians about 1890. Although cult beliefs varied somewhat from tribe to tribe, converts generally were persuaded that if they followed certain prescribed rituals, including the dance, they would soon return to their old ways of living. Even their dead relatives would be restored to life. Most Indians were too conscious of their military weakness to challenge their white masters directly. Ghost Dancers among the Dakota Sioux, however, influenced by the militant proselyter Sitting Bull, became convinced that true believers could not be harmed by the white man's bullets and that Sioux warriors would drive the intruders from Indian lands. Their dreams were rudely smashed at the massacre of Wounded Knee Creek in December 1890.[8]

The Boxer movement in China, 1898 to 1900, resembled in many respects the Indian Ghost Dance cults; however, the Boxers, more numer-

---

[6] Wallace, "Revitalization Movements." For a recent verification of Wallace's theories see Thomas Rhys Williams, "The Form of a North Borneo Nativistic Behavior," *American Anthropologist*, LXV (1963), 543–51. On the psychological results of socially caused stress, Wallace, "Stress and Rapid Personality Change"; William Caudill, *Effects of Social and Cultural Systems in Reactions to Stress*, Social Science Research Council Pamphlet No. 14 (New York, 1958); Caudill, "Cultural Perspectives on Stress," Army Medical Service Graduate School, *Symposium on Stress* (Washington, D.C., 1953); Hans Selye, *The Stress of Life* (New York, 1956); Roland Fischer and Neil Agnew, "A Hierarchy of Stressors," *Journal of Mental Science*, CI (1955), 383–86; Daniel H. Funkenstein, Stanley H. King, and Margaret E. Drolette, *Mastery of Stress* (Cambridge, 1957); M. Basowitz *et al.*, *Anxiety and Stress: An Interdisciplinary Study of a Life Situation* (New York, 1955).

[7] Alexander Lesser, *The Pawnee Ghost Dance Hand Game. A Study of Cultural Change* (New York, 1933), 44.

[8] Cora DuBois, *The 1870 Ghost Dance*, Anthropological Records, III (Berkeley, 1946); Leslie Spier, *The Ghost Dance of 1870 Among the Klamath of Oregon*,

ous and perhaps less demoralized than the Indians, aimed more directly at removing foreign influences from their land. The movement erupted first in Shantung province where foreigners, especially Japanese, British, and Germans, were most aggressive. A flood of the Yellow River had recently deprived about a million people in the province of food and shelter. Banditry was rampant, organized government ineffective. The Boxer movement, based on the belief that these tragic conditions were due almost entirely to the "foreign devils" and their agents, determined to drive the enemy out of China. Boxers went into action carrying charms and chanting incantations supposed to make them invulnerable to the foreigners' bullets. The first object of the Boxers' nativistic fury were Chinese who had converted to Christianity, the intruders' religion. The patriots then attacked railroad and telegraph lines, leading symbols of foreign influence. Finally, the Boxers turned against the foreigners themselves, slaughtering many. Not until after the Boxers carried on a two-month siege of the foreign community in Peking did American, European, and Japanese armies crush the movement.[9]

Other revitalization attempts proved more successful than the Boxers or Ghost Dancers. The Gaiwiio movement, for example, helped the Iroquois Indians of western New York State to retain their identity as a culture while adjusting successfully to an encroaching white civilization during the first decade of the nineteenth century. The movement implanted a new moral code among the Indians, enjoining sobriety and family stability and encouraging acceptance of Western technology, while revivifying cohesive Indian traditions.[10]

Dominant as well as conquered peoples, Ralph Linton has pointed

---

University of Washington Publications in Anthropology, II (Seattle, 1927); Lesser, *Ghost Dance;* A. L. Kroeber, *Handbook of the Indians of California,* Bureau of American Ethnology Bulletin 78 (Washington, D.C., 1925). Anthropologists recently have argued about the origins of the Ghost Dance cults. Both sides agree, however, that whatever their origins, the cults took the form they did because of intolerable cultural conditions caused largely by white encroachments. David F. Aberle, "The Prophet Dance and Reactions to White Contact," *Southwest Journal of Anthropology,* XV (1959), 74–83; Leslie Spier, Wayne Suttles, and Melville Herskovits, "Comment on Aberle's Thesis of Deprivation," *Southwest Journal of Anthropology,* XV (1959), 84–88.

[9] The best account of the Boxer movement is Chester C. Tan, *The Boxer Catastrophe* (New York, 1955). Also, George N. Steiger, *China and the Occident, the Origin and Development of the Boxer Movement* (New Haven, 1927); Peter Fleming, *The Siege at Peking* (New York, 1959).

[10] Wallace, "Handsome Lake." Wallace compared the Gaiwiio with a Chinese attempt to accommodate their society to Western civilization in "Stress and Rapid Personality Change." For a successful movement in the South Pacific see Mean, *New Lives for Old.*

out, undergo nativistic movements. Dominant groups, he observed, are sometimes threatened "not only by foreign invasion or domestic revolt but also by the invidious process of assimilation which might, in the long run, destroy their distinctive powers and privileges." Under such circumstances, Linton concluded, "the frustrations which motivate nativistic movements in inferior or dominated groups" are "replaced by anxieties which produce very much the same [nativistic] result" in dominant groups.[11]

Communist "brainwashers" have consciously attempted to achieve results comparable to those obtained by prophets of movements like the Ghost Dance cult and the Boxers. They create intolerable stress within individuals, not through rapid societal change, but by intentional physical debilitation and continual accusations, cross-examinations, and use of other anxiety-provoking techniques. Then they offer their prisoners an escape from the induced psychological torment: conversion to the new gospel.[12]

The similarity in the mental processes involved in "brainwashing" and in the formation of nativistic movements becomes even clearer upon examination of the Chinese Communist attempt to establish their doctrines in mainland China. Again, the Communists intentionally have created conditions like those out of which nativistic cults have arisen more spontaneously in other societies. In addition to the stress which ordinarily would accompany rapid industrialization of an economically backward society, the Chinese leaders have provoked additional anxiety through the systematic use of group confessions and denunciations and have intentionally disrupted family life. Hostility toward the American enemy has been purposely aroused and used to unify the masses, as well as to justify the repression of millions of alleged internal enemies. The whole population has been continually urged to repent their sins and to adopt wholeheartedly the Communist gospel, which has a strong nativistic component. As a psychologist has remarked, to a large extent the Chinese Communists provide both the disease and the cure.[13]

---

[11] Linton, 237. Also, Carroll L. Riley and John Hobgood, "A Recent Nativistic Movement Among the Southern Tepehuan Indians," Southwest Journal of Anthropology, XV (1959), 355–60.

[12] Robert J. Lifton, "Thought Reform in Western Civilians in Chinese Communist Prisons," Psychiatry, XIX (1956), 173–95; Edgar H. Schein, "The Chinese Indoctrination Program for Prisoners of War, A Study of Attempted Brainwashing," Psychiatry, XIX (1956), 149–72.

[13] Edgar H. Schein, with Inge Schneier and Curtis H. Bark, Coercive Persuasion (New York, 1961); William Sargent, Battle for the Mind (New York, 1957), 150–65; Robert J. Lifton, Thought Reform and the Psychology of Totalism (New York, 1961); R. L. Walker, China Under Communism (London, 1946).

The ferocious outbreak of nativism in the United States after World War I was not consciously planned or provoked by any individual or group, although some Americans took advantage of the movement once it started. Rather, the Red Scare, like the Gaiwiio and Boxer movements described above, was brought on largely by a number of severe social and economic dislocations which threatened the national equilibrium. The full extent and the shocking effects of these disturbances of 1919 have not yet been adequately described. Runaway prices, a brief but sharp stock market crash and business depression, revolutions throughout Europe, widespread fear of domestic revolt, bomb explosions, and an outpouring of radical literature were distressing enough. These sudden difficulties, moreover, served to exaggerate the disruptive effects already produced by the social and intellectual ravages of the World War and the preceding reform era, and by the arrival, before the war, of millions of new immigrants. This added stress intensified the hostility of Americans strongly antagonistic to minority groups, and brought new converts to blatant nativism from among those who ordinarily were not overtly hostile toward radicals or recent immigrants.

Citizens who joined the crusade for one hundred per cent Americanism sought, primarily, a unifying force which would halt the apparent disintegration of their culture. The movement, they felt, would eliminate those foreign influences which the one hundred per centers believed were the major cause of their anxiety.

Many of the postwar sources of stress were also present during World War I, and the Red Scare, as John Higham has observed, was partly an exaggeration of wartime passions.[14] In 1917–18 German-Americans served as the object of almost all our nativistic fervor; they were the threatening intruders who refused to become good citizens. "They used America," a patriotic author declared in 1918 of two million German-Americans, "they never loved her. They clung to their old language, their old customs, and cared nothing for ours. . . . As a class they were clannish beyond all other races coming here."[15] Fear of subversion by German agents was almost as extravagant in 1917–18 as anxiety about "reds" in the postwar period. Attorney General Thomas Watt Gregory reported to a friend in May 1918 that "we not infrequently receive as many as fifteen hundred letters in a single day suggesting disloyalty and the making of investigations."[16]

Opposition to the war by radical groups helped smooth the transition among American nativists from hatred of everything German to

---

[14] Higham, 222.

[15] Emerson Hough, *The Web* (Chicago, 1919), 23. Hough was a rabid one hundred per center during the Red Scare also.

[16] T. W. Gregory to R. E. Vinson, May 13, 1918, Papers of Thomas Watt Gregory (Library of Congress, Washington, D. C.).

fear of radical revolution. The two groups of enemies were associated also for other reasons. High government officials declared after the war that German leaders planned and subsidized the Bolshevik Revolution.[17] When bombs blasted homes and public buildings in nine cities in June 1919, the director of the Justice Department's Bureau of Investigation asserted that the bombers were "connected with Russian bolshevism, aided by Hun money."[18] In November 1919, a year after the armistice, a popular magazine warned of "the Russo-German movement that is now trying to dominate America. . . ."[19]

Even the wartime hostility toward German-Americans, however, is more understandable when seen in the light of recent anthropological and psychological studies. World War I disturbed Americans not only because of the real threat posed by enemy armies and a foreign ideology. For many citizens it had the further effect of shattering an already weakened intellectual tradition. When the European governments decided to fight, they provided shocking evidence that man was not, as most educated members of Western society had believed, a rational creature progressing steadily, if slowly, toward control of his environment. When the great powers declared war in 1914, many Americans as well as many Europeans were stunned. The *New York Times* proclaimed a common theme—European civilization had collapsed: The supposedly advanced nations, declared the *Times*, "have reverted to the condition of savage tribes roaming the forests and falling upon each other in a fury of blood and carnage to achieve the ambitious designs of chieftains clad in skins and drunk with mead."[20] Franz Alexander, director for twenty-five years of the Chicago Institute of Psychoanalysis, recently recalled his response to the oubreak of the World War:

---

[17] Subcommittee of Senate Committee on the Judiciary, *Hearings, Brewing and Liquor Interests and German and Bolshevik Propaganda,* 66th Congress, 1st Session, 1919, 2669 ff.: *The New York Times,* July 7, August 11 and 29, September 15–21, 1918.

[18] *Washington Post,* July 3, 1919. Bureau Director William J. Flynn produced no evidence to back this assertion. Later he claimed to have conclusive proof that the bombers were Italian anarchists. Flynn to Attorney General Harry Daugherty, April 4, 1922, Department of Justice Records, File 202600, Sect. 5 (National Archives, Washington, D. C.).

[19] *Saturday Evening Post,* CXCII (November 1, 1919), 28. For similar assertions in other publications, Meno Lovenstein, *American Opinion of Soviet Russia* (Washington, D.C., 1941), Chap. 1, *passim.*

[20] Quoted in William E. Leuchtenburg, *The Perils of Prosperity, 1914–32* (Chicago, 1958), 13. There is no comprehensive study of the effects of the war on the American mind. For brief treatments, Henry F. May, *The End of American Innocence* (New York, 1959), 361–67; Merle Curti, *The Growth of American Thought* (New York, 1951), 687–705; Ralph Henry Gabriel, *The Course of American Democratic Thought* (New York, 1956), 387, 404; André Siegfried, *America Comes of Age* (New York, 1927), 3; Walter Lord, *The Good Years, From 1900 to the First World War* (New York, 1960), 339–41.

The first impact of this news is [*sic*] unforgettable. It was the sudden intuitive realization that a chapter of history had ended. . . . Since then, I have discussed this matter with some of my contemporaries and heard about it a great deal in my early postwar psychoanalytic treatments of patients. To my amazement, the others who went through the same events had quite a similar reaction. . . . It was an immediate vivid and prophetic realization that something irrevocable of immense importance had happened in history.[21]

Americans were jolted by new blows to their equilibrium after entering the war. Four million men were drafted away from familiar surroundings and some of them experienced the terrible carnage of trench warfare. Great numbers of women left home to work in war industries or to replace men in other jobs. Negroes flocked to Northern industrial areas by the hundreds of thousands, and their first mass migration from the South created violent racial antagonism in Northern cities.

During the war, also, Americans sanctioned a degree of government control over the economy which deviated sharply from traditional economic individualism. Again, fears aroused before the war were aggravated, for the reform legislation of the Progressive era had tended to increase government intervention, and many citizens were further perturbed by demands that the federal government enforce even higher standards of economic and social morality. By 1919, therefore, some prewar progressives as well as conservatives feared the gradual disappearance of highly valued individual opportunity and responsibility. Their fears were fed by strong postwar calls for continued large-scale government controls—extension of federal operation of railroads and of the Food Administration, for example.

The prime threat to these long-held individualistic values, however, and the most powerful immediate stimulus to the revitalistic response, came from Russia. There the Bolshevik conquerors proclaimed their intention of exporting Marxist ideology. If millions of Americans were disturbed in 1919 by the specter of communism, the underlying reason was not fear of foreign invasion—Russia, after all, was still a backward nation recently badly defeated by German armies. The real threat was the potential spread of communist ideas. These, the one hundred per centers realized with horror, possessed a genuine appeal for reformers and for the economically underprivileged, and if accepted they would complete the transformation of America.

A clear picture of the Bolshevik tyranny was not yet available; therefore, as after the French Revolution, those who feared the newly successful ideology turned to fight the revolutionary ideals. So the

---

[21] Franz Alexander, *The Western Mind in Transition* (New York, 1960), 73–74. Also see William Barrett, *Irrational Man* (Garden City, N. Y., 1961), 32–33.

Saturday Evening Post declared editorially in November 1919 that "History will see our present state of mind as one with that preceding the burning of witches, the children's crusade, the great tulip craze and other examples of softening of the world brain." The *Post* referred not to the Red Scare or the impending Palmer Raids, but to the spread of communist ideology. Its editorial concluded: "The need of the country is not more idealism, but more pragmatism; not communism, but common sense."[22] One of the most powerful patriotic groups, the National Security League, called upon members early in 1919 to "teach 'Americanism.' This means the fighting of Bolshevism . . . by the creation of well defined National Ideals." Members "must preach Americanism and instil the idealism of America's Wars, and that American spirit of service which believes in giving as well as getting."[23] New York attorney, author, and educator Henry Waters Taft warned a Carnegie Hall audience late in 1919 that Americans must battle "a propaganda which is tending to undermine our most cherished social and political institutions and is having the effect of producing widespread unrest among the poor and the ignorant, especially those of foreign birth."[24]

When the war ended Americans also confronted the disturbing possibility, pointed up in 1919 by the struggle over the League of Nations, that Europe's struggles would continue to be their own. These factors combined to make the First World War a traumatic experience for millions of citizens. As Senator James Reed of Missouri observed in August 1919, "This country is still suffering from shell shock. Hardly anyone is in a normal state of mind. . . . A great storm has swept over the intellectual world and its ravages and disturbances still exist."[25]

The wartime "shell shock" left many Americans extraordinarily susceptible to psychological stress caused by postwar social and economic turbulence. Most important for the course of the Red Scare, many of these disturbances had their greatest effect on individuals already antagonistic toward minorities. First of all, there was some real evidence of danger to the nation in 1919, and the nation provided the chief emotional support for many Americans who responded easily to charges of an alien radical menace. Violence flared throughout Europe after the war and revolt lifted radicals to power in several

---

[22] *Saturday Evening Post,* CXCII (November 1, 1919), 28.

[23] National Security League, *Future Work* (New York, 1919), 6.

[24] Henry Waters Taft, *Aspects of Bolshevism and Americanism, Address before the League for Political Education at Carnegie Hall, New York, December 6, 1919* (New York, 1919), 21.

[25] U. S., *Congressional Record,* 66th Congress, 1st Session, August 15, 1919, 3892.

Eastern and Central European nations. Combined with the earlier Bolshevik triumph in Russia these revolutions made Americans look more anxiously at radicals here. Domestic radicals encouraged these fears; they became unduly optimistic about their own chances of success and boasted openly of their coming triumph. Scores of new foreign language anarchist and communist journals, most of them written by and for Southern and Eastern European immigrants, commenced publication, and the established radical press became more exuberant. These periodicals never tired of assuring readers in 1919 that "the United States seems to be on the verge of a revolutionary crisis."[26] American newspapers and magazines reprinted selections from radical speeches, pamphlets, and periodicals so their readers could see what dangerous ideas were abroad in the land.[27] Several mysterious bomb explosions and bombing attempts, reported in bold front page headlines in newspapers across the country, frightened the public in 1919. To many citizens these seemed part of an organized campaign of terror carried on by alien radicals intending to bring down the federal government. The great strikes of 1919 and early 1920 aroused similar fears.[28]

Actually American radical organizations in 1919 were disorganized and poverty-stricken. The Communists were inept, almost without contact with American workers and not yet dominated or subsidized by Moscow. The IWW was shorn of its effective leaders, distrusted by labor, and generally declining in influence and power. Violent anarchists were isolated in a handful of tiny, unconnected local organizations.[29] One or two of these anarchist groups probably carried out the

---

[26] Robert E. Park, *The Immigrant Press and Its Control* (New York, 1922), 214, 230–38, 241–45; R. E. Park and Herbert A. Miller, *Old World Traits Transplanted* (New York, 1921), 99–101; Daniel Bell, "The Background and Development of Marxian Socialism in the United States," in Donald Drew Egbert and Stow Persons, *Socialism in American Life* (Princeton, 1952), I, 334; Lovenstein, 7–50; Leuchtenburg, 67–68; Murray, 33–36.

[27] The Justice Department distributed pamphlets containing such material to all American newspapers and magazines; *Red Radicalism, as Described by Its Own Leaders* (Washington, D. C., 1920); National Popular Government League, *To the American People, Report Upon the Illegal Practices of the Department of Justice* (Washington, D. C., 1920), 64–66. The staunchly antiradical *New York Times* published translations from a large sample of foreign language radical newspapers on June 8, 1919.

[28] Murray, Chaps. 5, 7–10. Asked by a congressional committee a few weeks after the spate of bombings in June 1919 whether there was real evidence of an organized effort to destroy the federal government, Assistant Attorney General Francis P. Garvan replied, "Certainly." Garvan was in charge of federal prosecution of radicals. *Washington Post,* June 27, 1919.

[29] Theodore Draper, *The Roots of American Communism* (New York, 1957), 198–200, 302, 312–14; David J. Saposs, *Left Wing Unionism, A Study in Policies and Tactics* (New York, 1926), 49–50, 152–57; Selig Perlman and Philip Taft

"bomb conspiracy" of 1919; but the extent of the "conspiracy" can be judged from the fact that the bombs killed a total of two men during the year, a night watchman and one of the bomb throwers, and seriously wounded one person, a maid in the home of a Georgia senator.[30]

Nevertheless, prophesies of national disaster abounded in 1919, even among high government officials. Secretary of State Robert Lansing confided to his diary that we were in real peril of social revolution. Attorney General A. Mitchell Palmer advised the House Appropriations Committee that "on a certain day, which we have been advised of," radicals would attempt "to rise up and destroy the Government at one fell swoop." Senator Charles Thomas of Colorado warned that "the country is on the verge of a volcanic upheaval." And Senator Miles Poindexter of Washington declared, "There is real danger that the government will fall."[31] A West Virginia wholesaler, with offices throughout the state, informed the Justice Department in October 1919 that "there is hardly a respectable citizen of my acquaintance who does not believe that we are on the verge of armed conflict in this country." William G. McAdoo was told by a trusted friend that "Chicago, which has always been a very liberal minded place, seems to me to have gone mad on the question of the 'Reds.'" Delegates to the Farmers National Congress in November 1919 pledged that farmers would assist the government in meeting the threat of revolution.[32]

The slight evidence of danger from radical organizations aroused such wild fear only because Americans had already encountered other threats to cultural stability. However, the dislocations caused by the war and the menace of communism alone would not have produced such a vehement nativistic response. Other postwar challenges to the social and economic order made the crucial difference.

Of considerable importance was the skyrocketing cost of living. Retail prices more than doubled between 1915 and 1920, and the price

(eds.), *Labor Movements* in John R. Commons (ed.), *History of Labour in the United States 1896–1932*, IV (New York, 1935), 621, 431–32; Jerome Davis, *The Russian Immigrant* (New York, 1922), 114–18; Kate Holladay Claghorn, *The Immigrant's Day in Court* (New York, 1923), 363–73; John S. Gambs, *The Decline of the I.W.W.* (New York, 1932), 133; Murray, 107–10.

[30] *The New York Times,* May 1, June 3, 4, 1919.

[31] "The Spread of Bolshevism in the United States," private memorandum, dated July 26, 1919, Papers of Robert Lansing (Library of Congress, Washington, D. C.); "One Point of View of the Murders at Centralia, Washington," private memorandum, dated November 13, 1919, Lansing Papers; U. S., *Congressional Record,* 66th Congress, 1st Session, October 14, 1919, 6869; *Washington Post,* February 16, 1919; New York *World,* June 19, 1919.

[32] Henry Barham to Palmer, October 27, 1919, Justice Department Records, File 202600; unidentified correspondent to McAdoo, February 10, 1920, McAdoo Papers (Library of Congress, Washington, D. C.); A. P. Sanders to Palmer, November 12, 1919, Justice Department Records, File 202600; *The New York Times,* October 31, 1919.

rise began gathering momentum in the spring of 1919.[33] During the summer of 1919 the dominant political issue in America was not the League of Nations; not even the "red menace" or the threat of a series of major strikes disturbed the public as much as did the climbing cost of living. The *Washington Post* early in August 1919 called rising prices, "the burning domestic issue...." Democratic National Chairman Homer Cummings, after a trip around the country, told President Woodrow Wilson that more Americans were worried about prices than about any other public issue and that they demanded government action. When Wilson decided to address Congress on the question the Philadelphia *Public Ledger* observed that the administration had "come rather tardily to a realization of what is uppermost in the minds of the American people."[34]

Then the wave of postwar strikes—there were 3,600 of them in 1919 involving over 4,000,000 workers[35]—reached a climax in the fall of 1919. A national steel strike began in September and nationwide coal and rail walkouts were scheduled for November 1. Unions gained in membership and power during the war, and in 1919 labor leaders were under strong pressure to help catch up to or go ahead of mounting living costs. Nevertheless, influential government officials attributed the walkouts to radical activities. Early in 1919, Secretary of Labor William B. Wilson declared in a public speech that recent major strikes in Seattle, Butte, Montana, and Lawrence, Massachusetts, had been instituted by the Bolsheviks and the IWW for the sole purpose of bringing about a nationwide revolution in the United States.[36] During the steel strike of early fall, 1919, a Senate investigating committee reported that "behind this strike there is massed a considerable element of I.W.W.'s, anarchists, revolutionists, and Russian soviets...."[37] In April

---

[33] U. S. Bureau of the Census, *Historical Statistics of the United States, Colonial Times to 1952, A Statistical Abstract Supplement* (Washington, D. C., 1960), 91, 92, 126; U. S. Department of Labor, Bureau of Labor Statistics, Bulletin Number 300, *Retail Prices 1913 to December, 1920* (Washington, D. C., 1922), 4; Daniel J. Ahearn, Jr., *The Wages of Farm and Factory Laborers 1914–1944* (New York, 1945), 227.

[34] *Washington Post*, August 1, 4, 1919; *The New York Times*, July 30, August 1, 1919; Philadelphia *Public Ledger*, August 5, 1919.

[35] Florence Peterson, *Strikes in the United States, 1880–1936*, U. S. Department of Labor Bulletin Number 651 (Washington, D. C., 1938), 21. More employees engaged in strikes in 1919 than the total over the ten-year period 1923–32.

[36] *Washington Post*, February 21, 1919. As late as April 1920, Secretary Wilson agreed with Palmer during a Cabinet meeting that the nationwide rail walkout had been caused by Communists and the IWW. Entry in Josephus Daniels' Diary for April 14, 1920, Papers of Josephus Daniels (Library of Congress, Washington, D. C.).

[37] U. S. Senate, Committee on Education and Labor, *Report, Investigation of Strike in Steel Industry*, 66th Congress, 1st Session, 1919, 14.

1920 the head of the Justice Department's General Intelligence Division, J. Edgar Hoover, declared in a public hearing that at least fifty per cent of the influence behind the recent series of strikes was traceable directly to communist agents.[38]

Furthermore, the nation suffered a sharp economic depression in late 1918 and early 1919, caused largely by sudden cancellations of war orders. Returning servicemen found it difficult to obtain jobs during this period, which coincided with the beginning of the Red Scare. The former soldiers had been uprooted from their homes and told that they were engaged in a patriotic crusade. Now they came back to find "reds" criticizing their country and threatening the government with violence, Negroes holding good jobs in the big cities, prices terribly high, and workers who had not served in the armed forces striking for higher wages.[39] A delegate won prolonged applause from the 1919 American Legion Convention when he denounced radical aliens, exclaiming, "Now that the war is over and they are in lucrative positions while our boys haven't a job, we've got to send those scamps to hell." The major part of the mobs which invaded meeting halls of immigrant organizations and broke up radical parades, especially during the first half of 1919, was comprised of men in uniform.[40]

A variety of other circumstances combined to add even more force to the postwar nativistic movement. Long before the new immigrants were seen as potential revolutionists they became the objects of widespread hostility. The peak of immigration from Southern and Eastern Europe occurred in the fifteen years before the war; during that period almost ten million immigrants from those areas entered the country. Before the anxious eyes of members of all classes of Americans, the newcomers crowded the cities and began to disturb the economic and social order.[41] Even without other postwar disturbances a nativistic movement of some strength could have been predicted when the wartime solidarity against the German enemy began to wear off in 1919.

In addition, not only were the European revolutions most successful in Eastern and to a lesser extent in Southern Europe, but aliens from

---

[38] *The New York Times,* April 25, 1920, 23.

[39] George Soule, *Prosperity Decade, From War to Depression: 1917–1929* (New York, 1947), 81–84; Murray, 125, 182–83.

[40] *Proceedings and Committees, Caucus of the American Legion* (St. Louis, 1919), 117; *The New York Times,* May 2, 1919; *Washington Post,* May 2, 1919. Ex-servicemen also played major roles in the great Negro-white race riots of mid-1919. *Washington Post,* July 20–23, 28–31.

[41] *Historical Statistics of the United States,* 56. On the causes of American hostility to recent immigrants see John Higham's probing and provocative essay "Another Look at Nativism," *Catholic Historical Review,* XLIV (1958), 147–58. Higham stresses status conflicts, but does not explain why some competitors on the crowded social ladder were more antagonistic to the new immigrants than were others.

these areas predominated in American radical organizations. At least ninety per cent of the members of the two American Communist parties formed in 1919 were born in Eastern Europe. The anarchist groups whose literature and bombs captured the imagination of the American public in 1919 were composed almost entirely of Italian, Spanish, and Slavic aliens. Justice Department announcements and statements by politicians and the press stressed the predominance of recent immigrants in radical organizations.[42] Smoldering prejudice against new immigrants, and identification of these immigrants with European as well as American radical movements, combined with other sources of postwar stress to create one of the most frenzied and one of the most widespread nativistic movements in the nation's history.

The result, akin to the movements incited by the Chinese Boxers or the Indian Ghost Dancers, was called Americanism or one hundred per cent Americanism.[43] Its objective was to end the apparent erosion of American values and the disintegration of American culture. By reaffirming those beliefs, customs, symbols, and traditions felt to be the foundation of our way of life, by enforcing conformity among the population, and by purging the nation of dangerous foreigners, the one hundred per centers expected to heal societal divisions and to tighten defenses against cultural change.

Panegyrics celebrating our history and institutions were delivered regularly in almost every American school, church, and public hall in 1919 and 1920. Many of these fervent addresses went far beyond the usual patriotic declarations. Audiences were usually urged to join a crusade to protect our hallowed institutions. Typical of the more moderate statements was Columbia University President Nicholas Murray Butler's insistence in April 1919 that "America will be saved, not by those who have only contempt and despite for her founders and her history, but by those who look with respect and reverence upon the great series of happenings extending from the voyage of the Mayflower. . . ."[44]

---

[42] Draper, 189–90; *Annual Report of the Attorney General for 1920* (Washington, D. C., 1920), 177; Higham, *Strangers in the Land*, 226–27.

[43] The word "Americanism" was used by the nativists of the eighteen-forties and eighteen-fifties. During World War I, the stronger phrase "100 per cent Americanism" was invented to suit the belligerent drive for universal conformity.

[44] Horace M. Kallen, *Culture and Democracy in the United States* (New York, 1924), Chap. 3, 154–55; Edward G. Hartman, *The Movement to Americanize the Immigrant* (New York, 1948), Chap. 9; Nicholas Murray Butler, *Is America Worth Saving? An Address Delivered Before the Commercial Club of Cincinnati, Ohio, April 19, 1919* (New York, 1919), 20.

What one historian has called "a riot of biographies of American heroes—statesmen, cowboys, and pioneers"[45] appeared in this brief period. Immigrants as well as citizens produced many autobiographical testimonials to the superiority of American institutions. These patriotic tendencies in our literature were as short-lived as the Red Scare, and have been concealed by "debunking" biographies of folk heroes and skeptical autobiographies so common later in the nineteen-twenties. An unusual number of motion pictures about our early history were turned out immediately after the war and the reconstruction of colonial Williamsburg and of Longfellow's Wayside Inn was begun. With great fanfare, Secretary of State Lansing placed the original documents of the Constitution and the Declaration of Independence on display in January 1920, and the State Department distributed movies of this ceremony to almost every town and city in the United States.[46] Organizations like the National Security League, the Association for Constitutional Government, the Sons and the Daughters of the American Revolution, the Colonial Dames of America, with the cooperation of the American Bar Association and many state Bar Associations, organized Constitution Day celebrations and distributed huge numbers of pamphlets on the subject throughout the country.

The American flag became a sacred symbol. Legionnaires demanded that citizens "Run the Reds out from the land whose flag they sully."[47] Men suspected of radical leanings were forced to kiss the stars and stripes. A Brooklyn truck driver decided in June 1919 that it was unpatriotic to obey a New York City law obliging him to fly a red cloth on lumber which projected from his vehicle. Instead he used as a danger signal a small American flag. A policeman, infuriated at the sight of the stars and stripes flying from a lumber pile, arrested the driver on a charge of disorderly conduct. Despite the Brooklyn patriot's insistence that he meant no offense to the flag, he was reprimanded and fined by the court.[48]

Recent immigrants, especially, were called upon to show evidence of real conversion. Great pressure was brought to bear upon the foreign-born to learn English and to forget their native tongues. As Senator William S. Kenyon of Iowa declared in October 1919, "The time has come to make this a one-language nation."[49] An editorial in the

---

[45] Emerson Hunsberger Loucks, *The Ku Klux Klan in Pennsylvania* (New York, 1936), 163.

[46] Kallen, Chap. 3, 154–55; Division of Foreign Intelligence, "Memorandum about Constitution Ceremonies," January 19, 1920, Lansing Papers; *The New York Times,* January 18, 1920.

[47] *American Legion Weekly,* I (November 14, 1919), 12.

[48] Sullivan, VI, 118; New York *World,* June 22, 1919.

[49] *The New York Times,* October 14, 1919.

American Legion Weekly took a further step and insisted that the one language must be called "American. Why, even in Mexico they do not stand for calling the language the Spanish language."[50]

Immigrants were also expected to adopt our customs and to snuff out remnants of Old World cultures. Genteel pre-war and wartime movements to speed up assimilation took on a "frightened and feverish aspect."[51] Welcoming members of an Americanization conference called by his department, Secretary of the Interior Franklin K. Lane exclaimed in May 1919, "You have been gathered together as crusaders in a great cause. . . . There is no other question of such importance before the American people as the solidifying and strengthening of true American sentiment." A Harvard University official told the conference that "The Americanization movement . . . gives men a new and holy religion. . . . It challenges each one of us to a renewed con-secration and devotion to the welfare of the nation."[52] The National Security League boasted, in 1919, of establishing one thousand study groups to teach teachers how to inculcate "Americanism" in their foreign-born students.[53] A critic of the prevailing mood protested against "one of our best advertised American mottoes, 'One country, one language, one flag,'" which, he complained, had become the basis for a fervent nationwide program.[54]

As the postwar movement for one hundred per cent Americanism gathered momentum, the deportation of alien nonconformists became increasingly its most compelling objective. Asked to suggest a remedy for the nationwide upsurge in radical activity, the Mayor of Gary, Indiana, replied, "Deportation is the answer, deportation of these leaders who talk treason in America and deportation of those who agree with them and work with them." "We must remake America," a popular author averred, "We must purify the source of America's

---

[50] *American Legion Weekly*, I (November 14, 1919), 12.

[51] Higham, *Strangers in the Land*, 225.

[52] United States Department of the Interior, Bureau of Education, *Organization Conference, Proceedings* (Washington, D. C., 1919), 293, 345–50.

[53] National Security League, 4.

[54] *Addresses and Proceedings of the Knights of Columbus Educational Convention* (New Haven, 1919), 71. Again note the family resemblance between the attempt to protect America through absolute conformity in 1919–20 and the more drastic, centrally-planned Chinese Communist efforts at national indoc-trination. A student of Chinese "coercive persuasion" described the "elaborate unanimity rituals like parades, . . . 'spontaneous' mass demonstrations and society-wide campaigns, the extensive proselytizing among the 'heretics' or the 'infidels,' the purges, programs of re-education, and other repressive measures aimed at deviants." In China, also, past national glory is invoked as evidence of present and future greatness. Schein *et al.*, 62; Lifton, *Thought Reform and the Psychology of Totalism*; Walker, *China Under Communism*.

population and keep it pure. . . . We must insist that there shall be an American loyalty, brooking no amendment or qualification."[55] As Higham noted, "In 1919, the clamor of 100 per centers for applying deportation as a purgative arose to an hysterical howl. . . . Through repression and deportation on the one hand and speedy total assimilation on the other, 100 per centers hoped to eradicate discontent and purify the nation."[56]

Politicians quickly sensed the possibilities of the popular frenzy for Americanism. Mayor Ole Hanson of Seattle, Governor Calvin Coolidge of Massachusetts, and General Leonard Wood became the early heroes of the movement.[57] The man in the best political position to take advantage of the popular feeling, however, was Attorney General A. Mitchell Palmer.[58] In 1919, especially after the President's physical collapse, only Palmer had the authority, staff, and money necessary to arrest and deport huge numbers of radical aliens. The most virulent phase of the movement for one hundred per cent Americanism came early in 1920, when Palmer's agents rounded up for deportation over six thousand aliens and prepared to arrest thousands more suspected of membership in radical organizations. Most of these aliens were taken without warrants, many were detained for unjustifiably long periods of time, and some suffered incredible hardships. Almost all, however, were eventually released.[59]

After Palmer decided that he could ride the postwar fears into the presidency, he set out calculatingly to become the symbol of one hundred per cent Americanism. The Palmer raids, his anti-labor activities, and his frequent pious professions of patriotism during the campaign were all part of this effort. Palmer was introduced by a political associate to the Democratic party's annual Jackson Day dinner in January 1920 as "an American whose Americanism cannot be misunderstood." In a speech delivered in Georgia shortly before the primary election (in which Palmer won control of the state's delegation to the Democratic National Convention), the Attorney General asserted: "I am myself an American and I love to preach my doctrine before undiluted one hundred per cent Americans, because my platform is, in a word, undiluted Americanism and undying loyalty to the republic." The

---

[55] Emerson Hough, "Round Our Town," *Saturday Evening Post*, CXCII (February 21, 1920), 102; Hough, *The Web*, 456.

[56] Higham, *Strangers in the Land*, 227, 255.

[57] Murray, 62–65, 147–48, 159–60.

[58] For a full discussion of Palmer's role, Stanley Coben, *A. Mitchell Palmer: Politician* (New York, 1963).

[59] Coben, *Palmer*, Chaps. 11, 12; Claghorn, Chap. 10; Constantine Panunzio, *The Deportation Cases of 1919–1920* (New York, 1920); Zechariah Chafee, Jr., *Free Speech in the United States* (Cambridge, 1941), 204–17; Murray, Chap. 13.

same theme dominated the address made by Palmer's old friend, John H. Bigelow of Hazelton, Pennsylvania, when he placed Palmer's name in nomination at the 1920 National Convention. Proclaimed Bigelow: "No party could survive today that did not write into its platform the magic word 'Americanism.' . . . The Attorney General of the United States has not merely professed, but he has proved his true Americanism. . . . Behind him I see a solid phalanx of true Americanism that knows no divided allegiance."[60]

Unfortunately for political candidates like Palmer and Wood, most of the social and economic disturbances which had activated the movement they sought to lead gradually disappeared during the first half of 1920. The European revolutions were put down; by 1920 communism seemed to have been isolated in Russia. Bombings ceased abruptly after June 1919, and fear of new outrages gradually abated. Prices of food and clothing began to recede during the spring. Labor strife almost vanished from our major industries after a brief railroad walkout in April. Prosperity returned after mid-1919 and by early 1920 business activity and employment levels exceeded their wartime peaks.[61] At the same time, it became clear that the Senate would not pass Wilson's peace treaty and that America was free to turn its back on the responsibilities of world leadership. The problems associated with the new immigrants remained; so did the disillusionment with Europe and with many old intellectual ideals. Nativism did not disappear from the American scene; but the frenzied attempt to revitalize the culture did peter out in 1920. The handful of unintimidated men, especially Assistant Secretary of Labor Louis F. Post, who had used the safeguards provided by American law to protect many victims of the Red Scare, found increasing public support. On the other hand, politicians like Palmer, Wood, and Hanson were left high and dry, proclaiming the need for one hundred per cent Americanism to an audience which no longer urgently cared.

It is ironic that in 1920 the Russian leaders of the Comintern finally took charge of the American Communist movement, provided funds and leadership, and ordered the Communist factions to unite and participate actively in labor organizations and strikes. These facts were reported in the American press.[62] Thus a potentially serious foreign

---

[60] Coben, *Palmer*, Chap. 13; *The New York Times*, January 9, 1920; Atlanta *Constitution*, April 7, 1920; *Official Report of the Proceedings of the Democratic National Convention, 1920* (Indianapolis, 1920), 113–14. Palmer also launched a highly publicized campaign to hold down soaring prices in 1919–20, by fixing retail prices and bringing suits against profiteers and hoarders.

[61] Bell, 334; Soule, 83–88; *Seventh Annual Report of the Federal Reserve Board for the Year 1920* (Washington, D.C., 1920), 7.

[62] Draper, 244, 267–68; New York *World*, March 29, 1920.

threat to national security appeared just as the Red Scare evaporated, providing a final illustration of the fact that the frenzied one hundred per centers of 1919–20 were affected less by the "red menace" than by a series of social and economic dislocations.

Although the Red Scare died out in 1920, its effects lingered. Hostility toward immigrants, mobilized in 1919–20, remained strong enough to force congressional passage of restrictive immigration laws. Some of the die-hard one hundred per centers found a temporary home in the Ku Klux Klan until that organization withered away during the mid-twenties. As its most lasting accomplishments, the movement for one hundred per cent Americanism fostered a spirit of conformity in the country, a satisfaction with the *status quo,* and the equation of reform ideologies with foreign enemies. Revitalization movements have helped many societies adapt successfully to new conditions. The movement associated with the American Red Scare, however, had no such effect. True, it unified the culture against the threats faced in 1919–20; but the basic problems—a damaged value system, an unrestrained business cycle, a hostile Russia, and communism—were left for future generations of Americans to deal with in their own fashion.

Part 2

THE PROBLEMS OF PEACE
AND WAR, SINCE 1920

20

What Happened to the
Progressive Movement in the 1920's?
ARTHUR S. LINK

Reform is a major theme in twentieth-century American history. The revamping of social institutions during the 1900's and 1910's, one of the most prominent manifestations of this reform spirit, has generally been called the progressive movement. The big question about the progressive movement, as indeed about any large-scale attempt to reorder society, is how and why it occurred. In general, as we have already noted, the answer is that existing institutions were not adequate to meet the needs of a society undergoing rapid and extensive change. The vitality of the progressive movement was, if a formula may be suggested, inversely proportional to the ability of institutions to meet the problems of an increasingly industrial and urban society. In this light, it may be seen that there is a link between the reform movements of all of the decades of our century, between the Square Deal of Theodore Roosevelt, the New Freedom of Woodrow Wilson, and the New Deal of Franklin Roosevelt. In this light, it may also be seen that a progressive movement continued during the 1920's, although its vitality had abated somewhat and its role become considerably weaker.

The following analysis of the progressive movement of the 1920's is the work of Professor Arthur S. Link of Princeton University, who is also the author of a multi-volume biography of Woodrow Wilson and of other volumes on the recent history of the United States, as well as editor of the Woodrow Wilson papers (presently being published). Professor Link is, to-

SOURCE: *The American Historical Review*, LXIV (July, 1959), 833–51. Reprinted by permission of the author.

gether with such other eminent historians as John M. Blum, Eric Goldman, Frank Freidel, Richard Hofstadter, and Arthur M. Schlesinger, Jr., among the major historians of reform in twentieth-century America. In the following article, Professor Link stresses not only the reasons for the relative decline of progressivism during the 1920's but also the measure of its survival and effectiveness. In the process, he answers some very important questions. What has been the prevalent myth about reform during the 1920's? What were the fundamental features of the progressive movement of the 1900's and 1910's? What accounts for its relative decline during the 1920's? In what significant respects, however, and for what reasons, did progressivism survive? What larger synthesis may be tentatively suggested concerning the progressive movement of the 1920's?

The answers given by Professor Link to these questions will in turn raise further questions. If the main point of his analysis is to challenge the governing hypotheses about the 1920's, it is fair to ask how much he has, as he himself suggests, overdrawn these hypotheses in order to advance his argument. Secondly, why were these hypotheses formulated to begin with? It may very well be that the myth they contain was integral to the national view of the 1920's: to the reaction from the trials of the earlier decade, to the hopes of a people for peace, prosperity, and isolation. If so, the myth is part of the reality of the 1920's. It cannot be negated by so-called facts. What people believe to be true about themselves and their age is a fact.

An equally interesting question for the student is the nature of reform in our times. To what extent is this an age of social discontents, and what are their forms and substance, why have they arisen? How are they related to the discontents of the earlier decades, to those which generated the progressive movement? To what extent was the decade of World War II and of the cold war a watershed for an essentially new age of social self-consciousness? Are we now in a decade of social equipoise and satisfaction or has the nature of our discontent been substantially altered? In sum, where do we stand, and for what reasons, in the larger course of American reform?

If the day has not yet arrived when we can make a definite synthesis of political developments between the Armistice and the Great Depression, it is surely high time for historians to begin to clear away the accumulated heap of mistaken and half-mistaken hypotheses about this important transitional period. Writing often without fear or much research (to paraphrase Carl Becker's remark), we recent American historians have gone on indefatigably to perpetuate hypotheses that either reflected the disillusionment and despair of contemporaries, or once served their purpose in exposing the alleged hiatus in the great continuum of twentieth-century reform.

Stated briefly, the following are what might be called the governing hypotheses of the period under discussion: The 1920's were a period made almost unique by an extraordinary reaction against idealism and reform. They were a time when the political representatives of big business and Wall Street executed a relentless and successful campaign in state and nation to subvert the regulatory structure that had been built at the cost of so much toil and sweat since the 1870's, and to restore a Hanna-like reign of special privilege to benefit business, industry, and finance. The surging tides of nationalism and mass hatreds generated by World War I continued to engulf the land and were manifested, among other things, in fear of communism, suppression of civil liberties, revival of nativism and anti-Semitism most crudely exemplified by the Ku Klux Klan, and in the triumph of racism and prejudice in immigration legislation. The 1920's were an era when great traditions and ideals were repudiated or forgotten, when the American people, propelled by a crass materialism in their scramble for wealth, uttered a curse on twenty-five years of reform endeavor. As a result, progressives were stunned and everywhere in retreat along the entire political front, their forces disorganized and leaderless, their movement shattered, their dreams of a new America turned into agonizing nightmares.

To be sure, the total picture that emerges from these generalizations is overdrawn. Yet it seems fair to say that leading historians have advanced each of these generalizations, that the total picture is the one that most of us younger historians saw during the years of our training, and that these hypotheses to a greater or lesser degree still control the way in which we write and teach about the 1920's, as a reading of textbooks and general works will quickly show.

This paper has not been written, however, to quarrel with anyone or to make an indictment. Its purposes are, first, to attempt to determine the degree to which the governing hypotheses, as stated, are adequate or inadequate to explain the political phenomena of the period, and, second, to discover whether any new and sounder hypotheses might be suggested. Such an effort, of course, must be tentative and above all imperfect in view of the absence of sufficient foundations for a synthesis.

Happily, however, we do not have to proceed entirely in the dark. Historians young and old, but mostly young, have already discovered that the period of the 1920's is the exciting new frontier of American historical research and that its opportunities are almost limitless in view of the mass of manuscript materials that are becoming available. Thus we have (the following examples are mentioned only at random) excellent recent studies of agrarian discontent and farm movements by Theodore Saloutos, John D. Hicks, Gilbert C. Fite, Robert L. Morlan, and James H. Shideler; of nativism and problems of immigration and assimilation by John Higham, Oscar Handlin, Robert A. Devine, and Edmund D. Cronon; of intellectual currents, the social gospel, and religious controversies by Henry F. May, Paul A. Carter, Robert M. Miller, and Norman F. Furniss; of left-wing politics and labor developments by Theodore Draper, David A. Shannon, Daniel Bell, Paul M. Angle, and Matthew Josephson; of the campaign of 1928 by Edmund A. Moore; and of political and judicial leaders by Alpheus T. Mason, Frank Freidel, Arthur M. Schlesinger, Jr., Merlo J. Pusey, and Joel F. Paschal.[1] Moreover, we can look forward to the early publication of studies that will be equally illuminating for the period, like the biographies of George W. Norris, Thomas J. Walsh, and Albert B. Fall now being prepared by Richard Lowitt, Leonard Bates, and David Stratton, respectively, and the recently completed study of the campaign and election of 1920 by Wesley M. Bagby.[2]

---

[1] Theodore Saloutos and John D. Hicks, *Agrarian Discontent in the Middle West, 1900–1939* (Madison, Wis., 1951); Gilbert C. Fite, *Peter Norbeck: Prairie Statesman* (Columbia, Mo., 1948), and *George N. Peek and the Fight for Farm Parity* (Norman, Okla., 1954); Robert L. Morlan, *Political Prairie Fire: The Nonpartisan League, 1915–1922* (Minneapolis, Minn., 1955); James H. Shideler, *Farm Crisis, 1919–1923* (Berkeley, Calif., 1957); John Higham, *Strangers in the Land: Patterns of American Nativism, 1860–1925* (New Brunswick, N.J., 1955); Oscar Handlin, *The American People in the Twentieth Century* (Cambridge, Mass., 1954); Robert A. Devine, *American Immigration Policy, 1924–1952* (New Haven, Conn., 1957); Edmund D. Cronon, *Black Moses: The Story of Marcus Garvey and the Universal Negro Improvement Association* (Madison, Wis., 1955); Henry F. May, "Shifting Perspectives on the 1920's," *Mississippi Valley Historical Review,* XLIII (Dec., 1956), 405–27; Paul A. Carter, *The Decline and Revival of the Social Gospel* (Ithaca, N.Y., 1956); Robert M. Miller, "An Inquiry into the Social Attitudes of American Protestantism, 1919–1939," doctoral dissertation, Northwestern University, 1955; Norman F. Furniss, *The Fundamentalist Controversy, 1918–1931* (New Haven, Conn., 1954); Theodore Draper, *The Roots of American Communism* (New York, 1957); David A. Shannon, *The Socialist Party of America: A History* (New York, 1955); Daniel Bell, "The Background and Development of Marxian Socialism in the United States," *Socialism and American Life,* ed. Donald D. Egbert and Stow Persons (2 vols., Princeton, N.J., 1952), I, 215–405; Paul M. Angle, *Bloody Williamson* (New York, 1952); Matthew Josephson, *Sidney Hillman: Statesman of American Labor* (New York, 1952); Edmund A. Moore, *A Catholic Runs for President: The Campaign of 1928* (New York, 1956); Alpheus Thomas Mason, *Brandeis: A Free Man's Life* (New York, 1946), and *Harlan Fiske Stone: Pillar of the Law* (New York, 1956); Frank Freidel, *Franklin D. Roosevelt: The Ordeal* (Boston, 1954); Arthur M. Schlesinger, Jr., *The Age of Roosevelt: The Crisis of the Old Order* (Boston, 1957); Merlo J. Pusey, *Charles Evans Hughes* (2 vols., New York, 1951); Joel Francis Paschal, *Mr. Justice Sutherland: A Man against the State* (Princeton, N.J., 1951).

[2] Wesley M. Bagby, "Woodrow Wilson and the Great Debacle of 1920," MS in the possession of Professor Bagby; see also his "The 'Smoke-Filled Room' and the Nomination of Warren G. Harding," *Mississippi Valley Historical Review,* XLI (Mar., 1955), 657–74, and "Woodrow Wilson, a Third Term, and the Solemn Referendum," *American Historical Review,* LX (Apr., 1955), 567–75.

Obviously, we are not only at a point in the progress of our research into the political history of the 1920's when we can begin to generalize, but we have reached the time when we should attempt to find some consensus, however tentative it must now be, concerning the larger political dimensions and meanings of the period.

In answering the question of what happened to the progressive movement in the 1920's, we should begin by looking briefly at some fundamental facts about the movement before 1918, facts that in large measure predetermined its fate in the 1920's, given the political climate and circumstances that prevailed.

The first of these was the elementary fact that the progressive movement never really existed as a recognizable organization with common goals and a political machinery geared to achieve them. Generally speaking (and for the purposes of this paper), progressivism might be defined as the popular effort, which began convulsively in the 1890's and waxed and waned afterward to our own time, to insure the survival of democracy in the United States by the enlargement of governmental power to control and offset the power of private economic groups over the nation's institutions and life. Actually, of course, from the 1890's on there were many "progressive" movements on many levels seeking sometimes contradictory objectives. Not all, but most of these campaigns were the work of special interest groups or classes seeking greater political status and economic security. This was true from the beginning of the progressive movement in the 1890's; by 1913 it was that movement's most important characteristic.

The second fundamental fact—that the progressive movements were often largely middle class in constituency and orientation—is of course well known, but an important corollary has often been ignored. It was that several of the most important reform movements were inspired, staffed, and led by businessmen with very specific or special-interest objectives in view. Because they hated waste, mismanagement, and high taxes, they, together with their friends in the legal profession, often furnished the leadership of good government campaigns. Because they feared industrial monopoly, abuse of power by railroads, and the growth of financial oligarchy, they were the backbone of the movements that culminated in the adoption of the Hepburn and later acts for railroad regulation, the Federal Reserve Act, and the Federal Trade Commission Act. Among the many consequences of their participation in the progressive movement, two should be mentioned because of their significance for developments in the 1920's: First, the strong identification of businessmen with good government and economic reforms for which the general public also had a lively concern helped preserve the good reputation of the middle-class business community (as opposed to its alleged natural enemies, monopolists, male-factors of great wealth, and railroad barons) and helped to direct the energies of the progressive movement toward the strengthening instead of the shackling of the business community. Second, their activities and influence served to intensify the tensions within the broad reform movement, because they often opposed the demands of farm groups, labor unions, and advocates of social justice.

The third remark to be made about the progressive movement before 1918 is that despite its actual diversity and inner tensions it did seem to have unity; that is, it seemed to share common ideals and objectives. This was true in part because much of the motivation even of the special-interest groups was altruistic (at least they succeeded in convincing themselves that they sought the welfare of society rather than their own interests primarily); in part because political leadership generally succeeded in subordinating inner tensions. It was true, above all, because there were in fact important idealistic elements in the progressive ranks—social gospel leaders, social justice elements, and intellectuals and philosophers—who worked hard at the task of defining and elevating common principles and goals.

Fourth and finally, the substantial progressive achievements before 1918 had been gained, at least on the federal level, only because of the temporary dislocations of the national political structure caused by successive popular uprisings, not because progressives had found or created a viable organization for perpetuating their control. Or, to put the matter another way, before 1918 the various progressive elements had failed to destroy the existing party structure by organizing a national party of their own that could survive. They, or at least many of them, tried in 1912; and it seemed for a time in 1916 that Woodrow Wilson had succeeded in drawing the important progressive groups permanently into the Democratic party. But Wilson's accomplishment did not survive even to the end of the war, and by 1920 traditional partisan loyalties were reasserting themselves with extraordinary vigor.

With this introduction, we can now ask what happened to the progressive movement or movements in the 1920's. Surely no one would contend that after 1916 the political scene did not change significantly, both on the state and national levels. There was the seemingly obvious fact that the Wilsonian coalition had been wrecked by the election of 1920, and that the progressive elements were divided and afterward unable to agree upon a program or to control the national government. There was the even more "obvious" fact that conservative Republican presidents and their cabinets controlled the executive branch throughout the period. There was Congress, as Eric F. Goldman had said, allegedly whooping through pro-corporation legislation, and the

Supreme Court interpreting the New Freedom laws in a way that harassed unions and encouraged trusts.[3] There were, to outraged idealists and intellectuals, the more disgusting spectacles of Red hunts, mass arrests and deportations, the survival deep into the 1920's of arrogant nationalism, crusades against the teaching of evolution, the attempted suppression of the right to drink, and myriad other manifestations of what would now be called a repressive reaction.[4]

Like the hypotheses suggested at the beginning, this picture is overdrawn in some particulars. But it is accurate in part, for progressivism was certainly on the downgrade if not in decay after 1918. This is an obvious fact that needs explanation and understanding rather than elaborate proof. We can go a long way toward answering our question if we can explain, at least partially, the extraordinary complex developments that converge to produce the "obvious" result.

For this explanation we must begin by looking at the several progressive elements and their relation to each other and to the two major parties after 1916. Since national progressivism was never an organized or independent movement (except imperfectly and then only temporarily in 1912), it could succeed only when its constituent elements formed a coalition strong enough to control one of the major parties. This had happened in 1916, when southern and western farmers, organized labor, the social justice elements, and a large part of the independent radicals who had heretofore voted the Socialist ticket coalesced to continue the control of Wilson and the Democratic party.

The important fact about the progressive coalition of 1916, however, was not its strength but its weakness. It was not a new party but a temporary alliance, welded in the heat of the most extraordinary domestic and external events. To be sure, it functioned for the most part successfully during the war, in providing the necessary support for a program of heavy taxation, relatively stringent controls over business and industry, and extensive new benefits to labor. Surviving in a crippled way even in the months following the Armistice, it put across a program that constituted a sizable triumph for the progressive movement—continued heavy taxation, the Transportation Act of 1920, the culmination of the long fight for railroad regulation, a new child labor act, amendments for prohibition and woman suffrage, immigration restriction, and water power and conservation legislation.

---

[3] Eric F. Goldman, *Rendezvous with Destiny* (New York, 1953), 284. The "allegedly" in this sentence is mine, not Professor Goldman's.

[4] H. C. Peterson and Gilbert C. Fite, *Opponents of War, 1917–1918* (Norman, Okla., 1957); Robert K. Murray, *Red Scare: A Study in National Hysteria, 1919–1920* (Minneapolis, Minn., 1955).

Even so, the progressive coalition of 1916 was inherently unstable. Indeed, it was so wracked by inner tensions that it could not survive, and destruction came inexorably, it seemed systematically, from 1917 to 1920. Why was this true?

First, the independent radicals and antiwar agrarians were alienated by the war declaration and the government's suppression of dissent and civil liberties during the war and the Red scare. Organized labor was disaffected by the administration's coercion of the coal miners in 1919, its lukewarm if not hostile attitude during the great strikes of 1919 and 1920, and its failure to support the Plumb Plan for nationalization of the railroads. Isolationists and idealists were outraged by what they thought was the President's betrayal of American traditions or the liberal peace program at Paris. These tensions were strong enough to disrupt the coalition, but the final one would have been fatal even if the others had never existed. This was the alienation of farmers in the Plains and western states produced by the administration's refusal to impose price controls on cotton while it maintained ceilings on the prices of other agricultural commodities,[5] and especially by the administration's failure to do anything decisive to stem the downward plunge of farm prices that began in the summer of 1920.[6] Under the impact of all these stresses, the Wilsonian coalition gradually disintegrated from 1917 to 1920 and disappeared entirely during the campaign of 1920.

The progressive coalition was thus destroyed, but the components of a potential movement remained. As we will see, these elements were neither inactive nor entirely unsuccessful in the 1920's. But they obviously failed to find common principles and a program, much less to unite effectively for political action on a national scale. I suggest that this was true, in part at least, for the following reasons:

First, the progressive elements could never create or gain control of a political organization capable of carrying them into national office. The Republican party was patently an impossible instrument because control of the GOP was too much in the hands of the eastern and midwestern industrial, oil, and financial interests, as it had been since about 1910. There was always the hope of a third party. Several progressive groups—insurgent midwestern Republicans, the railroad brotherhoods, a segment of the AF of L, and the moderate Socialists under

---

[5] On this point, see Seward W. Livermore, "The Sectional Issue in the 1918 Congressional Elections," *Mississippi Valley Historical Review*, XXXV (June, 1948), 29–60.

[6] Arthur S. Link, "The Federal Reserve Policy and the Agricultural Depression of 1920-1921," *Agricultural History*, XX (July, 1946), 166–75; and Herbert F. Margulies, "The Election of 1920 in Wisconsin: The Return to 'Normalcy' Reappraised," *Wisconsin Magazine of History*, XXXVIII (Autumn, 1954), 15–22.

Robert M. La Follette—tried to realize this goal in 1924, only to discover that third party movements in the United States are doomed to failure except in periods of enormous national turmoil, and that the 1920's were not such a time. Thus the Democratic party remained the only vehicle that conceivably could have been used by a new progressive coalition. But that party was simply not capable of such service in the 1920's. It was so torn by conflicts between its eastern, big city wing and its southern and western rural majority that it literally ceased to be a national party. It remained strong in its sectional and metropolitan components, but it was so divided that it barely succeeded in nominating a presidential candidate at all in 1924 and nominated one in 1928 only at the cost of temporary disruption.[7]

Progressivism declined in the 1920's, in the second place, because, as has been suggested, the tensions that had wrecked the coalition of 1916 not only persisted but actually grew in number and intensity. The two most numerous progressive elements, the southern and western farmers, strongly supported the Eighteenth Amendment, were heavily tinged with nativism and therefore supported immigration restriction, were either members of, friendly to, or politically afraid of the Ku Klux Klan, and demanded as the principal plank in their platform legislation to guarantee them a larger share of the national income. On all these points and issues the lower and lower middle classes in the large cities stood in direct and often violent opposition to their potential allies in the rural areas. Moreover, the liaison between the farm groups and organized labor, which had been productive of much significant legislation during the Wilson period, virtually ceased to exist in the 1920's. There were many reasons for this development, and I mention only one—the fact that the preeminent spokesmen of farmers in the 1920's, the new Farm Bureau Federation, represented the larger commercial farmers who (in contrast to the members of the leading farm organization in Wilson's day, the National Farmers' Union) were often employers themselves and felt no identification with the rank and file of labor.

It was little wonder, therefore (and this is a third reason for the weakness of progressivism in the 1920's), that the tension-ridden progressive groups were never able to agree upon a program that, like the Democratic platform of 1916, could provide the basis for a revived coalition. So long as progressive groups fought one another more fiercely than they fought their natural opponents, such agreement was impossible;

---

[7] For a highly partisan account of these events see Karl Schriftgiesser, *This Was Normalcy* (Boston, 1948). More balanced are the already cited Freidel, *Franklin D. Roosevelt: The Ordeal,* and Schlesinger, *The Age of Roosevelt: The Crisis of the Old Order.*

and so long as common goals were impossible to achieve, a national progressive movement could not take effective form. Nothing illustrates this better than the failure of the Democratic conventions of 1924 and 1928 to adopt platforms that could rally and unite the discontented elements. One result, among others, was that southern farmers voted as Democrats and western farmers as Republicans. And, as Professor Frank Freidel once commented to the author, much of the failure of progressivism in the 1920's can be explained by this elementary fact.

A deeper reason for the failure of progressives to unite ideologically in the 1920's was what might be called a substantial paralysis of the progressive mind. This was partly the result of the repudiation of progressive ideals by many intellectuals and the defection from the progressive movement of the urban middle classes and professional groups, as will be demonstrated. It was the result, even more importantly, of the fact that progressivism as an organized body of political thought found itself at a crossroads in the 1920's, like progressivism today, and did not know which way to turn. The major objectives of the progressive movement of the pre-war years had in fact been largely achieved by 1920. In what direction should progressivism now move? Should it remain in the channels already deeply cut by its own traditions, and, while giving sincere allegiance to the ideal of democratic capitalism, work for more comprehensive programs of business regulation and assistance to disadvantaged classes like farmers and submerged industrial workers? Should it abandon these traditions and, like most similar European movements, take the road toward a moderate socialism with a predominantly labor orientation? Should it attempt merely to revive the goals of more democracy through changes in the political machinery? Or should it become mainly an agrarian movement with purely agrarian goals?

These were real dilemmas, not academic ones, and one can see numerous examples of how they confused and almost paralyzed progressives in the 1920's. The platform of La Follette's Progressive party of 1924 offers one revealing ilustration. It embodied much that was old and meaningless by this time (the direct election of the president and a national referendum before the adoption of a war resolution, for example) and little that had any real significance for the future.[8] And yet it was the best that a vigorous and idealistic movement could offer. A second example was the plight of the agrarians and insurgents in Congress who fought so hard all through the 1920's against Andrew

---

[8] For a different picture see Belle C. La Follette and Fola La Follette, *Robert M. La Follette* (2 vols., New York, 1953); and Russel B. Nye, *Midwestern Progressive Politics, 1870–1950* (East Lansing, Mich., 1951). Both works contribute to an understanding of progressive politics in the 1920's.

Mellon's proposals to abolish the inheritance tax and to make drastic reductions in the taxes on large incomes. In view of the rapid reduction of the federal debt, the progressives were hard pressed to justify the continuation of nearly confiscatory tax levels, simply because few of them realized the wide social and economic uses to which the income tax could be put. Lacking any programs for the redistribution of the national income (except to farmers), they were plagued and overwhelmed by the surpluses in the federal Treasury until, for want of any good arguments, they finally gave Secretary Andrew Mellon the legislation he had been demanding.[9] A third and final example of this virtual paralysis of the progressive mind was perhaps the most revealing of all. It was the attempt that Woodrow Wilson, Louis D. Brandeis, and other Democratic leaders made from 1921 to 1924 to draft a new charter for progressivism. Except for its inevitable proposals for an idealistic world leadership, the document that emerged from this interchange included little or nothing that would have sounded new to a western progressive in 1912.

A fourth reason for the disintegration and decline of the progressive movement in the 1920's was the lack of any effective leadership. Given the political temper and circumstances of the 1920's, it is possible that such leadership could not have operated successfully in any event. Perhaps the various progressive elements were so mutually hostile and so self-centered in interests and objectives that even a Theodore Roosevelt or a Woodrow Wilson, had they been at the zenith of their powers in the 1920's, could not have drawn them together in a common front. We will never know what a strong national leader might have done because by a trick of fate no such leader emerged before Franklin D. Roosevelt.

Four factors, then, contributed to the failure of the progressive components to unite successfully after 1918 and, as things turned out, before 1932: the lack of a suitable political vehicle, the severity of the tensions that kept progressives apart, the failure of progressives to agree upon a common program, and the absence of a national leadership, without which a united movement could never be created and sustained. These were all weaknesses that stemmed to a large degree from the instability and failures of the progressive movement itself.

There were, besides, a number of what might be called external causes for the movement's decline. In considering them one must begin with what was seemingly the most important—the alleged fact that the 1920's were a very unpropitious time for any new progressive revolt because of the ever-increasing level of economic prosperity, the mate-

---

[9] Here indebtedness is acknowledged to Sidney Ratner, *American Taxation: Its History as a Social Force in Democracy* (New York, 1942).

rialism, and the general contentment of the decade 1919 to 1929. Part of this generalization is valid when applied to specific elements in the population. For example, the rapid rise in the real wages of industrial workers, coupled with generally full employment and the spread of so-called welfare practices among management, certainly did much to weaken and avert the further spread of organized labor, and thus to debilitate one of the important progressive components. But to say that it was prosperity per se that created a climate unfriendly to progressive ideals would be inaccurate. There was little prosperity and much depression during the 1920's for the single largest economic group, the farmers, as well as for numerous other groups. Progressivism, moreover, can flourish as much during periods of prosperity as during periods of discontent, as the history of the development of the progressive movement from 1901 to 1917 and of its triumph from 1945 to 1956 prove.

Vastly more important among the external factors in the decline of progressivism was the widespread, almost wholesale, defection from its ranks of the middle classes—the middling businessmen, bankers, and manufacturers, and the professional people closely associated with them in ideals and habits—in American cities large and small. For an understanding of this phenomenon no simple explanations like "prosperity" or the "temper of the times" will suffice, although they give some insight. The important fact was that these groups found a new economic and social status as a consequence of the flowering of American enterprise under the impact of the technological, financial, and other revolutions of the 1920's. If, as Professor Richard Hofstadter had claimed,[10] the urban middle classes were progressive (that is, they demanded governmental relief from various anxieties) in the early 1900's because they resented their loss of social prestige to the *nouveaux riches* and feared being ground under by monopolists in industry, banking, and labor—if this is true, then the urban middle classes were not progressive in the 1920's for inverse reasons. Their temper was dynamic, expansive, and supremely confident. They knew that they were building a new America, a business civilization based not upon monopoly and restriction but upon a whole new set of business values —mass production and consumption, short hours and high wages, full employment, welfare capitalism. And what was more important, virtually the entire country (at least the journalists, writers in popular magazines, and many preachers and professors) acknowledged that the nation's destiny was in good hands. It was little wonder, therefore, that the whole complex of groups constituting the urban middle classes,

---

[10] Richard Hofstadter, *The Age of Reform: From Bryan to F.D.R.* (New York, 1955), 131 ff.

whether in New York, Zenith, or Middletown, had little interest in rebellion or even in mild reform proposals that seemed to imperil their leadership and control.

Other important factors, of course, contributed to the contentment of the urban middle classes. The professonalization of business and the full-blown emergence of a large managerial class had a profound impact upon social and political ideals. The acceleration of mass advertising played its role, as did also the beginning disintegration of the great cities with the spread of middle- and upper-middle-class suburbs, a factor that diffused the remaining reform energies among the urban leaders.

A second external factor in the decline of the progressive movement after 1918 was the desertion from its ranks of a good part of the intellectual leadership of the country. Indeed, more than simple desertion was involved here; it was often a matter of a cynical repudiation of the ideals from which progressivism derived its strength. I do not mean to imply too much by this generalization. I know that what has been called intellectual progressivism not only survived in the 1920's but actually flourished in many fields.[11] I know that the intellectual foundations of our present quasi-welfare state were either being laid or reinforced during the decade. Even so, one cannot evade the conclusion that the intellectual-political climate of the 1920's was vastly different from the one that had prevailed in the preceding two decades.

During the years of the great progressive revolt, intellectuals—novelists, journalists, political thinkers, social scientists, historians, and the like—had made a deeply personal commitment to the cause of democracy, first in domestic and then in foreign affairs. Their leadership in and impact on many phases of the progressive movement had been profound. By contrast, in the 1920's a large body of this intellectual phalanx turned against the very ideals they had once deified. One could cite, for example, the reaction of the idealists against the Versailles settlement; the disenchantment of the intellectuals with the extension of government authority when it could be used to justify the Eighteenth Amendment or the suppression of free speech; or the inevitable loss of faith in the "people" when en masse they hounded so-called radicals, joined Bryan's crusade against evolution, or regaled themselves as Knights of the Ku Klux Klan. Whatever the cause, many alienated intellectuals simply withdrew or repudiated any identification with the groups they had once helped to lead. The result was not fatal to progressivism, but it was serious. The spark plugs had been removed from the engine of reform.

---

[11] *Ibid.*, 5, 131, 135 ff. For a recent excellent survey, previously cited, see Henry F. May, "Shifting Perspectives on the 1920's." Schlesinger's previously cited *Age of Roosevelt* sheds much light on the economic thought of the 1920's.

The progressive movement, then, unquestionably declined, but was it defunct in the 1920's? Much, of course, depends upon the definition of terms. If we accept the usual definition for "defunct" as "dead" or "ceasing to have any life or strength," we must recognize that the progressive movement was certainly not defunct in the 1920's; that on the contrary at least important parts of it were very much alive; and that it is just as important to know how and why progressivism survived as it is to know how and why it declined.

To state the matter briefly, progressivism survived in the 1920's because several important elements of the movement remained either in full vigor or in only slightly diminished strength. These were the farmers, after 1918 better organized and more powerful than during the high tide of the progressive revolt; the politically conscious elements among organized labor, particularly the railroad brotherhoods, who wielded a power all out of proportion to their numbers; the Democratic organizations in the large cities, usually vitally concerned with the welfare of the so-called lower classes; a remnant of independent radicals, social workers, and social gospel writers and preachers; and finally, an emerging new vocal element, the champions of public power and regional developments.

Although they never united effectively enough to capture a major party and the national government before 1932, these progressive elements controlled Congress from 1921 to about 1927 and continued to exercise a near control during the period of their greatest weakness in the legislative branch, from 1927 to about 1930.

Indeed, the single most powerful and consistently successful group in Congress during the entire decade from 1919 to 1929 were the spokesmen of the farmers. Spurred by an unrest in the country areas more intense than at any time since the 1890's,[12] in 1920 and 1921 southern Democrats and midwestern and western insurgents, nominally Republican, joined forces in an alliance called the Farm Bloc. By maintaining a common front from 1921 to 1924 they succeeded in enacting the most advanced agricultural legislation to that date, legislation that completed the program begun under Wilsonian auspices. It included measures for high tariffs on agricultural products, thoroughgoing federal regulation of stockyards, packing houses, and grain exchanges, the exemption of agricultural cooperatives from the application of the antitrust laws, stimulation of the export of agricultural commodities, and the establishment of an entirely new federal system of intermediate rural credit.

---

[12] It derived from the fact that farm prices plummeted in 1920 and 1921, and remained so low that farmers, generally speaking, operated at a net capital loss throughout the balance of the decade.

When prosperity failed to return to the countryside, rural leaders in Congress espoused a new and bolder plan for relief—the proposal made by George N. Peek and Hugh S. Johnson in 1922 to use the federal power to obtain "fair exchange" or "parity" prices for farm products. Embodied in the McNary-Haugen bill in 1924, this measure was approved by Congress in 1927 and 1928, only to encounter vetoes by President Calvin Coolidge.

In spite of its momentary failure, the McNary-Haugen bill had a momentous significance for the American progressive movement. Its wholesale espousal by the great mass of farm leaders and spokesmen meant that the politically most powerful class in the country had come full scale to the conviction that the taxing power should be used directly and specifically for the purpose of underwriting (some persons called it subsidizing) agriculture. It was a milestone in the development of a comprehensive political doctrine that it was government's duty to protect the economic security of all classes and particularly depressed ones. McNary-Haugenism can be seen in its proper perspective if it is remembered that it would have been considered almost absurd in the Wilson period, that it was regarded as radical by nonfarm elements in the 1920's, and that it, or at any rate its fundamental objective, was incorporated almost as a matter of course into basic federal policy in the 1930's.

A second significant manifestation of the survival of progressivism in the 1920's came during the long controversy over public ownership or regulation of the burgeoning electric power industry. In this, as in most of the conflicts that eventually culminated on Capitol Hill, the agrarian element constituted the core of progressive strength. At the same time a sizable and well-organized independent movement developed that emanated from urban centers and was vigorous on the municipal and state levels. Throughout the decade this relatively new progressive group fought with mounting success to expose the propaganda of the private utilities, to strengthen state and federal regulatory agencies, and to win municipal ownership for distributive facilities. Like the advocates of railroad regulation in an earlier period, these proponents of regulation or ownership of a great new monopoly failed almost as much as they had succeeded in the 1920's. But their activities and exposures (the Federal Trade Commission's devastating investigation of the electric power industry in the late 1920's and early 1930's was the prime example) laid secure foundations for movements that in the 1930's would reach various culminations.

Even more significant for the future of American progressivism was the emergence in the 1920's of a new objective, that of committing the federal government to plans for large hydroelectric projects in the Tennessee Valley, the Columbia River watershed, the Southwest, and the

St. Lawrence Valley for the purpose, some progressives said, of establishing "yardsticks" for rates, or for the further purpose, as other progressives declared, of beginning a movement for the eventual nationalization of the entire electric power industry. The development of this movement in its emerging stages affords a good case study in the natural history of American progressivism. It began when the Harding and Coolidge administrations attempted to dispose of the government's hydroelectric and nitrate facilities for the production of cheap fertilizer—a reflection of its exclusive special-interest orientation. Then, as new groups joined the fight to save Muscle Shoals, the objective of public production of cheap electric power came to the fore. Finally, by the end of the 1920's, the objective of a multipurpose regional development in the Tennessee Valley and in other areas as well had taken firm shape.

In addition, by 1928 the agrarians in Congress led by Senator George W. Norris had found enough allies in the two houses and enough support in the country at large to adopt a bill for limited federal development of the Tennessee Valley. Thwarted by President Coolidge's pocket veto, the progressives tried again in 1931, only to meet a second rebuff at the hands of President Hoover.

All this might be regarded as another milestone in the maturing of American progressivism. It signifies a deviation from the older traditions of mere regulation, as President Hoover had said in his veto of the second Muscle Shoals bill, and the triumph of new concepts of direct federal leadership in large-scale development of resources. If progressives had not won their goal by the end of the 1920's, they had at least succeeded in writing what would become perhaps the most important plank in their program for the future.

The maturing of an advanced farm program and the formulation of plans for public power and regional developments may be termed the two most significant progressive achievements on the national level in the 1920's. Others merit only brief consideration. One was the final winning of the old progressive goal of immigration restriction through limited and selective admission. The fact that this movement was motivated in part by racism, nativism, and anti-Semitism (with which, incidentally, a great many if not a majority of progressives were imbued in the 1920's) should not blind us to the fact that it was also progressive. It sought to substitute a so-called scientific and a planned policy for a policy of laissez faire. Its purpose was admittedly to disturb the free operation of the international labor market. Organized labor and social workers had long supported it against the opposition of large employers. And there was prohibition, the most ambitious and revealing progressive experiment of the twentieth century. Even the contemned antievolution crusade of Bryan and the fundamentalists and the surging drives for conformity of thought and action in other fields should be mentioned. All these movements stemmed from the conviction that organized public power could and should be used purposefully to achieve fundamental social and so-called moral change. The fact that they were potentially or actively repressive does not mean that they were not progressive. On the contrary, they superbly illustrated the repressive tendencies that inhered in progressivism precisely because it was grounded so much upon majoritarian principles.

Three other developments on the national level that have often been cited as evidences of the failure of progressivism in the 1920's appear in a somewhat different light at second glance. The first was the reversal of the tariff-for-revenue-only tendencies of the Underwood Act with the enactment of the Emergency Tariff Act of 1921 and the Fordney-McCumber Act of 1922. Actually, the adoption of these measures signified, on the whole, not a repudiation but a revival of progressive principles in the realm of federal fiscal policy. A revenue tariff had never been an authentic progressive objective. Indeed, at least by 1913, many progressives, except for some southern agrarians, had concluded that it was retrogressive and had agreed that the tariff laws should be used deliberately to achieve certain national objectives—for example, the crippling of noncompetitive big business by the free admission of articles manufactured by so-called trusts, or benefits to farmers by the free entry of farm implements. Wilson himself had been at least partially converted to these principles by 1916, as his insistence upon the creation of the Federal Tariff Commission and his promise of protection to the domestic chemical industry revealed. As for the tariff legislation of the early 1920's, its only important changes were increased protection for aluminum, chemical products, and agricultural commodities. It left the Underwood rates on the great mass of raw materials and manufactured goods largely undisturbed. It may have been economically shortsighted and a bad example for the rest of the world, but for the most part it was progressive in principle and was the handiwork of the progressive coalition in Congress.

Another development that has often been misunderstood in its relation to the progressive movement was the policies of consistent support that the Harding and Coolidge administrations adopted for business enterprise, particularly the policy of the Federal Trade Commission in encouraging the formation of trade associations and the diminution of certain traditional competitive practices. The significance of all this can easily be overrated. Such policies as these two administrations executed had substantial justification in progressive theory and in precedents clearly established by the Wilson administration.

A third challenge to usual interpretations concerns implications to be drawn from the election of Harding and Coolidge in 1920 and 1924. These elections seem to indicate the triumph of reaction among the mass of American voters. Yet one could argue that both Harding and Coolidge were political accidents, the beneficiaries of grave defects in the American political and constitutional systems. The rank and file of Republican voters demonstrated during the preconvention campaign that they wanted vigorous leadership and a moderately progressive candidate in 1920. They got Harding instead, not because they wanted him, but because unusual circumstances permitted a small clique to thwart the will of the majority.[13] They took Coolidge as their candidate in 1924 simply because Harding died in the middle of his term and there seemed to be no alternative to nominating the man who had succeeded him in the White House. Further, an analysis of the election returns in 1920 and 1924 will show that the really decisive factor in the victories of Harding and Coolidge was the fragmentation of the progressive movement and the fact that an opposition strong enough to rally and unite the progressive majority simply did not exist.

There remains, finally, a vast area of progressive activity about which we yet know very little. One could mention the continuation of old reform movements and the development of new ones in the cities and states during the years following the Armistice: For example, the steady spread of the city manager form of government, the beginning of zoning and planning movements, and the efforts of the great cities to keep abreast of the transportation revolution then in full swing. Throughout the country the educational and welfare activities of the cities and states steadily increased. Factory legislation matured, while social insurance had its experimental beginnings. Whether such reform impulses were generally weak or strong, one cannot say; but what we do know about developments in cities like Cincinnati and states like New York, Wisconsin, and Louisiana [14] justifies a challenge to the assumption that municipal and state reform energies were dead after 1918 and, incidentally, a plea to young scholars to plow this unworked field of recent American history.

Let us, then, suggest a tentative synthesis as an explanation of what happened to the progressive movement after 1918:

First, the national progressive movement, which had found its most effective embodiment in the coalition of forces that reelected Woodrow Wilson in 1916, was shattered by certain policies that the administration pursued from 1917 to 1920, and by some developments over which the administration had no or only slight control. The collapse that oc-

---

[13] Much that is new on the Republican preconvention campaign and convention of 1920 may be found in William T. Hutchinson, *Lowden of Illinois: The Life of Frank O. Lowden* (2 vols., Chicago, 1957).

[14] See, e.g., Allen P. Sindler, *Huey Long's Louisiana: State Politics, 1920–1952* (Baltimore, Md., 1956).

curred in 1920 was not inevitable and cannot be explained by merely saying that "the war killed the progressive movement."

Second, large and aggressive components of a potential new progressive coalition remained after 1920. These elements never succeeded in uniting effectively before the end of the decade, not because they did not exist, but because they were divided by conflicts among themselves. National leadership, which in any event did not emerge in the 1920's, perhaps could not have succeeded in subduing these tensions and in creating a new common front.

Third, as a result of the foregoing, progressivism as an organized national force suffered a serious decline in the 1920's. This decline was heightened by the defection of large elements among the urban middle classes and the intellectuals, a desertion induced by technological, economic, and demographic changes, and by the outcropping of certain repressive tendencies in progressivism after 1917.

Fourth, in spite of reversals and failures, important components of the national progressive movement survived in considerable vigor and succeeded to a varying degree, not merely in keeping the movement alive, but even in broadening its horizons. This was true particularly of the farm groups and of the coalition concerned with public regulation or ownership of electric power resources. These two groups laid the groundwork in the 1920's for significant new programs in the 1930's and beyond.

Fifth, various progressive coalitions controlled Congress for the greater part of the 1920's and were always a serious threat to the conservative administrations that controlled the executive branch. Because this was true, most of the legislation adopted by Congress during this period, including many measures that historians have inaccurately called reactionary, was progressive in character.

Sixth, the progressive movement in the cities and states was far from dead in the 1920's, although we do not have sufficient evidence to justify any generalizations about the degree of its vigor.

If this tentative and imperfect synthesis has any value, perhaps it is high time that we discard the sweeping generalizations, false hypotheses, and clichés that we have so often used in explaining and characterizing political developments from 1918 to 1929. Perhaps we should try to see these developments for what they were—the normal and ordinary political behavior of groups and classes caught up in a swirl of social and economic change. When we do this we will no longer ask whether the progressive movement was defunct in the 1920's. We will ask only what happened to it and why.

The Days of Boom and Bust
JOHN KENNETH GALBRAITH

There are events in history which are of transcendent importance, because they cleave the continuity of human experience, because they summarize the direction of one age and herald the advent of another, because they are dramatic, immediate, brief, and irreversible. Such events clearly include Caesar's crossing of the Rubicon, the conversion of Paul to Christianity, the pronouncement of Luther to the Diet of Worms, the signing of the Declaration of Independence, and the Bolshevik Revolution of November, 1917. Such an event certainly was the great stock market crash of October, 1929.

But what were the nature and importance of the crash? What had caused it? What were the basic flaws in the American economy which the crash summarized? To what degree were Americans conscious of these flaws? To what extent were American political leaders culpable for not taking action to prevent the crash? To what extent could their action have prevented it? To what extent was the crash responsible for ushering in the age of the Great Depression, which continued in effect until the outbreak of World War II in Europe?

These are the questions on which Professor John Kenneth Galbraith of Harvard University undertakes to throw some light in the following essay. As a perceptive critic of some of the basic deficiencies of American capitalism, Professor Galbraith is particularly well qualified to point out the most glaring and disastrous instance of its deficiencies. His books, each of them devoted to revaluating the premises of our economic way of life, include: American Capitalism: The Concept of Countervailing Power *(1952),* Economics and the Art of Controversy *(1955),* The Affluent Society *(1958), and* The New Industrial State *(1967). An especially relevant and significant volume among his writings is, as one might have surmised, on the subject of* The Great Crash, 1929 *(1955).*

Professor Galbraith is convinced that there are valuable lessons to be learned from economic history, and this conviction is basic to his careful study of the great crash. The question for us, obviously, is what exactly did

SOURCE: *American Heritage, The Magazine of History,* IX (August, 1958), 28–33, 101–102. Reprinted by permission of the author and publisher.

the crash teach us? What deficiencies of American capitalism did it reveal? What measures have we since taken to remedy those deficiencies? In The Great Crash, *Professor Galbraith concludes that while there may conceivably be another crash, because of steps we have since taken it is likely that its consequences would be nowhere near so disastrous. Regarding the larger issue of the future of American capitalism, Professor Galbraith appears to be less certain. In* The Affluent Society, *he seriously questioned the premises guiding our economy. To what extent, he asked, is our productive capacity geared to purposes that are valid in the world of today? The question is important, because of the challenge to our economic ways presented by nations with "socialist" or managed economies. More than important, it is vital, because of the challenge to our economic goals that is urged upon us by a world whose peoples are, in an overwhelming majority, hungry and wanting.*

The decade of the twenties, or more precisely the eight years between the postwar depression of 1920–21 and the stock market crash in October of 1929, were prosperous ones in the United States. The total output of the economy increased by more than 50 per cent. The preceding decades had brought the automobile; now came many more and also roads on which they could be driven with reasonable reliability and comfort. There was much building. The downtown section of the mid-continent city—Des Moines, Omaha, Minneapolis—dates from these years. It was then, more likely than not, that what is still the leading hotel, the tallest office building, and the biggest department store went up. Radio arrived, as of course did gin and jazz.

These years were also remarkable in another respect, for as time passed it became increasingly evident that the prosperity could not last. Contained within it were the seeds of its own destruction. The country was heading into the gravest kind of trouble. Herein lies the peculiar fascination of the period for a study in the problem of leadership. For almost no steps were taken during these years to arrest the tendencies which were obviously leading, and did lead, to disaster.

At least four things were seriously wrong, and they worsened as the decade passed. And knowledge of them does not depend on the always brilliant assistance of hindsight. At least three of these flaws were highly visible and widely discussed. In ascending order, not of importance but of visibility, they were as follows:

First, income in these prosperous years was being distributed with marked inequality. Although output per worker rose steadily during the period, wages were fairly stable, as also were prices. As a result, business profits increased rapidly and so did incomes of the wealthy and the well-to-do. This tendency was nurtured by assiduous and successful efforts of Secretary of the Treasury Andrew W. Mellon to reduce income taxes with special attention to the higher brackets. In 1929 the 5 per cent of the people with the highest incomes received perhaps a third of all personal income. Between 1919 and 1929 the share of the one per cent who received the highest incomes increased by approximately one-seventh. This meant that the economy was heavily and increasingly dependent on the luxury consumption of the well-to-do and on their willingness to reinvest what they did not or could not spend on themselves. Anything that shocked the confidence of the rich either in their personal or in their business future would have a bad effect on total spending and hence on the behavior of the economy.

This was the least visible flaw. To be sure, farmers, who were not participating in the general advance, were making themselves heard; and twice during the period the Congress passed far-reaching relief legislation which was vetoed by Coolidge. But other groups were much less vocal. Income distribution in the United States had long been unequal. The inequality of these years did not seem exceptional. The trade-union movement was also far from strong. In the early twenties the steel industry was still working a twelve-hour day and, in some jobs, a seven-day week. (Every two weeks when the shift changed a man worked twice around the clock.) Workers lacked the organization or the power to deal with conditions like this; the twelve-hour day was, in fact, ended as the result of personal pressure by President Harding on the steel companies, particularly on Judge Elbert H. Gary, head of the United States Steel Corporation. Judge Gary's personal acquaintance with these working conditions was thought to be slight, and this gave rise to Benjamin Stolberg's now classic observation that the Judge "never saw a blast furnace until his death." In all these circumstances the increasingly lopsided income distribution did not excite much comment or alarm. Perhaps it would have been surprising if it had.

But the other three flaws in the economy were far less subtle. During World War I the United States ceased to be the world's greatest debtor country and became its greatest creditor. The consequences of this change have so often been described that they have the standing of a cliché. A debtor country could export a greater value of goods than it imported and use the difference for interest and debt repayment. This was what we did before the war. But a creditor must import a greater value than it exports if those who owe it money are to have the wherewithal to pay interest and principal. Otherwise the creditor must either forgive the debts or make new loans to pay off the old.

During the twenties the balance was maintained by making new foreign loans. Their promotion was profitable to domestic investment houses. And when the supply of honest and competent foreign borrowers ran out, dishonest, incompetent, or fanciful borrowers were invited to borrow and, on occasion, bribed to do so. In 1927 Juan Leguia, the son of the then dictator of Peru, was paid $450,000 by the National City Company and J. & W. Seligman for his services in promoting a $50,000,000 loan to Peru which these houses marketed. Americans lost and the Peruvians didn't gain appreciably. Other Latin American republics got equally dubious loans by equally dubious devices. And, for reasons that now tax the imagination, so did a large number of German cities and municipalities. Obviously, once investors awoke to the character of these loans or there was any other shock to confidence, they would no longer be made. There would be nothing with which to pay the old loans. Given this arithmetic, there would be either a sharp reduction in exports or a wholesale default on the outstanding loans, or more likely both. Wheat and cotton farmers and others who depended on exports would suffer. So would those who owned the bonds. The buying power of both would be reduced. These consequences were freely predicted at the time.

The second weakness of the economy was the large-scale corporate thimblerigging that was going on. This took a variety of forms, of which by far the most common was the organization of corporations to hold stock in yet other corporations, which in turn held stock in yet other corporations. In the case of the railroads and the utilities, the purpose of this pyramid of holding companies was to obtain control of a very large number of operating companies with a very small investment in the ultimate holding company. A $100,000,000 electric utility, of which the capitalization was represented half by bonds and half by common stock, could be controlled with an investment of a little over $25,000,000—the value of just over half the common stock. Were a company then formed with the same capital structure to hold *this* $25,000,000 worth of common stock, it could be controlled with an investment of $6,250,000. On the next round the amount required would be less than $2,000,000. That $2,000,000 would still control the entire $100,000,000 edifice. By the end of the twenties, holding-company structures six or eight tiers high were a commonplace. Some of them— the utility pyramids of Insull and Associated Gas & Electric, and the railroad pyramid of the Van Sweringens—were marvelously complex. It is unlikely that anyone fully understood them or could.

In other cases companies were organized to hold securities in other companies in order to manufacture more securities to sell to the public. This was true of the great investment trusts. During 1929 one investment house, Goldman, Sachs & Company, organized and sold nearly a billion dollars' worth of securities in three interconnected investment trusts—Goldman Sachs Trading Corporation; Shenandoah Corporation; and Blue Ridge Corporation. All eventually depreciated virtually to nothing.

This corporate insanity was also highly visible. So was the damage. The pyramids would last only so long as earnings of the company at the bottom were secure. If anything happened to the dividends of the underlying company, there would be trouble, for upstream companies had issued bonds (or in practice sometimes preferred stock) against the dividends on the stock of the downstream companies. Once the earnings stopped, the bonds would go into default or the preferred stock would take over and the pyramid would collapse. Such a collapse would have a bad effect not only on the orderly prosecution of business and investment by the operating companies but also on confidence, investment, and spending by the community at large. The likelihood was increased because in any number of cities—Cleveland, Detroit, and Chicago were notable examples—the banks were deeply committed to these pyramids or had fallen under the control of the pyramiders.

Finally, and most evident of all, there was the stock market boom. Month after month and year after year the great bull market of the twenties roared on. Sometimes there were setbacks, but more often there were fantastic forward surges. In May of 1924 the New York *Times* industrials stood at 106; by the end of the year they were 134; by the end of 1925 they were up to 181. In 1927 the advance began in earnest— to 245 by the end of that year and on to 331 by the end of 1928. There were some setbacks in early 1929, but then came the fantastic summer explosion when in a matter of three months the averages went up another 110 points. This was the most frantic summer in our financial history. By its end, stock prices had nearly quadrupled as compared with four years earlier. Transactions on the New York Stock Exchange regularly ran to 5,000,000 or more shares a day. Radio Corporation of America went to 573¾ (adjusted) without ever having paid a dividend. Only the hopelessly eccentric, so it seemed, held securities for their income. What counted was the increase in capital values.

And since capital gains were what counted, one could vastly increase his opportunities by extending his holdings with borrowed funds—by buying on margin. Margin accounts expanded enormously, and from all over the country—indeed from all over the world—money poured into New York to finance these transactions. During the summer, brokers' loans increased at the rate of $400,000,000 a month. By September they totaled more than $7,000,000,000. The rate of interest on these loans varied from 7 to 12 per cent and went as high as 15.

This boom was also inherently self-liquidating. It could last only so long as new people, or at least new money, were swarming into the market in pursuit of the capital gains. This new demand bid up the stocks and made the capital gains. Once the supply of new customers began to falter, the market would cease to rise. Once the market stopped rising, some, and perhaps a good many, would start to cash in. If you are concerned with capital gains, you must get them while the getting is good. But the getting may start the market down, and this will one day be the signal for much more selling—both by those who are trying to get out and those who are being forced to sell securities that are no longer safely margined. Thus it was certain that the market would one day go down, and far more rapidly than it went up. Down it went with a thunderous crash in October of 1929. In a series of terrible days, of which Thursday, October 24, and Tuesday, October 29, were the most terrifying, billions in values were lost, and thousands of speculators— they had been called investors—were utterly and totally ruined.

This too had far-reaching effects. Economists have always deprecated the tendency to attribute too much to the great stock market collapse of 1929: this was the drama; the causes of the subsequent depression really lay deeper. In fact, the stock market crash was very important. It exposed the other weakness of the economy. The overseas loans on which the payments balance depended came to an end. The jerry-built holding-company structures came tumbling down. The investment-trust stocks collapsed. The crash put a marked crimp on borrowing for investment and therewith on business spending. It also removed from the economy some billions of consumer spending that was either based on, sanctioned by, or encouraged by the fact that the spenders had stock market gains. The crash was an intensely damaging thing.

And this damage, too, was not only foreseeable but foreseen. For months the speculative frenzy had all but dominated American life. Many times before in history—the South Sea Bubble, John Law's specu-lations, the recurrent real-estate booms of the last century, the great Florida land boom earlier in the same decade—there had been similar frenzy. And the end had always come, not with a whimper but a bang. Many men, including in 1929 the President of the United States, knew it would again be so.

The increasingly perilous trade balance, the corporate buccaneering, and the Wall Street boom — along with the less visible tendencies in income distribution— were all allowed to proceed to the ultimate disaster without effective hindrance. How much blame attaches to the men who occupied the presidency?

Warren G. Harding died on August 2, 1923. This, as only death can do, exonerates him. The disorders that led eventually to such trouble had only started when the fatal blood clot destroyed this now sad and deeply disillusioned man. Some would argue that this legacy was bad. Harding had but a vague perception of the economic processes over which he presided. He died owing his broker $180,000 in a blind account—he had been speculating disastrously while he was President, and no one so inclined would have been a good bet to curb the coming boom. Two of Harding's Cabinet officers, his secretary of the interior and his attorney general, were to plead the Fifth Amendment when faced with questions concerning their official acts, and the first of these went to jail. Harding brought his fellow townsman Daniel R. Crissinger to be his comptroller of the currency, although he was qualified for this task, as Samuel Hopkins Adams has suggested, only by the fact that he and the young Harding had stolen watermelons together. When Crissinger had had an ample opportunity to demonstrate his incompetence in his first post, he was made head of the Federal Reserve System. Here he had the central responsibility for action on the ensuing boom. Jack Dempsey, Paul Whiteman, or F. Scott Fitzgerald would have been at least equally qualified.

Yet it remains that Harding was dead before the real trouble started. And while he left in office some very poor men, he also left some very competent ones. Charles Evans Hughes, his secretary of state; Herbert Hoover, his secretary of commerce; and Henry C. Wallace, his secretary of agriculture, were public servants of vigor and judgment.

The problem of Herbert Hoover's responsibility is more complicated. He became President on March 4, 1929. At first glance this seems far too late for effective action. By then the damage had been done, and while the crash might come a little sooner or a little later, it was now inevitable. Yet Hoover's involvement was deeper than this—and certainly much deeper than Harding's. This he tacitly concedes in his memoirs, for he is at great pains to explain and, in some degree, to excuse himself.

For one thing, Hoover was no newcomer to Washington. He had been secretary of commerce under Harding and Coolidge. He had also been the strongest figure (not entirely excluding the President) in both Administration and party for almost eight years. He had a clear view of what was going on. As early as 1922, in a letter to Hughes, he expressed grave concern over the quality of the foreign loans that were being floated in New York. He returned several times to the subject. He knew about the corporate excesses. In the later twenties he wrote to his colleagues and fellow officials (including Crissinger) expressing his grave concern over the Wall Street orgy. Yet he was content to express himself—to write letters and memoranda, or at most, as in the case of the foreign loans, to make an occasional speech. He could with propriety have presented his views of the stock market more strongly to the Congress and the public. He could also have maintained a more vigorous and persistent agitation within the Administration. He did neither. His views of the market were so little known that it celebrated his election and inauguration with a great upsurge. Hoover was in the boat and, as he himself tells, he knew where it was headed. But, having warned the man at the tiller, he rode along into the reef.

And even though trouble was inevitable, by March, 1929, a truly committed leader would still have wanted to do something. Nothing else was so important. The resources of the Executive, one might expect, would have been mobilized in a search for some formula to mitigate the current frenzy and to temper the coming crash. The assistance of the bankers, congressional leaders, and the Exchange authorities would have been sought. Nothing of the sort was done. As secretary of commerce, as he subsequently explained, he had thought himself frustrated by Mellon. But he continued Mellon in office. Henry M. Robinson, a sympathetic Los Angeles banker, was commissioned to go to New York to see his colleagues there and report. He returned to say that the New York bankers regarded things as sound. Richard Whitney, the vice-president of the Stock Exchange, was summoned to the White House for a conference on how to curb speculation. Nothing came of this either. Whitney also thought things were sound.

Both Mr. Hoover and his official biographers carefully explained that the primary responsibility for the goings on in New York City rested not with Washington but with the governor of New York State. That was Franklin D. Roosevelt. It was he who failed to rise to his responsibilities. The explanation is far too formal. The future of the whole country was involved. Mr. Hoover was the President of the whole country. If he lacked authority commensurate with this responsibility, he could have requested it. This, at a later date, President Roosevelt did not hesitate to do.

Finally, while by March of 1929 the stock market collapse was inevitable, something could still be done about the other accumulating disorders. The balance of payments is an obvious case. In 1931 Mr. Hoover did request a one-year moratorium on the inter-Allied (war) debts. This was a courageous and constructive step which came directly to grips with the problem. But the year before, Mr. Hoover, though not without reluctance, had signed the Hawley-Smoot tariff. "I shall approve the Tariff Bill. . . . It was undertaken as the result of pledges given by the Republican Party at Kansas City. . . . Platform promises must not be empty gestures." Hundreds of people—from Albert H. Wiggin, the head of the Chase National Bank, to Oswald Garrison Villard, the editor of the *Nation*—felt that no step could have been more directly designed to make things worse. Countries would have even more trouble earning the dollars of which they were so desperately short. But Mr. Hoover signed the bill.

Anyone familiar with this particular race of men knows that a dour, flinty, inscrutable visage such as that of Calvin Coolidge can be the mask for a calm and acutely perceptive intellect. And he knows equally that it can conceal a mind of singular aridity. The difficulty, given the inscrutability, is in knowing which. However, in the case of Coolidge the evidence is in favor of the second. In some sense, he certainly knew what was going on. He would not have been unaware of what was called the Coolidge market. But he connected developments neither with the well-being of the country nor with his own responsibilities. In his memoirs Hoover goes to great lengths to show how closely he was in touch with events and how clearly he foresaw their consequences. In his *Autobiography,* a notably barren document, Coolidge did not refer to the accumulating troubles. He confines himself to such unequivocal truths as "Every day of Presidential life is crowded with activities" (which in his case, indeed, was not true); and "The Congress makes the laws, but it is the President who causes them to be executed."

At various times during his years in office, men called on Coolidge to warn him of the impending trouble. And in 1927, at the instigation of a former White House aide, he sent for William Z. Ripley of Harvard, the most articulate critic of the corporate machinations of the period. The President became so interested that he invited him to stay for lunch, and listened carefully while his guest outlined (as Ripley later related) the "prestidigitation, double-shuffling, honey-fugling, hornswoggling, and skulduggery" that characterized the current Wall Street scene. But Ripley made the mistake of telling Coolidge that regulation was the responsibility of the states (as was then the case). At this intelligence Coolidge's face lit up and he dismissed the entire matter from his mind. Others who warned of the impending disaster got even less far.

And on some occasions Coolidge added fuel to the fire. If the market seemed to be faltering, a timely statement from the White House—or possibly from Secretary Mellon—would often brace it up. William Allen White, by no means an unfriendly observer, noted that after one such comment the market staged a 26-point rise. He went on to say that a careful search "during these halcyon years . . . discloses this fact: Whenever the stock market showed signs of weakness, the President or the Secretary of the Treasury or some important dignitary of the administration . . . issued a statement. The statement invariably declared that business was 'fundamentally sound,' that continued prosperity had arrived, and that the slump of the moment was 'seasonal.'"

Such was the Coolidge role. Coolidge was fond of observing that "if you see ten troubles coming down the road, you can be sure that nine will run into the ditch before they reach you and you have to battle with only one of them." A critic noted that "the trouble with this philosophy was that when the tenth trouble reached him he was wholly unprepared. . . . The outstanding instance was the rising boom and orgy of mad speculation which began in 1927." The critic was Herbert Hoover.

Plainly, in these years, leadership failed. Events whose tragic culmination could be foreseen—and was foreseen—were allowed to work themselves out to the final disaster. The country and the world paid. For a time, indeed, the very reputation of capitalism itself was in the balance. It survived in the years following perhaps less because of its own power or the esteem in which it was held, than because of the absence of an organized and plausible alternative. Yet one important question remains. Would it have been possible even for a strong President to arrest the plunge? Were not the opposing forces too strong? Isn't one asking the impossible?

No one can say for sure. But the answer depends at least partly on the political context in which the Presidency was cast. That of Coolidge and Hoover may well have made decisive leadership impossible. These were conservative Administrations in which, in addition, the influence of the businessman was strong. At the core of the business faith was an intuitive belief in *laissez faire*—the benign tendency of things that are left alone. The man who wanted to intervene was a meddler. Perhaps, indeed, he was a planner. In any case, he was to be regarded with mistrust. And, on the businessman's side, it must be borne in mind that high government office often nurtures a spurious sense of urgency. There is no more important public function than the suppression of proposals for unneeded action. But these should have been distinguished from action necessary to economic survival.

A bitterly criticized figure of the Harding-Coolidge-Hoover era was Secretary of the Treasury Andrew W. Mellon. He opposed all action to curb the boom, although once in 1929 he was persuaded to say that bonds (as distinct from stocks) were a good buy. And when the depression came, he was against doing anything about that. Even Mr. Hoover was shocked by his insistence that the only remedy was (as Mr. Hoover characterized it) to "liquidate labor, liquidate stocks, liquidate the farmers, liquidate real estate." Yet Mellon reflected only in extreme form the conviction that things would work out, that the real enemies were those who interfered.

Outside of Washington in the twenties, the business and banking community, or at least the articulate part of it, was overwhelmingly opposed to any public intervention. The tentative and ineffective steps which the Federal Reserve did take were strongly criticized. In the spring of 1929 when the Reserve system seemed to be on the verge of taking more decisive action, there was an anticipatory tightening of money rates and a sharp drop in the market. On his own initiative Charles E. Mitchell, the head of the National City Bank, poured in new funds. He had an obligation, he said, that was "paramount to any Federal Reserve warning, or anything else" to avert a crisis in the money market. In brief, he was determined, whatever the government thought, to keep the boom going. In that same spring Paul M. Warburg, a distinguished and respected Wall Street leader, warned of the dangers of the boom and called for action to restrain it. He was deluged with criticism and even abuse and later said that the subsequent days were the most difficult of his life. There were some businessmen and bankers—like Mitchell and Albert Wiggin of the Chase National Bank—who may have vaguely sensed that the end of the boom would mean their own business demise. Many more had persuaded themselves that the dream would last. But we should not complicate things. Many others were making money and took a short-run view—or no view—either of their own survival or of the system of which they were a part. They merely wanted to be left alone to get a few more dollars.

And the opposition to government intervention would have been nonpartisan. In 1929 one of the very largest of the Wall Street operators was John J. Raskob. Raskob was also chairman of the Democratic National Committee. So far from calling for preventive measures, Raskob in 1929 was explaining how, through stock market speculation, literally anyone could be a millionaire. Nor would the press have been enthusiastic about, say, legislation to control holding companies and investment trusts or to give authority to regulate margin trading. The financial pages of many of the papers were riding the boom. And even from the speculating public, which was dreaming dreams of riches and had yet to learn that it had been fleeced, there would have been no thanks. Perhaps a President of phenomenal power and determination might have overcome the Coolidge-Hoover environment. But it is easier to argue that this context made inaction inevitable for almost any President. There were too many people who, given a choice between disaster and the measures that would have prevented it, opted for disaster without either a second or even a first thought.

On the other hand, in a different context a strong President might have taken effective preventive action. Congress in these years was becoming increasingly critical of the Wall Street speculation and corporate piggery-pokery. The liberal Republicans—the men whom Senator George H. Moses called the Sons of the Wild Jackass—were especially vehement. But conservatives like Carter Glass were also critical. These men correctly sensed that things were going wrong. A President such as Wilson or either of the Roosevelts (the case of Theodore is perhaps less certain than that of Franklin) who was surrounded in his Cabinet by such men would have been sensitive to this criticism. As a leader he could both have reinforced and drawn strength from the contemporary criticism. Thus he might have been able to arrest the destructive madness as it became recognizable. The American government works far better—perhaps it only works—when the Executive, the business power, and the press are in some degree at odds. Only then can we be sure that abuse or neglect, either private or public, will be given the notoriety that is needed.

Perhaps it is too much to hope that by effective and timely criticism and action the Great Depression might have been avoided. A lot was required in those days to make the United States in any degree depression-proof. But perhaps by preventive action the ensuing depression might have been made less severe. And certainly in the ensuing years the travail of bankers and businessmen before congressional committees, in the courts, and before the bar of public opinion would have been less severe. Here is the paradox. In the full perspective of history, American businessmen never had enemies as damaging as the men who grouped themselves around Calvin Coolidge and supported and applauded him in what William Allen White called "that masterly inactivity for which he was so splendidly equipped."

22

The Sources of the New Deal
ARTHUR M. SCHLESINGER, JR.

23

The New Deal in Historical Perspective
FRANK FREIDEL

24

The Roosevelt Reconstruction
WILLIAM E. LEUCHTENBURG

The age of Franklin Delano Roosevelt and the New Deal was certainly one of the most dramatic and controversial the American republic has experienced. If the controversy has now begun to settle, the drama still remains, intensified perhaps by the perspective in which we are coming to view it. In gaining that perspective, we are inevitably concerned with answering some probing questions about both the movement and its leader. What were the essential nature and meaning of the New Deal? What did it owe to the premises of American life? What did it owe to earlier reform movements, particularly to the progressive movement? Was it essentially conservative, or was it a radically new departure? To what extent did President Roosevelt direct the forces and events of his age, to what extent was he merely their instrument? Would our history in the 'thirties have been "markedly different" (as Professor Leuchtenburg concludes) without him?

How did Roosevelt alter the American presidency? In conducting his office, how much did he make use of the concepts and practices of his predecessors, particularly such "strong" presidents as Theodore Roosevelt and Woodrow Wilson? In what ways did the American presidency, responding to similar historical phenomena in other areas of the Western world, begin to take on the attributes of executive leadership in those areas?

Different but complementary approaches to these questions will be found in the following essays by three of our most notable writers on the age of Roosevelt and the New Deal. Arthur M. Schlesinger, Jr. was Professor of History at Harvard before he served as Special Assistant to President Kennedy during the years 1961 to 1963. In A Thousand Days (1965), he presented a lively and profound account of the Kennedy administration, for which he was awarded the Pulitzer Prize in biography in 1966. Two decades earlier, he had received the Pulitzer Prize for his study of The Age of Jackson. He has also been engaged in a multi-volume study entitled The Age of Roosevelt, of which three volumes have appeared: The Crisis of the Old Order (1957), which portrays American society and politics during the decade before Roosevelt's accession to power; The Coming of the New Deal (1958), a panoramic and brilliant canvas of Roosevelt's first two years in office; and The Politics of Upheaval (1960), which brings the epic narrative to the election of 1936.

Frank Freidel, Professor of History at Harvard, has taught at several universities, and was Harmsworth Professor of American History at Oxford in 1955–56. He has been writing the major Roosevelt biography of our times, of which three volumes have thus far been published: The Apprenticeship (1952), The Ordeal (1954), and The Triumph (1956). William E. Leuchtenburg, Professor of History at Columbia University, is the author of Flood Control Politics (1953), which deals with Connecticut River Valley conservation problems in recent decades, and The Perils of Prosperity, 1914–1932 (1958), a very bright and perceptive contribution to the Chicago History of American Civilization Series. The essay of Leuchtenburg's that is reprinted here is the final chapter of Franklin D. Roosevelt and the New Deal, a volume in the New American Nation Series and winner of the Bancroft Prize for 1963. Based on the latest researches and on a remarkably extensive canvassing of the manuscript sources, the book is considered by many critics to be the best single-volume analysis of its subject.

Various aspects of Roosevelt's achievement come under consideration in the essays that follow. But the theme that binds them together is the relevance of the New Deal to earlier American values and to the reform movements which sought to realize those values. What Roosevelt did, submits Professor Schlesinger, was in concert with the rhythm of American political life, which has alternating beats of reform and conservatism. What he did, submits Professor Freidel, represented in many respects a continuity from the progressive era and World War I, but also occurred as a response to political pressures that threatened Roosevelt's rule. What he did, submits Professor Leuchtenburg, amounted to a new and radical departure, one that was substantially different from progressivism.

Roosevelt's New Deal inevitably suggests questions concerning comparable reform movements both in our country and elsewhere. Are such movements inherent in the development of modern industrial society? How similar was the American response to the problems of depression to that of other Western societies? In what respect was Roosevelt's role comparable to that of his notable contemporaries in European democracies and dictatorships: Ramsay MacDonald, Léon Blum, Benito Mussolini? In what ways has American reform resisted ideology and in what sense has it been "pragmatic"? And an important final question: Do reform movements ever succeed, or is it that the tensions that produce them are absorbed in the greater tensions of external danger, as they seem to have been, for example, when both the progressive movement and the New Deal washed themselves into the vast deluge of world crises and world wars?

ARTHUR M. SCHLESINGER, JR.

In the background of any historical episode lies all previous history. The strands which a historian may select as vital to an understanding of the particular episode will vary widely according to his interest, his temperament, his faith and his time. Each man must unravel the seamless web in his own way. I do not propose here any definitive assessment of the sources of the New Deal. I doubt whether a final assessment is possible. I want rather to call attention to certain possible sources which may not have figured extensively in the conventional accounts, including my own—to the relation of the New Deal to the ebb and flow of American national politics and then its relation to the international dilemma of free society in this century.

Such relationships are speculative; nonetheless, an attempt to see them may perhaps cast light on some of the less discussed impulses behind the New Deal itself. To begin—and in order to make a sharp issue—let me ask this question: would there have been a New Deal if there had been no depression? Without a depression, would we have had nothing but a placid continuation, so long as prosperity itself continued, of the New Era of the Twenties?

I would answer that there would very likely have been some sort of New Deal in the Thirties even without the Depression. I think perhaps our contemporary thinking has come too unreflectively to assume depression as the necessary preliminary for any era of reform. Students of American history know better. The fight against depression was, to be sure, the heart of the New Deal, but it has not been the central issue of traditional American reform: it was not the heart of Jeffersonian de-

SOURCE: *Columbia University Forum*, II (Fall, 1959), 4–12. Reprinted by permission.

mocracy nor of Jacksonian democracy nor of the anti-slavery movement nor of the Progressive movement.

What preceded these other epochs of reform was an accumulation of disquietudes and discontents in American society, often non-economic in character, and producing a general susceptibility to appeals for change—this and the existence within society of able men or groups who felt themselves cramped by the status quo and who were capable of exploiting mounting dissatisfaction to advance policies and purposes of their own. This combination of outsiders striving for status and power and a people wearying of the existing leadership and the existing ideals has been the real archetype of American reform.

The official order in the Twenties presented perhaps the nearest we ever came in our history to the identification of the national interest with the interests, values and goals of a specific class—in this case, of course, the American business community. During the generation before Harding, the political leaders who had commanded the loyalties and the energies of the American people—Theodore Roosevelt and Woodrow Wilson—expressed strains in American life distinct from and often opposed to the dominant values of business. They represented a fusion of patrician and intellectual attitudes which saw in public policy an outlet for creative energy—in Lippmann's phrase, they stood for mastery as against drift. In the service of this conception, they led the people into great national efforts of various sorts, culminating in the convulsive and terrible experience of war. Two decades of this—two decades under the glittering eyes of such leaders as Roosevelt and Wilson, Bryan and La Follette—left the nation in a state of exhaustion.

By 1920 the nation was tired of public crisis. It was tired of discipline and sacrifice. It was tired of abstract and intangible objectives. It could gird itself no longer for heroic moral or intellectual effort. Its instinct for idealism was spent. "It is only once in a generation," Wilson himself had said, "that a people can be lifted above material things. That is why conservative government is in the saddle two-thirds of the time." And the junior official to whom he made this remark, the young Assistant Secretary of the Navy, also noted soon after his unsuccessful try for the Vice-Presidency in 1920, "Every war brings after it a period of materialism and conservatism; people tire quickly of ideals and we are now repeating history." John W. Davis, the Democratic candidate in 1924, said a few years later: "The people usually know what they want at a particular time . . . In 1924 when I was a candidate what they wanted was repose."

A nation fatigued with ideals and longing for repose was ready for "normalcy." As popular attention receded from public policy, as values and aspirations became private again, people stopped caring about politics, which meant that political power inevitably gravitated to society's powerful economic interests—the government of the exhausted nation quite naturally fell to the businessmen. And for nearly a decade the business government reigned over a prosperous and expanding country.

Yet, for all the material contentment of the Twenties, the decade was also marked by mounting spiritual and psychological discontent. One could detect abundant and multiplying symptoms of what Josiah Royce, after Hegel, used to call a self-estranged social order. The official creed began to encounter growing skepticism, and even opposition and ridicule, in the community at large. Able and ambitious groups, denied what they considered fitting recognition or opportunity, began to turn against the Establishment.

If the economic crash of 1929 astonished the experts, a spiritual crash was diagnosed well in advance. "By 1927," reported Scott Fitzgerald, "a widespread neurosis began to be evident, faintly signalled, like a nervous beating of the feet, by the popularity of crossword puzzles." In the same year Walter Lippmann pointed more soberly to the growing discrepancy between the nominal political issues of the day and the actual emotions of the people. If politics took up these real issues, Lippmann said, it would revolutionize the existing party system. "It is not surprising, then, that our political leaders are greatly occupied in dampening down interest, in obscuring issues, and in attempting to distract attention from the realities of American life."

What was wrong with the New Era was not (as yet) evidence of incompetence or stupidity in public policy. Rather, there was a profound discontent with the monopoly of power and prestige by a single class and the resulting indifference of the national government to deeper tensions. Those excluded from the magic circle suffered boredom, resentment, irritation and eventually indignation over what seemed the intolerable pretensions and irrelevances of their masters. Now it is the gravest error to underrate the power of boredom as a factor in social change. Our political scientists have pointed out convincingly how the human tendency toward inertia sets limits on liberalism; I wish they would spend equal time showing how the human capacity for boredom sets limits on conservatism. The dominant official society—the Establishment—of the Twenties was an exceedingly boring one, neither bright nor witty nor picturesque nor even handsome, and this prodded the human impulse to redress the balance by kicking up heels in back streets.

All this encouraged the defection of specific groups from a social order which ignored their needs and snubbed their ambitions. Within the business community itself there were dissident individuals, especially in the underdeveloped areas of the country, who considered that opportunities for local growth were unduly restrained by Wall Street's control of the money market. The farmers felt themselves shut out from the prevailing prosperity. Elements in the labor movement resented their evident second-class citizenship. Members of foreign nationality groups, especially the newer immigration and its children, chafed under the prevalent assumption that the real America was Anglo-Saxon, Protestant, middle-class and white. In time some of the younger people of the nation began to grow restless before the ideals held out to them; while others, in accepting these ideals, acquired a smug mediocrity which even depressed some of their elders.

Gravest among the symptoms was the defection of the intellectuals: writers, educators, newspapermen, editors—those who manned the machinery of opinion and who transmitted ideas. The fact of their particular estrangement and discontent guaranteed the articulation, and thus, to a degree, the coordination of the larger unrest. The intellectuals put the ruling class in its place by substituting for its own admiring picture of itself a set of disrespectful images, which an increasing number of people found delightful and persuasive; the insiders, who had before been seen in the reverent terms of Bruce Barton and the *American Magazine,* were now to be seen less reverently through the eyes of H. L. Mencken and Sinclair Lewis. Satire liberated people from the illusion of business infallibility and opened their minds to other visions of American possibility. The next function of the intellectuals was precisely to explore and substantiate those other visions. They did so with zest and ingenuity; and the result was that, beneath the official crust, the Twenties billowed with agitation, criticism and hope. Dewey affirmed man's capability for social invention and management; Beard argued that intelligent national planning was the irresistible next phase in history; Parrington insisted that Jeffersonian idealism had a sound basis in the American past, and indeed, expressed a truer Americanism than did materialism. Together the satirists and the prophets drew a new portrait of America—both of the American present and of the American promise—and the increasingly visible discrepancy between what was and what might be in America armed the spreading discontent.

The well of idealism was rising again; energies were being replenished, batteries recharged. Outsiders were preparing to hammer on the gates of the citadel. The 1928 election, in which an Irish Catholic challenged Yankee Protestant supremacy, illustrated the gathering revolt against the Establishment. And, though Hoover won the election, Samuel Lubell has pointed out that "Smith split not only the Solid South but the Republican North as well." Smith carried counties which had long been traditionally Republican; he smashed the Republican hold on the cities; he mobilized the new immigrants. In losing, he polled nearly as many votes as Calvin Coolidge had polled in winning four years before. He stood for the vital new tendencies of politics; and it is likely that the prolongation of these tendencies would have assured a national Democratic victory, without a depression, in 1932 or certainly by 1936. And such a Democratic victory would surely have meant the discharge into public life of able and ambitious people denied preference under a business administration—much the same sort of people, indeed, who eventually came to power with the New Deal; and it would have meant new opportunities for groups that had seen the door slammed in their faces in the Twenties—labor, the farmers, the ethnic minorities, the intellectuals.

The suspicion that a political overturn was due even without a depression is fortified, I think, by the calculations of my father in his essay of some years back "The Tides of National Politics." In this essay he proposed that liberal and conservative periods in our national life succeed themselves at intervals of about fifteen or sixteen years; this alternation takes place, he wrote, without any apparent correlation with economic circumstances or, indeed, with anything else, except the ebb and flow of national political psychology. By this argument, a liberal epoch was due in America around 1934 or 1935, depression or no.

In short, the New Deal was, among other things, an expression of what would seem—to use a currently unfashionable concept—an inherent cyclical rhythm in American politics. The Depression did not cause the cycle: what the Depression did was to increase its intensity and deepen its impact by superimposing on the normal cycle the peculiar and unprecedented urgencies arising from economic despair. One might even argue—though I do not think I would—that the Depression coming at another stage in the cycle would not necessarily have produced a New Deal. It is certainly true, as I said, that depressions did not induce epochs of reform in 1873 or in 1893. I think myself, however, that the magnitude of the shock made a political recoil almost certain after 1929. Still, the fact that this recoil took a liberal rather than a reactionary turn may well be due to the accident that the economic shock coincided with a liberal turn in the political cycle.

In any event, the fact remains that the historical New Deal, whether or not something like it might have come along anyway, was after all brought into being by the Depression. It assumed its particular character as it sought to respond to the challenge of economic collapse. And, in confronting this challenge, it was confronting a good deal more than merely an American problem. Mass unemployment touched the very roots of free institutions everywhere. "This problem of unemployment," as Winston Churchill said in England in 1930, "is the most torturing that can be presented to civilized society." The problem was more than torturing; it was something civilized society had to solve if it were to survive. And the issue presented with particular urgency was whether representative democracy could ever deal effectively with it.

Churchill, in the same Romanes lecture at Oxford in 1930, questioned whether it could: democratic governments, he said, drifted along the lines of least resistance, took short views, smoothed their path with platitudes, and paid their way with sops and doles. Parliaments, he suggested, could deal with political problems, but not with economic. "One may even be pardoned," Churchill said, "for doubting whether institutions based on adult suffrage could possibly arrive at the right decisions upon the intricate propositions of modern business and finance." These were delicate problems requiring specialist treatment. "You cannot cure cancer by a majority. What is wanted is a remedy."

The drift of discussion in the United States as well as in Britain in the early Thirties revealed an increasingly dour sense of existing alternatives; on the one hand, it seemed, was parliamentary democracy with economic chaos; on the other, economic authoritarianism with political tyranny. Even more dour was the sense that history had already made the choice—that the democratic impulse was drained of vitality, that liberalism was spent as a means of organizing human action. Consider a selection of statements from American writers at the time, and their mortuary resonance:

> The rejection of democracy is nowadays regarded as evidence of superior wisdom. (Ralph Barton Perry)
> The moral and intellectual bankruptcy of liberalism in our time needs no demonstration. It is as obvious as rain and as taken for granted. (Nathaniel Peffer)
> To attempt a defense of democracy these days is a little like defending paganism in 313 or the divine right of kings in 1793. It is taken for granted that democracy is bad and that it is dying. (George Boas)
> 'Liberalism is dead.' So many people who seem to agree upon nothing else have agreed to accept these three sweeping words. (Joseph Wood Krutch)
> Modern Western civilization is a failure. That theory is now generally accepted. (Louise Maunsell Fields)
> Why is it that democracy has fallen so rapidly from the high prestige which it had at the Armistice? . . . Why is it that in America itself—in the very temple and citadel of democracy—self-government has been held up to every ridicule, and many observers count it already dead? (Will Durant)

Only the most venerable among us can remember the creeping fear of a quarter of a century ago that the free system itself had run out of energy, that we had reached, in a phrase Reinhold Niebuhr used as a part of the title of a book in 1934, the "end of an era." What this pessimism implied for the realm of public policy was that democracy had exhausted its intellectual and moral resources, its bag of tricks was played out, and salvation now lay in moving over to a system of total control.

In affirming that there was no alternative between laissez-faire and tyranny, the pessimists were endorsing a passionate conviction held by both the proponents of individualism and the proponents of collectivism. Ogden Mills spoke with precision for American conservatives: "We can have a free country or a socialistic one. We cannot have both. Our economic system cannot be half free and half socialistic . . . There is no middle ground between governing and being governed, between absolute sovereignty and liberty, between tyranny and freedom." Herbert Hoover was equally vehement: "Even partial regimentation cannot be made to work and still maintain live democratic institutions." In such sentiments, Hoover and Mills would have commanded the enthusiastic assent of Stalin and Mussolini. The critical question was whether a middle way was possible—a mixed system which might give the state more power than conservatives would like, enough power, indeed, to assure economic and social security, but still not so much as to create dictatorship. To this question the Hoovers, no less than the Stalins and Mussolinis, had long since returned categorical answers. They all agreed on this, if on nothing else: no.

As I have said, economic planning was not just an American problem. Great Britain, for example, was confronting mass unemployment and economic stagnation; moreover, she had had since 1929 a Labor government. In a sense, it would have been hard to select a better place to test the possibilities of a tranquil advance from laissez-faire capitalism to a managed society. Here was a Labor leadership, sustained by a faith in the "inevitability of gradualness," ruling a nation committed by tradition and instinct to the acceptance of empirical change. How did the British Labor government visualize its problem and opportunity?

The central figures in the Labor government of 1929 were Ramsay MacDonald, now Prime Minister for the second time, and Philip Snowden, his sharp and dominating Chancellor of the Exchequer. Both were classical Socialists who saw in the nationalization of basic industry the answer to all economic riddles. Yet in the existing political situation, with a slim Labor majority, nationalization was out of the question. With socialism excluded, MacDonald and Snowden—indeed, nearly all the Labor party leaders—could see no alternative to all-out socialism but nearly all-out laissez-faire. A capitalist order had to be operated on capitalist principles. The economic policy of the Labor government was thus consecrated as faithfully as that of Herbert Hoover's Republican administration in the United States to the balanced budget and the gold standard—and, far more faithfully than American Republicanism, to free trade.

Socialism across the Channel was hardly more resourceful. As the German Social Democrat Fritz Naphtali put it in 1930, "I don't believe that we can do very much, nor anything very decisive, from the point of view of economic policy, to overcome the crisis until it has run its course." In this spirit of impotence, the democratic Socialists of Europe (until Léon Blum came to power some years later) denied the possibility of a middle way and concluded that, short of full socialization, they had no alternative but to accept the logic of laissez-faire.

The assumption that there were two absolutely distinct economic orders, socialism and capitalism, expressed, of course, an unconscious Platonism—a conviction that the true reality lay in the theoretical essences of which any working economy, with its compromises and confusions, could only be an imperfect copy. If in the realm of essences socialism and capitalism were separate phenomena based on separate principles, then they must be kept rigorously apart on earth. Nor was this use of Platonism—this curious belief that the abstraction was somehow more real than the reality, which Whitehead so well called the "fallacy of misplaced concreteness"—confined to doctrinaire capitalists and doctrinaire socialists. The eminent Liberal economist Sir William Beveridge, director of the London School of Economics, braintruster for the Lloyd George welfare reforms before the First World War, spoke for enlightened economic opinion when he identified the "inescapable fatal danger" confronting public policy in the Depression as "the danger of mixing freedom and control. We have to decide either to let production be guided by the free play of prices or to plan it socialistically from beginning to end . . . Control and freedom do not mix." Beveridge, encountering Donald Richberg in Washington in the glowing days of 1933, asked a bit patronizingly whether Richberg really believed that there was "a halfway between Wall Street and Moscow." As for Britain, "there is not much that anyone can do now to help us," Beveridge said. "We must plan to avoid another crisis later. We shall not by conscious effort escape this one."

So dogma denied the possibility of a managed capitalism. But could dogma hold out in Britain against the urgencies of depression? Some Englishmen dissented from the either/or philosophy. In the general election of 1929, for example, John Maynard Keynes and Hubert Henderson had provided the Liberal party with the rudiments of an expansionist policy, based on national spending and public works. As unemployment increased in 1930, so too did the pressure for positive government action. That year Sir Oswald Mosley, a member of the Labor government, proposed to a cabinet committee on unemployment an active program of government spending, accompanied by controls over banking, industry and foreign trade. But he could make no impression on the capitalist orthodoxy of the Socialist leaders; Snowden rejected the Mosley memorandum. Another minister suggested leaving the gold standard; Snowden covered him with scorn. To the party conference of 1930, MacDonald said, "I appeal to you to go back to your Socialist faith. Do not mix that up with pettifogging patching, either of a Poor Law kind or Relief Work kind." In other words, socialism meant all or—in this case—nothing!

As economic pressure increased, more and more had to be sacrificed to the balancing of the budget; and the implacable retrenchment meant more governmental economy, reduction in salaries, reduction in normal public works, until, in time, the frenzy for economy threatened the social services and especially the system of unemployment payments on which many British workers relied to keep alive. The summer crisis of 1931, after the failure of *Kreditanstalt,* weakened the pound; and to Snowden and the Labor government nothing now seemed more essential than staying on the gold standard. To keep Britain on gold required American loans; American loans would not be forthcoming unless satisfactory evidence existed of a determination to balance the budget; and the evidence most likely to satisfy J. P. Morgan and Company, which was arranging the American credit, was a cut in unemployment benefits.

In August 1931, MacDonald and Snowden confronted the cabinet with this dismal logic. Arthur Henderson made it clear that the whole cabinet absolutely accepted Snowden's economic theory: "We ought to do everything in our power to balance the Budget." But MacDonald's proposal for a cut in the dole seemed downright wrong; the Labor government fell. MacDonald soon returned to office as head of a National government. The new government, slightly more adventurous than its predecessors, took Britain off gold in a few weeks. Sidney Webb, Labor's senior intellectual, provided the Labor government its obituary: "No one ever told *us* we could do that!"

The Labor government having immobilized itself by its intellectual conviction that there was no room for maneuver, no middle way, now succeeded through its collapse in documenting its major premise. Then the experience of 1931 displayed the Right as too hardboiled ever to acquiesce in even the most gradual democratic change. "The attempt to give a social bias to capitalism, while leaving it master of the house," wrote R. H. Tawney, "appears to have failed."

If piecemeal reforms were beyond the power of the Labor government, as they were beyond the desire of a Tory government, then the only hope lay in the rapid achievement of full socialism; the only way socialism could be achieved seemed to be through ruthlessness on the Left as great as that on the Right. Such reasoning was responsible for the lust for catastrophic change that suffused the British Left and infected a part of the American Left in the early Thirties. No one drew more facile and sweeping conclusions than Harold Laski. The fate of the MacDonald government, Laski wrote, was "tantamount to an insistence that if socialists wish to secure a state built upon the principles of their faith, they can only do so by revolutionary means."

From this perspective Laski and those like him quite naturally looked with derision on the advocate of the middle way. In December 1934, for the perhaps somewhat baffled readers of *Redbook* magazine, Laski debated with Maynard Keynes whether America could spend its way to recovery. Public spending, Laski said with horror, would lead to inflation or heavy taxation or waste; it would mean, he solemnly wrote, "an unbalanced budget with the disturbance of confidence (an essential condition of recovery) which this implies": it would bequeath a "bill of staggering dimensions" to future generations. "Government spending as anything more than a temporary and limited expedient," he concluded, "will necessarily do harm in a capitalist society." This was, of course, not only the argument of Ramsay MacDonald but of Herbert Hoover; Laski's novelty was to use it to defend, not a balanced budget and the gold standard, but—socialist revolution.

One way or another, the British Left began to vote against liberal democracy. Sir Oswald Mosley, who had championed the most constructive economic program considered within the MacDonald government, indicated the new direction when, with John Strachey and others, he founded the authoritarian-minded New Party in 1931. Mosley's excesses soon led him toward fascism and discredit; but plenty of others were reaching similar conclusions about the impossibility of reform under capitalism. Sidney and Beatrice Webb abandoned Fabianism for the mirage of a new civilization in the Soviet Union. All peaceful roads to progress seemed blocked. After a visit with Roosevelt in Washington, Cripps wrote, "My whole impression is of an honest anxious man faced by an impossible task—humanizing capitalism and making it work." "The one thing that is not inevitable now," said Cripps, "is gradualness."

Both Right and Left—Hoover and Stalin, John W. Davis and Mussolini, Ogden Mills and Stafford Cripps—thus rejected the notion of a socially directed and managed capitalism, of a mixed economy, of something in between classical free enterprise and classical socialism. And the either/or demonstration commanded considerable respect in the United States—self-evidently on the American Right; and to some degree on the American Left. So Laski had made clear in *Democracy in Crisis* that the American ruling class would be as tough and hopeless as any other:

> What evidence is there, among the class which controls the destiny of America, of a will to make the necessary concessions? Is not the execution of Sacco and Vanzetti, the long indefensible imprisonment of Mooney, the grim history of American strikes, the root of the answer to that question?

In 1932 both Right and Left thus stood with fierce intransigence on the solid ground of dogma. In so doing, they were challenging an essential part of the American liberal tradition. When Professor Rexford G. Tugwell of the Columbia University economics department, on leave in Washington, revisited his campus in 1933, he rashly bragged of the New Deal's freedom from "blind doctrine," and the *Columbia Spectator,* then edited by a brilliant young undergraduate named James Wechsler, seized on this boast as the fatal weakness of Tugwell's argument and of the whole New Deal. "This is the crux of the problem," the *Spectator* said; "the blind stumbling in the most chaotic fashion—experimenting from day to day—without any anchor except a few idealistic phrases—is worthless. It is merely political pragmatism."

Merely political pragmatism—to ideologists, whether of Right or of Left, this seemed conclusive evidence of intellectual bankruptcy. As the conservatives had said that any attempt to modify the capitalist system must mean socialism, so the radicals now said that any attempt to maintain the capitalist system must mean fascism. "Roosevelt's policies can be welded into a consistent whole," wrote I. F. Stone, "only on the basis of one hypothesis . . . that Mr. Roosevelt intends to move toward fascism." "The essential logic of the New Deal," wrote Max Lerner, "is increasingly the naked fist of the capitalist state."

Convinced of the fragility of the system, the radicals saw themselves as the forerunners of apocalypse. "American commercial agriculture is doomed," wrote Louis Hacker; capitalism was doomed, too, and the party system, and the traditional American way of life. In 1934 Sidney Hook, James Burnham, Louis Budenz, V. F. Calverton, James Rorty and others addressed "An Open Letter to American Intellectuals." "We cannot by some clever Rooseveltian trick," the letter warned,

> evade the unfolding of basic economic and political developments under capitalism . . . Let us not deceive ourselves that we shall not have to face here also the choice between reaction, on the one hand, and a truly scientific economy under a genuine workers' democracy on the other.

In 1935 *The New Republic* stated with magisterial simplicity the argument of the radicals against the New Dealers, of New York against Washington, of the Marxists against the pragmatists.

> Either the nation must put up with the confusions and miseries of an essentially unregulated capitalism, or it must prepare to supersede capitalism with socialism. *There is no longer a feasible middle course.*

Both radicalism and conservatism thus ended in the domain of either/or. The contradictions of actuality, which so stimulated the pragmatists of Washington, only violated the proprieties and offended the illusions of the ideologists. While they all saw themselves as hardheaded realists, in fact they were Platonists, preferring essence to existence and considering abstractions the only reality.

The great central source of the New Deal, in my judgment, lay precisely in the instinctive response of practical, energetic, and compassionate people to those dogmatic absolutes. This passion to sacrifice reality to doctrine presented a profound challenge to the pragmatic nerve. Many Americans, refusing to be intimidated by abstractions or to be overawed by ideology, responded by doing things. The whole point of the New Deal lay in its belief in activism, its faith in gradualness, its rejection of catastrophism, its indifference to ideology, its conviction that a managed and modified capitalist order achieved by piecemeal experiment could combine personal freedom and economic growth. "In a world in which revolutions just now are coming easily," said Adolf Berle, "the New Deal chose the more difficult course of moderation and rebuilding." "The course that the new Administration did take," said Harold Ickes, "was the hardest course. It conformed to no theory, but it did fit into the American system—a system of taking action step by step, a system of regulation only to meet concrete needs, a system of courageous recognition of change." Tugwell, rejecting laissez-faire and communism, spoke of the "third course."

Roosevelt himself, of course, was the liberal pragmatist *par excellence.* His aim was to steer between the extremes of chaos and tyranny by moving always, in his phrase, "slightly to the left of center." "Unrestrained individualism" he wrote, had proved a failure; yet "any paternalistic system which tries to provide for security for everyone from above only calls for an impossible task and a regimentation utterly uncongenial to the spirit of our people." He constantly repeated Macaulay's injunction to reform if you wished to preserve.

Roosevelt had no illusions about revolution. Mussolini and Stalin seemed to him, in his phrase, "not mere distant relatives" but "blood brothers." When Emil Ludwig asked him his "political motive," he replied, "My desire is to obviate revolution . . . I work in a contrary sense to Rome and Moscow." He said during the 1932 campaign:

> Say that civilization is a tree which, as it grows, continually produces rot and dead wood. The radical says: 'Cut it down.' The conservative says: 'Don't touch it.' The liberal compromises: 'Let's prune, so that we lose neither the old trunk nor the new branches.' This campaign is waged to teach the country to march upon its appointed course, the way of change, in an orderly march, avoiding alike the revolution of radicalism and the revolution of conservatism.

I think it would be a mistake to underestimate the extent to which this pragmatic attitude was itself a major source of New Deal vitality. The exaltation of the middle way seems banal and obvious enough today. Yet the tyranny of dogma was such in the early years of the Great Depression that infatuation with ideology blocked and smothered the instinctive efforts of free men to work their own salvation. In a world intoxicated with abstractions, Roosevelt and the New Dealers stood almost alone in a stubborn faith in rational experiment, in trial and error. No one understood this more keenly than the great English critic of absolutes; Keynes, in an open letter to Roosevelt at the end of 1933, stated the hopes generated by the New Deal with precision and eloquence. "You have made yourself," Keynes told Roosevelt,

> the trustee for those in every country who seek to mend the evils of our condition by reasoned experiment within the framework of the existing social system. If you fail, rational choice will be gravely prejudiced throughout the world, leaving orthodoxy and revolution to fight it out. But, if you succeed, new and bolder methods will be tried everywhere, and we may date the first chapter of a new economic era from your accession to office.

The question remains: why did the New Deal itself have the pragmatic commitment? Why, under the impact of depression, was it not overborne by dogma as were most other governments and leaders in the world? The answer to this lies, I suspect, in the point I proposed earlier—in the suggestion that the New Deal represented, not just a response to depression, but also a response to pent-up frustration and needs in American society—frustrations and needs which would have operated had there been no depression at all. The periodic demand for forward motion in American politics, the periodic breakthrough of new leadership—these were already in the works before the Depression. Depression, therefore, instead of catching a nation wholly unprepared, merely accelerated tendencies toward change already visible in the national community. The response to depression, in short, was controlled and tempered by the values of traditional American experimentalism, rather than those of rigid ideology. The New Deal was thus able to approach the agony of mass unemployment and depression in the pragmatic spirit, in the spirit which guaranteed the survival rather than the extinction of freedom, in the spirit which in time rekindled hope across the world that free men could manage their own economic destiny.

FRANK FREIDEL

In less than a generation, the New Deal has passed into both popular legend and serious history. The exigencies of American politics long demanded that its partisans and opponents paint a picture of it either in the most glamorous whites or sinister blacks. Long after the New Deal was over, politicians of both major parties tried at each election to reap a harvest of votes from its issues.

SOURCE: Frank Freidel, *The New Deal in Historical Perspective*, 2nd ed., No. 25 (1965), pp. 1–20. This article is part of a series of pamphlets published in Washington, D.C. by the Service Center for Teachers of History of the American Historical Association. Reprinted by permission of author and publishers.

Gradually a new generation of voters has risen which does not remember the New Deal and takes for granted the changes that it wrought. Gradually too, politicians have had to recognize that the nation faces new, quite different problems since the second World War, and that campaigning on the New Deal has become as outmoded as did the "bloody shirt" issue as decades passed after the Civil War. At the same time, most of the manuscript collections relating to the New Deal have been opened to scholars so rapidly that careful historical research has been possible decades sooner than was true for earlier periods of United States history. (The Franklin D. Roosevelt papers and the Abraham Lincoln papers became available for research at about the same time, just after the second World War.)

It has been the task of the historians not only to analyze heretofore hidden aspects of the New Deal on the basis of the manuscripts, but also to remind readers of what was once commonplace and is now widely forgotten. A new generation has no firsthand experience of the depths of despair into which the depression had thrust the nation, and the excitement and eagerness with which people greeted the new program. Critics not only have denied that anything constructive could have come from the New Deal but they have even succeeded in creating the impression in the prosperous years since 1945 that the depression really did not amount to much. How bad it was is worth remembering, since this is a means of gauging the enormous pressure for change.

Estimates of the number of unemployed ranged up to thirteen million out of a labor force of fifty-two million, which would mean that one wage-earner out of four was without means of support for himself or his family. Yet of these thirteen million unemployed, only about a quarter were receiving any kind of assistance. States and municipalities were running out of relief funds; private agencies were long since at the end of their resources. And those who were receiving aid often obtained only a pittance. The Toledo commissary could allow for relief only 2.14 cents per person per meal, and the Red Cross in southern Illinois in 1931 was able to provide families with only seventy-five cents a week for food. It was in this crisis that one of the most flamboyant members of the Hoover administration suggested a means of providing sustenance for the unemployed: restaurants should dump left-overs and plate scrapings into special sanitary cans to be given to worthy unemployed people willing to work for the food. It was a superfluous suggestion, for in 1932 an observer in Chicago reported:

> Around the truck which was unloading garbage and other refuse were about thirty-five men, women, and children. As soon as the truck pulled away from the pile, all of them started digging with sticks, some with their hands, grabbing bits of food and vegetables.

The employed in some instances were not a great deal better off. In December 1932 wages in a wide range of industries, from textiles to iron and steel, averaged from a low of 20 cents to a high of only 30 cents an hour. A quarter of the women working in Chicago were receiving less than 10 cents an hour. In farming areas, conditions were equally grim. In bitter weather on the Great Plains, travelers occasionally encountered a light blue haze that smelled like roasting coffee. The "old corn" held over from the crop of a year earlier would sell for only $1.40 per ton, while coal cost $4 per ton, so many farmers burned corn to keep warm. When Aubrey Williams went into farm cellars in the Dakotas in the early spring of 1933 farm wives showed him shelves and shelves of jars for fruits and vegetables—but they were all empty. Even farmers who could avoid hunger had trouble meeting payments on their mortgages. As a result a fourth of all farmers in the United States lost their farms during these years.

Despairing people in these pre-New Deal years feared President Herbert Hoover had forgotten them or did not recognize the seriousness of their plight. As a matter of fact he had, more than any other depression president in American history, taken steps to try to bring recovery. But he had functioned largely through giving aid at the top to prevent further collapse of banks and industries, and the concentric rings of further collapses and unemployment which would then ensue. Also he had continued to pin his faith upon voluntary action. He felt that too great federal intervention would undermine the self-reliance, destroy the "rugged individualism" of the American people, and that it would create federal centralization, thus paving the way for socialism.

President Hoover was consistent in his thinking, and he was humane. But it would have been hard to explain to people like those grubbing on the Chicago garbage heap, why, when the Reconstruction Finance Corporation was loaning $90,000,000 to a single Chicago bank, the President would veto a bill to provide federal relief for the unemployed, asserting, "never before has so dangerous a suggestion been seriously made in this country." It was not until June 1932 that he approved a measure permitting the RFC to loan $300,000,000 for relief purposes.

It seems shocking in retrospect that such conditions should have existed in this country, and that any president of either major party should so long have refused to approve federal funds to alleviate them. It adds to the shock when one notes that many public figures of the period were well to the right of the President—for instance, Secretary of the Treasury Andrew Mellon—and that almost no one who was likely to be in a position to act, including Governor Roosevelt of New York, was ready at that time to go far to the left of Hoover.

Roosevelt, who was perhaps the most advanced of the forty-eight governors in developing a program to meet the depression, had shown little faith in public works spending. When he had established the first state relief agency in the United States in the fall of 1931, he had tried to finance it through higher taxes, and only later, reluctantly, abandoned the pay-as-you-go basis. He was, and he always remained, a staunch believer in a balanced budget. He was never more sincere than when, during the campaign of 1932, he accused the Hoover administration of having run up a deficit of three and three-quarters billions of dollars in the previous two years. This, he charged, was "the most reckless and extravagant past that I have been able to discover in the statistical record of any peacetime Government anywhere, any time."

Governor Roosevelt's own cautious record did not exempt him from attack. In April 1932, seeking the presidential nomination, he proclaimed himself the champion of the "forgotten man," and talked vaguely about raising the purchasing power of the masses, in part through directing Reconstruction Finance Corporation loans their way. This little was sufficient to lead many political leaders and publicists, including his Democratic rival, Al Smith, to accuse Roosevelt of being a demagogue, ready to set class against class.

Smith and most other public figures, including Roosevelt, favored public works programs. A few men like Senators Robert F. Wagner of New York and Robert M. La Follette of Wisconsin visualized really large-scale spending on public construction, but most leaders also wanted to accompany the spending with very high taxes which would have been deflationary and thus have defeated the program. None of the important political leaders, and none of the economists who had access to them, seemed as yet to visualize the decisive intervention of the government into the economy of the sort that is considered commonplace today. The term "built-in stabilizers" had yet to be coined.

The fact was that Roosevelt and most of his contemporaries, who like him were products of the Progressive Era, were basically conservative men who unquestioningly believed in the American free enterprise system. On the whole, they were suspicious of strong government, and would indulge in it only as a last resort to try to save the system. This was their limitation in trying to bring about economic recovery. On the other hand, part of their Progressive legacy was also a humanitarian belief in social justice. This belief would lead them to espouse reforms to improve the lot of the common man, even though those reforms might also take them in the direction of additional government regulation. Roosevelt as governor had repeatedly demonstrated this inconsistency in his public statements and recommendations. He had ardently endorsed states rights and small government in a truly Jeffersonian way. Then in quite contrary fashion (but still in keeping with Jeffersonian spirit applied to twentieth century society) he had pointed out one or another area, such as old age security, in which he believed the government must intervene to protect the individual.

At this time, what distinguished Governor Roosevelt from his fellows were two remarkable characteristics. The first was his brilliant political skill, which won to him an overwhelming proportion of the Democratic politicians and the general public. The second was his willingness to experiment, to try one or another improvisation to stop the slow economic drift downward toward ruin. During the campaign of 1932, many a man who had observed Roosevelt felt as did Harry Hopkins that he would make a better president than Hoover, "chiefly because he is not afraid of a new idea."

Roosevelt's sublime self-confidence and his willingness to try new expedients stood him in good stead when he took over the presidency. On that grim March day in 1933 when he took his oath of office, the American economic system was half-paralyzed. Many of the banks were closed; the remainder he quickly shut down through presidential proclamation. Industrial production was down to 56 per cent of the 1923–25 level. Yet somehow, Roosevelt's self-confidence was infectious. People were ready to believe, to follow, when he said in words that were not particularly new, "The only thing we have to fear is fear itself." He offered "leadership of frankness and vigor," and almost the whole of the American public and press—even papers like the Chicago *Tribune* which soon became bitter critics—for the moment accepted that leadership with enthusiasm.

For a short period of time, about one hundred days, Roosevelt had behind him such overwhelming public support that he was able to push through Congress a wide array of legislation which in total established the New Deal. It came in helter-skelter fashion and seemed to go in all directions, even at times directions that conflicted with each other. There was mildly corrective legislation to get the banks open again, a slashing of government costs to balance the budget, legalization of 3.2 beer, establishment of the Civilian Conservation Corps, of the Tennessee Valley Authority, and of a wide variety of other agencies in the areas of relief, reform, and, above all in those first months, of recovery.

What pattern emerged in all of this legislation? How sharply did it break with earlier American political traditions? The answer was that it represented Roosevelt's efforts to be president to all the American people, to present something to every group in need. And it was based squarely on American objectives and experience in the Progressive Era and during the first World War. It went beyond the Hoover program in that while the word "voluntary" remained in many of the laws, they now had behind them the force of the government or at least strong economic incentives.

It has been forgotten how basically conservative Roosevelt's attitudes remained during the early period of the New Deal. He had closed the banks, but reopened them with relatively little change. Indeed, the emergency banking measure had been drafted by Hoover's Treasury officials. What banking reform there was came later. His slashing of the regular government costs was something he had promised during his campaign, and in which he sincerely believed and continued to believe. He kept the regular budget of the government low until the late thirties. While he spent billions through the parallel emergency budget, he did that reluctantly, and only because he felt it was necessary to keep people from starving. He was proud that he was keeping the credit of the government good, and never ceased to look forward to the day when he could balance the budget. For the first several years of the New Deal he consulted frequently with Wall Streeters and other economic conservatives. His first Director of the Budget, Lewis Douglas, parted ways with him, but late in 1934 was exhorting: "I hope, and hope most fervently, that you will evidence a real determination to bring the budget into actual balance, for upon this, I think, hangs not only your place in history but conceivably the immediate fate of western civilization." (Douglas to FDR, November 28, 1934)

Remarks like this struck home with Roosevelt. Douglas's successors as Director of the Budget held much the same views, and Henry Morgenthau, Jr., who became Secretary of the Treasury at the beginning of 1934, never failed to prod Roosevelt to slash governmental expenditures.

We should add parenthetically that Roosevelt always keenly resented the untrue newspaper stories that his parents had been unwilling to entrust him with money. As a matter of fact he was personally so thrifty when he was in the White House that he used to send away for bargain mail-order shirts, and when he wished summer suits, switched from an expensive New York tailor to a cheaper one in Washington. This he did despite the warning of the New York tailor that he might thus lose his standing as one of the nation's best-dressed men.

Financial caution in governmental affairs rather typifies Roosevelt's economic thinking throughout the entire New Deal. He was ready to go much further than Hoover in construction of public works, but he preferred the kind which would pay for themselves, and did not think there were many possibilities for them in the country. His estimate before he became president was only one billion dollars worth. In 1934, he once proposed that the government buy the buildings of foundered banks throughout the nation and use them for post-offices rather than construct new buildings. This is how far he was from visualizing huge public works expenditures as a means of boosting the country out of the depression. His course in this area was the middle road. He wished to bring about recovery without upsetting the budget any further than absolutely necessary. He did not launch the nation on a program of deliberate deficit financing.

When Roosevelt explained his program in a fireside chat at the end of July 1933, he declared:

> It may seem inconsistent for a government to cut down its regular expenses and at the same time to borrow and to spend billions for an emergency. But it is not inconsistent because a large portion of the emergency money has been paid out in the form of sound loans. . . . ; and to cover the rest . . . we have imposed taxes. . . .
>
> So you will see that we have kept our credit good. We have built a granite foundation in a period of confusion.

It followed from this that aside from limited public works expenditures, Roosevelt wanted a recovery program which would not be a drain on governmental finances. Neither the Agricultural Adjustment Administration nor the National Recovery Administration were. He had promised in the major farm speech of his 1932 campaign that his plan for agricultural relief would be self-financing; this was achieved through the processing tax on certain farm products. The NRA involved no governmental expenditures except for administration.

Both of these programs reflected not the progressivism of the first years of the century, but the means through which Progressives had regulated production during the first World War. This had meant regulation which would as far as possible protect both producers and consumers, both employers and employees. Here the parallel was direct. The rest of Roosevelt's program did not parallel the Progressives' wartime experience, for, during the war, in terms of production regulation had meant channeling both factories and farms into the maximum output of what was needed to win the war. Now the problem in the thirties was one of reducing output in most areas rather than raising it, and of getting prices back up rather than trying to hold them down.

Certainly the nation badly needed this sort of a program in 1933. The products of the fields and mines and of highly competitive consumers' goods industries like textiles were being sold so cheaply that producers and their employees alike were close to starvation. The overproduction was also wasteful of natural resources. In an oilfield near Houston, one grocer advertised when 3.2 beer first became legal that he would exchange one bottle of beer for one barrel of oil. They were worth about the same. In other heavy industries like automobiles or farm machinery, production had been cut drastically while prices remained high. One need was to bring prices throughout industry and agriculture into a more equitable relationship with each other, and with the debt structure.

The NRA scheme in theory would help do this. Its antecedents were in the regulatory War Industries Board of the first World War, and indeed it was run by some of the same men. The War Industries Board had functioned through industrial committees; in the twenties these committees had evolved into self-regulatory trade associations. Unfortunately, as Roosevelt had found when he headed the association created to discipline one of the largest and most chaotic of industries, the American Construction Council, self-regulation without the force of law behind it, had a tendency to break down. When the depression had hit, some businessmen themselves had advocated the NRA scheme, but Hoover would have none of it. Roosevelt was receptive.

The theory was that committees in a few major fields like steel, textiles, bituminous coal and the like, would draw up codes of fair practice for the industry. These would not only stabilize the price structure, but also protect the wages and working conditions of labor. Even consumers would benefit, presumably through receiving more wages or profits, and thus enjoying larger purchasing power with which to buy goods at somewhat higher prices.

In practice, the NRA program went awry. Too many committees drew up too many codes embodying many sorts of unenforceable provisions. There was a code even for the mopstick industry. What was more important, some manufacturers rushed to turn out quantities of goods at the old wage and raw material level before the code went into effect, hoping then to sell these goods at new higher prices. Consequently during the summer of 1933 there was a short NRA boom when industrial production jumped to 101 per cent of the 1923–25 level, and wholesale prices rose from an index figure of 60.2 in March to 71.2 by October. The crop reduction program of the AAA led to a corresponding rise in agricultural prices.

Had consumers at the same time enjoyed a correspondingly higher purchasing power, the recovery scheme might well have worked. Some of its designers had visualized pouring the additional dollars into consumers' pockets through a heavy public works spending program. Indeed the bill which created the NRA also set up a Public Works Administration with $3,300,000,000 to spend. This money could have been poured here and there into the economy where it was most needed to "prime the pump." But Roosevelt and his most influential advisers did not want to give such an enormous spending power to the administrator of the NRA, nor had they really accepted the deficit spending school of thought. Hence while some of the money being spent by the New Deal went for immediate relief of one form or another, it went to people so close to starvation that they were forced to spend what they received on bare necessities. This was of little aid in priming the pump. The public works fund, which could have served that purpose, went to that sturdy old Progressive, "Honest Harold" Ickes. He slowly went about the process of allocating it in such a way that the government and the public would get a return of one hundred cents (or preferably more) on every dollar spent. Raymond Moley has suggested that if only the cautious Ickes had headed the NRA and the impetuous Johnson the Public Works Administration the scheme might have worked.

Without a huge transfusion of dollars into the economy, the industrial and agricultural recovery programs sagged in the fall of 1933. Roosevelt turned to currency manipulation to try to get prices up. He explained to a critical Congressman, "I have always favored sound money, and do now, but it is 'too darned sound' when it takes so much of farm products to buy a dollar." Roosevelt also accepted a makeshift work relief program, the Civil Works Administration, to carry the destitute through the winter.

Already the New Deal honeymoon was over, and in 1934 and 1935 a sharp political struggle between Roosevelt and the right began to take form. To conservatives, Roosevelt was shattering the constitution with his economic legislation. Al Smith was attacking the devaluated currency as "baloney dollars," and was writing articles with such titles as "Is the Constitution Still There?" and "Does the Star-Spangled Banner Still Wave?" Former President Hoover published his powerful jeremiad, *The Challenge to Liberty*.

Many businessmen complained against the NRA restrictions, the favoritism allegedly being shown to organized labor, and the higher taxes. Although some of them had advocated the NRA, the significant fact was that the thinking of most businessmen seems to have remained about what it had been in the 1920's. They were eager for aid from the government, as long as it involved no obligations on their part or restrictions against them. They wanted a government which could protect their domestic markets with a high tariff wall, and at the same time seek out foreign markets for them, a court system which could discipline organized labor with injunctions, and a tax structure which (as under Secretary of the Treasury Mellon) would take no enormous bite of large profits, and yet retain disciplinary levies on the lower-middle income groups. All these policies they could understand and condone. The New Deal, which would confer other benefits upon them, but require corresponding obligations, they could not.

This hostile thinking which began to develop among the business community was sincere. Businessmen genuinely believed that under the New Deal program too large a share of their income had to go to organized labor, and too much to the government. They freely predicted federal bankruptcy as the deficit began to mount. If they had capital to commit, they refused to expend it on new plants and facilities (except for some introduction of labor-saving machinery). They were too unsure of the future, they complained, because they could not tell what that man in the White House might propose next. Business needed a "breathing spell," Roy Howard wrote Roosevelt, and the President promised one. Nevertheless, the legislative requests continued unabated.

All this, important though it is in delineating the ideology of businessmen, is not the whole story. The fact is that during the long bleak years after October 1929 they had slipped into a depression way of thinking. They regarded American industry as being over-built; they looked upon the American market as being permanently contracted. By 1937 when industrial production and stock dividends were up to within ten per cent of the 1929 peak, capital expenditures continued to drag along the depression floor. Industrialists did not engage in the large-scale spending for expansion which has been a significant factor in the boom since 1945. As late as 1940 to 1941, many of them were loathe to take the large defense orders which required construction of new plants. Unquestionably the pessimism of businessmen during the thirties, whether or not linked to their hatred of Roosevelt and fear of the New Deal, was as significant a factor in perpetuating the depression, as their optimism since the war has been in perpetuating the boom.

The paradox is that some of the New Deal measures against which the businessmen fought helped introduce into the economy some of the stabilizers which today help give businessmen confidence in the continuation of prosperity. These came despite, not because of, the businessmen. Roosevelt long continued to try to cooperate with the leaders of industry and banking. Their anger toward him, and frequently-expressed statements that he had betrayed his class, at times bewildered and even upset him. For the most part he laughed them off. He hung in his bedroom a favorite cartoon. It showed a little girl at the door of a fine suburban home, apparently tattling to her mother, "Johnny wrote a dirty word on the sidewalk." And the word, of course, was "Roosevelt."

To some of his old friends who complained to him, he would reply with patience and humor. Forever he was trying to point out to them the human side of the problem of the depression. Perhaps the best illustration is a witty interchange with a famous doctor for whom he had deep affection. The doctor wired him in March 1935:

> Pediatricians have long been perplexed by difficulty of weaning infant from breast or bottle to teaspoon or cup. The shift often establishes permanent neurosis in subsequent adult. According to report in evening paper twenty-two million citizen infants now hang on federal breasts. Can you wean them doctor and prevent national neurosis?

Roosevelt promptly replied:

> As a young interne you doubtless realize that the interesting transitional process, which you describe in your telegram, presupposes that the bottle, teaspoon, or cup is not empty. Such vehicles of feeding, if empty, produce flatulence and the patient dies from a lack of nutrition.
> The next question on your examination paper is, therefore, the following:
> Assuming that the transitional period has arrived, where is the Doctor to get the food from to put in the new container?

As time went on, and the attacks became virulent from some quarters, at times even passing the bounds of decency, Roosevelt struck back vigorously. During his campaign in 1936 he excoriated the "economic royalists." When he wound up the campaign in Madison Square Garden, he declared:

> We had to struggle with the old enemies of peace—business and financial monopoly, speculation, reckless banking, class antagonism, sectionalism, war profiteering. They had begun to consider the Government of the United States as a mere appendage to their own affairs. And we know now that Government by organized money is just as dangerous as Government by organized mob.
> Never before in all our history have these forces been so united against one candidate as they stand today. They are unanimous in their hate for me—and I welcome their hatred.

To these sharp words Roosevelt had come from his position early in the New Deal as the impartial arbiter of American economic forces. He had come to them less because of what he considered as betrayal from the right than through pressure from the left. How had this pressure applied between 1934 and the campaign of 1936?

Back in 1934, while the economic temperature chart of the near frozen depression victim had fluctuated up and down, still dangerously below normal, the dispossessed millions began to look at the New Deal with despair or even disillusion. Those workers going on strike to obtain the twenty-five or thirty-five cents an hour minimum wage or the collective bargaining privileges promised by the NRA began to wisecrack that NRA stood for the National Run-Around. Some of them and of the unemployed millions in northern cities still dependent upon meager relief handouts began to listen to the stirring radio addresses of Father Charles Coughlin. Old people began to pay five cents a week dues to Dr. Francis Townsend's clubs, which promised them fantastically large benefits. Throughout the South (and even in parts of the North) the dispossessed small farmers listened with enthusiasm to the exhortations of the Louisiana Kingfish, Huey Long, that he would share the wealth to make every man a king.

Many Democratic politicians were surprisingly oblivious to these rumblings and mutterings. Much of the private conversation of men like Vice President John Nance Garner sounded like the public demands of the Liberty Leaguers: cut relief and balance the budget. Garner, who spent the 1934 campaign hunting and fishing in Texas, predicted the usual midterm loss of a few congressional seats back to the Republicans. Instead the Democrats picked up a startling number of new seats in both houses of Congress. The dispossessed had continued to vote with the Democratic party—but perhaps because there was no alternative but the Republicans who offered only retrenchment. Charles Beard commented that the 1934 election was "thunder on the left."

President Roosevelt, who was brilliantly sensitive to political forces, sensed fully the threat from the left. At the beginning of that crisis year 1935 he proposed in his annual message to Congress the enactment of a program to reinforce "the security of the men, women, and children of the nation" in their livelihood, to protect them against the major hazards and vicissitudes of life, and to enable them to obtain decent homes. In this increased emphasis upon security and reform, Professor Basil Rauch sees the beginnings of a second New Deal.

Certainly the pattern as it emerged in the next year was a brilliant one. Roosevelt neutralized Huey Long with the "soak the rich" tax, "holding company death sentence," and with various measures directly of benefit to the poorer farmers of the South. Before an assassin's bullet felled Long, his political strength was already undercut. Similarly Roosevelt undermined the Townsend movement by pressing passage of the Social Security Act, which provided at least small benefits for the aged, at the same time that a congressional investigation disclosed how men around Townsend were fattening themselves on the nickels of millions of the aged. As for Father Coughlin, the Treasury announced that money from his coffers had gone into silver speculation at a time he had been loudly advocating that the government buy more silver at higher prices. More important, Coughlin had less appeal to employed workers after the new National Labor Relations Act raised a benign federal umbrella over collective bargaining. For the unemployed, a huge and substantial work relief program, the Works Progress Administration, came into existence.

Partly all this involved incisive political counterthrusts; partly it was a program Roosevelt had favored anyway. In any event, combined with Roosevelt's direct and effective appeal in radio fireside chats, it caused the dispossessed to look to him rather than to demagogues as their champion. Millions of them or their relations received some direct aid from the New Deal, whether a small crop payment or a WPA check. Millions more received wage boosts for which they were more grateful to Roosevelt than to their employers. Others through New Deal mortgage legislation had held onto their farms or homes. All these people, benefitting directly or indirectly, looked to Roosevelt as the source of their improved economic condition, and they were ready to vote accordingly. Roosevelt, who had been nominated in 1932 as the candidate of the South and the West, the champion of the farmer and the middle-class "forgotten man," after 1936 became increasingly the leader of the urban masses and the beneficiary of the growing power of organized labor.

What happened seems sharper and clearer in retrospect than it did at the time. Secretary Ickes, recording repeatedly in his diary during the early months of 1935 that the President was losing his grip, was echoing what many New Dealers and part of the public felt. They did not see a sharp shift into a second New Deal, and that is understandable. Roosevelt ever since he had become president had been talking about reform and from time to time recommending reform measures to Congress. He seems to have thought at the outset in two categories, about immediate or short-range emergency recovery measures to bring about a quick economic upswing , and also in terms of long-range reform legislation to make a recurrence of the depression less likely. Some of these reform measures like TVA had been ready for immediate enactment; others, like a revision of banking legislation and the social security legislation, he had planned from the beginning but were several years in the making. Frances Perkins has vividly described in her memoirs the lengthy task she and her associates undertook of drafting and selling to Congress and the public what became the Social Security Act of 1935.

Then Roosevelt had to face the additional factor that the emergency legislation had not succeeded in bringing rapid recovery. He had to think in terms of more permanent legislation with which to aim toward the same objectives. That meant he ceased trying to save money with a temporary program of cheaper direct relief, and switched instead to work relief (in which he had always believed) to try to stop some of the moral and physical erosion of those unfortunates who had been without employment for years.

In part the Supreme Court forced the recasting of some of his legislation. It gave a mercy killing in effect to the rickety, unwieldy NRA code structure when it handed down the Schechter or "sick chicken" decision of May 1935. On the whole the NRA had been unworkable, but it had achieved some outstanding results—in abolishing child labor, in bringing some order in the chaotic bituminous coal industry, and the like. Roosevelt was furious with the court, since the decision threatened to undermine all New Deal economic regulation. He charged that the justices were taking a horse and buggy view of the economic powers of the government. There followed six months later the court invalidation of the Triple-A processing tax, which for the moment threw out of gear the agricultural program.

The answer to these and similar Supreme Court decisions was Roosevelt's bold onslaught against the court after he had been re-elected in the great landslide of 1936. He had carried every state but Maine and Vermont; he considered himself as having a great mandate from the people to continue his program. Nor had he any reason to doubt his ability to push a court reform program through Congress, since the already bulging New Deal majorities had become still bigger. He was wrong; he failed. His failure came as much as anything through a great tactical error. He disguised his program as one to bring about a speedier handling of cases, when he should have presented it frankly as a means of ending the court obstruction of the New Deal. This obstruction was real. Many corporations openly flouted the National Labor Relations Act, for example, they were so confident that the Supreme Court would invalidate it.

However laudable the end, to many a well-educated member of the middle class who had supported Roosevelt even through the campaign of 1936, Roosevelt's resort to subterfuge smacked of the devious ways of dictators. In 1937, Americans were all too aware of the way in which Hitler and Mussolini had gained power. It was not that any thinking man expected Roosevelt to follow their example, but rather that many objected to any threat, real or potential, to the constitutional system including the separation of powers. After Roosevelt, they argued, the potential dictator might appear. It may be too that times had improved sufficiently since March 1933 so that constitutional considerations could again overweigh economic exigencies. In any event, Roosevelt lost his battle—and won his war.

While the struggle was rocking the nation, the justices began exercising the judicial self-restraint which one of their number, Harlan F. Stone, had urged upon them the previous year. They surprised the nation by upholding the constitutionality of the National Labor Relations Act and the Social Security Act. In large part this eliminated the necessity for the New Dealers to make any change in the personnel of the court, and thus helped contribute to Roosevelt's defeat in Congress. Further, the fight had helped bring into existence a conservative coalition in Congress which from this time on gave Roosevelt a rough ride. Many old-line Democratic congressmen now dared proclaim in public what they had previously whispered in private. All this added up to a spectacular setback for Roosevelt—so spectacular that it is easy to overlook the enormous and permanent changes that had come about.

In the next few years the Supreme Court in effect rewrote a large part of constitutional law. The federal and state governments were now able to engage in extensive economic regulation with little or no court restraint upon them. The limits upon regulation must be set for the most part by the legislative branch of the government, not the judiciary. Not only were the National Labor Relations Act and Social Security constitutional, but a bulging portfolio of other legislation.

These laws were not as spectacular as the measures of the Hundred Days, but in the bulk they were far more significant, for they brought about lasting changes in the economic role of the federal government. There was the continued subsidy to agriculture in order to maintain crop control—based upon soil conservation rather than a processing tax. There were all the agricultural relief measures which came to be centralized in the Farm Security Administration. Although that agency has disappeared, most of its functions have continued in one way or another. There was a beginning of slum clearance and public housing, and a continuation of TVA, held constitutional even before the court fight. There was a stiffening of securities regulation. There was a continuation of much that Roosevelt had considered beneficial in the NRA through a group of new laws usually referred to as the "little NRA." These perpetuated the coal and liquor codes, helped regulate oil production, tried to prevent wholesale price discriminations and legalized the establishment of "fair trade" prices by manufacturers. Most important of all, the Fair Labor Standards Act of 1937 set a national minimum of wages and maximum of hours of work, and prohibited the shipping in interstate commerce of goods made by child labor. These are lasting contributions of the New Deal, either substantial laws in themselves or the seeds for later legislation.

What then, is to be said of the recession and the anti-monopoly program? A Keynesian point of view is that public works spending, the other New Deal spending programs, and the payment of the bonus to veterans of the first World War (over Roosevelt's veto, incidentally), all these together had poured so much money into the economy that they brought about a substantial degree of recovery, except in employment, by the spring of 1937. At this point Roosevelt tried to balance the budget, especially by cutting public works and work relief expenditures. The result was a sharp recession. Roosevelt was forced to resort to renewed pump-priming, and in a few months the recession was over.

Even this recession experience did not convert Roosevelt to Keynesianism. Keynes once called upon Roosevelt at the White House and apparently tried to dazzle him with complex mathematical talk. Each was disappointed in the other. In 1939, after the recession when a protégé of Mrs. Roosevelt's proposed additional welfare spending, Roosevelt replied by listing worthwhile projects in which the government could usefully spend an additional five billions a year. Then he pointed out that the deficit was already three billions, which could not go on forever. How, he inquired, could an eight-billion-dollar deficit be financed?

As for economists, many of them saw the answer in the enormous spending power which would be unleashed if the government poured out billions in time of depression. To most of them the lesson from the recession was that the only way to right the economy in time of upset was through spending.

As for businessmen, they could see in the recession only the logical outcome of Roosevelt's iniquitous tinkering with the economy. They had been especially angered by the protection the Wagner act had given to collective bargaining with the resulting militant expansion of organized labor. Roosevelt reciprocated the businessmen's feelings and blamed the recession upon their failure to cooperate. To a considerable degree he went along with a powerful handful of Progressive Republicans and Western Democrats in the Senate, like William E. Borah of Idaho and Joseph O'Mahoney of Wyoming, in attacking corporate monopoly as the villain. There are some indications, however, that the anti-monopoly program that he launched in the Department of Justice through the urbane Thurman Arnold was intended less to bust the trusts than to forestall too drastic legislation in the Congress. Roosevelt gave his strong backing to Arnold's anti-trust division only for the first year or two, and Arnold functioned for the most part through consent decrees. These in many instances allowed industries to function much as they had in the NRA days. The new program was in some respects more like a negative NRA than the antithesis of the NRA.

Thus from the beginning of the New Deal to the end, Roosevelt functioned with a fair degree of consistency. He heartily favored humanitarian welfare legislation and government policing of the economy, so long as these did not dangerously unbalance the budget. He preferred government cooperation with business to warfare with it.

Many of the New Dealers went far beyond Roosevelt in their views, and sometimes saw, in his reluctance to support them, betrayal rather than a greater degree of conservatism. They had valid grievances some of the time when Roosevelt stuck to a middle course and seemed to them to be compromising away everything for which they thought he stood, in order to hold his motley political coalitions together. It is a serious moral question whether he compromised more than necessary, and whether at times he compromised his principles. It has been charged that his second four years in the White House represented a failure in political leadership.

In terms of gaining immediate political objectives, like the fiasco of the court fight, and the abortive "purge" in the 1938 primaries, this is undoubtedly true. In terms of the long-range New Deal program, I think the reverse is the case. These were years of piecemeal unspectacular consolidation of the earlier spectacular changes. It was many years before historians could say with certainty that these changes were permanent. By 1948 various public opinion samplings indicated that an overwhelming majority of those queried, even though Republican in voting habits, favored such things as social security and the TVA. The election of a Republican president in 1952 did not signify a popular repudiation of these programs. In the years after 1952 they were accepted, and in some instances even expanded, by the Republican administration. The only serious debate over them concerned degree, in which the Republicans were more cautious than the Democrats. The New Deal changes have even come for the most part to be accepted by the business community, although the United States Chamber of Commerce now issues manifestoes against federal aid to education with all the fervor it once directed against Roosevelt's proposals. The fact is that the business community in part bases its plans for the future upon some things that began as New Deal reforms. It takes for granted such factors as the "built-in stabilizers" in the social security system—something, incidentally, that Roosevelt pointed out at the time the legislation went into effect.

In January 1939 Roosevelt, concerned about the threat of world war, called a halt to his domestic reform program. What he said then, concerning the world crisis of 1939, is remarkably applicable to the United States more than two decades later:

> We have now passed the period of internal conflict in the launching of our program of social reform. Our full energies may now be released to invigorate the processes of recovery in order to preserve our reforms, and to give every man and woman who wants to work a real job at a living wage.
>
> But time is of paramount importance. The deadline of danger from within and from without is not within our control. The hour-glass may be in the hands of other nations. Our own hour-glass tells us that we are off on a race to make democracy work, so that we may be efficient in peace and therefore secure in national defense.

WILLIAM E. LEUCHTENBURG

In eight years, Roosevelt and the New Dealers had almost revolutionized the agenda of American politics. "Mr. Roosevelt may have given the wrong answers to many of his problems," concluded the editors of *The Economist.* "But he is at least the first President of modern America who has asked the right questions." In 1932, men of acumen were absorbed to an astonishing degree with such questions as prohi-

source: William E. Leuchtenburg, *Franklin D. Roosevelt and the New Deal, 1932–1940* (New York: Harper and Row, 1963), pp. 326–48. Copyright © 1963 by William E. Leuchtenburg. Reprinted by permission of the publishers.

bition, war debts, and law enforcement. By 1936, they were debating social security, the Wagner Act, valley authorities, and public housing. The thirties witnessed a rebirth of issues politics, and parties split more sharply on ideological lines than they had in many years past. "I incline to think that for years up to the present juncture thinking Democrats and thinking Republicans had been divided by an imaginary line," reflected a Massachusetts congressman in 1934. "Now for the first time since the period before the Civil War we find vital principles at stake." Much of this change resulted simply from the depression trauma, but much too came from the force of Roosevelt's personality and his use of his office as both pulpit and lectern. "Of course you have fallen into some errors—that is human," former Supreme Court Justice John Clarke wrote the President, "but you have put a new face upon the social and political life of our country."

Franklin Roosevelt re-created the modern Presidency. He took an office which had lost much of its prestige and power in the previous twelve years and gave it an importance which went well beyond what even Theodore Roosevelt and Woodrow Wilson had done. Clinton Rossiter has observed: "Only Washington, who made the office, and Jackson, who remade it, did more than [Roosevelt] to raise it to its present condition of strength, dignity, and independence." Under Roosevelt, the White House became the focus of all government—the fountainhead of ideas, the initiator of action, the representative of the national interest.

Roosevelt greatly expanded the President's legislative functions. In the nineteenth century, Congress had been jealous of its prerogatives as the lawmaking body, and resented any encroachment on its domain by the Chief Executive. Woodrow Wilson and Theodore Roosevelt had broken new ground in sending actual drafts of bills to Congress and in using devices like the caucus to win enactment of measures they favored. Franklin Roosevelt made such constant use of these tools that he came to assume a legislative role not unlike that of a prime minister. He sent special messages to Congress, accompanied them with drafts of legislation prepared by his assistants, wrote letters to committee chairmen or members of Congress to urge passage of the proposals, and authorized men like Corcoran to lobby as presidential spokesmen on the Hill. By the end of Roosevelt's tenure in the White House, Congress looked automatically to the Executive for guidance; it expected the administration to have a "program" to present for consideration.

Roosevelt's most important formal contribution was his creation of the Executive Office of the President on September 8, 1939. Executive Order 8248, a "nearly unnoticed but none the less epoch-making event in the history of American institutions," set up an Executive Office staffed with six administrative assistants with a "passion for anonymity." In 1939, the President not only placed obvious agencies like the White House Office in the Executive Office but made the crucial decision to shift the Bureau of the Budget from the Treasury and put it under his wing. In later years, such pivotal agencies as the Council of Economic Advisers, the National Security Council, and the Central Intelligence Agency would be moved into the Executive Office of the President. Roosevelt's decision, Rossiter has concluded, "converts the Presidency into an instrument of twentieth-century government; it gives the incumbent a sporting chance to stand the strain and fulfill his constitutional mandate as a one-man branch of our three-part government; it deflates even the most forceful arguments, which are still raised occasionally, for a plural executive; it assures us that the Presidency will survive the advent of the positive state. Executive Order 8248 may yet be judged to have saved the Presidency from paralysis and the Constitution from radical amendment."

Roosevelt's friends have been too quick to concede that he was a poor administrator. To be sure, he found it difficult to discharge incompetent aides, he procrastinated about decisions, and he ignored all the canons of sound administration by giving men overlapping assignments and creating a myriad of agencies which had no clear relation to the regular departments of government. But if the test of good administration is not an impeccable organizational chart but creativity, then Roosevelt must be set down not merely as a good administrator but as a resourceful innovator. The new agencies he set up gave a spirit of excitement to Washington that the routinized old-line departments could never have achieved. The President's refusal to proceed through channels, however vexing at times to his subordinates, resulted in a competition not only among men but among ideas, and encouraged men to feel that their own beliefs might win the day. "You would be surprised, Colonel, the remarkable ideas that have been turned loose just because men have felt that they can get a hearing," one senator confided. The President's "procrastination" was his own way both of arriving at a sense of national consensus and of reaching a decision by observing a trial by combat among rival theories. Periods of indecision —as in the spring of 1935 or the beginning of 1938—were inevitably followed by a fresh outburst of new proposals.

Most of all, Roosevelt was a successful administrator because he attracted to Washington thousands of devoted and highly skilled men. Men who had been fighting for years for lost causes were given a chance: John Collier, whom the President courageously named Indian Commissioner; Arthur Powell Davis, who had been ousted as chief engineer of the Department of the Interior at the demand of power interests; old conservationists like Harry Slattery, who had fought the naval oil interests in the Harding era. When Harold Ickes took office as Secretary of the Interior, he looked up Louis Glavis—he did not even know whether the "martyr" of the Ballinger-Pinchot affair was still alive—and appointed him to his staff.

The New Dealers displayed striking ingenuity in meeting problems of governing. They coaxed salmon to climb ladders at Bonneville; they sponsored a Young Choreographers Laboratory in the WPA's Dance Theatre; they gave the pioneer documentary film maker Pare Lorentz the opportunity to create his classic films *The Plow That Broke the Plains* and *The River*. At the Composers Forum-Laboratory of the Federal Music Project, William Schuman received his first serious hearing. In Arizona, Father Berard Haile of St. Michael's Mission taught written Navajo to the Indians. Roosevelt, in the face of derision from professional foresters and prairie states' governors, persisted in a bold scheme to plant a mammoth "shelterbelt" of parallel rows of trees from the Dakotas to the Panhandle. In all, more than two hundred million trees were planted—cottonwood and willow, hackberry and cedar, Russian olive and Osage orange; within six years, the President's visionary windbreak had won over his former critics. The spirit behind such innovations generated a new excitement about the potentialities of government. "Once again," Roosevelt told a group of young Democrats in April, 1936, "the very air of America is exhilarating."

Roosevelt dominated the front pages of the newspapers as no other President before or since has done. "Frank Roosevelt and the NRA have taken the place of love nests," commented Joe Patterson, publisher of the tabloid New York *Daily News*. At his very first press conference, Roosevelt abolished the written question and told reporters they could interrogate him without warning. Skeptics predicted the free and easy exchange would soon be abandoned, but twice a week, year in and year out, he threw open the White House doors to as many as two hundred reporters, most of them representing hostile publishers, who would crowd right up to the President's desk to fire their questions. The President joshed them, traded wisecracks with them, called them by their first names; he charmed them by his good-humored ease and impressed them with his knowledge of detail. To a degree, Roosevelt's press conference introduced, as some observers claimed, a new institution like Britain's parliamentary questioning; more to the point, it was a device the President manipulated, disarmingly and adroitly, to win support for his program. It served too as a classroom to instruct the country in the new economics and the new politics.

Roosevelt was the first president to master the technique of reaching people directly over the radio. In his fireside chats, he talked like a father discussing public affairs with his family in the living room. As he spoke, he seemed unconscious of the fact that he was addressing millions. "His head would nod and his hands would move in simple, natural, comfortable gestures," Frances Perkins recalled. "His face would smile and light up as though he were actually sitting on the front porch or in the parlor with them." Eleanor Roosevelt later observed that after the President's death people would stop her on the street to say "they missed the way the President used to talk to them. They'd say 'He used to talk to me about my government.' There was a real dialogue between Franklin and the people," she reflected. "That dialogue seems to have disappeared from the government since he died."

For the first time for many Americans, the federal government became an institution that was directly experienced. More than state and local governments, it came to be *the* government, an agency directly concerned with their welfare. It was the source of their relief payments; it taxed them directly for old age pensions; it even gave their children hot lunches in school. As the role of the state changed from that of neutral arbiter to a "powerful promoter of society's welfare," people felt an interest in affairs in Washington they had never had before.

Franklin Roosevelt personified the state as protector. It became commonplace to say that people felt toward the President the kind of trust they would normally express for a warm and understanding father who comforted them in their grief or safeguarded them from harm. An insurance man reported: "My mother looks upon the President as someone so immediately concerned with her problems and difficulties that she would not be greatly surprised were he to come to her house some evening and stay to dinner." From his first hours in office, Roosevelt gave people the feeling that they could confide in him directly. As late as the Presidency of Herbert Hoover, one man, Ira Smith, had sufficed to take care of all the mail the White House received. Under Roosevelt, Smith had to acquire a staff of fifty people to handle the thousands of letters written to the President each week. Roosevelt gave people a sense of membership in the national community. Justice Douglas has written: "He was in a very special sense the people's President, because he made them feel that with him in the White House they shared the Presidency. The sense of sharing the Presidency gave even the most humble citizen a lively sense of belonging."

When Roosevelt took office, the country, to a very large degree, responded to the will of a single element: the white, Anglo-Saxon, Protestant property-holding class. Under the New Deal, new groups took their place in the sun. It was not merely that they received benefits they had not had before but that they were "recognized" as having a place in the commonwealth. At the beginning of the Roosevelt era, charity organizations ignored labor when seeking "community" representation; at the end of the period, no fund-raising committee was complete without a union representative. While Theodore Roosevelt had founded a lily-white Progressive party in the South and Woodrow Wilson had introduced segregation into the federal government, Franklin Roosevelt had quietly brought the Negro into the New Deal coalition. When the distinguished Negro contralto Marian Anderson was denied a concert hall in Washington, Secretary Ickes arranged for her to perform from the steps of Lincoln Memorial. Equal representation for religious groups became so well accepted that, as one priest wryly complained, one never saw a picture of a priest in a newspaper unless he was flanked on either side by a minister and a rabbi.

The devotion Roosevelt aroused owed much to the fact that the New Deal assumed the responsibility for guaranteeing every American a minimum standard of subsistence. Its relief programs represented an advance over the barbaric predepression practices that constituted a difference not in degree but in kind. One analyst wrote: "During the ten years between 1929 and 1939 more progress was made in public welfare and relief than in the three hundred years after this country was first settled." The Roosevelt administration gave such assistance not as a matter of charity but of right. This system of social rights was written into the Social Security Act. Other New Deal legislation abolished child labor in interstate commerce and, by putting a floor under wages and a ceiling on hours, all but wiped out the sweatshop.

Roosevelt and his aides fashioned a government which consciously sought to make the industrial system more humane and to protect workers and their families from exploitation. In his acceptance speech in June, 1936, the President stated: "Governments can err, Presidents do make mistakes, but the immortal Dante tells us that divine justice weighs the sins of the cold-blooded and the sins of the warm-hearted in different scales.

"Better the occasional faults of a Government that lives in a spirit of charity than the constant omission of a Government frozen in the ice of its own indifference." Nearly everyone in the Roosevelt government was caught up to some degree by a sense of participation in something larger than themselves. A few days after he took office, one of the more conservative New Deal administrators wrote in his diary: "This should be a Gov't of humanity."

The federal government expanded enormously in the Roosevelt years. The crisis of the depression dissipated the distrust of the state inherited from the eighteenth century and reinforced in diverse ways by the Jeffersonians and the Spencerians. Roosevelt himself believed that liberty in America was imperiled more by the agglomerations of private business than by the state. The New Dealers were convinced that the depression was the result not simply of an economic breakdown but of a political collapse; hence, they sought new political instrumentalities. The reformers of the 1930's accepted almost unquestioningly the use of coercion by the state to achieve reforms. Even Republicans who protested that Roosevelt's policies were snuffing out liberty voted overwhelmingly in favor of coercive measures.

This elephantine growth of the federal government owed much to the fact that local and state governments had been tried in the crisis and found wanting. When one magazine wired state governors to ask their views, only one of the thirty-seven who replied announced that he was willing to have the states resume responsibility for relief. Every time there was a rumored cutback of federal spending for relief, Washington was besieged by delegations of mayors protesting that city governments did not have the resources to meet the needs of the unemployed.

Even more dramatic was the impotence of local governments in dealing with crime, a subject that captured the national imagination in a decade of kidnapings and bank holdups. In September, 1933, the notorious bank robber John Dillinger was arrested in Ohio. Three weeks later, his confederates released him from jail and killed the Lima, Ohio, sheriff. In January, 1934, after bank holdups at Racine, Wisconsin, and East Chicago, Indiana, Dillinger was apprehended in Tucson, Arizona, and returned to the "escape-proof" jail of Crown Point, Indiana, reputedly the strongest county prison in the country. A month later he broke out and drove off in the sheriff's car. While five thousand law officers pursued him, he stopped for a haircut in a barber shop, bought cars, and had a home-cooked Sunday dinner with his family in his home town. When he needed more arms, he raided the police station at Warsaw, Indiana.

Dillinger's exploits touched off a national outcry for federal action. State and local authorites could not cope with gangs which crossed and recrossed jurisdictional lines, which were equipped with Thompson submachine guns and high-powered cars, and which had a regional network of informers and fences in the Mississippi Valley. Detection and punishment of crime had always been a local function; now there seemed no choice but to call in the federal operatives. In July, 1934, federal agents shot down Dillinger outside a Chicago theater. In October, FBI men killed Pretty Boy Floyd near East Liverpool, Ohio; in November, they shot Baby Face Nelson, Public Enemy No. 1, near Niles Center, Illinois. By the end of 1934, the nation had a new kind of hero: the G-man Melvin Purvis and the chief of the Division of Investigation of the Department of Justice, J. Edgar Hoover. By the end of that year, too, Congress had stipulated that a long list of crimes would henceforth be regarded as federal offenses, including holding up a bank insured by the Federal Deposit Insurance Corporation. The family of a kidnaped victim could call in the federal police simply by phoning National 7117 in Washington.

Under the New Deal, the federal government greatly extended its power over the economy. By the end of the Roosevelt years, few questioned the right of the government to pay the farmer millions in subsidies not to grow crops, to enter plants to conduct union elections, to regulate business enterprises from utility companies to air lines, or even to compete directly with business by generating and distributing hydroelectric power. All of these powers had been ratified by the Supreme Court, which had even held that a man growing grain solely for his own use was affecting interstate commerce and hence subject to federal penalties. The President, too, was well on his way to becoming "the chief economic engineer," although this was not finally established until the Full Employment Act of 1946. In 1931, Hoover had hooted that some people thought "that by some legerdemain we can legislate ourselves out of a worldwide depression." In the Roosevelt era, the conviction that government both should and could act to forestall future breakdowns gained general acceptance. The New Deal left a large legacy of antidepression controls—securities regulation, banking reforms, unemployment compensation—even if it could not guarantee that a subsequent administration would use them.

In the 1930's, the financial center of the nation shifted from Wall Street to Washington. In May, 1934, a writer reported: "Financial news no longer originates in Wall Street." That same month, *Fortune* commented on a revolution in the credit system which was "one of the major historical events of the generation." "Mr. Roosevelt," it noted, "seized the Federal Reserve without firing a shot." The federal government had not only broken down the old separation of bank and state in the Reserve system but had gone into the credit business itself in a wholesale fashion under the aegis of the RFC, the Farm Credit Administration, and the housing agencies. Legislation in 1933 and 1934 had established federal regulation of Wall Street for the first time. No longer could the New York Stock Exchange operate as a private club free of national supervision. In 1935, Congress leveled the mammoth holding-company pyramids and centralized yet more authority over the banking system in the federal government. After a tour of the United States in 1935, Sir Josiah Stamp wrote: "Just as in 1929 the whole country was 'Wall Street-conscious' now it is 'Washington-conscious.'"

Despite this encroachment of government on traditional business prerogatives, the New Deal could advance impressive claims to being regarded as a "savior of capitalism." Roosevelt's sense of the land, of family, and of the community marked him as a man with deeply ingrained conservative traits. In the New Deal years, the government sought deliberately, in Roosevelt's words, "to energize private enterprise." The RFC financed business, housing agencies underwrote home financing, and public works spending aimed to revive the construction industry. Moreover, some of the New Deal reforms were Janus-faced. The NYA, in aiding jobless youth, also served as a safety valve to keep young people out of the labor market. A New Deal congressman, in pushing for public power projects, argued that the country should take advantage of the sea of "cheap labor" on the relief rolls. Even the Wagner Act and the movement for industrial unionism were motivated in part by the desire to contain "unbalanced and radical" labor groups. Yet such considerations should not obscure the more important point: that the New Deal, however conservative it was in some respects and however much it owed to the past, marked a radically new departure. As Carl Degler writes: "The conclusion seems inescapable that, traditional as the words may have been in which the New Deal expressed itself, in actuality it was a revolutionary response to a revolutionary situation."

Not all of the changes that were wrought were the result of Roosevelt's own actions or of those of his government. Much of the force for change came from progressives in Congress, or from nongovernmental groups like the C.I.O., or simply from the impersonal agency of the depression itself. Yet, however much significance one assigns the "objective situation," it is difficult to gainsay the importance of Roosevelt. If, in Miami in February, 1933, an assassin's bullet had been true to its mark and John Garner rather than Roosevelt had entered the White House the next month, or if the Roosevelt lines had cracked at the Democratic convention in 1932 and Newton Baker had been the compromise choice, the history of America in the thirties would have been markedly different.

At a time when democracy was under attack elsewhere in the world, the achievements of the New Deal were especially significant. At the end of 1933, in an open letter to President Roosevelt, John Maynard Keynes had written: "You have made yourself the trustee for those in every country who seek to mend the evils of our condition by reasoned experiment within the framework of the existing social system. If you fail, rational change will be gravely prejudiced throughout the world, leaving orthodoxy and revolution to fight it out." In the next few years, teams of foreigners toured the TVA, Russians and Arabs came to study the shelterbelt, French writers taxed Léon Blum with importing "Rooseveltism" to France, and analysts characterized Paul Van Zeeland's program in Belgium as a "New Deal." Under Roosevelt, observed a Montevideo newspaper, the United States had become "as it was in the eighteenth century, the victorious emblem around which may rally the multitudes thirsting for social justice and human fraternity."

In their approach to reform, the New Dealers reflected the tough-minded, hard-boiled attitude that permeated much of America in the thirties. In 1931, the gangster film *Public Enemy* had given the country a new kind of hero in James Cagney: the aggressive, unsentimental tough guy who deliberately assaulted the romantic tradition. It was a type whose role in society could easily be manipulated; gangster hero Cagney of the early thirties was transformed into G-man hero Cagney of the later thirties. Even more representative was Humphrey Bogart, creator of the "private eye" hero, the man of action who masks his feelings in a calculated emotional neutrality. Bogart, who began as the cold desperado Duke Mantee of *Petrified Forest* and the frightening Black Legionnaire, soon turned up on the right side of anti-Fascist causes, although he never surrendered the pose of noninvolvement. This fear of open emotional commitment and this admiration of tough-ness ran through the vogue of the "Dead End Kids," films like *Nothing Sacred*, the popularity of the St. Louis Cardinals' spike-flying Gas House Gang, and the "hardboiled" fiction of writers like James Cain and Dashiell Hammett.

Unlike the earlier Progressive, the New Dealer shied away from being thought of as sentimental. Instead of justifying relief as a humanitarian measure, the New Dealers often insisted it was necessary to stimulate purchasing power or to stabilize the economy or to "conserve manpower." The justification for a better distribution of income was neither "social justice" nor a "healthier national life," wrote Adolf Berle. "It remained for the hard-boiled student to work out the simple equation that unless the national income was pretty widely diffused there were not enough customers to keep the plants going." The reformers of the thirties abandoned—or claimed they had abandoned—the old Emersonian hope of reforming man and sought only to change institutions. This meant that they did not seek to "uplift" the people they were helping but only to improve their economic position. "In other words," Tugwell stated bluntly, "the New Deal is attempting to do nothing to *people,* and does not seek at all to alter their way of life, their wants and desires."

Reform in the 1930's meant *economic* reform; it departed from the Methodist-parsonage morality of many of the earlier Progressives, in part because much of the New Deal support, and many of its leaders, derived from urban immigrant groups hostile to the old Sabbatarian-ism. While the progressive grieved over the fate of the prostitute, the New Dealer would have placed Mrs. Warren's profession under a code authority. If the archetypical progressive was Jane Addams singing "Onward, Christian Soldiers," the representative New Dealer was Harry Hopkins betting on the horses at Laurel Race Track. When directing FERA in late 1933, Hopkins announced: "I would like to provide orchestras for beer gardens to encourage people to sit around

drinking their beer and enjoying themselves. It would be a great unemployment relief measure." "I feel no call to remedy evils," Raymond
Moley declard. "I have not the slightest urge to be a reformer. Social
workers make me very weary. They have no sense of humor."

Despite Moley's disclaimer, many of the early New Dealers like
himself and Adolf Berle did, in fact, hope to achieve reform through
regeneration: the regeneration of the businessman. By the end of 1935,
the New Dealers were pursuing a quite different course. Instead of
attempting to evangelize the Right, they mobilized massive political
power against the power of the corporation. They relied not on con-
verting industrial sinners but in using sufficient coercion. New Dealers
like Thurman Arnold sought to ignore "moral" considerations altogether; Arnold wished not to punish wrongdoers but to achieve price
flexibility. His "faith" lay in the expectation that "fanatical align-
ments between opposing political principles may disappear and a
competent, practical, opportunistic governing class may rise to power."
With such expectations, the New Dealers frequently had little patience
with legal restraints that impeded action. "I want to assure you,"
Hopkins told the NYA Advisory Committee, "that we are not afraid of
exploring anything within the law, and we have a lawyer who will
declare anything you want to do legal."

In the thirties, nineteenth-century individualism gave ground to a
new emphasis on social security and collective action. In the twenties,
America hailed Lindbergh as the Lone Eagle; in the thirties, when
word arrived that Amelia Earhart was lost at sea, the *New Republic*
asked the government to prohibit citizens from engaging in such "useless" exploits. The NRA sought to drive newsboys off the streets and
took a Blue Eagle away from a company in Huck Finn's old town of
Hannibal, Missouri, because a fifteen-year-old was found driving a
truck for his father's business. Josef Hofmann urged that fewer musi-
cians become soloists, Hollywood stars like Joan Crawford joined the
Screen Actors Guild, and Leopold Stokowski canceled a performance
in Pittsburgh because theater proprietors were violating a union contract. In New York in 1933, after a series of meetings in Heywood
Broun's penthouse apartment, newspapermen organized the American
Newspaper Guild in rebellion against the dispiriting romanticism of
Richard Harding Davis. "We no longer care to develop the individual as a unique contributor to a democratic form," wrote the mor-
dant Edgar Kemler. "In this movement each individual sub-man is
important, not for his uniqueness, but for his ability to lose himself
in the mass, through his fidelity to the trade union, or cooperative
organization, or political party."

The liberals of the thirties admired intellectual activity which had
a direct relation to concrete reality. Stuart Chase wrote of one govern-

ment report: "This book is live stuff—wheelbarrow, cement mixer, steam dredge, generator, combine, power-line stuff; library dust does not gather here." If the poet did not wish to risk the suspicion that his loyalties were not to the historic necessities of his generation, wrote Archibald MacLeish, he must "soak himself not in books" but in the physical reality of "by what organization of men and railroads and trucks and belts and book-entries the materials of a single automobile are assembled." The New Dealers were fascinated by "the total man days per year for timber stand improvement," and Tugwell rejoiced in the "practical success" of the Resettlement Administration demonstrated by "these healthy collection figures." Under the Special Skills Division of the RA, Greenbelt was presented with inspirational paintings like *Constructing Sewers, Concrete Mixer,* and *Shovel at Work.* On one occasion, in attempting to mediate a literary controversy, the critic Edmund Wilson wrote: "It should be possible to convince Marxist critics of the importance of a work like 'Ulysses' by telling them that it is a great piece of engineering—as it is." In this activist world of the New Dealers, the aesthete and the man who pursued a life of contemplation, especially the man whose interests centered in the past, were viewed with scorn. In Robert Sherwood's *The Petrified Forest,* Alan Squier, the ineffectual aesthete, meets his death in the desert and is buried in the petrified forest where the living turn to stone. He is an archaic type for whom the world has no place.

The new activism explicitly recognized its debt to Dewey's dictum of "learning by doing" and, like other of Dewey's ideas, was subject to exaggeration and perversion. The New Deal, which gave unprecedented authority to intellectuals in government, was, in certain important respects, anti-intellectual. Without the activist faith, perhaps not nearly so much would have been achieved. It was Lilienthal's conviction that "there is almost nothing, however fantastic, that (given competent organization) a team of engineers, scientists, and administrators cannot do today" that helped make possible the successes of TVA. Yet the liberal activists grasped only a part of the truth; they retreated from conceptions like "tragedy," "sin," "God," often had small patience with the force of tradition, and showed little understanding of what moved men to seek meanings outside of political experience. As sensitive a critic as the poet Horace Gregory could write, in a review of the works of D. H. Lawrence: "The world is moving away from Lawrence's need for personal salvation; his 'dark religion' is not a substitute for economic planning." This was not the mood of all men in the thirties—not of a William Faulkner, an Ellen Glasgow—and many of the New Dealers recognized that life was more complex than some of their statements would suggest. Yet the liberals, in their desire to free themselves from the tyranny of precedent and in their ardor for social achievement, sometimes walked the precipice of superficiality and philistinism.

The concentration of the New Dealers on public concerns made a deep mark on the sensibility of the 1930's. Private experience seemed self-indulgent compared to the demands of public life. "Indeed the public world with us has *become* the private world, and the private world has become the public," wrote Archibald MacLeish. "We live, that is to say, in a revolutionary time in which the public life has washed in over the dikes of private existence as sea water breaks over into the fresh pools in the spring tides till everything is salt." In the thirties, the Edna St. Vincent Millay whose candle had burned at both ends wrote the polemical *Conversation at Midnight* and the bitter "Epitaph for the Race of Man" in *Wine From These Grapes.*

The emphasis on the public world implied a specific rejection of the values of the 1920's. Roosevelt dismissed the twenties as "a decade of debauch," Tugwell scored those years as "a decade of empty progress, devoid of contribution to a genuinely better future," Morris Cooke deplored the "gilded-chariot days" of 1929, and Alben Barkley saw the twenties as a "carnival" marred by "the putrid pestilence of financial debauchery." The depression was experienced as the punishment of a wrathful God visited on a nation that had strayed from the paths of righteousness. The fire that followed the Park Avenue party in Thomas Wolfe's *You Can't Go Home Again,* like the suicide of Eveline at the end of John Dos Passos' *The Big Money,* symbolized the holocaust that brought to an end a decade of hedonism. In an era of reconstruction, the attitudes of the twenties seemed alien, frivolous, or—the most cutting word the thirties could visit upon a man or institution—"escapist." When Morrie Ryskind and George Kaufman, authors of the popular *Of Thee I Sing,* lampooned the government again in *Let 'em Eat Cake* in the fall of 1933, the country was not amused. The New York *Post* applauded the decision of George Jean Nathan and his associates to discontinue the *American Spectator:* "Nihilism, dadaism, smartsetism —they are all gone, and this, too, is progress." One of H. L. Mencken's biographers has noted: "Many were at pains to write him at his new home, telling him he was a sophomore, and those writing in magazines attacked him with a fury that was suspect because of its very violence."

Commentators on the New Deal have frequently characterized it by that much-abused term "pragmatic." If one means by this that the New Dealers carefully tested the consequences of ideas, the term is clearly a misnomer. If one means that Roosevelt was exceptionally anti-ideological in his approach to politics, one may question whether he was, in fact, any more "pragmatic" in this sense than Van Buren or Polk or even "reform" Presidents like Jackson and Theodore Roosevelt. The "pragmatism" of the New Deal seemed remarkable only in a decade tortured by ideology, only in contrast to the rigidity of Hoover and of the Left.

The New Deal was pragmatic mainly in its skepticism about utopias and final solutions, its openness to experimentation, and its suspicion of the dogmas of the Establishment. Since the advice of economists had so often been wrong, the New Dealers distrusted the claims of orthodox theory—"All this is perfectly terrible because it is all pure theory, when you come down to it," the President said on one occasion—and they felt free to try new approaches. Roosevelt refused to be awed by the warnings of economists and financial experts that government interference with the "laws" of the economy was blasphemous. "We must lay hold of the fact that economic laws are not made by nature," the President stated. "They are made by human beings." The New Dealers denied that depressions were inevitable events that had to be borne stoically, most of the stoicism to be displayed by the most impoverished, and they were willing to explore novel ways to make the social order more stable and more humane. "I am for experimenting . . . in various parts of the country, trying out schemes which are supported by reasonable people and see if they work," Hopkins told a conference of social workers. "If they do not work, the world will not come to an end."

Hardheaded, "anti-utopian," the New Dealers nonetheless had their Heavenly City: the greenbelt town, clean, green, and white, with children playing in light, airy, spacious schools; the government project at Longview, Washington, with small houses, each of different design, colored roofs, and gardens of flowers and vegetables; the Mormon villages of Utah that M. L. Wilson kept in his mind's eye—immaculate farmsteads on broad, rectangular streets; most of all, the Tennessee Valley, with its model town of Norris, the tall transmission towers, the white dams, the glistening wire strands, the valley where "a vision of villages and clean small factories has been growing into the minds of thoughtful men." Scandinavia was their model abroad, not only because it summoned up images of the countryside of Denmark, the beauties of Stockholm, not only for its experience with labor relations and social insurance and currency reform, but because it represented the "middle way" of happy accommodation of public and private institutions the New Deal sought to achieve. "Why," inquired Brandeis, "should anyone want to go to Russia when one can go to Denmark?"

Yet the New Deal added up to more than all of this—more than an experimental approach, more than the sum of its legislative achievements, more than an antiseptic utopia. It is true that there was a certain erosion of values in the thirties, as well as a narrowing of horizons, but the New Dealers inwardly recognized that what they were doing had a deeply moral significance however much they eschewed ethical pretensions. Heirs of the Enlightenment, they felt themselves part of a broadly humanistic movement to make man's life on earth more tolerable, a movement that might someday even achieve a co-operative commonwealth. Social insurance, Frances Perkins declared, was "a fundamental part of another great forward step in that liberation of humanity which began with the Renaissance."

Franklin Roosevelt did not always have this sense as keenly as some of the men around him, but his greatness as President lies in the remarkable degree to which he shared the vision. "The new deal business to me is very much bigger than anyone yet has expressed it," observed Senator Elbert Thomas. Roosevelt "seems to really have caught the spirit of what one of the Hebrew prophets called the desire of the nations. If he were in India today they would probably decide that he had become Mahatma—that is, one in tune with the infinite." Both foes and friends made much of Roosevelt's skill as a political manipulator, and there is no doubt that up to a point he delighted in schemes and stratagems. As Donald Richberg later observed: "There would be times when he seemed to be a Chevalier Bayard, *sans peur et sans reproche,* and times in which he would seem to be the apotheosis of a prince who had absorbed and practiced all the teachings of Machiavelli." Yet essentially he was a moralist who wanted to achieve certain humane reforms and instruct the nation in the principles of government. On one occasion, he remarked: "I want to be a *preaching President*—like my cousin." His courtiers gleefully recounted his adroitness in trading and dealing for votes, his effectiveness on the stump, his wicked skill in cutting corners to win a point. But Roosevelt's importance lay not in his talents as a campaigner or a manipulator. It lay rather in his ability to arouse the country and, more specifically, the men who served under him, by his breezy encouragement of experimentation, by his hopefulness, and—a word that would have embarrassed some of his lieutenants—by his idealism.

The New Deal left many problems unsolved and even created some perplexing new ones. It never demonstrated that it could achieve prosperity in peacetime. As late as 1941, the unemployed still numbered six million, and not until the war year of 1943 did the army of the jobless finally disappear. It enhanced the power of interest groups who claimed to speak for millions, but sometimes represented only a small minority. It did not evolve a way to protect people who had no such spokesmen, nor an acceptable method for disciplining the interest groups. In 1946, President Truman would resort to a threat to draft railway workers into the Army to avert a strike. The New Deal achieved a more just society by recognizing groups which had been largely unrepresented—staple farmers, industrial workers, particular ethnic groups, and the new intellectual-administrative class. Yet this was still a halfway revolution; it swelled the ranks of the bourgeoisie but left many Americans—share-croppers, slum dwellers, most Negroes—outside of the new equilibrium.

Some of these omissions were to be promptly remedied. Subsequent Congresses extended social security, authorized slum clearance projects, and raised minimum-wage standards to keep step with the rising price level. Other shortcomings are understandable. The havoc that had been done before Roosevelt took office was so great that even the unprecedented measures of the New Deal did not suffice to repair the damage. Moreover, much was still to be learned, and it was in the Roosevelt years that the country was schooled in how to avert another major depression. Although it was war which freed the government from the taboos of a balanced budget and revealed the potentialities of spending, it is conceivable that New Deal measures would have led the country into a new cycle of prosperity even if there had been no war. Marked gains had been made before the war spending had any appreciable effect. When recovery did come, it was much more soundly based because of the adoption of the New Deal program.

Roosevelt and the New Dealers understood, perhaps better than their critics, that they had come only part of the way. Henry Wallace remarked: "We are children of the transition—we have left Egypt but we have not yet arrived at the Promised Land." Only five years separated Roosevelt's inauguration in 1933 and the adoption of the last of the New Deal measures, the Fair Labor Standards Act, in 1938. The New Dealers perceived that they had done more in those years than had been done in any comparable period in American history, but they also saw that there was much still to be done, much, too, that continued to baffle them. "I believe in the things that have been done," Mrs. Roosevelt told the American Youth Congress in February, 1939. "They helped but they did not solve the fundamental problems. . . . I never believed the Federal government could solve the whole problem. It bought us time to think." She closed not with a solution but with a challenge: "Is it going to be worth while?"

"This generation of Americans is living in a tremendous moment of history," President Roosevelt stated in his final national address of the 1940 campaign.

"The surge of events abroad has made some few doubters among us ask: Is this the end of a story that has been told? Is the book of democracy now to be closed and placed away upon the dusty shelves of time?

"My answer is this: All we have known of the glories of democracy—its freedom, its efficiency as a mode of living, its ability to meet the aspirations of the common man—all these are merely an introduction to the greater story of a more glorious future.

"We Americans of today—all of us—we are characters in the living book of democracy.

"But we are also its author. It falls upon us now to say whether the chapters that are to come will tell a story of retreat or a story of continued advance."

25

Pearl Harbor:
The Debate Among Historians
JOHN E. WILTZ

26

Roosevelt as War Leader
MAURICE MATLOFF

27

Japanese Policy and Strategy in Mid-War
LOUIS MORTON

It is inevitable that World War II should command our attention. It was the costliest war we have ever fought, in terms of the casualties we suffered and the resources we expended. It was also the most momentous war we have fought, in the sense that it marked the termination of our diplomatic separateness and compelled us into an irreversible involvement in European affairs. Advancing by several degrees the type of war introduced by France during the revolution of the 1790's, World War II was startling and new: it was total war, its technology was radically destructive, its premises were more ideological than material, and its consequences were revolutionary. It ended not with peace but with cold war, with armed camps, wartime budgets, ideological conflict, continued revolutions throughout the world, and a very precariously maintained balance of power. It is vital for us yet, because it is in so many ways still unresolved. Our crises in Europe and wars in Asia have led us back to study World War II, urging us to reconsider steps we took and perhaps should not have taken or steps we did not take and perhaps should have taken.

What led to World War II? How discerning was the conduct of American diplomacy, particularly in the Far East, during the years before Pearl Harbor? What evidence have the "revisionist" historians cited to support their thesis that President Roosevelt conspired to involve the United States in war? How have "anti-revisionist" historians defended Roosevelt against the charge of conspiracy? Could the coming of World War II have been averted? What was the nature of Roosevelt's leadership during the war? What goals did he seek to achieve, and by what means? How successful was he in achieving his goals? If he was, as he has been called, a great war president, what were the qualities that made him great? What was the strategy of our enemies? How accurate was our view of their strategy and their view of ours?

The following essays by John E. Wiltz, Maurice Matloff, and Louis Morton undertake, respectively, to answer these questions. Professor Wiltz, of Indiana University, is one of our most promising young writers of diplomatic history. His first book, In Search of Peace: The Senate Munitions Inquiry, 1934–36 *(1963), was an excellent study of the findings and influence of the Nye Committee. Among his other writings is a brilliant survey of American diplomacy during the depression decade,* From Isolation to War, 1931– 1941 *(1968), and it is from the last chapter of this book that the selection reprinted below has been taken. In it, Professor Wiltz offers a dispassionate and fascinating inquiry into the question of whether a conspiracy on the part of Franklin Delano Roosevelt and his cohorts led us into World War II.*

Maurice Matloff and Louis Morton have made signal contributions to the multi-volume series entitled United States Army in World War II, *whose chief historian had been Dr. Kent Roberts Greenfield. Dr. Matloff has written two volumes dealing with the War Department and its role in wartime national planning and military strategy:* Strategic Planning for Coalition Warfare, 1941–1942 *(with Edwin M. Snell, 1953) and* Strategic Planning for Coalition Warfare, 1943–1944 *(1959). He has also contributed to two other volumes:* Command Decisions *(1959) and* Total War and Cold War *(1962). The essay below was delivered in 1964 as the sixth of the Harmon Memorial Lectures in Military History at the United States Air Force Academy in Colorado. In attempting to assess the plans and policies of Franklin Delano*

Roosevelt as war leader, Dr. Matloff affords us deep insight into both the qualities of Roosevelt's leadership and the presidential role in war.

Dr. Morton, *Professor of History at Dartmouth, is the author of* Robert Carter of Nomini Hall *(1941), a volume in the* Williamsburg Restoration Historical Studies *series; the book is a revaluation, from the point of view of an eminent member of Virginia's aristocracy, of the plantation economy in the late colonial period. As a participant in the massive cooperative history,* United States Army in World War II, *Professor Morton directed and supervised the preparation of "The War in the Pacific," a subseries of the larger enterprise. To this subseries he has contributed two volumes,* The Fall of the Philippines *(1953) and* Strategy and Command: The First Two Years *(1962). His essay on "Japanese Policy and Strategy in Mid-War" is a fascinating case study in military planning. It takes us, as it were, behind enemy lines, to the very heart of imperial command; and it assaults the myth that the Japanese command was inflexible and unable to make rapid and effective adjustments to the changing circumstances of war.*

If history has any lessons to teach, then we should very much wish to learn what we can from the history of American wars in general and from that of World War II in particular. Why have we fought our wars? How much has our entry into war been motivated by national ideology, how much by private concerns and material interests? Does our social psychology predispose us, as a nation, to war? Is it fair to say that we have fought our wars to fulfill our sense of destiny and our mission, and thus have been sustaining, in one way or another, the Puritan conviction that we have been on an errand into the wilderness, building for the world a model city upon a hill? And is it the defect of our polity that the ideology which, by reinforcing the national will, contributes to our winning a war is also one which, by beclouding our view of realities, contributes no less to our losing the peace? How far are liberal democracies such as ours transformed by war? Do times of crisis usually produce, as Tocqueville feared they would, more democracy but less liberalism?

Is the elected leader of a civil polity qualified to be the commander-in-chief of its wartime activities? Is it a major flaw in our constitution that, at the time of the most profound crisis, the nation may be led by a man of questionable abilities? What were the qualities of our great wartime presidents, and how much was their being considered great due to their having been presidents during wartime? What were the respective goals of our wartime presidents? How far did these goals also express national opinion, and how far were they realized?

If World War II is alive with significance for our own age, it is because it never really ended. It signaled the full arrival of an era when war or the imminence of war became the rule and peace the exception. A hydra of international conflict, it resulted in more and greater tensions than it had re-

moved. Taking place in an atmosphere vibrant with the possibility of nuclear war, relations between the Western and Communist powers posed seemingly insuperable problems at every turn. For Americans, thrust irrevocably into a position of leadership in world affairs, the problems were particularly meaningful and demanding.

What policy should the United States pursue in its intercourse with the world of nations? Stephen Decatur would surely be no guide for us—nor, for that matter, would McKinley, Theodore Roosevelt, or Wilson. But who would be? Caught against our will in a maelstrom of international change, unable to return to that apartness from world politics which we have regarded as part of our tradition, are we assuming our new role with sense and balance? Or are we assuming it with a dangerous national pride, with little understanding of other ways, with the presumption that the world has to be remade in our image? How valid, for example, is the allegation of Senator J. William Fulbright of Arkansas that our diplomacy has been proceeding from an arrogance of power? And how valid is the assertion of the historian Theodore Draper that, in recent years, we have been conducting our foreign affairs less by the usual instruments of politics and increasingly by those of militarism?

What exactly is the nature of our struggle with the Communist world? Is it a struggle of armaments, of ideologies, of gross national products, of institutional patterns? Are we correct in our estimate of it? Is it possible, as George F. Kennan has seriously urged upon us, that we have been attempting to meet the international realities of the world today with a sense of international reality that is traditional and utopian? Is it possible, in other words, that we have been basing our diplomacy on premises that are notably obsolete? Indeed, is there such a monolithic entity as "the Communist world," or is this description no more correct than would be a description of the liberal Western world as an integrated, uniformly minded political order?

What have been the respective contributions of the Truman, Eisenhower, Kennedy, and Johnson administrations toward solving our postwar diplomatic problems? Do the wars we have been waging in Asia bespeak the dismal failure of our diplomacy? Do they perhaps reflect a tacit understanding between the Communist world and ours that the cold war may become hot only in the borderlands of the major powers and only if it is limited to conventional armaments? Or has the cold war been fundamentally transformed? Have we arrived, as Maurice Goldbloom has suggested, at the age of the atomic stalemate? Or are we moving, as George Lichtheim has called it, toward an age of "Pax Russo-Americana"?

The war continuum in which we have been living these past two decades has informed every aspect of our national being. It has been so pervasively a strain upon us that we have, in a way, become numb to its presence and blocked it out of our daily consciousness. Whatever other lessons history may have to teach about war, there is one lesson that would seem to take precedence over all others: There has never been a generation without war, despite the growing improvement in the technology of destruction and the universal awareness of that improvement. In this age of the atomic bomb, it is a lesson well worth pondering.

JOHN E. WILTZ

Of the Japanese attack on Hawaii in December 1941, Robert E. Sherwood *(Roosevelt and Hopkins)* several years later wrote: "Millions of words have been recorded by at least eight official investigating bodies and one may read through all of them without arriving at an adequate explanation of why, with war so obviously ready to break out *somewhere* in the Pacific, our principal Pacific base was in a condition of peacetime Sunday morning somnolence instead of in Condition Red." Many Americans in the 1940's and after shared Sherwood's amazement, and in this atmosphere of historical bafflement perhaps the appearance of a devil theory was inevitable—a theory that Pearl Harbor was a monstrous plot hatched in the dark recesses of Washington.

According to the conspiracy idea, Roosevelt by 1940–41 was afire with one thought, to take the United States to war with Germany. His purpose? To save Britain and Russia and increase his own prestige and power. The destroyer deal and lend-lease were part of the presidential scheme to provoke Hitler. But the dictator would not accommodate the President by declaring war. Whereupon Roosevelt, ever the Machiavelli of American politics, found the strategy of getting the United States in war against the "real" enemy, Germany, via the "back door." In the words of the revisionist writer Charles C. Tansill *(Back Door to War)*, "when the President perceived that Hitler would not furnish the pretext for a war with Germany, he turned to the Far East and increased his pressure upon Japan." War with one Axis power would mean war with the other.

To carry out their design—so revisionists have written—Roosevelt and his fellow-conspirators (Secretaries Hull, Stimson, and Knox, and the army's chief of staff General George C. Marshall) pushed the Japanese to a position where they had to retreat from the Asian mainland to their home islands, or fight. They knew the Japanese would fight. But the master plotters in Washington did not stop there. To unite the country they determined that Japan should strike the first blow, and as a lure for a "sneak" attack—a "stab in the back"—the President exposed the Pacific fleet at Pearl Harbor. The price of presidential treachery? Destruction of two battleships, immobilization of six others, loss of several lesser vessels, elimination of 188 army and navy planes, and the death of 2,403 Americans.

SOURCE: John E. Wiltz, *From Isolation to War, 1931–1941* (New York: Thomas Y. Crowell Company, 1968), pp. 98–105. Reprinted by permission.

The best-known Pearl Harbor revisionists have been Charles A. Beard (*President Roosevelt and the Coming of the War*), Charles C. Tansill (*Back Door to War*), and Harry Elmer Barnes (*Perpetual War for Perpetual Peace*). Others are William Henry Chamberlin (*America's Second Crusade*), George Morgenstern (*Pearl Harbor: The Story of the Secret War*, 1947), Rear Admiral Robert A. Theobald (*The Final Secret of Pearl Harbor*, 1954), and Admiral Husband E. Kimmel (*Admiral Kimmel's Story*, 1955). Like prewar isolationists (which several of them were), revisionists have believed there could be no rational argument against the idea that war in Europe and Asia was not the business of the United States. The President, who was no dupe, understood the isolationist logic, and therefore knew what was best for the country. Still, as Barnes puts it, "to promote Roosevelt's political ambitions and his mendacious foreign policy some three thousand American boys were quite needlessly butchered."

Evidence for the revisionist case is purely circumstantial; no clear-cut documentary proof to support the theory of conspiracy has ever appeared. In the revisionist view the economic boycott of Japan, completed in summer 1941, and Roosevelt's refusal to meet the Japanese prime minister demonstrate that leaders in Washington were seeking war in the Pacific. But the revisionist case centers around Pearl Harbor: the idea that Roosevelt lured the Japanese to Hawaii by exposing the fleet and let the raid come without tipping off army and navy commanders. Revisionists saw that if they could establish this part of their thesis it would be easy enough to accept the argument that Roosevelt was maneuvering the Japanese via diplomacy.

As for Pearl Harbor, revisionists ask questions for which they think there are no satisfactory answers except conspiracy in Washington. Did not intercepted messages (American cryptanalysts had broken Japan's highest diplomatic code, the Purple Cipher) show unmistakable interest in warships at Pearl Harbor, a clear indication of Japanese intentions? What else except conspiracy could explain Secretary Stimson's remark at a White House meeting in November 1941, that the problem of Japanese-American relations was "how we should maneuver them [the Japanese] into the position of firing the first shot"? Why did leaders in Washington fail to provide Hawaii with one of the machines called "Magic" for decoding the Purple Cipher (the Philippines had one), unless they feared that army and navy commanders there would figure out for themselves what was up? And what about the "east-wind rain" code? "Magic" had revealed that the words "east-wind rain" in weather broadcasts would be the Tokyo government's signal to embassies that a break with America was imminent. Revisionists are sure that a monitor picked up the signal but that officials in Washington suppressed the information. Since intercepted messages in the first days of December 1941 indicated that war was about to break out in the Pacific, why did leaders in Washington fail to reiterate the warning to Pacific commanders in the most forceful language—unless Washington wanted surprise? Why did Roosevelt, knowing war to be at hand, fail to send the battleship fleet to sea— unless he wanted it to come under attack? Why were the Pacific fleet's aircraft carriers absent from Pearl Harbor on the fateful Sunday morning? Was it because the President was willing to sacrifice battleships but wanted to save the carriers? And why did General Marshall, on learning from an intercept that a Japanese attack might come at 1:00 P.M. December 7 (Washington time), transmit an alert to Hawaii by commercial telegraph instead of using the "scrambler" telephone on his desk— unless he wanted the message to arrive too late?

In the view of such writers as Herbert Feis (*The Road to Pearl Harbor*), William L. Langer and S. Everett Gleason (*The Undeclared War*), Julius W. Pratt (*Cordell Hull*), Elting E. Morison (*Turmoil and Tradition*), Basil Rauch (*Roosevelt: From Munich to Pearl Harbor*), Walter Millis (*This is Pearl!*), Samuel Eliot Morison (*The Two-Ocean War*, 1963), Forrest C. Pogue (*George C. Marshall*, II, *Ordeal and Hope*, 1966), Ladislas Farago (*The Broken Seal: "Operation Magic" and the Secret Road to Pearl Harbor*, 1967), and Roberta Wohlstetter (*Pearl Harbor: Warning and Decision*, 1962), the idea of conspiracy has no foundation. Feis, Langer and Gleason, Rauch, and Pratt have shown that each of America's diplomatic moves in the Pacific in 1940–41 was consistent with the Roosevelt administration's estimate of the national interest and requirements of international morality. As for the "back door" thesis, they note that the Axis alliance was defensive, and just as Japan had been under no obligation to declare war when Germany attacked the Soviet Union in June 1941, Germany was under no obligation if Japan should attack the United States. Roosevelt could have had no assurance that a "back door" strategy would take America into the European war. Regarding Pearl Harbor, anti-revisionists (or "court historians," as revisionists contemptuously call them) consider it understandable that the Japanese achieved surprise. Attention in official Washington had been fixed on Southeast Asia and the western Pacific, where Japanese troop concentrations and naval activity indicated a possible attack. In the words of Langer and Gleason, leaders in Washington "had been living from hour to hour with the problem of how to meet the virtual certainty of a Japanese attack in Southeast Asia. . . . Of Hawaii there was apparently no thought. This tragic oversight may be a classic example of human frailty, but it provides no evidence whatsoever to support the thesis that the President or any other responsible American official courted a Japanese attack on the Pearl Harbor base in order to enable them to lead the country into the European war by the Pacific back door."

Regarding revisionist questions about Pearl Harbor, anti-revisionists have nonconspiratorial answers for each. On Japan's interest in ships at Pearl Harbor, intercepts revealed that Japanese agents were collecting information on ships at several points, including the Canal Zone and Singapore; there seemed nothing unusual about interest in those based in Hawaii (although Ladislas Farago, in a chapter entitled "The Missed Clue," thinks a cumulative study by naval intelligence would have revealed a heavier emphasis on ship movements at Pearl Harbor). As for the "eastwind rain" signal, Farago found evidence that Japanese authorities executed it but doubts the testimony of the naval officer (also disputed by other navy men) who said monitors picked it up two days before the raid. On Stimson's "maneuver" statement, Richard N. Current in "How Stimson Meant to 'Maneuver' the Japanese" (*Mississippi Valley Historical Review,* XL, June 1953) contended that Stimson's remark did not prove conspiracy. Anticipating a Japanese strike somewhere in Southeast Asia, the secretary was seeking an announcement, perhaps a presidential declaration, that such a blow would constitute a threat to American interests. If it fell the President could claim that Japan had fired the first shot and ask Congress for war. On failing to provide Hawaii with a "Magic" decoding device: such machines were difficult to assemble, and of course the more machines about, the greater the chance the Japanese would realize that the United States had broken the Purple Cipher.[1] As for giving war alerts, the Washington government had issued commanders a "war warning" on November 27, and as Stimson later said (*On Active Service*), "we assumed that . . . it would not be necessary to repeat that warning over and over again during the ensuing days." As for the President's failure to send the battleships to sea, his naval advisers, thinking nobody could launch aerial torpedoes in a channel as shallow as that at Pearl, believed Hawaii the safest place in the Pacific for the fleet. On absence of the carriers: those "flat-tops" available for duty were off delivering planes for defense of Wake and Midway, under the circumstances a legitimate enterprise. On Marshall's failure to use the scrambler telephone, the general's biographer Forrest C. Pogue says that nobody suggested using the phone: "If anyone had, Marshall would not have risked revealing that the United States had broken the Japanese diplomatic code by relying on the dubious security of the scrambler then in use."

Perhaps Roberta Wohlstetter has given the best explanation, apart from the fixation on Southeast Asia, for failure of leaders in Washington and commanders in Hawaii to read "signals" pointing to an attack at

---

[1] One may note that the Philippines had a "Magic" machine, but commanders there did not conclude from intercepts that Pearl Harbor was about to come under attack.

Pearl Harbor: "It is much easier *after* the event to sort the relevant from the irrelevant signals. After the event, of course, a signal is always crystal clear; we can now see what disaster it was signaling, since the disaster has occurred. But before the event it is obscure and pregnant with conflicting meanings. . . . In short, we failed to anticipate Pearl Harbor not for want of the relevant materials, but because of a plethora of irrelevant ones."

To this one might add the view of Ladislas Farago that ability to de-code the Purple Cipher filled American leaders in autumn 1941 with a smug feeling of security: "Mr. Roosevelt and his associates . . . assumed that thanks to the 'Magics,' they could learn well in advance every-thing the Japanese were planning, enabling them to apply whatever preventive or counter measures they deemed advisable and neces-sary." Thus "Magic" was "partly responsible for the complacency with which American authorities approached the final crisis in Novem-ber and December 1941."

Though most historians reject the idea of conspiracy, the question remains of the wisdom of America's Far Eastern policy during the year or so before Pearl Harbor. Using general studies as a measure, the pre-vailing view parallels that set forth in the writings of Feis, Langer and Gleason, and Rauch, *i.e.,* most historians think the Roosevelt admin-istration made the proper responses to Japanese moves in East Asia in 1940–41. As explained by Feis ("War Came at Pearl Harbor: Suspi-cions Considered," *The Yale Review,* XLV, Spring 1956): "Our Govern-ment did obstruct Japanese efforts, believing them to be unjust, cruel, and a threat to our national security, especially after Japan became a partner with Hitler's Germany and Mussolini's Italy and bent its efforts toward bringing the world under their combined control." As for the revisionist idea that Roosevelt forced Japan into war by unreasonable demands, Feis *(The Road to Pearl Harbor)* retorts that it is absurd to claim that compliance with American demands would have meant extinction of Japanese nationality. The United States insisted that Japan give up no territories or resources except those held by force. The Japanese government would have remained independent and there would have been no limits on Japanese military power. In Feis's words, "extinction threatened the plan for expansion in Asia, but not Japan or the Japanese."

Not everyone agrees. While rejecting the conspiracy theory, a few writers have considered America's policy in the Far East in 1941 poorly conceived, claiming that it brought a war in the Pacific which the United States with honor and profit might have avoided. The first clear expression of this view appeared in 1952 in the memoirs of Joseph C. Grew *(Turbulent Era),* America's ambassador to Japan in 1932–41. Books by the British scholar Francis C. Jones *(Japan's New Order in East*

Asia, 1954) and Paul W. Schroeder (*The Axis Alliance and Japanese-American Relations*, 1958) have offered support. According to these men, the United States and Japan in 1941 might have struck a truce: Japan breaking away from the Axis alliance and pledging no new aggression in East Asia, the United States lifting restrictions on trade with Japan. As for other issues, including Japan's presence in China, they could await outcome of the war in Europe. Instead, the United States insisted on total surrender—withdrawal from the East Asian mainland to the home islands. Japan of course had invested too much blood and treasure in the China adventure to make such a retreat.

The Grew-Jones-Schroeder thesis is a heady wine and a large draught can send the imagination soaring. If the government in Washington could have postponed a showdown in the Far East the United States could have put all its strength in the balance against Hitler. Not only would the European war have ended sooner; the Anglo-American armies could have gone ashore in France a year or so before they did, swept eastward, and saved much of Eastern Europe from the Red Army and communism. After defeating Hitler the triumphant Allies could have wheeled around to the Pacific and compelled the Japanese, perhaps without a fight, to disgorge their empire. The deadly campaigns on Guadalcanal and Iwo Jima would never have taken place, the United States would not have gained the dubious distinction of dropping the first atomic bomb, and spared from continuous fighting Chiang Kai-shek's government in China might have brought the regeneration of Chinese life that would have kept the world's most populous country out of the communist orbit. And Japan? Though wounded in pride, it would have remained a force in the Far East, a bastion against the Soviet Union and the ideas of communism. A heady wine indeed!

MAURICE MATLOFF

Let me begin by going back to 1 March 1945, when a weary President, too tired to carry the ten pounds of steel that braced his paralyzed legs, sat down before the United States Congress to report on the Yalta Conference—the summit meeting in the Crimea with Marshal Stalin and Prime Minister Churchill—from which he had just returned.

"I come from the Crimea Conference," he said, "with a firm belief that we have made a good start on the road to a world of peace. . . .

"This time we are not making the mistake of waiting until the end of the war to set up the machinery of peace. This time, as we fight

SOURCE: Maurice Matloff, *Roosevelt as War Leader* (Colorado: United States Air Force Academy, 1964), pp. 1–21. Dr. Matloff's lecture is part of the Lt. General Hubert R. Harmon Memorial Lectures in Military History—USAF Academy, Colorado. Reprinted by permission.

together to win the war finally, we work together to keep it from happening again."

Forty-two days later—12 April 1945—Franklin Delano Roosevelt was dead. Not long afterward, Allied forces pounded Germany and Japan into defeat. Thereupon began a great controversy over the way President Roosevelt had directed his three wars—the war against Germany, the war against Japan, and war against war itself.

No problem of World War II is more fascinating to the historian, none more difficult, than the question of President Roosevelt's leadership. This subject has stirred violent debate ever since the war and, from all indications, will continue to do so. Two extreme views have appeared. One portrays a President who blundered into war, bungled its conduct, and lost the peace. The other presents a picture of a President who was drawn into a war he did not want, rallied the free world, won a great victory, and moved the United States to the center of the world stage. One school of thought emphasizes blunders and mistakes—and on this list Pearl Harbor, the unconditional surrender policy, the Yalta Conference usually stand high. Indeed, in the early postwar days, writers seemed to be vying with each other in a numbers game—to see how many major mistakes they could find. The other school has called this approach "Monday morning quarterbacking" and refutes the charges, discounts the so-called mistakes, and stresses constructive achievements.

The controversy extends not only to the President's policies but also to his plans and methods. Some have argued that FDR had a master plan and a strategy to match. Others counter that he played strictly by ear. Some have contended he was the ready tool of his military staff, others that he manipulated that staff to his will. Interestingly enough, the two most recent accounts of revisionist writing on American strategy have attempted to make out a case for a strong activist role of the President in military strategy and to downgrade the role of the staff. Contrary to Robert Sherwood's findings that on "not more than two occasions" in the war did FDR overrule his staff, the latest account, just off the press, suggests there were more than twenty cases. We may be in for a new numbers game in the continuing controversy.

Where does the truth lie? Why all the controversy? It cannot be explained as simply a case of the "fog of war" or of partisan prejudices. In part the controversy stems from preconceived notions about Mr. Roosevelt—a carryover of stereotyped views about the myth and the man as New Dealer to war leader. In part it arises out of Mr. Roosevelt's highly personalized ways of doing business. He could be direct, he could be indirect, he could even be devious—and we shall have more to say about his methods as we go along. Those who stress Mr. Roosevelt as the "fox" and the "artful dodger" in domestic politics find it hard to believe he could be a genuine do-gooder and idealist in international affairs. The debate has also been fed by the disillusionment and frustration of the postwar years—the cold war—and the tendency to look backward for scapegoats. Furthermore, there are problems of perspective, evidence, and motivation. World War II history merges into current history, but the most difficult part of current history is to find the current. Many of the trends set in motion during the war are still open-ended and our perspective is blurred. We cannot always be sure what is important, and it is difficult to evaluate with certainty what we identify. We have tons of records. No war was better recorded than World War II. Never have historians made such a concentrated assault on war documents so soon after a conflict. But all too often the historian who has struggled through mountains of paper finds the trail disappearing, at the crucial point of decision-making, somewhere in the direction of the White House. Nor can we always be certain of Mr. Roosevelt's motives. He rarely recorded his reasons. He did not leave us the memoirs we have come to expect from our Presidents. Though he was historically minded, he permitted no historian to peer over his shoulder in the White House. As a result the historian has to pick and choose, interpret and reinterpret; he must distinguish between appearances and realities and try to fit the pieces into a proper pattern. Above all, he must beware of creating new myths in place of those he destroys.

To do justice to all the facets of FDR's war leadership would take far more time than we have at our disposal today. I would like to focus attention principally on FDR's roles as Commander-in-Chief and war statesman after Pearl Harbor. We shall be especially interested to see what use he made of military power and how he viewed its relationships to foreign policy—problems of central importance to his war leadership.

I

Long before the attack on Pearl Harbor plunged the nation into war, Mr. Roosevelt's apprenticeship for war leadership had begun. Intensely interested in naval affairs from his youth, he had had firsthand experience, as Assistant Secretary of the Navy in World War I, in preparing for war. Extremely conscious of Wilson's experiences during and after World War I with Allies, enemies, and the U.S. Congress, he was determined to avoid Wilson's mistakes. Roosevelt himself had fought for the League of Nations, on which Wilson had staked so much of his war policy. He knew that victory had to be won on Capitol Hill as well as on the battlefield. A year before Pearl Harbor—in his "arsenal of democracy" speech—he had spoken out against the folly of a negotiated peace with the Nazis. During that same year he appointed two

Republicans—Frank Knox and Henry L. Stimson—to be Secretaries of the Navy and War Departments, respectively—the first of a series of steps toward bipartisanship. The Commander-in-Chief would also serve as the politician-in-chief.

Between 1939 and 1941, under President Roosevelt's leadership, the country gradually awakened to the dangers from without and began to mobilize. His efforts during the prewar period to join military power to national policy were, however, only partially successful. Simply put, that policy was to try to avert war but to be prepared for it should it come. He used power to avert war—what we would today call the deterrent. Calls for planes, "now—and lots of them," keeping the fleet at Pearl Harbor, extending naval patrols, garrisoning Atlantic bases, reinforcing the Philippines did not avert war. Nor did he succeed in harnessing that military power—such as it was—to an effective diplomacy to develop an alternative to war. But he did succeed in getting rearmament started. He went as far as he dared in letting foreign powers know that America would aid those fighting tyranny. By the time of Pearl Harbor, we were, in effect, a nonbelligerent ally. He reached for his Commander-in-Chief's baton early and used it actively. He gathered in the reins of military power, harnessed his team, and began to educate his staff even as they were educating him for the tasks ahead. The relatively prolonged "short of war" period gave him an invaluable "dry run" and by late 1941 he was ready.

Enemy action, not the President's wish or design, put an end to the three years of peacetime preparation. The measures he had instituted to stop Japanese aggression may have narrowed the choices for Japan, but Japan made the decision for war. FDR's campaign for preparedness was still far from complete, but so far as advance military planning was concerned, the nation never entered a war so well prepared. The armed forces were being built up, weapons were beginning to flow, the basis of coordinated action with Britain had been set. Pearl Harbor exposed weaknesses in America's preparations, but the steps that had already been taken enabled the United States within less than a year to take the offensive against Germany and Japan. As events were to show, the President had successfully converted the peaceful democracy to war purposes.

With American entry into the war, the Grand Alliance really came into being. In the year following Pearl Harbor, the President devoted himself to consolidating the hard-pressed Alliance. There was both need and opportunity to shape that alliance, composed of such diverse sovereign states as Great Britain and the Soviet Union, both fighting desperately, and the still untried United States. And, unlike Wilson, Roosevelt personally participated in the important wartime conferences of the Allies.

This coalition was really a polygamous marriage. It represented different degrees of partnership. With Churchill and the British, Roosevelt had a special relation—and the Anglo-American partnership was an alliance within an alliance. Wearing both a political and a military hat, Roosevelt sometimes found himself more in agreement with Churchill than with his own military staff. Throughout the war, and particularly in the early defensive stage, Churchill exercised a strong influence on him. The doughty British statesman-warrior, whose conversation always charmed Roosevelt even when his ideas did not, was a perfect foil for FDR. As FDR once told Churchill, "It is fun to be in the same decade with you."

With the Soviet Union—the half ally involved almost to the end only in Europe—relations were never so intimate, and Roosevelt early took over the role of mediator between Churchill and Stalin in this "Strange Alliance." From the beginning, he strove to win the friendship of the Soviet Union. "The only way to have a friend," he once quoted Emerson, "is to be one." To bring the Soviet Union out of isolation, even as the United States had been drawn away from its isolationism, became one of his major goals.

Roosevelt's relationship with China's Chiang Kai-shek, who was involved only on the Japanese side of the war, was also a special one. In this role FDR did not always find himself in agreement with the British or with his own staff. From the beginning he hoped to raise China to recognition as a great power.

To Roosevelt the alliance presented a grand opportunity to "win friends and influence people"; to get allied nations, united by the common bond of danger, to know one another better and break down legacies of suspicion. To FDR the summit meetings from Washington to Yalta were more than assemblies to iron out war strategy and policy; they were historic chapters in international cooperation. To this end he early essayed the role he played throughout the war—guardian of the good relations of the coalition.

This attitude colored his approach to military strategy. Usually he went along with his staff on military strategy and was content to have the British and the Joint Chiefs of Staff settle it or to allow events to shape it. But wherever differences with major allies threatened to strain the coalition, he stepped in. Thus in the summer of 1942 he intervened to break a deadlock between the American Joint Chiefs— intent on preparing for an early cross-Channel operation in force—and the British Prime Minister and his staff intent on launching a North African operation. The decision for North Africa reversed the approval he had earlier given to the cross-Channel operation. He justified this decision on the ground that he wanted American troops in action in 1942, but he was also very much aware that the British were faltering and that the Russians were having a disastrous summer. The North African operation would provide a timely demonstration of Allied solidarity. Not only did he overrule his staff on this occasion—as he was to do on several others—but he refused to permit the staff to give an ultimatum to the British, a threat to go all-out in the Pacific should the cross-Channel operation be canceled. Indeed in this connection in mid-July 1942 he used an imperative tone that was quite unusual to put down the stirrings of protest of his staff. Note, too, that throughout the war he steadfastly backed the "Europe first" decision—the basic coalition decision in strategy confirmed at the Anglo-American Conference in Washington soon after Pearl Harbor—a decision in which major allies found common political as well as military grounds.

It is difficult, on the face of available evidence, to ascribe strong strategic convictions to Mr. Roosevelt. Well into midwar he continued to show what his staff regarded as diversionist tendencies. When the invasion of North Africa proved successful, he could hardly repress a note of personal triumph to General Marshall. "Just between ourselves," he declared, "if I had not considered the European and African fields of action in their broadest geographic sense, you and I know we would not be in North Africa today—in fact, we would not have landed either in Africa or in Europe!" The Mediterranean fascinated him almost as much as it did Winston Churchill. The American staff spent a good part of its wartime efforts trying to win him—and seeing to it that he stayed won—to a strategy based on a scheduled cross-Channel operation in force. It is not generally realized that Mr. Roosevelt as late as the summer of 1943 toyed with the idea of a campaign through the Iberian peninsula in place of the cross-Channel attack and even at Teheran in November 1943 showed interest in Adriatic ventures.

This does not mean that FDR was opposed to the cross-Channel operation. Far from it. It does mean that he permitted his staff wide latitude in the day-to-day conduct of the strategic business of the war. But it also means that he reserved to himself the determination of the choice and timing of important decisions. Once determined—and no one could be more stubborn when his mind was made up—Mr. Roosevelt stood fast at Teheran for a cross-Channel operation and in the summer of 1944 for a southern France operation. By his interest in the Mediterranean and his desire to meet the British at least halfway, the President in effect compelled American strategists—in midwar—to broaden their strategic thinking and to consider various permutations and combinations of Mediterranean, cross-Channel and strategic bombing operations. The rigidity of American strategists has been much exaggerated.

Mr. Roosevelt's flexible approach to strategy gave his staff military advisers considerable problems. In the spring of 1942 he breezily tossed off a promise to Mr. Molotov for an early second front—to his staff's consternation. At times he adopted a cautious "wait and see" attitude, reluctant to commit himself in advance of an international conference. Occasionally he prodded the planners to do more for the Mediterranean. In this connection he once chided General Marshall, declaring that planners were "always conservative and saw all the difficulties." Small wonder that for a long time—in midwar—the staff could not work out a united front with him for the great conference with the British. FDR played off one school of thought against the other, for example those advocating ground offensives in the China theater versus those advocating more air operations there. Spectacular actions that promised fast results also appealed to him—send an air force to the Caucasus to help the hard-pressed Russians, he proposed in late 1942, an offer the Russians refused; let Chennault mount a daring air campaign to bolster limping China, he ruled in 1943. At a conference he could take a strategic strand from Churchill, one from General Marshall, and another from General Chennault and come up with a position of his own. He could also reverse himself even during a conference—witness the decision by default in the case of a large-scale operation on the mainland of Asia at Cairo-Teheran. The chiefs became accustomed to seeing "OK-FDR" on their papers; at least once he also wrote "Spinach."

Yet when all is said and done, there is nothing to indicate that he had a thought-out strategic military plan of his own—separate from that of his staff. This was a working partnership. If he pulled the rug from under his staff on occasion, he could also back them strongly. They freed him from immersing himself in details—details bored him. They enabled him to play his favorite mediatory role at the conferences. The precise number of times he overruled his staff is not really important. For every case offered there are literally hundreds where he did not intervene—as a glance at JCS minutes of the war would show. What is important is the area of differences and these we have suggested lie in the realm of keeping the alliance in harness to get on with the war. Note how little, in contrast to European strategy, he intervened in Pacific strategy—basically in an American theater where Allies played a relatively small role and where he gave the JCS a comparatively free hand within the context of the "Europe first" decision.

As Commander-in-Chief Mr. Roosevelt was fortunate in his choice of staff and commanders. Unlike Lincoln, he found his general early. General Marshall soon won his confidence and carried much of the burden of debate with Churchill and the British Chiefs of Staff over European strategy, permitting Mr. Roosevelt to play his favorite mediatory role. The reliance he placed on Marshall is reflected in his decision not to release Marshall for the top command in Europe. As Roosevelt put it, "I . . . could not sleep at night with you out of the country." In Admirals King and Leahy he found strong naval advisers; Leahy, his personal link with the JCS, also became his "leg-man." Each could get his ear, as could also the Air Force's General "Hap" Arnold, via Harry Hopkins. The working relationship that grew up among them justified his confidence and produced an orderly administration in the day-to-day conduct of the war that was in marked contrast to Roosevelt's personalized methods in other fields. His system of administration during the war may have appeared haphazard and his relationship with his staff loose, but that system and relationship worked for him.

As time went on, FDR's respect for the complexities of military planning grew along with his knowledge. "You can't imagine how tired I sometimes get," he once stated, "when something that looks simple is going to take three months—six months to do. Well, that is part of the job of a Commander-in-Chief. Sometimes I have to be disappointed, sometimes I have to go along with the estimates of the professionals." The JCS system, which came into existence soon after Pearl Harbor and to which, characteristically, Roosevelt never gave a charter, remained his bulwark in the military field. Unlike the ubiquitous Churchill, he did not hang over the shoulders of his staff and commanders; nor did he harry them with messages, overwhelm them in debate, and give them no rest. Weeks would go by when he did not see General Marshall and for a long period after the North Africa decision, to which Stimson had objected strongly, the President did not see his Secretary of War. While much advice from nonmilitary sources reached him informally through various members of his inner circle, as Commander-in-Chief he preserved formal but friendly relations with commanders in the field through accepted military channels. Only once, at Pearl Harbor in July 1944, did he see General MacArthur during the war, and it is doubtful that even then he intervened in strategic decisions that were pending.

To sum up, in general the Commander-in-Chief exercised a loose control over military strategy but preserved an independent role in it. He kept his cards close to his chest, persuaded rather than commanded, or let events make the decisions. He conducted grand strategy through the JCS and outside of it. He used any and all instruments at hand; as usual, he was not too much concerned with system and form. He assimilated and synthesized strategic ideas and then used his power of leadership to translate them into reality. His flexibility in military strategy was entirely consistent with his desire to defeat the enemies decisively and to keep the alliance solidified. He was wedded to no strategic doctrine except victory. To the President, military strategy, like politics, was the art of the possible. Through lend-lease he gave the coalition bricks and mortar. He used strategy to cement the alliance.

But he refused to use strategy to achieve strictly political objectives overseas. When the question of a possible Balkan operation came up in August 1943, he declared it was "unwise to plan military strategy based on a gamble as to political results." To the American President, strategy had to serve larger and nobler purposes.

So far we have been talking about the President as Commander-in-Chief. The time has come to ask the most important question of all— what was FDR after—what were his objectives in the war and after the war?

To answer this question we must first consider the role of the war President in his other important capacity, as manager of foreign relations. From the beginning, Roosevelt, like Wilson before him, was his own Secretary of State. He did not give the State Department the exceptionally free hand he permitted the Pentagon. He turned down Cordell Hull's proposal, after Pearl Harbor, that the Secretary of State participate in the President's war councils, particularly those involving diplomatic matters. Indeed, the Secretary of State's plea to be taken along to international summit conferences is one of the most poignant notes in all the literature of World War II. Only once, at the Quebec Conference of August 1943, did Secretary Hull attend a wartime summit meeting outside the United States; and even there he was not brought into the discussion by the Anglo-American Chiefs of Staff on the occupation of Germany. As a result, Roosevelt was his own quarterback. When on occasion he threw the ball to the Secretary of State, the latter was apt to be taken by surprise. By early 1942, a working division of labor had developed. FDR would be occupied with the JCS and with Allied political and military leaders in fighting the war; the Department of State would handle the more routine aspects of foreign relations and would work out the plans for the postwar settlement. The enunciation of higher aims in the struggle, FDR reserved to himself.

It is not surprising therefore that when President Roosevelt made his announcement of unconditional surrender as his war aim at the Casablanca Conference in January 1943, he had not threshed it out with the JCS or the Secretary of State. We know now that this momentous announcement did not come to him out of the blue—an impression he delighted in giving to the press on such occasions along with a flourish of his familiar long cigarette holder. The origins and the impact of the formula will long be debated. Here I should like to emphasize that the announcement was entirely consistent with his approach to war and peace and with the circumstances of the turn of the year 1942. Unconditional surrender, he stressed at the time, did not mean the destruction of the peoples of Germany, Italy, and Japan, but the destruction of the evil philosophies that had taken hold in those lands. There must be no compromise—no deals—with those who fomented war.

In effect this meant that a wedge must be driven between the enemy governments and their people—a moral offensive must be waged along with the fighting in the field. What he was offering was a simple dramatic slogan to rally the Allies for victory and to drive home to friend and foe that this time there would be no negotiated peace and no "escape clauses" offered by another Fourteen Points. This time the foe would have to admit he was thoroughly whipped.

We may conjecture that there were special circumstances at the time that reinforced his reading of World War I experience. In particular, the formula might reassure the Russians, disappointed in the delay of a second front in Europe, of the determination of the Western Powers to wage a fight to the finish with Germany. Also, since Pearl Harbor, he had been concentrating on defensive objectives of U.S. policy—essentially the security of the Atlantic and Pacific Oceans. By the time of Casablanca these objectives had been largely secured, and the President may have leaped ahead in his thinking, impatiently, to the peace conferences that would follow a clear-cut victory, at which he could appear, uncommitted, to emulate the purposes, while avoiding the mistakes, of President Wilson.

The unconditional surrender formula is as important for what it did not set forth as for what it implied. Significantly, the President did not set forth here as his war aim the objective of restoring the balance of power in Europe and Asia. This was never his stated objective in the war. Nor was he concerning himself here with the terms of the peace settlement. On the contrary, from the beginning of the war he spoke— as we have seen in his Arsenal of Democracy speech—of the folly of a negotiated peace with the Nazis. And from the beginning he wanted to postpone territorial and political settlements with the Allies until after the war. Indeed, in May 1942, he had intervened during Anglo-Russian treaty negotiations to oppose a guarantee of territorial concessions to the Soviet Union, even though at the time Churchill was willing to yield to the Soviet desire. Note that about the same time he had been willing to toss the Soviet Union a strategic bone—a promise for an early second front—he had not been willing to compromise the political settlement after the war.

The formula appears consistent, too, with his emerging views on an international security system after the war. Interestingly enough, and it may be more than coincidence, a recommendation for unconditional surrender that was brought to his attention shortly before the Casablanca Conference had been arrived at by a subcommittee of the State Department in the course of its own study of postwar organization for peace. In 1942 Mr. Roosevelt had been thinking of an armed alliance of big powers—"sheriffs" to keep order during the transition from war to peace, but in 1943 he definitely gave his support to a United

Nations organization. Certainly the President later openly called unconditional surrender the first step in the substitution for the old system
of balance of power a new community of nations. Whatever reason
bore most heavily with him in January 1943, unconditional surrender
promised to allow him to come to the peace settlement with his own
hands unbound by either enemies or allies, to keep the alliance in
war unfettered by political deals, and to set the stage for molding a
new environment of international relations after the war.

From Casablanca onward the President strove to achieve unconditional surrender and the establishment of a United Nations. For the
American military staff, unconditional surrender was to serve essentially as a military objective, reinforcing its own notions of a concentrated, quick war. Winning the war decisively obtained top priority.

For his part, the President in 1943–44 concerned himself with
cementing good relations with the Allies. The Grand Alliance must be
brought through the war intact, converted for peace purposes, and
housed in the United Nations. With the British, the close partners, this
meant seeing to it that somehow their notion of a cross-Channel operation was reconciled with that of the Americans. With the Russians, it
signified continued aid and the earliest possible establishment of a
second front in Europe. As a result, FDR fought a coalition war without
coalition politics in the narrow sense. The compromise nature of Allied
strategy, as it emerged from the great midwar conferences, stemmed in
considerable measure from his influence, as growing American power
in the field strengthened his hand at summit meetings. More and more
his attention at the conferences was taken up with the discussion of
the United Nations organization. Meanwhile, as from the beginning
of the conflict, he did nothing to jeopardize domestic public opinion or
bipartisanship.

During midwar, he followed his policy of postponing specific
political adjustments with the Allies and also sought to avoid American
involvement in postwar Europe's politics. From the beginning he did
not feel the American people would support a prolonged occupation in
Europe. Nor did he want American troops in Europe permanently.
He feared lest the United States be drawn into Europe's complex
wrangles and trouble spots—into "Pandora's box," to use Cordell
Hull's phrase. This concern came out sharply in his discussion with the
JCS, enroute to the Cairo Conference in November 1943, on the zones
of occupation in postwar Germany. As he told the JCS, "We should not
get roped into accepting any European sphere of influence." The British
had proposed dividing Germany into three zones, of which the United
States should take the southernmost. He objected to taking the southern zone lest the United States thereby become involved in a prolonged

task of reconstituting France, Italy, and the Balkans. "France," he declared, was "a British baby." It was at this time that he went so far as to suggest that the northwest zone be extended eastward to include Berlin and that the United States take over that zone. "The United States," he stated, "should have Berlin." Significantly, the President added that, "There would definitely be a race for Berlin. We may have to put the United States Divisions into Berlin as soon as possible." With a pencil on a National Geographic Society map he quickly sketched the zonal boundaries as he envisaged them, putting Berlin and Leipzig in the big American zone—one of the most unusual and hitherto little noticed records of the entire war. Later, in February 1944, he resorted to the jocular tone he sometimes used to get his point across to Churchill: "Do please don't ask me to keep any American forces in France. I just cannot do it! I would have to bring them all back home. As I suggested before, I denounce in protest the paternity of Belgium, France, and Italy. You really ought to bring up and discipline your own children. In view of the fact that they may be your bulwark in future days, you should at least pay for the schooling now." Eventually reassured by readjustments with the British in the zonal boundaries and lines of communication, the President broke the deadlock in September 1944 at the second Quebec Conference, and accepted the southern zone.

FDR's methods worked well in midwar; his main objectives seemed well on the road to realization. By Teheran the blueprint of quick, decisive military victory in Europe had finally been agreed upon by the Russians, the British, and the Americans, and the Allies had also agreed on the principle of a United Nations organization.

Teheran was the high point of the President's war leadership. He had met with Stalin face to face for the first time in the war and, as he put it, had "cracked the ice." The personal relationship he had enjoyed with Churchill might henceforth be extended to Stalin and, as we know, he had great faith in his ability to handle face-to-face contacts. So encouraged was he that in early March 1944 he commented:

> On international cooperation, we are now working, since the last meeting in Teheran, in really good cooperation with the Russians. And I think the Russians are perfectly friendly; they aren't trying to gobble up all the rest of Europe or the world. They didn't know us, that's the really fundamental difference. . .
> And all these fears that have been expressed by a lot of people here—with some reason—that the Russians are going to try to dominate Europe, I personally don't think there's anything in it. They have got a large enough "hunk of bread" right in Russia to keep them busy for a great many years to come without taking on any more headaches.

In June 1944 the Western Allies landed in Normandy and the Russians began to drive from the east in a giant nutcracker squeeze that promised to crush Germany quickly; in August the Allied representatives met at Dumbarton Oaks to spell out further their ideas on the international organization to keep the peace. By the time of the second Quebec Conference in September FDR could look forward with confidence to ending the war in Europe, gathering momentum to wind up the struggle with Japan, and getting on with the business of peace. Military strategy and national policy seemed to be well meshed; indeed, military strategy, in effect, was national policy in midwar.

II

In the final months of FDR's war leadership the picture changed and the problems multiplied. It is this period, more than the other war periods, that critics of his leadership have dealt with most harshly. The full impact of the President's methods and policies began to be felt even as the Allied armies overran Europe and fought their way into the heart of Germany. The demands of a policy of total victory and of total peace began to conflict. Never was his leadership more necessary; never was it more fitful.

As the strategy unrolled in the field and the American staff strove to end the war swiftly and decisively, Churchill, wary of the swift Soviet advance in eastern and central Europe, wished Western strength diverted to forestall the Soviet surge and the war steered into more direct political channels. The President, who had so often sided with the Prime Minister in the past, would not go along. Many reasons may account for the President's refusal to change course—for example, his desire to get on with the war against Japan—a compulsion he could never forget, and his desire to get on with the peace. What part, if any, the state of his health played, we shall never be able to measure precisely. But it is clear by 1945 the Commander-in-Chief was caught in a political dilemma. He was disturbed by the Soviet Union's efforts to take matters into its own hands and to put its own impress on the political shape of postwar Europe. As he had gauged domestic opinion, however, he had to fight a quick and decisive war. For to Americans war was an aberration—an unwelcome disturber of normality, a disagreeable business to be gotten over with as quickly as possible: "thrash the bullies and get the boys home" was the American approach. Moreover, the President's policy for peace centered in an international organization to maintain the peace not in reliance on the balance of power. To achieve this aim he had to take the calculated risk of being able to handle Stalin and keep the friendship of the USSR. In the event, American national policy in the final year placed no obstacles in the way of a decisive ending of the European conflict. The President did not choose to use for immediate political purposes the military power the United States had built up on the Continent. In the absence of political instructions to the contrary, the American military forces kept at the task of ending the war as quickly as possible.

It is one of the ironies of history that President Roosevelt, pragmatist that he was on most issues, should go down as almost inflexible on the Russian issue. To the end, he refused to use lend-lease as a bargaining weapon, or the armed forces as "levers for diplomacy"—to use Herbert Feis's apt phrase, vis-à-vis the Soviet Union. Nevertheless, Roosevelt's last exchanges with Stalin in March and April 1945—over the Polish problem and the negotiations for the surrender of German forces in Italy—were most sharp. His last message to Churchill, written an hour before his death, expressed the optimistic hope that the Polish problem, like others with the Soviet Union, would also pass and that the course toward the Russians had so far been correct, but at the same time urged firmness.

Ironically, too, in the final period, when winning the war decisively and establishing the United Nations—his two main goals—were clearly in sight, his dilemmas were piling up. And weaknesses in his leadership began to show up, along with growing divergences within the coalition he had tried to preserve and shape for larger postwar purposes. Immediate and harsh political problems were rising in the liberated countries of Europe for which his two main objectives provided no ready solution; the presence of armies and power—not principle—threatened to set the conditions of the peace.

Against this background, the much-debated conference of Yalta must be regarded not as the cause but as the symptom of the loosening bonds of the coalition. Yalta brought together three great powers with divergent approaches to the fundamental problems of war and peace. The common danger that had held them together was fading, the political declarations and principles to which the Allies had subscribed —notably the unconditional surrender formula—were beginning to show weaknesses as binding links. Military strategy as a bond of unity was proving a thin cement. Great Britain was growing weaker; the United States and the Soviet Union relatively stronger.

Yalta marked the growing intrusion of problems of victory and peace, the disunity of the West, and the emergence of the Soviet Union as a world power. The American military were conscious of the Soviet rise and troubled by it. Even before Yalta they were stiffening their stand in dealings with the Soviet forces in the field and calling for a *quid pro quo*. But they were also conscious that the war was not yet over in Europe—the Battle of the Bulge was fresh in their minds—and that the final campaigns against Japan were still to be fought. As their

Pacific drives had picked up momentum, China had declined in their plans against Japan and they wanted Russia as a substitute. Following military advice, Roosevelt's immediate objective at Yalta was to get the Russians into the war against Japan as soon as possible; his long-range objective remained—to come out with a working relationship to prevent another world catastrophe. This time, however, he had to pay a price—and that price was a breach in his policy of postponement.

All in all, Yalta marked an important transition. The balance of power in and out of the coalition had shifted without the full realization by the West—or by its leaders—of what the shift meant. The struggle between the West and the Soviet Union was beginning.

The growing disparity in power among the Allies as the war entered its final stages was not inconsistent with FDR's military policy so long as the enemies were beaten decisively. But it did raise serious problems for his political policy. From the beginning his political strategy rested on the survival of the United Kingdom, China's recognition as a great power, and the cooperation of the Soviet Union. In the closing months of the war the basic props of his larger political strategy began to reveal weaknesses. Britain was strained; Russia's cooperation was beginning to be questioned; China had been largely bypassed in the war and Roosevelt had become disillusioned with trying to make China a great power in the near future. At Malta on 2 February 1945 he told Churchill that he now believed "three generations of education and training would be required before China could become a serious factor." Neither FDR's military nor his political strategy was able to arrest the decline of the alliance as victory approached. Gaps began to open between his military strategy and his larger political goals. His political policy was not tuned to deal with what scholars have called the "middle range" of political problems that emerged between war and peace. Nor was he prepared to fill with American power the vacuums in Europe and the Orient that Allied strategic policy, intent on decisive military victory, had helped create.

III

In retrospect, it is apparent that President Roosevelt was not infallible. Before the war was over, his policies of concentrating on military victory and of laying the groundwork for a new postwar structure of international relations began to conflict and he had to yield on his policy of postponement. As we have seen, it is incorrect to say he had no political objectives. His political objectives remained general—a mixture of idealism and practicality, of optimism and reality. Flaws began to show up in his policies toward the USSR as well as toward China. He underestimated Soviet political ambitions. Certain policies introduced by the President in the early phases of the war were probably held too long and too rigidly—notably the generous lend-lease policy and the unconditional surrender concept. The limitations of unconditional surrender as a political formula began to show up in the last year of the war when the time had come—perhaps was long overdue—to replace a common war aim with a common peace aim.

No appraisal of FDR's failures and successes as a war leader would be complete without considering his attitude toward war and peace and America's place in world affairs. He saw war and peace in different compartments and as distinct phenomena. He did not appreciate that warfare in the twentieth century was undergoing a revolution, and that distinctions between war and peace were becoming blurred. Although FDR could wear his military hat jauntily, he disliked war intensely. Like Wilson, drawn into a conflict he did not seek, he expanded his war aims to accord with the great costs he knew it would involve. Not wanting American involvement in the feuds of Europe or the wrangles of Asia, he converted the war into a crusade for remaking the entire environment, if not the structure, of international relations. With the entry of the United States, he lifted the struggle, begun with the upsetting of the balance of power in Europe and Asia, into a world conflict against aggression and evil. Those who fomented war were evil; those who joined to end it would be purged. This view of the nature of war colored his thinking on the way the war was fought and on the peace to come. The driving purpose behind FDR's war policy was to create an instrumentality for peace as part of the conclusion of the war. He laid the foundations of a structure for international security intended to provide against the problems and dangers of the future; unfortunately the more urgent issues of the critical present still remained. He was willing to give the Soviet Union a chance to work out its problems and join with other nations in a new international security system. It is doubtful, however, that he really understood Marxist-Soviet politico-military strategy any more than did most of his generation.

He fought a war on two levels—one military, the other political. He fought the war as a pragmatist and as a crusader. It is incorrect to say he was oblivious to the political—that is a myth. It is also incorrect to believe that he had a well-worked-out, coherent military strategy of his own. He can be accused of not meshing the two closely.

He left his country military victory, power, and a vision. His use of power to achieve national policy was most successful during the war; his greatest success, harnessing power to military victory. His use of power to avert war before Pearl Harbor was not successful. To harness military power to a new international political order still remained his dream at death. His very success in war has led to the sharpest criticism of his war leadership—overconcentration on military objectives.

Once committed to the struggle, FDR set no brake on the waging of war and on the achievement of victory—total and complete. He set no limit on its strategic escalation. Whether he could have done so, once we were fully committed in Europe and against Japan, will remain a question for theorists of war. It appears more and more that the decision to develop the atomic bomb was the decision to use the bomb. Roosevelt began by waging a limited war in the Pacific. That struggle refused to stay limited. It almost caught up with the European war as American services vied with each other and the Allies began to compete for a place in the victory procession. It is ironical that the atomic bomb, whose development he fostered as a deterrent weapon against Germany, was used in the war against Japan and remains a fundamental element in the uneasy equilibrium of the postwar world. It is ironical that the power he generated and planned to dissipate has done as much to contain Communism as anything he had hoped for in the way of a new order.

The war-time President linked national with international security and staked all on the United Nations, as Wilson had on the League of Nations. Roosevelt had set as his political goal a new concert of power, not old-fashioned balance of power. He refused to the end to use military power and negotiate from strength to force the Soviet Union into a new international harness. Such an approach represented to him the very antithesis of the world he sought and furthermore might make the USSR retreat to isolationism. He was playing for bigger stakes and for the longer haul. He did not want to foreclose the future by mortgaging the present. To the end he was trying to avoid Wilson's mistakes. He still wanted to appear uncommitted at the peace conference. But the world of 1945 was not the world of 1919. A new colossus was already on the move in Europe. The strange ally was no longer shackled by the common bonds of danger any more than it was checked by FDR's vision of the future. At the close of his term as Commander-in-Chief, FDR's strength rested on two pillars—moral force and military power. He refused to make a virtue of power. He thereby laid himself open to the charge of relying too heavily on the power of virtue.

What, then, may we conclude about Franklin Roosevelt the war leader? His strength as a war president arose from many factors—the full powers residing in the Presidency, his long experience in that office, his dominant, persuasive personality, the mighty war machine he generated, and above all, his position as "arbiter in international affairs," as active but disinterested leader at the summit. He kept a firm, if outwardly loose, hold on the reins of national policy. Preoccupied with the mistakes of Wilson, when he put on his military hat he kept one eye on the domestic political front, the other on the postwar world. He was an extremely active and forceful Commander-in-Chief —one of the most active in American history. If at times the Commander-in-Chief yielded to the politician and at others to the statesman, he fought a nonpartisan war aimed at a nonpartisan peace. As a Commander-in-Chief and politician-in-chief he was highly successful.

He was a great war president but his greatness lay neither in the field of grand strategy nor of statesmanship. His greatness lay, rather, in rallying and mobilizing his country and the free world for war and in articulating the hopes of the common man for peace. He welded a great war alliance and managed to hold it together long enough to convert it to peaceful purposes. Without his wartime drive, it is doubtful that the United Nations organization would have come into existence. His war leadership demonstrated that the structure of the American Government, and of the office of the President, in the hands of an active and forceful Commander-in-Chief, was capable of meeting the greatest test in war the nation had yet faced. Though his power as war president came to rival Hitler's, he remained a champion of democratic ideals. The United States, he warned, would have to accept responsibility along with power on the world stage, but power would have to be joined with morality.

With all its cruel dilemmas, war abroad gave him the greatest challenge of his Presidency—an opportunity to project the vision of America on the world stage. He deliberately gambled all on a new international order that would guarantee peace and achieve the noblest aspirations of mankind. The war he waged was part of the never-ending struggle of mankind to banish war. He fell, as did Lincoln and Wilson before him, in the crusade he was waging. He was thus Commander-in-Chief in a very special sense. Whatever his mistakes in World War II, it is in the context of the struggle for his ideals that he largely staked his place in history.

Franklin Roosevelt had really fought three wars—the war against Germany, the war against Japan, and the war to end war. He had won the first two decisively. Had he really lost the third? Or had the war partners made a "good start on the road to a world of peace," as he reported to Congress after Yalta? Had he pointed succeeding generations in the correct direction? Were the years of tension and crisis that followed World War II only a low point in a world that moves "by peaks and valleys, but on the whole the curve is upward"—as he viewed human progress? Was the "fox" and the "artful dodger" really an innocent abroad? Or, in the long run, will the pragmatist and the idealist prove more realistic than his critics? The experience of your generation may help to supply the answers that await the judgment of history.

LOUIS MORTON

The assertion has been made frequently that during World War II Japanese military and naval staffs were inflexible, that, unlike the Allies, they were not able to adjust themselves to changed conditions. Their strategy, many believed, was fixed on the highest level without much awareness of the realities of the battlefield and was followed blindly by subordinates. This trait was regarded by Americans as characteristic of Japanese national life and of the Japanese military system. Contrasted to American flexibility in planning and rapid response to new situations, this view was often advanced as proof of the inherent virtues of the democratic system and the superiority of the American over the Japanese way of life. That the Japanese lost the war was for many the final proof of Japanese inflexibility and rigidity.

Gratifying as this view is to national pride, it hardly accords with the facts. It is true that Tokyo kept a closer control over commanders in the field than did Washington, but Japanese commanders had fairly wide discretion in the execution of strategy, made their own operational plans, and on occasion initiated change in orders from Tokyo when local conditions warranted. Army and Navy general staffs in Tokyo were as fully informed of the situation in the field as their American counterparts as a result of reports, informal correspondence, and personal visits. On the basis of this information, the Japanese High Command adjusted its plans, modified its strategy, drew up tentative military plans for the future, and coordinated these plans with other governmental agencies concerned with the prosecution of the war.

In exceptional circumstances, when a basic shift in strategy or what the Japanese termed "war-direction" was involved, the Japanese military could initiate a full-scale review of national policy on the highest governmental level, including even the Emperor himself. One such occasion came in September, 1943—midway in the war—after a series of dramatic reverses in the Solomons, New Guinea, and the Aleutians. Clearly foreshadowed was an Allied offensive of major proportions. How the Japanese High Command reacted to this situation, the appraisal it made of Japan's plight, and the measures it proposed to meet the threat furnish an excellent case study of Japanese staff work and planning on the highest level and an opportunity to examine the structure of the High Command itself.

THE JAPANESE HIGH COMMAND

Under the Japanese constitution, the civil and military functions of the Government were sharply separated. Only in the person of the Em-

SOURCE: From the U. S. Naval Institute Proceedings, LXXXV (February, 1959), 52–64. Copyright 1959 by the United States Naval Institute. Reprinted by permission.

peror himself, who had neither authority nor responsibility, were the two functions joined. Below him were two clearly delineated lines of authority—one through the Cabinet to the civil agencies of the Government, the other through the service chiefs to the military forces. Each was independent of the other and each acted in the name of the Emperor. In actual practice, however, the military exercised a veto over the civil government by virtue of the fact that the War and Navy Ministers, who were active officers nominated by the services, could force the resignation of the Prime Minister and the formation of a new Government simply by resigning, for no Cabinet could exist without the War and Navy Ministers.

Supreme Command of the military in Japan was vested in the Emperor and exercised in his name jointly by the Chiefs of the Army and Navy General Staffs. These officers were virtually the most important figures in Japan. As chiefs of their respective services, they controlled the armed forces, exercised a powerful influence over the War and Navy Ministers, and had direct access to the Emperor without reference to the Prime Minister or the Cabinet. No important decision affecting the size or employment of the military forces in Japan could be made without their consent. So great was their prestige and political power and so unlimited their capacity for independent action that they could virtually commit the nation to a course of action.

To provide effective direction and cooperation between the Army and Navy in time of war, a separate body known as Imperial General Headquarters was established in November, 1937, after the outbreak of war with China. Imperial General Headquarters was but the Supreme Command under another name. At its head was the Emperor and under him were the Chiefs of the Army and Navy General Staffs. Theoretically, this arrangement provided a unified command, but in actual practice the Army and Navy Sections of Imperial General Headquarters operated independently as separate, co-equal bodies. Strategy and policy were reached by agreement and cooperation, and no single group or individual could force decision.

The Japanese constitution made no provision for the coordination of political and military matters except in the person of the Emperor. To meet this need, the civil authorities and the Supreme Command established by informal agreement the Liaison Conference. The regular members of this Conference were the Prime Minister, the War and Navy Ministers, the Foreign Minister, and the Chiefs of the Army and Navy General Staffs. When necessary, other officials were invited to attend. As an extraconstitutional body, the Liaison Conference had no legal authority and its decisions were merely agreements having no force in law. But by virtue of the authority and official position of its members, agreements reached at the Liaison Conference became, in effect, national policy decisions.

The role of the Emperor was a passive one. Ordinarily he did not participate in the deliberations of Imperial General Headquarters or the Liaison Conference, but was kept informed by his various Ministers and by the service chiefs. But when particularly vital decisions on national policy were formulated, it was necessary to secure the Emperor's consent. Thus arose the institution of the Imperial Conference. This was nothing more than a meeting of the Liaison Conference, with the addition of the President of the Privy Council, in the presence of the Emperor. Its purpose was to inform His Majesty of the issues and of the decisions already reached by his chief advisers. Agreement was always obtained in advance, and no changes were ever made during the course of the conference.

Of all the institutions of wartime Japan, the most powerful was Imperial General Headquarters. Roughly comparable to the U. S. Joint Chiefs of Staff in the military sphere, Imperial General Headquarters exercised a political influence that has no parallel in the American system. And even in the realm of military decision, Imperial General Headquarters differed significantly from the Joint Chiefs of Staff organization. The Army and Navy Sections of Imperial General Headquarters operated independently, each issuing orders to subordinate service commanders. Joint action could be attained only by compromise; no machinery existed to compel interservice cooperation. While this was true also, to some degree, of the U. S. Joint Chiefs, the American system provided a procedure for obtaining interservice agreement that worked in all but exceptional cases. And if these means did not suffice, the President had the authority to make the decision. In this respect, the President was a more potent force than the Japanese Emperor, who had the form but not the substance of power.

There were, of course, real differences between the Japanese system for conducting the war and the American. On the Axis side there was virtually no coordination among the partners and Japan fought her own war in her own way. The military in Japan enjoyed a much greater influence and prestige than did the military and naval forces of the United States, and Japanese generals and admirals exercised considerable political authority in their own right. General Hideki Tojo, for example, was not only Prime Minister but also War Minister and after February, 1944, Chief of the Army General Staff as well. His naval colleague, Admiral Shigetaro Shimada, was at once the Navy Minister and Chief of the Navy General Staff. Furthermore, the Japanese Diet was in no sense comparable to the American Congress, and its control over military policy and appropriations was virtually nil.

Neither the Japanese nor the American system provided a truly joint staff, but there was not in the Joint Chiefs organization as clear a delineation between the services as there was in Imperial General

Headquarters. In the former, joint plans and action were achieved through a committee system; in the latter, each service prepared its own plans and then consulted with the other. Deadlocks were resolved by compromise, but since the Army was the more powerful of the services, it usually had its way where important Army interests were at stake.

In the area of unified command, the Americans—it would be more correct to say Allies—were far ahead of the Japanese. It is true that neither side attained a unified command on the highest level, except through the Chiefs of Staffs, but the Allies came much closer to this goal than the Japanese. At Rabaul, for example, the Japanese had two co-equal commanders. Admiral Mineichi Koga, commander of the Combined Fleet, could order the Navy commander at Rabaul to take a certain action, but he had no control over the corresponding Army commander, General Hitoshi Imamura. That officer's orders came from the Army Section of Imperial General Headquarters, and it was there that a coordinated plan had to be drawn.

The Japanese system had its shortcomings—as did the American system—but lack of flexibility and responsiveness to change were not among them. In an emergency, Imperial General Headquarters was capable of swift and drastic action, unencumbered by the restraints of Congressional investigation or Presidential authority. This was demonstrated dramatically in December, 1941, when the Japanese put into execution their plan for war. The adjustment and revisions made in this plan during the months that followed give no evidence of inflexibility. In March, 1942, Imperial General Headquarters extended its objectives and broadened its strategy. Later, after the defeats at Midway and Guadalcanal, it altered and narrowed its strategy to bring into harmony means and ends. Each time it made an exhaustive study of the situation and based its new "operational policy" on a realistic estimate of its own and the enemy's resources.

By September, 1943, twenty months after Pearl Harbor, Japan had reached a critical stage in the war. General MacArthur and Admiral Halsey had made serious inroads on the defenses of the strategic Southeast Area in the Solomons and eastern New Guinea, and showed every intention of continuing a drive from the south. In the north, American forces had taken Attu in May, 1943, and in July forced the Japanese to evacuate Kiska. And in the Central Pacific, American forces were becoming increasingly active. Only recently, fast carriers of the Pacific Fleet had struck Marcus Island, Wake, and Japanese bases in the Marshalls, and American forces had occupied islands in the Ellice Group, south of the Gilberts.

The Axis situation in Europe was no more encouraging. The German offensive in Eastern Europe had stalled and there was every sign of a

Soviet counteroffensive. In the Mediterranean, the Allies had followed up their success in North Africa with the landing in Sicily and, on September 8, Italy had surrendered. Any hopes the Japanese may have entertained for a negotiated settlement with Great Britain and the United States, based on a stalemate in Europe, now vanished. It was in these circumstances that Imperial General Headquarters undertook to reassess Japan's position in the global conflict, to appraise realistically the prospects for the future, and to adjust strategic plans to the new situation.

STRATEGIC PLANNING

The review of Japan's position in midwar opened early in September, 1943, with a comprehensive "Estimate of the Enemy Situation." Forecasting the enemy's intentions, even when his strength, dispositions, and capabilities are known, is usually little more than an educated guess. But this is a necessary part of military planning, and the Japanese planners at Imperial General Headquarters did not go far off the mark. During the remainder of 1943 and through 1944, the Allies, they thought, would make a concerted effort to capture Rabaul and other strategic positions in the south and Southwest Pacific, while opening offensives in Burma, Sumatra, and the Indian Ocean area. If the Allies succeeded in taking Rabaul, they would almost certainly drive next for the Philippines and the Mandated Islands. Oddly enough, the Japanese did not expect a "large-scale enemy offensive" in the Central Pacific that year because of the weakness in carrier strength. Just what the Japanese meant by a "large-scale" offensive is not clear. Certainly it did not mean operations against the Gilberts, Nauru, Wake, or Marcus, for these were definitely considered possible Allied moves to be undertaken in concert with the offensive against Rabaul. The Allies could be expected also, if the opportunity offered, to invade the Kuriles and the Netherlands East Indies, to disrupt Japanese sea communications, and to bomb the occupied areas and even Japan itself. Everywhere they turned, the Japanese faced the prospect of actual or potential Allied offensives. "In short," General Hikosahuro Hada, Deputy Chief of the Army General Staff, predicted gloomily, "the situation will develop steadily toward the decisive stage and we are rapidly approaching a crucial stage which may well decide the fate of our country."

The Japanese estimate of Allied forces gave little cause for optimism. "Front-line" strength they estimated at 23 divisions and 2,500 planes; total strength, including reserves, at 70 to 80 divisions and 6,000 aircraft. The rate of increase of these forces depended, the Japanese recognized, on a variety of factors: the situation in Europe, shipping, and U. S. production. But even assuming the Allies gave first priority to the war against Germany, the Tokyo planners reckoned that the Allies would have 4,000 aircraft and 35 divisions available for operations against Japan at the end of 1943. A year later, this total would have jumped to 7,000 aircraft and 60 divisions, assuming a shipping capacity of four to five million tons.

The main naval strength of the Allies, the Japanese knew, was concentrated in the U. S. Pacific Fleet operating out of Pearl Harbor. The nucleus of this fleet, they estimated correctly, consisted of about six aircraft carriers, fifteen battleships, and fifteen cruisers, organized into several forces. In addition, separate task forces, including ten converted aircraft carriers, were believed to be operating in the Alaska-Aleutians area and in the waters off Australia.

Japanese estimates of U. S. capability for the production of aircraft carriers showed a healthy respect for American industry. By the end of 1943, they estimated, the United States would have twelve carriers; at the end of the following year, eighteen. But it would be safer, the Japanese planners thought, to figure on a more rapid build-up of carrier strength by the United States than the number currently estimated.

Allied submarines, which were responsible for the bulk of their shipping losses, the Japanese placed at about 100. Of these, by far the greater number, about 80, were believed to be American; the remainder, British. Operating bases for the underwater craft were correctly located in Hawaii, Dutch Harbor, Alaska, and Ceylon. No mention was made of the Australian submarine base.

When they considered their own resources, the Japanese found little basis on which to predict an early change in the war. Their greatest weaknesses, they recognized, were in aircraft and in shipping, and without these they could not hope to halt the Allied drive, much less open an offensive of their own. The total number of aircraft that would be required by the Army and Navy during 1944, it was estimated, was 55,000, an impossible figure in view of the fact that total Japanese aircraft production in August, 1943, was only 1,360 and in September, 1,470. And even if the Japanese could produce as many as 55,000 planes, the effort would so strain the economy of the nation that it would be impossible to try to match American and British naval forces, or to build up the ground strength to a level adequate to meet a possible threat from the Soviet Union or to initiate large-scale offensive operations in China. But these the Japanese were apparently willing to sacrifice for air power, the Navy insisting only that it had to have special attack and antisubmarine craft.

The shipping problem was no less serious than the shortage of aircraft. Despite the best efforts of the Navy, ship losses had continued to mount. By the end of the year, the Japanese estimated, shipping losses from enemy submarines alone would be 100,000 tons a month. In a period of less than two years, 445 vessels totalling 1,754,400 tons had been sunk and another 414 (2,109,800 tons) damaged. By far the largest toll, over 2,000,000 tons, had been taken by Allied submarines; the action of Allied aircraft accounted for another 840,000 tons.

And there was every reason to expect that the number of sinkings would increase sharply unless drastic measures were taken. Above all else, escort vessels and aircraft were required to reduce the loss of ships, and these could only be obtained by a major effort involving allocations of steel and other natural resources as well as the industrial facilities engaged in other war production. "The Navy," declared Admiral Seiichi Ito, Deputy Chief of the Navy General Staff, "has been devoting all its efforts toward the speedy increase in escort vessels and planes . . . but it has sadly failed to reach the goal desired." In urging a major national effort to meet the problem, Admiral Ito had the strong support of General Hada, his opposite Army number, who called for the concentration of the nation's resources on the production of aircraft and ships. If this were done and if the Army and Navy cooperated closely, said Hada, then it might yet be possible to "crush the enemy counteroffensive and turn the tide of war."

But the production of aircraft and ships would take time. The problem facing the Japanese High Command, therefore, was to gain this time with a minimum loss, to trade space for time on the most advantageous terms. The solution proposed by the planners at Imperial General Headquarters was embodied in the "New Operational Policy." Convinced that the line eastern New Guinea—northern Solomons—Marshall and Gilbert Islands could not be held and was, indeed, on the verge of collapse, they recommended that a new line encompassing the "absolute national defense sphere" be established. Beyond this line there would be no retreat; along it would be built impregnable defenses. And while the Allies fought their way to this line, the Japanese could repair their losses in aircraft and shipping in preparation for a great counteroffensive.

The selection of a new defense line was based on the most careful calculation of Japan's resources and Allied capabilities. Extending from the Kurile Islands southward through the Bonins, Marianas, and Carolines, thence south and west to western New Guinea, the Sunda Islands in the Netherlands East Indies, and finally to Burma, this line comprised the minimum area considered essential for the attainment of Japan's war aims. Possession of this area would give Japan the advantage of interior lines and the raw materials and food she needed to meet military and civilian requirements. Since it corresponded also to the Greater East Asia Co-Prosperity Sphere, its security was an essential prerequisite to the political and economic control of the nations included within the Japanese orbit. Any reduction of the area, or the acquisition by the Allies of bases from which to strike important political and industrial targets within it, were bound to affect seriously Japan's political position and her capacity to wage war.

Based on these considerations, the Japanese planners formulated a strategy whose primary objective was the defense of this vital area. First, in recognition of their inability to hold the existing line in the Southeast Area, they would take a long backward step and establish a more restricted perimeter extending from the Carolines to western New Guinea. Next, they would erect an "undefeatable strategic position" along this new line, establishing advance bases in front of it to keep Allied air power at a safe distance and safeguard the line of communications. Finally, they would build up Japanese power within the absolute defense area, with special emphasis on air power. By utilizing the geographic advantages of this new line and their interior lines of communications, the Japanese hoped they would be able to repulse any large scale enemy offensive and ultimately launch a counteroffensive of their own.

In concrete terms, as enunciated by the Army Section of Imperial General Headquarters on September 15, 1943, this new strategy of "operational policy" would require:

1. Close cooperation with the Navy.

2. Strong delaying action in the Southeast Area. Allied forces advancing in this critical region were to be resisted fiercely and delayed as long as possible. The time thus gained was to be used to build up defenses along the new line from the Banda Sea to the Caroline Islands and to marshal the forces for a counteroffensive.

3. All-out defense in the Southwest Area, the Japanese designation for the region extending from the Banda Sea to Burma. This area was part of the absolute national defense sphere; therefore the complete destruction of any enemy forces seeking to invade the region was absolutely essential to Japan's successful prosecution of the war.

4. Preservation of the *status quo* in China, while increasing pressure against the enemy to destroy his will to fight. In North China, preparations would be made to meet the contingency of Soviet-American cooperation, but no step would be taken that might bring the Soviet Union into the war.

5. Strengthening the defenses of the home islands, the oil regions of the East Indies, and the shipping lanes to Japan. These measures were vital to the conduct of the war and the execution of the new operational policy.

6. Raiding operations deep behind enemy lines in every area.

7. All possible measures or operations that would bring into full play the combined fighting power of the air, ground, and naval forces; in short, any operation that promised success.

THE POLITICAL ESTIMATE

More than a revision of strategy was required to retrieve the losses Japan had suffered since the summer of 1942. A political and economic program to support this strategy was also needed. The basis of this program was a review of Japan's position by the civilian agencies of the Government, and on September 25 this review came before the Liaison Conference.

The meeting of the Liaison Conference opened with an "Estimate of the World Situation," the political counterpart of Imperial General Headquarters' military estimate of the situation. First the Japanese considered the war aims of the Allies. The United States and Great Britain, they were convinced, would be satisfied with nothing less than the complete defeat of Germany and Japan, the United States concentrating on Japan and Great Britain on Germany. The American aim, the Japanese believed, was a world organization in which the United States would be a dominant member; the aim of the English was the preservation of the Empire and the restoration of British prestige and influence.

In the Japanese view, the United States was anxious to end the war quickly and would therefore make an all-out effort at the earliest possible moment, probably in 1944. This effort would be characterized by the full application of America's overwhelming material superiority and by the cooperation of the British, Russians, and Chinese. The main offensive, the Japanese reasoned incorrectly but cautiously, would be made in East Asia. They concluded, therefore, that the United States would do everything possible to induce the Soviet Union to join the war against Japan and throw the weight of her military machine into the struggle for Asia. If this offensive failed or if the United States felt she could not gain a decisive victory over Germany and Japan, the Japanese thought the Americans might be willing to make peace. But the price, they believed, would be such as to leave the Axis Powers too weak to make war and the United States so strong that she could exercise a paramount influence on the policy of both the Axis and the Allied nations for years to come.

The Soviet Union loomed large in Japanese calculations. Peace with the Soviet Union was a basic goal of Japanese policy and a fundamental requirement for the prosecution of the war against the Allies. Fortunately Soviet war aims thus far had favored Japan's desire to remain at peace with the Soviet Union and, so far as the Japanese could anticipate, would continue to do so while the war lasted. Like the British, the Russians desired above all else the defeat of Germany and the recovery of their lost territory. To secure these, the Japanese were certain the Russians would concentrate all their resources in Europe while co-operating with the Americans and British as long as it suited their purpose. The Japanese were under no delusion that the Russian bear had changed its nature and predicted that the Soviet Union would utilize the war to unify the Slavs—an old dream of the Tsars—extend its influence into the Balkans and western Asia, and push its program for world revolution.

The capabilities of each of the Allies to achieve its war aims varied widely, but nowhere could the Japanese find any weakening of the will to fight or any sign of revolt against the political leadership of the nation. The position of President Roosevelt, they thought, would remain secure as long as the war situation remained favorable to the United States, but they thought his actions in 1944, an election year, needed to be watched carefully. Churchill's position was even more solid. Unlike Roosevelt's, it did not depend on optimistic war reports or on the improvement in the hard lot of the English people. The Japanese saw no evidence either that the influence and leadership of Stalin had been shaken in the least by the reverses suffered during the war. His position was considered extremely strong and not likely to change in the near future. The same was true for Hitler.

Realistically, the Japanese measured the capabilities of each nation to achieve its war aims largely in terms of industrial capacity and manpower. By these standards, the United States stood well on the top of the list, despite the limitations of its available manpower. According to Japanese calculations, the United States would reach its peak level of industrial production at the end of 1943. Thereafter, production would level off in all except certain critical war industries, such as aircraft and shipbuilding, where the rate of production would continue to mount. The Japanese did not foresee the development in the United States of any shortages so serious as to force the curtailment of the war production program. Raw materials and food were considered adequate, and even the manpower problem was not so serious as to prevent the United States from expanding its ground army to 123 divisions by the middle of 1944. American naval strength, the Japanese gloomily predicted, would also increase sharply, and in 1945 the United States could be expected to have 37 aircraft carriers and 23 battleships. These were figures that even the most optimistic Japanese could never hope to match. The following year would see a considerable increase in British ground, sea, and air forces, accomplished largely with the help of the United States and the Dominions.

On the basis of their estimate of the aims and capabilities of the Allies, the Japanese political and military leaders attempted to forecast the course of the war down to the end of 1944. From their point of view, there were three major theaters: the eastern front in Europe, the western front, and the Asiatic-Pacific front. In the first, they expected the Russians to continue their offensive and the Germans to withdraw gradually to the line of the Dnieper River and there to hold at all costs. The major effort of the western Allies—England and the United States—would be made in the Mediterranean area, the Japanese believed. The Allies could be expected also to support the Soviet offensive and intensify the air bombardment of Germany in an effort to weaken her ability to wage war. Nor did the Japanese overlook the possibility of an Anglo-American invasion of northwestern Europe sometime in 1944, probably during the spring or summer of the year. Beyond this they made no estimate as to the time and place of the invasion, for they recognized that the solution to these problems would depend largely on the "delicate relationship" between the western Allies and the Soviet Union.

The Japanese were under no illusion about the prospects for a German victory in Europe. That opportunity had been lost, and the best Germany could hope for was to keep the United States and England so engaged elsewhere that they would be unable to open the second front. When and if the Allies invaded, Germany would have to concentrate all its efforts on the destruction of the invading forces, for, in the view of the Japanese, the fate of Germany rested on the outcome of the war in western Europe.

The Japanese were not optimistic either about their own prospects. They fully expected that the United States and Great Britain acting under American pressure would push their advantage in the Far East and in the Pacific, no matter what happened in Europe, in order to defeat Japan at the earliest possible date. In this effort the Allies would utilize their resources to disrupt Japanese sea communications, destroy her shipping, bomb her cities and sources of raw materials, and isolate her by political means. But the immediate military threat, the Japanese believed, lay in the Southeast Area where the Allies (largely the Americans and Australians) had already begun a major offensive. This Allied effort, the Japanese expected, would be intensified during the late fall or winter of 1943 to coincide with large-scale operations in Burma and the Netherlands Indies.

There was one bright spot in this gloomy picture—the Soviet Union. According to Japanese calculations, there was little chance of Soviet intervention in the Far East during the coming year, either as an active participant or as a passive ally of the United States and Great Britain. Moreover the Japanese did not believe that the Russians would allow the Allies, either voluntarily or under pressure, to use Soviet airbases in the Maritime Provinces. This happy condition, the Japanese realized, might change suddenly, but they expected it to last while the war in Europe continued.

On the basis of this careful analysis of Allied war aims, capabilities, and intentions, the political leaders of Japan proposed a foreign policy to match the strategy of Imperial General Headquarters. First among the objectives of this policy was the preservation of peace with the Soviet Union. This was to be achieved in three ways: first, by maintaining Japanese military strength and, if possible, by winning military victories over the United States and Great Britain; second, by adopting positive measures designed to improve friendly relations between the two countries; and third, by exercising restraint but resolution in dealing with the Soviet Union over controversial matters.

To cope with the political offensive being waged by the Anglo-American allies in East Asia, the Japanese decided they must take stronger measures to convince the peoples of Asia that their destiny lay with Japan. The most effective argument, of course, was military victory, but the Japanese could not rely on that. They proposed therefore to secure the voluntary cooperation of the Asiatic people by fair and just treatment of the occupied nations and by propaganda emphasizing the evils of colonialism. The weakness in their argument, the Japanese realized, was the Japanese Army in China. Resistance by the Chungking government would by example encourage opposition to the Japanese everywhere in Asia. A primary aim of Japanese foreign policy, therefore, must be the settlement of the China Incident.

The possibility that Germany and the Soviet Union might suddenly conclude a separate peace treaty was a contingency the Japanese could not ignore. Such a move, they recognized, would undoubtedly have a profound effect on Japan's situation. Therefore, to insure that the effect was favorable and the dangers minimized, the Japanese agreed that they must follow the situation closely and be prepared at the first sign of peace to move in with an offer of mediation. The timing of this offer was considered of the utmost importance by the experts in Japan's Foreign Ministry. It should coincide, they said, with military success in the field, either by Germany or Japan, or with the successful completion of negotiations with Chungking.

Cooperation with Germany was a political rather than a military objective for the Japanese. What they wanted from Germany was war materials and technical information, and for these they were willing to make many concessions. One price they would not pay for this cooperation was a Japanese declaration of war against the Soviet Union. But they could not afford to reject such a proposal outright if it were made. Instead, they hoped to convince Hitler that Germany's interests would not be served by a Soviet-Japanese war. If Hitler insisted and made "final demands," the Japanese agreed that they would stand firm no matter what the consequences. Peace with the Soviet Union was evidently more important to Japan than cooperation with Germany. The political program, in its final form, consisted of six points:

1. Japan will strive to the utmost to prevent the outbreak of war with the Soviet Union, will take the initiative in improving Soviet-Japanese relations, and endeavor to mediate for peace between the Soviet Union and Germany at the proper opportunity.
2. Japan will maintain unremitting pressure against Chungking and will take the earliest possible opportunity to settle the Chinese problem.
3. Japan will take every possible measure to strengthen cooperation with Germany.
4. Japan will win the confidence of the nations and peoples of Greater East Asia and will guide them in order to receive and further encourage their cooperation with Japan's war efforts.
5. Resolute measures will be taken to build up the decisive military capability, especially air power, and a dauntless spirit to face the national crisis will be encouraged in order to bring the total national power into full play.
6. A propaganda effort against the enemy will be conducted under a consistent policy, and will be directed mainly toward propagation of the Axis cause, diffusion of Japan's policy in Greater East Asia, demoralizing our major enemy, the United States, alienation of the United States, Britain, China and the Soviet Union, and helping India achieve her independence.

The political program proposed by the Foreign Ministry and the comprehensive review and forecast on which it was based was accepted by the Liaison Conference of September 25 without dispute. At the same meeting, the assembled political and military chiefs approved the strategic policy presented by Imperial General Headquarters. These two, the military and political programs, were then blended into a single document called the "General Outline of War Direction Policy."

With agreement on a basic policy and a political program and military strategy designed to support that policy, the leaders of Japan were ready to go before the Emperor. His assent would sanctify the decisions already made and give them the powerful sanction of Imperial decree.

THE DECISION—SEPTEMBER 30, 1943

The Imperial Conference that fixed the course Japan would follow during the next year and a half opened at 10 o'clock on the morning of September 30, 1943. Assembled for this meeting with the Emperor, the "August Mind" of Japan, were the highest officials of the government— the Premier and War Minister, Hideki Tojo; the Navy, Foreign Affairs, Finance, Agriculture, and Commerce ministers; the chiefs and deputy chiefs of the Army and Navy General Staffs; the President of the Privy Council, Director of the Cabinet Planning Board, the Minister for Greater East Asia Affairs, and the heads of various government departments. In accordance with custom, Prime Minister Tojo presided.

For most if not all those present at the Imperial Conference, the proceedings offered nothing new. The purpose of the conference was to secure the Emperor's assent to decisions already made, not to present various proposals and policies for his decision. As the personification of national unity and the supreme symbol of Japanese life and thought, the Emperor stood above party and faction. Tradition limited his action to approval of the decisions of his ministers; precedent dictated silence. But by his presence alone, he set upon these decisions a finality and authority that could be achieved in no other way. Thereafter, there was no turning back; only another Imperial Conference could alter or reverse the course approved by the Emperor. This was the significance of the meeting of September 30; it witnessed, in solemn and historic fashion, a major shift in Japanese policy and strategy for the conduct of the war.

General Tojo opened the Conference with a reading of the political estimate adopted at the Liaison Conference of September 25. The Emperor listened gravely; there was no discussion. Next, the Secretary read the proposed "General Outline of the War Direction Policy," including the political, military, and economic measures required to support this policy. Then, with Tojo leading off, each of the more important officials stood up in turn to elaborate on the program and explain to Emperor Hirohito how his department expected to achieve the goals set out for it and pave the way to eventual victory.

Speaking for the Emperor as well as for several of the ministers, the Privy Council President, Yoshimichi Hara, asked a number of penetrating questions. What steps were being taken, he asked, to settle the outstanding issues between Japan and the Soviet Union specifically with regard to the dispute over Sakhalin and in the matter of fishing rights? The Foreign Minister, while admitting the importance of reaching agreement with the Soviet Union, could hold out no promise of any immediate settlement, whereupon Hara observed sharply that delay over minor details should not be permitted to interfere with negotiations. "The people are deeply concerned over the Soviet-Japanese relations," he remarked. "I strongly urge that relations between the two countries be improved promptly so that the people may be put at ease and our armed forces may devote themselves to the prosecution of the Greater East Asia War."

The Privy Council President emphasized also the great importance of aircraft production. In view of the fact that Japanese industry was currently building only about 17,000 planes annually, Hara wanted to know whether the goal of 40,000—the Army had asked for 55,000—was a realistic one. Both the President of the Planning Board and the Minister of Commerce and Industry asserted emphatically that it was, the latter claiming that he even expected to exceed that figure. Still somewhat skeptical, Hara observed dryly that there was a limit to a nation's productivity and pointed to the example of the United States and Germany. But he made it clear that he expected both men to make every effort to reach the goals they had set.

President Hara turned next to the Chiefs of the Army and Navy General Staffs, and the Conference took a sudden, more dramatic turn. What exactly did the term "absolute national defense sphere" mean? he asked. And when this was explained to him he wanted to know whether it would require the abandonment of territory already held by Japanese troops. Assured that it would not, Hara then asked whether this absolute national defense sphere could be held even if the 40,000-plane goal was reached. The Army answer expressed a commendable confidence and a determination to make up in mobility what it lacked in numbers. But Admiral Osami Nagano, Chief of the Navy General Staff, expressed no such confidence. The Navy would do its best, he said, but it could not promise success; too much in war depended upon fortune. Pointing to the failure of German plans in the war against the Soviet Union, Nagano declared: "I cannot predict the outcome of our war with any degree of accuracy."

This pessimistic view, realistic as it might be, came as a distinct surprise. Suddenly the atmosphere of the Conference became tense as everyone waited for the next move. Without hesitation, Tojo stepped into the breach. Japan, he declared, was engaged in a life and death struggle for its very existence. Whatever the future might hold and regardless of Germany's fate, every Japanese subject must carry on, firm in the determination to fight the war to a successful conclusion. In effect, Tojo's statement was a repudiation of Nagano, and the President of the Privy Council tactfully closed the incident with the remark that he was glad to note that Imperial General Headquarters seemed to have ample confidence in its ultimate success. It was on this note that the conference ended at 1530. There is no record that the Emperor spoke once during the entire meeting. His silence gave assent and placed the stamp of Imperial approval on the "New Operational Policy."

The plans so painfully made in September were scarcely put into effect when it became evident that they would have to be revised. Before the end of the year, MacArthur and Nimitz's forces had cracked through the outer defenses of the absolute national defense line and gave every indication of assaulting the line itself at an earlier date than the Japanese had estimated. The hopes for a great counteroffensive in the spring of 1944 were seen to be impossible, and the ambitious program for the production of planes and ships remained still to be achieved. By late December, Imperial General Headquarters had abandoned all plans for an early offensive and had accepted for the first time the possibility of an Allied penetration of the absolute national defense line. Time was running out for the Japanese.

The failure of the "New Operational Policy" should not blind us to the fact that it is often possible to learn as much from our former enemies as from our allies. The comprehensive review by the Japanese of their position in midwar was, perhaps, a futile gesture in view of the overwhelming superiority of American forces, but it should suffice to dispose once and for all of the myth of Japanese inflexibility. In a remarkably short time, the Japanese planners made a fairly correct reading of their own situation and of Allied intentions and on the basis of this review shaped for the nation new goals and a strategy designed to buy the time they so desperately needed. The process by which they arrived at the basic decisions underlying this new policy gives every indication of a high order of staff work by both military and civilian officials and a thorough appreciation of the political and military factors involved in the formulation of national policy. The fact that Japan lost the war should not prevent us from studying with profit a system which was able to produce quickly and efficiently reliable estimates and policy decisions on the very highest level.

28

Dilemmas of American Far Eastern Policy

JOHN K. FAIRBANK

As a consequence of our recent war in Asia we have been beset by one of the greatest crises ever in the conduct of our international affairs. The inescapable questions have been: how may we extricate ourselves from the crisis, and how indeed did we get involved to begin with? In its view of the world, America has faced two ways, toward the Atlantic and toward the Pacific. With respect to the Atlantic powers, our quest was disentanglement; with respect to the Pacific powers, our inclination was entanglement. Turning from the Atlantic world, in our relative weakness and backwardness, we sought respite and independence; turning to the Pacific, in our relative strength and modernity, we sought adventure and domain. American continentalism—the essential thrust of a full century of our history—surged naturally and inevitably to the Pacific. For the greater part of our history, we regarded Europe as our Nemesis, Asia as our opportunity. It would be too much to say that Europe has, in recent years, been our opportunity. But there can be no doubt at all that our Nemesis has been Asia.

We have not fathomed the meaning for us of recent developments in world affairs. We have not too well understood why European colonialism was disestablished in the years after World War II, and what its disestablishment signified. We have not been clear on how we became increasingly embroiled in Asia. Some of our political scientists have argued that we are entrapped in our ideals, that we have been victimized by pursuing a diplomacy that is moral rather than real. But the reasons for our entrap-

SOURCE: *Pacific Affairs*, XXXVI (Winter, 1963–64), 430–37. Reprinted by permission of the publisher.

ment and our victimization are historical as well. Two fundamental and closely interrelated processes have worked their way to fruition at the same time: one was our own sudden access to world leadership with World War II and its aftermath; the second was the Communist triumph in China and the rapid emergence of Communist China as a world power. The fact that the Communist victory in China was, in no small measure, part of the failure of American diplomacy brought confusion to our diplomats, and hysteria— in the so-called McCarthyite era—to our populace.

It is not so much that our diplomacy had until recent years been success-ful; it is that we had never before assumed responsibilities of power that could lead us to failure. Existentialism has no more been part of American diplomacy than it has been part of American life. We have lived instead by our myth of success, and we have shaped reality to its measure. The con-frontation with Asia has robbed us of the myth. We have been compelled to redefine the fundamentals that have governed American diplomacy and life these past two centuries. Such a confrontation has inevitably presented us with dilemmas that seem to be, within the framework of our traditional values, not only tremendous but also far beyond solution.

The dilemmas we have faced in the conduct of our relations with East Asia—particularly with China—are spelled out in the following article by John K. Fairbank of Harvard University. The article is a review essay on Tang Tsou's extensive and highly significant monograph, **America's Failure in China, 1941–1950** *(1963). Professor Tsou has been a member of the Department of Political Science at the University of Chicago and a research associate in the University's Center for the Study of American Foreign and Military Policy. Professor Fairbank is, of course, among the most renowned of our Sinologists. He has been in government service in a variety of capaci-ties, and he is the author of several volumes, including* **The United States and China** *(1948) and, with Edwin O. Reischauer, the imposing two-volume* **History of East Asian Civilization** *(1960, 1965).*

In his review of Tsou's study, Fairbank presents its basic theses and sub-mits them to close analysis. It becomes clear from Fairbank's comments that we made serious errors, of both omission and commission, in our Far East diplomacy during the critical decade of the 1940's. What makes the retro-spect painful is the awareness that our diplomats felt both that they were acting in our best interests and that they had a firm grip of the realities. What makes it almost insupportable is the sense that we are today suffering the consequences of those earlier errors and that, a modern Laocoön, we have been caught in the increasingly tighter coils of an East Asian involvement from which we cannot disengage ourselves. If and when we do, the disen-gagement will have brought us to a substantially new sense of our national ideals and of the conduct of our affairs in the rapidly transforming world of nations. The age of American innocence will, finally and irrevocably, have ended.

Suggestions that the government of South Vietnam should hold elections or otherwise pursue "reforms" in order to win back popular support are reminiscent of the United States' predicament in China in the late 1940's. In both cases the provision of American arms did little to endear the recognized government to the populace; the military build-up outstripped the growth of a stable polity; and skillful enemies exploited the resultant imbalance between the armament and the virtue of the ruling regimes. The complexities of Vietnam and China cannot be reduced to formulae, any more than those of Korea—even though American arms have achieved superior firepower and political frustration in all these three areas. South Vietnam in the 1960's, however, makes China in the 1940's all the more fascinating in retrospect and this lends added interest to a recent study* in which a professor of political science at the University of Chicago analyzes the disastrous gap between America's wartime aims in China and the means that were used. After a brief survey of the Open Door principles and the "traditional" American China policy, Dr. Tsou offers a narrative and analysis of three main phases—the initial policy and programs, conceived when the American war effort began, "to make China a great power"; the American reaction to China's domestic power struggle as it developed during the war, "to bring about a united and democratic China by peaceful means"; and finally the postwar mediation of General Marshall which encountered "the limits of a policy of limited assistance." The Korean War and the rise of Communist China form "the ironic fulfillment."

Dr. Tsou achieves a new level of perspective on Chinese and American attitudes both by his comprehensive grasp of the sources and by his analytic acumen. For example, excerpts from Chiang Kai-shek's diary, published by his son Ching-kuo on his seventieth birthday, make plain that he had no idea of the importance of agrarian reform in China and thought primarily in terms of patriotism and political control. On the U.S. side Dr. Tsou points up American unwillingness either to fight or to relinquish goals obtainable only by fighting—a dilemma inherited from the "traditional" Open Door policy which demanded the preservation of China's integrity but held that American interests in China were never worth a major war.

America's Failure in China builds upon Herbert Feis's *The China Tangle*, the CBI Theater history in three volumes by Romanus and Sunderland, and on other historical studies to present a systematic discussion of policy alternatives, aims, attitudes and assumptions during a succession of periods from 1941 to 1950. Since Dr. Tsou sets forth a vigorous and clearcut thesis with which many students of the subject will

---

* *America's Failure in China, 1941–50* by Tang Tsou with a foreword by Hans J. Morgenthau. Chicago: University of Chicago Press, 1963, 614 pp.

probably agree for some time to come, I should like to forego further praise and rather try to comment on certain major points, as a contribution to further discussion.

1. Whence came the Open Door, with its peculiar and unfortunate combination of demanding China's integrity and yet being unwilling to fight in the Far East? On this point of historical origins, Dr. Tsou seems to overlook the unusual circumstances in which American policy toward China developed during the era of the unequal treaty system from 1842 down to 1922. I refer to the fact that the treaty system as a particular type of international order was established by British naval power, which backed up the British consular establishment and even, for example, protected foreign trade against Chinese piracy. Thus the whole treaty port system in China and Japan in the nineteenth century was maintained by the obvious presence of gunboats, primarily British. Except for the American use of naval power in Perry's opening of Japan and in the less-publicized American naval fiasco in Korea in 1871, the Americans let the British take the lead, fight the two wars that set up the system in China, and thereafter underwrite it by force.

Another feature of the treaty system was the high degree of cooperation in it by the Ch'ing government of China, most evident in the Chinese Imperial Customs Service which supervised the functioning of the system on its commercial side through a joint Sino-foreign administration. Just as the Open Door notes of 1899 were inspired textually by the views of the Maritime Customs, so the second set of notes in 1900 demanding the preservation of China's territorial integrity may best be understood as an American effort to preserve the treaty system at a time of crisis.

In the end, however, the treaty system was underwritten after 1902 by the Anglo-Japanese alliance. Strangely, Dr. Tsou as a political scientist takes no note of the importance of this international power structure based on the British and Japanese fleets (see pages 14, 16, and 238). Rather than describing the balance of power in the Far East as "maintained by a shifting equilibrium among the conflicting policies and interests of the powers," he might well have analyzed the power structure represented by the Anglo-Japanese alliance, against which no combination of other powers could have availed in the period from 1902 to 1922.

Thus the American consecration of the Open Door idea was a luxury made possible by the fact that the United States could rely upon the stable maintenance of the treaty system in China underwritten by a naval power not its own. Once the Anglo-Japanese alliance was ended in 1922, the stable order of the treaty system, already outmoded by the rise of Chinese nationalism, quickly disintegrated. America's "traditional" Far Eastern policy had been compatible with her military isolationism because the balance of power in the Far East had been maintained, on the whole, by Britain.

2. Dr. Tsou makes one important point that deserves underlining by analogy to Europe. He points out that American political policy in World War II, to make China a great power capable of filling the power vacuum that the defeat of Japan would create in East Asia, required a parallel military policy, which originally aimed to make China the Allied base for the attack on Japan. If China had in fact become the Allied base, with National Government armies trained, supplied and battle-hardened in victory, the postwar dominance of the National Government could have been unchallengeable and its political and economic health might also have been far more vigorous. The possible analogy with Churchill's "soft underbelly" proposal for military action in southern Europe, which would create a postwar position of non-Communist strength there, may be worth suggesting. Both against Germany and against Japan the American concentration on winning the war, rather than on war-and-politics, led to the logistically more efficient approach straight at the enemy's heart. I would not attempt to argue with hindsight that this was basically unwise but certainly it is worth noting that both the Balkans and China—areas which later went Communist and into the Soviet orbit—were given low priority in the Allied military effort. It is often remarked that Communism has spread chiefly where Communist armies have gone; conversely, it might be argued that Communism would not have spread where Allied armies had gone. Specifically, if the Stilwell program for Chinese army training had been given high priority, the American influence in Free China after 1941 might have contributed to an improvement of the economic situation and of political morale and behavior, as well as to the performance of the Chinese government and its armed forces.

One of Dr. Tsou's main themes is the way in which the program to make China a great power, toward which Stilwell kept working, was dropped because of American strategic concentration on the naval reduction of Japan. Meanwhile Stilwell's efforts in training ground troops were resisted by Chiang Kai-shek as likely to get beyond his control and also by General Chennault as competing with air power. Dr. Tsou makes the further point that this fiasco in American planning was compounded by the imposition of the "Matterhorn" B-29 project for bombing Japan based at Chengtu. The slender Hump tonnage was extensively diverted to this Strategic Air Force project which aimed with single-minded intensity to hit the enemy, but in the process weakened the China theater. Even when the Japanese offensive in East China in the spring and summer of 1944 had destroyed the advanced American air bases, as Stilwell and Marshall had feared, the B-29's were not diverted to check it until late in the day. This is but one example of many in which the American capacity for fighting and winning the war had the effect of losing the peace. By V-J Day only one-third of the U.S. equipment of the 39-division army modernization program in China had been delivered and the Nationalist forces had not been built up as originally hoped.

3. Dr. Tsou is equally eloquent in painting the American dilemma, now familiar to us in Saigon, of trying to support a power-holder and get him to institute "reforms," both at once. The American support of Chiang in World War II was not accompanied by success in the American effort to make him broaden the base of his political power. Rather, U.S. support enabled him to suppress non-Communist political leaders of the very sort whose participation in the National Government might, in the U.S. view, have strengthened it.

Here it seems to me that Dr. Tsou as an American professor of political science suffers from the lack of understanding of Confucian government which has for so long typified his profession. American disappointment in Chiang Kai-shek, Syngman Rhee, and Ngo Dinh Diem, among others, has been so consistent a story of bad luck that we might well assume that something lies behind it other than personality. All these client rulers, holding power in parts of the "Chinese culture area" of East Asia, have been inheritors (as is Mao today) of the great tradition of Confucian government. As latter-day Sons of Heaven, their political behavior harks back to a different world that Western political scientists have only dimly perceived and even then seldom taken seriously.

The following features typify the Confucian ruler in the Chinese tradition. First, he tends to rule for life and pass his power to his offspring in a dynastic succession. Succession was to be arranged in the bedchamber and not by election of constituents, or any other show of popular opinion. A Son of Heaven had no terminal facilities by which to get out of the job once he had got it.

Secondly, he was an autocrat within the institutional limits set by the fact that his government was not a penetrating one but remained rather superficial to the life of the populace in the villages. Within his sphere, the Son of Heaven exercised arbitrary power even though he had to sanction it by use of the classical ideology.

Third, the maintenance of his power rested not only on the monopoly of military force but also on his maintenance of his ideological superiority in the established system of political thought. Confucian government had a very high ideological component. It was capable of controlling vast masses of people with a minimum of troops and a maximum of indoctrination—witness, for example, the examination system as only one of its institutional devices.

Fourth, one essential element of the ideology was the concept that the emperor brought men to accept his rule by his virtuous conduct and moral influence. The ruler must therefore be a sage and teacher as well as a commander and administrator, a very powerful executive, raised above the common man and accessible only to the "remonstrance" of officials speaking in terms of the accepted ideology.

In this system the ruler's prestige was absolutely all-important, not merely as a weather-gauge of his success as a ruler but also as an actual component of his power. Anything which detracted from his prestige, such as direct criticism, was as serious as outright rebellion. The rule of a Son of Heaven was preserved by the official myth that he was a sage and exemplar in his virtuous conduct without exception, not divine but still more-than-human in his abilities for benevolent rule and correct decision.

It follows from this last point that there could be no such thing as a "loyal opposition" in the Confucian government. Since the ruler held his position by his personal qualities and by the theory of Heaven's Mandate given to his family dynasty, there was no way that he could distinguish between his policies of state and his personal rule. Opposition to a policy was opposition to him and struck at the roots of his power. He could never submit his decisions to review or veto by others, least of all by the common herd. He had to take his position and stand upon it as a superior leader, not as a "servant of the people." He was the One Man at the top, carrying the burden of responsibility and decision, and could not delegate it without forfeiting his title to power. Even in the regimes in China today, popular participation is more symbolic than actual in the decision-making process. Communist "democracy" undoubtedly involves the people in the governmental process but certainly not in the position of final arbiters.

From this traditional point of view, the American demand for "democratization" and the broadening of the base of participation by bringing in other leaders, can only threaten the position of a Chiang or a Diem. On the contrary, such a man is inclined to feel that he must stand forth as an unshakable and all-wise potentate in form, and rely in fact upon the loyalty of persons who depend upon him for their careers and are not potential rivals. For him, it is "rule or ruin," and so he feels he has everything at stake in resisting the misguided American request. Chiang in Chungking could never see how to share his power and still perform his function as the old-style, monopolistic power-holder. Even later, when protected by the Seventh Fleet in Taiwan, he rejected Dr. Hu Shih's suggestion that the Kuomintang modernize its rule by splitting into two parties, one to be in office and one in opposition. Quite the contrary, when Lei Chen tried to form an opposition party, Western style, in 1960, he was jailed for ten years and the opposition party movement has remained suppressed, just as Diem felt compelled to suppress the Buddhists and all other rivals.

Thus the U.S. policy failure in the "Chinese culture area" has resulted from a conflict between modern Western and traditional Confucian concepts of government. This has been a failure in Americans' intellectual grasp, not merely in the fitting of military means to political ends.

4. Dr. Tsou stresses the point that the American government, assuming an unreal convergence of American and Chinese interests, failed to bargain to secure its own aims in China and turned against Stilwell's policy of seeking a *quid pro quo* for American aid. President Roosevelt sentimentally sought to be a "good neighbor" in China, did not demand contractual arrangements as to Chinese performance in return for American aid, and was even bluffed by Chiang's indirect suggestions of a separate Chinese peace with Japan. In the end Stilwell's policy of bargaining was supported, too late for effect, by Marshall, who eventually succeeded him as the chief American representative and held the same view. The whole story points up the skill of Chiang Kai-shek in manipulating Americans.

American incompetence undoubtedly reached its high point with the performance of Ambassador Hurley, a flamboyant individual who was entirely out of his depth and clung steadfastly, says Dr. Tsou, to three grievous errors: first, that the Soviet Union would follow the American lead in China; second, that the Chinese Communists were not hard-core Communists incapable of compromise; and third, that the Chinese Communists lacked popular support. Against these purblind views, the U.S. Foreign Service officers' estimates of the situation were correct. Dr. Tsou believes they went too far in assuming that the Chinese Communists could "be weaned from Moscow or at least encouraged to follow an independent and nationalistic policy," and this possibility may seem unlikely to most observers in retrospect, despite the big change in Sino-Soviet relations in 1963. However, the assumption was originally made in the context of the stated American effort to make China a great power, and this might conceivably have been carried through by the war-time military program as originally planned. On the other hand, this hopeful view does seem in retrospect to have given too little importance to the Chinese need for ideological orthodoxy, evident in the Confucian tradition mentioned above and in the true-believer dogmatism of Peking recently.

5. Dr. Tsou suggests that the line of "coalition government" may have had a parallel origin on the Chinese Communists' side as a manifestation of the united front concept but that its announcement was interwined with the American push in 1944 for Chiang Kai-shek to establish a "war council" and incorporate the Chinese Communists in

the war effort against Japan. Thus Ambassador Gauss advocated a war council on August 30, President Roosevelt having first raised it on July 14 in connection with the request that Stilwell take command in China. Chinese Communist representatives in Chungking came out for coalition government first on September 15 in the People's Political Council and the Party adopted this line formally on October 10, 1944. This parallelism of American and Chinese Communist efforts, each of which has its own backyard, deserves further study and investigation.

6. While Yalta was a compromise with the Open Door idea, it (and the subsequent Sino-Soviet treaty to which Stalin and Chiang agreed in August 1945) gave the Nationalists a good enough prospect to warrant its being welcomed by them. Russian gains would be limited and Russian support of Chinese unity could be expected, on the basis of this settlement in proportion as the National Government of China remained strong. The Yalta deal became a disaster only because Nationalist and American power in China later deteriorated so rapidly. It was the events *after* Yalta which made it a defeat, not the diplomatic agreement itself.

Ambassador Hurley's misconceived efforts (after the recall of Stilwell in November 1944) included several errors—for example, in the name of coalition, trying to force *both* the minor parties *and* the Chinese Communists on Chiang Kai-shek, instead of pushing the minor parties and non-Communist figures separately from the Communists. The result was to keep Chiang and his hard-core Kuomintang leaders aligned against all others and push the minor party and non-Communist groups into the Communist position. Later, in September 1945, when the Chinese Communist position had been weakened by the success of the American air-lift of Nationalist troops back to the former Japanese occupied areas and by the Sino-Soviet treaty between Moscow and Chungking, Hurley failed to press for negotiations in detail. His program of all-out support of Chiang in the name of the war effort discouraged a broadening of the political participation in the National Government. Here again the parallel with recent policy in Vietnam is striking. In the China of 1945, as in the South Vietnam of 1963, American policy slipped into the channel of looking upon politics as a means to win a war, not upon warfare as a means to political ends. Since politics are, one hopes, more permanent and pervasive than war, this is an upside-down approach.

7. In the background of General Marshall's mediation, Dr. Tsou points out that American policy was handicapped by a basic belief that "American interests in China were not worth a war," which was reinforced by the fact that the development of the crisis in Europe and the U.S. confrontation with Soviet power there, made it impossible to con-

template the use of American forces in China. The U.S. demobilization of six million troops in nine months also did not lend support to General Marshall's efforts.

After his almost impeccable display of objectivity Dr. Tsou's treatment of the Marshall mediation period discloses that he too is human, and as a scholar reconstructing the past can also be subject to wishful thinking. Repeatedly he lets himself express the hope that the United States could have got a "complete change" in Chinese leadership and that General Marshall by a different policy could have saved the situation. From all that has gone before, however, the reader is likely to feel that this is most unlikely. Dr. Tsou's discussion of a "program to build up a third force" and reorganize Chinese politics neglects the sadly deteriorating situation of the late 1940's in China as well as the fact that a Chinese regime in power becomes increasingly intent on holding power in proportion as power slips away. How, specifically, might a third force have been supported?

First of all, the rival forces, both Nationalist and Communist, were based on highly articulated and longstanding organizations (both military and administrative), with secret police and a tested inner group of power-holders. In these respects both the CC clique and the Whampoa military clique under Chiang were rather similar to the Chinese Communists. Such attributes of organization and power could not by any stretch of the imagination have been achieved in a short time by the so-called "liberals" or even by the "outside generals" in the Nationalist areas. It must not be forgotten that Chinese politics were not conducted within any framework of law such as Western political scientists are sometimes wont to assume.

How could an American or Chinese policy-maker in the period 1945–49 have advocated a specifically anti-Chiang program and yet avoided the charge of being pro-Communist, or at least subversive—at worst a knave, at best a fool? Dr. Tsou himself points up the fact of the Nationalists' influence in American politics, where Chiang Kai-shek already had many admirers, particularly in the Republican Party out of power—partly as a result of the American war-time propaganda build-up of his image as Free China's leader.

Was not General Marshall's contribution to the American "Failure" mainly that of a doctor receiving a dying patient? *America's Failure in China* vividly portrays his inability to raise the dead. Dr. Tsou, true to his thesis, attributes it to "the two inconsistent elements in the traditional pattern of American policy: the hope to preserve American influence and the incapacity to use force." Perhaps this is over-simple. Granting the doctor's limitations, how about the patient? The situation to be cured was inside the Chinese body politic, largely inaccessible to outsiders. America's failure was only a small aspect of China's general metamorphosis in this period. It must be understood in a broader context than that of the incompatibility of "ends and means" on the American side only. Below this operational level lay the incompatibility of two cultures, which remain incompatible still.

Tang Tsou's judicious summary of the vicissitudes of our China policy in the late 1940's, ending in the final disaster of war in Korea, sets the stage admirably for the study of Sino-American relations as contact-and-conflict between civilizations—an effort that is long overdue and increasingly needed.

29

Eisenhower's Popular Leadership
NORMAN A. GRAEBNER

As the decade of the 1950's recedes into history, it takes on an outline which blurs out the divergent lines by which it proceeded. In the foreshortened perspective of history, it may be seen as the decade of Eisenhower. But what does that mean? Who was the man and what was the age and to what extent did they converge? What were the major problems of the age and how did he meet them? What was his concept of the presidency and how did he articulate this concept in his various policies? What criteria should we use in estimating his success as a leader? And, in terms of those criteria, to what extent did Eisenhower succeed or fail?

These are the questions which Norman A. Graebner, Edward R. Stettinius Professor of Modern American History at the University of Virginia, undertakes to answer in the following essay. In addition to his studies on the ante-bellum and Civil War decades, Professor Graebner has written extensively on the years since World War II. In the essay below, he offers a perceptive appraisal of American politics during the 1950's and of Eisenhower's role in setting its course. This appraisal leaves us with some challenging questions. Will the American democracy be able to choose the leaders it must have to resolve its growing problems? Will these leaders be able to

SOURCE: *Current History*, XXXIX (October, 1960), 230–36, 244. Reprinted by permission of author and publisher.

make the right choices in an age when the margin for error appears to be growing ever more narrow? To what extent did Eisenhower's leadership prepare the nation for meeting the problems of the 1960's? Finally: How did the presidencies of Kennedy and Johnson, respectively, compare with that of Eisenhower: in their concepts of the presidency, the styles in which they conducted their office, their views of what America's major problems were, their success in solving these problems, their relationship with the American electorate, and the way they played their roles as prime leader of the nation?

After almost eight years in the White House, Dwight D. Eisenhower remains the most enigmatic phenomenon in the history of the American presidency. Never has a popular leader who dominated so completely the national political scene affected so negligibly the essential historic processes of his time. Never has a President so renowned for his humanitarian instincts avoided so assiduously all the direct challenges to the status of individual civil rights. Promoted in 1952 as the man best qualified to deal with the Russians, he has resolved or mitigated none of the cold war conflicts which existed when he assumed office. Elected with an unshakable reputation in military affairs, he has met expanding criticism from military experts for his primary decisions on national defense. Heralded as a man of peace, he has entered his last months in office with the United States subjected to humiliating and unprecedented abuse in many areas of the free world.

This evident dichotomy between the popular image of the President and the net gains of his leadership is a simple and disturbing expression of that traditional American philosophy which denies politics a distinct and honorable place in national affairs. American society has long admired personality more than political wisdom, technique more than substance, honesty more than judgment. In a nation where private virtues have become the measure for public as well as private action, the President's transparent goodness and integrity alone have permitted him to escape direct responsibility for the nation's performance at home and abroad.

But Eisenhower as a political phenomenon has also been the product of his times, for he has fit the 1950's like a glove. Prosperity, by 1953, had eliminated most of the direct economic and social challenges of the past and with them the hard contest of power which characterizes politics in periods of stress. This absence of pervading strife has contributed to the nation's complacency and sustained the illusion that good will is sufficient for successful leadership. When the President has failed to achieve what was expected of him, the country has excused the failure as either inconsequential or the product of perversity in others.   For Republican leaders, therefore, the task of maintaining Eisenhower's popularity has consisted largely in keeping the American people mindful of his personal attributes.   Republican editors, whether motivated by the President's obvious good intentions or by the knowledge that for a minority party he has been the greatest asset in over a generation, have given him the most adulatory press coverage in American history.   The principle that right intent is of the essence has permitted White House officials to isolate Eisenhower from his policies.   Indeed, even those Democratic leaders in Congress who have lampooned most things that the administration has done have been careful not to blame the President directly.

That Eisenhower's personality would become the dominant fact of American politics in the 1950's was apparent even before his nomination.   As a purely military figure he was clearly one of the most "available" candidates in the nation's experience.   His widely publicized and genuine personal charm, added to an illustrious military reputation at a time when such a reputation had some relevance to the requirements for successful leadership, made his selection by the Republican convention synonymous with his election to the White House.

Beyond Eisenhower's personal popularity nothing in the 1952 election was clear.   The Republican candidate was not offered to the nation as the exponent of any specific economic faith.   His personal "creed" had been published in the New York *Herald Tribune* prior to his nomination; it avowed a fundamental economic conservatism in which he warned that too much federal intervention would turn "the American dream into an American nightmare."   But such views were not publicized, and Republican campaigning avoided any open clash with established Democratic economic dogma.

EISENHOWER'S APPEAL IN 1952

In electing Eisenhower, the nation demanded nothing more than a kind of independent leadership from a great personality who could rise above the strife of party.   It was this quality in him that brought millions of stay-at-homes to the polls to produce a landslide victory. Eisenhower had not shattered the Democratic party.   Adlai Stevenson, his Democratic opponent, received 3,000,000 more votes than did Harry Truman in 1948.

Dominating the new administration in January, 1953, were representatives of the managerial class—the highly-paid men hired to manage the great industrial and commercial enterprises of the country.   This new class had thrown its corporate power behind Eisenhower in 1952: now it provided two-thirds of his original appointments to cabinet and key administrative posts.   This group interpreted the election as a clarion call to effect a conservative revolution.

Whatever the composition and intent of the new leadership, it could not ignore the twin legacies of the past—the New Deal and the cold war. Republican leaders might speak the rhetoric of free enterprise, but in the essential areas of national action they deviated scarcely from the Truman tradition. Secretary Humphrey could neither dismantle the budget nor halt the continuing inflation. Nor could Secretary Benson return the American farmer to free enterprise. Eventually he would hand out more in agricultural subsidies than any of his Democratic predecessors.

The "New Look" in military policy spelled out the administration's effort to fulfill its promise of tax reduction without endangering the nation. The President made it clear that he was tailoring military power to budgetary considerations. In May, 1953, he suggested a budget cut of $8 billion to achieve "maximum military strength within economic capacities." A healthy and functioning economy, he said, was inseparable from true defense.

Eventually the New Look resulted in the burgeoning emphasis on nuclear weapons, for with such weapons the nation could achieve maximum destructiveness at minimum cost. Military experts warned that the concentration on such weapons limited the nation's strategic flexibility and, in the event of aggression, narrowed the American response to inaction or the mushroom cloud. The President held his own simply by throwing his personal prestige behind the administration's basic military decisions.

Necessity had taken its toll of Republican ambitions. Occasional legislation like Tidelands Oil or the Dixon-Yates contract caught the old spirit, but most bills resembled the remnants of the New Deal. Never had a national leadership been forced to operate so completely outside its established philosophy. This, in essence, spelled out the Republican dilemma. With its deep allegiance to American business, the administration refused to modify or restate its neo-Hooverian beliefs. It talked the language of Main Street, but Main Street does not control elections.

What remained in the Republican arsenal were the alleged failures in Truman foreign policy that had been exploited effectively in the 1952 campaign. For the Taftites in Congress, foreign policy had become the pawn in the conservative revolution with American failures in the Far East attributed to Democratic subversion and even New Dealism itself. Through congressional investigation the Republican leadership in Congress proceeded to delve into everything from past treason and corruption to the decisions of the Korean War.

Eisenhower did nothing to prevent this continuing Republican assault on the Democratic past although Democratic support was essential for the success of his program in Congress. His administration quickly came to terms with Senator Joseph McCarthy of Wisconsin as the price of party unity. In exchange for administration silence the Wisconsin Senator agreed to attack nothing that occurred after January 20, 1953. Eventually the administration itself became implicated in offering the diet of "warmed-over spy" when Herbert Brownell, the Attorney General, resurrected the Harry Dexter White case in 1953. As the administration, under Executive Order 10450, relieved hundreds from the federal payroll, it never made clear the nature of the charges.

Democratic leaders never forced the President to pay the political price for silencing his own right wing for their support in Congress. The foreign aid bill of 1953, for example, passed an almost equally divided House with 160 Democratic and 119 Republican votes. On critical matters of foreign affairs it was the Democratic party that carried the administration's program. These Democratic votes, for which nothing was required, permitted Eisenhower to escape the internal warfare of his party.

THE NEW REPUBLICANISM

Sharp Republican reverses in November, 1953, demonstrated that the party leadership had not found a satisfactory formula. Republican chairman Leonard W. Hall admitted, "There is no question about it—as of today we are in trouble politically." To liberal Republicans there was an answer. The party required essentially a restatement of its philosophy that would form a better compromise between the past and present. Jacob K. Javits of New York suggested that liberal Republicanism contained the balance that would meet the challenge of American politics. "Republican progressives," he wrote in *The New York Times Magazine Section* of November 15, 1953,

> subscribe whole-heartedly to the principle of individual freedom and to the idea of an economic system of competitive, private enterprise functioning with government help and cooperation rather than under government domination. But they also hold that belief in free enterprise does not eliminate a wide area of activities in which government can and should protect the individual's welfare by providing him with greater opportunities for social improvement than he could otherwise obtain.

Eisenhower grasped at the new formula. The government, he explained, believed in a program that was liberal with respect to public needs but conservative in matters of finance. In his message of January, 1954, he promised the business community that it would be expected to meet the basic need of an expanding economy. But the government, he added, would face the issues of welfare, social security, health, education and housing. "Banishing of destitution and cushioning the shock of personal disaster on the individual," he said, "are proper concerns of all levels of government, including the federal government."

Republican writers such as Arthur Larson, author of *A Republican Looks at His Party*, accepted the challenge of giving the new consensus the stature of a philosophy which was neither old Republicanism nor New Dealism. They insisted that Eisenhower had become the architect and embodiment of a coherent political movement which had an entity of its own and which would continue after him. In a sense the new Republicanism reflected the President's amorphous vision of the general good which could best be achieved with moderation in everything. To describe his program, the President applied the terms "moderate progressivism" and "progressive moderation."

Essentially the new middle represented Republican conservatism which had made its bargain with the New Deal. As such it was an apt expression of the times, not a new philosophy of government. It simply reflected the conviction that policies of moderation are most suitable for times of prosperity. Efficiency and decentralization are natural goals in any post-crisis period.

Eventually the new Republicanism was reduced to an effort to explain the nation's high prosperity in terms of expanded economic freedom under the new Republican hegemony. At times it even identified prosperity with American virtues—a strong devotion to the family, the urge to work and save, the ambition to excel. Nowhere did Republican faith harbor the slightest doubt that the new balance had cured the business cycle. Assuming the persistence of prosperity, it contained no body of thought to guide the nation when things went wrong. It was not concerned with innovation or foreign affairs.

Actually the nation had long been moving toward what has been called the Eisenhower equilibrium. But the movement was prompted more by the mood of complacency and the conviction that enough had been done than by the attraction of any new economic doctrine. At the heart of the new center stood the conservative Democrats who after 1954 managed the affairs of Congress. With them were the Eisenhower Republicans of 1952 strengthened by the increasing conversion of Old Guard Republicans through political, economic and diplomatic necessity. Both groups agreed that the economy was basically sound and that the United States could not escape its challenges abroad. In the new consensus was an almost unprecedented feeling of interparty comradeship which blurred party distinctions. It left little room for the extremes in national political affairs. But the new center would last only as long as the nation's prosperity. Any serious cracking of the economy would again send politicians and the public scurrying to the edges of the political spectrum in search of answers and action.

THE EISENHOWER LEADERSHIP

Eisenhower's concept of his office was humble, even deferential, when compared to that of successful Presidents of the past. He had little taste for politics—the struggle for power among rival interests. Claiming no constitutional prerogatives for the executive branch, he pledged himself to restore confidence between the President and Congress so that both branches might work "with patience and good will to insure that the government is not divided against itself."

Eisenhower viewed his role as that of a presiding officer who exhorted and proposed, but who refused to enforce party discipline. Congressmen, he has said repeatedly, have a right to vote their own consciences.

Eisenhower was by training and habit a man of action, not of ideas. Abstractions never meant so much to him as things. For that reason the White House organization was designed to keep intellectual conflict within the administration to a minimum. Sherman Adams, White House Chief of Staff, controlled the information coming into the White House. James C. Hagerty, White House Press Secretary, controlled the information that came out. Together they managed to keep the President almost completely isolated. The President had never acquired the habit of reading the newspapers when he was in the Army; nor did he develop the habit after he entered the White House. He secured his news largely through the Army system of being "briefed" by spokesmen of Central Intelligence, the Pentagon, the State Department, or the White House staff.

Nor had the President any greater interest in other outside sources of information. Washington officials complained that they could not reach the President. Occasionally he conferred with Republican leaders in formal meetings, with White House aides sitting in.

Eisenhower once explained why he refused to become involved in details. "I do not believe," he informed a press conference, "that any individual . . . can do the best job just sitting at a desk and putting his face in a bunch of papers." It was his purpose, he added, "to keep his mind free of inconsequential details" so that he could make "clearer and better judgments." The President constructed his White House staff to eliminate the burden of detail.

Some writers have become ecstatic over Eisenhower's concept and use of his cabinet. They have prophesied that this organization, with its regularly scheduled meetings and carefully prepared agenda, will remain an integral part of the American governmental system. Perhaps the uniqueness of the system, relying on papers prepared by the executive departments, rests in the fact that it is admirably designed to achieve a broad consensus on administrative decisions. Eisenhower has viewed his administrative machine as partially a military staff, partially a board of directors.

The cohesion and loyalty of the White House team was a controlling factor in the President's willingness to run for a second term. "It's taken four years to get this outfit into top working shape," he told a friend. "It would be a shame to wash it out just as they are reaching their peak efficiency." If the staff system has secured the President's objectives of consensus and efficiency, it has also led to a diffusion of responsibility, illustrated most clearly in the U-2 incident of May, 1960.

Eisenhower has refused to permit his official duties to interfere with hunting, golfing and bridge. He has sought relaxation at every opportunity away from Washington, usually at his Gettysburg farm or at the Augusta National Golf Club. Occasionally he has taken a vacation in the West or New England. He once explained to a Washington press conference that recreation was essential to maintain the fitness necessary to meet the demands of the presidency. Hagerty has made it clear that when the President is absent from Washington a courier plane brings official papers every other day. In addition, the President often confers with officials in Washington by telephone, although more than once he has revealed extreme impatience at being disturbed by official calls from the capital.

Most Presidents have sought relief from the burdens of office. It was to the President's critics simply a matter of balance, and many believed that too often golf took precedence over matters of state. Edward P. Morgan of A.B.C. quipped characteristically in April, 1960: "President Eisenhower had hoped to helicopter to Gettysburg to cast his ballot today but found his schedule too tight. At the last minute, however, he did manage to squeeze in a round of golf."

Undoubtedly Eisenhower's concern for things material has had its effect on the intellectual climate of Washington. Many of the experts who drifted into Washington as economic and foreign policy advisers soon left. In every area of public policy the most impressive writers and thinkers are not only outside the government service but also almost totally ignored by those who make policy. Noting the absence of intellect in the nation's capital, James Reston of *The New York Times* Washington staff, complained in December, 1957:

> We are in a race with the pace of history. We are in a time when brain power is more important than fire power, but in the last five years, the President has gradually drifted apart from the intellectual opinion of the country, filled up his social hours with bantering locker-room cronies, and denied himself the mental stimulus that is always available to any President.

THE PRESIDENT'S NEW LOOK

Whatever the nature of Eisenhower's leadership, his personality remained the unquestioned phenomenon in presidential politics. His image was that of a well-meaning man standing at the center of American life. Never was its impact clearer than at the San Francisco convention of 1956. Eisenhower was the convention; he was the party. He was beyond challenge. Much of the President's power, ironically, resulted from his party's decline during his first term.

This commanding position was also the product of the President's new look. Under Hagerty's coaching Eisenhower had learned to dominate the Washington press conference—an exceedingly important method of shaping the public impression of the President. By 1954, he was completely at ease, often bantering with reporters. He was increasingly better informed. He had learned to dodge questions for which he had no ready answer, avoiding the "bloopers" of his early months. Republican professionals now called him the greatest instinctive politician since F.D.R.

Eisenhower's television style, assiduously cultivated by professionals, had become technically perfect. Television, in fact, provided party managers with the perfect medium for maintaining the Eisenhower image, for what mattered was not the intellectual content of his speeches, but the sincerity and warmth which he communicated to the public.

The Eisenhower personality overshadowed the presidency itself. The traditional duties and obligations of office appeared inconsequential when contrasted with the warm and easy smile, the beaming face, the informal, simple and unpretentious manner that captured the imagination of people everywhere. Even the most popular Presidents of the past had begun to lose much of their lustre long before they left the White House. But Eisenhower's stature continued to grow.

With the new look the President revealed more determination in office, more familiarity with issues. He spoke less of cooperation with Congress and more about defending the prerogatives of the executive. But energy and action are not the sole criteria for effective leadership. With his increased interest in the exercise of his powers the President demonstrated no new awareness of the great political forces in the world, no new evidence that he had any greater interest in ideas. Often he seemed to be placing his new leadership in the service of drift, providing, in the words of Richard H. Rovere, "the spectacle, novel in the history of the Presidency, of a man strenuously in motion yet doing essentially nothing—traveling all the time yet going nowhere."

The difficulty was not the President's firmness; it was the nature of his policies. It was less the decisiveness than the decisions themselves. Despite the energy behind them, Eisenhower's actions still suggested that there were no problems that good intentions would not cure.

Sustaining the Eisenhower image did little for the Republican organization. Party managers sought to exploit the President's personality. They succeeded merely in assuring the American people that whatever happened, the President, not the party, would assume the burdens of leadership. This accounts for the strange dichotomy between the President's growing popularity and the persistent decline in Republican strength. Republican Governor Theodore R. McKeldin of Maryland reminded a Republican audience in February, 1957, that the party "hasn't a thing that the country wants" except Eisenhower. Nowhere had the Republican party succeeded in turning the President's image into any genuine political gains.

What has characterized the Eisenhower foreign policies has been the substitution of principle and personality for the traditional ingredients of diplomacy. In large measure this approach was dictated by the successful Republican campaigning of 1952. For when the Republican leadership with its rhetoric of liberation, promised no less than the dismantling of both the Iron and Bamboo curtains, it denied itself the freedom to create future policy compatible with limited American power. Only when that leadership had disposed of its political symbols of Democratic iniquity and admitted publicly that it could not achieve what its key spokesmen, including the President, continued to promise during the months of party consolidation, could it formulate policy goals that had some relationship to the means at its disposal.

So completely had party objectives abroad over-reached American interest that the President's noteworthy achievements lay in *not* doing what members of his party demanded. His stature in the area of foreign affairs rested in his *refusal* to engage in war against mainland China, to become involved in the Indochinese civil war, to employ massive retaliation against Chinese cities.

It was the contribution of Secretary of State John Foster Dulles to translate American demands on Moscow and Peking, anchored to domestic political requirements, to the high realm of principle. If politics and principle converged, it was because both sought the retreat of the Soviet bloc. To that extent Dulles' principles appeared to square with American security interests, and the fact that through six years they exceeded what this nation's power could achieve and prevented the settlement of every outstanding issue in the cold war seemed to make no difference. If United States leadership could not secure what it wanted of others, it could at least take comfort in its ideals.

Unfortunately this reduced Mr. Dulles' diplomacy to rhetoric, for nothing else remained. As Hans J. Morgenthau wrote in December, 1956:

> When we heard spokesmen for the government propound the legal and moral platitudes which had passed for foreign policy in the interwar period, we thought that this was the way in which the government—as all govern-

ments must—tried to make the stark facts of foreign policy palatable to the people. . . . We were mistaken. Those platitudes *are* the foreign policy of the United States. . . .

If Dulles settled nothing, he also gave nothing away. The result of his tenure as Secretary of State was stalemate—a stalemate in which the cold war shifted to intense military and economic competition. Here Dulles' leadership could not prevent sharp reverses in Western power and prestige.

With Dulles' death in 1959 American policy became equated with the personality of the President. The rhetoric of liberation, now anchored to such homilies as "peace under freedom" or "peace with justice," continued, but even more important in the new diplomacy was the very person of the President. State visits abroad would give him the opportunity to demonstrate his good will before the world. Thereafter his success was measured not by diplomatic settlement but by the size and enthusiasm of the crowds that lined the thoroughfares of the cities of Europe, Asia and Latin America when he visited. These pressing throngs gave the impression that this nation was at last winning the cold war.

Unfortunately there was always the marked dichotomy between the cheers of the crowds and the lack of diplomatic progress in the chancelleries. Eisenhower's world travels were continuing expressions of American good intent, but they encompassed no action, commitments, or positive ideas to give permanent meaning to the tours. What remained after the experience was the evidence of personality and the absence of concrete achievement.

It was ironic that the President's good will tour of the Orient should be marred by Tokyo mobs, for the new diplomacy had been directed toward mobs. The President had been warned by writers, editors and even members of Congress, after the collapse of the Paris summit conference of May, 1960, not to run the risk of a trip around the fringes of the Communist world in the Far East. But to men who equated large crowds with diplomatic success here was the easiest method available to prove that the United States had lost nothing at Paris. What the cheers at Taipei and Tokyo might achieve was not clear. Had the President managed his trip to Japan he would have measured the triumph by the shouts of the people, for there was little to be gained in the quiet of the Japanese Foreign Office.

In a sense, Eisenhower's world tours comprised a final effort to create the illusion of peace when all genuine diplomacy had ceased to exist. What seemed to matter was the President's ability to draw larger and more enthusiastic crowds than Premier Khrushchev. But the visit of a president or premier to another land has no function other than to expose the visiting dignitary to the people that jam the thoroughfares.

It is a mutual demonstration of good will, but nothing more. For if actual diplomacy were the objective, that could be pursued more cheaply and effectively via normal diplomatic channels. Nothing better illustrates the ephemeral nature of state visits than Khrushchev's conviction that he had won over the support of the American public during his remarkable visit of September, 1959. In retrospect, the visit had no effect on Russian-American relations at all.

Eisenhower responded to his failures in Paris and Tokyo with an air of injured innocence. His own dignity amid the collapse of the summit created the impression that whatever went wrong he was not at fault. He continued to detach himself from personal responsibility or the opinion of the free world. For the loss of American prestige in the Far East he blamed the Communists, not the deep and reasonable doubts created by missiles and Soviet threats. He continued to identify world peace with his personal diplomacy, repeating this conviction after his return from the Orient in July, 1960:

> No consideration of personal fatigue or inconvenience, no threat or argument would deter me from once again setting out on a course that has meant much for our country, for her friends, and for the cause of freedom—and peace with justice in the world.

Always the sacrifice was to the person, not to the nation in the form of added strength or reduced ambitions. In equating the cause of peace with the enthusiasm he received abroad, the President forgot that it is this nation's relations with the governments at Moscow and Peking, not with the crowds of New Delhi, Paris, or Taipei, that matter. In denying any error in judgment or policy, the President permitted no official review of his record. This solved no problems, but merely swept them under the rug.

Eisenhower's leadership has given rise to a curious standard of appraisal. For almost eight years his adherents have measured his success by popularity, not achievement. As George E. Allen concluded in his *Saturday Evening Post* article on Eisenhower in April, 1960:

> The man who took office mistrusting politics and politicians will leave office having proved himself one of the most successful politicians ever to occupy the Presidency. He will leave the White House more popular than when he moved in, and this will be an unprecedented feat—a political feat.

By such standards of personal popularity Harding and Coolidge would rank among the most successful of American presidents; Washington, John Adams, Polk, Lincoln, and Wilson among the failures.

What matters far more in presidential success are, first, the intellectual alertness necessary to penetrate contemporary movements and, second, the political craftsmanship required to translate victory into political action which meets the challenge of the times. Measured by its adaptation of the Democratic past to the conditions of the 1950's, the Eisenhower leadership had been a success, indeed an historical necessity. But the permanent judgment of that leadership will hinge on the President's achievement in influencing, within the limits of his power, the fundamental trends of this age toward the protection of this nation's well-being.

The recent past is interlude. The dilemmas of the 1950's await their disposal in some future time. Only in that future will men be permitted to judge finally whether the present leadership has prepared the nation mentally and physically for the cataclysm that is sure to come.

30

The Radical Right and McCarthyism

SEYMOUR MARTIN LIPSET

If the 1950's were the decade of Eisenhower, they were also the decade of Senator Joseph R. McCarthy of Wisconsin. History does not take the full measure of men and institutions who do not succeed, and there is perhaps no effective way of estimating an impact which is essentially negative. But the age of Joe McCarthy, as he preferred to be known, was alive with his influence; evidences of it could be palpably felt in the fear to which he reduced his fellow Senators, in the dominion he exercised over executive leadership, in the threat to the civil liberties of anybody under suspicion of being subversive, in his considerable influence on American foreign policy.

That he found substantial support among many groups of Americans made him the subject of much study by scholars, for whom, as a group, Senator McCarthy entertained very little regard. Who were his followers? What were their beliefs? How did McCarthy articulate these beliefs? Scholars have tended to see McCarthyites and McCarthyism as part of a larger conservative movement in American politics. The nature of this movement

SOURCE: *The British Journal of Sociology,* VI (June, 1955), 197–201. Reprinted by permission of the author and publisher.

has been closely explored in several essays which, having originally ap-
peared in different periodicals, were collected by Daniel Bell in a volume
entitled The New American Right *(1955). Among the essays is one by*
Seymour Martin Lipset, Professor of Government and Social Relations at
Harvard University and author of a number of volumes which deal, in the
main, with important problems in American social development.

Professor Lipset's essay concerns itself with "The Sources of the 'Radical
Right.'" He terms the group radical because, as he says, "It desires to make
far-reaching changes in American institutions, and . . . it seeks to eliminate
from American political life those persons and institutions which threaten
either its values, or its economic interests. Needless to say, this movement is
opposed to the social and economic reforms of the last twenty years [i.e., the
New Deal and the Fair Deal], and to the internationalist foreign policy pur-
sued by the successive administrations in that period."

In the first section of his essay, Professor Lipset considers factors in
America's past which have continuously contributed to politics of extreme
conservatism. In the second section, he analyzes the groups which, at the
time he wrote his essay in the mid-fifties, were more prone than others to
support the radical right; these included economic extremists, "Tory" work-
ers, isolationists, Catholics, and people who sought in politics a realization
of their sentiments about status. In the final section, which is reprinted
below, Professor Lipset, to cite his own words, "deals with the specific char-
acter of McCarthyism as the principal expression of radical right ideology
on the current scene."

There is much to ponder in Professor Lipset's analysis. What, for exam-
ple, has happened to the radical right since the mid-fifties? To what extent
has its impact on civil liberties continued, as Professor Lipset suggested it
might, in the continuing atmosphere of the cold war? What other movements
in the American past have sought radical changes in our institutions? What
purposes motivated the various groups composing these movements? (The
first section of Professor Lipset's essay, as we have noted, draws a historical
pattern of ultra-conservative politics in America.) Why has radicalism
never succeeded in capturing control of American politics?

To understand McCarthyism one must also understand McCarthy. There
were significant points of convergence between the two, but there were also
significant points of divergence. An analysis of the groups whom McCarthy
attracted is most illuminating, yet note has to be taken that he did more than
speak for specific group interests or serve specific group motives. He was, as
Richard Rovere indicates so clearly in his brilliant study, Senator Joe Mc-
Carthy *(1959), a symbol of rebellion. He defied authority. He ruled Ameri-*
can politics by tantrums and melodrama. Publicly truculent, aggressive,
ill-mannered, and paranoiac, he served as surrogate to the many Americans
of no particular social group who projected onto him their response to the
besetting problems of the real world. In explaining McCarthyism, moreover,

some place has to be made, apart from a scheme of group motives, interests, and purposes, for those who really felt that McCarthy was speaking the truth, that in a world bristling with Communist expansion and threats there was validity in the warnings, however violent, of an anti-Communist.

If McCarthyism was a wider phenomenon than an analysis of group interests might indicate, it was conversely also a narrower one. McCarthyism hung ultimately on McCarthy, and in the deeper sociological sense McCarthy was not a McCarthyite. He did not lead a movement; rather, it tried to follow him. As Rovere suggests, he had no program, he did not wish to assume control of the state, he never encouraged direct action by his followers, he never attempted to set up an organization outside the prevailing party system. He was a rampant and strident ego, unattached to any social or economic plan. "If he was anything at all in the realm of ideas, principles, doctrines," says Rovere, "he was a species of nihilist; he was an essentially destructive force, a revolutionist without any revolutionary vision, a rebel without a cause." Here may be the real reason why the radical right was not able to make any headway in the mid-1950's. They were following not a leader, but a symbol of their own making.

One is left, of course, with the question of how the movement might have fared under a leader who could combine McCarthy's popularity with a positive program. The product of a crisis in America's adjustment to world politics, McCarthyism was a substantial threat to our tradition of civil rights and to our system of leadership. Would the threat recur as the crisis continued and perhaps deepened? And if it did recur, how well would our liberal and democratic institutions be able to sustain themselves?

MC CARTHYISM: THE UNIFYING IDEOLOGY

Extreme conservatism cannot ever hope to create a successful mass movement on the basis of its socio-economic programme alone. Except during significant crises, the majority of the traditional middle and upper class conservative elements are not likely to support extremist movements and ideologies, even when presented in the guise of conservatism, and the lower classes do not support movements in defense of privilege. The problem of the radical right is to locate a political philosophy which will have appeal to its traditionally rightist support, and will also enable it to win a mass base in the body politic. Nazism was able to do this in Germany by combining a strong nationalist appeal to the status-threatened German middle and upper classes, together with an "attack on Jewish international capitalism" designed to win over those most concerned with economic reform. As a number of European political commentators have suggested, anti-Semitism has often been the extreme rightist functional equivalent for the socialist attack on capitalism. The Jewish banker replaces the exploiting capitalist as the scapegoat.

In the United States, the radical right had to find some equivalent method of appealing to the groups which have a sense of being under-privileged, and McCarthy's principal contribution to the crystallization of the radical right in the 1950's has been to hit on the key symbols with which to unite all its potential supporters. McCarthy's crusade is not just against the liberal elements of the country, cast in the guise of "creeping socialists"; he is also campaigning against the same groups mid-west Populism always opposed, the eastern conservative financial aristocracy. In his famous Wheeling, West Virginia, speech of February 9, 1950, McCarthy began his crusade againt internal Communism by presenting for the first time an image of the internal enemy:

> The reason why we find ourselves in a position of impotency is not be-cause our only potential enemy has sent men to invade our shores, but rather because of the traitorous actions of those who have been treated so well by this nation. It is not the less fortunate, or members of minority groups who have been selling this nation out, but rather those who have had all the benefits the wealthiest nation on earth has had to offer—the *finest homes*, the *finest college educations*, and the *finest jobs* in the government that we can give. This is glaringly true in the State Department. There the *bright young men who are born with silver spoons in their mouths are the ones who have been worse.*

This defense of the minority groups and the underprivileged, and attack on the upper class, has characterized the speeches and writings of McCarthy and his followers from the beginning. In this McCarthy differs considerably from other anti-Communist investigators. He is rarely interested in investigating or publicizing the activities of men who belong to minority ethnic groups. The image which recurs time and again in his speeches is one of an easterner, usually of Anglo-Saxon Episcopalian origins, who has been educated in schools such as Groton and Harvard, and who is a member of the intelligentsia, the educated classes, not simply the intellectuals.

This pattern recurs again and again in the current writings of the radical right. The *Freeman* magazine writes that "Asian coolies and Harvard professors are the people . . . most susceptible to Red propa-ganda." *Facts Forum,* another vociferous exponent of radical right ideology, describes intellectuals as the group most vulnerable to Com-munism, and defines intellectuals, as "lawyers, doctors, bankers, teach-ers, professors, preachers, writers, publishers." In discussing the Hiss case, *Facts Forum* argued that the forces defending Hiss which were most significant were not the Communists, themselves, but "the Ameri-can respectables, *the socially pedigreed,* the culturally acceptable, the certified gentlemen and scholars of the day, dripping with college de-grees. . . . In general, it was the 'best people' who were for Alger Hiss." In discussing McCarthy's enemies, the *Freeman* stated: "He possesses, it seems, a sort of animal, negative-pole magnetism which repels alumni of Harvard, Princeton, and Yale. And we think we know what it is: *this young man is constitutionally incapable of deference to social status."*

These quotations could be extended indefinitely. Over and over again runs the theme, the common men in America have been victimized by members of the upper classes, by the prosperous, by the wealthy, by the well-educated, and when it is necessary to list names, these are almost invariably individuals whose names and backgrounds permit them to be identified with symbols of high status. Since he could attack other individuals and groups, this concentration on the Anglo-Saxon élite is no accident. What are the purposes it serves?

Initially McCarthy, coming out of a state, Wisconsin, which for over forty years had elected the two La Follettes with their isolationism and attacks on eastern business and Wall Street, may have been searching for an equivalent to the La Follette appeal. Much of the electorate of Wisconsin, and other sections of the Mid-West, the German-Americans and those who were sympathetic to their isolationist viewpoint, *have been smarting under the charge of disloyalty.* McCarthy has argued that it was not the isolationists but rather those who favoured our entry into the war with Germany who were the real traitors; because of backing Great Britain in World War II they had played into the hands of the Soviet Union and had been dupes as well as servants of Communism. The linkage between the attacks on Anglo-Saxon Americans and Great Britain may be seen in McCarthy's infrequent speeches on foreign policy, which invariably wind up with an attack on Great Britain, sometimes with a demand for action (such as economic sanctions, or pressure to prevent her from trading with Red China). Thus McCarthy is in fact attacking the same groups in the United States and on the world scene, as his liberal predecessors.

On the national scene, McCarthy's attacks are probably much more important in terms of their appeal to status frustrations than to resentful isolationism. In the identification of traditional symbols of status with pro-Communism the McCarthy followers, of non-Anglo-Saxon extraction, can gain a feeling of superiority over the traditionally privileged groups. Here is a prosperity-born functional equivalent for the economic radicalism of depressions. For the resentments of prosperity are basically not against the economic power of Wall Street bankers, or Yankees, but against their status power. An attack on their loyalty, on their Americanism, is quite clearly also an attack on their status. And this group also not only rejects the status claims of the minority ethnics, but also snubs the *nouveaux riches* millionaires.

Such an attack on the status system could conceivably antagonize groups within the radical right: such as the patriotic societies, the Daughters of the American Revolution, and members of old upper-status families like Archibald Roosevelt, who chaired the Roy Cohn testimonial dinner. Paradoxically, attacks on the Anglo-Saxon Yankee scapegoat do not have this effect because they are directed against majority elements in the society. An attack on Jews or the Irish, or Italians or Negroes, would have resulted in an immediate response from members of the attacked group. Anglo-Saxon white Protestants, as a majority group, however, are not sensitive to criticism, they are not vulnerable to being attacked, nor do they expect attack. McCarthy, on the one hand, can throw out symbols and images which appeal to the minority ethnics, to the Germans, to the Irish, and the Italians, and at the same time not secure the hostility of radical rightists who also are members of the D.A.R., the Sons of the American Revolution, the Patriotic Dames or any other comparable group. And in spite of his populist type symbols, he can retain the support or the cooperation of some big businessmen. This is his peculiar power. To the status-deprived he is a critic of the upper class, to the privileged he is a foe of social change and Communism.

ANTI-COMMUNISM: THE WEAKNESS OF A SINGLE ISSUE

In spite of its seeming successes in intimidating opponents, and gaining widespread support behind some of its leaders, the radical right has not succeeded in building even one organization of any political significance. And without organizing its backing, it cannot hope to secure any lasting power. This failure is not accidental, or a result of inept leadership, but rather stems from the fact that the only *political* issue which unites the various supporters of radical right politicians is anti-Communism. It is only at the leadership level that agreement exists on a programme for domestic and foreign policy. The mass base, however, is far from united on various issues. For example, as McCarthy well knows, the dairy farmers of Wisconsin want the government to guarantee 100 per cent parity prices. But this policy is an example of "creeping socialism" and government regimentation to some of the extremist elements on his side.

The Catholic working-class still remains committed to the economic objectives of the New Deal, and still belongs to C.I.O. trade unions. While McCarthy and other radical rightists may gain Catholic support for measures which are presented under the guise of fighting Communism, they will lose it on economic issues. And should economic issues become salient again as during a recession, much of the popular support for McCarthyism will fall away. As a result any attempt to build a radical right movement which has a complete political programme is risky, and probably will not occur.

The radical right also faces the problem that it unites bigots of various stripes. Although there is little available evidence, it seems true that most anti-Semites have become McCarthyites. In the South and other parts of the country, fundamentalist Protestant groups which are anti-Semitic and anti-Catholic back the radical right in spite of the fact that McCarthy is a Catholic.

One illustration of the way in which these contradictions among his supporters can cause difficulty, is a statement which recently appeared in the *New York Journal American:* "I think Joe owes the Army an apology but I doubt if our soldiers will get it. The Senator has sure lost his touch since he took up with those oil rich, anti-Catholic Texas millionaires. They are the very same gang which threw the shiv at Al Smith back in 1928."

Perhaps the greatest threat to the political fortunes of the radical right has been the election of the Republican Party in 1952. As long as the Republican Party was in opposition the radical right could depend upon the covert support, or at worst the neutrality, of most moderate conservative sections of the Republican Party. Republicans, even when they viewed the methods of the radical right with distaste, still saw the group as potential vote gainers for the Party. The frustration of twenty years in opposition reduced the scruples of many Republicans, especially those who were involved in party politics. The differences between the radical right and the moderate right are evident indeed and open factionalism existed in the party long before the election of Eisenhower. Nevertheless, the evidence is quite clear that a large proportion, if not the majority, of the moderate Republicans did not view McCarthy or the radical right as a menace to the party, until he began his attack upon them. Walter Lippmann once persuasively argued that when the Republicans were in office they would be able to control the radical right, or that the radical right would conform for the sake of party welfare. Most Republicans probably at the time agreed. However, the programme of Eisenhower Republicanism has not been one of turning the clock back, nor has it fed the psychic needs of the radical right in domestic or foreign policy. Eisenhower's policies in the White House have certainly not reduced the needs of radical right groups for political action, for scapegoatism. They have not reduced McCarthy's desires to capitalize upon popular issues to maintain power and prestige in the general body politic. As a result, the radical right is now forced to struggle openly with the moderate conservatives, essentially the Eisenhower Republicans (who in large measure represent established big business). This is a fight it cannot hope to win, but the danger exists that the moderates in their efforts to resist charges of softness to Communism, or simply to defeat the Democrats, will take over some of the issues of the radical right, in order to hold its followers, while destroying the political influence of its leaders.

It is extremely doubtful that the radical right will ever secure more power or influence than it has in the past. It has reached its optimum strength in a period of prosperity, and a recession will probably cripple its political power. It cannot build an organized movement. Its principal current significance, and perhaps permanent impact on the American scene, lies in its success in over-stimulating popular reaction to the problem of internal subversion, in supplying the impetus for changes which may have lasting effects on American life, e.g., the heightened security programme, political controls on passports, political tests for school teachers, and increasing lack of respect for the understanding of the Constitutional guarantees of civil and juridical rights for unpopular minorities and scoundrels. Whether these changes become institutionalized, however, depends on political developments of the next decade. And if the cold war and prosperity continue, the radical right, although organizationally weak, may play a decisive role in changing the character of American democracy. It is, therefore, a tendency in American life about which we need to know much more than we do.

31

John F. Kennedy as President
REXFORD G. TUGWELL

It is difficult to assess the presidency of John F. Kennedy. His tragic death inevitably fused the man and his office; it apotheosized the man, and invested his office with a charisma it never had when he was alive. A valid appraisal of President Kennedy's administration calls for honest answers to basic questions. We must begin by asking about each of the many roles a president plays: as chief of state, as Chief Executive, as director of foreign policy, as commander-in-chief of the armed forces, as legislative leader, as the leader of his political party, and as the leader of his nation. What does each of these roles involve? How far are they complementary? With what effectiveness did Kennedy discharge them?

Kennedy himself believed that "the presidency is peculiarly an office which is shaped by the individual who holds it." In what way? What traits best equip an individual to fill the office? What in particular were Kennedy's

SOURCE: *Political Science Quarterly*, LXXXII (June, 1967), 253–67. The original title of this article was "The President and His Helpers: A Review Article." Reprinted by permission of *Political Science Quarterly*.

traits, how did they shape his conduct of the presidency, and how much did they either promote or impede his effectiveness in conducting it? What have been the personal traits of our foremost presidents? Kennedy believed, moreover, that "greatness depends on the times as well as the man." What are the times that make for great presidents? Are they most often times of war, and have we tended to overestimate the men who led our nation in war and to underestimate those who led us in peace? If so, why? What role does the president play vis-à-vis the major problems of his day? How far is the presidency "merely a vehicle of the current status quo," as James MacGregor Burns thinks it often becomes (see Presidential Government, *1965)? In what respects, under what conditions, and for what ends may it serve (again in Professor Burns's words) as "an instrument of creative planning in the pursuit of new ways of realizing human and qualitative values in our public affairs"?*

How effective and powerful is the presidential office in providing leadership for so large and important a nation as ours, in times like these? Is the presidency of our own day essentially different from that construed by the Founding Fathers, and does it therefore need constitutional redefinition to make it truly workable? Is it, as Marcus Cunliffe asks, "a defective institution," badly in need of basic reforms, above all of a device to relate it closely and practicably to Congress (see Commentary, *February 1968)? Or should we listen to Clinton Rossiter's reiterated plea, in* The American Presidency *(1956, 1960), to "Leave Your Presidency Alone"? How far, indeed, do we subscribe to Professor Rossiter's presentation of the essential qualities of the presidency: that it balances power and liberty, that it offers a steady focus of leadership, that it symbolizes American continuity and destiny, that it has withstood the test of history, and that "it has been more responsive to the needs and dreams of giant democracy than any other office or institution in the whole mosaic of American life"?*

What makes a president great? Perhaps the most notable recent attempt to answer this question was made, in 1962, by Arthur M. Schlesinger, who polled seventy-five distinguished historians to find out both how they rated the presidents and what factors they considered most important in evaluating outstanding presidential leadership. The five presidents whom the historians called the greatest were, in the order they were ranked: Lincoln, Washington, Franklin D. Roosevelt, Wilson, and Jefferson. Certain common qualities and achievements were deemed to have given all five a distinct primacy over the other presidents. Each was president at a time of crisis and by timely action achieved enduring results. Each espoused the causes of liberalism and the general welfare and broke free from the status quo. Each was a constructive statesman in the conduct of American diplomacy, and a realistic politician in handling the affairs of his own party. Each strengthened the executive branch. And each was committed "to maintain and transmit to future generations the liberal and humane ideals of the past." *(Chap. 6, "Rating the Presidents," in* **Paths to the Present,** *1964.)*

In the following article, Rexford G. *Tugwell closely scrutinizes three portraits of Kennedy as president that have been drawn by different members of his administration. Tugwell is notably qualified to evaluate the presidency and its "helpers." One of Franklin D. Roosevelt's "brain-trusters," he was an intimate member of the New Deal administration. He has seen public service in a variety of capacities over his long career, perhaps most significantly as governor of Puerto Rico from 1941 to 1946. He has written many books on the relation between government and the national economy. He has taught at Columbia University and the University of Chicago, and is currently a senior fellow at the Center for the Study of Democratic Institutions at Santa Barbara. In the article below, Tugwell indicates the respects in which all three estimates of Kennedy's achievement share a common approach, noting too that each of them has failed to look at the basic institutional problems that have plagued the modern presidency.*

The most urgent problem seems to be that of properly using the presidency as an agency of innovation or renovation. Governmental institutions, like all others, become hard and unpliant, dictating their own interest and embodying their own rationale. They fail to accommodate new needs or bend in new directions. A strong president is, among other things, one who can create enough new institutions to bypass the old ones and can infuse the new institutions with enough energy to achieve what old ones could not. The paradox of the American presidency is that it can exercise great power in foreign affairs but can do relatively little at home. This paradox was enhanced for Kennedy because of the extremely narrow margin of his popular victory. How could he then proceed to build new frontiers with old institutions? How could he get America moving again in the face of immobilizing ways and means? The Kennedy presidency sums up both the promise and the inadequacy of presidential leadership. That we are the prime power in the world of nations in an age of perennial crisis, and that our domestic crisis is of no lesser magnitude or pressure, makes the American presidency a compelling problem for us to ponder.

In all probability the books considered here are only the first three of perhaps seven or eight likely to be written about the Kennedy presidency by his co-workers.[1] Even without others his brief regime can

---

[1] *Kennedy* by Theodore C. Sorensen, New York, Harper & Row, 1965.— viii, 783 pp.; *A Thousand Days: John F. Kennedy in the White House* by Arthur M. Schlesinger, Jr., Boston, Houghton Mifflin and Cambridge, Mass., The Riverside Press, 1965.—xiv, 1087 pp.; *With Kennedy* by Pierre Salinger, Garden City, N. Y., Doubleday, 1966.—xvi, 391 pp.

be said to have had a thorough apologia remarkably soon after its ending; when Galbraith, Bundy, Goodwin, Rostow, Bell, and others have had their say, the administration will have had a really formidable defense.

The word "formidable" is justified; these are all long and detailed books, written by competent expositors with the help of carefully kept notes and files. So is the word "defense"; the authors are all fierce Kennedy partisans.

Sorensen had worked for Kennedy since 1953 when he simply asked for and was given a job in the office of the new Senator from Massachusetts. Schlesinger's case was different. He was not an unknown young man but already a distinguished professor of history at Harvard, who had worked for liberal causes, was interested in politics, and had even been one of Stevenson's helpers in his contests with Eisenhower. For some reason not clearly explained, he had attached himself to the Kennedy cause and had been asked to join the White House staff.

Salinger came to Kennedy by way of the Senator's brother Robert. He was a San Francisco reporter who had graduated to writing special articles and was assigned (by *Colliers*) to write an exposé of the Teamsters Union about the time Robert was starting his work as counsel for Senator McClellan's Committee on Improper Activities in the Labor and Management Field. He offered to cooperate and, when *Colliers* suspended publication, was hired as an investigator. This was late in 1956; the committee's work went on for three years. At the end of that time the Kennedy candidacy had reached the organization stage, and Salinger began to work for the Senator in an office over a garage with Stephen E. Smith's name on the door. Smith was Kennedy's brother-in-law, and Salinger had been told "to set up a press operation."

The three, along with several others whose accounts are yet to come, worked through the campaign and were carried on into the White House to become members of the presidential staff. Salinger became press secretary and so had specified duties. Sorensen was special counsel, meaning that he was available for various assignments but was always in charge of the last draft of speeches. Schlesinger was given a watching brief and an office in the remote East Wing. He was occasionally assigned to some problem in the foreign field, but obviously was meant to be the administration's historian, something Kennedy anticipated with mixed feelings as the going got rough and mistakes were made.

All have written as might be expected of professionals, lucidly but with obvious reserve. There are some natural evidences of haste; Schlesinger, the historian, does not always distinguish what is important from what interested himself; Sorensen manages to be dull over long stretches, something unexpected for the author of so much luminous writing for the Kennedy signature; and Salinger's book suffers from lack of careful editing.

Still it is obvious that these three and their colleagues made up a wonderfully integrated presidential family; they were as much seized with the office as Kennedy himself, and all seem to have shared his dedication. It is no wonder that since his service was so tragically ended there has remained a widely felt sense of loss. Kennedy himself was a deeply engaged man who was able to look at himself with detached candor. He judged others in much the same way; he was cool and wry; and he learned his presidential lessons in a much shorter time than most of his predecessors. If he had lived he might well have been one of the most distinguished and honored of the line.

But he was not given time. And because he made terrible early mistakes, it cannot be claimed for him that he belongs among the select few—with Jefferson, whom he so much admired, with Lincoln, with Wilson, and with the Roosevelts. What can be said is that he was a most admirable individual. He was touched with grace; he never allowed himself the usual appeals to cheap sentiment; he worked unremittingly in spite of almost continuous pain from an old injury; his courage never failed; and he accepted fully his responsibility.

These qualities were part of a whole make-up that allowed him, nevertheless, to be ruthless, single-minded, and self-centered in his drive for power; and when he had that power, to dispose it according to his judgment, without sentiment, and always with first regard for its protection and its increase.

This, of course, was necessary. He was acutely aware that his support had been only a fraction of one per cent higher than that of his opponent. This is a crippling beginning for any president, and Kennedy did not even have the customary honeymoon. He could not bear down on the Congress as a popular leader; most of his proposals were rejected and during his time in office only one really major piece of legislation was accepted (it was not actually passed until after his death). It was as barren a time as that of Eisenhower who, in contrast, had not wanted very much of anything done; but anyone who says that now is attacked furiously by his partisans.

His chroniclers make a good deal of the better times that followed his election. He had promised to get the country moving again; and, they say, he did. What they have in mind is that a budget deficit was accepted as the means to this end. But his critics do not allow that any tremendous effort was needed to reduce taxes, congressmen being what they are.

Economics was not Kennedy's best subject and it took him some time—as it did many of those around him—to accept reduced taxes and increased public expenditure as a way to increase activity, especially when it might involve deficits. The idea had been similarly resisted by Roosevelt until slow recovery was interrupted by a sinking spell in 1937. Until that time such spending had been justified only as an effort to relieve the distress of the unemployed. But around Kennedy there were several economists who called themselves Keynesians— Walter Heller, for instance—and they convinced him that the release of purchasing power from reduced taxes would not only enlarge economic activity but would have the result of increasing employment. Eventually, also, revenue would be just as much or more from reduced rates on larger incomes than higher rates on smaller ones.

It was true that since the war the country had been in a sort of coma, afraid of more inflation such as had followed the Korean involvement, devoted to "sound" policies, and convinced that a high rate of unemployment together with unused industrial capacity was "normal." For all the nation's pride in past progress there was lacking the imagination to adapt to a high-energy economy. Kennedy had made much of this as a Republican characteristic when campaigning, but when elected he had no program for effecting a change and still had to be convinced that management was possible.

He confessed at one time that he could distinguish between monetary and fiscal policies only by recalling the initial of Chairman Martin of the Federal Reserve. But eventually he understood that orthodox monetary policy was effected by manipulating the interest rate, the supply of money, and market operations by the Federal Reserve. Business was kept from expanding by restricting loans or making them expensive; and these policies were supplemented by prudent management of public expenditures so that the budget balanced. There was something wrong about this; but what was it?

I

The newer economists pointed out that actually the budget had not been balanced during the Eisenhower years and that in spite of orthodox monetary policies the dollar had declined in purchasing power. The country, they said, was producing at much less than capacity and there was an intolerable rate of unemployment. This stagnation was unnecessary. The remedy was easier monetary policy, a release of purchasing power by reducing taxes, and increased public spending.

There were other reasons for a change and these appealed to Kennedy. Unemployment was not only a hardship for the unemployed but a social burden; restricted public expenditures for the last two decades had left the nation short of all sorts of facilities from schools to hospitals; the cities were rotting at the core—an enlargement of water supplies was needed, health statistics were frightening, and everyone was talking about the shortage of housing, school rooms, hospital beds, and utilities.

Schlesinger argues that Kennedy as a senator was "an incipient Keynesian."[2] And certainly as a representative of Massachusetts he had to be aware of declining industries, poverty-stricken cities, and distressed workers. But he had been more inclined to look for ways to improve New England's position than to consider the condition of the whole economy; and when he became president by so slim a margin, he began by being very cautious about criticism from the financial community. Walter Lippmann, in 1961, accused him of merely carrying on the Eisenhower policies.

He was, it is true, very much afraid of being called a "big spender," thinking that, if he was, he would have trouble getting anything at all out of a conservative congress. This problem was associated both with his lack of popular support and with an opposition from business that continued to grow. Sorensen refers to this in a chapter called "The Fight Against Recession": ". . . the sanctity of balanced budgets, moreover, made it politically impossible to convert overnight either the voters or Congress to the merits of budget deficits."

It was only in 1962 that he promised "tax reform" for the next year. But these chroniclers are right in saying that when it came, his fight for the use of fiscal measures was the boldest move of his presidency. For in that year another of the familiar Eisenhower recessions was obviously imminent. During the year before, all the indexes had turned downward, and his promise to get the country going again had begun to seem an empty one.

Galbraith, for one, thought the tax reduction a mistake. He called it a Keynesian reaction. The same effect, with a better result, he said, could be got by an increase of public spending for all those facilities so badly needed. The difference among Kennedy's associates was a heated one, especially since he felt it necessary to quiet what Paul Samuelson called "irrational opposition" by posing as an economical manager. It was widely publicized that he uniformly reduced the requests of agency heads, cutting away many billions before submitting his budget to the Congress. By various devices such as raising postal rates, reducing the cost of the farm program and putting the Interstate Highway project back on a self-financing basis by raising direct taxes, he was able to show that his own annual increases in domestic expenditures were

---

[2] The argument here goes back to 1952 when Kennedy was a newly elected congressman. It will be found in Chapter XXIII and cites a statement on "Meet the Press" in favor of enlarged purchasing power and, if necessary, an unbalanced budget.

smaller than those of the Eisenhower years. This Galbraith thought was nothing to be proud of; but in fact expenditures for welfare measures were increased—not nearly enough, but still by an appreciable amount.

It was a hard struggle, involving many devious recourses, and the dramatic vindication in the immediate response of the economy came too late for his political purposes. The argument for fiscal management was won. But the government lacked any means for actual control. The word management in this connection is deceptive. Government can increase or decrease its own taxing and spending and in this sense it does manage; but what goes on in the board rooms of corporations it has no way of reaching. And the decisions made there drastically affect the economy. Even prices, these days, are, most of them, "administered" privately and are quite unaffected by demand. It is unheard of to set prices calculated to tempt more consumers. If they do not buy, production schedules are reduced. This, unfortunately, causes unemployment and a further reduction in production. But the corporation is likely, in such circumstances, to *raise* prices. It is no great matter to it whether profits come from selling many goods or few, but it is a great matter to the economy.

Nevertheless it is Kennedy's contribution to domestic policy that monetary and fiscal management was made acceptable by him. It is already being made into a flexible and powerful defense against the recurrence of the hard times that for so long were a torment that seemed inevitable.

Presidents, as things are, sit in the center of the economic complex. They are expected to maintain prosperity (and are criticized if it declines), but what they can do about it is hardly more than peripheral. It is more correctly called influence than power, and influence has different sources than power, more uncertain, more easily eroded. Even the monetary controls are in independent hands. The Federal Reserve Board is not responsible to the chief executive.

Kennedy obviously had not assessed his situation realistically when he promised to "get things moving again." And he learned, when he did, that what he must do would gain him a reputation for recklessness. On the other hand, when he opposed price increases, he was "hostile to business." There was one period of stock-market decline when acidulous jokes circulated after an exchange with Roger Blough of U.S. Steel about an increase in steel prices. He was heard to repeat in the aftermath something his father had told him. All steel men, he had said, were S.O.B.'s; and now, the son said, he believed it. This was enlarged by some who overheard it to include *all* businessmen. He tried for correction in a press conference; Sorenson tells what happened: "His correction was ignored and his hope was unfulfilled. Buttons appeared bearing the caption 'S.O.B. Club.' Bumper stickers appeared reading 'Help Kennedy Stamp out Free Enterprise' or 'I miss Ike—Hell, I even miss Harry.'"

These exchanges in 1962 worried Kennedy the politician; but in spite of efforts at conciliation, involving some humiliation, he concluded that there was little he could do. A British cartoon at the time of his row with business about inflationary price increases pictured one furious executive saying to another, "This guy Kennedy thinks he's running the country!" Sorensen, commenting on this, says, "That caption was correct!" But, of course, Sorensen was wrong. He had not the means, if what was meant was the economy rather than the country.

II

Nor did Kennedy have a constitutional directive for doing so. Such a thing never entered any framer's mind. It was something come to informally in the twentieth century after bitter battles. And the mixed expectation and resentment accompanying such efforts had never been cleared away—as it should—by forthright amendment.

True, the president was given "the executive power" in the first words of Article II; but what was meant by this has to be understood in late eighteenth-century—and that means pre-industrial—terms. He is spoken of in modern commentaries as the *chief* executive, but this is not the language of the constitution. There is even doubt from a close reading of that document that he was meant to have more than a generally supervisory role in government. If it is recalled that there were in the beginning only three departments, each with a few clerks, and that government had very few responsibilities, the present position—without any constitutional recognition—is a startling transformation.

The curious fact is, however, that what the framers meant him to be, the president has become; he supervises but he does not manage the immense departments. What he does do is to manipulate the levers of central power, such of them as he controls, as best he can. Until recently these were largely conciliatory and negative except when he was acting as commander-in-chief. Cleveland was the first president to be confronted with the savage conflict of labor and management in an industrial system grown up without constitutional recognition. He unhesitatingly put down what seemed to him a simple rebellion. He was not expected to do more. That the conditions creating virtual civil war ought to be brought under control, with agreed rules, was still not something generally thought necessary. But the problems did not settle themselves; they rapidly grew worse. More and more often public intervention was necessary. There was a dangerous polarization, and

presidents from Theodore Roosevelt on had to struggle with complicated issues they had no mandate for and no effective means to use.
Kennedy had to confront all of them, and he was even without that
ultimate recourse of presidents—public support.

The gradual reaching back and reinterpreting of the constitution in
such matters had all the uncertainty of legislative and administrative
law and none of the certainty of constitutional agreement. When there
were emergencies the president, with a national constituency, acted
according to his judgment. The Congress was slow and contrary and
the Supreme Court was bound by its procedures; the whole responsibility devolved on the president.

What this impossible duty had become by Kennedy's time is detailed in these books. All the authors agree that he struggled manfully,
and all too often they incline to picture defeats as victories. He lost his
domestic battles because it was not clear what he might do, and even
more because he was met by a resistance he had no weapons for over-
coming. He was always conscious that he had to tread a narrow path
between the expectation that he would be the nation's protector and
the castigation that exploded when he used the means available to him.
He learned to be cautious about offending. He was a man of courage,
but a president's courage is not personal. He sometimes spoke of
"putting the presidency on the line," meaning that he risked diminishing his freedom to act. When he did this once or twice with business
or labor, he lost far more than he gained. When he went on the journey
to Texas that ended so fatally, it was because he knew he had lost too
much. He foresaw probable defeat in 1964 and was beginning a
campaign of recoupment.

III

In view of their sympathetic understanding of Kennedy's trials and of
his unremitting efforts to act as the people's surrogate, it seems strange
that none of his helpers gained perspective enough to unearth causes or
suggest remedies. There is no recognition that the presidency itself
had become impossible and that some sort of drastic overhauling had
become imperative. It is forgotten now, in the belated flowering of a
Kennedy cult, that he was a discouraged, not a triumphant, man in
1963. It was not because he failed in devotion or bravery; it was because
he was overwhelmed.

Sorensen does not admit this; everything, he says, was moving in
Kennedy's direction in November 1963: ". . . abroad after the Cuban
missle crisis and Test Ban Treaty, at home with the tax and civil rights
bills, in office with more complete mastery of the Executive Branch.
He was . . . neither wearied nor disillusioned by his burdens, more
respected and beloved than before, still growing, still striving. . . ."

Schlesinger is similarly affirmative: "He had so little time . . . yet he had accomplished so much. . . . He gave his country back to its best self, wiping away the world's impression of an old nation, of old men, played out, fearful of ideas, change and the future. . . ."

It is hard to take these dithyrambs seriously. He was no doubt an inspired leader for those who were close to him; but the rest of the country did not see it so and, if they read these encomiums now, will not find them believable.

He was a president who had little power because he had so small a majority and because he had so little influence as a legislative leader. He will be remembered, after some years, it may be guessed, for having participated in the disaster of the Bay of Pigs and for having faced down Khrushchev when the Russians attempted to establish a direct threat to American security in Cuba: one disaster and one triumph.

These last have to do with quite another phase of the presidency, one that presidents have really come to dominate as they have not the domestic scene. In one he failed; in the other he succeeded.

Actually both the Schlesinger and the Sorensen books have much more to say about Kennedy the world statesman than about Kennedy the chief executive. It was in foreign affairs that his talents—and his courage—could best be displayed. He, like other presidents, was allowed in such matters the most undisputed power—a power, again, that is not at all clearly conferred in the constitution but has been taken for granted since Washington's administration with, along the way, some embarrassing conflicts with a recalcitrant Senate. But one of the strangest—and longest—discussions in Schlesinger's account concerns the President's frustrations with the department in charge of foreign relations. In desperation he created a small duplicate State Department in his own office. This seems a feeble device to have been adopted by so inventive and intrepid a person. Actually it was an avoidance of trouble. Somewhat the same course was followed with Defense. In neither case was any attempt made to reduce these unruly bureaucracies—as they are pictured—to proper discipline. They were simply accepted as existing evils and left to function emptily in their own preferred ways, outside the presidential orbit.

Something is wrong here, very much wrong; but what it is we do not learn from these chronicles. The truth is that Kennedy did not function as an executive. He had only the most meager contacts with the secretaries of the domestic departments, largely because he had no interest in their operations. He had no cabinet, really, seeing no sense in discussing foreign policy with secretaries of Agriculture or Interior. This, of course, has been the habit of other presidents, but they were not executives either. Concerning this Sorensen admits that Freeman in Agriculture and Udall in Interior were "vigorous and progressive. . . .

But they were handicapped by the President's inability to give their departments and problems the same time and attention he gave to national security affairs."

This is putting first things first for a chief of state, but not for a chief executive. The neglect of domestic affairs is unfortunately not merely occasional; since the nation is continually in crisis now, made so by its position of overwhelming strength and by the challenge of newly risen nations with a missionary determination to humble the giant, the need for drastic change is underlined almost daily. No president, so long as this condition exists, will be able to act as chief executive.

What is needed is becoming obvious. National security is not, for instance, separable from the operations of at least three departments— Defense, State, and Treasury; and the president must certainly put together the budget and report on the state of the union. But why should he be called on to pretend that he is the administrator of the other departments (growing almost yearly more numerous) and agencies that so large, so complex, and so rich a nation needs to meet modern demands? There is agitation rising almost to furor about several issues—city deterioration, crime, pollution of air and water, transportation, and recreation, for instance—that, if they are mentioned at all in these memoirs, are mentioned only in passing. We are in danger of becoming a monstrous slum concentrated on our position in the world, concerned with the welfare of people in every nation but our own.

Of course the economy must be attended to. However much presidents regard themselves as world-strategists, they are forced to think of domestic management when hard times—or inflationary ones— threaten. Their attention is then jerked back from their main preoccupation somewhere abroad, but soon they are again diverted. Udall and Freeman did not often see Kennedy. No secretary of these vast conglomerations has for many years often seen his nominal chief.

IV

Kennedy's constant preoccupation was the one with which all modern presidents are forced to concern themselves. This, of course, is political leadership. It is properly the duty of the sole representative of all the people in a democratic state. Much of interest about it will be found in these books. All were involved with it and all understood its demands. Sorensen was most influential in this and Salinger was, as press secretary, its forward operative. Schlesinger often offered advice. But none of these was a real professional. The operative helpers were "the Irish Mafia"—O'Donnell, O'Brien, and the others, including Robert Kennedy.

This presidential responsibility, because it was not anticipated in the constitution, also has special difficulties that sometime and somehow must be remedied. A partisan nominee, an advocate, who suddenly on election becomes president, not only of his party, but of a whole people, but who, from time to time, must resume his partisan role, cannot be completely or satisfactorily chief of state. He may have a narrow majority, or he may not even have had a plurality of all the votes—something not only true of Kennedy but of his Democratic predecessors Cleveland and Wilson. He must always be conscious of having to earn the approval of something like half the electorate who preferred another candidate, or, at least, must be wary of their watchful skepticism. This was Kennedy's special cross, and it constricted his freedom of action. He was always, for instance, looking for Republicans, preferably realistic ones, to man his agencies—men like Dillon, McCone, McCloy, and Clay. This contributed to his safety from criticism; but it did not please members of his own party and enable him to influence the Congress and it did not give him intimates. The impression of him that lingers is that he was a very lonely man.

His calculations, however frustrated, were his alone to work out. They were intended to enhance his own powers and those of his office. But these are peculiar in nature and have become more peculiar with time. The theoretical ability to superintend the administrative establishment, when any novel initiations are undertaken, encounters the resistance of a huge bureaucracy; and if not resistance, then inertia. Orders from a president are smothered by interpretation as they pass down from desk to desk. There is delay, and, often, outright and organized opposition. Instructions affecting a private interest will, within hours, or certainly days, provoke a call from a senator or a congressman with protests. And mere changes in procedure or policy will simply be found not to happen. By pursuing the matter he can, of course, prevail, but he cannot pursue a hundred matters over a hundred days and with a hundred people.

The result of this is that the machine tends to run in its own way and at its own pace, more influenced by some interested legislator or a group of them, who make trouble if they are not listened to, than by the nominal chief executive.

The inability of a president—who must be political leader and chief legislator and who is sole custodian of the national security—to direct the domestic establishment has become almost total. Kennedy was reluctant to accept this disability and his helpers are reluctant to acknowledge it, but in his last year—1963—he was reduced to following up persistently no more than a few issues, and three particularly—civil rights for Negroes, the prevention or ending of serious strikes, and activating the economy.

These involved his duty as chief legislator; and at this he labored earnestly with the help of a formidable presidential lobby—that Irish Mafia—to extend federal investment in education, public housing, and other measures to expand purchasing power. He recognized his responsibility for leadership. But the struggles with a recalcitrant Congress were wearing and often only half-successful. He must have come to realize what seems never to have occurred to him in his years as a legislator, that congressional reforms were long overdue. Nor does it seem to have occurred to these chroniclers; either that, or reform seemed so remote as to be impractical.

These books dwell with pride on Kennedy's valiant bearing throughout his ordeals, but there is almost no suggestion that either he or they considered his frustrations to be institutional. In the sense that these are accounts only of the brief Kennedy years, there is, perhaps, no reason why there should have been such a questioning. Yet this was Kennedy's real trouble as it had been that of his predecessors. The Congress had fallen into the control of committee chairmen from safe districts, and nothing could disturb their immovability. They were reactionary and mostly Southern, and they treated presidential proddings with silent contempt. In these circumstances Kennedy got done only what this small cabal felt it must concede to prevent serious attempts to displace them.

As to this it is probable that congressional reform will never originate with a president. He must always try to get along as best he can because there are immediate things to be done. But the Congress will never itself initiate reform. It was given the advantage in the constitution of controlling the gateway to amendment. As a consequence, so far as congressional prerogative is concerned, there has never been any. As the original House of thirty-nine members, and Senate of twenty-four, grew to its present size, and debate gave way to committee operations, usually secret, the original notion of a legislature that made laws for the chief executive to carry out was reversed. The initiative passed to the president, with legislators holding back, bargaining for advantage and consenting only for extraneous reasons. The national interest gets a poor showing on Capitol Hill.

These rules do not apply to matters of foreign policy. Since the Congress has less interest, and lately because being commander-in-chief has become more important, the president's reputation is apt to be determined by his conduct of foreign affairs. Occasionally a treaty is not confirmed by the Senate, or the House attempts to interfere with military or diplomatic management as it does with domestic matters; but the president is indisputably chief of state, and interference with his assumed prerogatives has usually been extremely unpopular.

This is an unsatisfactory situation, too, in a democracy. A president cannot be king today, prime minister tomorrow, and permanent head of the civil service all the time. Yet even those caught up in constitutional obsolescences, as Kennedy was, struggle in the web without complaint. Not only he but these three extraordinarily competent helpers accepted things as they were, quite willing to lose tremendous battles without questioning the set conditions.

We are asked to agree that Kennedy was a great president. His accomplishments suffer by comparison with those of his successor, but this is somehow not accepted as the criterion. He was a man of grace, wit, courage, and devotion. His successor is notably less endowed with these qualities. It is submitted that these are the characteristics of a chief of state, not of a chief legislator or chief executive.

32

The South and the Reconstruction of American Politics

DEWEY W. GRANTHAM, JR.

The American South has always had its own identity. In The Mind of the South *(1940), probably the most widely known and influential volume on the South to appear in recent decades, W. J. Cash tried to define that identity. The South, he said, was sentimental and unrealistic, deeply rooted in its past, suspicious of new ideas, greatly attached to racial values. Its values were surely American, but they had been modified to a point where the South was almost a nation within a nation. It was, in Allen Tate's phrase, "Uncle Sam's other province."*

Some three decades later, it has become clear that the South is being fundamentally transformed. No one has done better to explain the transformation than C. Vann Woodward who, viewing it in historical perspec-

SOURCE: *The Journal of American History*, LIII (September, 1966), 227–46. Reprinted by permission.

tive, sees it as a Second Reconstruction. But unlike the first, says Woodward, the second is succeeding (see "From the First Reconstruction to the Second," Harper's, *April 1965). The basic difference between the two is that this time the Negro, rather than leaving his fate to the white man, has acted in his own behalf. Guided by his own leaders and organizations, impelled by a sense of his own power, he has himself been "a decisive participant, not an instrument of white purpose." The civil rights movement in all the areas of the old Confederacy is part of a larger social and economic transformation in which conditions in the South are increasingly approximating conditions in the rest of the country.*

A paramount feature of the Second Reconstruction has been the remaking of Southern politics, and it is this theme which Dewey W. Grantham, Jr., of Vanderbilt University deals with in the following essay. A specialist in the history of the South, Grantham is the author of two noteworthy books: Hoke Smith and the Politics of the New South *(1958), a study of the progressive governor and United States senator from Georgia, and* The Democratic South *(1963), a broad survey of Southern politics since the Civil War. In the essay below, Professor Grantham shows how Southern politics has, in the period since World War II, been altered by three significant factors: new economic and social conditions, the movement for Negro rights, and the increasing impact of the federal government on regional economics and politics. Grantham stresses the arrival of genuine two-party competition in presidential elections. In pursuing his theme, he points out that what is happening in Southern politics is closely related to what is happening in the politics of the nation.*

The interplay between the South and the rest of the nation poses challenging questions. How has the South related to the rest of America: in what ways has it shared national values and institutions, in what ways has it been a deviant, distant republic? Has the South been an America intensified and exaggerated, more heroic in its pursuit of the national myth, more pernicious in its intentness on achieving it? How far has the South's response to its social problems—above all, that of defining a role and status for its Negroes—dramatically diagrammed the inescapable tensions in all of American life between the ideal society and the real, the reach of our entrepreneurship and its grasp, the democratic principle and its actual practice, the appeal of golden opportunity and its miserably base attainment? In discussing the tendencies of recent decades, Grantham says that earlier Southern politics "was the perversion of the democratic process writ large." But he does not adequately convey what he means by the democratic process. Is it not by its nature subject to perversion? In what respect was it perverted in the South in an earlier era, and for what reason? The close tie between the South and the rest of the nation is central to Grantham's theme, but it is not really clear from what he is saying just how American politics is being reconstructed. The question, then, is how have the three forces he cites as central in the reconstruction of Southern politics also transformed American politics?

That new patterns are taking shape in Southern politics seems to be evident enough from recent events. In the elections of November 1966, which occurred a few months after Grantham's essay appeared, the resurgence of the Republicans in national politics was particularly strong in the South, where their congressional representation rose from 19 to 28. Southern Republicans elected governors in Florida and Arkansas and a United States senator in Tennessee for the first time since the days of the First Reconstruction. The South's politics was responding to larger forces at work throughout the nation.

But if the South was in these ways becoming American, could it not also be said that America was becoming Southern? The dynamics by which the South was coming to share American standards and modes—industrialization, internal migration, and urban growth—were also the dynamics by which the rest of the United States was coming to share the Southern problem. It was above all the migration northward of large elements of the South's black rural proletariat which at once diffused and altered the character of the Negro Revolution; and, by contributing to the creation of the inner cities of the larger metropolitan centers in the North and the West, infused awesome vitality into what had hitherto been a relatively contained, acquiescent Negro population. The tense dualism of black unrest and white backlash has now become a phenomenon of national, not merely regional, magnitude. Meeting the Negro's insistent demands for equality is now an American problem, not merely a Southern one. The problem, as we have seen, inheres in a larger transformation of American society and of American politics. The Second Reconstruction of the South is part of a vital and profound American Reconstruction.

The conflict between the forces of change and continuity in the southern part of the United States today is strikingly apparent in the region's politics. Although economic and social changes have contributed most notably to the South's recent transformation, it is clear that political affairs below the Potomac have been significantly altered during the last decade and a half. It appears not only that political practices within the region will be vastly different in the future but also that the changes now taking place will be profoundly important for American politics as a whole.

The elements responsible for change in the recent South are numerous and complex, but three factors should be emphasized in considering the evolution of southern politics since World War II. In the first place, federal intervention and the pressure of the national party system have steadily eroded the foundations of the South's political solidarity. Secondly, the industrialization, urbanization, and diversification of the regional economy have had a significant impact upon the course of southern politics. Finally, the movement for Negro rights, encompassing as it does the emergence of a compelling national issue, the Negro's political activation, and his own remarkable leadership, is having a far-reaching effect.

In some respects, of course, the emerging South is the product of developments that antedate the Great Depression and the New Deal. Early in the twentieth century a strong bifactionalism emerged along liberal-conservative lines, an important middle-of-the-road progressivism appeared with an urban leadership and philosophy, and a significant farm movement greatly influenced the making of public policy. The Wilson administration brought the region its first real involvement in the control of the national government since the Civil War. During the progressive era and the decade following World War I, state and municipal governments in the South began to adopt long-needed social reforms and introduced numerous public services. Meanwhile, the region was being differentiated in its economy and society by industrialization and urbanization, the rapid growth of Texas and Oklahoma, and the economic diversification of the upper South. Some of these tendencies were evident in the disruption of the South in the election of 1928, although they provided only a momentary threat to the continued solidarity of the section in national politics.

Franklin D. Roosevelt's leadership and the New Deal precipitated an extraordinary popular agitation over political and economic issues in the South, forced national issues into state and local political contests, and introduced codes and standards that did much to undermine the old faith in freedom of contract and states' rights. The New Deal also provided southern congressmen with an opportunity to contribute to the enactment of a momentous program of national reform and stimulated the liberalism of many southern leaders. But if the New Deal tended to nationalize southern politics and if it gave southern leaders a conspicuous place on the national stage, it also diminished the section's importance in the Democratic party. The repeal of the historic two-thirds rule for nominations in the national convention of 1936 and the consolidation of Roosevelt's national coalition in the election of that year made it impossible for the South to maintain as influential a role in the party's councils as had been true in the past. The revolution Alfred E. Smith began had been consummated.

Many things encouraged southerners to respond favorably to Roosevelt's leadership during the early 1930s. The manner in which the movement for his nomination in 1932 challenged the eastern domination of the Democratic party, the understanding he showed of the agrarian traditions of the South and West, his espousal of Jeffersonian principles, his enormous personal charm, and the way in which he identified himself with the southern region all struck a responsive chord among southerners. But somehow, as Frank Freidel has noted, Roosevelt's "states' rights and individualistic generalities seemed to lead him again and again to specifics involving positive government action." In time the unanimity of his southern support was destroyed and "the reservoir emptied—but only slowly." As men who felt strong personal ties of loyalty to each other and to the Democratic party, and as men who enjoyed the power provided by the party's majority position, southern congressional leaders were inclined, even after many of them had come to have doubts about the President's program, to give him what he wanted. For a time, moreover, some of them assumed that the New Deal was no more than a revival of the New Freedom— and would offer no greater threat to southern independence than had Wilson's administration. In addition, writes Freidel, the Roosevelt measures "represented a giant, nation-wide cornucopia from which federal aid poured into the desperately Depression-ridden South."

This is a point of transcendent importance. It goes far to explain the ambivalent response of the South to the New Deal as well as the increasing integration of the region into the framework of national politics in later years. The sudden infusion of money through the agricultural price-support system, federal credit agencies, and public works programs reanimated the old dream of a New South. The rescue of the agricultural economy and the rejuvenating effects of land reform, river development, reforestation, and new public buildings, roads, and schools can scarcely be overemphasized. But if this New Deal largess met with the approval of almost all southerners, many of them soon began to question such consequences of federal intervention as the growth of organized labor and the threat to regional wage differentials.

The New Deal also contained an implicit threat to the most vital element in the structure of southern solidarity—the dogma of white supremacy. The various New Deal expenditures designed to help the underprivileged inevitably went in considerable part to Negroes. Although the sharp opposition to Roosevelt's program provoked from southerners in the late 1930s stemmed largely from economic considerations, some southern congressmen expressed their racial concern from time to time, and a few of them foresaw how "the tiny shoots of civil rights controversy would burgeon in later years." The Supreme Court soon began to whittle away at the "separate but equal" doctrine, wartime innovations like the Fair Employment Practices Committee made their appearance, and racial tensions and dark rumors—of "Eleanor Clubs" and worse—swept the South in the wake of the Negro's economic advances and growing independence. By the end of the war it was easy for white southerners to speak of the New Deal's "coddling" of the Negro.

The New Deal's transformation of the Democratic party at the national level, its extensive involvement in the economy, and its modest contribution to the incipient movement for Negro rights represent aspects of governmental centralization in the United States which have been greatly accelerated during the last quarter century. And these developments have left their marks on recent southern politics.

If southern leaders expected Roosevelt's successor to turn aside from the path charted by the New Deal, they were quickly disillusioned. The reform program Harry S. Truman sponsored would not only expand the economic measures of the 1930s but would also enter boldly into the field of federal civil rights legislation. The revolt of the Deep South that resulted in 1948 carried South Carolina, Alabama, Mississippi, and Louisiana into the columns of the States' Righters, precipitating a bitter and continuing debate over the nature of the Democratic party as a national organization.

The most recalcitrant southern politicians argued that the Democratic party in the United States was confederate in nature, with the state parties being virtually autonomous. But this contention made little headway outside of the Dixiecrat states, and the dictates of the national party became more and more controlling in the years that followed. Even in the states they carried in 1948, the States' Righters appropriated the official Democratic label on the ballot. Following the election the question of party loyalty became an issue in several southern states, and in 1952 most state party organizations did not openly desert the national ticket. New party rules adopted in 1955–1956 involved the state parties and delegations to the national convention in good-faith commitments to work for the listing of the national ticket on the state ballot as the official Democratic party. Pressure for a more specific "loyalty pledge" mounted during the next eight years, and at the 1964 convention a plan was adopted to guarantee a broader base for the party's organizational politics. A majority of the state and congressional leaders in the South actively supported the national ticket in 1960, and this pattern was even more pronounced in 1964.

Many southerners had long assumed that, no matter how reform-minded a national administration might be, the South's essential position, particularly in the area of race relations, could always be protected because of its powerful voice in Congress. But this assumption has been greatly weakened as a result of liberal Democratic leadership in Washington and the force it has exerted through the party for the implementation of its platform. This situation reflects the strength of the Democratic party in other regions. Meanwhile, the rigidity and negativism of southern politicians weakened their effectiveness as sectional spokesmen. Southern congressmen were unable to prevent the passage of civil rights legislation in 1957 and 1960, and when the full resources of a Democratic administration were brought into play for the first time in 1963 and 1964, they found it impossible to prevent the enactment of a comprehensive civil rights law. Although the much-discussed conservative coalition of southern Democrats and non-southern Republicans continues to be effective after more than a quarter century of collaboration, it is significant that in 1964 most Republicans joined with the northern and western Democrats to pass the civil rights legislation, while the southern Democrats, especially in the House, did not combine with the Republicans in opposing the administration's antipoverty bill. The power of the Lyndon B. Johnson administration, the growth of southern Republicanism, and the eventual decline of the civil rights issue as the most compelling question confronting southern politicians may well lessen the significance of the interparty coalition in future years.

Since the mid-1930s the South's political defenses have crumbled one by one: the repeal of the two-thirds rule and the diminishing importance of the region in the Democratic national convention, the invalidation of the white primary and the liberalization of suffrage requirements, and the eventual weakening of the congressional seniority system. Nevertheless, it would be a mistake to overemphasize the element of coercion in the process of integrating the South into the Democratic party as a national organization. Southern leaders in Congress and in the various states have frequently been eager to respond in a positive way to some if not all of the progressivism inherent in a dynamic reform party in control of the national government. This was evident in the contribution of the more constructive southern congressmen to the enactment of the major New Deal measures, in the first presidential bid by a southerner in modern times on the basis of a genuine national appeal, and in the governorships of such men as Ellis G. Arnall of Georgia, Kerr Scott of North Carolina, and LeRoy Collins of Florida. A notable minority of congressmen from the South have not been true "southern coalitionists," and such men as Estes Kefauver, Albert A. Gore, Lister Hill, J. William Fulbright, and Russell B. Long have found opportunities in national Democratic administrations for service that goes beyond regional commitments.

Such considerations have contributed to the legislative successes of the Johnson administration and they played an important part in the presidential election of 1964 in the South, despite the unique factors in that campaign. In Arkansas, to take one example from the 1964 contest, the continued desire for federal assistance conspired with the pressure from national party leaders and the challenge of the Republicans at the state level to produce the best organized and most unified Democratic campaign in a generation. Governor Orval E. Faubus, while not outspoken in his support of the national ticket, discovered the merits of a Democratic campaign based on the "precinct to presidency" concept. One is reminded, in pondering the nationalizing effects of our new federalism, of the story told to James A. Michener by a newspaperman who traveled with Johnson through the South during the campaign of 1960. The vice-presidential nominee would invade a state capital, convene the two senators and the governor, and commence a lengthy political confab enlivened with plenty of liquid refreshments. After expressing his sympathy with the state leaders' repugnance for parts of the national platform, their doubts about John F. Kennedy's religion, and their fears growing out of the civil rights movement, "Good Ol' Lyndon" reminds his fellow Democrats that if the national campaign is lost both he and Kennedy would remain in the Senate.

> . . . and, Senator Buford and Senator Baxby, I just don't see how, if your defection is the cause of our defeat, you're ever going to get one little old bill through the Senate. Governor Beauregard, you say you have to have that new airport and you want to keep the Army base down here. How do you think you're going to get such bills through the Senate if Mr. Kennedy and I are sitting there solely because you didn't produce the vote that would have elected us?

If federal assistance in its myriad forms explains why many southerners approve and even welcome a dynamic government in Washington and are willing to come to terms with the centralizing tendencies of the party structure that accompany it, the economic development of the South, resulting in part from the aid of the national government, has greatly affected the region's politics. The South's relative position among the major regions has improved in almost every category of wealth since 1930. Factories and assembly plants have sprung up from Richmond to San Antonio; agriculture has been increasingly mechanized and diversified; sharecroppers and agricultural workers in large numbers have left the farms for the cities of the South and North, while a growing stream of technicians, managers, and businessmen has flowed into the region. The old agrarian South fell before the onslaught. The traditional staples in the southern economy steadily declined in relative importance, and the proportion of the labor force employed in agriculture dropped in the 1960s to less than 10 per cent (it had been more than 50 per cent in 1920). The region's relative urban population increased in the single decade of the 1950s almost as much as during the preceding thirty years. The migration that contributed to the urbanization of the South and other sections has accounted for a decline in the southern farm population of some eight million people since 1940. It has also reduced the Negro-white population ratio in the South to 1 in 5, and today less than 50 per cent of all American Negroes live in southern states.

Much of this change was painful, and many depressed farmers and unskilled inhabitants of towns and cities knew little of the region's new prosperity. Yet the prosperity was real and there was firm support for the buoyant economic outlook that lifted southern hopes. Southerners became healthier and better educated; the face of the land was remodeled as a result of improved agricultural methods, river development, and recreational programs; and modern roads and mass communication media destroyed the old isolation of the more remote areas. Changes in the social mobility and the class structure of the South are clearly diluting the homogeneity of the section and creating a society that will likely become more impervious to the debilitating effects of white-supremacy politics. Greater general prosperity and new modes of urban life will almost certainly have an impact upon a political system in which great numbers of people were traditionally too poor and apathetic to play any part. These developments may be expected to sharpen social and economic issues in such a way as to cut into the traditional domination of the black belts. Some states, particularly the so-called rim states, have moved much farther from the old regional patterns than have others, and their politics reflect this progressive shattering of the South.

In the long run the emergence of an urban politics may be among the most significant consequences of the new patterns of economic and social life in the region. The city makes it possible to mobilize group sentiment and to organize coalition campaigns. In the urban South workers have a better opportunity to join labor unions and Negroes have a better chance to vote. There is some evidence that the percentage of strict segregationists is smaller in urban than in rural areas of the South, that legislative contests are more competitive in metropolitan districts than elsewhere, and that congressmen from the urban South are less inclined to be influenced by sectional considerations in voting on foreign policy issues than are their rural colleagues. The pressure for municipal reform, for expanded public services at all levels, and for legislative reapportionment reflects the new urban politics in the region. In effect the city increasingly is providing the South's traditional underprivileged elements with a more democratic political setting.

But the process of economic growth and urbanization has proceeded at different rates of speed within the South as a whole and within each of the southern states. Ninety-eight of Georgia's 159 counties lost population in the 1940s, for example, and only 45 per cent of the region's counties experienced any population growth at all during the 1950s. The declining economic and social status of many rural and small-town southerners coupled with their disproportionate political power and reactionary policies have made them the great conservators of the South's traditions. It is this situation that accounts for much of the bitterness in the school desegregation controversy and the reapportionment struggle and that partially explains the upsurge of isolationism in the region.

The civil rights movement as a national issue and the growing importance of the Negro voter in the South have also helped to reshape the contours of southern politics. These developments are in considerable part the product of the great centralizing thrust in recent American politics and the vast change in the southern economy. Long before federal intervention, the collapse of the old agricultural economy in the South sent a broadening stream of Negroes northward, where their urban concentration and political power made them a significant factor in calling the civil rights movement into being. Meanwhile, the South's rapid urbanization and the economic advances of its Negro citizens combined with the opening of the primaries and the gradual removal of suffrage restrictions to give southerners of darker skin a new voice in political affairs. The political activation of the Negro and the broader movement for racial equality have become a mighty force in their own right and a major vehicle for the reconstruction of American politics. As a keen student of southern affairs points out, "Today, the Negro grip on the levers of social change is secure, and much more firm than the remnants of white direction."

The first significant increase of Negro voters in the modern South came in the wake of the Supreme Court decision in the case of *Smith* v. *Allwright* (1944), which opened the primaries to Negroes. By 1952 about 20 per cent of the Negro adults in the former Confederate states were registered to vote, and this percentage has slowly climbed since that time, reaching about 44 per cent (more than 2,174,000) early in 1965 as compared with a white registration of approximately 73 per cent. But Negro registration varies widely within the South (and within the individual southern states), ranging from a low of 6.7 per cent in Mississippi to a high of 69.4 per cent in Tennessee at the end of 1964. Intimidation, subterfuge, and various kinds of pressure applied by whites, as well as tradition, poverty, and illiteracy, have inhibited the political activation of Negroes in many parts of the region. Nevertheless, hundreds of registration drives and the new note of militancy among Negro leaders suggest that the ballot has become one of the most cherished symbols in the Negro's long quest for equality. The commitment of the Kennedy and Johnson administrations to the realization of this goal and the drive for federal legislation culminating in the voting law of 1965 will have a profound effect upon future southern politics. They foretell the emergence of a "new breed" of southern politicians.

Although the Negro vote in the South has not become the balance of power the demagogue perennially warned against, it has become too important to ignore. A student of Louisiana politics has pointed out, for instance, that Negro votes were "a crucial element in Adlai Stevenson's narrow victory in Lousiana in 1952; in Earl Long's first primary triumph in the 1956 Democratic gubernatorial primary; and in Eisenhower's precedent-shattering conquest of Louisiana's electoral vote in 1956." In 1960 Negro voters provided an indispensable contribution to Kennedy's narrow victory over Richard M. Nixon. The overwhelming Negro support (something like 95 per cent) Johnson received in 1964 made it possible for him to win just over half of the southern vote, and Negro votes made the difference in at least four of the southern states he carried.

Not only are Negroes becoming a vital consideration in presidential and statewide elections in the South, but they are also emerging as a major force in the liberalization of congressional districts and metropolitan areas. Negroes are now being elected to city councils and state legislatures, and they have suddenly begun to acquire an unaccustomed leverage in obtaining a fairer share of municipal services. Southern politicians are increasingly taking Negro voters into account. "Perhaps the most impressive new fact of Texas politics," commented the *Texas Observer* immediately after the election of 1964, ". . . is the politically coercive influence of Negro and Latin-American voters. It has become dangerous to the career of a statewide candidate to be known as an opponent of civil rights." The growing increment of Negro voters and the passage of the Civil Rights Act of 1964 and the voting rights legislation of 1965 will free many southern politicians from their long subservience to race and encourage economic liberals to adopt a more constructive approach to civil rights and related issues. The campaign for Negro enfranchisement will bring the ballot to many neglected whites in the section, reversing one of the side effects of Negro disfranchisement half a century ago. The possibility of a durable coalition between a portion of the white electorate and a substantial number of Negro voters below the Potomac is much more promising in the present situation than were the Reconstruction and Populist experiments.

No aspect of recent southern politics is more significant in its promise for the reconstruction of American politics than the rehabilitation of the Republican party and the arrival of genuine two-party competition in presidential elections in the South. This development, in its early stages at least, was related more to economic than to racial considerations, and it would seem that over a long period of time economic and social changes will provide the most lasting foundation for the growth of Republicanism in the region. But in the short run, and particularly in the Deep South, racial alienation has been an important factor in the erosion of traditional Democratic loyalties. There was, for example, a noticeable "Dixiecrat to Ike" trend in the states carried by J. Strom Thurmond, and in some cases the States' Rights ticket became a halfway house along the road to Republicanism. There was some evidence of this in the election of 1960 and it was massively demonstrated in the lower South in 1964. Mississippi, which was captured by a slate of unpledged electors in 1960, gave Barry M. Goldwater a stunning 87 per cent of its votes four years later. One wag was moved to remark that "we now have two parties in Mississippi but we're getting them one at a time."

Although the number of "Presidential Republicans" in the South increased during the 1940s, the election of 1952 was the event that set off the explosive forces long building up in the region. The basic explanation of the Republican party's southern victories in the 1950s lies in deep-seated economic and social forces, and in the growing dissatisfaction on the part of many southern Democrats with New Deal and Fair Deal economic policies. The Republicans retained their traditional strength in the upland regions of the South, but their most spectacular gains came in the urban areas. In city after city in the southern states Dwight D. Eisenhower carried the upper-income precincts by handsome majorities (and many of the middle-income precincts by less generous majorities), while Stevenson carried the lower-income districts by equally substantial margins. In 1956 the Republicans won no less than 60 of the approximately 100 urban counties in the 11 ex-Confederate states. While their percentages declined somewhat in 1960, the same pattern is evident in the returns from that election. In the 68 metropolitan counties and independent cities (those with an urban population of 50,000 or more) in the former Confederate states, Nixon received 49.3 per cent of the total vote as compared with 47.8 per cent for Kennedy. The Republican candidate undoubtedly benefited from the fact that Kennedy was a Catholic, and it should be noted that he ran better than Eisenhower in the black belts of 6 southern states.

This southern Republicanism reflected a strong liking for Republican conservatism and an intense dislike of Democratic liberalism. Southerners who had grown wealthy in the 1940s and 1950s often proved to be inordinately sensitive about threats to free enterprise, while many professional people and small businessmen were suspicious of big government and heavy public expenditures which they associated with Democratic control in Washington. Individualism remained strong in the flush industrial areas, many farmers and ordinary workers continued to respond to the incantation of states' rights, and large numbers of southerners agreed philosophically with conservative Republicanism. The process of siphoning off conservative Democrats was clearly under way. In Texas during the early 1960s there were reports of "Resignation Rallies"! Republicans benefited from the white migration into the region, the increase in the number of professional people and college graduates, the expanding middle class, and the rapid urbanization. As class and group differentials emerge in a two-party context, urban Republicanism in the South will probably level off, but the cities and suburban areas appear to provide the best hope for continued Republican gains in the southern states.

One scholar recently observed that

The GOP is discovering the wonders and infinite possibilities of leadership, organization, grass-roots contact, research, primaries, permanent headquarters, attractive candidates, contested elections on every level, the exploitation of dissatisfaction with Democratic one-party politics, issues, all-out, all-weather and all-year efforts, and grasping the impact of vast changes on traditional habits, loyalties, and images of the South.

The party's activity at the state and congressional levels did increase noticeably during the late 1950s and early 1960s. By 1964, according to party reports, all but 138 of 1,140 counties in the eleven Old South states were "organized." In 1958 Republican candidates for the United States House of Representatives from southern states polled only 609,108 votes; four years later the party's candidates obtained 2,083,971 votes. In 1964 Republican candidates ran in 84 of 119 congressional districts in the thirteen southern states, winning eighteen seats (as compared with fourteen in the previous Congress). Republicans have also become more active on the local scene, particularly in urban places, and they have won a scattering of offices. Although Republican victories in the South's local politics have scarcely rippled the waters of the long one-party calm, the grass-roots effects of economic change, urbanization, and reapportionment are becoming evident.

The forces of tradition, the vested interests making up the one-party structure, the obsession with race as a political issue, the conservative Democratic control of state and local government, and the prestige and influence of southern congressmen will all no doubt inhibit the emergence of a more thoroughgoing two-party system in the southern states. Nevertheless, millions of southerners in recent years have voted Republican for the first time, and that party has acquired a respectability—and even glamor—in some southern quarters that greatly enhances its competitive position. The shift from "postoffice Republicanism" to competitive Republicanism, the accelerating pace of GOP campaigning, and the increasing southern turnouts in presidential elections also augur well for the Republicans.

The deviant character of the national election of 1964 may have interrupted the emergence of a competitive Republican party in the rim states of the South, and the future of a Republicanism in the Deep South keyed to racism is clouded with uncertainty. But in some respects the election of 1964 may prove to be extraordinarily significant in its impact upon southern politics. A great many southerners supported the Republican party for the first time in their lives, and never before had the full implications of a national campaign reached into so many parts of the region. In states like Virginia and Florida the concept of party loyalty assumed new meaning and importance for Democratic leaders. And a majority of the southern states demonstrated their unwillingness to be dominated by racial or economic extremism.

Genuine two-partyism will probably develop in the inner South—the five states carried by Goldwater—more slowly than in the outer South. But the historical pattern of the border states may be duplicated by more and more southern states as they undergo social and economic changes. Following the Civil War, the Democrats captured control in all of the border states. But in each of them the Republicans were strong enough to pose a constant threat and occasionally to defeat the Democrats when the latter's factionalism flared up in bitter controversies. In time a party realignment, reflecting economic and demographic trends as well as New Deal politics, brought most of the Negroes, many of the upland inhabitants, and the laboring classes in the industrial region into the Democratic party, while the business interests and the old Democratic Bourbon element, originally Whig, increasingly went over to the Republican party.

The dynamic elements in the southern economy and the new wealth have heightened the conservative tendencies of southern politics, but the new society is also producing other groups that will eventually serve to counteract the dominant ones and to fragment and liberalize state and local politics. Such factors as socio-economic status, migration patterns, and issue orientation are not altogether absent even in the racially dominated politics of the Deep South, and the recurrent cleavages within the Democratic party in some areas are being translated into a Democratic-Republican division in national elections. The division of the electorate in the senatorial contest of 1962 between Lister Hill and James D. Martin may foreshadow a restructuring of the state's politics in a way that will align upland whites and enfranchised Negroes in partisan opposition to black-belt Bourbons and urban middle-class conservatives. In Texas, to take an even more promising case, the changing economic and social developments of the last quarter century and the impact of New Deal policies are clearly producing a system based on class and group politics.

As the urban populations come to exert greater weight in the political process through reapportionment and the political activation of the less affluent social elements, it is reasonable to expect southern politicians at all levels of government to broaden their programs. In Florida the governor increasingly speaks for the booming urban areas, and one result of reapportionment may well be a shift from the old struggle between the governor and the legislature to a conflict within the legislature, with the governor supporting one side or the other. In Virginia the rapidly growing urban corridor extending from the northern part of the state to the Tidewater cities has already diluted the power of the rural-based Byrd machine and the traditional Democratic dependence upon the Southside. The cities may provide much Republican support in future Virginia elections, but they are also likely to bring the Democrats recruits in the form of Negroes, organized labor, and the middle-class "swing vote."

The adjustment of state government to the demands of the modern era, halting and inadequate though it is, has proven nevertheless to be an innovating factor in southern politics. Responding to new social problems produced by rapid economic and population shifts, and also to the pressure of numerous federal programs that assimilated state and local governments into their machinery of operation, the states have greatly expanded their functions during the last two decades. One of the most notable features of state government in this period has been the emergence of the governor as a political and legislative leader, in part because of the lack of leadership in most legislatures. "With very few exceptions," says one student of state government, "the governor of a southern state is a program-oriented individual who sees the accomplishments of his administration in the light of program goals." In the future, as the effects of reapportionment and a broadened franchise become more obvious, governors in the South, as in other regions, are likely to prove increasingly responsive to the urban masses, including Negroes. The same will be true of a majority of southern legislators.

It is not too much to say that a political revolution, the end of which is not yet in sight, has swept the South since the 1930's. That revolution is intimately related to America's swiftly changing federalism and the Democratic dominance in our party system during the past generation. The federal government has probably had a greater impact upon the South than upon any other section—whether in the form of TVA, military and space installations, or court decisions and legislation in the field of civil rights. After conducting an intensive study of federal expenditures in Mississippi, the general counsel of the Civil Rights Commission observed in 1963, "We approached Mississippi as if it were pitted against the Federal government, but the most striking thing we found was the *presence* of the Federal government, in its aid programs and other activities, throughout the state." The national government has been the principal instrument in the broadening of the southern electorate, in making southerners more politically conscious, and in orienting them toward substantive issues. The growth of federal power since 1932 has served to liberate the states in important ways and to stimulate their administrative functions. The national parties have gradually extended their discipline into the South and have involved state and local units more completely in presidential campaigns. Democratic administrations in Washington have facilitated the appearance of "integrated liberals" in Congress from some southern metropolises and encouraged a selective liberalism on the part of more moderate leaders interested in public power, health, education, and other economic assistance from the federal government. National policies and issues, along with economic change and moderate leadership, have also contributed to the recession of racist politics in the outer states of the South. On the other hand, southern disaffection in and out of Congress with New Deal and Fair Deal reforms has been compounded by new currents in foreign affairs which weakened strong ties that once existed between many Democrats in the region and the national party on international questions. Economic and social changes have also had their effect. The South no longer possesses a distinct economic interest, and its well-to-do and rising middle classes find much in common with conservatives in other regions.

One of the consequences of the New Deal revolution was the assault on one-partyism through the resurgence of the Democratic party in many non-southern states. The erosion of sectionalism in other parts of the country deprived the Republican party of many safe congressional seats, and this situation encourages the GOP to compete with the Democrats in the South today. A slow convergence has taken place between "critical facets of mass-electoral behavior" as they appear in the South and elsewhere in the United States. Meanwhile, the geographical center of the race issue is rapidly shifting from South to North as a process of "de-regionalization of the problem" takes place.

Whether or not the "Negro problem" accelerates the process of party realignment in the region, it has surely been the most incendiary issue in recent southern politics and a major factor in the revolutionary character of political affairs in the contemporary South. The Second Reconstruction of the South has in fact come within sight of accomplishing what the First Reconstruction promised but failed to achieve: the full guarantee to the American Negro of his rights as a citizen. The Second Reconstruction, writes C. Vann Woodward, has "turned a corner." It is instructive to note how it differs from the first attempt at Reconstruction. In the current Reconstruction the Negro himself is a decisive participant, his voting power is more strategically located, the movement is sparked by Negro leaders and organizations, it is supported by white allies in the South as well as the North, and it is inspired by the pervasive awareness among Negroes of the enormous moral and political power of their cause.

The South has served in some measure as the nation's political conscience or, to use Leslie W. Dunbar's phrase, "America's exposed nerve." The region has provided the best example of the flouting of

America's most hallowed political traditions: the two-party system, the expression of minority and dissenting views, and responsible and broadly political leadership. Yet, fundamentally, what happened in the South was the perversion of the democratic process in America writ large. The recurrent dialogue that other parts of the country have carried on with the South suggests that Americans outside of the region have long recognized their own image in the mirror held up by that wayward section. But the South has changed in our time, changed enormously, and so has the rest of the United States. To understand the real meaning of the revolution the South is now experiencing, it is necessary to remember that the country as a whole has undergone a momentous change since 1929—a change grounded in the Great Depression, the New Deal, and the Second World War. The Second Reconstruction of the South, in its broadest dimensions, is only a part of that profound transformation in our national life.

33

The Limits of American Capitalism
ROBERT L. HEILBRONER

As we advance into the later decades of the twentieth century, we try to discern the direction in which the American polity is moving. We more clearly define the principal institutions of our society, liberal democracy and capitalism, by contrasting them with the authoritarian democracy and socialism of the Soviet Union, its satellites, and the People's Republic of China. We are aware that neither form of human polity purely articulates its central ideals. Indeed, we perceive that, in the dialectical process of history, both forms act and react upon each other, and that the confrontation between them may lead each one to assume some of the essential features of the other. The course of history involves the transformation of a society's institutions and ideas, and we accept as axiomatic that America will be substantially transformed during the next several decades. But how far can our polity change and still retain its identity? What are the limits within which American capitalism may be altered, without losing its basic character?

Robert L. Heilbroner undertakes to answer these questions in the essay below. His books, which translate the more difficult concepts of economic science into the language of the layman and which for this reason have found a wide audience, include: The Worldly Philosophers, The Future as

SOURCE: *Commentary*, XLI (April, 1966), 23–35. This article appeared in *Commentary* under the title "The Future of Capitalism," a condensation of pp. 3–4, 66–134 from Robert L. Heilbroner, *The Limits of American Capitalism* (New York: Harper & Row, 1966). Copyright © 1966 by Robert L. Heilbroner. Reprinted by permission of Harper & Row, Publishers.

History, The Making of Economic Society, *and* The Great Ascent. *The essay that follows is a slightly abridged version of the second of two essays that constitute his most recent volume,* The Limits of American Capitalism *(1966). In the five sections of this essay, Heilbroner addresses himself to the questions he considers central to his theme: 1) Why do societies resist change? 2) Within the limits of capitalism, to what extent is it possible to eliminate poverty and the maldistribution of income? 3) To what degree can capitalism accommodate planned production and overcome the problems of a market economy? What limits does "the capitalist imagination" impose on possible changes in capitalism? 4) How may the challenge of communism impel American capitalism to change? 5) In what ways may the "explosion of science and technology" transform the essential institutions of capitalism?*

To these questions Heilbroner has brought answers that are thoughtful and thought-provoking, so much so, indeed, that they compel us to turn to him with a series of our own questions. How correct is he in arguing that the basic force resisting change in capitalism is its inherent "system of privilege"? How can he reconcile his argument that the privileged capitalist class resists change with his statement that privilege is "invisible" and that the privileged are unaware of their being so? In what sense is capitalism a system of privilege, if the possession of wealth is widespread and the aspiration for possession almost universal?

Is there not a dialectic of interaction between the two predominant forms of contemporary economic philosophy that we ought to consider in estimating just what the limits of American capitalism are? It is fair enough to say that communism may pose a challenge to capitalism, but is it not specious to argue, as Heilbroner does, that communism's obvious shortcomings—its own system of privilege and its economic performance—do not significantly affect the impact of its challenge? How much more flexible, adaptive an economic system is capitalism than communism? What Heilbroner does not stress enough, indeed what he virtually glides over, is the degree to which communist ("socialist") ·societies are becoming capitalist. May we not say that the most remarkable phenomenon in the evolution of world economies is not so much how capitalism is being transformed by democratically expressed demands for social welfare and social responsibility, but how much communism is being transformed by massive popular insistence on material improvements—in goods and services—and by the resultant need to introduce elements of a market economy to satisfy this insistence? Is not Soviet Libermanism a backdoor capitalism, and does not Liberman represent for communist economic thought the kind of argument qua *rationalization that Adam Smith represented for late mercantilist economic thought?*

Heilbroner regards "economic man" as quintessential to capitalism and therefore as imposing limits on the changes possible within capitalism. But how far are the characteristics of "economic man," as Heilbroner defines them, really those of all men, and how much is he therefore confusing the limits of capitalism with those of human nature? His analysis is meaningful only to the degree that it posits a larger determinism. But is not the analysis substantially vitiated by his argument that scientific technology owed little to capitalism? Would it not have been more consistent with his theme to say that capitalism, for its own growth and survival, inevitably bred and fostered the technological advances that would in time radically transform it?

Both principal types of human polity today—the liberal capitalist and the authoritarian socialist—measure their success in terms of their effectiveness in meeting the internal and external problems they are facing. America's present crisis stems from our war in Vietnam and the plight of our central cities. The first has stirred a revolt of our college youth, the second a revolt of our black population. Because both revolts are concentrated and continuous, they seriously affect the course of our polity. Because both call into profound question the consensus on which our society rests, they may narrow the limits within which our socio-economic institutions can operate. If they do this, they would also be challenging the existence of American liberal capitalism itself.

For roughly the last century and a half the dominant system of economic organization in most of the West has been that of capitalism. In all likelihood, barring the advent of a catastrophic war, capitalism will continue as the dominant system of the Western world during the remainder of this century and well into the next. Although it will inevitably change, will likely suffer considerable duress over the next decades, and in the longer run will gradually give way to a very different kind of social order, for our lives and for those of our children, capitalism bids fair to confront us as the prevailing form of social organization in those nations where it is now solidly entrenched.

It seems to me that all serious social analysis and prediction must start from some such premise. At any rate, it is my premise, and I propose to explore—with all the uncertainties and risks inherent in such an enterprise—the social changes available to us within the limits of capitalism in the future.

But how can we establish these "limits"? Perhaps we can shed an initial light on the question if we imagine asking some perceptive observer in, say, 13th-century France what were the limits of feudalism. Our observer might be hard put to find an answer, particularly if he looked about him at the striking variety of forms that feudalism assumed in the various domains of Europe. Yet undoubtedly we could have suggested an answer to him that would have sounded reasonable: It is that certain kinds of economic and social change were unimaginable—indeed impossible—in 13th-century France because they would have implied the establishment of some totally different form of social organization. To take a central instance, it would have been impossible to have replaced the traditional ties, established customs, and fixed obligations by which the manorial economy hung together with some radically different system, such as the cash markets that were already disrupting the settled tenor of feudal economic life, because a change of this dimension would have critically undermined the power of the lord, elevated out of all proportion that of the parvenu class of merchants, and thereby destroyed the fixed hierarchy of status that was the very backbone of the feudal social structure. Thus, one meaning we can give to the idea of "limits" in a society is very simple: It is those boundaries of change that would so alter the functional base of a society, or the structure of privilege built on that base, as to displace a given social order by a new one.

In terms of the immediate subject of our essay, this draws the broad limits of American capitalism in the last third of the 20th century with reasonable fixity. To take a few examples: it is certainly beyond the present limits of capitalism to replace the guiding principle of production for profit by that of production for use; it is impossible to nationalize the great corporations or to end the private ownership of the means of mass communication; and it is impossible to end the concentration of wealth in private hands. One can debate whether all or any of these changes are desirable, but there is little point in debating whether they are realizable. Barring only some disaster that would throw open the gates to a radical reconstruction of society, they are not.

What we have established thus far, however, is only the first and most obvious answer to the question of what we mean by the "limits" of social change. For if we now return to the 13th century, we could imagine suggesting to our medieval observer another approach to the idea of feudal limits. Rather than pointing out to him the contemporary incompatibility of the market system, we might be able to show him the immense long-term historical momentum of the emergent forces of the monetized economy. Indeed, we might even be able to bring him to see that by the end of another four or five centuries, feudalism would have virtually disappeared, and that an economic organization of society once incompatible with feudalism would have triumphed over it.

From such a perspective, the task of delineating the limits of feudalism becomes a different one. It is no longer to discover what cannot be done in the short run, but to explore what *can* be done, and how, in doing it, the social structure may slowly and subtly alter, making possible still further change in the future.

It need hardly be said that one cannot project such a long evolutionary—or possibly revolutionary—advance in close detail. The precise route to be taken, the pace of progress, the roadblocks where the invading forces of a new society may be temporarily halted or even thrown back—all this surpasses any power of analysis we now have. But the grand line of march is not beyond our ability to foresee. Looking back at 13th-century France, we can see how defenseless were its castle walls against the insinuating influence of the market system. In similar fashion, it should be possible to explore the limits of capitalism in America, not alone in terms of changes that cannot now be accommodated by the business system, but in terms of those forces that are altering capitalism, like feudalism in an earlier day, in ways that will eventually cause its social and economic structure to be displaced by another.

I

We cannot, however, explore change until we answer a prior question: Why do societies resist change? A full explanation of social inertia must reach deep into the psychological and technical underpinnings of the human community. But in the process of gradual social adjustment it is clear enough where to look for the main sources of the resistance to change. They are to be found in the structure of privilege inherent in all social systems.

Privilege is not an attribute we are accustomed to stress when we consider the construction of *our* social order. When pressed, we are, of course, aware of its core institutions in capitalism—the right to reap private benefits from the use of the means of production and the right to utilize the dynamic forces of the marketplace for private enrichment. The element of privilege in these institutions, however—that is, their operative result in favoring certain individuals and classes—is usually passed over in silence in favor of their purely functional aspects. Thus, private property is ordinarily explained as being no more than a convenient instrumentality for the efficient operation of an economic system, or the market elements of Land, Labor, and Capital as purely neutral "factors of production."

Now these institutions and relationships do indeed fulfill the purposes for which they are advertised. But this is not the only use they have. Land, Labor, and Capital are not just functional parts of a mechanism but are categories of social existence that bring vast differences in life chances with them. It is not just Labor on the one hand, and Land or Capital on the other; it is the Bronx on the one hand and Park Avenue on the other. Similarly, private property is not merely a pragmatic arrangement devised for the facilitation of production, but a social institution that brings to some members of the community a style of life qualitatively different from that afforded to the rest. In a word, the operation of capitalism as a *functional* system results in a structure of wealth and income characteristic of capitalism as a *system of privilege*—a structure in which the top two per cent of American families own between two-thirds and three-quarters of all corporate stock, and enjoy incomes roughly ten times larger than the average received within the nation as a whole.

The mere presence of these concentrations of wealth or large disparities of income does not in itself differentiate the system of privilege under capitalism from those of most other societies in history. Rather, what marks off our system is that wealth and income within capitalism are not mainly derived from non-economic activity, such as war, plunder, extortionate taxation, etc., but arise from the activity of marketers or the use of property by its owners.

This mixture of the functional and the privileged aspects of capitalism has a curious but important political consequence. It is that privilege under capitalism is much less "visible," especially to the favored groups, than privilege under other systems. The upper classes in feudalism were keenly alive to the gulf that separated them from the lower classes, and perfectly open about the need for preserving it. The upper groups under capitalism, on the other hand, are typically unaware that the advantages accruing to them from following the paths of the market economy constitute in any sense or fashion a "privilege."

This lack of self-awareness is rendered even more acute by virtue of another differentiating characteristic of privilege under capitalism. It is that privilege is limited to the advantages inherent in the economic structure of society. That is, the same civil and criminal law, the same duties in war and peace, apply to both economically privileged and unprivileged. It would be a mistake to concentrate on obvious differences in the application of the law as being of the essence. Rather, one must contrast the single system of law and obligation under capitalism—however one-sidedly administered—with the *differing* systems that apply to privileged and unprivileged in other societies.

The divorce of economic from political or social privilege brings up the obvious fact that, at least in democratic societies like America, the privileged distribution of economic rewards is exposed to the corrective efforts of the democratic electorate. The question is, however, why the structure of privilege has remained relatively intact, despite so long an exposure to the potentially leveling influences of the majority.

In part, we can trace the answer to the very "invisibility" of privilege we have just described. Furthermore, in all stable societies the structure of privilege appears to the general public not as a special dispensation, but as the natural order of things, with which their own interests and sentiments are identified. This is especially true under capitalism, where the privileges of wealth are open, at least in theory, and to some extent in practice, to all comers. Finally, the overall results of capitalism, particularly in America during the entire 20th century and recently in Europe as well, have been sufficiently rewarding to hold anticapitalist sentiment to a relatively small segment of the population.

That the defense of privilege is the active source of resistance to social and economic change may appear so obvious as scarcely to be worth emphasizing. Obvious or not, it is a fact too often passed over in silence. It seems to me impossible to analyze the nature of the opposition to change without stressing the vulgar but central fact that every person who is rich under capitalism is a beneficiary of its inherent privileges. Taking the American system as it now exists, it seems fair to assert that the chance to own and acquire wealth constitutes a primary—perhaps even a dominating—social motivation for most men, and that those who enjoy or aspire to these privileges will not readily acquiesce in changes that will substantially lessen their chances of maintaining or gaining them.

II

The touchstone of privilege provides an indispensable key when we now return to our main theme. If it does not give us an exact calculus by which to compute what changes will and will not be acceptable, it does give us an angle of entry, a point of view, without which attempts to cope with the problem of social change are apt to have no relevance at all.

Take, for example, the problem of the poverty that now afflicts some 30 or 40 million Americans. One alleged cause of this poverty has always directly stressed the privileges of capitalism. This is the view that poverty under capitalism is largely ascribable to wage exploitation. There is clearly an element of truth here, in that the affluence of the favored groups in capitalism does indeed stem from institutions that divert income from the community at large into the channels of dividends, interest, rent, monopoly returns, etc. It is by no means clear, however, that the amount of this diversion, if redistributed among the masses, would spell the difference between their poverty and their well-being. On the contrary, it is now generally acknowledged that the level of wages reflects workers' productivity more than any other single factor, and that this productivity in turn is primarily determined by the quantity and the quality of the capital equipment of the economic system.

Certainly, the productivity of the great mass of workers under capitalism has steadily increased, and so have their real wages. Today, for example, industrial workers in America cannot be classified as "poor" by prevailing absolute standards, if we take $4,000 a year as defining a level of minimum adequacy for a small family. Although wage poverty is clearly present in capitalism, it is primarily restricted to the agricultural areas and to the lowest categories of skills in the service trades. No small part of it is accounted for by discrimination against Negroes, and by the really shocking levels of income of Negro farm and service labor. On the other hand, the proportion of the labor force that is afflicted with this poverty is steadily diminishing. Farmers, farm managers, and farm laborers together will probably constitute only 5 per cent of the labor force within a decade. The low-paid non-farm common laborer, who constituted over 12 per cent of the working force in 1900, makes up only 5 per cent of it today and will be a smaller percentage tomorrow.

There remains, nevertheless, the question of how much the existing level of wages could be increased if the categories of capitalist privilege did not exist. Since it is difficult to estimate accurately the total amount of "privileged" income under capitalism, let us take as its convenient representation the sum total of all corporate profits before tax. In the mid 1960's, these profits exceeded $70 billion a year. If this sum were distributed equally among the 70 million members of the work force, the average share would be $1,000. For the lowest-paid workers, such as migrant farm laborers, this would represent an increase in annual incomes of 100 per cent or more—an immense gain. For the average industrial worker, however, the gain would be in the neighborhood of 20–25 per cent, certainly a large increase but not one that would fundamentally alter his living standards.

Thus, insofar as the institutions of capitalism constitute a drain upon non-privileged groups, it can be fairly said that they are only marginally responsible for any inadequacy in the prevailing general level of income. Individual companies may indeed be capable of vastly improving the lot of their workers—General Motors makes nearly as much gross profit on a car as it pays out in wages, and "could," therefore, virtually double its wages. But for the economy as a whole, no such large margin of redistribution is possible. So long, then, as the defense of these privileges does not result in substantially *increasing* the share of national income accruing to the privileged elements of the nation, it seems fair to conclude that the level of material well-being under capitalism is limited mainly by the levels of productivity it can reach. If the trend of growth of the past century is continued, the average level of real wages for industrial labor should double in another two to three decades. This would bring average earnings to a level of about $10,000 and would effectively spell the abolition of wage poverty, under any definition.

This conclusion does not close our investigation into the relationship between poverty and privilege, but rather directs it toward what is now revealed as the principal cause of poverty. This is the fact that large groups within the population—the aged, the handicapped, the sick, the unemployed, the castaways in rural backwaters—have no active tie into the market economy and must therefore subsist at the very meager levels to which non-participants in the work process are consigned. There is only one way that their condition can be quickly alleviated, but that one way would be very effective indeed. This is to redistribute to them enough income earned or received by more favored members of the community to bring them to levels of economic decency. A program with this objective would require some $10 to $12 billion above the public assistance that the poor now receive in this country. Such a sum would amount to approximately a seventh of corporate profits before tax. Alternatively, shared among the 11- or 12-million consumer units who constitute the top 20 per cent of the nation's income receivers, it would require an average additional tax of roughly $1,000 on incomes that average $16,000.

In both cases, in other words, a program to eliminate sheer need among the poor would constitute a sizable incursion into the incomes enjoyed by favored groups, although hardly such an invasion as to constitute the elimination of these privileges. Thus, the failure to carry out such a program cannot be laid to the "objective" or functional difference that such a redistribution would entail, but simply to the general unwillingness of those who enjoy higher incomes to share their good fortune with those who do not. As Adam Walinsky has very aptly put it, "The middle class knows that the economists are right when they say that poverty could be eliminated if we only will it; they simply do not will it."

To what extent does that conclusion, then, lead to the prospect of alleviating poverty within the next generation or so? In the short run the outlook is not very hopeful. Given the temptations of luxury consumption and the general lack of deep concern in a nation lulled by middle-class images of itself, it is doubtful that very effective programs of social rescue can be launched within the next decade or two. Yet, of all the problems confronting capitalism, poverty seems the least likely to be blocked permanently by the resistance of privilege. Tax receipts are now growing at the rate of some $6 billion a year simply as a consequence of the growth of the level of output, and this flow of funds to the government will increase over the future. It may be that these receipts will be used for larger arms expenditures for some years, but assuming that full-scale war will be averted, sooner or later the arms budget must level off. Thereafter the funds will become available for use either in the form of tax reductions—an operation which normally favors the well-to-do—or as the wherewithal for a major assault on the slums, etc. In this choice between the claims of privilege and those of social reform, the balance is apt to be tipped by the emerging new national elites, especially from government. In addition, a gradual liberalization of the prevailing business ideology is likely to ease opposition to measures that clearly promise to improve the quality of society without substantially affecting its basic institutions of privilege.

It is idle to predict when Harlem will be reconstructed and Appalachia reborn, since so much depends on the turn of events in the international arena. Yet it seems to me that the general dimensions of the problem make it possible to envisage the substantial alleviation—perhaps even the virtual elimination—of massive poverty within the limits of capitalism three or four decades hence, or possibly even sooner.

The elimination of poverty is, however, only part of a larger problem within capitalism—the problem of income distribution. Hence, we might now look to the chances that capitalism will alter the moral anomalies of wealth as well as those of poverty.

Here it is not so easy to foresee a change in the operational results of the system of privilege. Since the 1930's, the political intent of the public has clearly been to bring about some lessening of the concentration of income that goes to the very rich, and some diminution of the enclaves of family wealth that have passed intact from one generation to the next. Thus, we have seen the introduction of estate taxes that levy imposts of about one-third on net estates of only $1 million, and of fully half on net estates of $5 million; and these rates have been supplemented by measures to prevent the tax-free passage of wealth before death by gift.

Since the enactment of these taxes, a full generation has passed, and we would therefore expect to see some impact of the legislation in a significant lowering of the concentration of wealth among the top families. Instead, we find that the share held by the top families has decreased only slightly—from 33 per cent of all personal wealth in 1922, to 29 per cent in 1953 (the last year for which such calculations exist). Concentration of stock—the single most important medium for the investment of large wealth—has shown no tendency to decline since 1922. Equally recalcitrant before egalitarian measures is the flow of income to topmost groups. Legal tax rates on top incomes have risen from 54 per cent under President Hoover to over 90 per cent in the 1940's and early 1950's, and to 72 per cent in the mid 1960's. The presumed higher incidence of taxes at the peak of the income pyramid has, however, been subverted by innumerable stratagems of trusts, family sharing of income, capital gains, deferred compensation, or other means of tax avoidance or outright tax evasion.

There is no indication that this resistive capacity of the system of privilege is likely to weaken, at least within the time span of a generation. Nor is there any sign that the "natural workings" of the system will lessen the flow of income to the top. The statistics of income distribution clearly show a slow but regular drift of income *toward* the upper end of the spectrum. Three per cent of all income was received by income receivers in the $15,000-and-up brackets in 1947; in 1963, in terms of constant dollars, this fraction had grown to eight. This determined self-perpetuation of large concentrations of private wealth is likely to continue—afflicting the social order with that peculiar irresponsibility that is the unhappy hallmark of the system. The power of wealth is by no means the only source of power in America and may, in fact, be expected to decline. But the voice of money still speaks very loudly, and the capacity of wealth to surmount the half-acquiescent opposition of a democratic political system promises that it will continue to resound in America for a long while to come.

III

The maldistribution of income and the social problems that spring from it can no longer be said to threaten the viability—although it may seriously jeopardize the social peace—of capitalism. This cannot be said, however, of a second problem—the economic malfunction that has periodically racked capitalism over the last hundred years and that nearly caused its demise in the 1930's.

The persistent breakdowns of the capitalist economy can all be traced to a single underlying cause: the anarchic or planless character of capitalist production. So long as the output of individual firms is guided solely by the profitable opportunities open to each, without regard to the state of the market as a whole, economic short-circuits must result whenever the output of all firms fails to dovetail with the structure of demand, or when the production plans of the business community as a whole are not adequate to cope with the independently formulated savings plans of the community at large. In a milieu of huge enterprises and enormous fixed investments, such miscalculations or imbalances carry the potential of a major disruptive impact.

Hence, it is not surprising that reformers have long advocated planning as the remedy for capitalist depressions or stagnation. The trouble has been, however, that much of the planning which its partisans have urged upon it has been incompatible with the institutions of capitalism. For example, proposals to nationalize the core of heavy industry or to convert the biggest corporations into quasi-public utilities, may have much to recommend them along strictly economic lines, but they all infringe the preserves of private property or of the market to a degree intolerable to the American business community.

This does not mean, however, that planning is therefore ruled out. On the contrary, a great deal of planning is virtually inevitable over the coming decades, but it is likely to be used in support of the main institutions of capitalism rather than as a means of replacing them.

One such planning instrument is certain to be the reliance on the government's fiscal powers to maintain aggregate demand. Although we are still only in the early stages of experience with public demand-creation, there is little doubt that a bold use of fiscal mechanisms can virtually guarantee a steady or rising level of total expenditure. Moreover, since demand-creation involves little or no interference with individual markets or business, it impinges little, if at all, on the preserves of privilege. Tax cuts, for example, are certain to be welcomed by business and upper-income groups. Additional spending, so long as it is within the established areas of public concern—arms, roads, schools, rivers and harbors, conservation, and perhaps now social welfare—is also welcomed as a source of new business.

There remains, to be sure, a body of ideological resistance to the use of fiscal measures of a compensatory sort, compounded of an ignorance of public finance and a shrewd foreboding that the assumption of public economic responsibility, no matter how useful at the moment, is freighted with serious long-term implications. Yet it seems likely that this is a view of dwindling importance. A very considerable segment of business backed the controversial Kennedy tax cut, and the undoubted success of that policy should pave the way for further measures of the same kind. In addition, the non-business elites, especially from the academic and government establishments, are strongly in favor of fiscal controls to buoy up the system, and their influence in securing the bold use of these measures may be very important or even decisive. Thus, there seems a reasonable expectation that measures to safeguard the economy against the collapse of effective demand lie well within the ambit of capitalism today.

What is more difficult to judge is the extent to which capitalism will be able to go beyond general fiscal planning into planning on a more detailed basis for the achievement of broad welfare objectives. Here the experience of Europe since the war is relevant. In nearly every nation of Europe we have seen the formulation of planning techniques that go considerably beyond the mere application of fiscal leverage, to the conscious "design" of the economic future. The very fact that European capitalism has taken this turn puts it beyond argument that a considerable amount of indirect planning is compatible with the main institutions of capitalism.

On the other hand, the growth of European planning owes much to the particular traditions of European capitalism, including the more or less formalized structures of employers' federations and the pronounced "*étatist*" tradition in many states. The absence of comparable institutions and history makes doubtful the possibility of a wholesale transplantation of European forms of planning to America. Furthermore, unlike its sister capitalisms across the Atlantic, the United States has not become accustomed to the public ownership of transportation or utilities, or to a large public-housing sector, or to the development of a strong system of public welfare.

As a result, the United States has always entertained an exaggerated suspicion of all invasions by the public authority into private terrain. Hence the extent and speed with which American capitalism may evolve in the direction of detailed economic planning would seem to depend primarily on whether circumstances arise that require such techniques. If, for example, the continued incursion of technology, coupled with a very large inflow of young people into the labor market, should create an employment crisis during the next decade, some form of industrial planning would quite possibly emerge as an instrument of social policy. In that case, policies designed deliberately to create employment through a substantial enlargement of public activities at state or local levels, or—looking farther ahead—the designation of a civil sector, such as the rebuilding of the cities, as the peacetime equivalent of the military sector, might well show up as part of the practicable social agenda.

Capitalism, then, can achieve considerable change within the boundaries imposed by its market mechanisms and privileges of private property. But there are also important limits beyond which it cannot go—at least within the foreseeable future. Primary among these is the continuing requirement that the economic participants in a capitalist world—even in a planned capitalist world—behave in the manner that is required of them if the market mechanism is to work. That is, they must act as "economic men," buying cheap and selling dear, allowing relative remunerations to weigh heavily in their choices of occupations or employment, setting acquisitive aims high in the hierarchy of life goals. These marketing traits are not merely pervasive private idiosyncrasies that can be dispensed with if they are no longer esteemed. They are integral to, and necessary for, the successful operation of a market system. In a setting of bare subsistence and newly-risen entrepreneurs there is little difficulty in adducing the acquisitive behavior required to run a capitalist economy. But in a more advanced and affluent society, where the primary drives of self-preservation begin to fail, the necessary marketing behavior must be sustained by supplementary motives of emulation and competitive striving. Thus, the endless and relentless exacerbation of economic appetites in advanced capitalism is not merely a surface aberration, but a deeply-rooted functional necessity to provide the motivations on which the market system depends.

This thralldom to an overweening economic imperative of sales and profits and its accompanying worship of a calculus of income are features of capitalism that cannot be eliminated by planning. A planned capitalism of the future, however rid of its gross malfunctions, will nonetheless be one in which men are subservient to the economic demands of a market environment.

Nowhere is this apt to pose a more serious problem than along the extended frontier where technology interacts with society. This interaction takes two forms. One, which we may call the *direct effect*, is revealed as the immediate change in the environment brought about by the application of a new technique such as the computerized control of production, or the use of a new product such as a jet transport. This effect, as we know from experience, may bring radical changes into economic or social life, but these changes have, at least, been consciously introduced into society (although often with inadequate appreciation of their immediate impact).

But there is as well an *indirect effect* of technology that diffuses throughout society as the secondary consequence of new machinery or new processes. Thus, the indirect effect of the new technology of automation is unemployment; the indirect effect of the new technology of medicine and health is an aging population; the indirect effect of the technology of war is the creation of a military-industrial economic sector. Not least we find, as a general indirect effect of all modern technology, an increasing complexity, size, and hierarchical organization of production, which gives rise in turn to a growing need for public intervention into the economic process itself.

Against this tremendous invasion of technology, a market economy offers but one instrument of control—the profit or loss stemming from the direct effect of a particular technology. As to its side-effects, the market mechanism proper has no controls whatsoever. As a result, the invasion of technology becomes an essentially disruptive force, continuously upsetting the patterns of life in a haphazard manner. Under a system that abdicates as much decision-making as possible to the rule of profit, the possibilities for a rational restraint over this force that rearranges our lives thus shrinks to a minimum. Capitalism is essentially defenseless before the revolutionizing impact of its technical drive. Of all the limits to which capitalism is subject, this is the most unyielding—although, as we shall see, it is this very helplessness of the system before the technological onslaught that holds out the most important promise for the long-term remaking of capitalism itself.

Our next concern lies with the reach and inhibitions of what we might call the *capitalist imagination*.

The quality of this imagination is most clearly revealed if we think for a moment of the "visionary" glimpses of the future often spelled out for us by business spokesmen—a future of enormous affluence, technical marvels, widespread leisure, etc. There is, in these vistas, much that is genuinely new and rich with possibilities for material betterment. But there is also something inherent in all these visions that remains unmentioned. It is that these imagined societies of the future still depend on "workers," however well off, who work for "businessmen," however enlightened, in a system motivated and directed by the commercial impulse, however tempered or refined. A society in which there were no workers or businessmen as we understand the terms; or in which the categories of privilege had been fundamentally altered; or where the pressures of the marketplace had been replaced by some other means of assuring economic continuity—all these possibilities are absent from the capitalist imagination. More than that, they are dismissed as "utopian."

Albeit unwittingly, this is set forth all too clearly in the peroration of a recent book by Frederick R. Kappel, President of A.T.&T.:

> We are involved in one of the great ideological struggles of all times. Essentially it is a contest between two quite basic concepts. One is that men are capable of faith in ideas that lift their minds and hearts, ideas that raise their sights and give them hope, energy, and enthusiasm. Opposing this is the belief that the pursuit of material ends is all that life on this earth is about.

The words are eloquent enough, but alas, what do they reveal? Which side, ours or theirs, is the side of "ideas that lift minds and hearts," which the side that believes "the pursuit of material ends is all that life on this earth is about"? In the breathtaking ambiguity of this intended affirmation of business faith, the unseeing confusion of identities meant to be so clearly polarized, lies an all too clear exposition of the weakness that inhabits the very center of the capitalist imagination.

We cannot be sure what effect such a constricted view of the future may have on the aspirations and attitudes of most American citizens. It is likely that for the majority who are understandably concerned with their material lot, it would make no difference whatsoever. But for a not unimportant minority—I think of college youth and of the intellectual community—the absence of any transcendent secular goal is apt to present an oppressive limitation to thought and spirit. Indeed, in my opinion the present anarchic mood of youth may well be due to just such a lack of a visionary future to which to bend its hopes and efforts.

IV

Whatever the ultimate effect of this stifling at home, there is another area where the limitations of the capitalist imagination are likely to be of very great importance. This is in the contest with Communism for the guidance of future world society.

It is hardly necessary to speak of the power of Communism as a force bearing on American capitalism. Yet in appraising that force, we often fail to articulate that which is most threatening about it to ourselves as members or protagonists of the capitalist way of life. This is the presence of Communism as a viable social system that has dispensed with our institutions of privilege, and that therefore faces capitalism with the living refutation of their necessity. In this fundamental sense, Communism puts capitalism on trial before the bar of history. In this trial it matters not that Communism has its own system of privilege, in some ways more primitive than our own. Nor does it count for much that capitalist performance on many fronts is manifestly superior to that of Communism. What matters is that Communism has demonstrated the mutability and historic transiency of our particular social order, and that that social order can never again feel entirely secure in its claims to permanence and legitimacy.

I believe it is this sense of historic unease that lies behind the deep, uncritical, and often unreasoning hostility of America toward Communism. The reasons we cite for our fear and hatred—the undeniable acts of cruelty and repression, of aggression and intolerance, of intrigue and untrustworthiness—can be duplicated in many non-Communist countries: in Portugal, in Spain, in the Union of South Africa, in various Latin American dictatorships, past and present. There, however, they have never roused in us the fervor or revulsion they do when discovered in the Communist world. In part, this is no doubt because these other nations are small and weak and do not constitute centers of national power comparable to Russia or China (although hardly Cuba); in part, because they do not seek to export their particular world-views. But more deeply, especially among the conservative interests of this country, I think it is because the existence of Communism frightens American capitalism, as the existence of Protestantism once frightened the Catholic Church; or the French Revolution the English aristocracy.

The fundamental threat of Communism is not likely to decline over the next generation. Rather, it is apt to grow. In Russia, the prospect is clearly for substantial economic expansion; for the gradual improvement of the still dreary life of its people; for a continuation of its massive scientific advances; for further intellectual, and perhaps political, liberalization. For China, no such sanguine assurances can be given, but its continuing emergence as the unquestioned leader of Asia seems hardly likely to be reversed. In Latin America and Africa, the outlook can only be for political turmoil as the aspirations of excited masses outdistance any conceivable pace of progress. In the ensuing unrest, radical leaders are bound to emerge, and it would be a miracle if they were not inclined, to some degree, toward Communism or some kind of national collectivism.

This tendency is apt to be reinforced by the very ideological limitations of capitalism we have been concerned with. If we look to the developing nations, we find in nearly all of them a yearning, not alone for material progress, but for a great social and political, even spiritual, transformation. However millennial these hopes, however certain to be dashed, they are not to be lightly disregarded. The leaders and elites of the young nations, like those of our own youth, are looking for a model of a society that will fire them to great efforts, and it is unlikely that they will find this model in the market-based and wealth-protecting philosophy of capitalism.

All these considerations point to the very great likelihood that Communism or radical national collectivism will make substantial inroads during the coming generation or two, perhaps by conquest or subversion, but more probably by the decay of existing orders unable to handle the terrible demands of political awakening and economic reformation.

Given this grave outlook, what would be its impact on America?

We have already witnessed the initial impact in the substantial militarization of American capitalism. The so-called military-industrial complex (to which should be added "political" as an equal partner) today contributes between eight and ten per cent to the Gross National Product. In the 1960's, military expenditure has regularly exceeded the sum total of all personal income taxes, has accounted for one-fourth of all federal public works, has directly employed some 3.2 million workers in defense industries and another 1.1 million as civilian employees of the Defense Department and the services, has subsidized about one-third of all research in the United States; and not least, has come to be accepted as a normal and permanent fixture of American life by all groups, including the academic. The fact is that American capitalism is now a semi-militarized economy and will very probably become even more so during the next decade.

In this dangerous situation, it is important for us to clarify the specific influence over the direction of events that can be ascribed to the business interest in society. According to Marxism—or more properly Leninism—the business structure itself inherently presses the state toward armed conflict. The fierce economic conflicts of capitalist nations prior to World War II, the long history of capitalist suppression of colonials continuing down to the present in some parts of Africa, the huge and jealously guarded interests of the United States and other capitalist nations in the oil regions of the Near East or Latin America— all make it impossible to dismiss such a picture of a belligerent capitalist imperialism. At the same time, even a cursory review of the nations initiating aggressive actions since 1945 should raise doubts as to the exclusive capitalist predisposition to war. More important, an analysis of the roots of belligerency in the more warlike capitalisms, specifically pre-war Germany or Japan, must emphasize the leading role played by purely military or lingering feudal elements, and the largely passive, although not always reluctant, part taken by capitalist groups.

On somewhat more Marxian lines, Victor Perlo has made a determination of the direct economic interest of the top American corporations in war or peace. He concludes that the economic self-interest of the biggest corporations is more or less evenly divided, with half profiting from a defense economy, and half—including such giants as General Motors and U.S. Steel—being penalized by it. Assuming that big businessmen would be motivated to oppose or support disarmament on such grounds, it is important to note that nothing like a monolithic "pro-war" economic interest can be said to exist within American capitalism.

Further, the imperialist thrust that increased both the chances and the causes of war in the late 19th century seems to be giving way to less dangerous forms of international relationship. Property interests that once had to be defended by force of arms are now protected by government insurance. International relationships that formerly allowed large capitalist enterprises to intervene directly into the economic and political life of colonial nations have been succeeded by relationships in which the independence of action of foreign companies is severely restricted. In a word, the politics of nationalism has asserted its preeminence over the economics of imperialism, with the salutary consequence of a diminution in the role of business as the active initiator of foreign economic policy.

Thus, the role of business proper in the struggle for world power does not seem intrinsically warlike. Unfortunately, that does not mean the chances for conflict are therefore small. Business is not the only power center within capitalist societies, and in America the military and the civil branches of government contain more than their share of belligerent-minded leaders who are in a position to influence foreign policy. Then, too, we must reckon with the generalized hatred of Communism among the lower and middle classes, a hatred that may originally have been implanted but that now flourishes as a self-maintaining source of aggression.

In this situation, given the reciprocal posture of the other side, it is difficult to see how a major conflict could be avoided, were not the consequences of all-out warfare so terrifying. On both sides, only the instinct of self-preservation—fortunately the single most powerful instinct—holds back the military-minded, the fundamentalist, the ambitious, or simply the self-righteous. As a result, the most probable outlook becomes a continuation of the military-political struggle on the scale of Korea or Vietnam. The danger is that a succession of such involvements may encourage the rise of a strict garrison state, one that is marked by an atmosphere of internal repression and external belligerence.

This grave possibility may well be the single most dangerous eventuality during the next decade or two, when the chances for Communist "takeovers" will be greatest. But the longer-term future is far from foreclosed along such lines. On both sides of the great divide, forces are at work that can lessen the intensity of hostilities. One of these is the enhanced prospect for international stabilization, once the worst is over and those nations that are going to go Communist or national-collectivist have done so. A second hopeful possibility is the growth of a greater degree of isolationism in American politics—or perhaps one should say a lesser degree of interventionism—compounded in part of disillusion, in part of fear, and in part of a more realistic appreciation of our inability to affect the unruly tides of world history. Yet another force for peaceful accommodation is the possibility that the specter of Communist "world domination" will be dispelled by the sight of Communist nations in intense rivalry, just as the Communist world may be relieved by the continuing evidence of inter-capitalist frictions.

And finally, we can hope that within a generation or so, new concerns posed by enormous world populations, interlocked global technical devices for communications, transport, power, and other uses, vanishing fossil fuel supplies, a worldwide polluted atmosphere, etc., will cause the present ideological fervor to subside under more pressing problems, just as did the great religious animosities of the past.

Not all the preconditions for such a turn of events lie in our own hands. Much depends on the continuation of the present trend toward the fragmentation and gradual liberalization of the Communist world. But given this opportunity, there seems at least a reasonable chance that American and European capitalism can find a *modus vivendi* with the other side. There again, I believe, the critical determination of direction is apt to reside with the new elites rising within capitalism. Indeed, if there are limits to the adaptability of capitalism before the untoward development of world events, these limits appear to reside, more than is the case with the other challenges before the system, in the quality of the "new men" who are rising to positions of power within it.

V

It is time to revert to the question we set ourselves at the outset. What limits, we asked, were inherent in the capitalist system as such? The answer at which we have arrived is necessarily of a speculative nature. Yet, it does not appear entirely fanciful. What seems possible is to bring about social change that stops short of a direct assault on the economic machinery of privilege that all elites—indeed, that even the general public—in a capitalist society are normally eager to protect. This enables us to draw the general boundaries of short-term evolution for capitalism. The distribution of wealth can be corrected at the bottom, albeit slowly, but not at the top. The control over output can be improved very greatly but the essential commercial character of a market system, with its surrender to the acquisitive impulse, is incorrigible. A considerable accommodation can be made with the non-capitalist world, but the imagination of that world cannot be captured by a basically conservative outlook. There are, in a word, deep-seated attributes to the quality of life that constitute an impregnable inner keep of the system of American capitalism as we know it.

And yet, if we now recall our earlier concern with feudalism, we will recall that despite the seeming impregnability of its institutions in the 13th century, by the 18th century, somehow, the system had nonetheless changed out of all recognition. How did feudalism expire? It gave way to capitalism as part of a subversive process of historic change in which a newly-emerging attribute of daily life proved to be as irresistibly attractive to the privileged orders of feudalism as it was to be ultimately destructive of them. This subversive influence was the gradual infiltration of commercial relationships and cash exchanges into the everyday round of feudal life, each act of marketing binding men more fully into the cash nexus and weakening by that degree the traditional duties and relationships on which feudalism was based. Against this progressive monetization the old order struggled in vain, for the temptations and pleasures of the cash economy were greater than the erosion of privileges that went with it.

Could there be in our day an equivalent of that powerfully disintegrative and yet constitutive force—a force sufficiently overwhelming to render impotent the citadel of capitalism, and yet as irresistibly attractive to it as the earlier current of change was to feudalism? I think there is such a force, and that it already bulks very large within our world. This revolutionary power is the veritable explosion of organized knowledge, and its applied counterpart, scientific technology.

The extraordinary rate of expansion of this explosion is sufficiently familiar to require only a word of exposition. There is, for instance, the often-quoted but still astonishing statement that of all the scientists who have ever lived in all of history, half are alive today. There is the equally startling calculation that the volume of scientific publication during the last ten to fifteen years is as large as, or larger than, that of all previous ages. Such examples serve accurately enough to convey the notion of the exponential growth of scientific inquiry in our day. As to the equally phenomenal growth of the powers of the technology, if that needs any demonstration, there is the contrast cited by Kenneth Boulding between the centuries needed to recuperate from the physical destruction that accompanied the collapse of the Roman Empire, and the scant twenty years in which the shattered and burned cities of modern Europe and Japan were rebuilt after the Second World War.

This explosion of science and technology is often thought of as a product *of* capitalism, insofar as it arose in an age dominated by capitalism. Yet the association was far more one of coexistence than of causal interrelation. At best we can say that the secular air of bourgeois culture was compatible with, perhaps even conducive to, scientific investigation, but we can hardly credit the acceleration of scientific activities around the middle of the 19th century to the direct stimulus or patronage of capitalism itself.

Even scientific technology exhibits but little debt to the existence of capitalism. The technology on which capitalism began its long course of growth was strictly of a pragmatic, intuitive, pre-scientific kind. Watt, for example, invented the steam engine over fifty years before the basic formulation of the law of thermodynamics. The English textile, iron and steel, or chemical industries were founded and prospered with no "scientific" underpinnings at all. The same is true for the young railroad industry, for canal building, or road-laying. The deliberate employment of scientific investigation to create or refine the technology of production was considerably delayed in arriving. In this country the first private industrial laboratory was not built until 1900 by the General Electric company, and organized research and development on a large scale did not really get under way until 1913.

Thus, we find the flowering of science and the application of science to technology—the very hallmarks of the modern era—to be currents that arose *within* capitalism, but that do not owe their existence directly to capitalism. Rather, science and its technology emerge as a great underground river whose tortuous course has finally reached the surface during the age of capitalism, but which springs from far distant sources. Having now surfaced, that river must cut its own channels through the existing social landscape. Indeed, if we ask what force in our day might in time be strong enough to undercut the bastions of privilege of capitalism and to create its own institutions and social structures in their place, the answer must surely be the one force that dominates our age—the power of science and of scientific technology.

There is, I suspect, little to argue about as to the commanding pressure of science in modern times. What is likely to be a good deal less readily accepted, however, is the contention that this force will cause drastic modifications in, or even the eventual supersession of, capitalism. For at first glance this new current of history seems to have imparted an immense momentum to capitalism by providing it with a virtually inexhaustible source of invention and innovation to insure its economic growth. Merely to review in our minds the broad areas of investment and economic output that owe their existence *entirely* to the laboratory work of the last three decades—the nuclear and space establishments, electronics, the computerization of industry, the creation of new materials such as plastics—is to reveal the breadth of this new gulf stream of economic nourishment.

Yet, like the attractions of the cash market for the feudal lord, the near-term advantages of science and technology conceal long-term conflicts and incompatibilities between this new force of history and its host society. Indeed, the insinuation of science and technology into the interstices of business enterprise promises to alter the fundamental working arrangements of capitalism.

At least one of these alterations is already familiar to us. This is the tendency of technology to create social problems that require public controls to correct or forestall. In part, these agencies of control are contained and concealed *within* the centers of production themselves, where they show up as rising echelons of corporate administration and supervision. In part, the controls show up in the familiar bureaus of government that cope, with greater or lesser success, with the social repercussions of transportation, nuclear energy, drugs, air pollution, etc. In still a different aspect, the controls invade areas of social life rather than production, as in the astonishing network of government required solely to manage the automobile (an effort that requires the labor of one out of every ten persons employed by all state and local governments). Meanwhile, in the background of the social system the controls are manifest as the growing apparatus of regulation over wages and prices, and over the total flow of economic activity—all ultimately traceable to the need to intervene more closely into an economy of increasing technological disruption.

Not that the disruptive effect of technology is itself a new phenomenon. The dislocations of the technology of the pre-scientific age—say the spinning jenny—were quite as great as those of the modern age. The difference is that in an earlier age the repair of technological disturbances was largely consigned to the adaptive powers of the individual and his family, to the ameliorative efforts of small-scale local government, and to the annealing powers of the market itself. Today, however, these traditional agencies of social repair can no longer cope effectively with the entrance of technology. The individual, now typically a member of a small urban family rather than of a large extended rural family, is much less capable of withstanding economic displacement without external assistance. The local community, faced with large-scale problems of unemployment or ecological maladjustment brought about by technical change, has no recourse but to turn to the financial help and expertise available only from larger government units. The market, which no longer "clears" when the marketers are enormous firms rather than atomistic business units, also discovers that the only antidote to grave economic disjunction is the countervailing influence or *force majeur* of the central governing authority. In a word, technology seems to be exerting a steady push from many levels and areas of the economy in the direction of a society of *organization*.

To this well-known effect of technical progress we must now add another—the capacity of technology to render redundant the physical energies of man. That is, machines do man's work for him, thereby freeing him from the bonds of toil and, not less important in the context of our inquiry, from the hegemony of the market process.

We see this disemployment effect most dramatically in the case of agriculture. But equally startling is the labor-displacing effect of modern technology in that congeries of activities associated with the extraction of basic materials from nature and their fabrication, assembly, conversion, or transport to point of sale. Since 1900, science and technology have given us a stupendous array of new products, each requiring large quantities of human effort—the automobile, the whole range of consumer durables, the communications industry, office machinery, new metals, fabrics, and materials of all kinds, to name but a few. Yet at the end of that period, the total requirements on the labor force for all these goods-centered industries had risen by only *two percentage points*. During the era of the greatest increase in factory production ever known, virtually no increase in the distribution of labor in favor of the goods sector was needed—indeed, since the hours of work fell, there was actually a *relatively decreased* need for human effort in the output of these goods.

Today we stand at the threshhold of a new stage in the application of scientific technology to human activities: automation. What is most threatening about this technology is that it has begun to invade a sanctuary of hitherto relatively unmechanized work—the vast numbers of jobs in the office, administrative, and service occupations. By 1960, more than half the labor force was in these jobs. And now, into this varied group of occupations, technology is starting to penetrate in the form of machines as complex as those that can read and sort checks, or as relatively simple as those that dispense coffee and sandwiches.

This is not to maintain that no new areas of employment exist. Certainly there remain very large and still untapped possibilities for work in the reconstruction of the cities; the provision of education; the improvement of health and recreation facilities; the counseling of the young and the care of the aged; the beautification of the environment. Provided only that demand can be marshaled for these activities, there is surely no dearth of job prospects for the coming generation.

But that is precisely the point. The incursion of technology has pushed the frontiers of work into a spectrum of jobs whose common denominator is that they require *public action and public funds* for their initiation and support. The employment-upsetting characteristics of technology thus act to speed capitalism along the general path of planning and control down which it is simultaneously impelled by the direct environment-upsetting impact of technological change.

If we look further ahead, the necessity for planning is apt to become still more pressing. The day of a "fully automated" society is by no means a fantasy, although its realization may well require another century, or more. That is to say, we can, without too much difficulty, imagine a time when as small a proportion of the labor force as now suffices to overprovide us with food, will serve to turn out the manufactured staples, the houses, the transportation, the retail services, even the governmental supervision that will be required.

What the leisured fraction of the population will then do with itself is an interesting and important question. It may possibly find avenues of remuneration that are resistive to mechanical duplication, so that instead of taking in one another's wash, we buy one another's paintings. But even in this best outcome, the underlying process of production, now enormously mechanized and intricately interconnected, would require some form of coordination other than the play of market forces. If we think of the network of controls over output and disposal that now characterize the agricultural sector, we catch some idea of the controls required to operate an economy where manpower requirements generally would have been reduced to a level comparable to that of farming today. And, if the leisured population does not find adequate remuneration in unmechanizable private employments, it will have to be given the direct right to share in society's output—another vital infringement on the market's function.

But the erosion of the market goes deeper yet. For the introduction of technology has one last effect whose ultimate implications for the metamorphosis of capitalism are perhaps greatest of all. This is the effect of technology in steadily raising the average level of well-being, thereby gradually bringing to an end the condition of material need as an effective stimulus for human behavior.

Everyone recognizes that the end to want would represent the passage over an historic watershed for mankind. But it must be equally clear that such a passage will also represent a basic revision of the existential situation that has hitherto provided the main impetus for work. As needs diminish, the traditional stimuli of capitalism begin to lose their force, occupations become valued for their intrinsic pleasures rather than for their extrinsic rewards. The very decision to work or not becomes a matter of personal preference rather than of economic necessity. More telling, the drive for profit—the nuclear core of capitalist energy—becomes blunted, as the purchasable distinctions of wealth decline. In a society of the imaginable wealth implicit in another hundred years of technical progress, who will wish to be the rich man's servant at any price?

All this is no doubt a gain in human dignity. But that is not an end to it. As a result of this inestimable gain in personal freedom, a fundamental assurance for social viability also vanishes, for the market stimuli that bring about social provisioning are no longer met with obedient responses. One has but to imagine employees in an industry of central importance going on strike, not with the slim backing of unemployment insurance and a small union supplement, as today, but with liquid assets sufficient to maintain them, if need be, for a year or more, to envisage the potential for social disorder inherent in the attainment of a genuinely widespread and substantial affluence.

Yet it is precisely such an affluence that is within clear sight, provided that the impetus of science and technology continue to propel the economy for another century. In this impasse there is but one possible solution. *Some authority other than the market must be entrusted with the allocation of men to the essential posts of society, should they lack for applicants.*

We have concerned ourselves so far only with the curious two-edged effect of science and technology on the functional aspects of capitalism. Now we must pay heed to a second and perhaps even more critical effect, the conquest of the capitalist imagination by science and scientific technology.

I think it is fair to say that capitalism as an *idea* has never garnered much enthusiasm. All efforts to raise money-making to the level of a positive virtue have failed. The self-interest of the butcher and the baker to which Adam Smith appealed in lieu of their benevolence may serve as powerful sources of social energy, but not as powerful avatars of the social imagination.

By way of contrast, I think it is also fair to say that science *is* the burning idea of the 20th century, comparable in its impact on men's minds to the flush of democratic enthusiasm of the late 18th century or to the political commitment won by Communism in the early 20th. The altruism of science, its "purity," the awesome vistas it opens and the venerable path it has followed, have won from all groups exactly that passionate interest and conviction that is so egregiously lacking to capitalism as a way of life.

It is not alone that science carries a near-religious ethos of conviction and even sacrifice. Within Communism as within capitalism, the new elites arising within the framework of the old society owe their ascendancy and their allegiance in large part to science. The scientific cadres proper, the social scientists, the government administrative personnel —even the military—look to science not merely as the vehicle of their expertise, but as the magnetic North of their compass of values. These new elites have not as yet divorced their social goals from those of the society to which they are still glad to pay allegiance, and no more than the 13th-century merchants huddled under the walls of a castle, do they see themselves as the potential architects and lords of a society built around their own functions. But as with the merchants, we can expect that such notions will in time emerge and assert their primacy over the aims of the existing order.

What sorts of notions are these apt to be?

One general direction of thought will surely be the primacy of scientific discovery as a central purpose of society, a *raison d'être* for its existence, perhaps even a vehicle for its religious impulses. No doubt the distribution of social resources and of privileges will reflect this basic orientation toward scientific exploration and application. Not less characteristic will be an emphasis on rational solutions to social problems. The key word of the new society is apt to be *control*. Not alone economic affairs (which should become of secondary importance), but the numbers and location of the population and its genetic quality, the manner of social domestication of children, the choice of life-work —even the very duration of life itself—are all apt to become subjects for scientific investigation and direction.

It is tempting, but idle, to venture beyond these few suggestions. What manner of life, what institutions, what ideologies may serve the purposes of a society dedicated to the accumulation of scientific knowledge and power, we cannot foretell; variations may well be as great as those observable in societies dedicated to the accumulation of material wealth. Nor does there seem to be much point in attempting to foresee by what precise stratagems the elites and ideas of the future may finally assert their claims. Historic projection is rarely, if ever, a matter of simple extrapolation from the present and recent past. Should there arise radical parties in America, broadly-based and aimed at a rational reorganization of economic affairs, the pace of transition would be quicker. Should there not, change will still occur, but more slowly. Veblen was too impatient for his engineers to take over; Schumpeter, more realistic when he advised the intelligentsia to be prepared to wait in the wings for possibly a century, a "short run" in affairs of this kind, he said.

So, too, the examples of the past discourage us from attempting to prophesy the manner of demise of the system to be superseded. The new protagonists of social and economic control will lack for some time an articulate conception of a purposively constituted and consciously directed social system. The old ideas of the proper primacy of economic aims will linger side-by-side with newer ideas of the priority of scientific interests. And no doubt the privileges of the older order will endure side-by-side with those of the new, just as titles of nobility exist to this very day. It is conceivable that violence may attend the transfer of power and responsibility from one elite to another, but more probably the transfer will be imperceptible; managed by the sons of the old elite entering the profession of the new.

All these are the merest speculations, difficult to avoid entirely, not to be taken too literally. Only one thing is certain. It is the profound incompatibility between the new idea of the active use of science within society and the idea of capitalism.

The conflict lies in the ideas that ultimately inform both worlds. The world of science as it is applied to society is committed to the idea of man as a being who shapes his collective destiny; the world of capitalism to an idea of man as one who permits his common social destination to take care of itself. The essential idea of a society built on scientific engineering is to impose human will on the social universe; that of capitalism to allow the social universe to unfold as if it were beyond human interference.

Before the activist philosophy of science as a social instrument, this inherent social passivity of capitalism becomes archaic, and eventually intolerable. The "self-regulating" economy that is its highest social achievement stands condemned by its absence of meaning and intelligence, and each small step taken to correct its deficiencies only advertises the inhibitions placed on the potential exercise of purposeful thought and action by its remaining barriers of ideology and privilege. In the end, capitalism is weighed in the scale of science and found wanting, not alone as a system but as a philosophy.

That an ascendant science, impatient to substitute reason for blind obedience, inquiry for ideology, represents a great step forward for mankind, I do not doubt. Yet it seems necessary to end on a cautionary note. Just as the prescient medievalist might have foreseen in capitalism the possibilities for the deformation of human life as well as for its immense improvement, so the approaching world of scientific predominance has its darker side. There lurks a dangerous collectivist tinge in the prospect of controls designed for the enlargement of man but inherently capable of his confinement as well. But beyond that, there is, in the vista of a scientific quest grimly pursued for its own sake, a chilling reminder of a world where economic gains are relentlessly pursued for their own sake. Science is a majestic driving force from which to draw social energy and inspiration, but its very impersonality, its "value-free" criteria, may make its tutelary elites as remote and unconcerned as the principles in whose name they govern.

Against these cold and depersonalizing tendencies of a scientifically organized world, humanity will have to struggle in the future, as it has had to contend against not dissimilar excesses of economic involvement in this painful—but also liberating—stage of human development. Thus, if the dawn of an age of science opens larger possibilities for mankind than it has enjoyed heretofore, it does not yet promise a society in which the overriding aim of mankind will be the cultivation and enrichment of all human beings, in all their diversity, complexity, and profundity. That is the struggle for the very distant future, which must be begun, nonetheless, today.

34

The Negro American Protest

THOMAS F. PETTIGREW

The so-called Negro Revolution is, apart from our war in Vietnam, the central fact of American life today. The war, however, appears as a distant commitment, with consequences that are for the most part felt remotely; the Negro Revolution is a vital presence, touching immediately upon the majority of our citizens, the inhabitants of urban America. The Negro protest commands our daily attention. It has been a major factor in American affairs since May 1954, when the Supreme Court, in the case of Brown v. Board of Education of Topeka, *declared that segregation in public education was unconstitutional, and by its declaration sparked the whole recent movement for giving black Americans their full measure of civil rights.*

A mass movement of increasing intensity, the Negro protest has its own character and dynamics, which correspond in some ways to other mass movements of social protest but which in other respects are unique. The

SOURCE: *The Journal of Negro Education*, XXXII (Fall, 1963), 493–506. Reprinted by permission.

drive for civil rights legislation, the sit-in demonstrations, the freedom rides, the boycotts of businesses owned by whites, the increasing appeal of Black Muslim ideology, the emergence of the concept of Black Power, the out- break of mass civil disorders—in Harlem, Watts, Detroit, Newark: these express a deeper development, governed by its own rationale and character- ized by increasing radicalization. It has progressed from attempts merely to alter the law to organized expressions of discontent, from legal gradualism to direct massive action.

To speak of the Negro Revolution is to identify it as such, certainly, but it is also to raise questions about it. Is it really a revolution, or is the nomen- clature a typically American device of having radical transformations in name rather than in fact, the former a substitute, safe yet resonant, for the latter? How far is the Negro Revolution consistent with earlier major changes in American society? Is it conservative in purpose and nature: that is, does it seek to realize ideas and values that have long prevailed and to do so by altering prevailing institutions? Or does it seek a radical change in American society, a basic redefinition of what our values are, of the way our ethnic groups are organized, and of our relation to a world that is largely non-white?

Is color indeed the heart of the problem, and is real equality a possibility for whites—perhaps even for certain whites—only? How far can we ac- commodate into our daily lives what has hitherto been, and in basic ways remains, a color caste? What is the essential nature of the Negro's passage through American life today? Is he part of a colonial sub-society, curiously deposited in the interstices of a dominant white society, which exploits its colonials more psychologically than economically? Is the Negro an internal migrant, seeking to make the transit from the "inner city" ghettoes of the great metropolitan areas? And if he is, how far will he come to regard his ethnicity, his identity, indeed his color and his separateness, as the elements he may retain, perhaps must retain, in order to achieve equality? In short, how much will he come to believe and insist that to be equal he must also be separate?

If the Negro Revolution is truly a revolution, what has been its course? What were its original aims, how have they been radicalized, and in what stages, by what means, for what reasons? How has the revolutionary leader- ship changed, and what in fact have been the role and impact of both the leaders and agencies of the whole protest movement during the 1950's and 1960's?

In considering the dynamics of the Negro Revolution, we ought to be aware, too, that it is part of a deeper tension, a greater antithesis, in Ameri- can society. It involves not merely Negro action, but also white reaction. The intents and acts of neither group can be simply defined. It is clear enough, however, that among a large number of whites, particularly the lower and lower-middle classes, there has been a "backlash" response to the Negro's claim to real equality. What has been the nature of this response? Are the whites anxious about their status, fearful that if they lose the superiority that attaches to whiteness they lose the only superiority they possess? Are they perpetuating prejudices they were raised to believe, or perhaps finding in Negro protest a realization of fears that have animated them and a justification of hostility they have long had? As neighbors to the black "central cities" of America, do they perhaps feel they are being called on to practice the equality that the safely removed white elites are preaching? Is the white response typical of the way groups only recently arrived, and still insecurely seeking to establish their own status in American society, respond to groups of new arrivals who are just beginning to run the whole course of acculturation and ascent in status? Is not know-nothingism endemic in a society of immigrants, and is not the white "backlash" essentially an expression of American know-nothingism?

A continuing movement in contemporary American life, the Negro Revolution is the subject of an ever-growing body of literature. One of the most valuable analyses of its nature and significance was the 1963 Yearbook of the Journal of Negro Education, *entitled "The Relative Progress of the American Negro Since 1950." A symposium of seventeen articles, the Yearbook dealt with several larger themes, including general characteristics of the Negro population in 1960, economic status and advancement, progress in the attainment of equal civil rights, and social and educational development. In the following essay, Thomas F. Pettigrew, Professor of Social Psychology at Harvard University, summarizes these articles (which he refers to as chapters) and advances his own view of the Negro protest movement. Professor Pettigrew is the author of* A Profile of the Negro American *(1964) and co-author of* Christians in Racial Crisis: A Study of Little Rock's Ministry *(1959).*

His central theme in the selection below is that the Negro's drive toward equality is not to be measured merely in terms of actual gains but, more significantly, in terms of psychological losses. The improvement the Negro has achieved, submits Professor Pettigrew, may be validly understood only in the light of his aspirations. The article concludes with five very perceptive observations about the future course of the Negro protest movement.

Since 1963, when Professor Pettigrew wrote the article, the movement has gained momentum and intensified. While it is fair to say that later events have not borne out all his predictions, they have validated many of them. Professor Pettigrew's article has the authenticity of its times. His predictions are important, basically, not as prophecy but as perception, not as guesses but as social commentary. His article is a statement on a central problem of our times, and its final sentence poses the problem in its essence, giving us deep insight into the expansion of the Negro Revolution during the years since 1963. One fundamental factor in that expansion could not too well have been anticipated by Professor Pettigrew: the extension of the

American war in Vietnam. How much has the burgeoning war overseas affected the burgeoning revolution at home? Both have been the dominant realities of our society in recent years and both belong to a larger direction in American life which it behooves us to contemplate and understand.

INTRODUCTION

The late Samuel Stouffer, one of America's greatest sociologists, always became incensed when a layman blithely reacted to a behavioral science finding with "Who didn't know that?" He countered with a simple true-false test of ten items, the "obvious, common sense" answers to which had all been demonstrated incorrect by rigorous social research. Most of those who take Stouffer's test miss every item. The moral is clear: many behavioral science findings appear obvious only after the fact.

Stouffer's favorite illustration involved the relative morale of the Air Corps and the Military Police in World War II. Promotions were rapid and widespread in the Air Corps, but slow and piecemeal in the Military Police. Conventional wisdom predicts that the Air Corpsmen should have been more optimistic about their chances for promotion, for the "obvious" reason that they were in *absolute* terms moving ahead faster in their careers. But, as a matter of empirical fact, Stouffer found in his famous studies of *The American Soldier* that the Air Corps-men were considerably more frustrated over promotions than the Military Police. What was not so obvious was that the fliers' wide-open system of promotions led them to assume exceedingly high aspirations; most of them expected such swift elevation that even the realistically generous promotions of their service left them *relatively* dissatisfied. By contrast, morale was reasonably high among the Military Police. They did not expect rapid promotions and learned to be content with what few advances they did achieve. It was not the absolute level of attainment that made for poor morale so much as *relative deprivation*— the discrepancy between what one expects and what one receives.

Likewise, conventional wisdom dictates that Negro Americans should have higher morale today than at any previous point in America's history. After all, have Negro gains not been faster in recent decades than any period since emancipation? Why, then, are many Negroes so unusually restive, so openly angry, so impatient for further gains? Relative, not absolute, deprivation once again provides a social psychological explanation. The great majority of Negroes in past years dared not cherish high aspirations for themselves. While never satisfied with their lot, they, like the Military Police, expected very little of life and had to be content with what crumbs they did receive. But Negro Americans in recent years hunger for much more than crumbs. Like the Air Corpsmen, they have tasted significant progress and can fully appreciate what further progress could mean. Indeed, Negro aspirations have risen far more swiftly than Negro advances. Thus, while better off in absolute terms than ever before, Negroes today are relatively more deprived than they were prior to the last 25 years of racial change.

This important social psychological principle underlies the Negro American protest of 1963. The present paper analyzes the preceding papers in terms of relative deprivation. It briefly summarizes the actual gains of recent years, lists the simultaneous psychological losses of these same years, and, finally, offers five predictions concerning the future of the Negro protest.

ACTUAL GAINS

The complexity of Negro progress, as Rayford Logan emphasizes in his chapter, makes it impossible to gauge such progress precisely. Nevertheless, virtually all observers agree that the past quarter-century has witnessed the most rapid actual gains in Negro American history. Consider this sampling of recent advances culled from the papers of this Yearbook:

The Negro's transition from rural Southerner to urbanite, North and South, continues apace (Preston Valien's chapter). Today's Negro Americans are more urban than white Americans, and are particularly concentrated in the largest of cities. By 1960, half of all Negroes lived in metropolitan areas of at least a half-million people. Although it raises new problems, this massive movement leads directly to a more sophisticated people capable of effective protest. It also leads to improvements in standards of living. Health offers one example (Marcus Goldstein's chapter). In part a consequence of urbanization, Negro mortality rates have notably declined. In relation to the nation as a whole, age-adjusted nonwhite total mortality rates improved from 1950 to 1960 virtually as much as they had in the previous half century.

Advances have also been registered in employment. Middle and high level federal employment has shown substantial growth within the last few years (John Hope II and Edward Shelton's chapter); employment opportunities for trained Negro youth have expanded in the professional, technical, and clerical categories, as well as the more traditional service field (William Amos and Jane Perry's chapter); and nonwhite males have made gains somewhat faster than white males in both the operative and professional job classifications (Walter Daniel's chapter). Some aspects of Negro-controlled business have also developed (Harding Young's chapter). The assets of Negro savings and loan associations, for instance, have multiplied over 32 times since 1947, a rate roughly three times that of all savings and loan associations combined.

These trends in turn generate economic and housing progress. From 1950 to 1960, median Negro family income climbed 73 per cent (Young's chapter); the Negro middle class swelled; and the percentage of non-whites residing in adequate, standard housing doubled (Marian Yankauer and Milo Sunderhauf's chapter). In addition, significantly fewer Negro households in 1960 included lodgers and three family generations than in 1950 (G. Franklin Edward's chapter).

Important changes have also occurred in political power. Over a million more Negroes voted in 1962 than in 1950; and the potency of this increased access to the ballot was demonstrated in elections for offices ranging from state legislator to the presidency (Harold Gosnell and Robert Martin's chapter). Three Southern states—North Carolina, South Carolina, and Texas—remained in the Democratic Party column in 1960 largely as a result of the Negro vote for John Kennedy. And in 1962 competent Negroes won a variety of posts, from State Senator in Georgia to high state posts in New England.

Educational progress has also been evident. The percentage increments of Negro youth of all ages attending school were dramatic between 1940 and 1960; indices of educational quality, such as expenditures per pupil, number of pupils per teacher, and the academic preparation of teachers, have all risen in Southern high schools for Negroes; and the median education of Negroes in the 25-to-29 age group jumped from seven years in 1940 to 11 years in 1959 (Eunice Newton and Earle West's chapter). Furthermore, the percentage of Negroes who have at least attended college more than doubled from 1940 to 1960 (Hurley Doddy's chapter).

These gains of the 1950s and early 1960s, combined with the gains of the 1940s, have had a profound psychological effect upon Negro Americans. Despair and hopelessness have declined, new and proud aspirations have taken hold, and a determined optimism about the future has developed. These trends became noteworthy by the early 1950s. A representative 1954 national public opinion poll asked: "On the whole, do you think life will be better for you or worse, in the next few years than it is now?" Of those with an opinion, 64 per cent of the Negro respondents felt life would soon be better. This figure compares with only 53 per cent of a white control sample equivalent to the Negro sample in region of residence, sex, age, education, and occupation.

The public school desegregation ruling of the Supreme Court, of course, made 1954 a vintage year for rising Negro aspirations. But recent poll data suggest that, if anything, this high level of optimism has risen further. The 1963 *Newsweek* opinion survey of Negro Americans uncovered revealing results: 73 per cent feels that the racial attitudes of whites will improve during the next five years; 63 per cent thinks whites will accept racial change without violence; 85 per cent desires to own a private home; and 30 per cent believes it is qualified for elevation now to professional or other white-collar employment.

This same poll finds that much of this renewed hope for the future centers upon education. Although one in five families interviewed had a child who had dropped out of school before completing high school, 97 per cent wants its children to finish high school. Negroes have traditionally placed great faith in education as a means of achieving full acceptance in American society, and several additional studies point to the intensity of this faith at the present time. One investigation conducted in the middle 1950s in the Northeast noted that a sample of Negro mothers strongly valued achievement in terms of an activistic, individualistic, and future orientation that usually accompanies high educational aspiration. Indeed, 83 per cent of these mothers intended for their sons to go to college.

Studies of the children themselves further confirm this emphasis upon education as a means for upward social mobility. One research project of the early 1950s tested and interviewed Negro and white children of matched intelligence from a desegregated elementary school. The Negro youngsters expressed higher levels of aspiration and more ambitious hopes for the future. And a recent investigation of Negro high school students throughout the South reveals that they, too, harbor a great desire for further education.

Some observers interpret such heightened educational aspirations as "unrealistic" and indicative that Negroes learn early to separate their hopes from the stark reality that generally confronts them. But another study done in the late 1950s of high school seniors in Kentucky discovered that most of the Negro children who had reached this level had surprisingly well conceived plans for the future. Negro seniors in this sample were not only more optimistic than the white seniors, but they shrewdly appraised their position in American society, their better chances for white-collar jobs in the North, and their need to end discriminatory barriers.

PSYCHOLOGICAL LOSSES

These rising expectations are increasingly framed in terms of the standards of the wider society, as Whitney Young emphasizes (Daniel Thompson's chapter). Negro protest today is shifting from an exclusive emphasis upon desegregation and equal opportunity to a broader demand for a "fair share" and advantages comparable to those of whites. Sensing this significant shift, the Yearbook explicitly set out to assess the 1963 status of Negro Americans in direct comparison with other Americans. And this assessment reveals that in general the Negro's situation in 1963 represents sharp improvement relative only to previous Negro conditions; it does not mark dramatic improvement relative to present white conditions. Consider once again each of the realms in which changes have been registered.

Despite the large-scale migration since 1915, substantial segments of the Negro population remain in the most hostile and deprived pockets of the nation (Valien's chapter). Mere mention of county names—such as Greene and Monroe in Alabama, Lee and Terrell in Georgia, Carroll and Tate in Mississippi, McCormick and Williamsburg in South Carolina, Fayette and Haywood in Tennessee, and Prince Edward in Virginia—serves to remind us that several millions of Negroes still reside in rural areas of the South which are resisting racial change by almost every means possible. The high promise of change is barely beginning in these Black Belt counties.

There is also another aspect to the recent improvements in Negro American health. Life expectancy at birth still lags behind that of white Americans, though the discrepancy has closed to six to eight years. And relative to white rates, nonwhite mortality rates for such diseases as diabetes mellitus and cirrhosis of the liver actually increased between 1950 and 1960, though much of this increase may well reflect better reporting and diagnosis rather than actual retrogression (Goldstein's chapter). These remaining disparities in health lead to phenomena such as proportionately greater numbers of young and middle-aged widows in the Negro community; thus, the percentage of widows among nonwhite women 54 years old or less is roughly twice that of white women.

Employment presents a similar picture. Even in government service, Negroes are still concentrated in the lower blue-collar brackets and sparse in the higher white-collar brackets (Hope and Shelton's chapter); in most unionized industries, basic racial employment patterns remained unchanged during the 1950's (Ray Marshall's chapter); Negro youth have about twice the unemployment rate of white youth (Amos and Perry's chapter); and Negro adults in general are still vastly underemployed, downgraded, and underpaid relative to comparably educated segments of the white community (Daniel's chapter). Norval Glenn has projected the slow occupational trends of the 1950s into the future. He calculates that at the 1950 to 1960 rate of change nonwhites in the United States would not attain their proportional representation among clerical workers until 1992, among skilled workers until 2005, among professionals until 2017, among sales workers until 2114, and among business managers and proprietors until 2730! Obviously, such a snail's pace is ridiculously slow to satisfy a people whose expectations for the immediate future are among the most optimistic in the nation; hence, the significant slogan of the March on Washington—*"jobs* and freedom now.*"

The projected eight centuries necessary to close the racial gap among business managers and proprietors illustrates once more the exclusion of Negroes from executive roles in the general society and the minuscule nature of Negro business. Even in the savings and loan field, a strong Negro business area, the assets of Negro-controlled institutions constitute only approximately three-tenths of one per cent of total assets; and in the insurance field, the strongest Negro business area, the assets of all Negro-controlled companies constitute only a fraction of any one of the very largest companies (Young's chapter). Though minor allowance must be made for publishing and insurance companies and financial institutions, the dour generalization of Franklin Frazier continues to hold true: ". . . 'Negro business', which has no significance in the American economy, . . . [is] a social myth . . ."

Changes in Negro income relative to white income provide the most disappointing trend of the past decade (Thompson's chapter). Daniel shows the failure of the median wage of Negro males to climb relative to the white figure; median family income data illustrate the same trend. The ratio of nonwhite to white median family income in 1959 (51.7%) was virtually the same as in 1949 (51.1%). Korean War prosperity elevated the ratio to its highest point (56.8%) in 1952, but it has since declined almost steadily. This means that, although the absolute level of Negro family income rose throughout the 1950s, white family income rose proportionately faster.

The sharp racial discrepancy in family income persists in spite of a larger average number of Negro family members working and larger families to support. Differential tax payments balance this racial inequity slightly; but Negroes typically obtain less for their consumer dollar. This is especially true in housing. While some housing gains occurred in the 1950s, the quality of Negro housing remains vastly inferior relative to that of whites (Yankauer and Sunderhauf's chapter). For example, in Chicago in 1960, Negroes paid as much for housing as whites, despite their lower incomes. Median rents for both groups were $88, yet Negroes received much poorer accommodations. The Taeubers attribute this fact to the existence of essentially two separate housing markets; and they point out that residential segregation that creates these dual markets "has increased steadily over past decades until it has reached universally high levels in cities throughout the United States, despite significant advances in the socio-economic status of Negroes."

Even the accelerated political advances of Negro Americans leave much undone. Negroes still vote as a group far less often than whites. Particularly in those Southern areas where racial change is most desperately needed, Negroes are least often found on the electoral rolls. Indeed, there is a massive denial of the franchise in most of Alabama and Mississippi and large parts of Louisiana, Georgia, and South Carolina (Gosnell and Martin's chapter). The voting title of the 1963 Civil Rights Act provides limited help, but does not offer a definitive solution.

Finally, Negro education has yet to approach that generally available to whites. To quote Newton, it remains in general "less available, less accessible, and especially less adequate." Negro college attendance is only about half that of whites (Doddy's chapter). These gaps are especially serious. Fourteen generations of Negro talent have already been wasted by American society; our technological society cannot afford to waste yet another. And, as we have seen, Negro hopes for the future are so centered upon education that training of poor quality at this stage could well undercut the determined thrust toward group uplift.

Thus, in each interrelated realm—health, employment, business, income, housing, voting, and education—the absolute gains of the 1950s pale when contrasted with current white standards. Numerous spokesmen have boasted of the present status of the Negro in glowing international comparisons. Negroes in the United States today, goes one boast, have a consumer buying power comparable to that of similarly-populated Canada. And a larger percentage of Negroes, goes another, attends college than the residents of the British Isles. But such glittering statements must not blind us to the fact of greatest psychological importance. Negro-American standards have their psychological meaning relative to the standards of other Americans, not Canadians or the British. The Negro American judges his living standards, his opportunities, indeed, even judges himself, in the only cultural terms he knows—those of the United States and its "people of plenty." Dr. Martin Luther King, Jr. bluntly made the point in his eloquent March-on-Washington address: "The Negro lives on a lonely island of poverty in the midst of a vast ocean of material prosperity and finds himself an exile in his own land."

The resulting relative deprivation is the fundamental basis of mass Negro American dissatisfaction today. But it is not the only factor. Special frustrations are created by the appearance of proud new African nations upon the world scene. Emerging Africa has a dual psychological effect upon Negro Americans. On the one hand, it generates racial pride and an elevated self-esteem—especially for the darkest members of the group. On the other hand, it lends a desperate urgency to protest at home. Heretofore, Negro Americans have been the most sophisticated and prestigeful black group in the Western world—regardless of their lowly position by American standards. But now many Africans can claim complete freedom, while Negroes still seek theirs. In this sense, then, independent African nations add to the Negro's keen sense of relative deprivation.

A similar phenomenon occurs regionally within the United States. Negro Northerners have typically prided themselves on being the products of the big-city North, on being superior to their Southern "country cousins." Yet Negro Southerners today lead the struggle for racial justice; many of them have willingly faced fire hoses, dogs, jail, and police brutality in order to demand and assert their rights; and one of them, Dr. King, has become the flesh-and-blood symbol of the protest movement throughout the country. A few Negro leaders in the South even hint wryly that the day may come when Negro Northerners will have to migrate southward to obtain true equality. And when Negroes in the North contrast their slow progress against de facto segregation in housing, schools, and employment with the dramatic desegregation of public facilities in many parts of the South, they must wonder if such wry hints do not possess some basis in truth.

Thus, the present-day Negro's feeling of being left behind springs from three sources. It derives partly from relating his situation to emerging Africa. For the Negro Northerner, it also stems from comparing his gains with those of his on-rushing Southern relatives. But its primary source is from contrasting his still meager lot with the abundance of other Americans.

"ALL, HERE, NOW!"

Intense relative deprivation in an age of rising expectations is the stuff out of which revolutions are made. But this revolution of 1963, with its ringing demand for "all, here, now," is a revolution in a sense special to the Negro's unique role in American society. An understanding of this special form of revolution is requisite to any meaningful projection of the Negro American's status into the future.

This revolution does resemble more violent revolutions in some ways. As August Meier asserts in his illuminating chapter, the present movement has shifted "in emphasis from legalism to direct action," from narrow objectives to a full-scale attack, from pockets of protest to a genuine mass movement cutting across divisions within the Negro community. And like other mass movements, it has achieved a heightened militancy and urgency, a new sense that "even yesterday was too late." It also exhibits some of the irrationality common to all revolutions.

Nevertheless, this is a revolution with a basic difference. It aims to modify, not to overturn, the society it confronts; it seeks to amend, not to ravage. Negro Americans are so firmly rooted in and shaped by their land that their revolution attempts merely to guarantee full participation in the society as it otherwise exists. In short, they do not wish to deprecate or destroy that which they wish to join. It is, then, a peculiarly conservative revolution, a fact that in many ways gives it a special force.

Such a conservative revolution acts out the culture's most cherished values; it dramatizes the "American dilemma" between high ideals and lowly practices. It does not offer new values, but demands that old values be realized. To suppress such a revolution would be to surrender the very foundations of the United States. There is in the long run, then, but one viable alternative—to move with history and achieve a racially integrated society in which skin color loses all relevance. This alternative is already recognized in the support given the protest by the federal government—a strange ally for true revolutionaries. Even if federal authorities have sometimes been too late with too little help, as in Albany, Georgia, the fact remains that the current Negro protest takes place within a generally permissive national atmosphere.

Moreover, this special type of revolution is supported to a considerable degree by white American opinion. There is a hard core of whites that marches in demonstrations, goes to jail, even faces death with Negroes. Though a small minority, it serves the vital function of keeping the confrontation from becoming a purely black versus white conflict. To be sure, there is also a hard core of white deadenders, those who resist even token desegregation by burning crosses, exploding bombs, and shooting others in the back. But the majority of white Americans ranges somewhere in between, and, while their attitudes often do not measure up to Negro expectations, they nevertheless contribute to the permissive atmosphere in a number of key ways.

To begin with, there is general approval outside of the South of the Supreme Court's 1954 school desegregation ruling. Gallup polls show that 62 per cent of the nation, Negro and white, approves of the decision, with the proportion among non-Southerners reaching almost three out of four. School desegregation itself wins general approval outside of the South, providing Negro children are not in the majority. In the South, although racial change is still widely opposed by white Southerners, such change is increasingly seen as inevitable. Gallup polls have repeatedly asked Southerners of both races if they thought "the day will ever come when white and Negro people will be going to the same schools, eating in the same restaurants, and generally sharing the same public accommodations." In 1957, only 45 per cent of the South answered "yes"; by 1958, 53 per cent did so; by 1961, 76 per cent; and by 1963, 83 per cent. In addition, among the 83 per cent who saw desegregation as inevitable in 1963, half believed it would come about completely within five years and another fourth believed it would occur within ten years. Thus, the majority of white Southerners clearly expects racial progress even while opposing it, and this widespread feeling of inevitability contributes importantly to the present milieu in which the Negro protest is operating.

The ground was prepared for these white opinions before the current revolution. During and since World War II, the stereotype of the Negro has undergone drastic modification. Witness the erosion of the racist contention that Negroes are innately stupid. The National Opinion Research Center asked Americans in a series of representative polls: "In general, do you think Negroes are as intelligent as white people— that is, can they learn just as well if they are given the same education and training?" In 1942, only 42 per cent of white Americans believed the two groups to be equally intelligent; by 1944, the figure was 44 per cent, by 1946, 53 per cent; by 1956, 78 per cent. This fundamental alteration of the image of the Negro acts to sharpen further white guilt over the "American dilemma."

There remain, however, serious limitations to white understanding of the Negro American. The majority of white Americans as yet neither identifies with Negro Americans nor senses the urgency of the present revolution. The majority of whites believes that Negroes are being treated fairly in the United States and that gradualism should be the rule in effecting desegregation. These beliefs assuage guilty consciences; thus, it is not surprising that Negro demonstrations which boldly challenge these beliefs are resented. In 1961, for example, national samples questioned by Gallup pollsters indicated that 64 per cent disapproved of the freedom rides and 57 per cent believed they would "hurt the Negro's chance of being integrated in the South." Similarly, 65 per cent of white Northerners and 73 per cent of white Southerners interviewed in 1963 think that "mass demonstrations by Negroes are likely to hurt the Negro's cause for racial equality." Without denying the basic justice of the protest, many whites handle their guilt by complaining that Negroes are "pushing too hard too fast." Yet some of these same people realize upon reflection that Negroes do in fact make maximum progress only when they confront the nation directly with their demands.

Within this social psychological context—severe relative deprivation among Negroes, an urgent, but basically conservative, protest revolution, a supportive federal government, and a guilty, if gradualistic, climate of dominant white opinion—five predictions for the future can be ventured. *First, Negro protest will continue to grow both in intensity and depth.* As demonstrations persist, advances will occur ever more rapidly. These advances serve to reward the protest and stimulate its continuance. "The leaders sitting down together would, of course, be the best way," confides one Negro lady, "but we found it didn't work and sit-ins did." Advances also serve to highlight further racial changes that are needed. These effects are part of a widely-studied psychological phenomenon known technically as "goal gradient" and popularly as "running for home." As subjects in an experiment approach their final goal, they typically gain a "second wind" and speed up their performance. Or in relative deprivation terms, protest success enlarges aspirations faster than actual gains can meet; the result is deeper frustration and more insistent demands. "The closer we come to the achievement of our ideals," shrewdly observes a Civil Rights Commissioner, "the more obvious and galling is the disparity."

Apart from its success, the current revolution will become increasingly intense because of the psychological effects of the demonstrations themselves. No protester, Negro or white, comes out of a racial demonstration the same person he was when he entered. Personal participation publicly commits the protester; it gives him a new sense of actively influencing events rather than passively accepting them; and it can provide him with greater confidence and an enhanced self-image. All of these changes aid him in undertaking additional protest. In short, demonstrations are both a symptom and a cause of psychological health. "My feets is tired," remarked an elderly Negro lady in the midst of the Montgomery bus boycott, "but my soul is rested."

Furthermore, demonstrations instruct both participants and bystanders that segregation is a two-way street, a process of role reciprocation. It takes two to tango, and it requires the complicity of both whites and Negroes to maintain patterns of segregation and discrimination. If Negroes disengage themselves from these patterns, racial barriers cannot long be maintained. This insight, achieved in the midst of demonstrations, also makes further protest inevitable. "We the Negro people are now not afraid," announces a grocery store owner in a small Alabama town, "we have woke up."

Second, the protests will increasingly attract a larger proportion of lower-income Negroes and shift from status to economic goals. The direct action phase of the revolution began in earnest when Southern college students initiated in 1960 a wave of mass sit-in demonstrations aimed at the desegregation of lunch counters. The fact that college students sparked this phase and that public facilities were the initial targets is of importance; but direct action weapons are now spreading and will continue to spread to diverse segments of the Negro population with primarily economic targets.

The fact that Negro college students ignited the direct action fuse involves a special irony. These youngsters benefited from the best schools the South ever provided Negroes. Though still not the equal of white education, this improved training produced a more sophisticated, self-confident generation. It also kindled, through the mechanism once again of relative deprivation, a greater frustration over racial barriers which exploded in militant social action. Like oil and water, education and oppression do not mix.

The student presented the perfect symbol as the initiator of public demonstrations. Well-dressed and well-behaved, the Negro student epitomized the group's aspirations for social mobility and integration. His nonviolent movement flew in the face of the contradictory racist stereotype of the Negro as violent yet subservient, degraded yet happy with his lot. The student was also less encumbered with fears from past mistreatment and less vulnerable to economic retaliation. In short, he was uniquely situated to transform public protest and going to jail into not only socially respectable acts but badges of high honor.

To become a full-fledged revolution, however, the movement had to incorporate elements of the Negro community. The Montgomery bus boycott in 1955–1956 provided a preview of the power of a unified effort across class lines. But it required Bull Connor's police dogs and fire hoses in Birmingham to capture the imagination of all segments of Negro America. Data from *Newsweek's* poll of Negroes in the summer of 1963 tell the story. Fifty per cent feels the pace of racial change is far too slow; 80 per cent is certain that demonstrations are effective; four per cent has already personally or has family members who have been jailed in the cause; 40 per cent has already personally or has family members who have taken part in a sit-in, marched in a mass protest or engaged in picketing; and 48 per cent reports a willingness to participate in mass protests even if it means going to jail. Clearly, the revolution is an authentic mass movement that unites many different Negro elements, and shows every promise of recruiting more adherents in the future.

As the proportion of lower-income participators climbs, the nature of the struggle's primary goals necessarily shifts from status to economic concerns. To illustrate with extreme examples, poor Negroes are not importantly affected by the desegregation of the opera, expensive restaurants, or golf courses. They are chiefly interested in getting good jobs and sharing in the material abundance surrounding them. "Freedom" for them inseparably signifies both dollars and dignity. Yet relative occupational and income gains, it will be recalled, were the most disappointing indices of the 1950s. Consequently, 1963's wave of building-site demonstrations against racial discrimination in the building trades is sure to be merely the forerunner of attacks upon a variety of employment realms and economic problems.

Third, a more extensive use of local and national boycotts of consumer products will be made. The consumer boycott is a weapon yet to be fully exploited. But a number of localities, such as Philadelphia and Nashville, have learned what well-organized Negro boycotting can accomplish. *Newsweek* reports that because of employment discrimination

29 per cent of its sample stopped buying in certain stores and 19 per cent stopped buying certain companies' products. But this barely touches the potential. Sixty-three per cent of the sample states it would stop buying at a store if asked, including over two-thirds of the highest-income Negroes.

This mass willingness to participate in boycotts stems from two factors. The first is economic; boycotts are unusually well-suited for achieving the employment breakthrough so desperately desired by low-income Negroes. The second factor is psychological. There are three major types of responses human beings can make to oppression: they can move toward the oppressor and seek acceptance as an equal; they can move against the oppressor and aggressively express their frustration; and they can move away from the oppressor and seek to minimize painful contacts. Boycotts have the distinct psychological advantage of appealing to all three of these basic responses. Such campaigns move toward the oppressor by seeking to achieve desegregation; they move against the oppressor by encouraging group unity and aggressively upsetting the white-controlled economy; and they move away from the oppressor by requesting the participators merely to avoid the scene of conflict. For these reasons, it seems highly probable that boycotts will soon increase in number and scope.

Fourth, as the revolution proceeds through the 1960s, some basic structural changes in American society will have to occur before viable solutions are possible. As Daniel Pollitt forcefully observes (Thompson's chapter), employment problems could prove to be a major bottleneck to significant Negro progress in the near future. This hard economic fact of life will become painfully obvious as this decade continues. The massive upgrading of Negroes—and many whites, too—at a time when the full effects of automation are starting to hit the labor force will require major societal surgery, not the aspirin-type palliatives so far considered by the United States Congress. Such surgery will be resisted by conservative forces more powerful and entrenched than those which have opposed desegregation; but it will become increasingly necessary for national development.

The most pressing need is a general expansion of the economy and a consequent expansion of the labor force. Negro employment gains have always come fastest during times of rapid growth—as in World War II; and significant gains in the 1960s are in large part dependent upon another period of rapid growth. All types of structural changes necessary to induce such economic growth responsibly are prerequisites, then, not just for national prosperity but for improved race relations as well. More specific samples of the required structural changes include the following:

(1) An extensive broadening of minimum wage legislation is needed by poorly-skilled Negroes who are employed. Many of the job categories in which Negroes are concentrated—service occupations, in particular—are not covered in the wage provisions of the Fair Labor Standards Act. Thus, the act as it now stands excludes those very people who most require its protection.

(2) Major tax cuts must be made at the bottom, rather than the top, of the income scale. At the very least, single persons with annual incomes below $2,000 and families with annual incomes below $4,000 should be exempt from federal income taxes (they will still bear an unduly heavy burden from sales taxes). These are levels widely regarded by economists as poverty-stricken by modern American standards, and relative deprivation considerations demand that these are the only realistic standards by which to judge the income of Americans. Present tax-cut proposals are inadequate in this regard.

(3) A great variety of federally-sponsored training and retraining programs are urgent necessities. Compared with present minuscule efforts, however, these future programs must be daringly new in both conception and magnitude. As Amos and Perry emphasize, automation requires more imaginative and flexible training than has typically been true in the past. The many boys now being taught cabinetmaking, to choose an absurd but actual example, should instead be taught the basic technological skills prerequisite for the jobs in greatest supply. Modern teaching methods must be applied, methods which utilize rather than magnify the special problems of disadvantaged individuals.

The size and complexity of this educational task invite attack from many directions—thoroughly revamped vocational training programs for the public schools, the proposed domestic equivalent of the Peace Corps, the Manpower Retraining programs, and a wider use of the educational potential of the armed forces. But if the unemployment and alienation in the depths of urban ghettoes today are to be remedied, a new conception of selection procedures will have to be adopted by these programs. As in the case of the minimum wage law, these programs are currently rejecting those unskilled persons who most desperately need the training. Of course, it is more expensive and difficult to prepare the most deprived segments of the population; but unless this is done, the fundamental educational problems of our time will be neglected.

And, fifth, steady progress—in relative as well as absolute terms— will be registered in the Yearbook which surveys the status of Negro Americans in the 1970s. The present revolution will probably enable Negroes during this decade to narrow, though not close, Negro-white disparities. Thus, in 1973, Goldstein might report that the life expectancy at birth of Negroes is only two or three years below that of whites; Hope and Shelton might report that the proportion of Negroes in the higher levels of government (GS and PFS 5 through 18) approximates the Negro population percentage; Marshall might report that the initial racial breakthroughs have finally occurred in such difficult areas as the building trades; Young might report that, while Negro-controlled business remains an insignificant factor in the American economy, increasing numbers of Negroes are assuming decision-making executive roles in previously all-white business; and Daniel might report that the pace of occupational upgrading of Negroes has sharply quickened, even among sales workers, and that the median Negro family income has inched up to almost two-thirds that of whites. Likewise, Yankauer and Sunderhauf might report a reversal in the residential segregation trends and additional gains in the quality of Negro housing; Gosnell and Martin might report a Negro voting percentage virtually as high as the white percentage and a developing political alliance in the South between Negroes and the working-class whites; and Newton, West, and Doddy might report that the education of Negroes at all levels has made appreciable gains in desegregation, availability, and quality.

This fifth prediction is predicated heavily upon the previous predictions. Should the protest movement cool, should the involvement of lower-income Negroes and the shift in emphasis to economic goals not take place, should nationwide boycotts not be effectively organized, should all types of necessary and decisive structural changes needed now by the American society be blocked, then obviously significant progress will not occur.

This is precisely what makes the 1960s such a crucial, yet promising, decade for American race relations. The gravest danger is not interracial violence, as the mass media endlessly assert, but that this golden opportunity will not be fully utilized. The nation is ripe for sweeping racial change and is in fact changing. Except for the Black Belt South, the formal desegregation of public facilities will soon be a mopping-up operation. The critical question, then, is: Can the revolution deal with de facto segregation and the vast educational and economic issues still impeding Negro progress as effectively as it has dealt with legal segregation?

The Student Left
in American Higher Education
RICHARD E. PETERSON

The 1960's were clearly a decade of disquietude and social change. The consensus that Eisenhower superintended, an amalgam of Roosevelt's domestic program and Truman's diplomacy, could not provide answers to new developments and new needs. Ushered in by a youthful president searching out new frontiers, the decade of the 60's bore its own distinctive characteristics, above all perhaps that of a younger generation's challenge of old values and its attempt through the instrument of new ideas to improve the quality of American life. Nowhere has the verve and spirit of the 1960's been more evident than in our colleges and universities, where student political activism has become a principal feature of campus life and where a left-wing student movement has emerged, dedicated to the overhauling and radical transformation of American society.

It is this student movement that Richard E. Peterson explores in the following essay. Acting chairman of the Higher Education Research Group in the Developmental Research Division of the Educational Testing Service at Princeton, New Jersey, Dr. Peterson is the author of The Scope of Organized Protest in 1964–65 *(1966) and of several monographs on college students. In his analysis of the left-wing student activism of the 1960's, he addresses himself to a series of basic questions. What have been the major varieties of contemporary student dissent? What are the essential tenets of the "new" student left? In what ways has American higher education been transformed since World War II? In terms of their orientation toward dominant social values, what major "analytic, ideal types" may be distinguished among American students? What are the particular personal characteristics of the student radicals? What correlation is there between the nature and outlook of a given college or university and the degree of radical student activity that is carried on there? What, in sum, has been the impact of*

SOURCE: *Daedalus,* Journal of the American Academy of Arts and Sciences, XCVII (Winter, 1968), 293–314. The subject of the Winter 1968 issue of *Daedalus* was "Students and Politics." Reprinted by permission.

on university life and on life in America outside the

*of the student left in our institutions of higher learning has
emely important and has inevitably attracted the attention of
able educators and writers. Their suggestions invite our critical
ion. How far, for example, shall we accept the thesis of Lewis S.
that the new student movement has "made no pretense at being rooted
economic issues," that it is élitist and populist, and that its ideology is one
of imposing the will of a band of activists on national policy* (Survey, *January 1967)? To what degree is Kenneth Keniston correct in saying that the
American student left concentrates more on process and tactics than on
program, that it is nonascetic, antitechnological, antiacademic, and above
all nonviolent* (The American Scholar, *Spring 1968)? What shall we make
of Irving Kristol's argument that campus activism is basically existentialist,
and that students rebel "not so much because things are bad for them, or for
others, but because things are what they are for them and for others"* (The
Atlantic Monthly, *November 1965)? For what reason has Herbert Mar-
cuse's attack on technological society and on "false" or "repressive" tolerance become the rallying cry of student radicals? (See Martin Peretz,
in the* Yale Review, *Summer 1968.) How valid are Nathan Glazer's observations that the position of the New Left has at least three basic flaws: that it
assumes that the problems of creating a better society are basically political,
that it cannot ultimately find an alternative to bureaucracy and institution-
alization, and that (despite its fondest aspirations) the overall tendency of
life in America and in other advanced industrial societies is not toward more
freedom and spontaneity but toward less* (Commentary, *July 1968)?*

*Heretofore, radicalism surged through the mainstream of American life
and only when it had reached a crest did it spill onto the campus and into the
classroom. Today it would seem that the reverse is true. Radicalism is
mainly the province of the young, and the young are mainly on the campus.
The university has become its own generator of social transformation. The
problem is why, and with what significance. The subject of contemporary
student radicalism immediately raises for us two larger questions. What have
been the nature and extent of radicalism in American life: in a society, in
effect, that is generally regarded as consensual and conformist? To what
extent have our schools been the conductors of social change, to what extent
merely its vehicles? Looking at the whole history of American education,
and bearing in mind that a nation to which ideals are central is also one to
which schools are central, we could learn much by examining these questions
closely and carefully.*

In striking contrast to students in many other countries, American college students have not been known until recently for their interest
in politics and national affairs. There has never been a tradition of

student politics, radical or otherwise, in American life, and it is in part because of the sharp break with the past that the surge in student political activism during the 1960's has so captured the fancy of observers of the American scene.

It may be useful at the outset to distinguish the student left from three other varieties of contemporary student dissent—student rightists, campus-issue protesters, and hippies. The student left is viewed as a movement that has emerged in the past seven or eight years on the basis of a shared rejection of many prevailing American institutions, a vaguely democratic-socialist political ideology, a faith in participatory democracy, and a commitment to direct social action. While the student left has grown out of an amalgam of shifting civil rights, peace, and anti-poverty sentiments and activities, its ultimate goal is radical reform of American society and the characteristic nature of human roles and relationships on which it rests.

The programmatic thrust for the student left has come chiefly from two organizations—the predominantly Negro, loosely structured Student Nonviolent Coordinating Committee and the almost totally white, nationally organized Students for a Democratic Society. SNCC, after last year's ironic shift in goals and tactics, seems to be weakening as an effective force for change. SDS is weighing new priorities in the hope of extending its grass-roots support and keeping the radical movement alive.

The student right, by comparison, directs its protest not so much at the *status quo,* but rather at what it perceives to be a rising tide of leftist influence ("liberal orthodoxy") on the campus and in the broader society. The educationally oriented tactics of the student conservatives are aimed chiefly at counteracting the efforts of both the student leftists and the nonideological campus-issue protesters.

Easily the most important conservative student organization is the Young Americans for Freedom (YAF), which claims a membership of twenty to thirty thousand spread across some two hundred campuses. From its founding in 1960, YAF grew to a peak in grass-roots support during the Goldwater-Johnson campaign of 1964. Since then, YAF has probably been best known for its efforts on behalf of the Administration's Vietnam policy—demonstrations of support for various escalations toward a military victory, blood donations, Christmas packages for the troops, and so forth.

Parents of conservative students are disproportionately Republican and Protestant, and they tend to be authoritarian and achievement-oriented in their child-rearing practices. Student rightists, heavily concentrated in business curricula, appear to be active not only at the large, prestigious, and visible institutions, but also at many smaller colleges—especially church-related ones, southern universities, and technical and other career-oriented institutions. As S. M. Lipset and Philip Altbach have observed, despite impressive financial and organizational backing, student conservatives "have not been successful in building a movement which has much commitment from its membership," nor has it "made any real impact on the campus."

Quite the contrary is true of campus-issue protesters. In the years "since Berkeley" (Fall, 1964), college campuses in many parts of the country have witnessed an unprecedented level of organized student protest over campus conditions, and the impact has been substantial. During the academic year 1964–65, there were more demonstrations about dormitory and other living-group regulations and campus food service, than about U.S. actions in Vietnam. Moreover, large numbers of students, most likely representing wider cross-sections of student bodies, were generally involved in protesting internal campus issues.

While many of the trouble spots are old and somewhat trivial, there is a new urgency and stridency. Often led by legitimate (elected) student leaders, the campus-issue activists have borrowed some of the tactics of the student leftists—the marches, sit-ins, and confrontation strategies of the civil rights movement, for example. Certainly the strategies of the FSM activists at Berkeley have not gone unnoticed by students on other campuses who generally seek more limited objectives. With the emergence of new models of higher learning—the experimental colleges and the free universities, for example—as well as the appeal of a politics of "student power," concern for *real* educational reform is unmistakably on the rise among these more conventional students.

There is some question as to whether discussion of hippies is relevant to a paper on college students. Collegiate life in its usual form is anathema for the confirmed hippie, whose characteristic response is aesthetic rather than intellectual. The hippies exist mostly on the periphery or in the underground of large urban colleges and universities—in a sense, dropping in and out. In contrast to the politically committed left-activists, real hippies have withdrawn from American culture and despair of any hopes that they, the "new lefties," or anyone else can alter the prevailing patterns of that culture.

THE ORGANIZED STUDENT LEFT: BRIEF NOTES

The "new" student left is not to be confused with the "old" left or, in Jack Newfield's words, the "hereditary" left—the student wing that is now chiefly represented by the Progressive Labor Party. Very weak numerically, the old left cannot be taken seriously as a political force mainly because—owing to its factionalism and ideological dogmatics (such as rigid reliance on economic variables)—it is not taken seriously by the new-left groups.

By way of further definition, it may be asserted that students on the new left share the belief that American society is so grossly defective that nothing short of a fundamental reconstruction of basic institutions will provide an adequate remedy, and they are willing to act on behalf of this belief. This definition would distinguish the leftists from the hippies, who are disinclined to act, as well as from the liberal groups whose goals are less radical. Among the latter would be the campus affiliates of ADA, SANE, ACLU, the College Young Democrats, and probably also the recently established University Christian Movement (UCM). By our definition, there would, of course, be many student leftists who are not dues-paying members of or active workers for leftist organizations. The student left, as defined, includes perhaps something on the order of 1 to 2 per cent of the total student population. The *organized* student left—formal affiliates of SDS, SNCC, SSOC, CORE—amounts to fewer than 15,000.

SNCC came into being at an October, 1960, meeting in Atlanta, the result of efforts by SCLU worker Ella Baker to bring together leaders of the various sit-ins that had occurred throughout the South since the original Greensboro and Nashville demonstrations earlier that year. Almost all of the early SNCC activists, both Negroes and whites, were of southern middle-class background. They shared a religious devotion to the ideals of nonviolence, love, and peace, along with a suspicion of formal organization and leadership. Early tactics emphasized direct confrontation—sit-ins, freedom rides, and the like.

Late in 1961, SNCC embarked on a new course and began sending full-time workers into rural communities in the South to help Negroes register to vote. The incredible heroism of individual SNCC organizers in Mississippi and Alabama has been movingly described by Newfield: "They were shot, beaten, gassed, whipped, jailed." The summer of 1964 saw the failure of the SNCC-inspired Mississippi Freedom Democratic Party and the tragedies of the SNCC-conceived Mississippi Summer Project (notably the murder of Goodman, Chaney, and Schwerner).

After a period of black-white populism, SNCC organizers began to lose faith in white liberals and federal civil rights measures. The belief emerged within SNCC that it was best for Negroes to make their own destiny rather than to integrate with a "sick" white society. In May of 1966, Stokely Carmichael replaced John Lewis, and a new SNCC was born out of a legacy of frustration and despair. Financially broken, its less than eighty paid workers are now seeking to stir the younger Negro generation toward open militancy and eventual Negro self-determination.

SDS also took shape soon after the original sit-ins. A small group of student intellectuals, mainly at the University of Michigan, established ties with the League for Industrial Democracy (LID) which was seeking to reconstruct its moribund student sector. Groups organized on eleven campuses, and Tom Hayden drafted SDS's manifesto, the *Port Huron Statement.* In June, 1962, fifty-nine people gathered for a founding convention at the F.D.R. Labor Center at Port Huron, Michigan.

After a year of organizing campus chapters and minor local polemicizing, SDS turned to community organization in northern urban ghettos, both black and white. ERAP (Economic Research and Action Projects) were under way in ten cities by 1965. "Community organization" has meant many things: fostering indigenous leadership, building a capacity to make decisions, initiating direct action, giving hope.

In 1965, SDS's focus was again on students, and the issues of Vietnam, the draft, and student power. In April, 1965, twenty thousand people came to Washington for a SDS-organized march to protest the war. SDS helped set up the first teach-in at Ann Arbor, and soon after initiated projects for draft resistance. SDSers in Cambridge helped guide the 1967 Vietnam Summer project. Many of the demonstrations against campus recruiters this past fall were organized by SDS chapters. According to Richard Blumenthal, SDS grew from 1,200 members and 30 chapters in 1965 to more than 6,000 and 227 chapters in 1967.

SDS is currently exploring new priorities and directions. To bring a larger element of rational analysis into its workings, it has established the Radical Education Project (REP) as an arm for research and theorizing. While aggressive efforts to influence student opinion continue on many fronts (as at the 1967 NSA Congress), there is also an emerging interest in ways to radicalize various middle-class adult groups.

Pluralistic (no one is excluded), nondogmatic, leaderless, and decentralized, the unifying bond for most SDSers seems to be a moral outrage at the hypocrisy in American society—the gap between the liberal democratic dream and the grim human reality of American life —and a commitment to work for radical social change.

THE SPECTRUM OF AMERICAN HIGHER EDUCATION

Since the end of World War II, the proportion of the college-age population (18–21) attending college has doubled—from 22 per cent in 1946 to 45 per cent in 1965. In the fall of 1967, approximately six million students were attending about 2,300 colleges and universities. Something over one third of these are public, tax-supported institutions; given their typically large size and egalitarian admissions policies, however, the public institutions presently enroll two thirds of the total student population.

American higher education, in short, has undergone a remarkable democratization. Perhaps its most contemporary expression is the local community supported and controlled "open door" two-year junior college. In 1945–46 there were 242 public junior colleges enrolling 110,000 students, while in 1965–66, there were 392 with enrollments totaling almost 700,000. Public junior colleges have assumed many functions. As evidence of a "cooling out" function, Lewis Mayhew has estimated that only 12 to 15 per cent of those who enter the junior colleges as freshmen eventually obtain Bachelor's degrees. (A sizable minority in the technical-vocational programs, perhaps 25 to 30 per cent, of course, at no time have BA aspirations.)

A second major theme in American higher education is its decentralization and consequent diversity. In 1965, there were 154 universities, 89 of which were public; 815 liberal-arts colleges, with six times as many private as public; 186 teachers' colleges, with all but 28 under public control; 55 technical institutions equally divided between public and private; 622 public and private junior colleges; 207 church-operated theological schools; with the balance of the 2,230 made up mostly of private professional and technical schools. In the private sector, 490 Protestant-controlled colleges enrolled 8 per cent of the total student population, 376 Roman Catholic-controlled institutions slightly over 7 per cent, and 490 independent institutions 18 per cent. In size, institutions range from over thirty thousand students on one campus, as at several midwestern universities, to the several hundred schools with enrollments of less than five hundred.

There are also huge differences in affluence, preparation of faculty, admissions selectivity, and other indices of institutional quality. Almost half of the colleges and universities are *not* accredited by an official accrediting organization. In California, the seventy-two generally well-financed and competently staffed junior colleges are open to all citizens of the state. (Not even a high-school diploma is needed if the applicant is over age eighteen.) On the other hand, some thirty or so institutions (rated as "most selective" by Cass and Birnbaum) comprise the "Paradise" of Kenneth Eble's cosmos; old, independently controlled, well-endowed, and concentrated mainly in the Northeast, they receive three or four applications for admissions for every freshman admitted. In intellectual sophistication, their student bodies stand well apart from the rest of the field.

With the exception of youths who live in states with poorly developed systems of higher education and lack the financial means to leave the state or the academic ability to obtain a scholarship, some form of higher education is available to all. Because of the many forms, prospective freshmen are often able, in Martin Meyerson's words, to "sort themselves according to their images of themselves and of the colleges to which they apply."

A TYPOLOGY OF AMERICAN COLLEGE STUDENTS FOR THE LATE-SIXTIES

Given an open, mass educational system, the diversity in student characteristics is extremely great. As a summarizing and expository convenience, recourse to some sort of typology is unavoidable. One typology that has proved to be particularly meaningful was proposed by Berkeley sociologists Burton Clark and Martin Trow in the form of four "sub-cultures"—the vocational, the academic, the collegiate, and the nonconformist. The model to be outlined clearly has roots in the Clark-Trow paradigm. It also draws on recent empirical studies, mainly the work of Harry Schumer and Robert Stanfield at the University of Massachusetts, the investigation by Jonathan Warren based on students from four southern California colleges, as well as data gathered with the College Student Questionnaires (CSQ), which contain a method for classifying students according to the Clark-Trow typology. In the past four years, the CSQ has been administered to over 120,000 students at some 250 colleges and universities.

The model posited here consists of eight student types distinguishable in terms of their dominant value commitment. It is useful to consider how the types might be arranged on a continuum of degree of acceptance-rejection of prevailing American institutions. Lacking pertinent data, this venture—summed up in the diagram below—is largely inferential and speculative.

Stance vis-à-vis American Institutions

Acceptance	Neutral	Rejection

←——→

Vocationalists Collegiates Ritualists Academics Intellectuals   Left-
Professionalists   Activists
                                                                   Hippies

It hardly needs to be said that the names refer to analytic, ideal types; they are oversimplified abstractions that mask the huge variability on many dimensions that unquestionably exists within each type.

Vocationalists. The basic commitment of the vocationally-oriented college student is to the training he is receiving for a specific occupational career. He views his college education chiefly in instrumental terms—as a means of acquiring a skill that will ensure the occupational security and social prestige that his family has lacked. Vocationalists are predominantly from working-class backgrounds, and they differ from what we will refer to as professionalists mainly in terms of socio-economic background. In college, they specialize in engineering, education, business, or other technical specialties. On various items in the CSQ, they evidenced a relatively firm and long-standing commitment to their vocational fields of choice, as well as a decidedly passive, dependent attitude toward learning. Students classified as vocationalists consistently score relatively low on the CSQ measures of cultural sophistication, social conscience, and liberalism. The vocationalist, in sum, is preparing himself to "make it" within the American system, which he accepts uncritically.

Professionalists. This type, the name borrowed from Kenneth Keniston, differs from the vocationalists in a number of important ways, but not, it is argued, in terms of the hypothetical dimension of acceptance-rejection of American institutions. Born of upper-middle-class and professional parents, he (this category is practically all male) aspires to much the same life pattern as his highly successful father—achievement, expertise, *noblesse oblige.*

Well-endowed intellectually, the professionalist was strongly motivated to succeed in secondary school (often one of the best), and in college he is bent on continuing his record of outstanding academic achievement toward early enrollment in a postgraduate professional school (law, medicine, business, government, and so forth). Professionalists would be disproportionately found in the best undergraduate colleges, a necessary springboard to the right graduate school and first job. Characteristically "staying cool," they are seldom excited by issues and ideas. While there clearly are attitudinal differences within this hypothetical category, the general political outlook of the professionalist is conservative to middle-of-the-road, and oriented toward the *status quo.*

Collegiates. The collegiate commitment is to popularity, play, and sex, as these proclivities may be realized through the various formalized extracurricular activities as well as informal off-campus events, such as spring-vacation congregations at beach resorts or fraternity weekends in the mountains, that define "college life."

Collegiates are from the middle classes. They are attracted to the relatively unselective public colleges and universities, especially the large and old ones in the South and Midwest, which are strongholds of big-time football and the national Greek-letter fraternities and sororities. Anti-intellectual, the collegiate's course work tends to center in fields that make relatively few intellectual demands. While particular subtypes of collegiates may exist on particular campuses, the common denominator seems to be an orientation toward the extracurriculum, broadly defined. Collegiates scored significantly higher on the extracurricular involvement scale in the CSQ than the other three Clark-Trow types, and they tend to be conformist and other-directed (low peer independence). Although the self-reported political attitudes of collegiates gravitate toward the conservative, politics—in the sense of adult partisanship and real issues—are simply not relevant.

Ritualists. The distinguishing attribute of the ritualist (the name suggested by Harry Schumer and Robert Stanfield) is his lack of commitment to anything. Possibly of less than average academic aptitude and usually from lower socio-economic strata, he has in a sense been swept into college by forces beyond his control—parental prodding, friends going on to college, a college within easy driving distance with admissions standards that can be met.

Schumer and Stanfield describe the ritualistic type as more strongly oriented toward home than the university, as preferring solitary rather than social activity, and as uninterested in either the academic or the collegiate environment. For the ritualist (as an ideal type), lack of commitment is total. He is apolitical, having no beliefs one way or another about the efficacy of American institutions.

Academics. The fundamental commitment of the academic type is to scholarly achievement within a specific subject field or academic discipline. Academics are concentrated in the selective and prestigious colleges and universities. They plan to go on to graduate school, a Ph.D., and a career of research and scholarship.

As identified in the CSQ, academics are broadly middle class in background and have relatively well-educated parents. In high school, by self-report, they studied extensively, received recognition for academic achievement, and found particular satisfaction from course work in the natural sciences. As a type, they are not critical of their college (mean scores on the four CSQ-2 satisfaction measures fall about at the norm) and are serious and organized in their study routines (study habits mean is the highest of the four types).

On the attitude scales in the CSQ, the academic type tends to score above the norm. We would infer that as an analytic type, the academic is slightly left of center in his politics. By nature and because of the pressure of other commitments, he is not an activist; he would, however, be a sympathizer and possibly even a participant in some future, broadly-based radical student movement.

Intellectuals. Whereas the academic pursues knowledge within the confines of a specific academic discipline, the intellectual, as a type, is oriented toward ideas and networks of ideas irrespective of the curriculum. In distinguishing the intellectual from the academic, Christopher Jencks and David Riesman have characterized the intellectual as being concerned with "questions of interest . . . to intelligent men everywhere." The prototype academic is a scientist, the prototype intellectual a philosopher or historian; the former seeks truth through the scientific method, the latter through an interplay of human insights.

These students tend to come from middle- and upper-class families, to be highly individualistic, liberal in their political outlook (but rather cool or unemotional about it), and aesthetically sensitive. Motivation for grades, a mark of the academic type, is not noticeable in the intellectual.

In view of the illustrious history of the alienation of intellectuals, we infer that the intellectual college student of the 1960's stands well over on our hypothetical acceptance-rejection of American institutions dimension.

Left-activists. The basic commitment of the left-activist, dues-paying and otherwise, is to personal involvement in action directed at reforming some facet of American life—be it political, economic, or cultural. His parents are prosperous and liberal in outlook. Highly intelligent, activists are found for the most part in the most selective and best-known colleges and universities, where their noncareer-oriented academic interests center in the social sciences and humanities. Activists share many of the personality traits of the intellectual, although the radical activists are characterized by a more passionate sense of outrage at perceived hypocrisy, injustice, and wrong-doing, and they have the courage to act.

Hippies. Of the eight types, the hippie's estrangement from American values and institutions is the most thoroughgoing. Unlike the left-activist who hopes for radical reform through political action, the hippie is pessimistically apolitical. The hippies who are enrolled in college would reject most of the usual student roles. On their respective campuses, they constitute, as Kenneth Keniston has put it, "a kind of hidden underground, disorganizing and shifting in membership, in which students can temporarily or permanently withdraw from the ordinary pressures of college life."

PERSONAL CHARACTERISTICS OF STUDENT RADICALS

The nine or so data-based studies of radical activists that have been published yield a remarkably consistent profile of the personal and background characteristics of these students.

In terms of the usual criteria, student leftists are upper-middle-class in their social origins. Their parents are politically liberal or radical, and many have been involved in radical politics. Both the students and their parents consider themselves to be either non-religious, or liberal and non-formalistic in their religious orientation. Parents of activists are permissive and democratic in their child-rearing practices, and their children are both highly intelligent and intellectually rather than career oriented. They are disproportionately concentrated in the social sciences and humanities and under-represented in preprofessional programs. They perceive themselves as independent from most sources of social influence and authority, and are interested in and sensitive to various forms of artistic expression. Radical activists perceive in themselves an altruistic sense of responsibility in relation to almost all people, and their interpersonal relationships stress empathy, openness, and honesty.

Student Activists at Michigan State University. As part of his doctoral work at Michigan State University, George Paulus gathered data during 1966 on three groups of students on that campus: 25 activist leaders, 25 student-government leaders, and a control group of 25 students carefully matched to the activist sample. The activist group consisted of leaders of the local SDS and SNCC organizations, as well as the leaders of a campus group called Committee for Student Rights (CSR). The student government leaders were elected ASMSU officials. These 75 students completed CSQ Parts 1 and 2.

Many commentators have spoken of the alienation and depersonalization of individual students at the multiversity. They often go on to reason that because of frustration many students seek identity and fulfillment through involvement in radical politics and larger political issues. Judging from the pattern of mean scores on the four CSQ satisfaction scales in Paulus's data, the relationship between dissatisfaction with college and radical politics is not a simple one. Taking SF (satisfaction with faculty and student-faculty relations) and SM (satisfaction with major field work) as indicators of *academic* satisfaction, and SA (satisfaction with administrative rules and practices) as a crude index of satisfaction with the *non-academic* side of college life, it appears that the MSU activists were generally *not* displeased by their academic experiences, but were highly provoked by the university's posture regarding student life outside the classroom. Specifically, SF and SM (and study habits) differences between the activist and matched control groups were not statistically significant; the gap on the SA scale, however, was fully two standard deviations. The activists, furthermore, roundly rejected the usual "collegiate" brand of extracurricular activities (low EI).

The pattern of mean scores on the other scales tends to agree with results of other studies in other settings. Judging from their high family-independence/peer-independence scores, the Michigan State University activists generally operate relatively independently of influence from parents or peers. The liberalism scale mean is the highest heretofore obtained with any student group. A standard deviation separated the Michigan State University activists from the matched controls on the social-conscience measure, a scale intended to tap moral concern over human injustice. The high cultural sophistication mean is in line with other research that has pointed to the aesthetic interests of activist students. Finally, the Michigan State University activists fell roughly a half a standard deviation above the "norm" on the CSQ-1 socio-economic index.

THE INSTITUTIONAL FACTOR: VARIATION IN STUDENT ACTIVISM AT DIVERSE COLLEGES AND UNIVERSITIES

Earlier we noted the diversity in American institutions of higher education—in purpose and curriculum, size, type of control, admissions selectivity, and the like. Additional institutional characteristics are also important in understanding the current status and future prospects of the student left: location of a college in a large urban center where the country's social ills tend to be focused; a tradition of student radicalism, as at Berkeley and the Universities of Michigan and Wisconsin; the degree to which a college—in both its explicit and informal policies —is closed and rigid or open and libertarian with regard to its students' personal and political lives. Many colleges and universities are known to prospective entrants in such terms. Institutions, in short, have reputations or images. The reasonably affluent student applies to or preselects three or four colleges whose images he thinks are compatible with his own interests, values, and aspirations.

This preselection mechanism is critical in understanding the variation in student activism from one college student body to another. In view of what is known about the personality and background of student leftists, the disposition to become involved in radical politics exists prior to entry into college. Such students select colleges where their disposition may find fruition. The activist-inclined student, it is suggested, is particularly mindful of the rigid-libertarian dimension of a college's image in his preselection deliberations.

INSTITUTIONAL VARIATION IN THE CLIMATE OF FREEDOM

Edmund Williamson and John Cowan's *The American Student's Freedom of Expression* will surely stand as a milestone in research on higher education. This study set out to describe the extent to which colleges allow their students freedom to express their beliefs on controversial issues. Questionnaires covering a host of policy manifestations were sent in the spring of 1964 to five officials at all the accredited four-year institutions in the country. Respondents included presidents, deans of students, chairmen of faculty committees on student affairs, student-body presidents, and editors of student newspapers. Eighty-five per cent of the colleges returned one or more of the five questionnaires, and almost 70 per cent returned all five.

The authors described private universities as being relatively permissive in regard to student freedom to discuss controversial topics, invite off-campus speakers, demonstrate actively, and engage in civil rights activity. Student-newspaper editors were exceptionally independent on these campuses, and there were many social- and political-action groups. Students clearly practice freedom more widely at private universities than they do at most other colleges.

Although students at private liberal-arts colleges enjoy freedom comparable to that in private universities, these colleges tend to be more in the "ivory tower" tradition, and students are less inclined to exercise their freedom or to engage in controversy about freedoms. Results for large public universities generally parallel those for private universities, except that administrators expressed only an "average" commitment to the principle of student freedom; student participation on policy-making committees was relatively greater, however, and there was less agreement among respondents than at private universities.

Student freedom to discuss or demonstrate at small public universities was not significantly above the average for all schools in the study. Student leaders, however, were independent and active in policy-making. The number of administrators committed to a philosophy of freedom was not unusually large, and respondents disagreed about the extent of freedom on respective campuses. The pattern of results for Protestant universities and liberal-arts colleges also did not differ substantially from the responses of all the schools as a group. There was, however, greater than average independence for the student editor. There was also exceptional disagreement among deans and student presidents concerning prohibition of liberal student organizations. Technical institutions were essentially at the national mean with respect to practice of academic freedom; administrators disagreed about whether freedom for students to address themselves to controversial social problems was essential to education. Students were seen as seeking competence in specialized fields, rather than interesting themselves in social issues.

An "average" amount of freedom for student groups to take controversial stands was thought to exist at Catholic universities. Student freedom to invite controversial speakers was significantly below the national mean. There was a great deal of supervision of student editors, and few student political organizations existed on these campuses. Administrators showed relatively little commitment to the concept of academic freedom. This pattern was much the same for the Catholic liberal-arts colleges, except that students were significantly restricted in freedom of expression.

There was less than average freedom to discuss topics, invite speakers, or demonstrate at teachers' colleges. Student newspaper editors were unusually dependent on the administration. There were few student political organizations. Student participation in policy-making, however, was about "average," but freedom seemed to be more preached than practiced.

INSTITUTIONAL VARIATION IN INCIDENCE OF STUDENT PROTEST

Planning for our survey of organized student protest got under way in the late spring of 1965, in the wake of the Berkeley crisis and reports of widespread student unrest. The general purpose of the study was to assemble some reasonably trustworthy information about the dimensions of discontent among America's college students.

In September, 1965, questionnaires were sent to deans of students at all the accredited four-year colleges in the country; the population of institutions, thus, was the same as that used by Williamson and Cowan. The deans were asked to indicate in relation to each of twenty-seven issues—class size, speakers regulations, dormitory rules, Vietnam, and so forth—whether there had been any occurrence of organized student protest during the preceding academic year (1964–65). They were requested to limit their judgments to planned, public expressions of disapproval on the part of groups and not to consider the usual complaints of individual students. Student personnel deans were surveyed on the assumption that among campus officials they are generally in closest touch with student protest activities. Based on an 85 per cent return, then, these survey results provide a picture of student activism as it is drawn by deans of students for the academic year 1964–65. The discussion that follows will be limited to the off-campus issues—civil rights and U. S. military policies—which, in contrast to the internal on-campus problems, most directly engage campus leftists.

Before turning to institutional variation in student activism, some mention of the over-all, national picture may be of interest. Of the twenty-seven issues considered, civil rights was the focus of student activism on the largest number of campuses. The year 1964, especially the summer, marked the heroic period in the civil rights struggle, at least insofar as the involvement of college students was concerned. Vietnam protests were reported at about one in five colleges (21 per cent), about the same as the number reporting protests about dress regulations (20 per cent). Agitation concerning food service and dormitory regulations was reported on 29 per cent and 28 per cent of the campuses respectively. While there was little geographical variation for the campus issues (dress regulations and so forth), proportionately fewer colleges in the South reported student activism in relation to the off-campus issues.

Percentages of nine different types of institutions indicating protest on the six off-campus issue-statements in the survey are given in Table 1. One can readily see the general parallel with the Williamson-Cowan results.

Civil rights involvement was most frequently reported by the independent universities. The deans at over half of these institutions reported that some of their students participated in civil rights activities locally or in the South during the summer of 1964. At the other extreme, about one in eight teachers' colleges reported student involvement in civil rights. A crude ranking of the eight types of student bodies in terms of civil rights activism would be: independent universities, independent liberal-arts colleges, public universities, and Catholic institutions—all standing above the "national norm"; ranged below the norm would be the public liberal-arts colleges, Protestant institutions, technical institutions, and teachers' colleges.

Variation by institutional type was more pronounced for the U. S. foreign-policy issues than for civil rights. On the Vietnam issue, the incidence of organized student protest ranged from a high of 61 per cent in the independent universities to 8 per cent in both the Protestant and Catholic institutions and 6 per cent at the teachers' colleges.

TABLE 1.   PERCENTAGES OF DIFFERENT TYPES OF INSTITUTIONS

	ALL	INDEP. UNIV.
	$N = 849$	$N = 51$
Civil rights: local area (off-campus)—protest and/or work	38	53
Civil rights: in the South during the summer of 1964—protest and/or work	28	51
Other civil rights protest or work	24	33
Disarmament, "ban-the-bomb," peace, etc.	12	26
U. S. policies regarding Vietnam	21	61
U. S. policies regarding the Dominican Republic	5	6

[N means number. Note that 34 of the total institutions reporting do not fall into any of the "types"

The deans were also asked (multiple-choice questions) to give the following information about their colleges: proportion of faculty doctorates, proportion of student body living on campus, proportion of student body belonging to leftist groups, and total enrollment (institutional size). Relationships between each of these variables, as well as the response to the question on civil rights activity in the South during the summer of 1964 and each of the protest issues were studied by means of product-moment correlation analysis.

Correlations involving the faculty-doctorates dimension (a crude index of institutional quality) and the six off-campus issues ranged from .18 on the Dominican Republic situation to .43 for the Vietnam issue; this last finding may be of some significance if the Vietnam war continues, since graduates from the "good" colleges will tend to be the opinion leaders of the coming generation. All six correlations with the commuter-residential dimension were negligible, which suggests that, in general, this factor is not related to campus activism. The range of correlations between estimated proportion of student body belonging to the organized left was from .22 (other civil rights) to .47 for Vietnam. Correlations for the response to the question concerning civil rights activities in the South ranged from .33 for the Dominican Republic situation, through .47 for Vietnam, to .54 for civil rights locally. The hypothesis here, of course, was that the presence on campus of highly committed civil rights activists would be associated with student militancy in behalf of other issues and problems.

REPORTING STUDENT PROTEST OVER SIX OFF-CAMPUS ISSUES

INDEP. L.A. COLL.	PUBLIC UNIV.	PUBLIC L.A. COLL.	PROT. INST.	CATH. INST.	TECH. INST.	T.C.
$N = 144$	$N = 133$	$N = 89$	$N = 160$	$N = 147$	$N = 28$	$N = 63$
46	44	30	30	45	36	13
35	37	22	25	23	14	11
33	29	16	13	30	11	14
18	20	14	5	5	7	2
27	36	17	8	8	25	6
6	11	6	1	1	7	3

listed and therefore do not appear separately in the above table. A.S.E.]

Size of student body proved to be unrelated linearly to organized student protest to any meaningful degree. Reasoning that the relationship may be curvilinear—that is, that student protest would occur most frequently at the *very* large institutions—a separate tabulation was made for the fifty largest public universities in the sample. (All have graduate and undergraduate student bodies exceeding ten thousand.) The figures for this subsample turned out to be considerably higher than those for any of the institutional types included in Table 1 (specifically: civil rights locally, 56 per cent; civil rights in the South, 54 per cent; other civil rights, 40 per cent; disarmament-peace, 44 per cent; Vietnam, 68 per cent [34 out of 50 universities]; and the Dominican Republic issue, 26 percent).

As we have argued elsewhere, the relative prevalence of organized student activism concerning off-campus political and social issues in the large institutions is probably less the result of multiversity-induced alienation than it is a reflection of the gross numbers of diverse individuals brought together at one time and place. The larger the student body is, the greater is the likelihood of there being some student who wishes to start something—an SDS chapter, a speech walk-out, a student strike—and of his being able to find others who will sympathize.

"Discovery" of the subjection of Negroes in democratic, enlightened America gave rise to the radical student movement. It took heart, until his assassination, in a young idealistic President. It was intensified by the discovery of grinding poverty in the world's wealthiest nation and by the thought of the world's greatest power being engaged in a war of attrition in a tiny, undeveloped country. It is sustained by the view that students themselves are being degraded in the university and, indeed, that citizens everywhere are leading "lives of quiet desperation." And it is supported by the belief that the social system that permits these hypocrisies cannot be tolerated and must be altered.

Only a small fragment of college students shares this powerful sense of outrage—no more than about 2 per cent. Intelligent, independent, noncareerist offspring of affluent parents, the student leftists tend to be enrolled in the "best" and most libertarian colleges and universities. In the general student population, student radicals would be greatly outnumbered by almost every "type" of student, probably including even the hippies who share the activists' moral revulsion, but not their willingness to act on behalf of a vision that goes beyond the self. The overwhelming majority of American college students are politically apathetic—caught up in their vocational, academic, or hedonistic pursuits.

Student leftists, working in league with various temporarily activated campus issue protesters, have already had a significant impact on university life, especially its nonacademic aspects. New freedoms have been granted students on many campuses—probably more often out of fear of the boat being rocked, however, than on the basis of some model linking personal freedom with intellectual and personality development. Professors, with little at stake in the nonacademic issues, have generally stood aside, often relishing the sight of administrators being manipulated by students.

By contrast, the impact of student radicals on the academic side of college life has been less noticeable. Here the professors do have a stake, and their conservatism on matters of instruction, curriculum development, and the like is well known. Such student-initiated alternative models as the free universities and experimental colleges, while they exist on upwards of forty of fifty campuses, enroll relatively small segments of the respective student bodies—mainly intellectuals, activists, and hippies. There are, however, some signs of reform. New grading practices such as pass-fail are, for example, being tried out (often as much because of the connection with the draft, however, as because of any presumed benefit to learning).

On balance, though, most signs indicate that the assault on the university is gathering steam. "Student power" was perhaps the salient catch phrase at the 1967 NSA Congress, and the great majority of the delegates there could in no sense be regarded as leftists. (SDSers began using the "student power" slogan soon after "black power" demands began to be heard.) New-left theorists regard issues in university reform as matters around which larger masses of students may be "radicalized" or "politicized" toward eventual reform of other social institutions. The university is also viewed as an increasingly pivotal and catalytic institution in American society; its reformation is expected to have wide repercussions.

So far, the impact of the student left on life in America outside the university seems to have been rather small. While lunch counters, bus terminals, and a few schools have been integrated, the lives of very few Negroes have been genuinely improved. New hopes may even have led to deeper frustrations and more desperate actions. While there appears to have been a dramatic shift in public opinion about the Vietnam situation in recent months, which must in part be attributed to student activism, the war in Vietnam goes on. Only token changes have been made in the draft law. The gap between the haves and the have-nots in America seems to be growing wider rather than narrower. Institutions, organizations, and relationships between people continue to be essentially bureaucratic in nature. In short, meaningful achievements have been few; all the conditions that spawned and nourished the radical movement still exist.

The future of the student left is contingent on many things: full-scale war, neo-McCarthyism, the capacity of the liberal establishment to co-opt radical ideas, the students' practical intelligence to deal with social and political complexities, and the temptation of materialism and careerism.

Students, by themselves, cannot effect major social changes. Student leftists must be willing to ally themselves with other radical and liberal elements: church people, various intellectuals (academic and professional), Negroes, the chronically unemployed and other elements of the excluded underclass, and some (maybe many) trade unionists. White student left groups have generally been willing to enter coalitions; black radicals, at the time this is being written, however, are pressing for positions that will strain even the loosest of coalitions.

Historians will credit the student leftist of the 1960's with being a major stimulus for reforms in higher education; these will mainly mean greater personal and academic freedom for students. New, highly open structural forms will have come into being to add to the total diversity of the system. Outside the university, however, the impact of the student left still largely remains to be seen.

36

The Place of Thought in American Life
DANIEL J. BOORSTIN

It is a commonplace that a nation's thinking is a mirror of the problems it is facing and of what it is doing to resolve them. Thought is society's commentary on the values by which it lives, its self-consciousness in defining its goals and pursuing them. To know American thought, therefore, is important, because it is also to know American life. It is to know the things that matter to us, the course we have taken in getting where we are, the way we construe reality and the way we address ourselves to the issues which reality presents. It is to know, moreover, what is distinctive about American life,

SOURCE: Daniel J. Boorstin, *America and the Image of Europe* (Cleveland, Ohio: Meridian Books, 1960). This article originally appeared in *The American Scholar*, XXV (Spring, 1956), 137–50. Reprinted by permission.

how it differs from European life, and the deeper circumstances which have given rise to the difference.

Such considerations are the subject of the following article by Daniel J. Boorstin, Professor of American History at the University of Chicago, and indeed are basic to all of Professor Boorstin's writings. These include The Mysterious Science of Law *(1939),* The Lost World of Thomas Jefferson *(1948),* The Genius of American Politics *(1953),* The Image: or, What Happened to the American Dream *(1962), and* The Americans, *of which two volumes* (The Colonial Experience, *1958, and* The National Experience, *1965) have thus far appeared. They are works of sophistication, originality, and insight, concerned mainly with the question of how and why the American experience has been unique. Professor Boorstin has, in fact, addressed himself to this larger question in all phases of his professional activity—as visiting professor of American history at foreign universities, as barrister-at-law of the Inner Temple, London, and as editor of the* Chicago History of American Civilization *Series. In the essay below, he analyzes the form and substance of American thought, underscoring the contrast it presents to the thought of Europe.*

His thesis regarding the place of thought in American life is comprehensive, illuminating, and challenging. His answers often pose further questions. What does he mean by thought? Is he talking about the place of thought in American life, or the place of living in American thought? Dealing only with American thought in its practical application, will he not inevitably conclude that it has been essentially practical? But is there not also a pragmatic aspect to European thought; is there not a larger body of European intellectual life which stands outside the metaphysical systems of its grand philosophers? Is Professor Boorstin fair, indeed, in his characterization of the role of these systems in European polity: does he not fail to take cognizance, first, of the breadth and universality by which they have sustained their meaning for successive generations and, second, of the practical issues in European life which have given the great philosophies their continuing vitality?

To argue conversely, in fact, is not our thought more systematic and that of Europe far less so than Professor Boorstin contends? Does he not tend to ignore our own system-makers, philosophers such as Cotton Mather, Thomas Jefferson, Ralph Waldo Emerson, John Fiske, William James, and John Dewey, to name the more obvious ones, each of whom saw American life in terms of a larger pattern? How different, indeed, is Professor Boorstin's own thesis from the philosophy of historical conservatism in any age, and from that of Edmund Burke in particular? Does he not proceed, in effect, from a metaphysic of pragmatism? And how correct is he in reducing American thought during the whole course of our history to the uniformity of his formulas? May it not be suggested, finally, that Professor Boorstin tends to push too hard the idea that in America thought has been a function of life, without sufficiently recognizing that life here has also been a function of thought? In other words, while we can accept the commonplace that social thought is a mirror of social life, we cannot ignore the less obvious but no less significant truth that social life is also a mirror of social theory.

But all these questions raised by Professor Boorstin's thesis merely testify to the imagination and importance of what he is saying. He is seeking to sweep up all the lines of our intellectual development into one larger design. He is concerned to find what is essentially American about the American experience. Identifying our intellectual life is a matter of consequence for understanding not only the paths the American mind has traveled in the past but also the crossroads at which it stands in the present—indeed, the particular direction it will follow.

No one can study the history of thought in Europe without taking account, at the outset, of two basic facts. First, there is the separation of the thought of the community into two streams: the stream of "high culture"—the thought, art and vocabulary of the aristocrats, priests, and all members of the privileged and ruling classes; and the stream of "popular culture"—the thought, art, customs, lore and folkways of the great mass of people. The gulf is so deep and the separation so wide between the two in most European countries, and has been for most of their history, that the definition of what is being talked about offers no problem to the historian of European thought. He is talking about either the "thinking class" or the "working class." It is a truism that in many periods the aristocracy of France felt a closer fellowship with the aristocrats of Germany than with the peasants of their own country. The folk culture of the English people is at least as remote from that of its aristocratic and educated classes as the culture of England is different from that of France or Italy.   When, for example, Sir Leslie Stephen wrote his *History of English Thought in the Eighteenth Century,* it was perfectly obvious that he was writing about the ideas which filled the heads of the small fraction of the English population who were literate, educated and close to the seats of power.

Second—and this feature is closely connected with the first—the history of European thought (by which is usually meant the thought of the only "thinking" people, that is the aristocratic classes) is on the whole reducible to the history of systems and schools of thought. It is the history of "Thomism," "Rationalism," "Transcendentalism," et cetera—terms which to most of the people of those days were as foreign as another language. It is the history of the specialized architecture of philosophies, rather than of the general physiology of thinking. The grander, the more filigreed and intricate a system, supposedly the greater its claim to treatment in the history of thought. Those elegant intellectual chapels built by Thomas Aquinas and Immanuel Kant thus have become the destinations of the historians' pilgrimage. Scholars find them a welcome refuge from the confusion of the market place.

But it is misleading to take these characteristics of European thought as the starting points for an American history. Our society, unlike most other modern nations, has not been marked by the separation into high culture and popular culture; nor has our thinking been dominated by systems and schools. On the contrary, there have been a number of other large and persistent characteristics of the place of thought in American life. There are those which concern the *form* of American intellectual life, and those which concern the *substance* of our way of thinking.

I

Beginning with the form of our intellectual life, we find two important and apparently contradictory characteristics: first, its unity or homogeneity; and second, its diffuseness.

The Unity of American Culture. From one point of view the history of culture in the most developed European countries in modern times has been rather uniform. For the growth of their liberal institutions has not removed their basic distinction between aristocratic culture and folk culture. What has happened is either that their aristocratic culture has been watered down piecemeal to make it more accessible and more palatable to the half-educated masses, or that a few places have been made available within the aristocracy for more talented and ambitious members of the lower classes ("the career open to talent"). A typical example of the first of these was the translation of the Greek and Latin classics into the vernacular languages, which was one of the major intellectual events of the European Renaissance. An example of the second was the growth of a system of scholarships which brought to Oxford and Cambridge some young men whose wealth and ancestry had not entitled them to that advantage. But the basic fact is that the modern intellectual and cultural life of the European community is still simply a modification and adaptation of the old aristocratic (high) culture to the sporadic demands of members of the rising classes. How little progress has yet been made is illustrated by the fact that throughout Western Europe (where alone true universities remain), with insignificant exceptions, a higher education is still the prerogative of the rich and the wellborn; but the student population in American colleges and universities is currently over two million. To say the very least, the culture of modern Europe bears the birthmark of its aristocratic origin: it was made by and for the very few, though it may gradually, in some places and to some extent, have become available to a few more.

American culture is basically different from all this. In this, as in so many other ways, here is something new under the sun. With due allowance for the influence of the European doctrine and example, one must not fail to see the vast importance of the peculiar American situation. For ours is a modern culture which skipped the aristocratic phase. While having the literary and vernacular resources of the European Renaissance and the Reformation behind us, we started our culture with some semblance of wholeness and homogeneity. We have been without that deep bifurcation into high and low, which was the starting point of the national cultures of Western Europe.

The student body of Harvard College in the seventeenth century was probably already more representative of the community at large than the universities of many European countries today. As Samuel Eliot Morison points out, in the earliest years of the College almost every Harvard student was the child of parents who actually farmed the soil, in addition to whatever else they did, and "it does seem that the College was fairly successful, after 1654, in recruiting boys of scholarly ambition from the plain people of New England." Part of the explanation of this phenomenon is found, for Massachusetts Bay at least, in the extraordinarily high proportion of university graduates to the whole population in those earliest years. But this was only one factor which happened to be important in that part of America. The more universal and characteristically American phenomenon was a homogeneity of thought and culture quite alien to the European experience. This was what Governor Thomas Hutchinson described, in the late eighteenth century, as the fact of "the generality of the colony being very near upon a level."

In Europe the progress of liberal and democratic movements has been measured by the extent to which they have broken down the barriers of the old aristocratic culture; anything which made the language and thought of the aristocracy available to more people was considered progressive. But in America the starting point has been the opposite: the unity of our society has been taken for granted. It is, rather, any failure to make culture available to all the people that has required justification.

While European liberals have tried to put the luxury of a classical education within the reach of members of the underprivileged classes, American democrats have attacked the very idea of a classical education because of its aristocratic overtones. Before the end of the eighteenth century, Benjamin Rush opposed the inclusion of Latin and Greek within the standard curriculum of a liberal education for the simple reason that these languages might be difficult for women to learn; and, he urged, nothing should be part of an American education which was not within the reach of all citizens. From the time of Rush and Jef-

ferson to that of John Dewey, our educators have been primarily interested in what Rush called "the mode of education proper in a Republic." Thus, foreign travel and study in a foreign university, basic
to the European aristocratic ideal of culture and congenial to the cosmopolitan and international allegiances of their educated classes, were
urged by the arbiters of European culture, at least from the seventeenth
century. But in 1798, Benjamin Rush asked (in words with which
Jefferson would have agreed) that Americans be educated at home
rather than in a foreign country. Only in the New World could the
unique republican principles of American life be properly reinforced in
the young, and only so could the equality of men and the unity of
American culture be encouraged. "I conceive the education of our
youth in this country to be particularly necessary in Pennsylvania,"
he wrote, "while our citizens are composed of the natives of so many
different kingdoms in Europe. Our schools of learning, by producing
one general, and uniform system of education, will render the mass of
the people more homogeneous, and thereby fit them more easily for
uniform and peaceable government." This desire for uniformity and
homogeneity has had, of course, a profound effect on our conception of
higher education, particularly in supporting movements to water it
down and flatten its flavor to suit everybody's palate. Thus, a profound
truth about our culture lurks in Bliss Perry's facetious suggestion that
the ideal of American education could most easily be attained by award-
ing every American citizen the degree of bachelor of arts at birth. There
is no denying that we started with the assumption that a society should
have a single culture whose highest thoughts should be accessible to
most men.

Even our geographic vastness and variety have contributed to
this. Because differences of region and climate are so overwhelming,
the differences of social classes in the several parts of the country have
actually seemed less important. The American who goes to England,
France or Italy cannot but note linguistic versatility as a mark of social
caste; the upper classes not only speak their national language with an
aristocratic accent, they actually speak several languages. In contrast
to this, in the United States, of course, accent is a sign not of class but
of regional origin. Even the regional dialects have been much less
marked here than in other countries of comparable size. English
travelers and American lexicographers noted this in the eighteenth and
early nineteenth centuries. "It is agreed," John Pickering observed in
1816, "that there is greater uniformity of dialect throughout the United
States (in consequence of the frequent removals of people from one part
of our country to another) than is to be found throughout England."
On the whole, it is the members of our lower classes who tend to know
another language—such as German or Italian or Yiddish—in addition

to English. It is partly by losing their cosmopolitan character, by forgetting all languages other than English that people become homogenized into American culture. In the United States we all try to speak the same language, and only a few know more than one.

Our ideal of equality has carried with it the fact of universal literacy, and in this and other ways has contributed to the ideal of cultural unity. The Protestant tradition, our lack of ancient institutions and the absence of a professional class of articulators—a "learned" or "cultured" class—all these have played their part. Unprecedented technological development, taken together with natural wealth, a high standard of living and a domestic mass-market for all kinds of products, has produced a uniformity of standards of consumption and a homogeneity in the particular articles consumed. In America, brand names (with all they imply of universal familiarity with a single product, of homogeneity of product, and of potentially universal consumption of the same product) are symbols of the unity of our culture. A Ford car and a Bendix washer are owned by the chairman of the board of directors as well as by the night watchman. Finally, our yen for orthodoxy has encouraged people both to wish for and to believe in a unity in our ways of thinking and acting.

The Diffuseness of American Intellectual Life. A feature complementary to the aristocratic starting point of European culture is the sharpness with which it is focused on one or a few centers. In modern Europe, the intellectual capital is almost as universal a phenomenon as the aristocracy. Almost every country has had its Paris, its mecca of culture, where one could sit and be at the center of things. One of Europe's main appeals to the American intellectual who has had even a taste of it is the ease with which the focus of intellectual influence and power can be discovered. The young American who goes to Oxford or Cambridge has the comfortable feeling of knowing—or being in a position to get to know—everybody who is anybody in English culture. The other day I talked with a young American student who had just returned from a couple of years in one of the English universities. Having been only another student in America, required to show what he could do in order to acquire a status, he had found himself suddenly offered a position of status and privilege simply because he was a student at Cambridge, England. "It's awfully comfortable," he said, "to be one of the ruling class." After such an experience, the young American cannot but feel a loss of privilege as well as a loss of bearings when, on return to the United States, he discovers that there is no such center.

Looking at our history as a whole, one sees a diffuseness and a shifting of intellectual life quite alien to the modes of culture in the great nations of Europe. True, different cities have had their days of glory: Boston, Philadelphia, Williamsburg, New York, Chicago and others.

But none has had much more than a day. Our cultural center has been nowhere because it has been everywhere. We are almost alone among nations in having found it necessary and possible to create, *ad hoc*, a special city to serve as the national political capital; that city has never been our cultural capital. From time to time we have had something like an elite, a group which took to itself the privileges—and claimed the immunities—of the intellectual ruling classes of Europe. The most recent and most striking (and the most difficult for our intellectuals to forget) was the New Deal, when American intellectuals had a taste of that sense of power and of sitting at the center which has been familiar to those of Europe. But as Bernard De Voto has described under the useful title of "The Literary Fallacy," American history and American culture, even more than those of other countries, are imperfectly and partially estimated if literature is confused with life, if our society is judged by its literary product. For many reasons, then, American intellectual history can be neither the history of our intellectuals nor the story of our philosophies.

II

Turning from the form of American intellectual life to the substance of our way of thinking, we find a number of equally striking characteristics. They describe the peculiar vitality and formlessness of our culture. The more rigid and dead the thought of a people, the more easily it is described and reduced to the systems which delight and comfort the academic mind. The more alive a culture and its ways of thought, the more elusive it is and the harder to capture it in systems and categories. The following characteristics are actually ways of describing the elusiveness of American culture.

Interest in Institutions Rather than Ideologies, in Process Rather than Product. Our most important and most representative thinkers have been more interested in institutions than in ideologies. For an ideology is something fixed and rigid: it is a posture of the truth which some men see in one age and which they seek to get other men to accept as the whole truth. But institutions live and grow and change. They have a life of their own as a philosophy cannot; and our major accomplishments have been in the realm of institutions rather than of thought.

At least since the eighteenth century, observers of our society have noted equality as a characteristic of American life. But it is the *fact* rather than the *theory* of equality which has flourished here. If European countries have been strong in theories of equality, as in other political theories, they have been feeble in developing equalitarian institutions. In the United States, on the contrary, where we have had unprecedented success in developing the institution of social equality, we have never been able to produce a pretty or an important theory about it. This is but an example, if one of the more spectacular, of how our talent for improving life has excelled our capacity for perfecting thought.

We have shown very little interest in producing things which would endure: monuments have not been in our line. We have been more concerned with whether an idea or a thing actually serves its purpose than whether it will continue to serve that purpose for a day or a century. We have been anxious not to freeze the categories of thought, for we are ready to believe that old purposes and old needs will be supplanted by new. In exhibiting his plant, an Italian businessman will show with pride the original workshop where his great-great-grandfather started and which is still in use; an American businessman points out with pride that not a brick of his original plant remains, that the old has been thoroughly replaced by superior modern materials.

Our lack of interest in systems of thought, in ideologies and philosophies, is but a particular illustration of our general lack of interest in perfecting the *product*. This goes with our special interest in improving the *process*. We have been more interested in how and whether things work than in how beautiful they can be in themselves. Our architecture has been concerned less with houses than with housing; our engineers, less with producing sturdy automobiles than with developing satisfactory transportation. We have been interested less in good food than in satisfactory diet. We have been worried less over the content of an education, the meaning of truth, knowledge and culture, than over understanding and improving the learning process. Our dramatic artists have been less anxious to produce rounded and enduring works of dramatic art than to provide moments and experiences of entertainment and amusement. The "movies"—from this point of view appropriately and significantly named—is the most characteristic of American art forms. It is an artistic object which from its very nature can never be grasped as a whole; the form is elusiveness itself. It cannot be held in the hand and examined for its perfection, like a play of Shakespeare or an oil painting. It can *only* be experienced; and its "meaning" is the accumulated sensation of many separate moments.

About a century ago, Sir Henry Maine made his famous suggestion that "the movement of the progressive societies has hitherto been a movement from Status to Contract." There is a great deal of truth in his observation, even when applied to American as contrasted with European society. But a more general principle, of which Maine's maxim is in this case but a corollary, is that the transit of civilization from Europe to America has been a movement from product to process, from art to institutions, from an interest in things to an interest in ways. The great wealth of America has actually had much to do with this. The abundance of our material resources has encouraged a wholesome unconcern for material things in themselves. We have been able to afford to experiment with the ways of doing a job without worrying about preserving any of the particular physical devices perfected for the purpose. If they no longer do, we throw them away and try others. Thus, our domestic architecture, unlike that of Europe, is not the production of inheritable estates, but the perfection of housing; our automobiles are not heirlooms (as they have become in England or in Italy), but transportation; our dress manufacturers, instead of producing garments which are beautiful and durable, aim to offer the wearer the sensation of being modish for a season.

Never has a people been more wasteful of the things of the earth, and never has that waste expressed greater contempt for the things of this world. America and Asia, as W. H. Auden observes, have in common the fact that they are built on waste: Asia on the waste of human life, America on the waste of material wealth. While scarcity has tempted people in Europe to treat physical means as if they were ends, to give them the reverence and the loving care which the objects of this world may not deserve, the people of the United States have tended to treat all means as expendable and have become preoccupied with getting the job done. In the second-hand-automobile market in Turin, Italy, when I went to sell a car which I had used for a year, the dealers felt its pulse, listened to its cough and pityingly, almost tenderly, remarked that it was *stanca*—"tired." When in Chicago I took my used car to such a market, the dealer looked hastily at his handbook, rather than the car, told me what a machine of that vintage was worth, and turned quickly to persuade me of the superior operating advantages of a new model. The printed word, in the form in which it reaches most people here, aims less to be a rounded literary product than a means of entertainment, of topical and relevant instruction, of information on the qualities and prices of all the other available means of living.

In this sense—contrary to current clichés about us—our willingness to waste things has expressed our unconcern for the things of life and our greater interest in the ways of life. Our distinctive interest in process has been expressed in myriad aspects of American culture which have enabled us to see through the object to the objective; to view art not as the perfection of artistic objects, but as a kind of experience; to see religiosity expressed not in the construction of religious monuments and churches, but in a "religious experience" for which the church building is only a more or less effective instrument.

In the realm of material things, all this has been encouraged basically by our great material wealth with all it has meant in the way of an indefinitely expandable market and a continuing demand for better ways of doing all sorts of things. The distinction here is crucial. We must not consider the growing demand for air conditioners in middle-class homes as just a simple expression of materialism and greed for more things of this world. It is more precise to recognize this as but another illustration of our passionate preference for the experience of being cool in summer and for being comfortable in many other ways.

In the realm of ideas, this frame of mind has carried a distinctive lack of interest in the form of thought, a cavalier indifference to whether our thought is consistent and systematic. We are immensely interested in ideas when they wear work clothes, when they are embodied in institutions. Even then we are less interested in how they look than in how they work. We are less interested in how they sound in the salon or from the lecture platform than in how they function in the market place.

The Success Criterion. The intellectual landscape of contemporary Europe is haunted by the ghosts of lost causes. There is hardly a movement in the checkered history of a European nation which does not have its active partisans today. A catalogue of living philosophies in Italy now is an index to Italian history. In those more metaphysically minded countries, which have possessed dominant intellectual classes, political parties are ideological. Philosophers classify themselves as disciples of dead centuries. And all intellectual life becomes a museum of past ideologies. Where ways of thought are judged by their intellectual consistency and by their aesthetic appeal, by their appeal to a distinctively intellectual ruling class rather than by their ability to become embodied in institutions, the intellectual life of the community becomes one with the speculations of its visionaries and the vagaries of its metaphysicians. And this is true in most of the countries of Europe.

But in the United States, almost from the beginning, our ideas have been tested by their ability to become embodied in institutions. Puritanism was to prove itself in Zion; Quakerism in a City of Brotherly Love. Where success is a test of truth, men lose interest in lost causes. They cannot be excited by ideas of philosophic systems (however symmetrical or well constructed or well argued) which do not still give promise of being put into practice. The feasibility of a philosophy becomes one with its validity. The intellectual vision of the community becomes confined by the limits of the practical. This may bound the speculative life, but it has its advantages.

Defeat and oblivion become a single fate. Somehow, systems of thought seem to lose their immortality; if only once proved unworkable, they die. Thus, intellectual life in the United States at any moment is both more and less cumulative than elsewhere. For our history is a process of elimination which has disposed of irrelevant ideas; and the living ideas at any particular time are all those remaining ideas with some reasonable prospect of adoption. If our intellectual life is a less rich museum for philosophers, it may be a richer tool house for cultivating our garden.

The Importance of Context: The Implicitness of Ideas. Never before was a culture so much nourished on the belief that values grow from the context, that the appropriate way of thinking grows out of the particular style of living. "We ever held it certain," declared Cabeza de Vaca in 1535, "that going toward the sunset we would find what we desired." The Puritans, too, believed that Westward the course of the Gospel would have its way: following Jesus' prophecy in Matthew 24:27, they were confident that, as the light of the Gospel had formerly shone out of the East, so now it would shine out of the West. Through the eighteenth and nineteenth centuries—from Crèvecoeur's notion that American had produced a new man, through Jefferson's belief in the wealth, promise and magnificence of the continent, and Turner's faith in a frontier-born culture and frontier-nourished institutions—runs the refrain that American values spring from the circumstances of the New World, that these are the secret of the "American Way of Life." This has been both an example of our special way of dealing with ideas and an encouragement to it. For lack of a better word, we may call this a leaning toward *implicitness,* a tendency to leave ideas embodied in experience and a belief that the truth somehow arises out of the experience.

This carries with it a preference for the relevance of ideas as against their form and a surprising unconcern for the separability of ideas. We have seldom believed that the validity of an idea was tested by its capacity for being expressed in words. The beliefs that values come out of the context and that truth is part of the matrix of experience (and hardly separable from it) become themselves part of the way of American thinking—hence, the formlessness of American thought, its lack of treatises, schools and systems.

The Nirvana of Success: Self-Annihilation through Mastery and Adaptation. All this has produced a quaint inversion of the Buddhist approach to life, or rather something like an American notion of Nirvana. For the Buddhist, bliss is attained by the loss of personal identity, by being absorbed into the universal oneness and nothingness. His self-annihilation is arrived at by transcending the physical environment, by rising above wind and rain, hunger, life and death. The characteristic notion of bliss developed on the American continent involves a comparable process of absorption and loss of identity. But here that oneness is attained by a complete adaptation to the environment which involves seizing the opportunities which it offers, by "fitting in." The objective is an almost mystic and naïvely sensed accord with everything about one. The oblivion of Nirvana and the oblivion of success have much in common. In both, the individual transcends his own personality to become part of what surrounds him. The desire to master the forces of nature, to wrest from the environment all the wealth it holds, to find all possible uses of every material—this has carried with it a willingness to adapt to the social situation, to make the social norm not the fulfillment of some preconceived, philosophy-sharpened ideal, but the fulfillment of the possibilities in the situation, the attainment of compromise. So, for the American, it is not Nirvana, but Rotariana.

Continuity and Conservatism of Ways of Thought. Perhaps never before has there been a society with such remarkable continuity in its ways of thought even from the time of its first settlement. The success criterion, the implicitness, the concern for institutions—all these have prevented abrupt breaks in the direction of our thought. For the chain of circumstances is not casually broken as the chain of ideas can be. A philosopher in his study can think up a new and sometimes attractive frame of ideas; he can propose an anarchy, a revolution or a new beginning; he is free as the air. But circumstances hold within them certain limits; every event somehow grows out of its predecessors. And American empiricism has tied our thinking to the slow, organic growth of institutions. By rejecting ideologies, we reject the sharp angles, the sudden turns, the steep up-and-down grades, which mark political life in many parts of the world, in favor of the slow curves, the imperceptible slopes of institutional life. If ever the circumstances of a culture have suited a people to think "institutionally," American history has done so. For us, fortunately, it is impossible to distinguish the history of our thought from the history of our institutions.

Part 3

CONCLUSION

America's Influence:
Our Ten Contributions to Civilization
ARTHUR M. SCHLESINGER

The present in which we are living is a point of arrival in the epic course of the American past. In the world of today we are under a compelling need, one that exceeds mere scholarship, to understand the meaning and direction of our national life. We can understand that life the more fully and accurately for looking at it in the perspective of our history. Setting the issue of today into the matrix of yesterday, we shall better be able to answer the questions posed by both of them. Such questions have, in recent years, evoked several significant appraisals of the American experience, including Frank Thistlethwaite's The Great Experiment *(1955), William Miller's* A New History of the United States *(1958), Daniel Boorstin's* The Americans *(2 vols., 1958, 1965), Carl Degler's* Out of Our Past *(1959), Samuel Eliot Morison's* The Oxford History of the American People *(1965), and John M. Blum's* The Promise of America *(1965). These the student would do well to consult in formulating his own appraisal, and in coming to grips with some of the central problems regarding the course of our republic, past and present. What, indeed, has the American past been all about? What are its dominant themes, its central features? What forces have charted the course of the republic? What has been the role of America in the world of nations? At what point, in the dramatic process of our becoming, have we presently arrived? What lines of the past run into the present and how far will they run into the future?*

In the following essay, the late Arthur M. Schlesinger, Sr., who taught at Harvard University for three decades before his retirement in 1954, addressed himself to a question which, in a way, represents a summary of all the foregoing ones: What have been America's seminal contributions to civilization? Professor Schlesinger's own studies, rich, varied, and numer-

SOURCE: *The Atlantic Monthly*, CCIII (March, 1959), 65–69. Copyright 1959 by *The Atlantic Monthly*. This article also appeared in Arthur M. Schlesinger, *Paths to the Present* (Boston: Houghton Mifflin Company, Sentry Editions, 1963). Reprinted by permission.

ous, afforded him an excellent basis for formulating an answer. Concerned in the main with the social development of the United States, they include The Colonial Merchants and the American Revolution *(1918),* New Viewpoints in American History *(1922),* The Rise of the City *(1933),* Paths to the Present *(1949, 1963),* The American as Reformer *(1950), and* Prelude to Independence *(1958). Professor Schlesinger also was co-editor, with Dixon Ryan Fox, of* A History of American Life *(13 volumes, 1927–44). In the essay below, he singles out the ideals which have consti-tuted our contribution. He indicates their impact on developments in other continents. And he defines the differences between the guiding principles of our civilization and those of Europe.*

Professor Schlesinger's observations throw a revealing light upon American life. An appraisal and an approval of our past, they are also a commentary on our present. Concerned with the pressing problem of the role we are to play in the world drama of our times, Professor Schlesinger's estimates inevitably invite further inquiries. The most important of these, certainly, concerns what Professor Schlesinger calls our "concept of the inherent and universal right of revolution." If our own age is moved by this concept, above all, it is fair enough that we try to understand what it has meant to us and to what extent we have held it and continue to hold it. Was not the American Revolution essentially a conservative one, cast in the image of the English Revolution of 1688? And was not that English Revolu-tion the model for Europeans during the eighteenth century, as indeed the dramatic changes in England were their model during the nineteenth cen-tury? To what extent did our relatively limited revolution serve to guide the more radical ones which took place on the continent from 1789 (in France) to 1917 (in Russia) and which are today proceeding throughout Asia, Africa, and Latin America? How extensive, in the worlds of yesterday and today, has been our understanding of the aspirations and the achievements of these more radical revolutions?

Our contributions to civilization, moreover, are not merely positive; they are also negative. We have also been known abroad for attitudes that have not commended us to world favor: our nativist movements, our xenophobia, our ethnocentricity, our refusal and inability to extend equality to colored peoples, our materialism without ideals, our self-suffi-ciency, our refusal to accept the responsibilities of leadership, our inability (both literally and figuratively) to talk the languages of other nations, our reluctance to admit that there are other values and other ways than ours or that whatever is American is not necessarily right. In the balance-book of our influence, some account must accordingly be made of the debits. We must understand, in addition, that even our virtues may not be a source of in-fluence. One nation's virtues are conceivably another nation's vices. Our grand principles may not be translatable into other tongues. We may have to grant, in assaying our influence, that we cannot make contributions of what others will not accept. As we review Professor Schlesinger's selection of our major achievements, we would do well to ask how meaningful each of them would be to the various polities of a world in turmoil. We must understand, finally, that leadership is a two-way relationship. To be truly successful, the leader must know how to be led. The momentous question before us is not merely how we shall influence but also how capable we are of being influenced—how responsive, that is, our own ways and values will be to those of the world around us.

The study of American history will help us understand these questions in their larger meaning, by giving them a deeper dimension. A study of the past is an act of self-consciousness. It is an act of coming to terms with one's society and one's age. Having a considered sense of the actualities of the past, we shall also have a more certain sense of the possibilities of the present. We shall become aware of the values and institutions of American society in evolution. We shall see more clearly the forces that have shaped our republic. We shall understand the role of the great leaders in our history, and their relation to those forces. We shall gain a sense of the evitability or inevitability of historical developments in America and of the part played by chance and by accident in producing them. We shall be able to perceive the pattern of continuity and change in American life. We shall also be able to perceive the whole process of becoming, whereby our society has grown and changed during the course of more than three and a half centuries. We shall achieve, finally, a deeper consciousness of what America is today and how it is proceeding into the later decades of the twentieth century.

Since the United States has now become the leader of the free world, our allies are asking, and we ourselves should be asking, what this portends for the future of civilization. The key to the answer, I suggest, lies in America's seminal contributions of the past. In my view these have been at least ten.

THE RIGHT OF REVOLUTION

First and foremost stands the concept of the inherent and universal right of revolution proclaimed in the Declaration of Independence: the doctrine that "all men are created equal" possessing "unalienable rights" to "life, liberty, and the pursuit of happiness," with the corollary that governments derive "their just powers from the consent of the governed" and that therefore the people have the right to supplant a government "destructive of these ends" with one which they believe "most likely to effect their safety and happiness." True, the history of England provided precedents for the men of 1776, and the Age of Enlightenment supplied intellectual support; but the flaming pronouncement, followed by its vindication on the battlefield, made the doctrine ever afterward an irrepressible agency in "the course of human events."

Europe was the first to respond. In 1789 occurred the great French Revolution, the forerunner of two later ones of the French people during the nineteenth century; and neighboring countries were not slow to follow. A series of revolts, centering in 1830 and 1848, drove the Turks from Greece, overturned or strove to overturn illiberal governments through most of the rest of the Continent, and hastened political reforms in other lands to forestall popular upheavals.

These convulsions all had their internal causes, but in every instance the leaders derived inspiration from America's achievement of popular rule as well as from its freely expressed interest in their similar aspirations. Presidents, Congresses, and civic gatherings applauded the uprisings, and American volunteers actually fought in the Greek war of liberation. After Russia helped Austria to suppress the Hungarian rebellion, a United States warship late in 1851 carried the Magyar patriot Kossuth away from the scene, and in this country he received the honors of an American hero. The citizens of Springfield, Illinois, for example, rallied to his cause in words which have a fresh and poignant significance for us today. Affirming "the right of any people . . . to throw off . . . their existing form of government, and to establish such other in its stead as they may choose," they condemned the "interference of Russia in the Hungarian struggle" as "illegal and unwarrantable" and asserted that "to have resisted Russia . . . would have been no violation of our own cherished principles . . . but, on the contrary, would be ever meritorious, in us, or any independent nation." Abraham Lincoln, then in private life, was one of the authors of the resolutions.

The doctrine of revolution, however, had still broader implications. The European eruptions in most instances sought merely to replace domestic regimes; the American revolt, to cast off a distant yoke. It was the first of the great colonial insurrections, an example all the more potent because Washington's ill-trained soldiers defeated the mightiest nation in the world. The Spanish dependencies to the south took heed and early in the nineteenth century won their freedom. Then, oddly enough, came a setback to the trend as a large part of Asia and Africa and many islands of the Pacific fell under the sway of Old World powers. And after a time even the United States, forgetful of its own once colonial status, followed suit.

But in the twentieth century the two world wars radically changed the situation, recalling the United States to its historic heritage, crippling the military strength of the European imperialist countries, and awakening subject peoples everywhere to their right of self-determination. America led the way by relinquishing its Caribbean protectorates and granting independence to the Philippines, and soon the Old World governments fell into line, some voluntarily to anticipate the inevitable, as in the case of England, and others because they were unable to quell native rebellions, as in the cases of France and Holland.

Although more than a century and a half has elapsed since America proclaimed the right of revolution, these events of our own day evidence its continuing vitality. Lest I be accused of claiming too much for a precedent so far in the past, consider the words of President Sukarno of Indonesia several years ago in his address of welcome to the Bandung Conference. This Asian-African gathering, the first of its kind in history, brought together delegates from twenty-nine nations, most of them newly free.

"The battle against colonialism [Sukarno declared] has been a long one, and do you know that today is a famous anniversary in that battle? On the eighteenth day of April, one thousand seven hundred and seventy-five, just one hundred and eighty years ago, Paul Revere rode at midnight through the New England countryside, warning of the approach of British troops and of the opening of the American War of Independence, the first successful anticolonial war in history. About this midnight ride the poet Longfellow wrote:

> A cry of defiance and not of fear,
> A voice in the darkness, a knock at the door,
> And a word that shall echo for evermore. . . .

Yes [he concluded], it shall echo for evermore . . . until we can survey this our own world, and can say that colonialism is dead."

THE PRINCIPLE OF FEDERALISM

Because of the difficulties experienced under the Articles of Confederation, the Constitution of 1787 established a partnership of self-governing commonwealths with an over-all elective government powerful enough to protect and promote their joint concerns and—what was no less important—with a provision for admitting later states on a plane of full equality. This was something new in history; Tocqueville called it "a great discovery in modern political science," for no other people had ever devised a federal structure over so large an area or with a central government chosen by popular vote or on such generous terms for future members. It offered mankind a key to the age-old problem of reconciling legitimate local interests with the general good.

Mexico, Argentina, and other Latin American countries adopted variants of the plan, and so did Germany and Austria-Hungary. Britain applied it to two of its largest colonies, Canada and Australia, and in the twentieth century recast most of its empire into a Commonwealth of Nations on the same basis. More dramatically, the principle caused men to conceive of some sort of federation of the world, first in the

League of Nations and then in the United Nations, both sponsored by American Presidents; and in the not too distant future it promises to bring about a United States of Western Europe.

THE CONSENT OF THE GOVERNED

Neither the doctrine of revolution nor the principle of federalism necessarily ensured that the government so established would rest on the consent of the governed. This was an entirely different matter, as the history of Latin American dictatorships as well as that of other nations proves. But, as we have seen, it was a basic tenet of the founders of the United States and may well be regarded as America's third contribution to humanity.

The framers of the Constitution spurned European tradition by rejecting a monarchy, a nobility, or a hereditary legislative chamber, placing their trust in a government of the people, by the people, and for the people, one which should rule by counting heads instead of breaking them. Starting with a somewhat limited number of voters but in better proportion than in any other country, the suffrage was broadened generation by generation until it came to include all adults of both sexes; and at every point America set the pace for the Old World. The underlying philosophy was not that the common man is all-wise, but only that he can govern himself better than anyone else can do it for him.

THE ROLE OF WOMEN

Women played a man's part as well as a woman's in taming the wilderness, and until very recently, moreover, they were fewer in number than the opposite sex and hence received a consideration unknown abroad. From early times foreign observers marveled at the unusual educational opportunities open to women, their immunity from molestation when traveling alone, their freedom to go out of the home to agitate for temperance, antislavery, and other reforms. "From the captain of a western steamboat to the roughest miner in California," wrote one visitor, "from north, south, east, and west, we hear but one voice. Women are to be protected, respected, supported, and petted."

The organized feminist movement arose earlier in the United States than in any other nation not because American women enjoyed so few privileges but because they had so many that they demanded more—in short, all those exercised by their husbands and brothers, including that of suffrage. The famous women's rights convention at Seneca Falls, New York, in 1848, the first in the history of the world, turned the Declaration of Independence to account by proclaiming "all men and women are created equal," with the same unalienable rights to "life, liberty, and the pursuit of happiness." It took the women many years to achieve that goal, but in time they succeeded, and every victory spurred their sisters in other lands to similar endeavors.

THE MELTING-POT CONCEPT

A fifth contribution of the United States has been the fusing of many different nationalities in a single society. America has been in the best sense of the term a melting pot, every ingredient adding its particular element of strength. The constant infusion of new blood has enriched our cultural life, speeded our material growth, and produced some of our ablest statesmen. Over seventeen million immigrants arrived in the single period from the Civil War to World War I—more than America's total population in 1840—and today English and Scottish blood, the principal strains in colonial times, constitutes considerably less than half the whole.

Many other peoples, it is true, are also of mixed origin; but the American achievement stands alone in the scale, thoroughness and rapidity of the process and, above all, in the fact that it has been the outcome not of forcible incorporation but of peaceful absorption. Significantly, the very nationalities which had habitually warred with one another in the Old World have lived together in harmony in the New. America has demonstrated for everyone with eyes to see that those things which unite peoples are greater than those which divide them, that war is not the inevitable fate of mankind.

Our most tragic failure has involved our Negro citizens, now a tenth of our number. Taken forcibly from Africa, trammeled in slavery for two and a half centuries, denied their constitutional rights after emancipation in the states where most of them lived, this ill-used race has been a standing reproach to our professions of democracy and has enabled Communist spokesmen as well as other foreign critics to impugn the very principle of human equality on which the Republic was founded. Nevertheless, even these injured people have not been unwilling Americans, as the Irish before winning their freedom were unwilling Britons: they have only been unwilling to be halfway Americans or second-class citizens. Hence they have unhesitatingly rejected the blandishments of Soviet propaganda. Fortunately they can now at long last look forward to the final rectification of the wrongs they have so patiently endured.

FREEDOM OF WORSHIP

The recognition that the relations between man and his Creator are a private affair into which government must not intrude contravened the age-long European practice of uniting church and state and imposing harsh restrictions on dissenters. The American system was a legacy of colonial times, when the theological motive for settlement was intense and the multiplicity of denominations suggested the need for mutual forbearance. Rhode Island, Maryland and Pennsylvania in the persons of Roger Williams, Lord Baltimore and William Penn set the pattern to which the Bill of Rights of the federal Constitution gave nationwide sanction. Religion by choice was the natural counterpart of government by consent, and, contrary to Old World belief, the separation of church and state did not in fact weaken either but strengthened both.

THE PUBLIC SCHOOL

The principle of government by consent made it imperative that the people be literate and well-informed if they were to vote intelligently. To ensure this essential condition, statesmen agreed that society must at its own initiative and expense supply the means of schooling. This, too, broke drastically with the Old World concept that education should be a privately financed undertaking for the upper classes, the rank and file supposedly having little need for any in what was deemed to be their permanently inferior station.

New England inaugurated the practice in colonial days; then, with the swift extension of the franchise during the first half of the nineteenth century, it was adopted throughout the North and later in the South. Free public education thus became the article of American faith it has continued to be ever since. From the United States the plan spread in modified form around the world. Japan, for example, in 1872 made it the cornerstone of its program of modernization. Probably America has conferred no greater boon on mankind, for popular education is the seedbed of virtually all other human aspirations. And akin to this system was the tax-supported free public library, in which America has also led the world.

THE SPIRIT OF PHILANTHROPY

Foreigners have always criticized the American for his pursuit of the Almighty Dollar, but have seldom gone on to note that he has in unparalleled degree returned the fruits of his labors to society. If he has been hardheaded about making money, he has, so to speak, been softhearted about spending it. This constitutes the American version of the Old World concept of *noblesse oblige* carried to a point the Old World has never approached. Even long before Carnegie and Rockefeller amassed their colossal fortunes, men and women of modest means gave freely to schools, churches, foreign missions, colleges, hospitals, charities and other projects for social betterment.

In the twentieth century this same concern has led men of wealth to set up some four thousand philanthropic foundations staffed with experts to administer the funds with maximum usefulness and for nearly every conceivable object of human benefit. Their programs, exceeding all earlier bounds, include the control of epidemic diseases and far-reaching researches in the natural and social sciences. Even so, the lion's share of the more than 7.8 billion dollars devoted to altruistic purposes in 1959 still derived from other than foundation sources.

And, increasingly, Americans have extended their beneficence to foreign peoples. Over a century ago popular subscriptions helped relieve Irish suffering during the terrible potato famines of the 1840's and later aided with equal generosity the victims of natural catastrophes in other lands. And, besides the work of the Red Cross in peace and war, the great foundations have in our own day improved health, educational and agricultural conditions in many countries. In the same tradition the private organization known as CARE has, since World War II, channeled gifts of food, clothing, medicine and the like to the needy of Europe, Asia, Africa and Latin America. Thanks to this ingrained trait of the national character, the government found it easy to mobilize our people behind the Marshall Plan, a tax-supported program for repairing the war-stricken economies of Western Europe, and later behind economic aid for backward countries all over the world. Though these official undertakings were in part designed to halt the spread of Communism, they arose from deeper springs of human compassion and have no parallel in history.

MECHANICAL INGENUITY

Mechanical ingenuity, or what today is called technological know-how, is, contrary to common belief, by no means a late development. From the mid-eighteenth century on, the people, confronted with a chronic shortage of labor and the problems arising from formidable distances and poor communications, devised means to overcome these handicaps as well as to ameliorate other conditions of life. The record is truly remarkable. Before the end of the nineteenth century Benjamin Franklin, Eli Whitney and their successors produced such epochal inventions as the lightning rod, the cotton gin, the steamboat, the metal plow, the harvester, vulcanized rubber, the sewing machine, the telegraph, the telephone and the electric light, among others. In still other instances they greatly improved on what had come to them from abroad.

The outcome was not only to transform American life but that of peoples everywhere. For the most part the machines, techniques and products made their way round the world by reason of their superiority to anything before known. As early as 1838 American locomotive builders were shipping their engines abroad, a few years later the Russian government employed American engineers to construct and equip a railroad between Moscow and St. Petersburg, and shortly Prussia sent a delegation to the United States to study this country's methods before launching her own rail system. At the international exposition in London in 1851 our inventors won so many awards as to amaze even informed Europeans. The Colt revolver, for example, was hailed by the British press as a weapon that would revolutionize the conduct of war as greatly as had the introduction of gunpowder, while a precision instrument for observing the stars earned the encomium of "the most wonderful achievement since the days of Newton." Thus, even before the era of great industrial expansion after the Civil War, American technology was well embarked on its international career.

Occasionally official United States missions lent a hand for diplomatic reasons. A notable instance occurred in the case of Japan after it abandoned its long isolation, while others involved taking the new discoveries and products to unprogressive Latin American countries. President Truman therefore was not occupying wholly new ground when in 1949 he proposed his Point Four Program to make "the benefits of our scientific advances and industrial progress available for the improvement and growth of underdeveloped areas" and thus "help them realize their aspirations for a better life." Under this program the United States has sent experts in industry, engineering and agriculture to many lands; built roads and bridges in Iran, irrigation works in India and fertilizer plants in Korea; and endeavored in countless other ways to remove the obstacles that have barred less enterprising countries from the advantages of modern civilization. Just as the government has made our philanthropic impulse a vital instrument of foreign policy, so also it has done with our technological skill.

EVOLUTIONARY PROGRESS

Our tenth contribution has been our way of meeting internal crises by bending without breaking our free institutions. The spirit of America has been empirical and pragmatic, dedicated to equalitarian ends but willing to realize them by flexible means. In the European sense of the term, America's major political parties are not parties at all, because they do not divide over basic ideologies. Neither wishes to overturn or replace the existing political and economic order; they merely desire to alter it at slower or faster rates of speed.

One of our proudest achievements has been the creation of a system of controlled capitalism that yields the highest living standards on earth and has made possible a society as nearly classless as man has ever known. The profit system as it has developed in America is a multiprofit system, sharing its benefits with all segments of society: capital, labor and the consuming masses. Yet even this was not due to a preconceived blueprint; it too was the result of trial and error. Unprincipled businessmen had first to be brought to heel by government restraints and the growing power of organized labor before they came to learn that they must serve the general good in pursuing their selfish interests. Now labor is in turn feeling the restraint.

Even our creed of democracy is no fixed and immutable dogma. Thus the statesmen of the early republic, though they were stalwart champions of private enterprise, chose to make the post office a government monopoly and to confide the schools to public ownership. Since then, by fits and starts, and most recently under the New Deal, the United States has taken on many of the characteristics of a welfare state. This has occurred, however, not under the banner of socialism or any other "ism," but simply because the Americans hold with Lincoln that "the legitimate object of government is to do for a community of people whatever they need to have done but cannot do at all, or cannot do so well for themselves, in their separate and individual capacities."

Viewed as a whole, the contributions of America to civilization will be seen to have been for the most part in the nature of methods or processes. They have aimed to release men from political and religious disabilities, from ignorance and poverty, from backbreaking toil. They have struck at the fetters which from time immemorial the Old World has fastened on human beings. They have opened the doors of opportunity for the many while still assuring them to the few, in the belief that everyone should have an equal chance to be as unequal as he can without denying the same right to others. In brief, they have sought to substitute fluidity for rigid class distinctions as the vital principle of social well-being. And the consequence has been a general leveling of society upward instead of downward.

But what of the future? I recall what a thoughtful Hollander said to me a few years after World War II. Observing that Europe's age of greatness was now over and that Americans must henceforth take the lead in the advancement of civilization, he wondered whether they would be equal to the task. Plainly he had grave doubts, for like most foreigners he thought of us as having been only beneficiaries of the bounty of the Old World without making any creative returns in kind. But for an American historian the answer is clear. The true measure of our past contributions lies in the very fact that they have become so woven into the life of mankind that my Dutch friend was unaware of them. If we can only preserve our free institutions and our faith in the untrammeled human spirit, we shall triumphantly meet the challenge now before us.

Correlation of American History: Recent
Interpretations, Book II,
with American History Texts

	John M. Blum et al., THE NATIONAL EXPERIENCE, 2nd ed.	Carman, Syrett, and Wishy, A HISTORY OF THE AMERICAN PEOPLE, 3rd ed., Vol. II	John A. Garraty, THE AMERICAN NATION
Text Chapters	Related selections in *American History: Recent Interpretations*		
1		1, 2, 10	
2		6	
3		4, 6–8	
4		4, 9, 11	
5			
6		5	
7		3, 5, 13	
8			
9		16	
10		12, 13, 14	
11		15	
12		16, 17	
13		18	
14			
15	1, 2	19, 21, 22	
16	10	21–24	1, 2
17		22, 23, 24	11
18	4, 6, 7, 8, 9	25	6, 7, 8
19	11, 12, 14	26, 27	9, 11, 12
20	3, 4, 5, 13	28	4, 14
21		29, 30, 31, 32	3, 4, 5, 13
22	15, 16	33–37	
23	15, 17, 18		15, 16
24	18		15, 17
25	19, 20		19, 20, 21, 22
26	20, 21, 22		21, 22, 23, 24
27	20, 21, 22		25, 26, 27
28	22, 23, 24		28, 29, 30, 31
29	25		29, 30, 31, 32
30	26, 27		33, 34, 35, 36, 37
31	28		
32	29, 30		
33	31–37		

Text Chapters	Oscar Handlin, AMERICA: A HISTORY	Hicks, Mowry, and Burke, A HISTORY OF AMERICAN DEMOCRACY, 3rd ed.	Hofstadter, Miller, and Aaron, THE UNITED STATES, 2nd ed.
	Related selections in *American History: Recent Interpretations*		
17			1, 2, 10
18			
19			6, 7, 8, 9
20		1, 2	3, 4, 5, 13
21		3, 13	11, 12
22			12, 13, 14
23		6, 7, 8	16
24		9, 11	15, 16, 17
25		5	18
26		12, 13, 14	19, 20, 21, 23
27		12	22, 23, 24
28			36
29		16	25, 26, 27
30		15, 16	28, 29, 30, 32
31		17	31, 33–37
32		18	
33	1, 2		
34	6	19, 20	
35	6, 14		
36	10		
37	9	21, 22, 23	
38	12	22, 23, 24	
39	13		
40	3	25, 26, 27	
41		28	
42	5	29, 30	
43	11	32, 33, 34, 35, 36	
44	6, 7, 8	31, 32, 37	
45			
46	15		
47	16		
48	17		
49			
50	18		
51			
52			
53	19, 20		
54			
55	21, 22		
56	22, 23, 24		
57	25, 26, 27		
58	28, 30		

	Oscar Handlin, AMERICA: A HISTORY	Hicks, Mowry, and Burke, A HISTORY OF AMERICAN DEMOCRACY, 3rd ed.	Hofstadter, Miller, and Aaron, THE UNITED STATES, 2nd ed.
Text Chapters	Related selections in *American History: Recent Interpretations*		
59			
60	28		
61	29, 31		
62	33		
63	34		
64	36		
65	31		
66	35, 36, 37		

	Williams, Current, and Freidel, A HISTORY OF THE UNITED STATES, 2nd ed., Vol. II	Williams, Current, and Freidel, AMERICAN HISTORY: A SURVEY, 2nd ed.	L. B. Wright *et al.*, THE DEMOCRATIC EXPERIENCE, revised
Text Chapters	Related selections in *American History: Recent Interpretations*		
1	1, 2, 10		
2	1		
3	6, 7, 8, 9		
4	12, 14		
5			
6	11		
7	3, 4		
8	5		
9			
10	15		
11	16		1, 2
12	16, 17		10, 11
13			6, 7, 8, 9
14	18		3, 4, 5, 13
15	18		4, 12, 14
16			15, 16, 17
17	19, 20		18
18	20, 21, 22		
19	21, 22		19, 20, 21, 22
20	22, 23, 24		21, 22, 23, 24
21	22, 23, 24	1, 2, 10	
22	25	3, 4	25, 26, 27
23	26		28–32
24	26, 27	6, 7, 8, 9, 11	33–37
25	28	5	
26	28		
27	32	12, 13, 14	
28		15	
29	29, 30	16, 17	
30	29	18	
31	31–37		
32		19, 20, 21	
33		21, 22	
34		22, 23, 24	
35		25	
36			
37		26, 27	
38		28	
39		29, 30, 32	
40		29	
41		31–37	

Index

Fourteenth Amendment (*cont.*)
  and Negro rights, 13, 166–67, 168
  and private contracts, 53–75
Fowler, Orson, 136–37
Frank, Henry, 228
Frankfurter, Felix, 51
Franklin, John H., 11*n*, 14
  on Reconstruction, 4–5, 22–34
Frazier, Franklin, 547
free banking, 38, 41
Freedmen's Bureau, 7, 8, 23
Freeman, Orville, 491
Freidel, Frank, 12*n*, 340, 499
  on New Deal, 363, 376–92
Freund, Paul, 74
Frick, Henry C., 106, 107
Fulbright, J. William, 412
Full Employment Act of 1946, 399

Gage, Lyman J., 134–35, 139
Gaiwiio movement, 312, 314
Galbraith, John Kenneth
  on economy in 1920's, 350–61
  on John F. Kennedy, 484, 487, 488
Garfield, James A., 211
Garland, Hamlin, 228
Garner, John Nance, 387, 400
Garraty, John A., 299
Garvan, Francis P., 318*n*
Gary, Elbert H., 352
General Managers' Association, 57, 58, 61
Genzmer, George Harvey, 124*n*
George, Alexander L., 299
George, Henry, 177
George, Juliette L., 299
Gerard, James W., 289
Germany
  American policy, 300–3
  anti-German sentiments toward, 289–93, 302–3, 314–15
  and Japan, 445, 446, 447–48
  submarines and World War I, 286, 293–94, 296, 299–303, 305
Ghost Dance cult, 311, 312, 313
Gibbs, Jonathan C., 24
Gilbert, Felix, 170
Glad, Paul W., on Election of 1896, 75–89
Gladden, Washington, 135
Gladstone, William, 206
Glass, Carter, 277, 281, 360
Glass bill, 278–79
Glavis, Louis, 395
Glazer, Nathan, 558
Gleason, S. Everett, 415, 417
Gleaves, Richard H., 24
Glenn, Norval, 546
Godkin, E. L., 120, 126, 134, 136, 201, 227
gold
  bank reserves of, 49–50
  issue in election of 1896, 86

gold (*cont.*)
  premium as tariff, 40
  speculation in, 43–44
Goldbloom, Maurice, 412
Goldman, Eric F., 336–37
Goldwater, Barry M., 506, 508
Gompers, Samuel, 151–52, 228, 265*n*
Gould, Jay, 121*n*, 124, 126
government
  authority over business, 62–68, 345–46, 601
  businessmen on, 134–35, 137–39
  consent of governed, 596, 598
  and federalism principle, 595–96
  and liberty of contract, 53–75
  municipal reform, 234–58
  New Deal and expansion, 396–400
  presidential concepts of, 362–63, 482–83, 489–90
  and Supreme Court, 389–90
Graebner, Norman A., on Eisenhower, 462–74
Granger Cases, 63–64, 68
Grant, Percy Stickney, 227
Grant, Ulysses S., 42, 165, 200, 201, 205
Grantham, Dewey W., Jr., on politics in South, 496–511
Gras, N. S. B., 128
Gray, William, 42
Great Britain, 291, 292
  economic problems of, 369–73
  Far Eastern policy of, 455, 456
  reform movement in, 206–7
  in World War I, 294, 296, 300, 301
  in World War II, 413, 422, 444, 446
Great Depression
  attitudes of businessmen during, 125–26
  economy in, 377–78, 379–92
  and New Deal, 364–65, 368–69
Greenback Expansion Bill, 41–42, 43
greenbackism, 45–50, 120
Greene, Fred, 291*n*
Greenfield, Kent Roberts, 410
Gregory, Thomas Watt, 314
Grenville, J. A. S., 291*n*
Grew, Joseph C., 417, 418
Grey, Sir Edward, 294, 298, 301
Grob, Gerald N., on labor movement, 143–56
Guggenheim family, 108
Gutman, Herbert, 252

Hacker, Louis, 374
Hada, Hikosahuro, 440, 442
Hagerty, James C., 468, 470
Hale, Robert L., 67
Hall, Leonard W., 466
Halsey, William, 439
Hamblen, Herbert, 220
Hampton, Wade, 32

Handlin, Mary F., 19
Handlin, Oscar, 19, 253
Hanna, Mark, 77–78
Hanson, Ole, 325, 326
Hara, Yoshimichi, 449–50
Harding, Warren G.
  economic policy of, 346, 347, 355–56
  election of, 347–48
  labor policies of, 352
Harlan, John M., 59, 60, 67, 72
Harriman, E. H., 127
Harris, James H., 24
Harrison, Benjamin, 80
Haskell, C. N., 123–24
Hawley, Joseph R., 213n
Hawley-Smoot tariff, 357
Hay, John, 261
Hayden, Tom, 562
Hayes, Rutherford B., 165, 175, 205
Haymarket bomb incident, 136, 144, 176, 177
Hays, Samuel P., 77
  on Progressivism, 234–58
Haywood, Big Bill, 262
Heilbroner, Robert L., on American capitalism, 512–39
Heinze, F. Augustus, 108
Heller, Walter, 486
Henderson, Arthur, 372
Henderson, Hubert, 371
Hepburn Act, 268, 335
Hershey, Amos S., 292
Hewitt, Abram S., 173
Hicks, John D., 12
Hidy, Muriel E., 105, 121n, 130
Hidy, Ralph W., 105, 121n, 130
Higginson, Henry Lee, 135, 136
Higham, John, 306, 307, 308n, 314, 321n
  on immigration restrictions, 170–77
Hill, J. W., 240
Hill, James J., 106
Hill, Lister, 508
Hindenburg, Paul von, 301
hippies, 559, 560, 567
Hirohito, Emperor of Japan, 437, 438, 449, 450
Hiss, Alger, 477
Hitchman Coal and Coke Co. v. *Mitchell*, 61–62
Hitler, Adolf, 389, 445
Hoar, Ebenezer R., 200, 205
Hoar, George F., 196
Hofmann, Josef, 402
Hofstadter, Richard, 12, 20
  on Charles Beard, 123, 124, 125n
  on elite reformers, 198–218
  on Progressivism, 22n, 123, 124, 236, 237, 238, 342
Holden v. *Hardy*, 70–71, 72, 74

holding companies, 99–100, 353
Hollingsworth, J. Rogers, 77
Holme, John, 224
Holmes, Oliver Wendell, 60, 62, 72–73
Holzman, Robert, 8n
Hood, James W., 24
Hoogenboom, Ari, 202n
Hook, Sidney, 374
Hoover, Herbert, 346, 359, 396
  economic policy of, 356–59, 370, 373, 377, 378, 381, 383
  election of, 367
  on government power, 399
  on New Deal, 384
Hoover, J. Edgar, 321, 398
Hopkins, Charles Howard, 179, 182
Hopkins, Harry, 380, 401–2, 405
Hopkins, W. R., 250n
Hough, Emerson, 314n, 325n
House, Edward M., 289, 294, 295, 297, 298, 302–3, 304
House-Grey Memorandum, 294, 298
Houston, David, 281
Howard, Roy, 385
Hudson, W. S., 196
Hughes, Charles Evans, 51, 61, 356
Hull, Cordell, 413, 426, 428
Humphrey, George M., 465
Hunnicut, James W., 32
Hurley, Patrick, 459, 460
Hurst, James Willard, 51
Hutchinson, Thomas, 580

Ickes, Harold, 375, 384, 388, 394–95, 397
Imamura, Hitoshi, 439
immigrants
  acculturation pressures on, 323–24
  alienation of, 367
  attitudes toward, 318, 321–25, 327
  immigration impact, 169, 171–72
  melting-pot concept, 597
  reformers and, 204
  restrictions on, 169–77, 265n, 327, 346
  voting patterns of, 84–85
immigration acts, 171, 172–73
imperialism
  and capitalism, 528–30
  and destiny concept, 194–96
  as issue in election of 1896, 87
  and white-supremacy movement, 167
In re Debs, 58
In re Jacobs, 70, 71
income
  distribution of, 351–52, 518–22
  in Great Depression, 378
  minimum wage legislation, 555
  of Negroes vs. whites, 544, 547
  New Deal attitudes on, 401